SUPREME COURT JUSTICES

A BIOGRAPHICAL DICTIONARY

Timothy L. Hall

Facts On File, Inc.

For Ben and Amy

Supreme Court Justices: A Biographical Dictionary

Facts On File, Inc.
132 West 31st Street
New York NY 10001

Library of Congress Cataloging-in-Publication Data
Hall, Timothy L.
Supreme Court justices: a biographical dictionary / Timothy L. Hall.
p. cm.
Includes bibliographical references and index.
ISBN 0-8160-4194-6
1. United States. Supreme Court—Officials and employees—Biography—Dictionaries. 2. Judges—United States—Biography—Dictionaries. I. Title.

KF8744.H35 2001
347.73'2634—dc21
[B] 00-065415

Facts On File books are available at special discounts when purchased in bulk quantities for businesses, associations, institutions, or sales promotions. Please call our Special Sales Department in New York at (212) 967-8800 or (800) 322-8755.

You can find Facts On File on the World Wide Web at http://www.factsonfile.com

Text design and layout by Rachel L. Berlin
Cover design by Cathy Rincon

Printed in the United States of America

VB FOF 10 9 8 7 6 5 4 3 2 1

This book is printed on acid-free paper.

Contents

Acknowledgments v
Introduction vi

James Wilson 1
John Jay 5
William Cushing 10
John Blair, Jr. 14
John Rutledge 17
James Iredell 21
Thomas Johnson 25
William Paterson 28
Samuel Chase 32
Oliver Ellsworth 36
Bushrod Washington 39
Alfred Moore 43
John Marshall 46
William Johnson 51
Henry Brockholst Livingston 55
Thomas Todd 59
Gabriel Duvall 62
Joseph Story 65
Smith Thompson 70
Robert Trimble 74
John McLean 78
Henry Baldwin 82
James Moore Wayne 86
Roger Brooke Taney 90
Philip Pendleton Barbour 95
John Catron 99
John McKinley 103
Peter Vivian Daniel 107
Samuel Nelson 111
Levi Woodbury 115
Robert Cooper Grier 119
Benjamin Robbins Curtis 123
John Archibald Campbell 127
Nathan Clifford 132
Noah Haynes Swayne 136
Samuel Freeman Miller 140
David Davis 144
Stephen Johnson Field 148
Salmon Portland Chase 153
William Strong 157
Joseph P. Bradley 161
Ward Hunt 165
Morrison Remick Waite 168
John Marshall Harlan 173
William Burnham Woods 178
Stanley Matthews 182
Horace Gray 186
Samuel Blatchford 190
Lucius Quintus Cincinnatus Lamar 194
Melville Weston Fuller 198
David Josiah Brewer 202
Henry Billings Brown 206
George Shiras, Jr. 210
Howell Edmunds Jackson 214
Edward Douglass White 218
Rufus Wheeler Peckham, Jr. 222
Joseph McKenna 226
Oliver Wendell Holmes, Jr. 230
William Rufus Day 235
William Henry Moody 239
Horace Harmon Lurton 243
Charles Evans Hughes 247
Willis Van Devanter 252
Joseph Rucker Lamar 256
Mahlon Pitney 259
James Clark McReynolds 262
Louis Dembitz Brandeis 267
John Hessin Clarke 271
William Howard Taft 275
George Sutherland 279
Pierce Butler 283
Edward Terry Sanford 287
Harlan Fiske Stone 290
Owen Josephus Roberts 295

Benjamin Nathan Cardozo 299
Hugo Lafayette Black 303
Stanley Forman Reed 307
Felix Frankfurter 311
William Orville Douglas 315
Frank Murphy 319
James Francis Byrnes 323
Robert Houghwout Jackson 326
Wiley Blount Rutledge 330
Harold Hitz Burton 334
Fred Moore Vinson 337
Thomas Campbell Clark 341
Sherman Minton 345
Earl Warren 349
John Marshall Harlan II 354
William J. Brennan, Jr. 358
Charles Evans Whittaker 362
Potter Stewart 365
Byron Raymond White 368
Arthur Joseph Goldberg 372
Abe Fortas 376
Thurgood Marshall 380
Warren Earl Burger 384
Harry Andrew Blackmun 388
Lewis Franklin Powell, Jr. 392
William Hubbs Rehnquist 396
John Paul Stevens 400
Sandra Day O'Connor 404
Antonin Scalia 408
Anthony McLeod Kennedy 412
David Hackett Souter 416
Clarence Thomas 420
Ruth Bader Ginsburg 424
Stephen Gerald Breyer 428

Glossary 433

Chronology 439

Appendix 1: Justices 446

Appendix 2: Presidents and Their Appointments to the Supreme Court 452

Appendix 3: Important Supreme Court Cases 455

Appendix 4: The Constitution of the United States 504

Bibliography 515

Index 549

ACKNOWLEDGMENTS

I am indebted to Dean Samuel Davis and the Lamar Order of the University of Mississippi Law School for supporting my work on this project. Stacy Prewitt and Archie Speights provided research and editorial assistance. Niler Franklin and Jennifer Barnes at the University of Mississippi Law School helped to prepare the manuscript for publication. The staff of the University of Mississippi Law School Library, especially Lynn Murray, supported my work on this project by assisting me in gathering more than two centuries' worth of biographical materials concerning the justices. I am grateful to Nicole Bowen, my editor at Facts On File, for conceiving and asking me to contribute to this biographical series, and to my friend Kent Rasmussen for recommending me and introducing me in the first place to the world of reference writing. Finally, I owe a debt beyond gratitude to my wife, Lee, and my children, Ben and Amy, for tolerating the frequent nights I spent in the company of Supreme Court justices rather than theirs.

Introduction

By the beginning of the 21st century, 108 men and women had served on the U.S. Supreme Court. They arrived there by paths as varied as their backgrounds. Before their careers as Supreme Court justices they were lawyers, politicians, bureaucrats, and judges. Samuel Freeman Miller, for example, practiced medicine briefly before turning to a legal career that ultimately brought him to the Supreme Court in 1862. William Howard Taft, who was president of the United States before becoming chief justice of the Supreme Court in 1921, viewed the transition from the office of chief executive to that of chief justice as a promotion. Many arrived on the Court after careers in politics, serving variously as mayors, governors, state legislative representatives, and senators. The presidents who appointed them to the Court did so to repay favors, to satisfy important political constituents, or to recognize loyalty and even merit. David Davis steered Abraham Lincoln's campaign for president, and though he would have preferred to be president himself, he settled for a seat on the nation's highest court instead. President Franklin D. Roosevelt promoted his attorney general, Frank Murphy, to the Supreme Court, partly because Murphy proved to be somewhat more of a reformer than Roosevelt found palatable for his continued political ambitions. Consequently, by nominating Murphy to the Court, Roosevelt removed a possible political liability from his administration.

During the 1930s, politicians who bristled at the Court's power to overturn laws referred caustically to the "nine old men." They have indeed been mostly old and mostly men. Newly appointed justices of the Supreme Court have typically been past the age of 50 when they arrive on the Court, and they labor there well into their 60s and beyond. Death has removed a good many of them from their posts. Some of them, such as Robert Grier and Stephen Fields, had to be sternly persuaded to relinquish their seats after old age had undermined their abilities to accomplish the Court's work. Early in his career on the Court, Justice Stephen Fields had been deputized by his colleagues to persuade Robert Grier to step down from the Court. Nearly 30 years later a similar delegation, lead by Justice John Marshall Harlan, arrived to urge Fields to retire. When Harlan reminded Fields of his earlier mission to Grier, the aging Fields replied, "Yes, and a dirtier day's work I never did in my life!"

Until the last two decades of the 20th century, the Court was the nation's most exclusive men's club. In 1981 President Ronald Reagan disturbed this fraternity by appointing Sandra Day O'Connor to become the Court's first female member. It took more than a decade until the appointment of Ruth Bader Ginsburg in 1992 increased the number of women on the Court to two. The color barrier on the Court had been broken somewhat earlier, when President Lyndon B. Johnson nominated Thurgood Marshall as an associate justice. Marshall had been a preeminent civil rights attorney prior to his appointment as the Court's first African-American justice. When he retired from the Court in 1991 after 24 years of service, President George Bush named another African American, Clarence Thomas, to replace Marshall.

In respects other than race and gender, the justices on the Supreme Court have been somewhat more diverse. Protestants have predominated on the Court, though Catholics managed to secure a seat as early as 1836, when President Andrew Jackson appointed Roger B. Taney as chief justice. Thereafter, a steady string of Catholic justices occupied seats on the Court: Joseph McKenna, Pierce Butler, Edward D. White, Frank Murphy, William J. Brennan,

Jr., Antonin Scalia, and Anthony M. Kennedy. Nearly eight decades after the appointment of the first Catholic justice to the Court, Woodrow Wilson nominated Louis D. Brandeis to become the Court's first Jewish justice. Brandeis, one of the most famous justices ever to have served on the Court, was followed by other Jewish justices: Benjamin Nathan Cardozo, Felix Frankfurter, Arthur J. Goldberg, Ruth Bader Ginsburg, and Stephen Breyer. In terms of wealth, justices on the Supreme Court have varied from the middle class upwards. Frequently, justices on the lower end of this spectrum gauged their decision on when to retire from the Court on when they would be entitled to retirement benefits. But the Court has known justices who were independently wealthy. Justice Stephen Breyer, for example, married the daughter of a wealthy British family. Nevertheless his fortuitous financial circumstances have not prevented Justice Breyer from riding a bus to his work on the Court and bringing his lunch with him. Though the members of the Court have generally been prosperous or at least financially secure, the Court has known justices whose finances were more troubled. One of the first Supreme Court justices, James Wilson, saw a series of real estate and business speculations collapse, and spent the last months of his life fleeing creditors. He could not escape them, though, and twice had to be rescued from jail by his son after creditors had him imprisoned for his debts.

The justices' educational backgrounds have varied as well. Some of the Court's early members had studied law at the Inns of Court in England before practicing in the colonies, but the Revolutionary War ended this commerce in legal ideas. Afterward, for the next century or so, justices came to the Court with the educational background typical of practicing lawyers in the United States. They generally had a college degree and a legal education that consisted of having apprenticed with some experienced lawyer. Formal legal education was not unheard of in the early years of the Republic. For example, Levi Woodbury studied briefly at the Tapping Reeve Law School in Litchfield, Connecticut, and in 1780 Chief Justice John Marshall, the Court's most famous jurist, attended the lectures of George Wythe, who taught law at the College of William and Mary. Overall, though, the system of legal apprenticeships dominated legal education until the end of the 19th century.

The country's elite law schools, such as those at Harvard, Yale, Columbia, and Stanford, have featured prominently among the alma maters of Supreme Court justices, especially in the 20th century. Justices have both graduated from and taught at some of the nation's most prestigious law schools. Justice Benjamin Curtis, for example, studied law at Harvard in the first part of the 19th century and was privileged to learn from the lectures of Associate Justice Joseph Story, who held an endowed chair at Harvard Law School for a time. The teacher-student relationship between justices of different generations occurred again when William O. Douglas studied under Harlan F. Stone at Columbia Law School and William J. Brennan, Jr., studied with Felix Frankfurter at Harvard Law School. The 20th century saw a number of justices arrive on the Court after having enjoyed careers as law school professors. William O. Douglas, Antonin Scalia, and Stephen Breyer are only a few of the many justices who have had academic backgrounds. Even in the 20th century, though, a law degree from an Ivy League school has not been a prerequisite for a seat on the Supreme Court. Chief Justice Warren E. Burger, for instance, earned his law degree by taking night courses at St. Paul College of Law (later to become the William Mitchell College of Law) while he sold insurance during the day.

The work of Supreme Court justices is demanding intellectually, and those men and women who have sat on the Court have varied a good deal in the mental gifts they have brought to this work. Some justices, such as Oliver Wendell Holmes, Jr., and Benjamin Nathan Cardozo, arrived on the Court with a reputation for judicial brilliance based on their prior service as state court judges, a reputation that was reinforced by their work on the Court. Others entered upon their responsibilities with great trepidation. Joseph McKenna, the last justice appointed to the Court in the 19th century, was so anxious about his preparation to serve on the Court that he spent a few months taking courses at Columbia Law School between the time of his confirmation and when he took his seat on the Court. Other justices might have benefited from the kind of modest self-understanding exhibited by McKenna, for the Court has had more than its share of intellectual pedestrians. A law clerk once asked Justice Oliver Wendell Holmes, Jr.—certainly one of the brightest intellectual stars in the Court's universe—what he thought of Rufus Peckham intellectually. Holmes is said to have responded, "Intellectually? I never thought of him in that connection. His major premise was, 'God damn it!'"

By the beginning of the 21st century, the Court had come to exercise a remarkable measure of power within the American political tradition. But it had not always been so. In 1790 the nation over whose laws the Court would preside was itself an infant, brought to life by the ratification of the U.S. Constitution on June 21, 1788. Article III of that founding document provided that "[t]he judicial Power of the United States, shall be vested in one supreme Court, and in such inferior Courts as the Congress may from time to time ordain and establish." The Court therefore needed a Congress to create it. Thus, the first Congress set out at once to erect the judicial structure ordained by the Constitution by passing the Judiciary Act of September 24, 1789. This act established a Supreme Court with a chief justice and five associate justices. The same day, President George Washington named six men to occupy the first seats on the Court: John Jay as chief justice, and John Rutledge, William Cushing, Robert Harrison, James Wilson, and John Blair, Jr., as associate justices. Harrison declined to serve, and in February 1790 Washington appointed James Iredell to fill the final seat on the Court.

On February 1, 1790, the Supreme Court of the United States met for its first session. The clamor of controversy that would frequently surround its later life made no appearance this first day. In fact, not all the justices were even in attendance at the Royal Exchange Building on Broad Street in New York City. The chief justice, John Jay, and two other associate justices were present, but Congress had set the Court's original number at six, and it would not be until the following day that a fourth justice arrived to make a quorum. Even then the Court had little business to attend to. By the end of the 20th century, some 7,000 appeals would find their way to the Court each year. But the press of that caseload lay far in the future.

Chief Justice John Jay, appointed by President Washington, remained on the Court only six years before departing to become governor of New York. After Jay had enjoyed two successful terms as New York governor, President John Adams tried to lure him back to the Supreme Court. Adams nominated Jay to replace Oliver Ellsworth, who had resigned from the Court in 1800. The Senate confirmed Jay's reappointment, but he was unwilling to return to the Court. "I left the bench," he explained in a letter to Adams, "perfectly convinced that under a system so defective it would not obtain the energy, weight, and dignity which was essential to its affording due support to the national government; nor acquire the public confidence and respect which, as the last resort of the justice of the nation, it should possess."

Jay famously underestimated the role that the Court would soon play—and would thereafter continue to play—in the life of the nation. When he turned down a chance to return to the Court as chief justice, President Adams turned to John Marshall to fill the position of chief justice. In the following years, Marshall secured the Court's place at the heart of the American political system and his own place at the head of the list of the Court's most influential justices. "Marshall found the Constitution paper; and he made it power," one observer has declared. "He found a skeleton, and he clothed it with flesh and blood."

Alexis de Tocqueville, whose *Democracy in America* famously described the United States a generation after its founding, noted that every political problem in the United States eventually became a legal problem. In the seminal decision of *Marbury v. Madison* (1824), Chief Justice John Marshall announced the doctrine of judicial review: the principle that the Supreme Court and other federal courts have the authority to judge the constitutionality of laws passed by Congress. The doctrine of judicial review eventually came to mean that the federal courts had power to determine the constitutionality of laws passed and other actions taken by both federal and state governments. By securing the power of judicial review, Marshall ensured that the Court would stand close to the center of American political life. The record of its decisions is a record of the most important and most controversial questions of American public life. Slavery, the income tax, segregation, school prayer, busing, abortion, sex discrimination, gay rights, term limits, capital punishment—all these subjects have arrived at one time or another for consideration by the nation's high court. Supreme Court decisions can influence Wall Street and death row and order the conduct of presidents and prisoners. In the disputed presidential election of 2000, the Court's decision in *Bush v. Gore* essentially determined who would be the nation's 42nd president.

The Supreme Court initially had six members, but the number of justices has varied from five to 10 over the years. In the main, this number has increased with the growth of the nation. After being briefly pared to five in 1801, the number of justices returned to six in 1802, became seven in 1807, nine in 1837, and 10 in 1863. For a time, when President Andrew Johnson and the Reconstruction Congress were at odds, Congress passed legislation that prevented the president from filling vacancies on the Court, and its numbers slipped to seven. But in 1869, new legislation fixed the number of justices at nine, where it has remained since. President Franklin D. Roosevelt briefly threatened to pack the Court with additional justices who would be more receptive to his New Deal agenda in the late 1930s. His plan would have swelled the Court to as many as 15 justices, but he abandoned it after it received a cool reception from Congress and after the Court itself became more respectful of Roosevelt's New Deal programs.

This is not to say that the Supreme Court has the last word on matters of public importance in the United States. Justice Robert Jackson once declared that "We are not final because we are infallible . . . we are infallible because we are final." But surely the justice exaggerated. On more than one occasion the nation has chosen to amend the Constitution rather than be ruled by particular Supreme Court decisions. In fact, the Court's first significant constitutional decision, *Chisholm v. Georgia* (1793), in which it held that the citizens of one state could sue another state, so dismayed the nation that Congress promptly proposed the Eleventh Amendment, which barred such suits; it was ratified in 1798. Similarly, the Fourteenth Amendment overruled the Court's infamous holding in the *Dred Scott* case that blacks were incapable of being U.S. citizens, and the Sixteenth Amendment overturned the Court's conclusion in *Pollock v. Farmers' Loan & Trust Company* (1895) that the federal income tax was unconstitutional. In the face of sustained and widespread dissatisfaction with its decisions, the Supreme Court has proved to be not so final as Justice Jackson's declaration suggests.

Article III of the Constitution specifies that the Supreme Court and such other, lower federal courts as Congress shall create, may hear a variety of cases and controversies. Congress, though, has power to prescribe the manner in which cases may reach the Supreme Court, and it has currently granted the Court a wide measure of discretion in deciding itself what cases to hear. The Supreme Court is required by law to hear only a small number of cases and accepts only a small fraction of the approximately 7,000 cases annually presented for its review. Normally the Court chooses to hear only those cases that present some issue of national importance or that involve significant legal issues on which lower courts have been divided in their results.

Parties wishing the Court to review the outcome of their case apply for a writ of certiorari. In the parlance of Supreme Court practice, when the Court agrees to hear a case, it grants the writ. The Court is technically in session continuously, but it accomplishes its most public work from the beginning of the term on the first Monday in October until the end of June, by which it has generally announced decisions in cases from that term. After the Court accepts a case for review, lawyers representing the various parties involved may be permitted to present an oral argument to the Court. Since the Court considers only the legal issues raised by a previous trial, it hears no new witnesses and its deliberations do not involve a jury. Instead, lawyers in a particular case appear before the justices and present arguments in support of their clients while also responding to questions that individual justices may ask. These sessions of the Court begin with the traditional call to order announced by the marshal of the Court:

> The Honorable, the Chief Justice and the Associate Justices of the Supreme Court of the United States. Oyez! Oyez! Oyez! All persons having business before the Honorable, the Supreme Court of the United States, are admonished to draw near and give their attention, for the Court is now sitting. God save the United States and this Honorable Court!

After the justices hear oral arguments in a case, they subsequently meet privately in conference to discuss and vote on the outcome of particular cases. Occasionally the justices will agree on the outcome and will provide a joint explanation of their reasoning in the form of a per curiam opinion. More commonly, the justices disagree among themselves about the resolution. When a majority of the justices agree on a particular result, one justice will be assigned to prepare a majority opinion explaining the legal basis for the majority's decision. The chief justice makes this assignment when he is in the majority; otherwise, the senior justice in the majority decides who will write the Court's opinion. Justices who agree with the result in a case but disagree with some or all of the reasoning expressed in the majority opinion may write a "concurring" opinion. Justices on the losing side of a case may express their views in a dissenting opinion.

No television cameras intrude upon the Court's public sessions. The opinions written by the justices and sometimes partially read when the Court announces a decision are the key vehicles through which it communicates with the American people. It is impossible to tell the story of the Court, or of its members, without considering these opinions, and the biographical essays that follow will discuss some of the more important opinions decided over the course of the Court's history. But the converse is also true. It is impossible to tell the story of the Court without telling the stories of its members, for they each bring their own history to the work of judging and are inexorably influenced by these histories.

JAMES WILSON (1742–1798)

Associate Justice, 1790–1798

Appointed by President George Washington

JAMES WILSON
(United States Supreme Court)

The first justice sworn to serve on the U.S. Supreme Court rose from modest circumstances in Scotland, the country of his birth, to become one of the founding generation's most influential figures. James Wilson accumulated, in rapid succession, wealth, political power, and, finally, a seat on the new nation's highest court. But financial reversals ultimately tempered his political and judicial successes, leaving the justice in his final years a desperate specter of the man he had once been and an unfinished portrait of what he had set out to paint of himself. He left a larger mark on his country than he did on the Court itself, and he is less to be remembered for his career as a justice of the Supreme Court than as one of the chief architects of the nation over whose legal disputes the Court would preside.

James Wilson was born on September 14, 1742, on a farm in Fifeshire, Scotland, to James Wilson and Alison Lansdale Wilson, devout Scottish Calvinists of meager means. His parents aspired for him to become a clergyman. To this end they sent him to a local parish school and, when he was 14 years of age, to the University of St. Andrews, which he attended with the help of a scholarship. In his fifth year at the university, he transferred to divinity school. But when his father died shortly thereafter, Wilson abandoned both his university studies and his plans for entering the ministry. He found work as a tutor and studied briefly to become an accountant, but he finally determined to cast his future with the New World. Thus, in 1765 he arrived in Pennsylvania, where he had relatives, and found work as a tutor at the College of Philadelphia, later to become the University of Pennsylvania.

Though consistent in some ways with Wilson's learned temperament, the life of an educator did not ultimately satisfy his copious ambitions. He therefore turned to a legal career by reading law under John Dickinson, an eminent colonial lawyer who had himself studied at the London Inns of Court. Within a short time Wilson established his own legal practice in the town of Reading, Pennsylvania. After a few years he transported his growing practice to Carlisle and eventually to Philadelphia in 1778. During this period, in 1771 Wilson married Rachel Bird, whose father had built the Hay Creek ironworks. Rachel gave birth to six children before her death 15 years later.

Wilson's mind, drawn to the study and practice of law, also gravitated to political matters. By 1768 he had written what would become one of the leading pamphlets of the pre-Revolutionary years. In *Considerations on the Nature and Extent of the Legislative Authority of the British Parliament,* Wilson argued that Parliament lacked any power to govern the colonies. For a rising lawyer, his pamphlet's sentiments were radical and calculated to offend at least some of the interests that might further his legal career. Perhaps for this reason, Wilson delayed publication of the pamphlet until 1774, when its temper was far more consistent with the rapidly developing spirit of the times. On the eve of the Revolution, Wilson served as a delegate from Carlisle to the Pennsylvania provincial convention, and by 1775 he had been named a delegate from Pennsylvania to the Second Continental Congress. Wilson and other Pennsylvania delegates at first were cool to the idea of separation from Britain, but eventually Wilson, at least, sided with the revolutionaries and signed the Declaration of Independence.

The decade that saw Wilson's expanding law practice and his entrance into the political field also found him launching into the speculative business ventures that would dominate the rest of his life and ultimately contribute to his financial ruin. Although he dabbled in a variety of ventures, he gravitated most to land speculation and became quite wealthy in short order. By 1778 he had moved to Philadelphia, where even more fertile business and law practice connections presented themselves. Though his principles made him a democrat of the first order, his legal and business associations branded him the friend of wealth and privilege. In Philadelphia he defended Quaker Tories from patriotic challenges and the Bank of North America against attempts to revoke its charter. In the latter defense, Wilson penned another influential pamphlet, titled *Considerations on the Bank of North America,* which championed the power of the Continental Congress to charter the Bank.

Through his defense of the Bank of North America, Wilson proved himself a vigorous advocate of a strong national authority. This position cast him at the forefront of the movement that would eventually replace the Articles of Confederation with the Constitution of the United States. Wilson served as a delegate to the 1787 Constitutional Convention, and among its august body he played a principal role, overshadowed only by James Madison in the importance of his contribution to the Constitution's framing. Wilson championed the principle of separation of powers, a political doctrine that would undergird crucial aspects of the new nation's formation. He was also a vigorous advocate of democratic principles such as the popular election of legislative representatives and of the president as well. On these points, at least, his political vision outstripped the times, since the Constitution proposed by the 1787 convention shielded both the Senate and the presidency from popular elections. Not until the 20th century was popular election of senators achieved, through ratification of the Seventeenth Amendment to the Constitution in 1913.

In 1789, after leading the drive to ratify the Constitution in Pennsylvania, Wilson proposed himself to President George Washington to become the first chief justice of the U.S. Supreme Court. Washington, though, named John Jay to this post instead and nominated Wilson to occupy one of the positions on the Court as associate justice. Wilson was confirmed to this position and took the oath of office in October 1789. His tenure on the Court was unremarkable, partly because the Court's role in the new national scheme was itself as yet unremarkable, and partly because his financial affairs became ever more precarious during the decade he served on the Court, consuming attention that he might otherwise have focused on his work as a justice. In spite of Wilson's expressed desire to serve as chief justice of the Court, President Washington passed over him for this position again in 1795 and 1796.

The official life of a Supreme Court justice finds its record chiefly in judicial opinions crafted by that justice. It is therefore not surprising that few opinions mark James Wilson's relatively undistinguished tenure. A single modern Supreme Court opinion sometimes spans more than 100 printed pages; Justice Wilson's entire corpus of opinions consumes only a fraction of that, barely 20 pages of printed text. His concurring opinion in *Chisholm v. Georgia* (1793) represents perhaps his most significant judicial craftsmanship. When a citizen of South Carolina brought suit against the state of Georgia for a debt, the resulting case presented the Court with the controversial issue of whether a state could be sued in federal court by the citizens of another state. For ardent advocates of state sovereignty, the suit represented an attack on that sovereignty. But for a majority of the justices on the Supreme Court, including Wilson, the possibility of suits by citizens of one state against another state in federal court was inherent in the idea of a national government. Wilson argued in his concurring opinion that Georgia was not a sovereign state but an element of the larger Union forged by the Constitution of the United States of America. As such, it was amenable to claims brought by other members of the Union, including claims from the citizens of other states in the Union. For Georgia to exempt itself from the judicial processes of the Union into which it had been merged by the sovereign act of its people was inconceivable. Wilson's view of the matter, though consistent with those of every other justice save James Iredell, proved not so consistent with the views of most Americans. Opponents of the result were many, and they effectively mustered the political will necessary to amend the Constitution to override the result in *Chisholm*. The Eleventh Amendment to the Constitution, ratified in 1798, repudiated *Chisholm* and converted Wilson's most careful writing into a minor tributary of historical curiosity.

In 1786 Wilson's wife Rachel died. He married again in 1793, this time to 19-year-old Hannah Gray, who was 32 years his junior. She would accompany him for the remaining years of his life, which proved to be numbered. By 1797 Wilson's business and real estate speculations had begun to collapse into judgments against him, forcing the justice to flee from creditors even as his work as a justice frequently required him to ride circuit, deciding mostly trivial cases. He could not elude all his creditors, however, and he was eventually arrested in Burlington, New Jersey, and jailed until his son was able to post bail. Wilson then escaped to Edenton, North Carolina, but he was discovered there and arrested again for failure to pay a $197,000 debt. His son rescued him again but could not rescue his health, on which jail and financial calamity had taken their toll. In July 1798, while lodged at an inn in Edenton, Wilson contracted malaria. The next month he suffered a stroke, and he died on August 21, 1798. His family could not afford to move the body back to Philadelphia and accepted the assistance of Justice James Iredell in having Wilson buried in North Carolina. His remains would stay there until history softened its verdict on the measure of his career and honored him in 1906 with a burial at Christ Church in Philadelphia.

We are left to wonder what impact Justice James Wilson would have made on a court whose influence was as capacious as his ambitions, or what judicial work he might have accomplished had his mind not been consumed with the management of collapsing financial fortunes. Wilson suffered the ignominy of riding circuit to tend to relatively minor judicial matters, all the while attempting to dodge the creditors who pursued him relentlessly. The Court on which he served was still in its infancy and would not reach its mature strength until after Wilson's inauspicious service had ended. Though he championed the idea of a strong national government with ancillary, strong federal courts, it would remain for Chief Justice John Marshall to fasten this idea on the American political tradition.

FURTHER READING

Hall, Mark David. *The Political and Legal Philosophy of James Wilson 1742–1798.* Columbia: University of Missouri Press, 1997.

———. "James Wilson: Democratic Theorist and Supreme Court Justice." In *Seriatim: The Supreme Court Before John Marshall.* Edited by Scott Douglas Gerber. New York: New York University Press, 1998.

Pascal, Jean M. *Political Ideas of James Wilson, 1742–1798.* New York: Garland Publishing, Inc., 1991.

Smith, Page. *James Wilson, Founding Father, 1741–1798.* Chapel Hill, N.C.: University of North Carolina Press for the Institute of Early American History and Culture, 1956.

Wilson, James. *The Works of James Wilson, Associate Justice of the Supreme Court of the United States . . . Being His Public Discourses Upon Jurisprudence and the Political Science, including Lectures as Professor of Law, 1790–2.* Edited by James DeWitt Andrews. Chicago: Callaghan and Company, 1896.

JOHN JAY (1745–1829)

Chief Justice, 1789–1795

Appointed by President George Washington

JOHN JAY
(Engraving, Library of Congress)

The first chief justice of the U.S. Supreme Court brought to his role immense stature as an American statesman and a wealth of political experience. His actual experience as a judge, though, was more limited. John Jay presided over an infant Court at a time when its prestige and authority were only dim foreshadowings of what they would eventually become. His one attempt to champion the sovereignty of the nation over that of the states suffered swift and emphatic rebuke at the hands of the American people. Not surprisingly, therefore, Jay soon abandoned his service on the Court for the more politically vigorous office of New York governor.

—ʍ—

John Jay was born in New York City on December 12, 1745, the eighth child of Peter Jay and Mary Van Cortlandt. His father had retired wealthy at the age of 40 from the family mercantile business; his mother was a member of an influential Dutch family in New York. To the privileges of his birth, Jay's parents added the privileges of a superior education, having him instructed first by a private teacher and then later securing his entrance into King's College, which would later become Columbia University. After his graduation in 1764, he worked for two years in the office of the noted New York lawyer Benjamin Kissam. When a strike by New York lawyers in response to the Stamp Act crisis deprived him of this work for a time, he supplemented his education by obtaining a master of arts from King's College in 1767. He then returned to serve as Kissam's chief clerk until he was admitted to the New York bar in 1768 and established his own practice. For the next seven years he built a thriving practice, won his first public office as a commissioner appointed to resolve a boundary dispute between New York and New Jersey in 1769, and in 1774 married Sarah Van Brugh Livingston, whose father would subsequently become governor of New Jersey.

The revolutionary fervor that ultimately transformed the colonies into a nation did not immediately grip John Jay. He possessed the conservative respect for stability characteristic of a wealthy mercantile family. But the tide of events ultimately captured him, first as a public servant and eventually as an advocate of independence. He served as a delegate to the First and Second Continental Congresses, though he was absent from the signing of the Declaration of Independence because of his service as a delegate to the New York Provincial Congress, where he played an important role in the drafting of the New York state constitution. By 1777 Jay had been appointed chief justice of the New York Supreme Court, a position he held until he was elected president of the Continental Congress in 1778. Within a year he traded this position for an appointment as minister to Spain, in which capacity he sought to secure Spanish support for the cause of independence. From this post he traveled to France in 1782 to assist in the negotiations with Great Britain for the Treaty of Paris (signed in September 1783), which ended the war for independence on favorable terms to the colonies. After he returned from this successful mission, in 1784 Congress appointed him secretary of foreign affairs, a position he occupied for the next five years.

Jay's diplomatic experience fostered in him a pessimistic regard for the future of the unruly confederation of states created in the wake of the American Revolution. Increasingly, he saw the need for a strong national government to replace the fractious state sovereignties, with legislative, executive, and judicial powers broad enough to allow the nation to take its place among the community of nations with which Jay was now on familiar terms. Once the Constitutional Convention had produced a draft Constitution to achieve these aims, Jay became an ardent supporter of the document's ratification. Together with James Madison and Alexander Hamilton, Jay contributed essays to the influential *Federalist Papers,* which urged ratification, even though a prolonged illness limited his contribution to only five papers (Nos. 2–5 and 64). In addition to this work, Jay authored an influential pamphlet in favor of ratification, titled "Address to the People of the State of New York," which highlighted the weaknesses of the Articles of Confederation and the strengths of the proposed Constitution.

On September 24, 1789, George Washington, the first president of the United States, nominated John Jay to be the first chief justice of the republic's Supreme Court. In the days following Washington's election as chief executive, Jay had proved to be an invaluable adviser and an ally trusted by the president to bring their shared vision to the new nation's highest judicial post. Washington conveyed Jay's commission with a letter that was full both of the formality of a solemn moment in the country's history and of a friend's high regard.

> In nominating you for the important station which you now fill, I not only acted in conformity to my best judgment, but I trust I did a grateful thing to the good citizens of these

> United States, and I have a full confidence that the love which you bear to our country, and a desire to promote the general happiness, will not suffer you to hesitate a moment to bring into action the talents, knowledge and integrity which are so necessary to be exercised at the head of that department which must be considered the keystone of our political fabric.

Jay was quickly confirmed, and on February 2, 1790, he called the inaugural session of the Supreme Court to order with a quorum of four justices. The Court held its first session in the Royal Exchange Building in New York City, but Washington's estimation of the Court's role as a "keystone" of the new republic did not seem immediately accurate. The justices' initial session lasted nine days before they adjourned for lack of legal business, and the years immediately following saw little improvement in the Court's stature. By the terms of the Judiciary Act of 1789, the justices of the Supreme Court were given responsibility not only for serving as members of that Court but also for riding circuit to serve with various district judges in circuit courts scattered across the new nation. The latter, especially, was onerous duty that would endure for nearly 100 years; justices then and later complained bitterly about the circuit riding.

For someone who had been among the chief midwives of the nation's birth, Jay found his new post an exercise in frustration. The power that the Court would eventually wield lay in its future. For the time, at least, the Court was no place for a statesman of Jay's caliber—that is, he was not able to make it such a place. His Court's most significant decision only confirmed its relative weakness within the national scheme. *Chisholm v. Georgia* (1793) presented Jay and his associate justices with their first significant constitutional issue: Does the Constitution prevent a state from being sued by the citizen of another state in federal court? The suit arose out of a claim against the state of Georgia by a citizen of South Carolina, who was serving as the executor of the estate of a South Carolina merchant, for money owed on a contract with Georgia to provide cloth and clothing to the state; the contract had been entered into during the Revolutionary War. Georgia refused to appear to defend the suit, claiming that it was a sovereign state and immune to suit in federal court. But Jay's court held that Georgia did not possess the sovereignty it imagined and was thus amenable to suit. Three other justices joined with Chief Justice Jay in concluding that the Constitution authorized such suits. Only Justice James Iredell dissented from this ruling.

In the Court's early years, each justice explained the reasons for his decision in a separate opinion. Jay's *Chisholm* opinion rejected Georgia's claim of sovereignty. It was the *people* of the United States who were sovereign, and these people had ratified the Constitution of the United States. According to Jay, when the preamble to this document declared that "We the people of the United States do ordain and establish this constitution," it testified that the people of the United States were "acting as sovereigns of the whole country; and in the language of sovereignty, establishing a constitution by which it was their will, that the state governments should be bound, and to which the state constitutions should be made to conform." The Constitution, by Jay's reading, permitted suits by the citizen of one state against another state, because Article III, Section 2 extended federal judicial power to cases between "a State and Citizens of another State."

The American public, however, viewed the result in *Chisholm v. Georgia* with alarm. Opponents of the decision included both those of an antifederalist temper who feared consolidation of the states into a single, undifferentiated national unity and those who predicted that the decision would foster ruinous litigation against the states. Congress soon proposed and the states ratified the Eleventh Amendment to the Constitution, which declared that federal judicial power did not extend to suits against a state by a citizen of another state or another country.

The same year that Jay's court decided *Chisholm v. Georgia*, it also considered another important constitutional issue. In summer 1793

President George Washington sought the Court's advice concerning the obligations imposed on the United States by the treaty of 1778 between France and the United States. This was not the first occasion in which Washington had solicited and the Court had provided informal legal advice. In 1790 the president had sought an opinion from the Court as to whether the federal law requiring the justices to ride circuit was unconstitutional. Jay and certain other justices responded that they thought the requirement was indeed unconstitutional, though Washington did not follow their advice by seeking to abolish the practice. In 1793, however, when Washington, through Secretary of State Thomas Jefferson, returned for additional advice, the Court was more reluctant to provide it. This time Jay and his fellow justices responded by letter that they deemed it unsuitable for them to render advice in a context not connected to an actual case before them, since such a practice would threaten the principle of separation of powers embodied in the Constitution.

By 1794 Jay's formidable political talents had begun to chafe within the narrow opportunities for their use presented by his role as chief justice. While still occupying this position, Jay accepted responsibility for traveling to England as an envoy to negotiate the resolution of lingering hostilities between England and the United States. This mission produced the 1794 Treaty of Amity, also known informally as Jay's Treaty. Upon his return, Jay received news of his nomination for governor of the state of New York. He had been similarly nominated for this position two years earlier in 1792, and though he did not campaign from his perch on the nation's highest court, he had nevertheless only narrowly lost the election. This time, however, he was elected, and he promptly resigned from his post on the Supreme Court on June 29, 1795.

Jay served for six years as New York's governor, winning reelection after his first three-year term. When President John Adams nominated him to fill the position on the Supreme Court vacated by Chief Justice Oliver Ellsworth in 1800, the Senate confirmed the nomination, but Jay refused to accept it. He explained his decision to Adams in the following terms:

> I left the bench perfectly convinced that under a system so defective it would not obtain the energy, weight, and dignity which was essential to its affording due support to the national government; nor acquire the public confidence and respect which, as the last resort of the justice of the nation, it should possess. Hence I am induced to doubt both the propriety and the expediency of my returning to the bench under the present system.

Jay left his post as governor and retired to his estate in Westchester County, New York, in 1801. This retirement would last for almost 30 years, a period which, though ultimately filled with productive activity, would begin with loss, through the death of his wife in 1802. He spent his remaining years pursuing agricultural interests and being active in the affairs of the Episcopal Church. He aided in the formation of the American Bible Society, serving as its president in 1821. Death closed the long years of his retirement on May 17, 1829, in Bedford, New York.

—~—

John Jay's brief tenure as chief justice of the Supreme Court failed to secure the prestige the Court would later own. Whether he lacked the qualities of judicial statesmanship necessary for such a task or whether the times failed to provide him sufficient opportunity, his Court would eventually lie beneath the constitutional shadow cast by Chief Justice John Marshall. Though Jay secured more of a place in the country's history through his service in other political roles, even in these arenas he never quite stepped to the center of the stage that would be occupied by contemporaries such as Madison and Jefferson. He did not attend the Constitutional Convention, and his initial political successes never yielded him the position of president of the United States. Had he accepted President John Adams's invitation to return to the position of chief justice in 1800, he would perhaps have presided over a Court of increasing stature. His refusal of this appointment, though, resulted in the nomination of John Marshall to this post; and Marshall, by convergence of ability and opportunity, would earn the reputation for judicial greatness that has been withheld from Jay.

FURTHER READING

Casto, William. *The Supreme Court in the Early Republic: The Chief Justiceships of John Jay and Oliver Ellsworth.* Columbia: University of South Carolina Press, 1995.

Jay, John. *The Correspondence and Public Papers of John Jay, 1763–1826.* Edited by Henry P. Johnston. New York: Da Capo Press, 1971.

Johnson, Herbert Alan. *John Jay. Colonial Lawyer.* New York: Garland, 1989.

———. *John Jay, the Nation, and the Court.* Boston: Boston University Press, 1967.

Pellew, George. *John Jay.* Boston: Bobbs-Merrill Company, 1898; Philadelphia: Chelsea House Publishers, 1997.

Smith, Donald L. *John Jay: Founder of a State and Nation.* New York: Teachers College Press, Columbia University, 1968.

William Cushing (1732–1810)

Associate Justice, 1790–1810

Appointed by President George Washington

William Cushing
(United States Supreme Court)

William Cushing, one of President George Washington's initial appointments to the newly created Supreme Court, arrived with more judicial experience than any of the other justices. He also remained on the Court longer than any of Washington's other appointments to the new Court, serving as an associate justice through the first decade of the 19th century. Steady service, rather than intellectual brilliance or profound influence, characterized a judicial career than began before the Revolutionary War and persevered through the birth and infancy of a new nation.

—\m—

If it were possible to imagine a person born to be a judge, then one might imagine William Cushing to be such a person. He was born on March 11, 1732, in Scituate, Massachusetts, into a family of judges: Both his father and grandfather served on the Massachusetts superior court. Cushing himself would one day occupy a post on this court as a result of his father's political influence. The elder Cushing saw to it that the judicial seat from which he eventually retired went to his son. William Cushing's heritage on his mother's side, though not dominated by judges, could nevertheless be traced to the Puritan preacher John Cotton, one of the most influential citizens of the early decades of the Massachusetts Bay Colony.

Cushing benefited from the educational privileges customary for children of influential Massachusetts families. From 1747 to 1751 he attended Harvard College, where he received the classical education thought appropriate for colonial gentlemen. After teaching grammar school for a year in Roxbury, Massachusetts, he returned to Harvard to study theology. But the traditional family ties to law soon tugged him away from this vocational path and into an apprenticeship with Boston lawyer Jeremiah Gridley that began in December 1754 and ended with Cushing's admission to the bar in 1757.

Cushing's career as a lawyer was lackluster. He began practicing in his hometown of Scituate, but when his practice there did not quickly blossom into prosperity, he moved to Pownalborough, an area that would eventually become Maine. This migration did little to improve Cushing's circumstances. He had an inability for holding onto clients that generally spells the ruin of a legal practice, and his career in law might have met a premature end had he not been appointed as a probate judge. This appointment did not secure him material success, but it nevertheless set him on the path that he would follow for the remainder of his days. When his father prepared to retire from the Massachusetts Superior Court of Judicature, the elder Cushing petitioned Lieutenant Governor Thomas Hutchinson to assign the vacancy to his son. Though Hutchinson seems not to have immediately preferred William Cushing for this post, he ultimately assigned it to Cushing in 1772, and thus perpetuated what now appeared to be a family dynasty of Massachusetts judges.

The years prior to the Revolutionary War posed acute challenges for those entrusted with colonial posts. Cushing, especially, lacked the financial wherewithal to offend his political patrons with impunity and so had to tread carefully to survive passage through the Scylla of British colonial authority and the Charybdis of rising revolutionary fervor. For this delicate maneuver, however, Cushing showed himself to be quite able. He had a lifelong facility for not saying much, and it served him well in the tumultuous years leading up to the American Revolution.

Eventually, though, even silence failed to provide a secure harbor. Scarcely a year after Cushing's appointment to the Massachusetts bench, Lieutenant Governor Hutchinson insisted that judges, whose salaries had previously been paid by the legislative assembly, be paid instead by the Crown. The Massachusetts legislative assembly responded by threatening to impeach any judge who accepted the Crown's stipend or failed to make a public declaration of willingness to be paid by the assembly. When Chief Justice Peter Oliver declared in favor of receiving payment from the Crown, the assembly promptly launched impeachment proceedings against him and threatened the same against Cushing if he failed to accept the assembly's salary. Forced to choose sides, Cushing elected to receive payment from the assembly, thus casting his lot with the growing revolutionary spirit. Cushing's decision to side with the Massachusetts assembly temporarily alienated him from Hutchinson and other colonial authorities, who refused to seat him on the Governor's Council, but it eventually secured his place in the postcolonial commonwealth of Massachusetts as an associate justice of the Superior Court.

In 1774 Cushing married Hannah Phillips, who became his companion on his rides through the circuit of the court. Within three years Cushing was elevated to chief justice of the Massachusetts Superior Court, a position he occupied for the next 12 years. Cushing filled the seat vacated by John Adams, who had been named to the Superior Court in 1775 but had not actually served, due to his work in the Continental Congress and a variety of other duties. In 1777, though, Adams was appointed commissioner to France. He therefore formally resigned from the Massachusetts Superior Court. As chief justice of Massachusetts's highest court, Cushing attended the Massachusetts Constitutional Convention in 1779 along with the other justices of that court. He seems to have played no significant role in the proceedings, though after the convention was over, he vigorously championed the new Massachusetts constitution on his circuit travels. The constitution's ultimate ratification resulted in his court earning a new name—the Supreme Judicial Court—but Cushing remained its chief justice.

During William Cushing's final decade of service as a state court judge, he found himself close to the center of a turmoil that would hasten the move to fashion a national constitution capable of establishing justice and ensuring "domestic Tranquillity." Severe economic depression during the 1780s ultimately sparked a riot among the farmers of western Massachusetts. Spanning six months at the end of 1786 and the beginning of 1787, it was named Shays's Rebellion for its leader, Daniel Shays. Many Massachusetts farmers, burdened with debt and lacking the hard currency necessary to lift it, resorted to violence after their initial petitions for paper currency, tax relief, and judicial reform went unheeded. Among their many grievances was a complaint against Cushing's court. The justices often traveled singly on circuit and not in the pairs necessary to constitute a quorum to determine cases. Under these circumstances, debt collection cases could not be heard. This delay in the resolution of cases did not, however, benefit the debtors, many of whom were farmers, since interest continued to accrue on the debt. When a sufficient number of justices finally arrived to hold court, debtors found themselves faced with greater debts than a more speedy resolution of their cases would have produced. When petition ripened accordingly into violence, the farmers led by Daniel Shays seized courthouses and prevented the operation of courts for a time. But the rebellion ultimately collapsed, and Cushing's court presided over treason trials against the insurgents. Cushing himself sentenced many of the defendants to hang, though John Hancock, the newly elected governor of Massachusetts, ultimately pardoned most of these.

In 1788 Cushing served as vice president of the Massachusetts ratifying convention, presiding over much of the convention while its president, John Hancock, suffered from illness. Thereafter, upon the Constitution's ratification and the election of George Washington as president, Cushing was nominated by Washington on September 24, 1789, to fill one of the first positions on the new nation's highest court. Confirmed by the Senate two days later, William Cushing took the oath of office on February 2, 1790, and joined Chief Justice John Jay, and associate justices James Wilson and John Blair in the Supreme Court's first session that day.

Cushing would occupy a seat on the Supreme Court for the next 21 years, and though his tenure would surpass those of all the justices with whom he initially served, his presence made no significant impact on the Court. He wrote 19 opinions while on the Court and these, like the man himself, were characterized by brevity and terseness. Like the other early justices of the Supreme Court, Cushing may have found its first years tedious through the onerous work of circuit riding and the relative insignificance of its work. He joined with a majority of the Court in the vastly unpopular decision of *Chisholm v. Georgia* (1793) and witnessed the country's quick rebuke of that decision through enactment of the 11th Amendment to the Constitution. Frustrated, perhaps, by the limitations of his seat on the Court, Cushing decided to run for governor of Massachusetts in 1794, while still on the Court. He lost by an embarrassingly wide margin to Samuel Adams. John Jay's subsequent election as governor of New York in 1795 offered Cushing the possibility of a consolation for his political defeat. After Jay's resignation, President Washington first nominated John Rutledge for the post of chief justice, but the

Senate refused to confirm him. Consequently, on January 26, 1796, Washington nominated Cushing for the position. Although Cushing attended one presidential dinner party as chief justice, he shortly declined the nomination, pleading financial circumstances as reason not to accept the added responsibilities of chief justice. He served out his days as an associate justice, bound to the bench even in old age because the decades of judicial service had left him with no private wealth on which to retire. Toward the end, he considered resignation from the Court and its arduous circuit-riding responsibilities, but he wavered in reaching a decision until his death made it for him. He died on September 13, 1810, in Scituate, Massachusetts, the town where he had been born.

Justice William Cushing provided a link between the administration of law under the British crown and under the independent commonwealths created by the American Revolution. In this respect his career testifies to the rule of law's necessity and durability even in the face of revolutionary change. Cushing also served as a sturdy but unspectacular bridge between the infant Supreme Court under the leadership of Chief Justice John Jay and the Court that came of age under the tutelage of Chief Justice John Marshall. He witnessed the Court's rebuke at the hands of the nation after the decision in *Chisholm v. Georgia* (1793), but also its ascendancy under the leadership of Chief Justice Marshall in cases such as *Marbury v. Madison* (1803), which established the Court's power to review the constitutionality of actions taken by the other branches of government.

Further Reading

Cushing, John D. "The Cushing Court and the Abolition of Slavery in Massachusetts." *American Journal of Legal History* 5 (1961): 118–144.

Gerber, Scott Douglas. "Deconstructing William Cushing." In *Seriatim: The Supreme Court Before John Marshall.* Edited by Scott Douglas Gerber. New York: New York University Press, 1998.

Johnson, Herbert Alan. "William Cushing." In *The Justices of the United States Supreme Court 1789–1969: Their Lives and Major Opinions,* vol. 1. Edited by Leon Friedman and Fred L. Israel. New York: R. R. Bowker Co., 1969.

O'Brien, F. William. "Justice William Cushing and the Treaty Making Power." *Vanderbilt Law Review* 10 (1957): 351–367.

Rugg, Arthur P. "William Cushing." *Yale Law Journal* 30 (1920): 120–144.

JOHN BLAIR, JR. (1732–1800)

Associate Justice, 1790–1795

Appointed by President George Washington

JOHN BLAIR, JR.
(United States Supreme Court)

A Virginian born to wealth and privilege, John Blair, Jr., brought extensive political and judicial experience to his appointment as one of the Supreme Court's first associate justices. Following in his father's political footsteps, Blair served in a variety of political positions for the commonwealth of Virginia and an even greater variety of judicial posts, first under the commonwealth and then for the state of Virginia. His tenure as an associate justice of the U.S. Supreme Court culminated a distinguished career as a judge, although ill health forced him to resign prematurely from this final position.

John Blair, Jr., was born in Wilmington, Virginia, in 1732, the son of John Blair, Sr., and Mary Monro Blair. The senior Blair was an important Virginia statesman, having served in the House of Burgesses, on the Governor's Council, and as acting governor of Virginia in 1758 and 1768. Blair's family also possessed significant wealth, and it enabled the junior Blair to procure an education at the College of William and Mary, which had been founded by Blair's great uncle. John Blair, Jr., graduated with honors in 1754. Thereafter, he traveled to England, where he studied law in the Middle Temple of the Inns of Court and was called to the bar in 1757. During his stay, he met and married Jean Blair in Edinburgh, Scotland, on December 26, 1756.

Upon his return to Virginia, Blair began a successful law practice. In 1765 his election as the delegate of the College of William and Mary to Virginia's House of Burgesses inaugurated his political career. He demonstrated conservative sensibilities when, for example, he opposed Patrick Henry's fiery denunciations of the Stamp Act, passed by Parliament the year Blair took his seat in the House of Burgesses. Blair resigned his legislative seat in 1771 to assume the position of clerk of the Governor's Council, a post his father had held 30 years earlier.

As events cascaded toward revolution, Blair increasingly favored independence. In 1769 he signed a nonimportation agreement in protest when the House of Burgesses was dissolved. In 1776 he attended the Virginia constitutional convention, which framed a new form of government for the independent commonwealth, and he served on the committee charged with drafting a constitution and declaration of rights. When the new constitution was ratified, Blair was elected a member of the Governor's Council.

By 1777, though, Blair had resigned this office after the Virginia legislature chose him to sit on the General Court of Virginia, the first of several judicial posts he would ultimately hold. Within two years he assumed the position of chief justice of this court, and in 1780 he was named one of three chancellors to Virginia's High Court of Chancery. Blair's political and judicial experience resulted in his appointment as a Virginia delegate to the 1787 Constitutional Convention in Philadelphia. He joined an illustrious company of Virginians—George Washington, Edmund Randolph, James Madison, George Mason, and George Wythe—and, though he did not participate actively in the debates of the Convention, he signed the final document on behalf of Virginia, together with George Washington and James Madison.

Blair returned home from Philadelphia to continue his judicial duties and was shortly appointed by the Virginia legislature to take a seat on the new Virginia Supreme Court of Appeals. But his fellow Virginian, George Washington—now president of the United States—soon turned to Blair as his choice to fill one of the first seats on the U.S. Supreme Court. On September 24, 1789, Washington named John Jay as chief justice, and John Blair, Jr., James Wilson, William Cushing, John Rutledge, and Robert H. Harrison to form the first Supreme Court. Blair, along with Jay, Wilson, Cushing, and Rutledge, accepted this commission. Only Harrison declined it; he was replaced by James Iredell. Blair's letter to President Washington accepting the position hinted at the circumstances that would ultimately cause him to resign his most important judicial post:

> When I considered the great importance, as well as the arduous nature of the duties, I could not but entertain some fears, that I might find them well adapted neither to my domestic habits, my bodily constitution, nor my mental capacity; in every other respect, the office promises me a very desirable situation, for which I know not how sufficiently to declare my gratitude.
>
> I have determined to make an experiment, whether I may be able to perform the requisite services, with some degree of satisfaction, in respect both to the Public and my self; . . .

Notwithstanding his reservations, Blair accepted the commission as an associate justice of the Supreme Court.

Few significant cases arrived at the Court during its early years. Of these, *Chisholm v. Georgia* (1793) was the most important. This case, involving a claim against Georgia by a citizen of another state, presented the Court with significant issues about the nature and structure of the new nation. Blair joined a majority of the Court in holding that the Constitution did not preclude federal courts from entertaining suits by citizens of one state against another state. Only Justice James Iredell dissented from this holding. Blair's opinion in the case anchored itself firmly to the text of the Constitution rather than to abstract discussions concerning the relative sovereignties of state and federal governments or to comparisons between the U.S. Constitution and various Europeans constitutions. Article II, Section 2 tendered jurisdiction over cases "between a State and Citizens of another State" to federal court. Although the state of Georgia argued that this clause applied only to suits in which a state was a plaintiff in a case against the citizen of another state, Blair saw no constitutional grounds for failing to apply the clause to situations in which a state was a defendant in a case brought by the citizen of another state. As to the suggestion that this construction of the Constitution undermine the sovereignty of states, Blair disagreed: "[W]hen a state, by adopting the constitution, has agreed to be amendable to the judicial power of the United States, she has, in that respect, given up her right of sovereignty."

The nation promptly overrode the Supreme Court's decision in *Chisholm v. Georgia* by ratifying the Eleventh Amendment to the Constitution. This repudiation of the Court's authority, along with the onerous circuit-riding duties required of all the justices, ultimately prompted Chief Justice Jay to resign from the Court in 1795 after being elected governor of New York. Associate Justice James Rutledge had already resigned in favor of a judicial commission in his home state of South Carolina. Justice Blair, however, seems not to have suffered from disillusionment concerning the prestige of his appointment. In his case, though, the poor health and domestic problems he had cited to President Washington in his initial, hesitant acceptance of the associate justice position eventually impaired his ability to continue the responsibilities of the post. By letter to President Washington dated October 25, 1795, Blair informed the chief executive that he was not able to remain in his position. "A strange disorder of my head," he wrote, had caused him to neglect the responsibilities of his office. "I knew the advantage of my situation; I had a just sense of the high obligation confer'd upon me thro your goodness, & perhaps I should say, too partial opinion of my merit; & I confess, it was with reluctance that I though of quiting such a station, flattering my self that by some happy turn I might be restored to a capacity of performing it's duties." Blair retired to his home in Williamsburg, where he died on August 31, 1800.

Some of the Justices appointed by President Washington to the nation's first Supreme Court eventually regretted their decision to accept a seat on the Court. The Court's early prestige was a bare shadow of what it would later become, and men such as John Jay and John Rutledge soon found their gaze wandering to more influential posts. Justice John Blair, Jr., though, seems not to have suffered from this dissatisfaction. His ambitions and abilities were well matched with a seat on the Court as an associate justice, and he might have served a greater tenure had not illness forced him to resign his responsibilities.

Further Reading

Drinard, J. Elliott. "John Blair." *Proceedings of the Virginia State Bar Association* 39 (1927): 436–449.

Holt, Wythe. "John Blair: 'A Safe and Conscientious Judge.'" In *Seriatim: The Supreme Court Before John Marshall.* Edited by Scott Douglas Gerber. New York: New York University Press, 1998.

Horner, Frederick. *History of the Blair, Banister and Braxton Families Before and After the Revolution.* Philadelphia: J. B. Lippincott Co., 1898.

Israel, Fred L. "John Blair, Jr." In *The Justices of the United States Supreme Court 1789–1969: Their Lives and Major Opinions,* vol. 1. Edited by Leon Friedman and Fred L. Israel. New York: R. R. Bowker Co., 1969.

JOHN RUTLEDGE (1739–1800)

Associate Justice and Chief Justice, 1790–1791, 1795

Appointed by President George Washington

JOHN RUTLEDGE
(United States Supreme Court)

The first justice to resign from his post on the nation's highest court, John Rutledge exemplified the frustrations that service on the early Court produced among its members. Having held a series of important political posts and served as a state judge prior to his appointment to the Supreme Court, Rutledge could not fail to find his new role irksome. The Court lacked both significant cases and national respect in its earliest years. Furthermore, the Judiciary Act of 1789, which had established a system of federal courts, imposed on the Supreme Court justices the arduous labor of riding circuit to preside over cases in the states of the new union. Rutledge was the first, though not the last, justice to abandon his service on the Supreme Court in exchange for more attractive opportunities—in his case a judicial post in his home state. Although he would return briefly to the Court in 1795 as its interim chief justice, a political gaffe ultimately deprived Rutledge of confirmation to the chief seat.

John Rutledge was born in Charleston, South Carolina, in September 1739 to Dr. John Rutledge and his 15-year-old wife, Sarah Hext Rutledge, a wealthy young heiress. A physician who had emmigrated from Ireland at an early age, the elder Rutledge died in 1750, leaving young John to be raised by his mother and mentored by his uncle, Andrew Rutledge, who served as Speaker of the South Carolina Commons House of Assembly. John received the rudiments of a classical education first from his father, then from an English clergyman who tutored him privately, and finally from a school in Charleston run by David Rhind. After these educational experiences, he studied law for a time with his uncle Andrew Rutledge and then, after his uncle's death in 1755, in the law office of James Parsons of Charleston. After two years of this apprenticeship, Rutledge journeyed to London, where he studied at the Middle Temple of the Inns of Court and was eventually called to the bar on February 9, 1760.

In December 1760 Rutledge returned to South Carolina and at once took possession of the fertile opportunities that family wealth and connections presented him. He was admitted to the South Carolina bar the next month and in March 1761 was elected to a seat in the South Carolina Assembly. The following year the colony's governor, Thomas Boone, appointed Rutledge attorney general, a post that the latter held for 10 months. In 1765 Rutledge traveled as one of South Carolina's delegates to the Stamp Act Congress in New York; at the age of 25, he was the youngest delegate present. His youth did not deter him from leadership, however, and Rutledge served as the chairman of the Resolutions Committee, which drafted a memorial to the House of Lords requesting repeal of the tax. A year later the Stamp Act was, in fact, repealed.

In the 15 years after Rutledge's return from England, his law practice developed steadily. His legal work included representing many of the South Carolina's wealthiest landowners and merchants. By 1763 he was able to announce that he would not even consider cases that did not provide him a retainer of at least 100 pounds. The same year he married Elizabeth Grimké; the couple eventually had 10 children, one of whom—John Rutledge, Jr.—later served in the U.S. House of Representatives from 1797 to 1803. Two of Elizabeth Grimké's nieces would achieve prominence in the 1830s and 1840s as abolitionists and reformers in South Carolina.

When events in the mid-1770s began to cascade toward what would become the struggle for independence, Rutledge played a central role. In September 1774 his state sent him to the Continental Congress as chairman of its delegation. There Rutledge championed a moderate course in the dealings of the colonies with Great Britain and sought to safeguard his home state's economic interests. He allied himself with other conservative delegates who steadfastly resisted more radical demands for independence from Britain. Furthermore, when the Congress moved to ban imports and exports from England, Rutledge secured an exemption for the sale of rice—South Carolina's principal export.

Rutledge attended the Second Continental Congress in Philadelphia the following May as one of South Carolina's delegates. Months had passed since the First Continental Congress, and Rutledge had become more hospitable to the idea of independence, though it would be some time before he accepted the notion of permanent severance from England. In his capacity as chairman of the Committee on Government, he helped to establish procedures for the states to form new governments. He also supported the appointment of George Washington as commander in chief of American forces and even contributed advice about building an American fleet and defending it against the British navy.

In December 1775 Rutledge returned to South Carolina and helped draft a state constitution that provided for a bicameral legislature and an executive chosen by this legislature. When the legislature met for the first time in March 1776, it promptly elected Rutledge the first president of the South Carolina Republic.

Though he announced that he trusted differences between American and Britain might yet be resolved, Rutledge immediately organized a militia, which in the summer of 1776, orchestrated South Carolina's repulsion of an attack by the British fleet against Fort Sullivan in Charleston harbor. A week after this victory, Rutledge's brother Edward signed the Declaration of Independence in Philadelphia on behalf of South Carolina.

Rutledge served as president of South Carolina until March 1778, when a dispute over a newly proposed constitution set him at odds with the South Carolina assembly. The new constitution weakened the executive's power and made both houses of the assembly elected by popular vote. No great friend of direct democracy, Rutledge opposed the document and eventually resigned. The constitution was ratified, and under its terms South Carolina became a state rather than a republic and its chief executive a governor rather than a president. In February 1779, however, facing the threat of British invasion, the South Carolina assembly elected Rutledge governor. But Rutledge could not repeat the victory that had saved Fort Sullivan in 1776. The British captured Charleston in May 1780, forcing Rutledge to flee the state until the defeat of Cornwallis at Yorktown, Virginia, in October 1781.

After the war, since John Rutledge could not succeed himself as governor, he was elected instead to the Continental Congress in 1782. When the South Carolina legislature created a new court of chancery in 1784, Rutledge accepted an appointment as its chief judge. His own political stature and his ties to other South Carolina leaders made him a natural choice to serve as one of South Carolina's delegates to the Constitutional Convention in Philadelphia in 1787. While there, he served on the Committee of Detail charged with producing a first draft of the Constitution. Still an opponent of direct democracy, Rutledge argued in favor of provisions that would place significant government power into the hands of those with wealth and property. He supported property requirements for public officials and would have withheld a salary from the upper house of Congress to assure that only the wealthy could serve as senators. He was no more successful in achieving these aims than he had been in opposing the democratic reforms embraced by South Carolina's 1778 constitution. He did, however, join with others in defeating a proposed ban on the slave trade in the new nation. Overall, he was recognized as a man of considerable importance at the Convention by other delegates. William Pierce, a delegate from Georgia, described him as "a Gentleman of distinction and fortune," though he added that Rutledge was "too rapid in his public speaking to be denominated an agreeable orator." Rutledge served on the important select committee that produced the Great Compromise, which gave states equal representation in the Senate and apportioned representation in the lower house according to population. He is also credited with having proposed the Constitution's Supremacy Clause in substantially the form in which it entered the text of the Constitution. After the Convention he returned to South Carolina and helped secure the Constitution's ratification there.

After George Washington's election as the nation's first president, John Rutledge was among the top contenders for the position of chief justice of the Supreme Court, established by the Judiciary Act of 1789. But numerous posts were already occupied by southerners in the new government; thus, Washington offered the chief seat to John Jay from New York, and Rutledge had to content himself with an appointment as associate justice. He did not hold the appointment for long, however. During his brief time as a justice, Rutledge never attended a session of the Court, though he did fulfill his circuit-riding responsibilities. Within a little more than a year, unhappiness with being passed over for chief justice, the lack of cases before the Court, and the arduous nature of circuit riding persuaded Rutledge to retire from his position on the Supreme Court in favor of becoming the chief justice of the South Carolina Court of Common Pleas. His resignation in March 1791 occasioned an attempt by President Washington to fill the vacancy that was unusual in its approach. He wrote a letter jointly to Edward Rutledge, the departing justice's brother, and C. C. Pinckney, inquiring as to whether one of them would accept the post: "Will either of you two Gentlemen accept it? And in that case, which of you?" Both declined the position.

A few years after Rutledge resigned from the Court, he learned that John Jay would soon be stepping down from the position of chief justice, after being elected governor of New York. The imminent vacancy prompted Rutledge to express his interest in returning to the Court as chief justice. He wrote privately to Washington in June 1795 to state his willingness to accept the position, and Washington immediately responded by forwarding Rutledge a temporary commission, dated July 1, 1795, as chief justice. Because the Senate was in recess, the commission was effective until the end of the next session. As a consequence of this appointment, Rutledge presided over the August term of the Court, during which it decided two cases. His permanent appointment was derailed, however, after he made an intemperate speech in opposition to the Jay Treaty with Britain, a treaty to which Washington and the Federalists were committed. When word of the speech, along with suggestions that Rutledge might be mentally unbalanced, reached the Capitol, the Senate, which convened in December 1795, declined to confirm him by a vote of 14-10. Upon hearing of this vote, Rutledge attempted suicide on December 26, 1795, by throwing himself off a wharf into Charleston Harbor. Two slaves managed to rescue him, however, and he lived five more years in relative seclusion before dying on June 21, 1800.

John Rutledge arrived at the Supreme Court after an illustrious legal and political career had made him one of the most important citizens of South Carolina and one of the leaders in establishing the new nation. His arrival, however, came at a time when the Court's stature was relatively slight, its important cases as yet nonexistent, and its responsibilities—through circuit riding—immensely arduous. Unlike some of his contemporaries, his successes before the nation's birth overshadowed the events of the rest of his life. His vacillation—first accepting an appointment that was less than he had hoped, then abandoning the post, then finally seeking and, for a short time obtaining, the chief seat on the nation's highest Court, only to lose it through a political miscalculation—ended his career on a tragic note.

Further Reading

Barry, Richard Hayes. *Mr. Rutledge of South Carolina.* New York: Duell, Sloan and Pearce, 1942.

Haw, James. *John & Edward Rutledge of South Carolina.* Athens: University of Georgia Press, 1997.

———. "John Rutledge: Distinction and Declension." In *Seriatim: The Supreme Court Before John Marshall.* Edited by Scott Douglas Gerber. New York: New York University Press, 1998.

Barnwell, Robert W. "Rutledge, 'The Dictator.'" *Journal of Southern History* 7 (1941): 215–224.

McCowan, George S. "Chief Justice John Rutledge and the Jay Treaty." *South Carolina Historical Magazine* 52 (1961): 10.

JAMES IREDELL (1751–1799)

Associate Justice, 1790–1799

Appointed by President George Washington

JAMES IREDELL
(United States Supreme Court)

The youngest of George Washington's appointments to the Supreme Court, James Iredell gained his seat after another nominee had declined a similar commission from the president. He was not yet 40 years old when he joined the Court, and death would remove him from his post before a decade had passed. While on the Supreme Court, Iredell championed a more vigorous vision of dual sovereignty within the new union than that embraced by the other justices on the Court. But Iredell's view would ultimately prevail when the nation added an amendment to the U.S. Constitution that made his perspective an important part of the fundamental law of the United States.

James Iredell was born in Sussex County, England, on October 5, 1751. His father, a not particularly successful merchant, suffered a stroke in 1766 that forced him to retire and made it necessary for James Iredell to find work that would assist in the support of his family. A relative subsequently secured Iredell a position in the colonies as comptroller of customs for Port Roanoke at Edenton, North Carolina. There Iredell worked for his cousin, Henry E. McCulloh, who was the collector of customs for the port and who, being absent frequently from Edenton, soon relied on Iredell both to collect the duties for the port and to manage McCulloh's real estate holdings. Iredell's salary for the post went to support his family; he cared for his own needs through fees he collected.

During this time Iredell met and began to study law under Samuel Johnson, an important Edenton lawyer. Under Johnson's tutelage, Iredell acquired the legal training necessary for admission to practice before the Inferior Courts of North Carolina in 1770 and before the Superior Courts the following year. This relationship with Samuel Johnson gained Iredell not only a professional career but also a wife. He married Johnson's sister Hannah in 1773, and the couple ultimately had two daughters and a son. Their son, James Iredell, Jr., eventually shared his father's political inclinations, becoming governor of North Carolina and a U.S. senator.

By the mid-1770s, James Iredell was juggling several responsibilities. In 1774 he succeeded his cousin as Collector of Port Roanoke and the same year was appointed deputy king's attorney to prosecute criminal cases in three North Carolina counties. That same year Iredell plunged into the political controversy over the relationship between England and the colonies. Warned not to side with colonial revolutionaries or risk being cut out of a wealthy relative's will, Iredell nevertheless sided with the colonial view—although not initially, at least, with those who demanded independence. Never a gifted speaker, in 1774 Iredell nonetheless took pen in hand to publish a tract called "To the Inhabitants of Great Britain," which argued that Parliament had no authority over the colonies. After the colonies declared their independence in 1776, Iredell joined in the spirited debates about what forms of government the newly independent commonwealths should adopt. He sided with other conservatives in favoring independent executives, judges with life tenure, and property requirements for voting and office holding, rather than with radicals and their more purely democratic aspirations.

In the following years, Iredell, still a relatively young man, took a leading role in the development of North Carolina's legal structure. He assisted in revising the state's laws in 1776, and the following year, when he was still only 27 years old, he was elected to one of the three positions on the state's highest court. He resigned after six months, however, to return to his law practice. In 1779 he was first appointed interim attorney general by the governor of North Carolina, then was formally elected to this position by the state legislature. With the conclusion of the Revolutionary War in 1881, Iredell left his public position to return to the private practice of law, and for the rest of the decade he worked mainly at establishing a prosperous legal practice.

When the Philadelphia Constitutional Convention produced the proposed U.S. Constitution in the fall of 1787, James Iredell became a vigorous advocate in favor of its ratification. Writing under the name "Marcus," Iredell published a series of letters in support of the Constitution. His first, appearing in the October 15, 1787, edition of the New York *Daily Advertiser,* briefly summarized the interests that would be supported by the new system of government. This article appeared in the same month that the first of the influential *Federalist Papers* was published in New York. A few months later, in February and March 1788, Iredell wrote some pieces that responded to the objections to the Constitution posed by George Mason, the respected Virginia statesman. Writing again as Marcus, James Iredell supplied point-by-point rejoinders to key objections voiced by Mason, under a general heading that described the Constitution as "A System of Government Which I Am Convinced Can Stand the Nicest Examination." Federalists warmly received this rejoinder to Mason, and it brought Iredell to the attention of national leaders such as George Washington.

The issue of ratification came before the North Carolina ratifying convention, which met in Hillsboro, North Carolina, beginning on July 21, 1788. Iredell sided with the Federalists in support of ratification, but antifederalist opposition to the Constitution dominated the convention. Iredell took to the convention floor to argue on behalf of the Constitution, but he failed to sway the antifederalists, who succeeded in defeating ratification by a lopsided vote of 184-84. When a second convention convened in Fayetteville in November 1789, however, it ratified the Constitution, joining the Union that had been established some seven months previously.

By the time North Carolina ratified the Constitution, George Washington had been elected president, and Congress had enacted the Judiciary Act, establishing the Supreme Court. In September 1789 Washington nominated six men to serve on the Court, but one of these—Robert H. Harrison—declined Washington's commission. On February 8, 1790, Washington nominated Iredell to fill the sixth seat on the Court, not only because of his abilities and Federalist sympathies, but also because North Carolina, so lately become a state, had not yet had any of its citizens nominated to fill important positions within the new national government. The Senate confirmed Iredell's appointment the same day, and at 39 years of age, Iredell became the youngest member of the nation's highest court.

Though Iredell joined the Court with great enthusiasm, he soon felt the demands of circuit riding onerous, especially because it fell to him to ride the southern circuit. With the addition of North Carolina to the nation, this circuit embraced North and South Carolina, as well as Georgia. The Judiciary Act of 1789 required Supreme Court justices to make two circuits of their assigned states each year and each, for the southern circuit, required in excess of 1,800 miles of travel. In addition to these circuit obligations, the justices also participated in two Supreme Court terms each year. By 1792 Iredell had complained to Chief Justice John Jay that the combined obligations were more than a justice could conscientiously fulfill. Congress the same year amended the Judiciary Act to rotate the responsibility for riding the southern circuit among the justices, but in his first four years of service on the Court, Iredell rode the circuit five times.

Justice Iredell participated in the most famous decision of the Court's first decade—*Chisholm v. Georgia* (1793)—and had the distinction of casting the only dissenting vote in the case. *Chisholm* presented the Court with a contract claim brought by a citizen of South Carolina against the state of Georgia for cloth and clothing sold during the Revolutionary War. The claimant filed the case in federal court, but the state of Georgia refused to answer it, arguing that the federal court had no jurisdiction in such a case. The case presented the Supreme Court with volatile issues regarding the nature of federal and state sovereignty within the new nation. All the other justices concluded that Article III, Section 2 of the Constitution gave the Court jurisdiction in the case, since it provided that the federal judicial power extended to controversies between a state and the citizens of another state. Iredell alone dissented.

In a lengthy opinion, Iredell explained the reasons for his refusal to join with the majority of the Court in allowing the suit against Georgia. Though the Constitution provided for a Supreme Court, Iredell believed that it also delegated to Congress the responsibility for establishing this Court and providing for the specifics of its operations. He thought it therefore crucial to inquire into the precise authority granted to the Court by Congress under the terms of the Judiciary Act of 1789, which had established the basic structure of federal courts. According to this Act, Iredell found, the federal courts—including the Supreme Court—were provided with power to exercise various powers so long as these were, in the words of the Act, "agreeable to the principles and usages of law." Furthermore, Iredell viewed the doctrine of sovereign immunity as a settled principle of law, one that forbade suits against a sovereign without its permission in most cases. Importantly, the justice reasoned that the states were sovereign except in the limited areas in which they had delegated sovereignty to the United States. As to suits by noncitizens, Iredell saw no cause to believe that states had surrendered their sovereign immunity in the formation of the union and therefore concluded that the Court had no authority under the Judiciary Act to entertain a suit so disagreeable to settled principles of law. The nation soon added its own dissent to Iredell's in the *Chisholm* case, by ratifying the Eleventh Amendment to the Constitution, which overruled the decision of the Court's majority.

Iredell served nearly 10 years on the Court before his health failed. While en route to Philadelphia for the fall term of the Court in 1799, he became ill. He returned to his home in Edenton, North Carolina, where he died on October 20.

James Iredell left a brief and partially puzzling record as a justice of the Supreme Court. His famous dissent in *Chisholm v. Georgia* (1793) has sometimes caused proponents of states' rights to adopt him as a patron saint. But his judicial activity as a whole resists ready categorization. Both as an attorney and as a judge, Iredell insisted that constitutions generally, and the U.S. Constitution in particular, superseded contrary laws and that courts had the power to declare such laws void. At least in the framing era, a strong commitment to judicial review normally allied itself with Federalist sympathies. Iredell, was in fact, a Federalist in his outlook, championing the cause of the new union and spearheading North Carolina's entry into that Union. His abiding commitment to a dual sovereignty that included both the national government and the governments of states was greater, though, than other members of the Court were prepared to embrace. But the nation's ratification of the Eleventh Amendment to the Constitution, which reversed the majority's result in *Chisholm*, also ratified a view more consistent with Iredell's than with the other early justices on the Supreme Court.

FURTHER READING

Connor, H. G. "James Iredell: Lawyer, Statesman, Judge." *University of Pennsylvania Law Review* 60 (1912): 225–253.

Fordham, Jeff B. "Iredell's Dissent in *Chisholm v. Georgia*." *The North Carolina Historical Review* 8 (1931): 155–167.

Graebe, Christopher T. "The Federalism of James Iredell in Historical Context." *North Carolina Law Review* 69 (1990): 251–272.

Israel, Fred L. "James Iredell." In *The Justices of the United States Supreme Court 1789–1969: Their Lives and Major Opinions,* vol. 1. Edited by Leon Friedman and Fred L. Israel. New York: R. R. Bowker Co., 1969.

McRee, Griffith John. *Life and Correspondence of James Iredell: One of the Associate Justices of the Supreme Court of the United States.* New York: Appleton, 1857–1873.

Whichard, Willis P. "James Iredell: Revolutionist, Constitutionalist, Jurist." In *Seriatim: The Supreme Court Before John Marshall.* Edited by Scott Douglas Gerber. New York: New York University Press, 1998.

THOMAS JOHNSON (1732–1819)

Associate Justice, 1792–1793

Appointed by President George Washington

THOMAS JOHNSON
(United States Supreme Court)

Perhaps no justice ever came to a seat on the U.S. Supreme Court more reluctantly than Maryland's Thomas Johnson, and no justice served on the Court for a shorter tenure than he did. By the last decade of the 18th century, age and bodily infirmity had persuaded Johnson to retire from what had been a busy public life. But at the request of President George Washington, a longtime acquaintance and business partner, Johnson made an attempt at the post of associate justice, only to discover shortly that "[t]he office and the man do not fit." He left his seat on the Court for a long retirement, leaving little record of his brief presence there.

Thomas Johnson was born on November 4, 1732, in Calvert County, Maryland, to parents of some local prominence. His father, Thomas Johnson, Sr., had served in the Maryland Assembly for several years in the third decade of the 18th century. The family was a large one. Johnson was the fifth child of 12, 11 of whom survived infancy. He was educated at home until he left to make his way in Annapolis, the colonial capital of Maryland. There he found work as a court clerk and studied law under the tutelage of Stephen Bordley, eventually gaining admission to the Annapolis Mayor's Court in 1756 and the Charles County and Provincial Courts in 1759. By 1762 Johnson had been elected a delegate to the lower house of the Maryland Assembly; he would continue to serve in the assembly repeatedly over the next 12 years. He married Ann Jennings in 1766, and the couple would eventually have eight children in the course of their 28 years of marriage.

By the early years of the decade that would yield American independence, Thomas Johnson had already gravitated toward revolutionary activism. In 1765 he led Maryland protests against the soon-to-be-repealed Stamp Act, passed by Parliament that year and rescinded the next. He counted among his friends several men who would sign the Declaration of Independence on behalf of Maryland, including Samuel Chase, a future Supreme Court justice, and Charles Carroll, a wealthy man who became one of Johnson's clients. In the early 1770s Johnson also became acquainted with George Washington, with whom he shared a keen interest in the Potomac River and the possibilities of making it navigable. In the following decade, the two would help form the Potomac Company for the purpose of making this dream a reality.

In the acceleration of congresses and conventions that ultimately severed the colonies from England, Johnson played an important role and earned the attention of national statesmen. Maryland sent him as one of its delegates to the First and Second Continental Congresses beginning in 1774, and at these gatherings he broadened his acquaintances to include men such as John Adams and John Jay. At the Second Continental Congress he nominated his friend George Washington as commander in chief of the Continental Army, but then he rushed back to Maryland without tarrying to sign the Declaration of Independence. Once there, he helped to gather arms and supplies for Washington's army and was appointed commander of Maryland's militia. Soon after marching his forces to New Jersey to reinforce Washington's army, he learned that he had been elected the first governor of the state of Maryland in February 1777. He therefore returned home again to take up that office. He was elected again to the governorship each of the following two years, and left the office in 1779 only because the Maryland constitution prevented him from holding another consecutive term.

When Johnson finished his final term as governor of Maryland in 1779, he attempted the first of several attempted retirements. He settled in Frederick, Maryland, where he built a house and turned down the chance to serve in Congress, although he did accept a seat in the Maryland state legislature and served there from 1780 to 1782. He resumed the practice of law and joined with Washington in 1785 to help found the Potomac Company. Toward the end of the decade, he served again in the Maryland House of Delegates and also represented his county in the Maryland ratifying convention, where he urged the state to ratify the Constitution and subsequently worked to see George Washington elected the first president of the United States. In April 1790 Maryland's governor appointed Johnson chief judge of the Maryland General Court.

His appointment to the Maryland court was not the first instance in which Johnson had been considered for a judicial post. President Washington had offered Johnson the position as Maryland's first federal district judge, and the Senate had in fact confirmed Johnson for this post on September 26, 1789, immediately after passage of the Judiciary Act of 1789 and the creation of the federal court system, but Johnson refused the appointment. A year and a half later, in March 1791, John Rutledge resigned from the Supreme Court, and President Washington turned again to Johnson. In July 1791 Washington wrote to Johnson: "Permit me to ask you with frankness, and in the fullness of friendship, whether you will accept of an appointment in the Supreme Judiciary of the United States?" Johnson responded to the president, but without definitely accepting

Washington's offer. He desired to make inquiry "whether the southern Circuit would fall to me; if it would at my Time of Life and otherwise circumstanced as I am it would be an insurmountable Objection." The difficulty he alluded to was the burdensome requirement that Supreme Court justices serve as judges of circuit courts and participate in circuit riding, which had been imposed by the Judiciary Act of 1789 and was not completely abandoned until 1869. Circuit courts conducted trials and heard appeals from district courts; they were superintended by federal district judges and Supreme Court justices riding circuit. Initially, the new nation was divided into three circuits, the most expansive of which was the southern circuit, consisting of North and South Carolina and Georgia. Supreme Court justices assigned to hear cases in the courts of the southern circuit had to travel 1,800 miles or more twice yearly. Johnson was, not surprisingly, worried that by becoming the junior member of the Court, he would be saddled with the exhausting responsibility of riding the southern circuit. Washington, though, continued to press Johnson to join the Court, and ultimately persuaded him to accept a temporary commission—while the Senate was out of session—on August 5, 1791. The Senate confirmed his appointment on November 7, 1791. The appointment was short-lived, however. As Johnson feared, he was assigned the southern circuit, and his health proved inadequate for the work of a Supreme Court justice. After illnesses interfered with his attendence at both sessions of the Supreme Court and with his circuit-riding obligations, Johnson resigned on January 16, 1793.

When Thomas Johnson left his position on the Supreme Court, he did not retire completely from public life. In January 1791 President Washington appointed him one of three commissioners to oversee the location and design of a new national capital; Johnson served in this position until 1794. He finally managed to extricate himself from this post as well, upon which he retired to his estate in Frederick, Maryland. Washington made one last attempt to entice Johnson back to public life by offering him the position of Secretary of State in 1795, but Johnson declined and settled into a long retirement that would end with his death in Frederick on October 26, 1819.

Thomas Johnson participated in no important decisions during his brief tenure on the U.S. Supreme Court. The year that he resigned the Court decided *Chisholm v. Georgia* (1793), but the justice from Maryland had already retired to his estate in Frederick by the time the case came before the Court. All told, he made his mark more as a state legislator and governor than as a Supreme Court justice. By the time President Washington lured Johnson into this last of his important offices, he had largely abandoned further plans for public life, having already served both his state and the nation he helped to form through nearly a quarter century of work. That Johnson held his position as associate justice of the Supreme Court for so short a tenure was unusual but did not otherwise mar a distinguished record of public service.

Further Reading

Delaplaine, Edward S. *The Life of Thomas Johnson: Member of the Continental Congress, First Governor of Maryland, and Associate Justice of the United States Supreme Court.* New York: Grafton Press, 1927.

———. *Thomas Johnson, Maryland and the Constitution.* Baltimore: Maryland State Bar Association, 1925.

Johnson, Herbert Alan. "Thomas Johnson." In *The Justice of the United States Supreme Court 1789–1969: Their Lives and Major Opinions,* Vol. 1. Edited by Leon Friedman and Fred L. Israel. New York: R. R. Bowker Co., 1969.

William Paterson (1745–1806)

Associate Justice, 1793–1806

Appointed by President George Washington

William Paterson
(United States Supreme Court)

Appointed by President Washington to fill an early vacancy on the Supreme Court, William Paterson brought a wealth of legal experience to his position as senior associate justice. Prior to joining the Court, Paterson had practiced law privately and as an attorney general for the state of New Jersey. In addition to this practical experience, Paterson had helped revise the laws of his state and, importantly, served as a principal architect of the federal judicial system through his role in drafting the Judiciary Act of 1789. To these accomplishments must be added the important role that Paterson played in the Constitutional Convention. In light of these achievements, it is not unreasonable to suggest that William Paterson may have had more influence on American law before he became a justice of the Supreme Court than after he assumed this position.

William Paterson was born on December 24, 1745, in Country Antrim, Ireland, but his family soon migrated to America, living briefly in New York and Connecticut before finally settling in Princeton, New Jersey. There his parents opened a general store, lived frugally, and invested wisely. In 1759 Paterson was able to attend the College of New Jersey (which eventually became Princeton University); he graduated in 1763. Over the next several years he pursued a master's degree, which he obtained in 1766, and studied law with Richard Stockton. By 1769 he had been admitted to the bar and moved to New Bromley, New Jersey, where he established his practice.

By the mid-1770s Paterson had earned one the first of many public posts that would fill most of his life. In 1775 Somerset County sent him as a delegate to the First Provincial Congress of New Jersey, where he assumed the position of assistant secretary. Within a short time he was named secretary of the New Jersey congress and played an important part in drafting the New Jersey constitution. In 1776 Paterson became New Jersey's first attorney general. He served in this position until 1783, when he returned to the private practice of law. In 1777 he married Cornelia Bell, who died in childbirth in 1783. The next year Paterson married one of Cornelia's close friends, Euphemia White.

In 1787, when the Constitutional Convention met in Philadelphia, Paterson attended as a delegate from New Jersey. There he played a crucial role in the proceedings by proposing the famous New Jersey Plan, offered to counter the proposal of the Virginia delegation. Virginia, a large state, had proposed a bicameral legislature for the new national government, in which the number of representatives in each house would be selected according to the population of their respective states. Smaller states such as New Jersey opposed this plan, so Paterson proposed in its stead a plan that would have created a legislature with a single chamber and given all the states given equal representation in this chamber. The ultimate bicameral scheme adopted in the Constitution reflected a compromise between the Virginia plan and Paterson's plan. Satisfied with this result, Paterson joined in signing the Constitution on September 17, 1787.

Paterson returned to New Jersey, where he advocated ratification of the Constitution. Once this was done, his state promptly elected him to a seat in the U.S. Senate. As a senator, Paterson's most memorable work was to help draft the Judiciary Act of 1789. Together with Oliver Ellsworth—himself a future chief justice of the Supreme Court—Paterson played a principal role in establishing the basic framework of the federal courts: a Supreme Court consisting of a chief justice and five associate justices, three circuit courts, and a district court for each of the original 13 states. To the great consternation of Supreme Court justices for the next century, the Judiciary Act specified that the justices were required not only to attend sessions of the Supreme Court but also to preside over circuit court proceedings held in various venues throughout the states. This provision burdened the justices with onerous circuit-riding responsibilities. Ironically, a decade later, after Paterson himself had joined the Court, he would complain to his wife that his circuit-riding duties had compelled him to travel "over stones and rocks and mountains."

Paterson did not serve long in the U.S. Senate. In 1790 the governor of New Jersey died, and the New Jersey legislature elected Paterson to fill the vacant position. He was subsequently reelected governor for three more one-year terms. As governor, Paterson codified the state's laws and revised the rules of practice and procedure for the state's common law and chancery courts. He also joined with his friend Alexander Hamilton in planning a city to be located on the Passaic River and proposing that it be named "Paterson." (Though the plan was not immediately successful, a town named "Paterson" would later be founded at the falls of the Passaic, and still later, in the 20th century, earn literary fame as the subject of William Carlos Williams's book-length poem, *Paterson.*)

President George Washington interrupted William Paterson's tenure as governor of New

Jersey in 1793 by nominating him to fill the seat on the Supreme Court so briefly occupied by Thomas Johnson, and before him John Rutledge. "I think it necessary," Washington wrote to Paterson, "to select a person who is not only professionally qualified to discharge that important trust, but one who is known to the public and whose conduct meets their approbation. . . . Under this impression, Sir, I have turned my thoughts upon you; and if you will permit me to nominate you for this Office, I shall have the satisfaction to believe that our Country will be pleased with, and benefitted by the acquisition." Paterson immediately agreed to be nominated for the position and was eventually confirmed as an associate justice, though his previous service as a senator occasioned a minor delay in the confirmation process. Washington had nominated Paterson to the Supreme Court on February 27, 1793, but the following day he withdrew the nomination on discovering that Paterson had served in the Senate that had passed the Judiciary Act of 1787 and that his term as a senator had not yet expired. Washington viewed these circumstances as violating Article I, Section 6 of the Constitution, which prevents members of the House and Senate from being appointed to a civil office created during their service as legislators. The president nominated Paterson again on March 4, 1793, and the Senate confirmed the nomination the same day. Paterson took the oath of office as an associate justice of the Supreme Court within a week and began one of the longest tenures on the Court of any Washington appointee. Only William Cushing and Samuel Chase would exceed Paterson's 13 years on the Court.

Under the terms of the Judiciary Act of 1789, Supreme Court justices had responsibility for sitting as circuit justices in one of the three circuits initially created under the Act. These courts both presided over trials and heard appeals. Paterson probably left his most memorable record, for good and for ill, in his role as a circuit judge. In *Van Horne's Lessee v. Dorrance* (1795), for example, he wrote an opinion for the circuit court that presaged the Supreme Court's important decision eight years later in *Marbury v. Madison* (1803). Both cases involved the seminal question of whether courts had the authority to declare null and void legislative acts that were inconsistent with a constitution. *Van Horne's Lessee* involved a state law in conflict with the state constitution; *Marbury* involved a federal law—the Judiciary Act of 1787—arguably in conflict with the U.S. Constitution. Both cases, though, posed a similar issue. Paterson's resolution of this issue—in favor of the power of courts to nullify unconstitutional legislation—would anticipate Chief Justice John Marshall's similar resolution in *Marbury*. In *Van Horne's Lessee*, Paterson charged the jury in the following terms:

> The Constitution is certain and fixed; it contains the permanent will of the people, and is the supreme law of the land; it is paramount to the power of the Legislature, and can be revoked or altered only by the authority that made it. . . . What are Legislatures: Creatures of the Constitution; they owe their existence to the Constitution; they derive their power from the Constitution; It is their commission; and, therefore, all their acts must be conformable to it, or else they will be void. The Constitution is the work or will of the People themselves, in their original, sovereign, and unlimited capacity. Law is the work or will of the Legislature in their derivative or subordinate capacity. The one is the work of the Creator, and the other of the Creature. The Constitution fixes limits to the exercise of legislative authority and prescribes the orbit within which it must move. In short . . . the Constitution is the sun of the political system; around which all Legislative, Executive, and Judicial bodies must revolve. Whatever may be the case in other countries, yet in this there can be no doubt, that every act of the Legislature, repugnant to the Constitution, is absolutely void.

In his capacity as a circuit judge, Paterson also presided over controversial prosecutions brought under the Alien and Sedition Act of 1789; his conduct as a judge in these cases has tended to dim somewhat the luster of his other accomplishments. The Alien and Sedition Act punished conduct that opposed the federal government as well as certain writings critical of the federal government. Though the act was inspired by fears that immigrants might spread popular unrest, it was eventually wielded by Federalists against Jeffersonian Republicans. Paterson presided over the case of Matthew Lyon, a Vermont congressman who became the first person convicted under the Act, and in this role he demonstrated himself more an ardent Federalist than a judge. This, of course, pleased Federalists greatly, but it earned him the disfavor of Republicans and the criticism of historians.

In 1795, shortly after Paterson joined the Court, President Washington offered him the post of Secretary of State, but he chose instead to remain on the Court. Five years later, when Chief Justice Oliver Ellsworth resigned in 1800, it was widely believed that Paterson would be nominated to succeed him. But President John Adams preferred his secretary of state, John Marshall, over Paterson for that post. Though the Senate briefly stalled Marshall's confirmation, hoping that Adams would relent and appoint Paterson chief justice, the president's adamancy ultimately secured the confirmation of John Marshall as chief justice. Paterson would not have occupied the chief seat on the Court for long in any event. The circuit riding took an inevitable toll on his health, and in 1804 he suffered severe injuries as a result of a carriage accident. His service on the Court was intermittent after this accident, and on September 9, 1806, while en route to his daughter's home in New York, he died.

Justice William Paterson's career on the Supreme Court has tended to be overshadowed by that of John Marshall, whose appointment as chief justice in 1800 is widely understood as having initiated an Olympian age in the Court's history. But Paterson, in his own way, had already contributed mightily to the role of the Court before he ever ascended to its lofty perch. He championed the cause of small states in the Constitutional Convention, thus facilitating the Great Compromise that eventually secured passage of the Constitution. And as a U.S. senator he, together with Oliver Ellsworth, played the principal role in fashioning the formative Judiciary Act of 1789, which established a vigorous role for federal courts in the new nation and guided the conduct of those courts for more than a century to come.

Further Reading

Degnan, Daniel A. "Justice William Paterson: Founder." *Seton Hall Law Review* 16 (1986): 313–338.

———. "William Paterson: Small States' Nationalist." In *Seriatim: The Supreme Court Before John Marshall*. Edited by Scott Douglas Gerber. New York: New York University Press, 1998.

Hickox, Charles F., III and Andrew C. Laviano. "William Paterson." *Journal of Supreme Court History Annual* (1992): 53–61.

O'Connor, John E. *William Paterson, Lawyer and Statesman, 1745–1806*. New Brunswick, N.J.: Rutgers University Press, 1979.

Paterson, William. *Glimpses of Colonial Society and the Life at Princeton College, 1766–1773, by One of the Class of 1763*. Edited by W. Jay Mills. Philadelphia: Lippincott, 1903; Detroit: Grand River Books, 1971.

SAMUEL CHASE (1741–1811)

Associate Justice, 1796–1811

Appointed by President George Washington

SAMUEL CHASE
(United States Supreme Court)

Samuel Chase has the distinction of being the only justice of the U.S. Supreme Court to have been impeached by the House of Representatives for "high crimes and misdemeanors." He avoided conviction before the Senate, but he did not escape the general—though by no means universal—consensus of legal historians that he was one of the worst justices ever to occupy a seat on the high court. Although Chase seems clearly to have possessed sufficient intellectual gifts to have served with distinction on the Court, he lacked the dispassionate character necessary to the office of judging. Intemperate and overtly partisan, he had a disposition better suited to a prize-fighter than a judge.

Samuel Chase was born in Somerset County, Maryland, on April 17, 1741, to the Reverend Thomas Chase and Martha Walker Chase. His father was an Episcopal clergyman from whom the young Chase received his early education. In 1759, at the age of 18, Samuel was apprenticed to study law at the office of John Hammand and John Hall in Annapolis, Maryland. He married Ann Baldwin in 1762 and was admitted to practice the following year.

In 1764 Chase was elected to the Maryland legislature, beginning a tenure of political office that lasted 20 years. Over the ensuing decade, he was borne along by the revolutionary currents that began to wash across the colonies. Parliament's infamous Stamp Act of 1765 prompted him to join the Sons of Liberty, and he was a relentless agitator against the Stamp Act and other British policies. Never one to suffer a grievance silently, he so annoyed the mayor and aldermen of Annapolis at one juncture that they branded him a "busy restless Incendiary—a Ringleader of Mobs, a foul mouth'd and inflaming son of Discord and Faction—a common Disturber of the public Tranquility, and a Promoter of the lawless excesses of the multitude." Not to be outdone in a war of words, Chase retorted that his accusers were nothing more than "despicable Pimps" and "Tools of Power." Nevertheless, with the onset of revolution, Chase earned recognition as a leader, and Maryland sent him to serve in the First and Second Continental Congresses. When the other revolutionary leaders signed their names to the Declaration of Independence in 1776, Chase arrived in time to add his own signature to the distinguished list after first having to hurry back to Maryland to persuade the assembly to support independence.

Chase threw himself into the work of the Continental Congress, serving on 21 committees in 1777 and 30 in 1778. He also threw himself into the more questionable project of trying, with a few others, to corner the market on flour with information he obtained as a member of the Congress. For this conduct Alexander Hamilton, writing as "Publius," excoriated him in the *New York Journal* and Maryland removed him as one of its delegates to the Continental Congress for two years. Sometime during this period his wife died, having given birth to seven children, four of whom survived infancy. Throughout the 1780s, Chase pursued a variety of business ventures and these, though not so tainted with the spectacle of self-dealing as his flour investments, nevertheless fared no better financially. In 1784 he married Hannah Kitty Giles of England. By the close of the decade, Chase was busy seeking legislative relief for his financial woes. In the 1786–87 term of the Maryland Assembly, Chase pressed unsuccessfully as a state legislator for paper money and debt relief. When these proposals failed to pass, he was forced to petition the Maryland legislature to declare him bankrupt in 1789.

During the same period, Samuel Chase took on the first of the judicial robes that would clothe him for the rest of his life. In 1788 he became a judge of the Baltimore Criminal Court; in 1791 he added to this position a seat on the General Court of Maryland as chief judge. The same controversy that had swirled around his career as a legislator also followed him onto the bench, however. At least some in the Maryland Assembly found his dual judgeships objectionable and his judicial manner imperious, and they sought, unsuccessfully, to oust him from his posts. Failing in this effort, Chase's opponents were left with name-calling, and the judge's normal red-faced countenance earned him the epithet "Old Bacon Face."

When the Philadelphia Convention proposed the Constitution in 1787, Chase quickly made himself known as an opponent of the proposed system. He charged that the Constitution would erect a government of the wealthy classes at the expenses of farmers and artisans. His objections were sufficiently weighty to prompt Chase to vote against ratification at the Maryland convention. But when the Constitution was ratified in spite of his opposition, Chase quickly became a Federalist, at least partially if not wholly for the pragmatic reason that he wished to obtain an appointment in the new government. Though his past improprieties and his agitation against the Constitution might have made any such prospect exceedingly dim, Chase had at least two factors in his favor. First, he had supported George Washington in the Continental Congress and thus earned the political gratitude of the future first president. Second, President Washington's secretary of war, James McHenry, himself a leading Federalist from Maryland, urged Washington to find a post for Chase. Though Washington seems to have eyed Chase briefly for the position of attorney general, he ultimately nominated Chase on January 26, 1796, to the seat on the Supreme Court recently vacated by James Blair of Virginia. On February 4, 1796, Chase formally took his seat on the Court.

Chase's early years on the Court suggested the potential for solid service and perhaps even distinction as a justice of the Supreme Court. Within little more than a month, the Court heard arguments and rendered a decision in two important cases. Chase's opinions in these cases, especially in *Ware v. Hylton* (1796), gave promise of significant judicial ability. In *Ware* the Court invalidated a Virginia law inconsistent with the 1783 Treaty of Paris; Chase's opinion firmly supported the supremacy of federal treaties over conflicting state laws. Two years later, in *Calder v. Bull* (1798), Chase gave a lasting construction to the Constitution's *ex post facto* clause by holding, with the rest of the Court, that it applied only to criminal proceedings.

Beginning in 1799, however, Justice Chase's actions while presiding over circuit court proceedings earned the abiding ire of Republicans. The passage of the Sedition Act of 1798 had made it a crime to publish "false, scandalous, and malicious" attacks on government officials. Federalist prosecutors soon wielded the Sedition Act against critics of the Adams administration, and Chase showed himself a vigorous ally of prosecutions brought under the act. In Philadelphia, Chase presided over the notorious treason trial of John Fries, and he conducted himself in such an offensive manner that Philadelphia lawyers, after investigating the proceedings, refused to appear before him on his further circuit visits to the city. Some of the opposition to Chase undoubtedly sprang from serious differences of opinion about the legality of the Sedition Act prosecutions and about the nature of federal power generally. Although Chase may have begun his political life with a spirit of popular democracy, by the close of the 18th century he had metamorphosed into a staunch Federalist, appalled at the ascendancy of Jeffersonian Republicanism and dedicated to protecting the nation from the heresies of this party. But political disagreements are not enough to account for the venom that Chase provoked from his opponents. That he cloaked prosecutorial zeal under judicial robes provoked talk of impeachment among those who would otherwise have been merely stern political opponents.

One last display of Federalist zeal was sufficient to harden opposition to Chase. In 1803, while presiding over a grand jury in Baltimore, Chase harangued the jury with his opinion of a new Maryland law that abolished property requirements for voting. The prospect of widespread male suffrage filled the justice with dread, and he made dire predictions about the loss to property rights and personal liberty that "mobocracy" would produce. In a veiled reference to Jefferson and his party, Chase concluded that "[t]he modern doctrines by our late reformers, that all men in a state of society are entitled to enjoy equal liberty and equal rights, have brought this mighty mischief upon us, and I fear that it will rapidly destroy progress, until peace and order, freedom and property shall be destroyed." President Jefferson, when he learned of Chase's tirade, was not amused, and he complained to Joseph H. Nicholson, a congressional representative from Maryland: "Ought this seditious and official attack on the principles of our Constitution, and the proceedings of a State, go unpunished?"

Thus prompted by the president, the House of Representatives appointed a committee to consider whether impeachment of Justice Chase was appropriate. The committee recommended impeachment, and the House concurred on

March 12, 1804, by a vote of 73 to 32, forwarding eight articles of impeachment to the Senate for trial. They detailed a variety of alleged misconduct in Sedition Act trials, the treason trial of Fries, and the Baltimore grand jury charge. The following year, trial commenced in the Senate on January 3, 1805, with Chase represented by an exceptional team of influential lawyers. In the end, votes taken on March 1, 1805, failed to produce a two-thirds majority on any of the articles of impeachment. The article complaining of Chase's Baltimore grand jury charge garnered the most votes—19 of 34—but even this vote fell short of the needed total. Chastened, but not removed from office, Chase's remaining years on the Supreme Court played out quietly. Chief Justice John Marshall assumed the task of writing opinions for the Court in all its major decisions; thus, the work of Chase and the other associate justices fell under Marshall's substantial shadow. Affliction with gout also caused Chase to miss much of the work of the Court during his final years. He died on June 19, 1811, in Baltimore.

"I never sat with him without pain, as he was forever getting into some intemperate and unnecessary squabble," Federal District Judge Richard Peters of Pennsylvania said of Justice Samuel Chase. Chase's defenders, then and now, have seen him as the victim of the politically motivated attacks of those who could not abide his high Federalist principles. His detractors—and these have been many—have seen rather an imperious and abusive justice, wholly lacking in judicial temperament. Whichever verdict is more nearly correct, it is fair to say that Chase brought no great credit to the Supreme Court during his tenure as an associate justice. In fact, if the more temperate Chief Justice John Marshall had not been able to convey a sense that the Supreme Court was above the ordinary political squabbles of the day, the Court might never have attained the powerful role that it did. If Chase contributed to this development at all, it was an exemplar of the road that the Supreme Court wisely chose not to follow.

Further Reading

Berger, Raoul. "The Transfiguration of Samuel Chase: A Rebuttal." *Brigham Young University Law Review* (Summer 1992): 559–596.

Elsmere, Jane Shaffer. *Justice Samuel Chase*. Muncie, Ind.: Janevar Pub. Co., 1980.

Haw, James A., et al. *Stormy Patriot: The Life of Samuel Chase*. Baltimore: Maryland Historical Society, 1980.

Presser, Stephen B. "The Verdict on Samuel Chase and His 'Apologist.'" In *Seriatim: The Supreme Court Before John Marshall*. Edited by Scott Douglas Gerber. New York: New York University Press, 1998.

Presser, Stephen B. and Becky Bair Hurley. "Saving God's Republic: The Jurisprudence of Samuel Chase." *University of Illinois Law Review* (Summer 1984): 771–822.

Rehnquist, William H. *Grand Inquests: The Historic Impeachments of Justice Samuel Chase and President Andrew Johnson*. New York: William Morrow, 1992.

OLIVER ELLSWORTH (1745–1807)

Chief Justice, 1796–1800

Appointed by President George Washington

OLIVER ELLSWORTH
(United States Supreme Court)

President George Washington's last appointment to the Supreme Court placed the Connecticut statesman Oliver Ellsworth in the chief seat on the nation's highest court. The four years Ellsworth occupied this position were uneventful, and like other Washington appointees, he earned his place in American history chiefly by his political accomplishments—in his case many and varied—before accepting a seat on the Court. As the principal drafter of the Judiciary Act of 1789, Ellsworth made a formative and lasting contribution to the American judicial system. That he briefly acted a part in the system he had played a chief role in scripting was a fitting climax to an illustrious career.

Oliver Ellsworth was born on April 29, 1745, in Windsor, Connecticut, to David Ellsworth and Jemima Leavitt Ellsworth. His parents wished him to become a clergyman and to this end arranged for him to study with Joseph Bellamy, a minister in Bethlehem, Connecticut. In 1762, when he was 17, he entered Yale. Ellsworth's sojourn at Yale was not long, owing to an overly mischievous nature. In his sophomore year a series of disciplinary infractions resulted in his dismissal, and he soon enrolled in the College of New Jersey (which eventually became Princeton University). There he met young men such as William Paterson, with whom he would later have close contact in public life. He graduated in 1766 and returned home to Windsor, where his father prevailed on him to study theology with the Reverend John Smalley. After a year, however, Ellsworth abandoned a ministerial career in favor of a career in law. He first studied under Matthew Griswold but soon had to accept a more affordable apprenticeship with Jesse Root. In 1771 he was admitted to the Connecticut bar.

Ellsworth's early years of practice did not immediately bring financial success. He married Abigail Wolcott, the niece of a former Connecticut governor, but the political and social ties he secured by this union did not alter his fortunes at once. The couple took up residence on a farm owned by Ellsworth's father near Windsor, and he struggled to develop his practice while cutting and selling timber from the farm to make ends meet. Lacking a horse, Ellsworth traveled 10 miles on foot to attend court sessions in nearby Hartford, but in the beginning industry alone did not secure him success: his total earnings from the practice of law for the first three years were a paltry three pounds.

Eventually, though, hard work, family connections, growing experience, and natural ability combined to make his law practice prosper. Soon he entered the field of politics when Windsor elected him its representative to the Connecticut General Assembly in 1773. Continuing in this post the following year, he was also appointed justice of the peace for Hartford County. By 1777 he had gained the post of state's attorney for Hartford County, and that same year he was elected to represent Connecticut in the Continental Congress. His service in these positions ultimately yielded an appointment to Connecticut's Supreme Court of Errors in 1785 and, a year later, to the state's Superior Court.

When the Constitutional Convention met in Philadelphia in 1787, Oliver Ellsworth arrived as one of three Connecticut delegates. In this capacity he helped negotiate the compromise that forged a union of both small and large states by creating a bicameral legislature that partially protected the interests of each. The House of Representatives favored the populous states, because their populations would guarantee them proportionately greater representation in the chamber. The Senate protected the interests of less populous states by giving them an equal voice there. Ellsworth is also credited with suggesting the title for the framework of government as "the government of the United States." After making these important contributions, though, Ellsworth's responsibilities in Connecticut forced him to leave the Constitutional Convention early and thus prevented him from signing the proposed Constitution.

Upon his return to Connecticut, Ellsworth labored vigorously for ratification of the Constitution, and when his state joined the others in the new union, it promptly selected Ellsworth as one of its first senators. He served in the U.S. Senate until 1796 and commanded such respect among the other legislators that Aaron Burr is said to have suggested that "If Ellsworth had happened to spell the name of the Deity with two d's, it would have taken the Senate three weeks to expunge the superfluous letter." While in the Senate, Ellsworth's most important legislative contribution was drafting, along with future Supreme Court justice William Paterson, the Judiciary Act of 1789, signed into law by President George Washington on September 24, 1789. This seminal act established the structure of the federal court system, providing for the Supreme Court to consist of a chief justice and five associate justices and creating 13 district and three circuit courts. The first nine sections of the act are written in William Paterson's hand, while the remaining sections—10 through 23—are in Ellsworth's.

Immediately after the Judiciary Act became law, President Washington nominated John Jay to serve as the Court's first chief justice. Jay served in this post for six years but resigned in 1795 after being elected governor of New York. Washington sought first to elevate Associate Justice John Rutledge to replace Jay as chief justice, but although Rutledge served temporarily in the position for a few months, the Senate ultimately refused to confirm his appointment. Washington then approached Associate Justice William Cushing to accept the chief seat, but Cushing refused the nomination. Finally, the president nominated Oliver Ellsworth to become chief justice of the Court. The Senate confirmed the appointment the following day, and a few days later Ellsworth took the oath of office.

Ellsworth served only three years as chief justice, and his tenure on the Court was uneventful. No landmark cases came before Court during these years. Like Jay before him, Ellsworth was also pressed into service as a diplomat, being sent by President John Adams as a minister to France at the end of 1799. This diplomatic venture, which partially resolved growing differences between the United States and France, took a heavy toll on Ellsworth's physical well-being. When he finally arrived in Paris in March 1800, his health was ruined. In October 1800 he wrote to President John Adams from France, informing the president that he would not be returning immediately to the United States, and that he was therefore resigning his position as chief justice:

> Constantly afflicted with the gravel, and the gout in my kidnies, the unfortunate fruit of sufferings at sea, and by a winters journey through Spain, I am not in a condition to undertake a voyage to America at this late season of the year; nor if I were there, would I be able to discharge my official duties. I must therefore pray you, Sir, to accept this my resignation of the office of Chief Justice of the United States.

Ellsworth returned home to Connecticut the following spring to a partial retirement, though he served for a time on the Governor's Council. He briefly considered undertaking an appointment as chief justice of the Connecticut Supreme Court but ultimately declined the position. He died in Windsor on November 26, 1807.

Oliver Ellsworth's career exhibited the breadth of political and judicial experience common among many of the earliest justices on the Supreme Court, who ascended to that Court only after lengthy political careers. As was often the case in the years before the Supreme Court achieved a prominent place within the American political system, Oliver Ellsworth's accomplishments as a politician outshone his accomplishments as a justice of the Supreme Court. The Court he briefly shepherded was still in its infancy, in search of its own identity within the national system. That Ellsworth was not able to secure a prominent place for it around the American table did not obscure his otherwise substantial contributions to the life of his country.

Further Reading

Brown, William G. *The Life of Oliver Ellsworth.* New York: Macmillan, 1905; New York: Da Capo Press, 1970.

Casto, William R. *Oliver Ellsworth and the Creation of the Federal Republic.* New York: Second Circuit Committee on History and Commemorative Events, 1997.

———. "Oliver Ellsworth's Calvinism: A Biographical Essay on Religion and Political Psychology in the Early Republic." *Journal of Church and State* 36 (1994): 507–525.

———. *The Supreme Court in the Early Republic: The Chief Justiceships of John Jay and Oliver Ellsworth.* Columbia, S.C.: University of South Carolina Press, 1995.

Lettieri, Ronald John. *Connecticut's Young Man of the Revolution: Oliver Ellsworth.* Hartford: American Bicentennial Commission of Connecticut, 1978.

Bushrod Washington (1762–1829)

Associate Justice, 1799–1829

Appointed by President John Adams

Bushrod Washington
(United States Supreme Court)

Bushrod Washington, nephew of President George Washington, was a man of significant ability whose historical reputation suffers the misfortune of his having dwelled within the long shadows cast by his uncle and by a famous friend, Chief Justice John Marshall. His tenure on the U.S. Supreme Court roughly coincided with that of Marshall, who dominated the Court during the first three decades of the 19th century. Marshall's preeminence therefore left Washington and the other associate justices of this period to carry out their work far from public attention, little noticed by their contemporaries and by historians of the Court.

George Washington was present at the birth of Bushrod Washington to John Augustine Washington and Hannah Bushrod Washington on June 5, 1762, in Westmoreland County, Virginia. Bushrod's father was a member of the Virginia legislature and a county magistrate. George Washington had no children, and Bushrod, his favorite nephew, became the object of considerable attention from the man who would eventually be the first president of the United States. Bushrod's education included private tutoring at the home of Richard Henry Lee, followed by attendance at the College of William and Mary, beginning in 1775. After graduating from William and Mary in 1778, Bushrod returned home for a short period, but in 1780 he joined with other aspiring law students at his alma mater to study with the first American professor of law, George Wythe. Among his fellow students during this period was John Marshall, future chief justice of the Supreme Court.

British general Cornwallis's invasion of Virginia in the first part of 1781 inspired Washington to join the Continental Army. He served in the cavalry under John Mercer, seeing action at Green Spring and witnessing Cornwallis's surrender at Yorktown. Subsequently, Washington studied law in Philadelphia, Pennsylvania, under James Wilson, an eminent lawyer. Bushrod's uncle, George Washington, appears to have paid the necessary fee for this study with Wilson, who would play a leading role in the 1787 Constitutional Convention and would later be one of President George Washington's first appointments to the Supreme Court.

In 1784 Bushrod Washington established a law practice, first in Westmoreland County, then in Alexandria, and finally, around 1790, in Richmond, Virginia. In 1785 he married Julia Ann Blackburn, whose father, Thomas Blackburn, had been aide-de-camp to General George Washington during the Revolutionary War. Like his famous uncle, Bushrod and his wife were childless.

In 1787, the year that the luminaries of American politics met in Philadelphia for the Constitutional Convention, Bushrod Washington inaugurated his own political career by winning a seat in the Virginia House of Delegates. He served there with John Marshall, and the two also participated in the Virginia convention that ratified the U.S. Constitution. During the following decade, Washington developed a thriving legal practice in Richmond, Virginia. His reputation grew to the point that students clamored to apprentice with him to study law. Washington trained a number of them, including Henry Clay. He appeared regularly to argue cases before the Virginia Court of Appeals, often against his future colleague on the Supreme Court, John Marshall. He served as a reporter for this court and ultimately published a two-volume summary of the cases argued there from 1700 to 1796, titled *Reports of Cases Argued in the Court of Appeals of Virginia.*

Despite his kinship with George Washington and his favored-nephew status, Bushrod gained no overt political preferences from this connection. In fact, his one attempt to petition the president for an appointment as a district attorney in Virginia met with terse rejection. President Washington responded to the request bluntly: "Do you think yourself worthy of the office, and even if you do, do you suppose I would use the patronage of my office for the benefit of anyone, however worthy, connected with me?" By the same token, Bushrod's uncle does not appear to have used his influence with President John Adams to secure his nephew's nomination for a seat on the Court when one came open in 1798.

Bushrod Washington's old legal mentor, James Wilson, died in August 1798. He had served almost a decade as an associate justice of the Supreme Court, having been appointed to that position by President Washington upon the initial creation of the Court. Following Wilson's death, President Adams decided to find a Virginian to fill the vacant seat on the Court. He therefore focused his attention on John Marshall and Bushrod Washington, both of whom had followed the urging of George Washington and announced candidacies for the U.S. Congress. When President Adams offered the seat first to Marshall, he declined in favor of pursuing his congressional election campaign. Bushrod Washington, however, ever more the student of law than of politics, happily abandoned his own campaign when Adams approached him about the vacant position on the Supreme Court. The Senate confirmed his nomination on December 20, 1798, and Washington thereupon began a judicial career that would span more than three decades.

Two years after Washington joined the Court, its chief justice, Oliver Ellsworth, resigned while serving the United States on a diplomatic mission to Europe. To fill this chief seat, President Adams nominated John Marshall, who, once confirmed, would serve until his death in 1835. The tenure of the two Virginians, Chief Justice Marshall and Associate Justice Washington, would thus roughly coincide; and Marshall, by reason of his dominance on the Court over the decades, would eclipse Washington's own presence there.

Marshall was able to eliminate, for the most part, the practice of having the members of the Court publish *seriatim* opinions, in which the various justices explained their reasons for reaching a particular decision in separate opinions. In place of this practice, the chief justice began a new one of announcing Court decisions largely by means of joint opinions expressing the majority view. Moreover, Marshall generally chose to write the opinions of the Court himself. These innovations had the effect of diminishing the public role played by other justices on the Court. Washington, for instance, wrote relatively few opinions over the course of his three decades as a justice—81 in all—and only rarely dissented from a decision by the Court.

Washington's chief distinction during his long tenure on the Court was unflattering, though not concerning his work as a justice but rather his attitudes and practices concerning slaveholding. As George Washington's heir, Bushrod inherited Mount Vernon with instructions to free the slaves who worked there upon the death of the former president's wife, Martha Washington. Though he did so, he later brought more slaves to Mount Vernon in an attempt to rescue the estate from dilapidation. This attempt failed, and Washington ultimately sold many of the Mount Vernon slaves in 1821 under circumstances that separated some families at the auction block. On hearing of this abolitionists clamored that Washington should have freed the slaves, but he insisted that they were his property and that he had every right to dispose of them as he saw fit. As president of the American Colonization Society, Washington favored the emancipation of slaves and their recolonization in Africa, but only on terms that protected the rights of present slaveholders.

Like other justices on the Court, Washington not only attended sessions of the full Court but also participated in circuit court proceedings. He began initially on the southern circuit, but beginning in 1802 and for the rest of his life, he rode the third circuit, which included Pennsylvania and New Jersey. Bushrod Washington died in Philadelphia on November 26, 1829; his wife, Julia, died three days later, while attempting to transport her husband's body back to Mount Vernon for burial. Justice Joseph Story delivered the following eulogy:

> He was a learned judge. Not that every-day learning which may be gathered up by a hasty reading of books and case; but that which is the result of long-continued laborious services, and comprehensive studies. He read to learn, and not to quote; to digest and master, and not merely to display. He was not easily satisfied. If he was not as profound as some, he was more exact than most men. But the value of his learning was, that it was the keystone of all his judgments. He indulged not the rash desire to fashion the law to his own views; but to follow out its precepts, with a sincere good faith and simplicity. Hence, he possessed the happy faculty of yielding just the proper weight to authority; neither, on the one hand, surrendering himself to the dictates of other judges, nor, on the other hand, overruling settled doctrines upon his own private notions of policy or justice.

Bushrod Washington brought to his position as an associate justice a single-minded passion for the study of law, and he used his considerable legal skills to support quietly, yet insistently, the efforts of Marshall to enhance the Court's power and prestige. As is so often the case of quiet allies, history rewarded Washington's unseen support of Marshall's leadership with obscurity. Nevertheless, this support undoubtedly aided Marshall in crafting a vigorous role for the federal courts within the new nation.

Further Reading

Binney, Horace. *Bushrod Washington.* Philadelphia: C. Sherman & Son, 1858.

Blaustein, Albert P. and Roy M. Mersky. "Bushrod Washington." In *The Justices of the United States Supreme Court 1789–1969: Their Lives and Major Opinions,* vol. 1. Edited by Leon Friedman and Fred L. Israel. New York: R. R. Bowker Co., 1969.

Stoner, James R. Jr. "Heir Apparent: Bushrod Washington and Federal Justice in the Early Republic." In *Seriatim: The Supreme Court Before John Marshall.* Edited by Scott Douglas Gerber. New York: New York University Press, 1998.

Custer, Lawrence B. "Bushrod Washington and John Marshall: A Preliminary Inquiry." *American Journal of Legal History* 4 (1960): 34–48.

Dunne, Gerald T. "Bushrod Washington and the Mount Vernon Slaves." *Supreme Court Historical Society Yearbook, 1980.* Washington, D.C.: Supreme Court Historical Society, 1980.

ALFRED MOORE (1755–1810)

Associate Justice, 1800–1804

Appointed by President John Adams

ALFRED MOORE
(United States Supreme Court)

Alfred Moore served four years as an associate justice of the U.S. Supreme Court, but little historical record remains of his brief tenure on the Court. He passed quickly onto the national scene and then, just as quickly, departed from it, leaving scarcely a ripple in the wake of his passage. Even while he was on the Court, circumstances prevented him from participating in *Marbury v. Madison* (1803), one of the most important decisions ever rendered by the Supreme Court. If the Court has a most shadowy corner, little illuminated by the attention of historians, then Moore surely occupies a place there.

Alfred Moore was born on May 21, 1755, in Brunswick, North Carolina. He did not always know the obscurity that cloaked his abbreviated sojourn on the

Court. In fact, Moore was born into an influential political family and his years before joining the Court exhibited a steady course of significant, if not preeminent, accomplishments. Moore received his early education in Boston, and then returned to North Carolina, where he studied law with his father and was admitted to the bar in 1775. That same year he married Susanna Elizabeth Eagles and joined the fight against the British by accepting a commission as captain with the First North Carolina Continental Regiment, commanded by his uncle, Colonel James Moore.

The Revolutionary War, though, took a heavy toll on the Moore family. James Moore died in January 1777; Alfred's father, Maurice, and his brother died soon after. These tragedies prompted Alfred to resign his commission in March 1777 in order to care for his mother and the family plantation. But Moore continued some measure of military activity by serving in the militia, where he helped harass the British lines; perhaps in retaliation, the British plundered the Moore family plantation on Eagles Island, near Wilmington. After the British finally retreated from the area, Moore spent the rest of the war serving as judge advocate of the North Carolina military forces.

When the war was over, North Carolina rewarded Moore's service by electing him to the state legislature. Soon after, beginning in May 1782, he replaced James Iredell as attorney general of North Carolina. Over the following years Moore earned a reputation as one of the state's top triumvirate of lawyers, joined by James Iredell and William R. Davie. Toward the end of this period, the Constitutional Convention met in Philadelphia and proposed a constitution for ratification by the states; North Carolina did not include Moore as one of its delegates to the Convention. As a Federalist, Moore supported ratification, but he failed to win a delegate's slot in the first North Carolina ratifying convention, which met in July 1788 and declined to ratify the Constitution. The following year, after he won a seat as a delegate to a second ratifying convention, he joined James Iredell and William R. Davie in persuading the convention to ratify the U.S. Constitution in November 1789.

In 1791 the North Carolina legislature passed a law creating the post of solicitor general. Moore viewed this act as an unconstitutional intrusion on his powers, and he resigned from his position as attorney general in protest. But unable to abandon political life for good, he successfully ran for a seat in the North Carolina legislature in 1792. A few years later he narrowly lost his election bid for the U.S. Senate. By the end of the decade, however, he had gained the attention of President John Adams, who appointed him in 1798 as one of the commissioners delegated to negotiate a treaty with the Cherokee Nation. Moore did not complete his service in this position, owing to his election to a seat on the North Carolina Superior Court in 1799. He served on this court for a year; then the death of James Iredell in the fall of 1799 created a vacancy on the U.S. Supreme Court that President John Adams sought to fill with an appointment from North Carolina. William R. Davie had perhaps the better credentials for the post, but Adams had only recently appointed him as a plenipotentiary to France (with Oliver Ellsworth, who was chief justice of the Supreme Court at the time). Thus, on December 4, 1799, Moore won the nomination instead. He was confirmed by the Senate shortly thereafter and took the oath of office on April 21, 1800, inaugurating a most inauspicious career as a justice of the Supreme Court.

Alfred Moore joined the Court on the eve of its transformation from a little-regarded institution in American life into a co-equal branch of government. Within a year after Moore had been sworn in as a justice, President Adams appointed a new chief justice: John Marshall. Marshall secured the Court's authority as a final arbiter of the Constitution's meaning and would thus give it a powerful voice within the structure of American law. Time and circumstance, though, deprived Moore of any real part in this transformation.

Moore wrote only one opinion during his four years on the Court, and though it raised a firestorm of protest at the time, it established no enduring legal principle but only stoked the flames of discord between Federalists and Republicans. The case, *Bas v. Tingy* (1800), involved an American ship that had been captured by the French in 1799 and then, within a few weeks, recaptured by an American ship. Applicable law rewarded the recapturing ship according to whether the original capture had been by an "enemy." The issue in the case, over which anti-French Federalists and pro-French Republicans were in sharp disagreement, was whether France amounted to an "enemy" at the time. The Supreme Court held that a limited state of war did, in fact, exist between the United States and France at the time. This ruling infuriated Republicans, prompting one Republican newspaper to call for the impeachment of the entire court. Moore's opinion in the case—written at a time when justices still announced their individual decisions through separate or *seriatim* opinions—was the only one he would ever write while on the Court. It spanned a mere handful of paragraphs and in straightforward terms expressed his agreement that France was indeed an enemy.

Moore missed the Court's main event during his brief tenure: the decision in *Marbury v. Madison* (1803). *Marbury* presented the Court with an opportunity to address the question of whether it had authority to declare acts of Congress void for violating the Constitution. In early February 1803, when the Court heard evidence and argument in the case, travel delays prevented Moore from arriving at the Court from North Carolina in time to hear most of the presentations in the case. He was therefore not able to participate in the Court's decision, announced by Marshall on February 24, holding that the Court did indeed have the power to decide the constitutionality of federal laws.

Circuit riding, the bane of many early Supreme Court justices, took its toll on Moore's health. All the justices were responsible not only for attending and participating in sessions of the Supreme Court but also for presiding over sessions of the Circuit Courts of Appeals. This latter responsibility required significant travel that strained the health of many justices. On January 26, 1804, Moore resigned his seat on the Supreme Court and returned home to North Carolina, where he died six years later, on October 15, 1810.

The leadership of John Marshall on the Supreme Court eclipsed the presence of most other justices during the first few decades of the 19th century, and perhaps none more so than the North Carolina lawyer Alfred Moore. Though successful as a lawyer and politician, Moore was not able to create a name for himself on the Supreme Court. He was physically a small man, described as standing a mere 4′5″tall, easily dwarfed by taller men; and—at least on the Supreme Court—his diminutive physical stature mirrored his influence.

Further Reading

Davis, Junius. *Alfred Moore and James Iredell, Revolutionary Patriots.* Raleigh: North Carolina Society of the Sons of the Revolution, 1899.

Friedman, Leon. "Alfred Moore." In *The Justices of the United States Supreme Court 1789–1969: Their Lives and Major Opinions,* Vol. 1. Edited by Leon Friedman and Fred L. Israel. New York: R. R. Bowker Co., 1969.

Mason, Robert. *Namesake: Alfred Moore 1755–1810, Soldier and Jurist.* Southern Pines, S.C.: Moore County Historical Association, 1989.

JOHN MARSHALL (1755–1835)

Chief Justice, 1801–1835

Appointed by President John Adams

JOHN MARSHALL
(Engraving, Library of Congress)

John Marshall piloted the Supreme Court through the first three and a half decades of the 19th century and set a course for the Court's position within the national order that endures to the present day. On formative national issues he penned judicial opinions still studied today, not simply as specimens of history but as living charters for present political and legal realities. It is no wonder, then, that Justice Oliver Wendell Holmes, himself among the greatest jurists ever to have occupied a seat on the Court, named Marshall as the nation's preeminent judge: "If American law were to be represented by a single figure, skeptic and worshipper alike would agree that the figure could be one alone, and that one, John Marshall." James A. Garfield was even more descriptive of Marshall's formative influence on the Court and the Constitution. "Marshall found the Constitution paper; and he made it power," Garfield declared. "He found a skeleton, and he clothed it with flesh and blood."

—∞—

When John Marshall was born in Germantown, Virginia, on September 24, 1755, the birth of the nation whose laws he would eventually superintend lay more than three decades in the future. Marshall's family, though, already occupied a prominent place within the existing social and political order. Thomas Marshall, the father of the future justice, was a member of colonial Virginia's House of Burgesses and ultimately served as a delegate to the Virginia Provincial Convention of 1775. Mary Randolph Keith Marshall, the justice's mother, traced family ties to the wide and prosperous Randolph family, which also claimed Thomas Jefferson as a member. Marshall was educated first at home by his mother and later with local Anglican clergy. But the Revolutionary War intruded itself on his studies, and he gained a commission as lieutenant in the Culpepper Minute Men, with whom he fought at the battle of Great Bridge. Marshall later served as an officer in the Virginia Continental Regiment, where he saw action at the battles of Brandywine, Germantown, and Stony Point.

In 1780, after the conclusion of his military service, John Marshall resumed his studies, this time under George Wythe, who taught law at the College of William and Mary. His legal instruction was of brief duration, however. After three months he left the college, returned to Fauquier County, and was admitted to practice law before the Virginia bar. In 1783 he married Mary Willis Ambler of Richmond, Virginia, and established a home with her there; they eventually had a total of 10 children. For the next 15 years, Marshall practiced law and participated in Virginia politics, serving in the Virginia House of Delegates, on the Virginia Privy Council of State from 1782 to 1784, and as the Recorder of the Richmond Hustings Court from 1785 to 1788. In the latter position Marshall assisted in meting out justice in a variety of minor civil and criminal matters; this would be his only judicial experience prior to ascending to the chief seat on the nation's highest court.

In June 1788 Marshall attended the Virginia convention that ultimately ratified the U.S. Constitution, lending his voice in support of ratification. After the Constitution became effective, though, Marshall avoided the steady stream of federal posts offered to him. He concentrated instead on building his legal practice, finding a solid business in defending Virginia debtors from their British creditors. This work eventually placed him before the newly created Supreme Court in 1796, where he argued—unsuccessfully—the case of *Ware v. Hylton* (1796), in which the Court invalidated a debtor-favoring Virginia law held to be inconsistent with the Treaty of Paris. President John Adams finally coaxed Marshall into federal service on a diplomatic mission to France, with Charles Pinckney and Elbridge Gerry. The unofficial French attempt to solicit a bribe from the American diplomats as the price of entering into negotiations with France, referred to as the XYZ Affair, ultimately made the mission unsuccessful. But Marshall found his national reputation increased among fellow citizens outraged at the French offense. Former president George Washington thereupon persuaded Marshall to run for Congress, and Marshall won election to the House of Representatives in 1799. The following year President Adams appointed him secretary of state.

When Chief Justice Oliver Ellsworth announced his resignation from the Supreme Court in late 1800, Marshall's service in the Adams administration made him a likely candidate for the post. Adams, though, offered the position first to John Jay, a former chief justice, but Jay declined the opportunity to return to the Court from which he had resigned to become governor of New York. After Jay's refusal, Adams came under significant pressure to elevate Associate Justice William Paterson to the chief seat on the Court. He finally named Marshall for the position on January 20, 1801, however, and the Senate somewhat reluctantly confirmed the nomination on January 27.

Marshall's name would be written prominently across the ensuing years of the Court's history, chiefly because he persuaded his colleagues on the Court to abandon the practice of writing separate or *seriatim* opinions in favor of a single joint opinion of the Court, which Marshall routinely undertook to write himself. One observer of this revolution viewed it unhappily. In a letter to Thomas Jefferson, Associate Justice William Johnson, whom Jefferson had appointed to the Court, described Marshall's practice of writing opinions for the full Court:

> When I was on our State Bench, I was accustomed to delivering seriatim opinions in an Appellate Court, and was not a little surprised to find our Chief Justice in the Supreme Court delivering all the opinions. . . . But I remonstrated in vain; the answer was, he was willing to take the trouble, and it is a mark of respect to him. I soon, however, found the real cause. Cushing was incompetent, Chase could not be got to think or write, Patterson was a slow man and willingly declined the trouble, and the other two judges [Marshall and Washington] you know are commonly estimated as one judge.

Whatever the origin of the practice, however, it would ascribe Marshall's name to the leading opinions of his years on the Court, and these would profoundly shape the course of American law.

Early in his tenure as chief justice, John Marshall crafted the opinion that would most secure his place in the Court's history. In *Marbury v. Madison* (1803), the Supreme Court confronted the controversial attempt by departing Federalist lawmakers to appoint Federalist justices of the peace who would carry on their political principles even after President Thomas Jefferson's Democratic-Republicans had swept into power. When Jefferson's administration declined to deliver commissions for these positions, one of the appointed justices of the peace—William Marbury—sought relief in the Supreme Court, seeking an order commanding James Madison, Jefferson's secretary of state, to deliver his commission. Though Marshall's opinion for the Court concluded that Marbury had a right to the commission that had been denied him, it focused attention on the question of whether the Court had the power to order delivery of the commission. The Judiciary Act of 1789, which had given initial shape to the system of federal courts established in broad outlines by Article III of the Constitution, purported to grant the Court authority to issue orders such as the one sought by William Marbury. But the Court concluded that this grant of authority contravened the terms of the Constitution. More important, the Court determined that *it* had constitutional power to declare this fact: that it had power to declare an act of Congress—such as the Judiciary Act of 1789—unconstitutional, insofar as the Court found that its provisions violated the Constitution. Thus, the Federalist Court surrendered the narrow field at issue to the Jeffersonians. The Federalist appointee, William Marbury, went away empty-handed, because the Court found that it lacked the power to help him. Nevertheless, Marshall's opinion in *Marbury* captured for the Court the far more important power of *judicial review*—that is, the power to rule on the constitutionality of legislative enactments. By seizing this power, Marshall immeasurably enhanced the prestige and power of the Court, moving it from a position of weakness with respect to the other two coordinate branches of government into a position of equal prominence.

In general, John Marshall championed a wide scope for the exercise of national power. In *McColloch v. Maryland* (1819), Marshall's opinion for the Court secured a solid foundation for such national power by construing the "necessary and proper" clause of Article I of the Constitution as granting Congress broad latitude to choose among a variety of means to carry out its enumerated powers. At issue in *McColloch* was whether Congress had the authority to charter a national bank. When Alexander Hamilton first proposed the bank in 1791, James Madison and Thomas Jefferson argued that legislation chartering it would exceed Congress's power under the Constitution. But Congress disagreed and subsequently chartered the First Bank of the United States. At the end of 20 years, however, when the charter expired, a Jeffersonian Congress declined to renew it. After the War of 1812, Congress considered the issue again, and in 1816 the Second Bank of the United States was chartered. Many Jeffersonians, however, continued to oppose the Bank, which some states attempted to tax. When Maryland did so, and the Bank's cashier refused to pay the state tax, the matter eventually landed before the Supreme Court.

Marshall's opinion found that Congress had power to charter the Bank. Not impressed with appeals pointing out the lack of any specific authority to create a bank in the U.S. Constitution, Marshall insisted instead that the Constitution by its nature spoke in broad, sweeping terms, and one should not expect it to provide detailed descriptions of legislative power. "We must never forget," he wrote, "that it is a *a constitution* we are expounding." Marshall concluded that the power to create a national bank was implicitly authorized by the Constitution, and that it furthermore fell within the constitutional authority of Congress to pass "all laws which shall be necessary and proper for carrying into execution" Congress's enumerated powers. As to the issue of whether a state was authorized to tax the Bank of the United States, Marshall's opinion for the Court concluded that the power to tax was the power to destroy and that no state had the power to undermine Congress's legislative work through punitive taxes.

Through *McColloch,* the Marshall court interpreted the Constitution as granting broad scope to national power. During the same decade, Marshall and his colleagues addressed the scope of what would become the most important of all congressional powers: the power to regulate interstate commerce. In *Gibbons v. Ogden* (1824), conflicting federal and state laws relating to navigation on a state's waterways forced the Court to consider the breadth of congressional authority to regulate commerce among the states. In a landmark decision, the Court concluded that Congress did properly regulate traffic on state's waterways, because the regulation of navigation along state waterways affected interstate commerce. This ruling would eventually arm Congress with power to make laws on an immense range of subjects and provide a key underpinning for Congress's modern legislative authority.

By 1812 Democratic appointments to the Supreme Court had deprived Federalists of their advantage there, but Marshall succeeded in dominating the Court's decisions for more than a decade after this point. Up until 1825, when his influence on the Court finally began to decline, he authored a majority of the Court's opinions. In the last decade of his tenure, Marshall's leadership waned and health problems sapped his strength. He underwent gall bladder surgery in 1831 and suffered the death of his wife the following year. In February 1835 he attended his last session of the Court before seeking medical attention for an intestinal blockage. He died six months later, on July 6, 1835.

History has robed Chief Justice Marshall in superlatives. The Virginian found the Supreme Court lacking in the preeminence necessary to attract and—especially—retain the services of superior jurists. The decade before his ascension to the Court's chief post saw men such as John Jay and Oliver Ellsworth briefly hold the same position, only to abandon it for more lively political occupations. Marshall, however, forged an institutional reputation for the Court that would elevate it in the pantheon of American institutions to a position as a co-equal branch of government. He did this even after shifting political currents surrounded him with fellow justices who were not initially aligned with his Federalist principles but who, by the force of his leadership and his powers of reason, came eventually to be his allies in creating a Court with the stature by which it is known today.

Further Reading

Baker, Leonard. *John Marshall: A Life in Law.* New York: Macmillan, 1974.

Faulkner, Robert Kenneth. *The Jurisprudence of John Marshall.* Princeton. N.J.: Princeton University Press, 1968.

Hobson, Charles F. *The Great Chief Justice: John Marshall and the Rule of Law.* Lawrence: University Press of Kansas, 1996.

Johnson, Herbert Alan. *The Chief Justiceship of John Marshall, 1801–1835.* Columbia: University of South Carolina Press, 1997.

Smith, Jean Edward. *John Marshall: Definer of a Nation.* New York: H. Holt and Co., 1996.

William Johnson (1771–1834)

Associate Justice, 1804–1834

Appointed by President Thomas Jefferson

William Johnson
(United States Supreme Court)

The son of a South Carolina blacksmith, William Johnson forged the tradition of dissent on the Supreme Court. Appointed by President Thomas Jefferson in the wake of a Democratic ascendancy over the Federalists, Johnson served his tenure on a Court dominated by Chief Justice John Marshall. And though Marshall successfully wielded both his position and the force of personality to present a largely united face for the Court in most cases, Johnson remained a frequent renegade. Not convinced that the Court's stature as a democratic institution required invariable unanimity, Justice Johnson regularly voiced a contrary determination in important cases.

William Johnson was born in Charleston, South Carolina, on December 27, 1771, on the eve of the Revolutionary War. His father was a blacksmith, a longtime state lawmaker, and a Revolutionary patriot. Through William's mother, Sarah Nightingale Johnson, the Johnson family would eventually inherit substantial wealth. But the elder Johnson's patriotic activities made him an enemy of the British, and after their capture of Charleston, he became a prisoner of war, held for a time in Florida and only united with his family after two and a half years.

The Revolutionary War seems not to have greatly unsettled Johnson's educational opportunities. He graduated in 1790 from the College of New Jersey (now Princeton University) first in his class. Thereafter he studied law with Charles Cotesworth Pinckney, the prominent South Carolina Federalist who had himself studied law at the Inns of Court in England. Johnson was admitted to the bar in 1793. The following year he married Sarah Bennett and was elected to serve the first of three two-year terms in the South Carolina House of Representatives. While serving as a state legislator, Johnson fell under the sway of Jeffersonian principles. By 1798 he had been made speaker of the House of Representatives. The following year he earned an appointment to the newly created South Carolina Court of Common Pleas.

After Thomas Jefferson won the presidential election of 1800, he quickly found himself at odds with a Federalist Supreme Court. Jefferson had to endure Chief Justice Marshall's opinion in *Marbury v. Madison* (1803), in particular its declaration that Jefferson's administration had unlawfully deprived a justice of the peace—a Federalist—of his commission. Though Marshall's opinion ultimately concluded that the Court lacked the power to compel Jefferson's secretary of state James Madison to convey the commission, it was chastisement enough to have the Court declare in sober terms that Jefferson and his party had inflicted a wrong, even if the Court was powerless to right it. Even more grievous to Jeffersonians was *Marbury*'s principle of judicial review, which armed federal courts with the power to void the product of popular democratic will. When Associate Justice Alfred Moore resigned his seat on the Supreme Court in 1804, Jefferson quickly moved to fill the vacant seat with a jurist more inclined to the president's political philosophy. William Johnson seemed well suited to penetrate the Federalist citadel with Jeffersonian principles. He was nominated by the president on March 22, 1804, and confirmed by the Senate within two days.

President Jefferson no doubt hoped that he had chosen a man of resolute and independent spirit, capable of resisting Marshall's attempt to unify the Court along lines amenable to Marshall's own judicial philosophy. On this point, at least, Jefferson had correctly gauged the temper of his first appointment to the Court. Johnson would eventually leave his mark as a justice willing to air disagreements with his brethren through dissenting opinions. He was not successful, though, in challenging Marshall's attempt to persuade the other justices on the Court to present a single face to the nation through the adoption—whenever possible—of an opinion for the Court, rather than having each announce opinions separately. If Marshall was willing to write the most important opinions of the Court himself, then the other justices were inclined to let him do so, to the great consternation of observers such as Thomas Jefferson. In 1820 the former president complained in a letter that judges were "the subtle corps of sappers and miners constantly working under ground to undermine the foundations of our confederated fabric." In Jefferson's mind, this hidden demolition of democratic principles worked under the cloak of such "opinions of the Court" as Marshall had successfully championed. Jefferson, though, saw them as engines of antidemocratic destruction: "An opinion is huddled up in conclave, perhaps by a majority of one, delivered as if unanimous, and with the silent acquiescence of lazy or timid associates, by a crafty chief judge, who sophisticates the law to his mind, by the turn of his own reasoning."

However much he may have chafed at the practice of substituting an opinion of the Court for seriatim opinions by the various justices, Johnson ultimately acquiesced to this practice, at least partially. He tried to explain to Jefferson the delicate position he occupied:

> Some case soon occurred in which I differed from my brethren, and I thought it a thing of course to deliver my opinion. But, during the rest of the session I heard nothing but lectures on the indecency of judges cutting at each other, and the loss of reputation which the Virginia appellate court had sustained by pursuing such a course. At length I found that I must either submit to circumstances or become such a cypher in our consultations as to effect no good at all.

Though Johnson reported to Jefferson that he had "bent with the current" on the issue of writing separate opinions, he nevertheless amassed an impressive record of dissent. Not only was he quick to announce his disagreement with the majority's result in particular cases, but he was ready to distance himself from the others' reasoning in a case, even when he agreed with the particular result; thus, he frequently authored concurring opinions. Between 1805 and 1822, Johnson authored roughly half of both dissenting and concurring opinions filed by justices of the Court.

The fierce independence that made William Johnson the first great dissenter also made him willing to frustrate the administration that had appointed him. In the first decade of his service on the Court, Johnson earned the ire of President Jefferson in a decision he rendered while acting as a circuit court judge. Jefferson had successfully obtained legislation imposing a trade embargo against France and England as a means of avoiding American entanglement in the Napoleonic Wars. His administration interpreted the embargo as allowing U.S. authorities to detain any ships at port suspected of attempting to violate the embargo. Adam Gilchrist found his ship detained in Charleston, South Carolina, after port authorities suspected that his stated plan for transporting cotton and rice to Baltimore was nothing more than a ruse to evade the trade embargo. Gilchrist petitioned Johnson, acting as a circuit judge, to free his ship from the grasp of Jeffersonian policy and Johnson, after reportedly boarding the vessel himself and inspecting its cargo, issued orders to the captain of the ship allowing him to depart from Charleston Harbor. In *Gilchrist v. Collector of Charleston* (1808), Johnson argued that Congress had not meant to interfere with normal trade on the mere suspicion that a vessel was seeking to violate the embargo with England and France. Jefferson's administration, he concluded, had exceeded its authority in its adoption of the policy by which Gilchrist's vessel had been detained; and the principle of judicial review established in *Marbury v. Madison* authorized Johnson to exercise judicial power to overturn Jefferson's executive action. An irate Jefferson instructed his attorney general, Caesar A. Rodney, to launch a public attack on Johnson's *Gilchrist* opinion, about which Rodney had complained that Johnson had contracted a fatal case of "leprosy of the bench." Johnson himself felt compelled to justify his decision in a published letter.

The independence that Johnson exhibited in the *Gilchrist* case would feature prominently throughout much of his judicial career. The willingness to tread a solitary course applied not only to disagreements with his brethren on the high court but also to disagreements with other southerners. By the last years of his service on the Court, Johnson had become an exile from his home state of South Carolina, residing permanently in New York City. While riding circuit in Charleston in 1823, Johnson authored the opinion in *Elkison v. Deliesseline* (1823), which involved a South Carolina law that required black sailors to be jailed until claimed by a captain or else sold into slavery. Johnson, a slave owner himself, nevertheless thought that the South Carolina law intruded on matters of interstate and foreign commerce over which Congress had exclusive power.

Johnson arrived at the Supreme Court a young man of 32 years, and his tenure there would occupy the remainder of his life. He managed, though, to pursue several other interests beyond the scope of his judicial responsibilities. In 1822 he published a two-volume biography of Revolutionary general Nathanael Greene, and he participated in the founding of the University of South Carolina. His wife, Sarah Bennett Johnson, gave birth to eight children, but only two of these—Anna Hayes and Margaret Bennett—survived to adulthood. William and Sarah later adopted two children who were refugees from Santo Domingo, John and Madeleine L'Engle. Toward the middle of his service on the Supreme Court, Johnson sought some other political appointment that would allow him to leave the Court, but none was forthcoming, and in 1819 the justices received an increase in salary that apparently steeled Johnson to another decade and a half of work on the Court. At the end of that period Justice Johnson underwent surgery for a jaw infection and died shortly thereafter on August 4, 1834, in Brooklyn, New York.

Like the other justices who served on the Marshall court, Johnson's contributions during these years are inevitably eclipsed by those of the chief justice under which he served. He was a miniature spoiler of Marshall's grand project of increasing the Supreme Court's institutional stature within the nation by presenting a common face to its citizens. As it now appears, Marshall succeeded in spite of the steady stream of dissents and concurrences authored by Justice Johnson. Johnson's accomplishments as a jurist can scarcely equal those of Marshall, but they can perhaps be said to supplement the achievements of the chief justice. If Marshall partially tamed the separate justices to secure the Court's prestige, Johnson demonstrated that the position won by Marshall for the Court within the new republic was durable enough to withstand a vigorous public dialogue among its members.

FURTHER READING

Greenberg, Irwin F. "Justice William Johnson: South Carolina Unionist, 1823–1830." *Pennsylvania History* 36 (1969): 307–34.

Huebner, Timothy S. "Divided Loyalties: Justice William Johnson and the Rise of Disunion in South Carolina, 1822–1834." *Journal of Supreme Court History Annual* (1995): 19–30.

Kolsky, Meredith. "Justice William Johnson and the History of the Supreme Court Dissent." *Georgetown Law Journal* 83 (1995): 2069–2098.

Morgan, Donald. *Justice William Johnson: The First Dissenter.* Columbia: University of South Carolina Press, 1954.

Schroeder, Oliver, Jr. "Life and Judicial Work of Justice William Johnson, Jr." *University of Pennsylvania Law Review* 95 (1946): 164–201; 344–86.

Henry Brockholst Livingston (1757–1823)

Associate Justice, 1807–1823

Appointed by President Thomas Jefferson

Henry Brockholst Livingston
(United States Supreme Court)

President Thomas Jefferson's second appointment to the Supreme Court was the son of a wealthy and politically influential New York family. He rose to prominence in New York politics during the final decade of the 18th century, served for a time on the prestigious New York Supreme Court, and eventually won a seat on the U.S. Supreme Court. But President Jefferson's attempt to make appointments to the Court that would undermine the dominance of its Federalist chief justice, John Marshall, proved—in the case of Livingston—a marked failure. Livingston quickly came under Marshall's considerable influence and spent the greater part of his tenure on the Court in quiet acquiescence to the leadership provided by the chief justice.

Henry Brockholst Livingston was born into a celebrated New York family, though he spent part of his childhood in New Jersey, where his father had transplanted the family's prestige by serving as governor of New Jersey during the Revolutionary War. Henry Brockholst Livingston—who ultimately abandoned use of his first name and chose to be known as "Brockholst"—graduated from the College of New Jersey (now Princeton University) in 1774, on the eve of the Revolutionary War. While at Princeton, Brockholst Livingston had James Madison as a classmate. When the war began, he served under General Philip Schuyler and General Benedict Arnold and ultimately progressed from his initial rank of captain to that of lieutenant colonel. A different service intruded on a further military career, however, and in 1779 Livingston traveled abroad to serve as secretary to John Jay, his sister's husband, American diplomat to Spain, and future chief justice of the U.S. Supreme Court.

The association between Livingston and Jay soon turned bitter and poisoned the relationship between the two men for years. In 1782 Jay departed Spain for France as one of the American commissioners delegated to negotiate the end of the Revolutionary War. Livingston set out for home, bearing dispatches for Congress, but was captured by the British on the return voyage. He managed to destroy the dispatches prior to his capture, but the British held him for a time as a prisoner of war in New York. Eventually, though, he was paroled. He was soon able to undertake the study of law in 1783 with Peter Yates in Albany, New York. Thereafter, Livingston set up a law practice in New York City, where his work included successfully defending the accused in the famous "Manhattan well mystery" case. In that murder trial, Livingston served as co-counsel with Alexander Hamilton and Aaron Burr for the accused, the fiancé of a woman whose body had been found in a well. The ensuing years also saw him enter the arena of politics, winning election in 1786 to the New York Assembly.

Toward the end of the 1780s, Brockholst drifted from the Federalist fold into that of the Democratic Republicans. Unyielding hostility toward his brother-in-law John Jay may have partially fueled this transformation—a hostility given full vent during Jay's 1795 gubernatorial campaign in New York, when Livingston actively opposed Jay's election. Jay won the election of 1795 and again in 1798, but popular sentiment soon veered toward Democratic Republicanism, and Livingston rode the rising tide of political support for the new party to successes of his own. He won election to two more terms in the New York Assembly, and in 1802 he was appointed to a seat on the New York Supreme Court.

Though Livingston eventually earned a reputation as a congenial man, during the early years of his adulthood he appears to have been burdened with a more violent temper. He participated in several duels, with such regularity that one female relative wrote to Livingston's sister at the time he left the country to serve as John Jay's secretary in Spain, warning her to restrain Livingston from his practice while on foreign soil. "Tell Harry to beware of engaging in a quarrel with the Dons in Spain. This dueling is a very foolish way of putting oneself out of the world." Whether this caution had any effect during Livingston's sojourn in Spain is unclear. It did not deter him from further duels, however, and in 1798 he killed a man during one. Livingston's temper also seems to have inspired other forms of enmity against him; in 1785 he was the object of an unsuccessful assassination attempt.

Livingston's appointment to the New York Supreme Court placed him in close association with the eminent jurist James Kent, whose *Commentaries on American Law* (1826—30), would become a classic legal treatise. Also, due to New York's important commercial status, Livingston gained experience in the resolution of business and maritime issues that he would carry forward into his service on the U.S. Supreme Court. While on the state court he was a vigorous participant in the legal disputes that were the court's diet; in four years he authored 149 opinions.

As early as 1804, Livingston's judicial service and Democratic sensibilities had attracted the attention of President Thomas Jefferson, who appears to have considered him for the seat on the Supreme Court that eventually went to Thomas Johnson of South Carolina. Two years later, however, Jefferson seized the opportunity presented by the death of Associate Justice William Paterson to nominate Brockholst Livingston to fill the vacant seat. The Senate confirmed his nomination in December 1806, and Livingston arrived at the Court in time to participate in the February 1807 term.

Livingston's migration away from the Federalist party largely reversed itself once he fell under the influence of the Court's chief justice, John Marshall. He seems to have briefly resisted Marshall's successful effort to assume the major role in announcing the Court's judgments. But he did not become a regular dissenter, as Jefferson's first appointment to the Court, Thomas Johnson, had become. Even when he may have seriously disagreed with the result in a particular case, Livingston seems to have been willing to suppress his own contrary views. For example, as a circuit court justice Livingston wrote an opinion in *Adams v. Storey* (1817) insisting that state insolvency legislation passed retroactively did not offend the Constitution of the United States. Two years later, however, the Court held in *Sturges v. Crowninshield* (1819) that a similar insolvency law discharging a preexisting debt violated the Contracts Clause of the Constitution. Despite the earlier conflicting position Livingston had taken in *Adams v. Storey,* he expressed not a word of dissent to Chief Justice Marshall's opinion for a unanimous Court.

In 17 years on the Court that Jefferson had hoped to pry away from Chief Justice Marshall's dominant federalism, Justice Livingston dissented only eight times. In addition to these dissents, Livingston wrote 38 majority opinions and six concurrences. If he had a particular niche on the Court, it was not in the articulation of decisions in questions of great constitutional moment but in the commercial and maritime cases that had been the steady diet of the New York Supreme Court on which he had briefly served. Here, according to the official eulogy delivered on his death and apparently written by his friend and eminent jurist Associate Justice Joseph Story, Livingston's judicial talents found room for expression:

> His genius and taste had directed his principal attention to the maritime and commercial law; and his extensive experience gave to his judgements in that branch of jurisprudence a peculiar value, which was enhanced by the gravity and beauty of his judicial eloquence.

Justice Livingston was married three times, to Catharine Keteltas, Ann Ludlow, and Catharine Kortright. He had a total of eleven children: five by Catharine Keteltas, three by Ann Ludlow, and three by Catharine Kortright, who survived him. In addition to his work on the Supreme Court, Livingston found time and energy to pursue a variety of public services. He helped found the New-York Historical Society and was a trustee of Columbia University for nearly 40 years. On March 18, 1823, in his 66th year, he died of pleurisy in Washington, D.C. As he had been preceded on the Court by a family relation—his brother-in-law John Jay—so he would be immediately followed by another: Smith Thompson, married twice to Livingstons.

—m—

Justice Joseph Story, before he followed Livingston onto the Supreme Court, had occasion to describe the man who would become his close friend. "Livingston," he wrote,

> has a fine Roman face; an aquiline nose, high forehead, bald head, and projecting chin, indicate deep research, strength, and quickness of mind. I have no hesitation in pronouncing him a very able and independent Judge. He evidently thinks with great solidity and seizes on the strong points of argument. He is luminous, decisive, earnest and impressive on the bench.

In private society he is accessible and easy, and enjoys with great good humor the vivacities, if I may coin a word, of the wit and moralist.

With whatever luminousness Livingston impressed his future colleague, history has left him largely within the shadows of the Marshall court, outshone by the chief justice and by Story himself. Livingston's importance to the history of the Supreme Court lies less in his own individual prominence than in his silent support of Marshall's leadership—a support that helped to fashion the Court's enduring prominence within the American political order.

Further Reading

Dunne, Gerald T. "Brockholst Livingston." In *The Justices of the United States Supreme Court 1789—1969: Their Lives and Major Opinions,* vol. 1. Edited by Leon Friedman and Fred L. Israel. New York: R. R. Bowker Co., 1969.

———. "The Story-Livingston Correspondence, 1812–1822." *American Journal of Legal History* 10 (1966): 224–236.

Livingston, Edwin Brockholst. *The Livingstons of Livingston Manor.* New York: The Knickerbocker Press, 1910.

THOMAS TODD (1765–1826)

Associate Justice, 1807–1826

Appointed by President Thomas Jefferson

THOMAS TODD
(United States Supreme Court)

Associate Justice Thomas Todd was the first justice on the Supreme Court from west of the Appalachian Mountains. He occupied the newly created seventh seat on the Court, established by Congress in 1807 to preside over the circuit covering Tennessee, Kentucky, and Ohio. Todd himself was an emblem of the possibilities for social and economic advancement made possible as the country spilled westward across the Appalachians. After family misfortunes left him an orphan, Todd migrated from Virginia to Kentucky, where he made a name for himself as a lawyer and a judge. Eventually he attracted the attention of President Thomas Jefferson and was appointed to a seat on the nation's highest court.

Thomas Todd began life in circumstances roughly as prosperous as those in which he ended it, though childhood reversals temporarily cast him far from the happy prospects that accompanied his birth. Born January 23, 1765, in King and Queen County, Virginia, to Richard Todd and Elizabeth Richard Todd, Thomas was descended from a wealthy 17th-century Virginia landholder. His father inherited a sizable portion of this wealth but died within two years after Thomas was born. Existing law deposited Richard Todd's estate into the hands of his oldest son and Thomas's brother, William, leaving Thomas and his mother to fend for themselves. When Thomas was 10 years old, the two moved to Manchester, Virginia, where his mother ran a boardinghouse. From this income she was able to provide the money for her son's education, but loss struck Thomas's life for the second time when she died shortly after the move to Manchester, leaving him an orphan at the age of 11. A family friend undertook Thomas's guardianship and managed to see that he received a classical education before losing his remaining inheritance from his mother through mismanagement.

When Thomas Todd was 16, the British invaded Virginia, and he managed to serve in the Continental army for six months prior to the war's conclusion. Afterward he attended Liberty Hall in Lexington, Virginia, which would eventually become Washington and Lee University, and received his degree from that institution in 1783. Upon graduation, he received an offer from Harry Innes, a relation of his mother, to serve as a tutor for Innes's daughters. Innes was a respected member of the Virginia bar and legislature, and he promised Todd instruction in the law, as well as room and board, for his tutoring services. Todd accepted this offer, which eventually carried him to Kentucky, after Innes earned an appointment as a district judge and moved to that territory in 1784 with his family and his young legal student.

With Innes's assistance, Todd immediately plunged into regional politics. In 1784 Kentucky held the first of several conventions designed to create a state separate from Virginia; Todd served as the clerk for this and subsequent conventions. The final convention produced a constitution for the new state. The document survives today, written in Thomas Todd's hand. Along with this political activity Todd established a thriving law practice specializing in the land title work that soon flooded the new state. For nearly a decade following 1792, Todd also served as secretary to the Kentucky legislature and, beginning in 1799, as the clerk of the Kentucky Supreme Court. In 1801 he was appointed to serve as a justice of this court, and he became its chief justice in 1806. During these years of state judicial service, Thomas Todd continued to devote substantial attention to the same kind of land title issues that had made him a wealthy lawyer. On the basis of his previous legal work in this area, he brought significant expertise to his work on the Kentucky Supreme Court—expertise that would soon serve him as an associate justice of the U.S. Supreme Court.

The spread of the country westward across the Appalachians prompted Congress in 1807 to amend the Judiciary Act of 1789, which had established the federal court system, to create a new circuit court of appeals covering Tennessee, Kentucky, and Ohio. A seventh seat would also be added to the Supreme Court and a justice appointed to oversee the newly created circuit. When President Jefferson asked the congressional representatives from these states about suitable candidates for the new post, Thomas Todd's name was prominently mentioned. Jefferson consequently nominated him for the post of associate justice. The Senate immediately confirmed the appointment, and Todd attended his first session of the Court in the February 1808 term.

Although Todd's political principles were solidly Democratic before he ascended to his seat on the Supreme Court, he became almost immediately one of Marshall's surest allies in the attempt to have the Court speak with a single voice. Todd dissented only once during his 19 years on the Court, a bare handful of lines disagreeing with the majority's resolution of *Finley v. Lynn* (1810), a case involving an indemnity bond. Far from becoming a Jeffersonian challenger to Marshall's leadership, Todd capitulated almost completely to the authority of the chief justice. After his one expression of judicial independence, Associate Justice Todd became a mostly silent member of the Marshall court. Of the 644 cases decided while he was on the Court, Todd wrote only 14 opinions: 11 majority opinions, two concurrences, and his *Finley* dissent. Most of the majority opinions he authored concerned the kind of land and title issues that had been the staple of his legal practice and of the cases decided by the Kentucky Supreme Court. He was frequently absent from the Court during the years of his tenure, and this may have contributed to his apparent disinclination to forge the kind of dissenting tradition that President Jefferson's first appointee, William Johnson, had created on the Court.

Todd married Elizabeth Harris in 1788, and the two had five children. One of their sons, Charles Stewart, would be minister to Russia in the mid-19th century. Elizabeth died in 1811, a few years after Todd joined the Court, and the justice married Lucy Payne the following year. Payne was one of Dolley Madison's sisters as well as the widow of George Steptoe Washington, a nephew of President George Washington. Together, the couple had three more children. Associate Justice Thomas Todd died in Frankfort, Kentucky, on February 7, 1826. He left a substantial inheritance for the era, totaling some $70,000 even after distributions had been made to his children.

Justice Todd remains one of the Supreme Court's lesser lights, shadowed by the ever-imposing figure of the chief justice with which he served. In fact, his greatest contribution to the Court may have consisted precisely of his willingness to defer to John Marshall's leadership. By this deference he aided Marshall in strengthening the Court in its early decades, allowing a more talented jurist to craft a powerful position for the Court within the American political order. This kind of contribution is not the sort to attract biographers, such as those that have flocked to the study of John Marshall. It is nonetheless important in spite of its obscurity.

FURTHER READING

Currie, David P. "The Most Insignificant Justice: A Preliminary Inquiry." *University of Chicago Law Review* 50 (1983): 466–480.

Easterbrook, Frank H. "The Most Insignificant Justice: Further Evidence." *University of Chicago Law Review* 50 (1983): 481–503.

Gardner, Woodford L., Jr. "Kentucky Justices on the U.S. Supreme Court." *Register of the Kentucky Historical Society* 70 (1972): 121–142.

Israel, Fred L. "Thomas Todd." In *The Justices of the United States Supreme Court 1789–1969: Their Lives and Major Opinions,* vol. 1. Edited by Leon Friedman and Fred L. Israel. New York: R. R. Bowker Co., 1969.

Levin, H. "Thomas Todd." In *The Lawyers and Law Makers of Kentucky.* Chicago: Lewis Publishing Co., 1897.

O'Rear, Edward C. "Justice Thomas Todd." *Kentucky State Historical Society Record* 38 (1940): 112–119.

GABRIEL DUVALL (1752–1844)

Associate Justice, 1811–1835

Appointed by President James Madison

GABRIEL DUVALL
(United States Supreme Court)

No justice ever sat so long on the Supreme Court with less of a discernable impact than Gabriel Duvall. Appointed simultaneously with one of the Court's legendary figures, Justice Joseph Story, Duvall would become a stalwart but utterly inconspicuous ally of Chief Justice Marshall and Story. When he attracted notice during the last half of his time on the Court, it was because ill health and deafness had made him into something of an embarrassment for his fellow justices. His resignation from the Court and his death nearly a decade later eliminated even this notice, however, and his tenure on the Court for nearly a quarter of a century was promptly forgotten. The first edition of the monumental *Dictionary of American Biography* (1872) included entries for every Supreme Court justice save one: Gabriel Duvall. Closer attention to the Supreme Court's history eventually rectified this omission, but Duvall remains one of the Court's lesser lights.

The life that ended with relative obscurity began prominently enough. Gabriel Duvall was born December 6, 1752, at Marietta, a 3,000-acre family plantation in Prince Georges County, Maryland; he was the sixth child of Benjamin Duvall and Susannah Tyler Duvall. The history of his early years, including his education, remains obscure, but he embarked on the study of law in Annapolis, Maryland, shortly before the start of the Revolutionary War. The war intruded on a prospective legal career, but Duvall plunged into its turmoil with vigor. He served as muster master and commissary of stores for the Maryland army and as a volunteer in the state militia. He was also a clerk for the Maryland revolutionary convention from 1775 to 1777 and for the Maryland House of Delegates for a decade beginning in 1787.

Duvall was admitted to the bar in 1778, and like many lawyers of his day he labored to establish a legal practice while also participating into political affairs. He won election to the Maryland State Council in 1782 and to the Maryland House of Delegates in 1787. In the latter year he was also chosen to represent Maryland at the Philadelphia Constitutional Convention, though he and the other delegates declined to serve—they for reasons that can only be the subject of conjecture, he apparently because he had arranged to be married to Mary Brice on July 24, 1787, while the Convention was still under way. This union proved tragically short, for Mary died in 1790 following the birth of their first and only child. His subsequent marriage to Jane Gibbon in 1795 lasted until she died nearly 40 years later.

In 1794 Gabriel Duvall entered the arena of national politics after being elected to serve out the term of a Maryland congressman who had resigned. Duvall himself resigned this position in 1796 to accept a position as chief justice of the Maryland General Court, the seat previously occupied by Samuel Chase, who had himself been appointed as an associate justice of the U.S. Supreme Court. That year, and in 1800, Duvall also served as an elector in the presidential elections. After six years on the Maryland General Court, he accepted an appointment to serve in President Jefferson's administration as the first comptroller of the U.S. Treasury. He continued in this post after James Madison had assumed the presidency.

In 1810 President Madison had his first opportunity to make appointments to the Supreme Court when Justice William Cushing of Massachusetts died. Before he could find a successor for Cushing, Justice Samuel Chase of Maryland also died, leaving two seats on the Court vacant. The president's early attempts to fill Cushing's position produced no success. Levi Lincoln, former attorney general, declined to accept the post; Alexander Wolcott failed to be confirmed by the Senate; and John Quincy Adams, minister to Russia at the time, also refused the nomination. Madison eventually nominated Joseph Story and Gabriel Duvall to fill the two vacancies on November 15, 1811. The Senate promptly confirmed the nominations, and Story and Duvall joined the Court of Chief Justice John Marshall.

In spite of their appointment by a Democratic-Republican president, both Story and Duvall would become close allies of the chief justice, steadfastly supporting his federalism. Justice Story, though, would occupy a more prominent place on the Court than Duvall in the years that followed. Justice Duvall sided with Marshall in most of the great constitutional questions that came before the Court and seems to have wholeheartedly acquiesced in Marshall's wish to author the Court's important opinions himself. During Duvall's quarter century on the Court, he wrote only 17 opinions, these generally in minor commercial and maritime cases. He was loyal to the chief justice, even when Marshall failed to secure a majority of the Court to support his view of the case in *Ogden v. Saunders* (1827); the triumvirate of Marshall, Story, and Duvall joined in a dissent written by Marshall. In *Ogden,* the only important constitutional case in which Marshall dissented, the majority rejected the chief justice's contention that a New York insolvency law violated the contracts clause of the Constitution, even as applied to contracts entered into after the enactment of the statute.

Duvall declined to follow Marshall's lead in only one important case: *Dartmouth College v. Woodward* (1819), in which a majority of the Court agreed with Daniel Webster, lead attorney for Dartmouth College, that a New Hampshire law that attempted to convert the college from a private into a public university under public control violated the Contracts Clause. Only Justice Duvall dissented from this holding, but, perhaps in deference to the chief justice, he chose not to write an opinion explaining the reasons for his dissent.

When Gabriel Duvall took his seat as an associate justice on the Supreme Court, he was nearly 60 years old. He served on the Court into his 80s, and the latter half of his tenure on the Court found him increasingly debilitated by illness and deafness. As he grew older, his appearance became strikingly venerable. One observer described him as having a head as "white as a snow-bank, with a long white cue hanging down to his waist." His deafness, though, gradually destroyed his ability to participate meaningfully in or profit from oral arguments before the Court. The chief justice appears to have treated his aging confederate kindly, commenting once to Story in a letter concerning lodging arrangements for the Court that "Brother Duvall must be with us or he will be unable to attend consultations." Nevertheless, Duvall's impairment was increasingly apparent and the source of regular speculation concerning his possible retirement from the Court. During his last decade on the bench, observers constantly predicted his imminent resignation, but Duvall, like many justices after him, worried about leaving his seat on the Court to be filled with an overly political appointment. He therefore clung to his seat, until he was assured in the mid-1830s that President Andrew Jackson wished to replace him with a fellow Maryland lawyer, Roger Brook Taney. Only then did Duvall resign, on January 14, 1835. Chief Justice John Marshall died, however, in the summer of 1835, and President Jackson appointed Taney to assume this seat instead of Duvall's. The Virginian Philip Barbour would ultimately replace Justice Duvall in 1836.

After he retired from the Supreme Court, Gabriel Duvall returned to Marietta, his family plantation in Maryland. There he lived for almost another decade before dying on March 6, 1844, in his 92nd year.

Modern historians of the Court tend to credit Gabriel Duvall with being an indispensable ally of the great chief justice, John Marshall, even though his public contribution to the Court was slight. Marshall's dominance of the Court, and his own indisputably important contribution to the Court's power and prestige relied in significant part on the confederacy of justices who would follow his leadership. Duvall was one such justice. For that, if nothing more, the venerable Marylander deserves credit.

FURTHER READING

Currie, David P. "The Most Insignificant Justice: A Preliminary Inquiry." *University of Chicago Law Review* 50 (1983): 466–480.

Dilliard, Irving. "Gabriel Duvall." In *The Justices of the United States Supreme Court 1789–1969: Their Lives and Major Opinions,* vol. 1. Edited by Leon Friedman and Fred L. Israel. New York: R. R. Bowker Co., 1969.

JOSEPH STORY (1779–1845)

Associate Justice, 1812–1845

Appointed by President James Madison

JOSEPH STORY
(United States Supreme Court)

Few of the justices who served on the Supreme Court with Chief Justice John Marshall managed to escape the shadow cast by his leadership. Men who enjoyed conspicuous prominence in the political or judicial roles they held prior to ascending to the nation's high bench seemed inevitably to recede into the background of the Court that was decisively Marshall's. Associate Justice Joseph Story, more than any other justice who sat on the Marshall Court, managed to escape the fate of prestigious anonymity that tended to afflict his other brethren. On the Court, he proved himself Marshall's most reliable lieutenant. Off the Court, he created a reputation as a prominent scholar whose influence on American law proved remarkably enduring.

Joseph Story was born on September 18, 1779, in Marblehead, Massachusetts, the son of a prominent physician. Story was the eldest child of his father's second marriage, to Mehitable Pedrick Story, and the eighth of his father's total 18 children. Story's grandfather and his father had modest claims to fame—his grandfather for having served as assistant deputy registrar of the British Vice Admiralty Court in Boston and clerk of the American Navy Board and his father for having participated in the Boston Tea Party. Educated at a private academy in Marblehead, Story left the school early, after being disciplined for brawling, and entered Harvard College in 1795. He graduated second in his class from Harvard in 1798 and turned to the study of law, apprenticing himself first with Samuel Seward and later with Samuel Putnam in Salem. He was admitted to the bar in 1801.

In these early years after graduating from Harvard, the law did not claim absolute dominion over Story's intellect. He labored at length to establish a reputation as a poet, contributing pieces to local newspapers and crafting a long poem titled *The Power of Solitude,* which he eventually published in book form in 1805. Whatever pleasure Story may have achieved by this publication paled in the face of tragedy, however. Near the end of 1804, he married Mary Lynde Oliver, a woman who shared a love of poetry with her spouse. But seven months later, he endured his young wife's untimely death and then, in the same year, the death of his father. The grieving Story promptly turned against his own poetic work, purchasing all the copies of *The Power of Solitude* he could find and destroying them.

The legal practice he began after 1801 also seemed destined at first for failure. Like many lawyers of the time, he combined legal work with political engagement. Owing to his father's influence, however, Story inclined to Democratic-Republican politics and thus for a time found himself alienated from opportunities in Federalist-dominated Massachusetts. But 1805, a year of great personal tragedy for the young lawyer, was also a year in which his political and legal fortunes brightened. Increasing Democratic power in Massachusetts spurred the growth of his legal practice and also won him election to the Massachusetts House of Representatives. He served as a legislative representative from 1805 to 1808. This political experience led to his election to Congress in 1808 to serve out the term of Jacob Crowninshield, who had died in office. With his election to this post, Story demonstrated—not for the last time—that his Democratic-Republican inclinations were perhaps not so securely fastened to his character as might have been supposed. He earned the ire of party leaders—President Thomas Jefferson in particular—by opposing Jefferson's embargo against foreign trade.

After a brief tenure in Congress, Story returned to Massachusetts, winning election again as a state representative and ultimately becoming speaker of the Massachusetts House of Representatives in 1811. During the same period he attracted national attention by representing investors in the famous land fraud case of *Fletcher v. Peck* (1810). The case originated in the corrupt sale of 35 million acres of land in the Yazoo area (present-day Mississippi and Alabama) by Georgia legislators. When these lawmakers lost in subsequent elections, the Georgia legislature attempted to invalidate the previous land transfers. The original purchasers had by this time sold tracts of the land to new purchasers who, with Story's assistance, protested the attempt to unseat their title. Story ultimately pursued the case to the Supreme Court, securing a controversial victory for his clients when Chief Justice Marshall concluded for a majority of the Court that the Contracts Clause of the Constitution prevented the Georgia legislature from invalidating the land titles, no matter the fraud with which the original sale had been tainted.

The same year that the Court decided *Fletcher,* Justice William Cushing died. Story possessed the experience and Republican credentials necessary to win appointment to the Court as Cushing's successor. Nevertheless, he was young for the post—a mere 32 years of age—and, more significantly, had earned the distrust of Jefferson, who, though no longer president, still dominated party affairs. Jefferson frankly counseled President James Madison against nominating Story; Madison therefore made a diligent effort to find a more suitable candidate. His first and third choices—Levi Lincoln and John Quincy Adams—declined to serve, and his second choice—Alexander Wolcott—failed to receive confirmation by the Senate. Thus, Madison turned at last to Joseph Story, who chose to relinquish a more lucrative career as an advocate to pursue the vocation of a jurist. By this time he had married Sarah Waldo Wetmore (in August 1808), and he had increasing financial obligations for his family. (This union also would know its share of sorrow, as five of the seven children born to the couple died before reaching adulthood.) But Story's scholarly inclinations could find no better venue for pursuit than the highest court of the land, and he therefore accepted Madison's nomination. The Senate confirmed him to the position of associate justice in November 1811; he took the oath of office on February 3, 1812.

Jefferson's premonition concerning Story's devotion to Republican principles almost immediately proved itself correct. The new associate justice—confirmed to the Court together with Gabriel Duvall—demonstrated himself, as Jefferson surmised, only a "pseudo-republican." He quickly aligned himself with the federalism of Jefferson's great nemesis, Chief Justice John Marshall, and championed, more than any other justice on the Court, a broad scope of authority for federal courts. In his zeal for this cause, he even outstripped Marshall himself at times. Early in his tenure on the Court, Story launched a campaign to recognize a federal common law of crimes. This issue had been settled shortly after Story took his seat on the Court in *United States v. Hudson & Goodwin* (1812), in which the Court denied the power of federal courts to enforce federal common-law—or judge-made—criminal sanctions. But the pseudo-Republican Story refused for a time to accept this decisively Republican holding. As a circuit judge he insisted that the issue was still open and lobbied his brethren—unsuccessfully, as it turned out—to reconsider *Hudson*. What Story could not accomplish through judicial action, though, he was able to accomplish politically. He drafted a code of federal criminal laws and in 1825, with the legislative assistance of Daniel Webster, saw it enacted by Congress as law.

Marshall took the lead in authoring most of the Court's important decisions during this period. But in *Martin v. Hunter's Lessee* (1816), the chief justice had to recuse himself because he had a financial interest at stake in the case and had been involved in the case as counsel at one point. In this important Federalist triumph, Associate Justice Story stood in for the chief justice, authoring the opinion for a unanimous Court. It was his most significant and most controversial opinion. The case arose from a Virginia statute, passed during the Revolutionary War, that confiscated the property of Loyalists. One such individual, Thomas Lord Fairfax, had willed his substantial properties to a British subject. This inheritance was frustrated by the Virginia law, however, even though the law itself was in conflict with the subsequently ratified Treaty of Paris and Jay Treaty, both of which protected Loyalists from the kind of confiscation the Virginia law had effected. When the Virginia law was challenged before the Supreme Court in *Fairfax's Devisee v. Hunter's Lessee* (1813), the Court, in an opinion by Justice Story, found the Virginia law was superseded by the federal treaties.

The decision played poorly in Virginia, where states' rights advocates denounced it as an assault on state sovereignty and where the Virginia Supreme Court soberly pronounced itself under no obligation to abide by the decision of the U.S. Supreme Court, claiming that the section of the 1789 Judiciary Act that authorized the Court to review state court decisions inconsistent with federal laws and treaties was itself unconstitutional. In this posture the case returned again to the Supreme Court as *Martin v. Hunter's Lessee*, and Justice Story again wrote the majority opinion for the Court. In it, he insisted that the Supreme Court was the final arbiter of questions involving the interpretation of the Constitution of the United States. Thus, just as the Court possessed the power of judicial review over federal laws—the principle announced in *Marbury v. Madison* (1803) by which the Court was declared the final authority as to whether a law violated the Constitution—so it also possessed this power with respect to state laws that were inconsistent with federal law.

Story championed a vision of federal judicial authority that would preside over unified principles of commerce. He denied that federal courts were bound to enforce practices that conflicted with these unified principles. Thus, in *Swift v. Tyson* (1845), he authored the Court's opinion granting federal courts the ability to apply general commercial principles to resolve cases involving suits between citizens of different states, rather than being bound by the law of a particular state. Story's decision in the case would survive until the 20th century, when the Court overturned *Swift* in *Erie Railroad v. Tompkins* (1938). More controversially, while acting as a circuit judge, Story—a longtime foe of slavery—held in *United States v. La Jeune Eugenie* (1822) that the international slave trade violated the law of nations. His brethren on the Court would not follow him to this controversial conclusion, however, and in *The Antelope* (1825), Marshall's opinion for the Court overruled Story's holding.

Justice Story served as Chief Justice Marshall's most vigorous ally on the Court until the latter died in the summer of 1835. Andrew Jackson's election as president in 1828 presaged a political climate increasingly hostile to the federalism of the Marshall Court at its height. Story characterized the inauguration of Jackson as "the reign of King Mob triumphant." Toward the end of the great fraternity of minds between Marshall and Story, the latter found an outlet for his opinions about the law that would eventually prove as enduring as his work on the Court, even as surrounding political circumstances made the nationalist ideals shared by the two justices ever more unpopular.

In 1829 Nathan Dane endowed a chair in law at Harvard University, stipulating that Justice Story be its first holder, that he lecture on a variety of legal topics, and that these lectures be published. It was a most fortuitous endowment for American law, because Justice Story seized the opportunity to commence an impressive and voluminous scholarly investigation of the law virtually unparalleled in the American legal tradition. Over the next 15 years he would produce legal commentaries of breathtaking scope: *Bailments* (1832), *Commentaries on the Constitution* (1833), *Conflicts* (1834), *Equity Jurisprudence* (1836), *Equity Pleadings* (1838), *Agency* (1839), *Partnership* (1841), *Bills of Exchange* (1843), and *Promissory Notes* (1845).

While Story wrote his great commentaries on the law, he also fought an increasingly rearguard action to uphold the federalist principles propounded by the Marshall court. Passed over for the position of chief justice when Marshall died in 1835, he soon found himself surrounded by Jackson appointees to the Court, not the least of which was Chief Justice Roger B. Taney. Over the next decade Story was often in disagreement with a majority of the Taney court, but he had taken to heart John Marshall's lessons regarding the importance of unity to the Court's institutional reputation; thus, he seldom dissented. By the early 1840s, Story was experiencing failing health and had begun to contemplate retirement. Illness forced him to miss the 1843 term of the Court, and though he returned in 1844, the following year he began his judicial duties with the hopes of serving only until his replacement could be identified. Illness intervened again, however, and Story died on September 10, 1845.

If John Marshall is the Court's preeminent justice, then his friend Joseph Story must be named its preeminent scholar. Erudite, perhaps even overly so in some of his judicial opinions,

Story was the first great champion of the scientific study of American law. Reason, if rightly applied, might distinguish law from the rough and tumble of politics; and federal courts, if only given authority, might preside over the national triumph of law's reason. History allied Story's vision of the law with that of Chief Justice Marshall, the Court's most accomplished judicial craftsman. Together, they laid a foundation for American law that continues, in important ways, to support the superstructure that passing years have erected upon it.

FURTHER READING

Dunne, Gerald T. *Justice Joseph Story and the Rise of the Supreme Court.* New York: Simon & Schuster, 1970.

McClellan, James. *Joseph Story and the American Constitution: A Study in Political and Legal Thought with Selected Writings.* Norman: University of Oklahoma Press, 1971.

Newmyer, R. Kent. *Supreme Court Justice Joseph Story: Statesman of the Old Republic.* Chapel Hill: University of North Carolina Press, 1985.

Story, Joseph. *The Miscellaneous Writings of Joseph Story.* Edited by William W. Story. Boston: C. C. Little and J. Brown, 1852. Reprint. New York: Da Capo Press, 1972.

Story, Joseph. *Joseph Story: A Collection of Writings by and about an Eminent American Jurist.* Edited by Mortimer D. Schwartz and John C. Hogan. New York: Oceana Publications, 1959.

SMITH THOMPSON (1768–1843)

Associate Justice, 1823–1843

Appointed by President James Monroe

SMITH THOMPSON
(United States Supreme Court)

President James Monroe made only one appointment to the U.S. Supreme Court. By many estimations at the time and subsequently, he elevated mediocrity over ability when he passed over James Kent, one of the most eminent jurists of the day, in favor of Smith Thompson, a man of insatiable political appetites and only modest judicial ability. Thompson spent the early years of his adult life clambering after the position of chief executive, both of his country and his state. He failed in each of these quests and settled instead for the career of a judge, first in New York and eventually on the U.S. Supreme Court. Once on the nation's high court, he tendered a mostly unremarkable service, distinguished in the main by his willingness to chart a judicial path independent of Chief Justice John Marshall.

Smith Thompson was born in Dutchess County, New York, on January 17, 1768, the son of Ezra Thompson and Rachel Smith Thompson. His father was a prosperous farmer and minor political figure, serving as an anti-Federalist delegate to the New York convention assembled in the summer of 1788 to consider ratification of the U.S. Constitution. The future Supreme Court justice attended the College of New Jersey (later to become Princeton University), graduating in 1788. Thereafter, he taught school for a time while also studying law in the offices of James Kent and Gilbert Livingston for three years. Thompson began his own law practice in 1792 and connected himself to a minor tributary of the prominent New York Livingston family two years later by marrying Sarah Livingston, the daughter of his former legal mentor, Gilbert Livingston. This family tie aided his political aspirations, contributing to his election to the New York Assembly in 1800 and to the New York Constitutional Convention of 1801. By the beginning of 1802, Thompson had ascended to a seat on the New York Supreme Court. He joined the court in the same year as Brockholst Livingston, his wife's cousin and the man Thompson would eventually succeed on the U.S. Supreme Court. In 1804 Thompson's former teacher, James Kent, also joined the New York court as its chief justice, a position that Thompson later gained after Kent became chancellor of New York in 1814. In all, Smith Thompson served 16 years on the New York court.

Thompson's years on the New York Supreme Court brought him in contact with a variety of legal issues, many of them relating to commercial matters and some involving constitutional questions. While serving on the state court, Thompson formed the basis of a constitutional philosophy that would eventually put him at odds with John Marshall, the chief justice of the U.S. Supreme Court. This philosophy championed state authority to regulate broadly in the commercial area, even in cases that conflicted with federal law. For example, in *Livingston v. Van Ingen* (1812), he wrote an opinion upholding a state steamboat monopoly granted by New York to Robert Livingston and dismissed the contention that this state law violated Congress's power to regulate interstate commerce. A decade later, when the dispute arrived at the Supreme Court in *Gibbons v. Ogden* (1824), Chief Justice John Marshall held to the contrary for the Court shortly before Thompson himself took a seat as an associate justice. On the New York Supreme Court, however, and later on the nation's high court, Smith Thompson developed the view that the U.S. Constitution contemplated concurrent powers by Congress and the states over matters affecting interstate commerce.

During his years on the New York bench, Thompson remained active in the intricate machinations of New York politics. His involvement in partisan maneuverings brought him into association with Martin Van Buren, a relationship of such amiableness that the Van Burens named their fourth son Smith Thompson Van Buren. The following years, however, would place the two men at odds as their separate political aspirations collided. But for the time, at least, Thompson's political alliances seemed to hold out the promise of ever more attractive possibilities.

In 1818 Thompson's reputation attracted the attention of President James Monroe, who sought to fill the cabinet position of secretary of the Navy with an appointment from the mid-Atlantic states. Monroe gave the post to Thompson, who joined the president's cabinet at the beginning of 1819. In his four years of service on the cabinet, Thompson so earned President Monroe's confidence that when Brockholst Livingston's death in 1823 created a vacancy on the Supreme Court, the president viewed Thompson as the leading candidate for the position. Other contenders for the seat included James Kent, Thompson's former teacher and colleague on the New York bench; and Martin Van Buren, his sometime friend, U.S. senator, and future president. Thompson, though, coveted the presidency himself, as a result of which he succeeded in alienating Van

Buren. Apparently knowing that a seat on the high court was his if he desired it, Thompson nevertheless sought to secure Van Buren's support for a presidential bid by dangling the possibility that Van Buren might secure the Court appointment. The relationship between the two men never recovered after Thompson abandoned his presidential hopes and accepted the post on the Supreme Court that President Monroe had reserved for him. The Senate confirmed his nomination on December 19, 1823, and Thompson took the oath of office on February 10, 1824. Thus began a 20-year career as an associate justice of the Supreme Court.

In his first few years on the Court, Thompson did not seem destined to challenge the leadership of Chief Justice Marshall. Toward the end of the 1820s, though, he demonstrated that his judicial attitudes fell closer to those of Associate Justice William Johnson, who had already forged a reputation as the Court's preeminent dissenter, than to those of Marshall. Thompson's presence on the Court, in fact, tilted the balance of judicial opinion enough to cast Marshall into the role of dissenter himself in *Ogden v. Saunders* (1827). Thompson, together with three other justices, joined in holding that a state insolvency law granting relief for debts created after the effective date of the law did not violate the Constitution's requirement that contractual obligations not be impaired. Marshall, together with Associate Justices Story and Duvall, joined in dissenting against this challenge to the Court's previous holding in *Sturges v. Crowinshield* (1819). Although *Sturges* involved a state law that attempted to relieve debtors of liability for debts incurred prior to the enactment of the law, the dissenters thought the essential principle of the case applicable to *Ogden v. Saunders.* For the first and only time in his career as a chief justice, Marshall found himself a dissenter in a significant constitutional case.

Thompson's early years on the Court did not purge him of other political aspirations. Taking a lead from the example of John Jay, who three decades before had successfully run for governor of New York while seated as chief justice of the Supreme Court, Thompson sought the same position himself in 1828. Earlier in the decade, when Thompson and Martin Van Buren were still on friendly terms, Van Buren attempted to persuade Thompson to give up his seat in Monroe's cabinet in favor of an attempt to run for the governor of New York. Thompson declined at that time, but in 1828 he agreed to submit himself to the race. Now, however, his former friend Van Buren stood opposite him in the contest. Van Buren, known as "the Little Magician" for his remarkable adroitness in political maneuvering, had endured his former friend's duplicity at the time of Thompson's appointment to the Supreme Court, but he would not be bested again. Van Buren won the gubernatorial election, claiming the prize that Thompson had coveted, and the governor would eventually claim a further object of Thompson's unfulfilled ambition: the presidency of the United States.

Thompson, on the other hand, remained on the Supreme Court. He wrote one of his most famous opinions—a dissent—a few years after the failed gubernatorial attempt. In *Cherokee Nation v. Georgia* (1831), the Court faced the issue of whether it had authority to hear a claim brought by the Cherokee Indians. The state of Georgia had attempted to control lands that had been protected by treaty for the benefit of the Cherokee, who requested an order from the Supreme Court to prevent this interference. Writing for the majority, Chief Justice Marshall insisted that the Court had no power to hear the case, since the Cherokee did not amount to the kind of foreign nation authorized to bring a claim before the Court under Article III of the Constitution. Justice Thompson, in dissent, argued to the contrary, saying that the Cherokee were a sovereign nation and thus entitled to seek relief from the Supreme Court in their conflict with the state of Georgia. Within a year the status of the Cherokee in the United States returned to the Supreme Court. This time the position that Thompson had expressed in dissent won over a majority of the Court, including the chief justice. In *Worcester v. Georgia* (1832), the Court was called on to consider whether a Georgia law that attempted to regulate missionary activity in Cherokee country and that was inconsistent with federal treaties was enforceable. In agreeing to consider the case, a majority of the Court retreated from the reasoning of *Cherokee Nation v. Georgia,* decided the previous year. This time, Marshall determined that the Cherokee were, in fact, a sovereign nation and entitled to seek relief for their grievances before the U.S. Supreme Court. This victory for the Cherokee, however, proved illusory. President Andrew Jackson supported the removal of the Cherokee to Indian Territory and refused to enforce the Court's *Worcester* decision. In the end, the Cherokee were forcibly evicted from their Georgia lands and relocated by a harsh journey—eventually named the Trail of Tears—that killed many of them.

Justice Smith Thompson sat on the Court for 20 years. During this period, he suffered the death of his wife Sarah, but he promptly renewed his attachment to the New York Livingston family by marrying Eliza Livingston, a cousin of his first wife. In addition to the two sons and two daughters born of his marriage with Sarah, his union with Eliza produced two more daughters and a son. Besides his service on the Supreme Court, Thompson, a Presbyterian, was a longtime member of the American Bible Society. He died at his home, Rust Plaetz ("Resting Place"), in Poughkeepsie, New York, on December 18, 1843.

Justice Smith Thompson continued the dissenting tradition that had been begun by William Johnson, Chief Justice Marshall's great Jeffersonian antagonist. His career overlapped the end of Marshall's tenure and the beginning of Marshall's successor, Roger B. Taney. His presence on the Court engineered Marshall's only significant constitutional defeat, and it spelled—in larger terms—the gradual eclipse of John Marshall's momentous influence over the course of American law. With a firm dedication to the importance of state power, Thompson presaged the political currents that would influence the Court over the following turbulent decades.

Further Reading

Dunne, Gerald T. "Smith Thompson." In *The Justices of the United States Supreme Court 1789–1969: Their Lives and Major Opinions,* vol. 1. Edited by Leon Friedman and Fred L. Israel. New York: R. R. Bowker Co., 1969.

Hammond, J. *The History of Political Parties in the State of New York.* Albany: n.p., 1842.

Lobingier, Charles S. "The Judicial Opinions of Mr. Justice Thompson." *Nebraska Bar Bulletin* 12 (1924): 421–426.

Roper, Donald Malcolm. *Mr. Justice Thompson and the Constitution.* 1963. Reprint. New York: Garland, 1987.

ROBERT TRIMBLE (1776–1828)

Associate Justice, 1826–1828

Appointed by President John Quincy Adams

ROBERT TRIMBLE
(United States Supreme Court)

Associate Justice Robert Trimble's service on the nation's highest court was tragically brief. Sudden illness and death deprived him of the opportunity of devoting more than two terms to the Court's business. Nevertheless, Trimble participated vigorously, authoring more than his share of opinions and joining a majority of the Court in the only significant constitutional case in which Chief Justice Marshall found himself in the minority. Altogether, Justice Trimble's untimely death left historians of the Court intrigued by the possible role he might have played on the Court had he been able to serve a longer tenure.

Born on November 17, 1776, in Berkeley County, Virginia (now West Virginia), to William and Mary McMillan Trimble, Robert Trimble migrated with his family to Kentucky when he was about three years of age. The Trimble family settled on Howard's Creek in Clark County, Kentucky, where farming and hunting brought its members a modest living. The details of the future justice's early education remain unclear, but he eventually studied law at Transylvania University in Lexington, Kentucky, under George Nicholas, Kentucky's first attorney general, and, after his death, under James Brown, who would later become U.S. minister to France. The beginning of the 19th century saw him admitted to the bar, and he was elected to the Kentucky legislature in 1802. The following year he married Nancy Timberlake, with whom he produced a sizable family, though several of their numerous children failed to survive to adulthood. Political activity seems not to have appealed to Trimble, and over the following decade he turned down a string of political opportunities, including further service in the Kentucky legislature and, most significantly, the chance to become a U.S. senator. Instead he accepted an appointment to the Kentucky Court of Appeals, on which he was commissioned in April 1807. Trimble's growing family necessitated an income more substantial than the $1,000 salary paid for his judicial position. He therefore resigned from the court in 1808 and concentrated instead on expanding his legal practice while continuing to turn aside most proffered appointments to public positions. When nominated to serve as chief justice of Kentucky in 1810, he declined to serve. He did the same in 1813 when he was approached to resume service on the Kentucky Court of Appeals. In 1813, though, he did accept a part-time appointment as Kentucky district attorney, since this position still allowed him to pursue his law practice.

Finally, in 1817 President James Madison was able to coax Trimble into federal service by appointing him a federal district judge for Kentucky. Trimble promptly accepted the position and held it until his appointment to the Supreme Court in 1826. Though he was nominally a Democratic-Republican, Trimble's judicial instincts, which strongly supported national political and judicial power, aligned themselves closely with those of Chief Justice Marshall on the U.S. Supreme Court. Trimble's tendency to support the legitimacy of national power earned him enemies within his home state of Kentucky. When he declared a state insolvency law ineffective to bind a federal court, one Kentucky newspaper reminded him publicly of the fate tempted by judges who displayed their nationalistic sympathies too aggressively. The impeachment proceedings launched against Supreme Court Justice Samuel Chase could as easily be targeted at the lesser lights of the federal bench, including upstarts such as Trimble.

Robert Trimble's dedication to a strong national government and his imperturbability in the face of criticism by champions of states' rights no doubt contributed to his 1826 appointment to the U.S. Supreme Court. Upon the death of Associate Justice Thomas Todd, another Kentuckian, on February 7, 1826, President John Quincy Adams made his only appointment to the Court when he nominated Trimble to the seat vacated by Todd. After relatively lengthy confirmation proceedings in which Senator John Rowan of Kentucky opposed the nomination, the Senate finally confirmed Trimble's appointment on May 9, 1826, by a vote of 25–5.

Associate Justice Robert Trimble arrived on a Court still clearly dominated by Chief Justice John Marshall. Upon his appointment two decades earlier, the chief justice had bent his colleagues on the Court to his desire to present a unified face as much as possible, through the issuance of a single opinion for the Court in many cases and through the reduction of the number of separate opinions authored by the justices. Marshall had taken on himself the work of writing most of the Court's opinions, and when Trimble joined the Court the chief justice still maintained this practice. Of the other justices on the Court, Joseph Story—Marshall's most dedicated ally—authored the most opinions after the chief justice. Justice Trimble, though, immediately plunged into work on the

Court, in two years writing more opinions than any other justice on the Court save Marshall himself. The 50-year-old Kentuckian wrote nine opinions for the Court out of 48 decided in his first term on the Supreme Court, and seven out of the 55 decided the following term.

Justice Trimble generally found himself in harmony with Marshall's federalism. But in one crucial case, Trimble departed from the chief justice and contributed to a result that placed Marshall in dissent for the first and only time in a significant constitutional case: *Ogden v. Saunders* (1827). At issue before the Court was a state insolvency law designed to evade the result of *Sturges v. Crowninshield* (1819), in which the Court had declared unconstitutional a state law that had protected debtors from obligations entered into prior to the passage of the law. Marshall held for the Court that this law violated the contracts clause of the Constitution, which prohibits state laws from impairing the obligations of contracts. *Ogden* involved debtor relief applied to obligations entered into *after* the enactment of the insolvency law. The chief justice, along with Associate Justices Story and Duvall, contended that this law also violated the contracts clause. Nevertheless, Associate Justice Trimble, writing for himself and three other justices, denied that this was the case. As long as states did not trespass on the holding of *Sturges* by attempting to provide for retroactive debt relief, they were left free to enact insolvency legislation until such time that Congress passed a federal bankruptcy law. As it happened, Congress did not craft permanent bankruptcy legislation until the very end of the 19th century, and the *Ogden* result accordingly became the charter for state insolvency legislation for the rest of the century.

Most of the opinions that Trimble wrote while on the Court involved relatively minor disputes about land titles and procedural matters. But in *The Antelope* (1827), Trimble's opinion for the Court ventured into the increasingly controversial subject of slavery. The case had actually appeared for the first time before the Court in 1825, before Trimble's appointment, and presented the justices with the issue of whether the slave trade violated international law. Sitting as a circuit judge, Associate Justice Story had ruled in *United States v. La Jeune Eugenie* (1822) that the slave trade violated natural law and was therefore illegal. When the issue arrived before the high court, however, the justices—without dissent, even from Story—upheld the legality of slave trade. Two years after the original decision, the case returned to the Court for a determination of whether their original decision on the disposition of the slaves involved had been carried out. Writing for the Court, Justice Trimble—himself a slave owner—pronounced the disposition of the slaves at issue in the case complete. Declared lawful property under principles of international law, the slaves had fought in vain against the Court's unwillingness to declare illegal what it found immoral.

Shortly after the conclusion of his second term on the Court, Robert Trimble contracted a "malignant bilious fever" and died on August 25, 1828, at the relatively youthful age of 52. The sudden tragedy, matched with the promise Trimble had demonstrated in two terms on the Court, elicited a glowing eulogy from Justice Story:

> [P]erhaps no man ever on the bench gained so much in so short a period of his judicial career . . . no man could bestow more thought, more caution, more candor, or more research upon any legal investigation than he did. . . . He loved the Union with an unflattering love and was ready to make any sacrifice to ensure its perpetuity. He was a patriot in the pure sense.

Unlike other justices on the Marshall court who receded quickly into the shadows of the Court's institutional life, Associate Justice Robert Trimble carved for himself an active role in his two short terms of service. He proved himself not only an important ally of Marshall's centralizing judicial philosophy; he was also capable of tempering the chief justice's nationalism in favor of a constitutionalism that reserved an important role for states in the nation's commercial life—a role made explicit in his opinion in *Ogden v. Saunders* (1827). What impact Trimble's contribution to the Court might have produced over a more extended career remains a matter of tantalizing conjecture.

FURTHER READING

Goff, John S. "Mr. Justice Trimble of the United States Supreme Court." *Kentucky Historical Society Register* 58 (1960): 6–28.

Israel, Fred L. "Robert Trimble." In *The Justices of the United States Supreme Court 1789–1969: Their Lives and Major Opinions,* vol. 1. Edited by Leon Friedman and Fred L. Israel. New York: R. R. Bowker Co., 1969.

Levin, H. "Robert Trimble." In *Lawyers and Lawmakers of Kentucky.* 1897. Reprint. Easley, S.C.: Southern Historical Press, 1982.

Schneider, Alan N. "Robert Trimble: A Kentucky Justice on the Supreme Court." *Kentucky State Bar Journal* 12 (1947): 21–30.

•

JOHN MCLEAN (1785–1861)

Associate Justice, 1830–1861

Appointed by President Andrew Jackson

JOHN MCLEAN
(United States Supreme Court)

John McLean served more than 30 years on the Supreme Court, all the while coveting the presidency of the United States. But his political ambition, though far from fanciful, never gained for him the elusive prize he sought. He remained on the Court through its transition from the leadership of Chief Justice John Marshall to that of Roger B. Taney. Though, like Taney, McLean had been appointed by President Andrew Jackson, his judicial philosophy had more in common with John Marshall than with Taney. In fact, history takes most note of McLean for his historic dissent in the infamous *Dred Scott* case, opposite the majority aligned with Taney.

John McLean was born in Morris County, New Jersey, on March 11, 1785, the son of Fergus McLean and Sophia Blackford McLean. A decade before John's birth, his Ulsterman father, originally Fergus McLain, immigrated to New Jersey and married Sophia. During John's early years his family migrated from New Jersey to western Virginia, then on to Kentucky and finally in 1797 to Warren County, Ohio, some 40 miles from Cincinnati. McLean began his study of law in 1804 at the age of 19, after attending a local school and receiving instruction from two local Presbyterian ministers who served as schoolmasters. He received his legal instruction from John S. Gano and Arthur St. Clair, Jr. By 1807 he had been admitted to the bar.

McLean married Rebecca Edwards soon afterward, and the two settled in Lebanon, Ohio, where the future justice labored to establish a law practice and briefly pursued a career as a printer and a newspaper owner. The newspaper McLean established, the Lebanon *Western Star,* displayed the partisan spirit customary for newspapers of the time, lending its journalistic voice to the cause of Jeffersonian politics. McLean's newspaper days did not last long, however, and by 1810 he had turned the paper and his printing business over to his brother Nathaniel in order to concentrate full-time on the practice of law. The following year he experienced two conversions: the one from a young man of Presbyterian background and skeptical temper to an ardent Methodist, the second from private practice of law to politics, through his appointment as examiner of the U.S. Land Office in Cincinnati. Both conversions affected the rest of his life. Thereafter, McLean was active in Methodist affairs, contributing Bible studies to church magazines, being named honorary president of the American Sunday School Union in 1849, and becoming one of the leading Methodist laymen of his day. His appointment to the Land Office post whetted a political appetite that remained virtually undiminished until his death a half century later.

The Land Office could not satisfy McLean's capacious political ambition for long. By 1812 he had been elected to Congress, and he served two terms in the House of Representatives before resigning in 1816, only to be elected immediately to the Ohio Supreme Court. Before he left Congress, McLean campaigned vigorously for James Monroe's nomination to the presidency, securing a gratitude that would produce important fruit six years later. For the time being, though, McLean undertook the arduous circuit-riding responsibilities that went with being a justice on the Ohio Supreme Court. He also wrote one judicial opinion that would foreshadow the most famous opinion of his career, written 40 years latter. In *Ohio v. Carneal* (1817), McLean considered the case of a Kentucky slave whose master caused him to work in Cincinnati each day and then return to Kentucky—a slave state—at night. Though McLean decided the case on other grounds, he expressed his own belief that slavery was inconsistent with "immutable principles of natural justice." While he did not deem it appropriate to free slaves based purely on his own moral opposition to slavery and was not prepared to say that merely bringing a slave into free territory should result in his emancipation, McLean did suggest that a master who used slave labor in a free state "forfeits the right of property in slaves."

A year after James Monroe's inauguration as president, he returned the favor of McLean's earlier support in Congress by appointing the Ohio judge commissioner of the General Land Office in 1822 and postmaster general in 1823. The latter post especially gave McLean ample scope to demonstrate his managerial skill and his political adroitness. Under his direction, the postal service expanded radically, increasing service routes and swelling the number of employees of the postal service until it became the largest executive department. McLean not only proved himself an able and vigorous administrator but also a skillful political operative. He held onto his position as postmaster after John Quincy Adams won the presidential election in

1824, even though he had initially thrown such influence as he possessed in the direction of Adams's opponent, John C. Calhoun. In the face of pressure from Adams's administration to use postal positions for political patronage, McLean preached the necessity of being above partisan politics even as he covertly made friends with Andrew Jackson, Adams's newest political rival. President Adams sensed that McLean was engaged in double dealing, but he could not lay his finger on any overt evidence of political treachery. McLean, the president declared, "plays his game with so much cunning and duplicity that I can fix upon no positive act that would justify the removal of him." Secure within a web of cordial ties to many of Adams's allies and reputed to have significant influence with Methodist voters, McLean managed to hold onto his position throughout Adams's administration.

When Andrew Jackson became president in 1829, McLean immediately reaped the harvest of his shrewd dealings during the Adams administration. The Kentuckian Robert Trimble had died suddenly and tragically in September 1828, leaving the so-called western seat on the Supreme Court vacant. Adams had failed to find a replacement before leaving office, and Jackson had scarcely taken up the reins of the presidency before he nominated John McLean for the seat. The Senate promptly confirmed the nomination in March 1829. McLean took the oath of office and began service in the first part of 1830.

In spite of his appointment by Jackson, McLean proved to be closer in judicial philosophy to Chief Justice John Marshall and Associate Justice Joseph Story than he was to Marshall's successor, another Jackson appointee, Roger B. Taney. McLean sided frequently, though not inevitably, with claims of national power over those of state authority. Thus, while he joined with Chief Justice Marshall in declining to consider the claim of the Cherokee in *Cherokee Nation v. Georgia* (1831), he also followed the chief justice a year later in reversing course by holding that the state of Georgia lacked the power to pass laws affecting the Cherokee in *Worcester v. Georgia* (1832). When Roger Taney replaced Marshall as chief justice, McLean broke ranks with him at once in *Charles River Bridge v. Warren Bridge* (1837), joining associate justices Joseph Story and Smith Thompson in dissent. Although he determined that the Court lacked jurisdiction to hear the case, McLean nevertheless suggested in his dissenting opinion that the Constitution's contracts clause prevented a state from granting permission to one group of investors to build a bridge and collect tolls on it and then authorizing a competing group of investors to build a new bridge and collect their own tolls. Similarly, 15 years later he demonstrated again his regard for congressional authority over interstate commerce by dissenting in *Cooley v. Board of Wardens* (1852). In this case a majority of the Court upheld a state law imposing a piloting fee for the port of Philadelphia that burdened interstate commerce.

Justice McLean penned his most famous opinion in *Dred Scott v. Sandford* (1857), a case which for McLean was a reprise of his earlier decision in *Ohio v. Carneal* (1817) on the Ohio Supreme Court. With Associate Justice Benjamin Curtis, McLean dissented from the Taney majority, which refused to hear the case of *Dred Scott* on the basis that blacks could not be citizens of the United States and thus were not entitled to invoke the Court's jurisdiction. The majority also declared the 1820 Missouri Compromise unconstitutional insofar as it attempted to abolish slavery in the territories. McLean bristled at the majority's willingness to conclude that the Constitution deprived blacks of U.S. citizenship on account of their presumed inferiority. He was not willing to infer from the original flourishing of the slave trade in North America any design by the framers of the Constitution to strip African Americans forever of the possibility of citizenship.

> I prefer the lights of Madison, Hamilton, and Jay, as a means of construing the Constitution in all its bearings, rather than to look behind

> that period, into a traffic which is now declared to be piracy, and punished with death by Christian nations. I do not like to draw the sources of our domestic relations from so dark a ground.

McLean also insisted that Congress clearly had power to ban slavery in the territories.

In more than 30 years on the Supreme Court, Justice John McLean seems never to have relinquished the hope that he might eventually win the presidency of the United States. In his quest for this high post, McLean's unswerving ambition proved more constant than his loyalty to any particular party. He first courted nomination as a moderate Democrat in the 1830s, then as an anti-Mason, then later as a potential standard-bearer for the Free-Soil Party or the Whigs in 1848, and finally as a potential Republican nominee for president in 1854 and 1860. Generally, McLean's name was floated as a potential candidate in party conventions and then withdrawn before the voting began. In 1854, though, he received 196 votes on the first ballot of the newly created Republican party convention but withdrew in the face of John C. Fremont's 359 first-ballot votes. McLean's dissent in the *Dred Scott* case generated renewed support for his possible Republican candidacy in 1860, even though he was 75 years old at the time. A picture from the time in *Harper's Weekly* displayed the leading Republican candidates for the nomination, with William F. Seward, favored to win, in a center position, McLean to his immediate right, and the dark horse candidate, Abraham Lincoln, below and to the left. But death finally overtook the man who had by then become the "Politician on the Supreme Court." McLean died in Cincinnati, Ohio, on April 4, 1861, in the spring after Lincoln had been inaugurated president of the United States.

Associate Justice John McLean largely inherited the enthusiasm for national power originally championed on the Court by Chief Justice John Marshall. Together with other federalist allies such as Joseph Story and James Moore Wayne, McLean interpreted the Constitution in ways largely hospitable to the growth and expansion of national power, even after such interpretations declined in their influence during the turbulent years of the mid-19th century. He is remembered chiefly for his antislavery views, expressed most memorably in his *Dred Scott* dissent, and for his boundless ambition to trade his judicial robes for the mantle of chief executive.

Further Reading

Gattel, Frank O. "John McLean." In *The Justices of the United States Supreme Court 1789–1969: Their Lives and Major Opinions,* vol. 1. Edited by Leon Friedman and Fred L. Israel. New York: R. R. Bowker Co., 1969.

Kahn, Michael A. "The Appointment of John McLean to the Supreme Court: Practical Presidential Politics in the Jacksonian Era." *Journal of Supreme Court History, Annual* (1993): 59–72.

Weisenburger, Francis Phelps. *The Life of John McLean: A Politician on the United States Supreme Court.* Reprint. New York: Da Capo Press, 1971.

HENRY BALDWIN (1780–1844)

Associate Justice, 1830–1844

Appointed by President Andrew Jackson

HENRY BALDWIN
(United States Supreme Court)

The image of the Supreme Court as a calm, collegial body of jurists deciding momentous questions has probably never been entirely accurate. But the Court's preeminent chief justice, John Marshall, labored diligently to give substance to this image in the early decades of the 19th century. By the force of his personality and intellect, he succeeded at least partially in this attempt. When he arrived on the Court, its members commonly published separate opinions to announce their individual reasons for deciding particular cases. Marshall persuaded his fellow justices to join in a single opinion for the Court whenever possible, and he wielded his influence to suppress the inclination of justices to dissent regularly from opinions declared by the majority. Though Marshall could not entirely prevent dissents from men such as Associate Justice Thomas Johnson—an appointee of President Thomas Jefferson and a frequent critic of Marshall's decisions—nevertheless, he was able to manufacture substantial harmony among his brethren. Henry Baldwin arrived on the Court toward the end of Marshall's long and historic tenure as chief justice, and with an irascible temper and an independent spirit, he came to exemplify the waning of the congenial Marshall court. The appearance of the Court as an institution that rose above partisan politics—an appearance carefully cultivated by John Marshall—would shortly be replaced by the image of a Court helpless to escape the ideological conflict that would eventually plunge the country into a bitter civil war. Baldwin remains a minor figure on the Court, but his fractiousness illustrated in miniature the spirit of the times, from which the Supreme Court proved unable to distance itself.

The son of Michael Baldwin and Theodora Wolcot Baldwin, Henry was born in New Haven, Connecticut, on January 14, 1780. He attended Yale University and graduated in 1797, upon which he completed an apprenticeship in the law office of Alexander J. Dallas in Philadelphia. He was admitted to the bar in Philadelphia but shortly headed west to join his brother Michael in Ohio. Baldwin did not complete this migration, however, for he eventually settled in Pittsburgh, and in 1801 he was admitted to the Allegheny County Bar. The following year he married Marianna Norton, his third cousin; she died in 1803 shortly after giving birth to their only child, a son. Two years after her death, Baldwin remarried, this time to Sally Ellicott.

Over the next decade, Baldwin established a reputation as one of Pittsburgh's preeminent lawyers, practicing together with Tarleton Bates, until Bates's death in 1806, and Walter Forward. With them, he became co-owner of a local Republican newspaper called *The Tree of Liberty.* Baldwin also invested in a variety of business ventures with mixed success. By 1816 his reputation had won him election to the U.S. Congress, where he demonstrated himself a vigorous advocate for tariff increases, an opponent of attempts to curtail slavery, and—most important for his future career—a defender of General Andrew Jackson, whose invasion of Florida in 1818 during the Seminole War had stirred national controversy and threatened Jackson's court-martial. When Baldwin resigned from Congress in 1822 because of ill health, he continued to support Jackson's presidential ambitions, which were realized in the election of 1828.

After Jackson became president, Baldwin expected that his loyalty to the general would result in a significant appointment in the Jackson administration. In fact, Jackson originally slated Baldwin to become secretary of the treasury. But Vice President John C. Calhoun was able to persuade the president to appoint another candidate to this position, rather than Baldwin. Not satisfied when Jackson offered him various diplomatic appointments, Baldwin complained privately to friends of his mistreatment by the president. When Justice Bushrod Washington died in the latter part of 1829, Jackson used the opportunity to reward Baldwin's loyalty by choosing him as the new associate justice to replace Washington. Over the protests of the two South Carolina senators who shared Calhoun's opposition to Baldwin, the Senate confirmed him after the first day of the new year. On January 18, 1830, Henry Baldwin took the oath of office and began what would be a 14-year career on the Court.

Having been admitted into the Court's inner sanctum, Justice Baldwin seemed at first to have taken on himself the role of an irascible outsider. In 1831, his second term of service, Baldwin dissented seven times, a rather remarkable display of contrariness for a recently appointed justice. He also let it be known to his political friends that he found himself so out of place on the Court that he had contemplated resigning his seat at once. Martin Van Buren recorded Baldwin's unhappiness: "Judge Baldwin is dissatisfied with the situation, for reasons which it is unnecessary to explain further than they grow out of opposition to what he regards as an unwarrantable extension of its powers by the Court, and has given the president notice of his intention to resign." President Jackson, though, persuaded his appointee to remain on the Court, although the coming years would often give him cause to regret his selection of Baldwin.

Baldwin proved himself an undependable ally of Jacksonian policy. He was, to be sure, often critical of attempts to increase federal power at the expense of state prerogatives, but he could not be relied on to translate this attitude into concrete defeats for federal power in every instance. In particular, he did not share the president's often-stated opposition to any renewal of the charter of the Bank of the United States. He also infuriated the president by his opinion for the majority of the Court in *United States v. Arredondo* (1831), which involved a title dispute dating back to an old Spanish land grant in Florida. Jackson opposed the venerable title claim but Baldwin, for the Court, insisted that the government had the burden of disproving the claim and that the security of real estate ownership required a vigorous protection of land titles.

But however irksome Baldwin might have been to Jackson at times, he could, on other occasions, prove himself quite capable of defying Chief Justice Marshall's leadership on cases important to the Jackson administration. In the Cherokee cases of 1831 and 1832, for example, Baldwin hewed to a course unswervingly favorable to Jackson's desire to relocate the Cherokee. In *Cherokee Nation v. Georgia* (1831), Baldwin found himself aligned with a majority of the Court, led by Marshall, who refused to hear a claim brought by the Cherokee against the state of Georgia, after concluding that the Cherokee were not a sovereign nation entitled to invoke the Court's jurisdiction. The next term, however, the majority realigned itself, again behind Marshall, leaving Baldwin alone to dissent when the Court held in *Worcester v. Georgia* (1832) that states had no power to interfere with the Cherokee people or lands. President Andrew Jackson refused to enforce the new majority opinion and supported the removal of the Cherokee to Indian Territory, a forced relocation that resulted in the deaths of many Cherokee and would become known as the Trail of Tears.

In Justice Baldwin's own view, his judicial philosophy occupied a middle ground between two unreasonable extremes. Other justices, he believed, tended to champion either federal or state power, respectively, without adequate reflection. Baldwin imagined that he had crafted a middle way between these two polar positions. Inspired perhaps by Justice Joseph Story, his court colleague, whose *Commentaries on the Constitution* had been published in 1833, Baldwin decided to publish a pamphlet containing a series of concurrences he had written during the 1837 term. The pamphlet was titled *A General View of the Origin and Nature of the Constitution and Government of the United States. . . . Together with Opinions in the Cases decided at January Term, 1837, Arising on the Restraints on the Powers of the States.* Curiously, Justice Baldwin insisted that his middle way had been the one applied by "the late venerated Chief Justice"—that is, John Marshall—thus eulogizing the man under whose leadership Baldwin had initially chafed. In fact, before Marshall's death in 1835, Baldwin had grown to respect the chief justice immensely. Justice Story observed at the time: "I rejoice that Judge Baldwin took such an interest in the chief justice's dying hours. I had no doubt he would, for there is no person on earth (I believe) for whom he felt so much reverence and respect."

In the years following the publication of his pamphlet, Baldwin continued to take every opportunity to express his views on important cases, even those in which he joined the majority. He was especially happy to make his views well known on the issue of slavery, about which he demonstrated a consistently proslavery mind set. In *Groves v. Slaughter* (1841), the Court dealt with Mississippi's 1832 constitution, which had prohibited the importation of slaves into the state for sale but had not passed legislation enforcing this prohibition. A majority of the Court held the Mississippi provision to be in violation of the U.S. Constitution, but Baldwin wrote separately to emphasize the protection accorded under the Constitution for rights of slaveholders. Similarly, when Justice Story's majority opinion in *Prigg v. Pennsylvania* (1842) upheld the Fugitive Slave Law and held that state laws inconsistent with it were invalid, Baldwin wrote separately to deny that any significant constitutional issue was presented by the case. At issue in *Prigg* were the actions of a defendant accused of kidnapping a runaway slave living in Pennsylvania. Although a majority of the Court treated the case as raising the core issue of whether state laws inconsistent with the Fugitive Slave Law were unconstitutional, Baldwin saw a more direct route to the defendant's acquittal: Since the person whose abduction triggered the case was a slave, there could be no crime of kidnapping. In essence, one could not kidnap property.

Overall, Henry Baldwin's years on the Court were characterized by contrariness as often as concordance. Rumors circulated regularly that he was mentally unstable, so eccentric was his temper. To these alienating factors was added the embarrassment of financial problems in his later years. He died in Philadelphia on April 21, 1844, after a lengthy illness, in death departing a Court on which he had never quite been at home.

An abrasive man, perhaps afflicted by a mental illness, Henry Baldwin disturbed the peace of the Marshall court in the waning years of its famous chief justice. Ironically, Baldwin grew to respect John Marshall in the closing years of Marshall's life, but by then he had already unsettled the collegial environment that Marshall had worked so hard to create on the Court. After Marshall's death, Baldwin continued to follow his own path, seemingly uninterested in efforts to craft consensus on the Court, always ready to speak his own mind. He possessed a temper not generally respected as a qualifying trait among jurists, and perhaps for that reason Baldwin failed to secure any significant position in the institutional history of the Supreme Court.

FURTHER READING

Baldwin, Henry. *A General View of the Origin and Nature of the Constitution and Government of the United States.* 1837. Reprint. New York: Da Capo Press, 1970.

Gattell, Frank Otto. "Henry Baldwin." In *The Justices of the United States Supreme Court 1789–1969: Their Lives and Major Opinions,* vol. 1. Edited by Leon Friedman and Fred L. Israel. New York: R. R. Bowker Co., 1969.

Taylor, Flavia M. "The Political and Civil Career of Henry Baldwin." *Western Pennsylvania Historical Magazine* 24 (March 1941): 37–50.

*J*AMES MOORE WAYNE (1790–1867)

Associate Justice, 1835–1867

Appointed by President Andrew Jackson

JAMES MOORE WAYNE
(United States Supreme Court)

James M. Wayne joined the Supreme Court the year that Chief Justice John Marshall died. He thus participated in the partial reorientation of constitutional law brought about by a Court presided over by Roger B. Taney. He served as an associate justice during the tumultuous years preceding the Civil War, and he participated briefly in the judicial affairs of the tattered nation that emerged from that war. Though often at odds with Taney and frequently imbued with a nationalist spirit more in keeping with Marshall's philosophy than with Taney's, Wayne nevertheless supported Taney in the one case that would become the century's most infamous: the *Dred Scott* case. A Southerner by birth and at heart, James Wayne was nevertheless a Unionist to the end, so much so that the South read his support for the Union as a sign of treachery, stripped him of citizenship, and confiscated his property.

—∞—

James Moore Wayne was born in 1790 in Savannah, Georgia, to Richard Wayne and Elizabeth Clifford Wayne. His father had migrated to the colonies from England in 1759 to serve in the British Army, settling originally in Charleston, South Carolina, where he married Elizabeth. During the Revolutionary War, he served first in the South Carolina Regiment of Volunteer Militia, but after being captured and paroled by the British, he eventually joined the British military. His wife's family connections saved him from the fate common to Loyalists, and the pair moved in 1789 to Savannah, where Elizabeth gave birth to James the following year.

James's father rapidly established himself in Savannah, gradually acquiring plantations, slaves, a wharf, and a store. The family secured a tutor to provide the early education of the future justice, and the boy proceeded so rapidly in his studies that he was able to enter the College of New Jersey (later to become Princeton) in 1804 at the age of 14; he graduated four years later. Thereafter he studied law, first under the direction of a prominent Savannah attorney and then under Judge Charles Chauncey of New Haven, Connecticut. In 1810 Wayne returned to Savannah after his father died and pursued law studies with his brother-in-law, Richard Stites. He was admitted to practice in 1811 and subsequently began a legal partnership with Samuel M. Bond. After the two lawyers parted company in 1816, Wayne set up his own practice. In these early years he also served in a volunteer cavalry company during the War of 1812, eventually becoming a captain in the unit. In 1813 he married Mary Johnson Campbell.

James Wayne took his first step into politics in 1815, when he was elected a representative to the Georgia legislature from his county. At the conclusion of his second term, Wayne turned his hand next to local politics, serving as mayor of Savannah from 1817 to 1819. From this post he returned to the practice of law, his income supplemented by a part-time position as a judge in Savannah's Court of Common Pleas. This job immersed him in a variety of minor civil and criminal matters. His ambition lay higher, though, and in 1822 he won a seat on the Georgia Superior Court. He served on this court until 1828, when he began the first of four terms of service in the U.S. House of Representatives, where he proved himself a vigorous supporter of President Andrew Jackson. He agreed with Jackson's plan to deny the Cherokee an independent sovereignty within the state of Georgia and to remove them instead to Indian Territory, and he agreed as well with Jackson's fierce opposition to renewal of the charter for the Bank of the United States. In the nullification controversy over South Carolina's opposition to the "tariff of abominations" of 1828, Wayne supported the president's "force bill," which authorized Jackson to use military force if necessary to collect the tariff in South Carolina. Though himself opposed to the tariff, Wayne demonstrated his allegiance to the Union by denying that South Carolina could legitimately nullify the federal tariff law or secede if federal authorities moved to collect the tariff by force.

By the time Justice William Johnson of North Carolina died in 1834, James Wayne had shown himself to be a loyal Jacksonian with both political and judicial experience. President Jackson therefore promptly nominated him to the vacant seat of the Supreme Court on January 6, 1835, and Wayne was confirmed at once by the Senate.

Associate Justice James Wayne arrived on the Court a few months before Chief Justice John Marshall died. He thus became a charter member of the Court presided over by Marshall's successor, Roger B. Taney. In many ways, though, Wayne proved to be more Marshall's successor than Taney did. He demonstrated—unusually for a Southerner of his time—a Marshall-like commitment to a strong national government, most particularly in his conviction that Congress had exclusive power to regulate matters affecting interstate commerce. He would eventually be called by Benjamin Curtis, his colleague on the Supreme Court, one of the "most high-toned federalists on the bench."

Wayne's federalism prompted him to dissent in the most important commercial case decided by the Taney court: *Cooley v. Board of Wardens* (1852). At issue in *Cooley* was a Pennsylvania statute that required ships using the port of Philadelphia to pay a fee if they did not utilize the services of a local pilot, with the fee being used to support a relief fund for pilots and their widows and children. A majority of the Taney court upheld this law against a challenge that it intruded on Congress's power to regulate interstate commerce, concluding that piloting laws were by their very nature matters of local rather than national concern. Justice Wayne dissented, arguing that Congress's power over interstate commerce was exclusive and clearly applied to the law in question.

A slave owner himself, Wayne regarded the issue of slavery as amendable only to such federal laws as supported the constitutional rights of slaveholders. Thus, he applied his generally nationalistic principles in *Prigg v. Pennsylvania* (1842) to join in the Court's holding that Congress had exclusive power to pass regulations involving the recapture of fugitive slaves. But when Congress wielded its power to restrict the introduction of slavery into new territories, such as in the Missouri Compromise of 1820, Wayne perceived an intrusion on the rights of slaveholders. He therefore joined in Chief Justice Roger Taney's infamous opinion in *Dred Scott v. Sandford* (1857), in which Taney found that blacks were disqualified per se from the possibility of being U.S. citizens and that the Missouri Compromise, insofar as it deprived slaveholders of their lawful property in slaves, was unconstitutional. In fact, when it appeared that the Court might attempt to bypass the constitutionality of the Missouri Compromise and resolve the case instead on a more narrow, technical ground, Wayne was an advocate for settling the slavery question decisively, a course that the majority of his brethren ultimately followed.

The Court's resolution of the *Dred Scott* case failed to accomplish the national resolution of the slavery question that the majority had sought to obtain through its authoritative voice. If anything, the decision in *Dred Scott* hardened the resolve of both sides in the bitter conflict, and by removing the core issue from the political battlefield through the declaration that the Missouri Compromise was unconstitutional, it invited the bloody battlefields that the Civil War contributed to the nation's history.

The war placed James Wayne, both a Unionist and a Southerner, in a precarious position. Unlike his fellow Southerner on the Court, Associate Justice John Archibald Campbell of Alabama, Wayne refused to resign his seat once war broke out. His own son, Major Henry C. Wayne, resigned from the United States Army and returned to Georgia to fight for the Confederacy. Justice Wayne, however, continued to serve on the Court, both out of conviction that the secession of the Southern states was illegitimate and out of a desire to represent the interests of those states on the Court. In the turmoil of the times, however, his home state failed to see any Georgian loyalty in Wayne's continuance on the Court. According to the South, he was, in the words of one newspaper attack, "no more of us." The Confederate District Court for Georgia declared him an "Alien Enemy" and seized his property: "Lots, parts of Lots & parcels of land and also said Stocks & negro slaves," all having been collectively valued at around $50,000. Only the industry of his son Henry, Adjutant General in Georgia after his resignation from the U.S. Army, managed to save the family property. Henry Wayne filed a petition with the court to recover his father's property and was granted it, subject to the condition that Justice Wayne satisfy from it any debts due to "faithful citizens of any of the Confederate States." Justice Wayne, for his part, continued to prove himself most "un-Southern" in his support of President Lincoln's attempts to preserve the Union by the force of arms. In the *Prize Cases* (1863), Wayne joined the slender majority of five out of nine justices who upheld Lincoln's order commanding a naval blockade of Southern ports.

After the war ended, Justice Wayne's commitment to the vanquished South became more pronounced. He returned home to Georgia at once to repair ties there, and on the Court he was vigorous in resisting postwar efforts to punish the South. He voted with the majority of the Court in *Cummings v. Missouri* (1867) and *Ex parte Garland* (1867), holding unconstitutional those state and federal laws that disqualified Southerners from practicing various occupations unless they swore that they had not supported the Confederacy. Furthermore, Justice Wayne refused to act as a circuit judge in Southern states subjected to military reconstruction rule. These acts of loyalty to the South would climax his long career on the Court. After contracting typhoid fever in the summer of 1867, Wayne died in Washington, D.C., on July 5 and was buried in Savannah.

Associate Justice James Wayne served during the Supreme Court's second significant period of history, under the direction of Chief Justice Roger B. Taney. But he was in many ways a jurist of a temper far more in keeping with Taney's predecessor, John Marshall. His respect for the national government was sturdy enough to bind him to the Union even when his Southern countrymen attempted to depart it. He illustrated, though, the blindness common to his age: the moral astigmatism that failed to recognize slavery's evil and the legal myopia that imagined the Supreme Court capable of resolving peaceably the nation's greatest crisis by the mere fiat of judicial declaration.

Further Reading

Battle, George G. "James Moore Wayne: Southern Unionist." *Fordham Urban Law Journal* 14 (1964): 42–59.

Lawrence, Alexander A. *James Moore Wayne, Southern Unionist.* Westport, Conn.: Greenwood Press, 1943. Reprint. 1970.

O'Connor, Sandra Day. "Supreme Court Justices from Georgia." *The Georgia Journal of Southern Legal History* 1 (1991): 395–405.

ROGER BROOKE TANEY (1777–1864)

Chief Justice, 1836–1864

Appointed by President Andrew Jackson

ROGER BROOKE TANEY
(Engraving from a painting by Alonzo Chappel, Library of Congress)

Made infamous by his opinion in the case of *Dred Scott v. Sandford,* Chief Justice Roger Brooke Taney nevertheless earns frequent mention as one of the greatest justices ever to have served on the Court. He inherited from Chief Justice John Marshall a constitutional system tilted prominently in favor of an expansive scope of national power and sharp restraints on the abilities of state to regulate commercial topics. Without repudiating this system in a fundamental way, Taney's court adjusted it to give a greater latitude for state power within the federal system. History has excoriated him for his *Dred Scott* opinion but also has been forced to admit grudgingly that he, as much as any other chief justice save Marshall himself, affected the course of constitutional development in the United States.

Roger Taney was born on a tobacco plantation in Calvert County, Maryland, on March 17, 1777, to Michael Taney and Monica Brooke Taney. Roger attended Dickinson College in Pennsylvania, graduating in 1795 as valedictorian of his class. Thereafter, he studied law in Annapolis, Maryland, with Judge Jeremiah Chase, who served on Maryland's General Court. Following this study he was admitted to the bar in 1799. That same year he served a term in the Maryland legislature as a member of the Federalist Party. After suffering defeat in his reelection attempt, he moved to Frederick and established a law practice there. In 1806 he married Ann Key, the sister of Francis Scott Key, an attorney friend of Taney's remembered by American history as the author of the lyrics to "The Star-Spangled Banner." Taney, who was Roman Catholic, and his wife, Ann, who was Episcopalian, settled on a compromise for the religious education of their children. Sons were to be raised according to the Catholic faith of their father, daughters according to the mother's Episcopalianism. As it turned out, the couple had only one son, who died in infancy, but their six daughters were dutifully raised as Episcopalians by their mother.

In Frederick, Taney's law practice steadily expanded, even as he continued to attend to political affairs, though, this attention yielded no tangible political position until 1816, when he was elected to the state senate for a five-year term. Two years after this term ended, he made another strategic career move by leaving Frederick to establish a new home in Baltimore. Here the one-time Federalist Roger Taney became a supporter of Andrew Jackson. Taney's new political affiliation as a Jacksonian Democrat soon secured him the post of state attorney general in 1826. After five years in this position, his continued loyalty to Jackson sent him to Washington as attorney general of the United States. In this cabinet position, Taney demonstrated the commitment to Jacksonian principles that would later characterize his decisions as the chief justice of the Supreme Court: a robust appreciation for states' rights and the divided sovereignty of federal and state governments, as well as a firm persuasion that the states were the primary repository of power to regulate slavery. He even delivered an official opinion as attorney general that foreshadowed his infamous declaration 30 years later in the *Dred Scott* case that blacks were by nature a "degraded" class disqualified from being U.S. citizens.

Taney's legal talent was matched by his loyalty to President Jackson when the controversy over the Bank of the United States placed a premium on loyalty. Vehemently opposed to the Bank, Jackson vetoed Congress's attempt to recharter it in the early 1830s, asserting the Bank to be unconstitutional, in direct repudiation of John Marshall's conclusion to the contrary some 10 years earlier in *McColloch v. Maryland* (1819). After the veto, Jackson immediately ordered his secretary of the treasury, Louis McLane, to remove federal deposits from the "moneyed Monster," only to be opposed by McLane. Jackson appointed another secretary, William J. Duane, but met with a similar response when he ordered the new secretary to strip the Bank of federal deposits. Finally, Jackson moved Taney to the post of treasury secretary in a temporary appointment. In so doing he found at last a receptive ear for his presidential command. Taney removed the federal deposits and placed them in a series of designated state banks to hold the federal deposits. He increased the criticism already directed at Jackson's administration by designating the Union Bank of Maryland, with which Taney had prior professional and continuing financial ties (he owned stock in the bank), as one of the "pet banks." In the summer of 1834, nine months after Taney had received his interim appointment as secretary of the treasury, Jackson finally asked the Senate to confirm Taney's appointment. But the confirmation was denied, and Taney returned home to Baltimore and the practice of law. He would not remain there long, however.

Upon the death of Associate Justice Gabriel Duvall in January 1835, President Jackson turned again to Taney and forwarded to the Senate his nomination to fill the vacancy on the Supreme Court. Having said no to a Taney appointment before, the Senate was prepared to turn down the president again. It ultimately postponed any action on Taney's nomination, effectively blocking his appointment to the Court. Then, Chief Justice John Marshall died during the summer of 1835. Jackson promptly nominated Taney to fill Marshall's vacant seat and Philip P. Barbour to occupy Duvall's still-vacant seat. On March 15, 1836, the Senate met in executive session and confirmed both men to the Supreme Court. Taney thus became not only the fifth chief justice of the Supreme Court but its first Roman Catholic and the man who would lead the Court during the period of the country's greatest crisis. With the appointment of Chief Justice Taney and Associate Justice Philip Barbour to the Court, President Jackson had managed to fill five seats on the Court—a majority—with his appointments.

The transition from the leadership of Marshall, the Federalist, to Taney, the Jacksonian Democrat, exhibited itself in matters of style as well as in matters of constitutional interpretation. The Marshall court's practice of having the justices room together during terms of the Court expired under Taney. Moreover, Taney proved himself not so jealous of the power to author the Court's significant opinions as did Marshall, and he regularly shared this responsibility with other members of the Court. Thus, in 1837, when the Taney court produced a troika of opinions that significantly altered the course of constitutional interpretation—*New York v. Miln* (1837); *Briscoe v. Bank of the Commonwealth of Kentucky* (1837); and *Charles River Bridge v. Warren Bridge* (1837)—Taney retained only one of these, the *Charles River Bridge* opinion, for himself.

The decentralization that occurred in the Court's institutional life mirrored the partial retreat from Marshall's high federalism, which had characterized the Court's jurisprudence during the early decades of the 19th century. Chief Justice Marshall had wielded the contracts clause of the Constitution to provide protection for a variety of vested rights from state interference. But Taney immediately demonstrated that the clause would provide less vigorous—or at least less consistently vigorous—protection for such rights under his Court. In *Charles River Bridge v. Warren Bridge* (1837), the Court was called on to consider the action of a state that had licensed one set of proprietors to build a bridge and collect tolls from it and then subsequently licensed a competing enterprise to build a newer bridge and also collect tolls from its users. The first set of proprietors challenged the grant of the competing licensee, arguing that it impaired their original contract with the state in violation of the Constitution's contracts clause. Taney, though, writing for a majority of the Court, refused to give such reach to the contracts clause, preferring instead to narrowly construe any rights granted by the states in favor of a broad reservation of power for the state to regulate property in ways suited to serve the public's interest. "While the rights of private property are sacredly guarded," Taney wrote, "we must not forget, that the community also have rights, and that the happiness and well-being of every citizen depends on their faithful preservation."

Although Taney's *Charles River Bridge* opinion granted a greater latitude to states to intrude on property interests that Marshall's court would have protected during its heyday, Taney's court is primarily remembered more for having made minor pragmatic adjustments to Marshall's federalism than for having repudiated it in any fundamental sense. It tamed Marshall's rigid axioms in favor of vested property rights to suit the burgeoning economic development of the mid-19th century. Moreover, by supporting a view of the Constitution that gave both Congress and the states power to regulate commercial affairs concurrently, in the absence of an outright conflict between the two, Taney and his colleagues encouraged state participation in economic development.

These contributions to the constitutional tradition would have earned Taney a chief place in the annals of the Court's great jurists, even had he not authored the most infamous opinion in the Court's history: the *Dred Scott* case. His role in the decision of this momentous case still threatens to tarnish beyond repair a reputation that would have otherwise been among the Court's most glittering.

Dred Scott v. Sandford (1857) presented the Court with the claim of Scott, a slave whose master had taken him from the state of Missouri into the free state of Illinois and later into the upper Louisiana Territory, which was itself free by the terms of the Missouri Compromise of 1820. Scott claimed that his sojourn in a free territory had made him free, and he sued the executor of his former master's estate (John F. A. Sanford, officially misnamed "Sandford" in court records) for a declaration of his freedom. Scott claimed to be a free citizen of Missouri, where he had at last returned after the travels with his former master, and entitled to sue Sanford, a citizen of New York, under the provision of Article III of the Constitution, which grants federal courts the power to hear cases between citizens of different states.

On March 6, 1857, the day after President James Buchanan's inauguration, the Supreme Court announced its decision in the case of *Dred Scott v. Sandford*. Although a majority of the Court had intended originally to dispose of the case on narrow, technical grounds, it ultimately determined to plunge into the thick of the slavery controversy in hopes of accomplishing a national resolution of the issue. Every justice wrote a separate opinion, but Chief Justice Taney's opinion was designated the opinion of the Court and his was the one that opponents of the case would revile with the most intense fervor.

Taney's opinion reached two key conclusions: first, that *Dred Scott* had no right even to present his claim because he was not a U.S. citizen; and second, that Congress could not constitutionally ban slavery in the territories. Taney's first conclusion, that Scott was not a citizen of the United States because he was black, was perhaps the most astonishing. As a race, African Americans were, Taney declared, inferior and never intended by the Constitution's framers to participate in the fraternity of U.S. citizenship. But the chief justice added an additional declaration to the one that stripped *Dred Scott*, and every person of his race, of citizenship: Congress lacked the power to prohibit slavery in the territories. By this conclusion Taney made it impossible for Congress to resolve the issue of slavery through the kind of mutual concessions that had produced the Missouri Compromise of 1820. The *Dred Scott* decision was the first occasion in which the Court had invalidated major federal legislation on constitutional grounds since the power of judicial review had been established in *Marbury v. Madison* (1803). Accordingly, Dred Scott, a black slave, had no right to present a claim in federal court because he was black; and even were the Court of a mind to entertain Scott's claim, he was still a slave. His sojourn in a free territory had not altered this terrible fact.

Taney had managed to avoid intense criticism for most of his long career as chief justice of the Supreme Court. But *Dred Scott* sparked vitriolic attacks on him. Taney's opinion also saddled constitutional law with two pernicious principles that required the process of constitutional amendment to undo. The Fourteenth Amendment eventually exterminated Taney's declaration that blacks were not—and could not be—citizens of the United States. It established that all persons "born or naturalized in the United States, and subject to the jurisdiction thereof, are citizens of the United States and of the State wherein they reside." Furthermore, the Thirteenth Amendment accomplished an abolition of slavery, thus making irrelevant Taney's conclusion that Congress had no power to abolish slavery even in the territories.

Chief Justice Roger Taney lived for seven years after the *Dred Scott* decision. In his remaining years he endured the sorrow of losing his wife and youngest daughter to yellow fever in the epidemic of 1855 and suffered the stream of criticism that his opinion in the *Dred Scott* case called down on himself and his Court. Taney died before the end of the Civil War, on October 12, 1864. He was 87 years old and had sat on the Court for 28 years. But for his opinion in *Dred Scott v. Sandford,* Taney would certainly be numbered among the greatest of the Supreme Court's justices. Even in spite of this decision, many historians continue to recognize Taney's other substantial contributions to the course of American law. He received and perpetuated Chief Justice John Marshall's principle of judicial review, confirming that the Supreme Court would be the final arbiter of the Constitution's meaning. He also confirmed Marshall's commitment to a strong national government, although he tempered Marshall's devotion to exclusive Congressional power over interstate commerce and vigorous protection of vested property rights with a more pragmatic appreciation of the role of states in regulating commerce and of the interests of the public in limiting property rights.

Further Reading

Freedman, Suzanne. *Roger Taney: The Dred Scott Legacy.* Springfield, N.J.: Enslow Publishers, 1995.

Lewis, Walker. *Without Fear or Favor: A Biography of Chief Justice Roger Brooke Taney.* Boston: Houghton Mifflin, 1965.

Newmyer, R. Kent. *The Supreme Court under Marshall and Taney.* 1968. Reprint. Arlington Heights, Ill.: Harlan Davidson, 1986.

Siegel, Martin. *The Taney Court, 1836–1864.* Millwood, N.Y.: Associated Faculty Press, 1987.

Steiner, Bernard Christian. *Life of Roger Brooke Taney, Chief Justice of the United States Supreme Court.* Westport, Conn.: Greenwood Press, 1970.

Philip Pendleton Barbour (1783–1841)

Associate Justice, 1836–1841

Appointed by President Andrew Jackson

Philip Pendleton Barbour
(United States Supreme Court)

Philip Pendleton Barbour personified the traits of conservative Virginia gentry in the first half of the 19th century. Alarmed at the prospect of increasing national power, he championed the rights of states to exercise legislative power free of federal interference, including the interference of federal judges wielding the Constitution. He supported the rights of slaveholders and, far from wishing the institution of slavery to wither away gradually, was a fierce advocate for the spread of slavery to the new Western territories. He carried these attitudes with him onto the Supreme Court and exhibited them in his opinions, though an untimely death ultimately made his brief tenure on the Court relatively lacking in any great significance.

Philip Pendleton Barbour was born on March 25, 1783, in Orange County, Virginia, to the family of a planter whose financial fortunes had suffered decline. His father, Thomas Barbour, served in the Virginia House of Burgesses before the American Revolution, and afterward in the Virginia General Assembly. His mother, Mary Pendleton Thomas Barbour, was herself a member of an influential Virginia family. The family's financial circumstances did not permit the kind of private education for Philip that was customary for Virginia gentry. Instead, he attended a local public school, where he demonstrated himself an exceptional student.

In 1800, at the age of 17, Philip determined to set off for Kentucky, where he intended to establish a law practice on the basis of his own study of the law. He proved inadequately equipped for the challenge, however. Within a year he returned to Virginia, borrowed money, and enrolled in the College of William and Mary, where he studied law for a few months. Afterward, he remained in Virginia and set up a law practice. He soon prospered sufficiently to marry Frances Johnson in 1804; together the couple had seven children.

In 1812 the 29-year-old Philip Barbour followed family tradition when he was elected to the Virginia House of Delegates, where he rapidly obtained influential assignments to the judiciary and finance committees. Two years later, in 1814, he leapt from state politics onto the national stage by winning election to Congress. His service in the House was mirrored by that of his older brother James, who was a U.S. senator from Virginia. The two brothers followed different political trajectories in spite of their kinship, however. In the Senate, James leaned toward a nationalistic view that would ultimately make him at home as a member of President John Quincy Adams's cabinet. Philip, in the House, lost no opportunity to trumpet the rights of states and the perils of excessive federal power.

Philip Barbour's position on the Bonus Bill of 1817 was in accord with his general attitude. The bill proposed to subsidize the construction of roads and canals, including a road from New York to Washington, D.C., and on to New Orleans. Indignant at the prospect of such governmental overreaching, Barbour lambasted the proposed law as "a bill to construct a road from the liberties of the country by way of Washington to despotism." Though his protests did not prevent the proposed legislation from winning passage in the House and the Senate, Barbour's fellow Virginian, President James Madison, shared the congressman's constitutional scruples concerning the bill and vetoed it.

During his tenure in the House, Philip Barbour participated in debates concerning the proposed censure of General Andrew Jackson for his conduct of the Florida campaign against the Seminole Indians, especially his summary execution of two British subjects accused of having incited the Seminole against the United States. When the House debated the censure motion at the beginning of 1819, Barbour proved himself one of Jackson's more vigorous defenders. His defense of the general foreshadowed his subsequent political alignment with Jacksonian Democrats. In February that same year, Barbour also participated in debates concerning the admission of Missouri to the Union. A states' rights conservative and a fierce supporter of slave owners' rights, Barbour had no doubt that attempts to limit slavery in Missouri were unconstitutional. In 1821 Barbour's reputation among Southern members of the House earned him the post of Speaker. He held the position for two years, until Henry Clay returned to the position.

With Clay's return as Speaker of the House, Barbour declined to run for another congressional term in 1824, choosing instead to return to the private practice of law. Thomas Jefferson failed to lure his fellow Virginian into a teaching post at the University of Virginia soon thereafter, though Barbour did agree to an appointment as a judge for the Virginia General Court. Two years later, however, Barbour won election again to his old seat in Congress and resigned his judicial appointment to return to the House of Representatives in December 1827. Over the next three years he gained increasing national stature as a leader of southern conservatives. In an action prescient of later Jacksonian policy, Barbour launched an aborted attempt to have the federal government rid itself of an ownership interest in the Bank of the United States, firing the first salvo in a battle that would ultimately overthrow the financial institution. During this period he also served as president of the Virginia Constitutional Convention, where he lent his conservative voice to a voting scheme that would have included slaves in apportionment ratios and restricted voting rights to males who owned land.

When Andrew Jackson was elected president in 1828, Philip Barbour might have expected to receive some significant appointment in the new administration. But Jackson disappointed Barbour, offering him no other post than a position as federal district judge for Eastern District of Virginia. Though it was less than Barbour might have hoped for, he nevertheless accepted the judicial seat and held it from 1830 to 1836. He briefly toyed with a possible candidacy for vice president under Jackson at the time of the 1832 election. Many southerners distrusted Jackson's personal choice for the position—the "Little Magician" from New York, Martin Van Buren—and proposed instead a Jackson-Barbour ticket. But Democratic party leaders ultimately dissuaded Barbour from pursuing this course, and the Virginian decided to bide his time for the future.

Throughout the first half of the 1830s, speculation abounded concerning the likely retirement of John Marshall, chief justice of the U.S. Supreme Court. More than one observer feared that Philip Barbour might have poised himself to win the nomination as chief justice if Marshall's seat came open. John Quincy Adams viewed Marshall's retirement with dread: "if [Marshall] should be now withdrawn, some shallow-pated wild-cat like Philip P. Barbour, fit for nothing but to tear the Union to rags and tatters, would be appointed in his place." In 1835 Associate Justice Gabriel Duvall resigned from the Court, after being assured that President Jackson planned to nominate Roger B. Taney to fill the vacant seat. In the summer of the same year, Chief Justice Marshall died, leaving Jackson with two seats on the Court. With Marshall's seat now open, Jackson nominated Taney to become the new chief justice and Philip P. Barbour as an associate justice. The Senate eventually confirmed both nominations.

Barbour participated in the "revolution" in constitutional law accomplished by the Taney court. From a vantage point more than a century and a half later, though, the "revolution" appears more akin to a relatively minor adjustment in constitutional trajectory than a wholesale repudiation of the foundation established by the Court of Chief Justice John Marshall. Roger Taney and his colleagues reasserted the importance of state government in the constitutional system, retreating somewhat from the strong nationalistic tendencies of the Marshall court. But even as the Taney court tempered Marshall's devotion to exclusive congressional control over interstate commerce, for example, it reasserted Marshall's parallel devotion to the authority of the Court to resolve the nation's constitutional disputes. Thus, justices such as Philip Barbour championed the cause of state participation in the emerging commercial landscape of the 19th century by vigorously asserting the Court's own power to preside over the interpretation of the Constitution.

Barbour himself authored one of the triumvirate of cases that set the new tone for the Taney court in 1837. In *Charles River Bridge v. Warren Bridge* (1837), for which Chief Justice Taney wrote the Court's opinion, and in *Briscoe v. Bank of Kentucky* (1837), for which Associate Justice John McLean wrote the majority opinion, the Court expanded the power of states to control banking and other forms of commercial development. Justice Barbour's opinion for the Court in *New York v. Miln* (1837) similarly upheld the power of a state to require shipmasters to reveal information about passengers arriving in New York ports from other states or countries. Against the claim that this law intruded on congressional power to regulate commerce among the states, Barbour concluded for a majority of the Court that the law represented instead a valid exercise of the state's police power—that is, its power to pass legislation to protect the health and welfare of its citizens. This power, Barbour insisted, had not been surrendered by states under the Constitution. It was, rather, "complete, unqualified, and exclusive." After this beginning on the Court, Barbour settled into a relatively minor role as a supporter of Chief Justice Taney's leadership, which was generally consistent with his own states' rights inclinations. His sudden death from a heart attack on February 25, 1841, in Washington, D.C., though, robbed him of the opportunity to forge any significant legacy as a jurist.

According to his detractors—and these were many—Philip Barbour scarcely ever encountered a state law that violated, in his eyes, the Constitution of the United States. Daniel Webster, the great American lawyer, orator, and statesman, described Barbour in sympathetic terms but noted his peculiar myopia in the area of states' rights and in his suspicion of the power of the national government:

> Barbour, I really think is honest & conscientious; & he is certainly intelligent; but his fear, or hatred, of the powers of this government is so great, his devotion to State rights so absolute, that perhaps [a situation] could hardly arise, in which he would be willing to exercise the power of declaring a state law void.

Barbour was not the first southerner to exhibit these habits of mind, nor would he be the last. In fact, measured by the southerners who followed him—including Peter Vivian Daniel, the man who would occupy the Supreme Court seat left vacant by his sudden death—Barbour was not so radical as he sometimes appeared in his own lifetime.

Further Reading

Cynn, Paul P. "Philip Pendleton Barbour." *John P. Branch Historical Papers of Randolph-Macon College* 4 (1913): 67–77.

Gatell, Frank Otto. "Philip Pendleton Barbour." In *The Justices of the United States Supreme Court 1789–1969: Their Lives and Major Opinions*, vol. 1. Edited by Leon Friedman and Fred L. Israel. New York: R. R. Bowker Co., 1969.

JOHN CATRON (CA. 1786–1865)

Associate Justice, 1837–1865

Appointed by President Andrew Jackson

JOHN CATRON
(United States Supreme Court)

John Catron of Tennessee served alongside Chief Justice Roger B. Taney on the Supreme Court for almost 30 years. He brought to the Court the basic mind-set of a Jacksonian Democrat, suspicious of national power but supportive of the Union, agreeable with the principles of states' rights but not with a right of nullification or secession. He participated in the Taney court's moderation of John Marshall's vigorous nationalism and in the Court's infamous attempt to settle the slavery question in the *Dred Scott* case. At the end of his life, loyalty to the Union made him an outcast in his home state.

The circumstances and date of John Catron's birth remain uncertain, though historians customarily assign his birth around 1786, probably in Pennsylvania to a family with Germanic origins. The name Catron appears to have been derived from the German "Kettenring," itself Americanized to "Kettering" and finally, "Catron." Modest family circumstances deprived John Catron of a private education, and such knowledge as he managed to acquire was self-taught. He grew up in Virginia, moved later to Kentucky, and finally migrated to Tennessee in 1812. He studied law briefly before undertaking military service for Tennessee and eventually serving under General Andrew Jackson during the War of 1812. After this military career he resumed legal studies and was admitted to the practice of law in 1815. Sometime during this period, Catron married Maltida Childress. The union produced no children.

For his first few years of work as an attorney, John Catron engaged in a general practice, supplemented by part-time work as a prosecuting attorney. In 1818 he moved to Nashville. Legal practice in Tennessee during this period typically involved substantial attention to the land disputes that plagued a state in which early land grants had been documented only casually and in which land values had climbed precipitously. Catron quickly became an expert in this area of the law, and by 1824 his increasing political connections and acknowledged expertise in the area of land titles had contributed to his being elected to Tennessee's highest court, the Court of Errors and Appeals. After seven years of service on the court, he was appointed its chief justice in 1831. During the same period, Catron became part owner of a profitable iron works; the eventual sale of his share in this business in 1833 earned him $20,000. While on the Court of Errors and Appeals, he demonstrated his political affinity with General Andrew Jackson, under whom he had served during the War of 1812, by publishing a series of attacks on the Bank of the United States that would presage Jackson's own subsequent war against the Bank after he became president.

As a state court judge, Catron penned memorable judicial diatribes against such social ills as dueling and in support of the South's "peculiar institution" of slavery. In *State v. Smith* (1829), a case involving a Tennessee lawyer disbarred for having traveled to Kentucky where he killed a man in a duel, Catron sternly defended the power of the state to discourage such behavior. It had every right, he declared, to "restrain the blind and criminal passions that drive to ruin the fearless and valuable man; to restrain the wicked vanity of the noisy coxcomb; and to protect from his misguided fears of giddy and idle ridicule the physically weak and nervous man." Catron also demonstrated the social attitudes toward slavery and African Americans that would align him with a majority of the Supreme Court 20 years later in the decision of the now-infamous *Dred Scott* case. *Fisher's Negroes v. Dabbs* (1834) presented Tennessee's highest court with the issue of whether a manumission clause in a will was enforceable. Could a master free his slaves on his death? Certainly not without the approval of the state in which manumission occurred, Catron believed. "Degraded by their color and condition in life, the free negroes are a very dangerous and most objectionable population where slaves are numerous. Therefore no slave can be safely freed but with the assent of the government where the manumission takes place." Absent the assent of the state of Tennessee to the manumission, which Catron would not imply, any slaves freed by the operation of the will in question could not remain in the state but must be sent to Liberia. Even their removal to a free state in the Union did not seem an adequate remedy for Catron, who argued that free negroes in free states were actually more inferior than slaves living in slave states. He felt it was only a pitiful fantasy that manumission actually improved the lot of a former slave; on the contrary, the manumitted slave was "a degraded outcast, and his fancied freedom a delusion."

Amendments to the Tennessee constitution abolished John Catron's judicial seat in 1834, sending him back to the private practice of law. Catron kept his hand in political affairs, though, by managing the 1836 election campaign of

Martin Van Buren, President Andrew Jackson's vice president and Jackson's choice as his successor. When Van Buren won the election, Jackson did not neglect to demonstrate gratitude for Catron's political service and for his sound Jacksonian views. Early in 1837, Congress amended the Judiciary Act to create a new circuit for the federal court of appeals—the Ninth—and increased the number of seats on the Supreme Court from seven to nine. As one of his last official acts before the inauguration of his successor, President Jackson nominated John Catron to fill one of the newly created seats on the Court. The Senate confirmed Catron's appointment to the high court on March 8, 1837, and he took the oath of office on May 1, 1837. Thus, at the age of 51, Associate Justice John Catron began a career on the Court that would last until his death in 1865, just over 28 years later.

As a member of the Court led by Chief Justice Roger B. Taney, Catron contributed to the new majority's modest revision of the strong nationalism characteristic of decisions during the John Marshall era of the Court. This revision emphasized the legitimate power of states to regulate some matters affecting interstate commerce, especially in cases involving the protection of public health and welfare. The power over health and welfare—often referred to as the "police power" of a state—was, according to Catron, "not touched by the Constitution, but left to the States as the Constitution found it." Thus, Catron joined a majority of the Court in the *Licence Cases* (1847), upholding the power of a state to limit the importation of liquor into that state from foreign countries and other states. Catron's deference to state police power in the *Licence Cases* did not represent an unthinking states' rights absolutism, however; two years later, in the *Passenger Cases* (1849), he joined a majority of the Court in holding invalid certain state laws taxing immigrants when these laws conflicted with federal statutes on this subject.

The most famous case decided by the Taney court was *Dred Scott v. Sandford* (1857), one in which Associate Justice Catron played a significant role behind the scenes. As the Court deliberated the case internally, Catron served as a conduit of information to James Buchanan on the eve of his inauguration, advising Buchanan of the likely result in the case. Catron even suggested that Buchanan encourage Justice Robert Grier to use the case as an opportunity to make some substantive resolution of the slavery issue rather than decide it on narrow, technical grounds. With Catron's inside information, Buchanan was able to promise at his inauguration that he would uphold the decision of the Supreme Court in the *Dred Scott* case, "whatever this may be." The Supreme Court ultimately ruled against Dred Scott's claim that his travels into free territory had made him free, but the justices announced their respective decisions in a variety of opinions. Chief Justice Taney argued that Scott had no right to present a claim in federal court, because he was—by reason of his race—disqualified per se from holding U.S. citizenship. In addition, Taney ruled that the Missouri Compromise of 1820 was unconstitutional. Catron, though his early state court opinion in *Fisher's Negroes v. Dabbs* (1834) suggested a clear affinity with Taney's conclusion about Dred Scott's citizenship, nevertheless declined to address this issue. Instead, he based his conclusion chiefly on the observation that the original terms of the Louisiana Purchase Treaty protected the property rights of slaveholders and thus superseded any contrary provisions of the Missouri Compromise. Furthermore, slaveholders' rights were also protected constitutionally by the privileges and immunities clause, which guaranteed to the citizens of each state the privileges and immunities possessed by citizens of other states.

The members of the majority in the *Dred Scott* case hoped to settle the slavery issue by lending the weight of the Court's authority to a resolution of the question. This hope proved illusory, however. With the onset of the Civil War, Catron found himself at odds with his home state, which ultimately joined the Confederacy. Even before Tennessee formally asserted its decision to depart the Union, Catron was forced to leave the state when he attempted to hold circuit court there. Stripped of property in Tennessee worth $100,000 and exiled for a time from his wife, Catron supported Union military authority by declining to grant writs of habeas corpus to release Confederate sympathizers. His view of the emergency powers of Union authorities during wartime was limited, though; he dissented in the *Prize Cases* (1863), which upheld President Abraham Lincoln's blockade of Southern ports shortly after the Civil War began. John Catron lived just long enough to see the Union preserved by the South's surrender. He died on May 30, 1865, a year after the death of Chief Justice Roger Taney.

As a young man, John Catron served under General Andrew Jackson, and he would be, for the rest of his life, a loyal Jacksonian Democrat. Along with other members of the Taney court, he helped forge a distinctive constitutional philosophy that partially perpetuated and partially altered the nationalism of the Court's former chief Justice, John Marshall. In the Court's continued assertion of power to decide the great constitutional questions of the day, Catron and his colleagues upheld Marshall's opinion in *Marbury v. Madison,* reaffirming the doctrine of judicial review. But in the balance the Court struck between federal and state legislative power, the Taney court tempered Marshall's federalism with a more vigorous appreciation of state legislative power. Catron epitomized the difficulty of finding an enduring resolution to the tension this produced. Overly confident in the power of the Court to resolve such tension in the area of slavery, Catron and his colleagues produced the ignominious *Dred Scott* decision. When this decision failed to secure a peaceful resolution of the slavery issue, the Unionist Catron became an outcast from his state. Only after his death would a weary nation be forced to amend the Constitution to remove the stain of the *Dred Scott* decision. The Union to which Catron rendered unceasing loyalty survived—but only by repudiating the institution of slavery with which he and his colleagues had tried to burden it.

Further Reading

Chandler, Walter. *The Centenary of Associate Justice John Catron of the United States Supreme Court.* Washington, D.C.: U.S. Government Printing Office, 1937.

Gattell, Frank Otto. "John Catron." In *The Justices of the United States Supreme Court 1789–1969: Their Lives and Major Opinions,* vol. 1. Edited by Leon Friedman and Fred L. Israel. New York: R. R. Bowker Co., 1969.

Livingston, John. "Biographical Letter from Justice Catron." In *Portraits of Eminent Americans Now Living.* New York: R. Craighead, Printer, 1854.

JOHN MCKINLEY (1780–1852)

Associate Justice, 1838–1852

Appointed by President Martin Van Buren

JOHN MCKINLEY
(United States Supreme Court)

Numbered among the lesser lights of the Taney court, Justice John McKinley of Alabama served a total of 14 years on the U.S. Supreme Court, seven of them displaying solid but unexceptional judicial talent and seven made ineffective by ill health that culminated in McKinley's death. History remembers him most for one eccentric opinion in a case from his native Alabama. He is otherwise notable only for having arrived on the Court just after the "Revolution of 1837," in which Taney and his Jacksonian colleagues distinguished themselves from the Marshall court; and for having died just before the Court's opinion in the *Dred Scott* case would robe the Taney court in ignominy.

Born on May 1, 1780, in Culpepper County, Virginia, John McKinley grew up in Lincoln County, Kentucky, where his father, Andrew McKinley, practiced medicine and where his mother, Mary Logan McKinley, had influential family connections. No details survive concerning John McKinley's early education. He studied the law on his own and won admission to the Kentucky bar in 1800. He then practiced law for a time in Kentucky before moving to Huntsville, Alabama, in 1818. There he established a legal practice and aspired to elected office, though his political aspirations at first bore no fruit. He lost an election for circuit judge in 1819 and also lost his more ambitious bid for the U.S. Senate in 1822. Finally, in 1826 the transference of McKinley's political allegiance from Henry Clay to Andrew Jackson secured him a seat in the U.S. Senate when Alabama Senator Henry Chambers died in office. While in the Senate, McKinley supported policies that favored the interests of small landowners over wealthy speculators. Feeling that settlers would actually improve the land, McKinley also favored transfers of federal lands to the states to be developed by its settlers.

McKinley's career in the Senate lasted until 1831, when he narrowly lost a reelection bid. He returned home to Alabama, moving his residence to Florence, where its citizens promptly elected him to represent them in the state legislature. Here he continued to support Jackson's policies—for example, by sternly condemning the Bank of the United States and by rejecting South Carolina's nullification threats against the tariff. By 1832 McKinley had again secured a national forum for his political talents after winning election to the House of Representatives. He served there from 1833 through 1835, opposing efforts to defy President Jackson's removal of federal deposits from the Bank of the United States. He also demonstrated typical Southern indignation at attempts to curtail slavery. When petitions were circulated calling for the abolition of slavery in the District of Columbia, McKinley voiced his opposition to the proposal. Slaves were property, he argued, and their owners should be free to take their property wherever they chose.

Two years in the House was enough for McKinley. Rather than run for reelection, he returned to the Alabama legislature in 1836. That same year he stood again for election to the U.S. Senate, and this time he won the post. As events would have it, however, McKinley did not return to Washington as a U.S. senator. At the close of President Jackson's term in office, Congress increased the number of justices on the Supreme Court from seven to nine. Jackson initially offered one of the new seats on the Court to William Smith of Alabama, who declined to accept the appointment. After Martin Van Buren's inauguration, in fall 1837, the newly elected president offered the seat to John McKinley. The Senate confirmed his nomination shortly thereafter, and McKinley took the oath of office as an associate justice of the Supreme Court on January 9, 1838. In addition to his participation in Court deliberations, McKinley also undertook the onerous duty of acting as a circuit judge for the new judicial circuit Congress had created when it had increased the number of seats on the Court. The Ninth Circuit, for which Justice McKinley had responsibility, included Alabama, Mississippi, Louisiana, and Arkansas.

Shortly after McKinley joined the Court, he decided a series of cases as a circuit judge in Alabama that drew national attention. In what would eventually arrive at the Supreme Court as *Bank of Augusta v. Earle* (1839), three banks that had been chartered outside of the state bought bills of exchange in Alabama. When the makers of the bills refused to pay, the banks brought suit against them. The makers defended themselves by arguing that the banks had not been authorized to do business in Alabama and thus had no right to buy or sell bills of exchange in the state. As a circuit judge, McKinley ruled against the out-of-state banks, stating that no corporation had power to do business in a state without that state's authorization. Thus, the out-of-state banks could not buy or sell bills of exchange in Alabama.

Commercial interests responded to McKinley's circuit opinion with panic, insisting that the national economy nurtured by the Marshall court was threatened by calamitous ruin if the opinion stood. According to Supreme Court Justice Joseph Story, McKinley had "frightened half the lawyers and all the corporations of the country out of their proprieties." Daniel Webster, who represented the banks in their eventual argument before the Supreme Court, minced no words at the time of McKinley's opinion; it was, he said, "anti-commercial, and anti-social, new and unheard of in our system, and calculated to break up the harmony which has so long prevailed among the states and people of the Union." When the case finally arrived before the Court, Webster argued that corporations had the Constitution's protection from state laws designed to treat out-of-state citizens unfavorably. The privileges and immunities clause of Article IV stipulated that "the citizens of each state shall be entitled to all privileges and immunities of citizens in the several states." Webster posited that since corporations were organizations of citizens, then they should be entitled to protection from the kind of hostile treatment inflicted on them by the state of Alabama.

Although a majority of the Supreme Court declined to grant corporations the protection of the privileges and immunities clause sought by Webster, every justice but McKinley determined that the Alabama justice's circuit opinion should be overturned. Writing for the majority, Chief Justice Roger B. Taney insisted that McKinley had been part right and part wrong. A state could restrain out-of-state corporations from doing business in that state; on this, Taney suggested, McKinley was correct. Nevertheless, Taney insisted with a majority of the Court that any restraint on out-of-state corporations had to be clearly imposed by a state's law—a point on which the majority parted ways with McKinley. That Alabama had not authorized a Georgia bank to do business in its state was not a sufficient reason to prevent the bank from engaging in business; Alabama had to explicitly exclude any out-of-state bank from conducting transactions in the state. This, Taney found, Alabama had not done. Therefore it could not prevent foreign corporations from conducting affairs in the state. The lone dissenter in the case, McKinley stood by his circuit opinion. Alabama responded to the Court's decision by passing the kind of exclusionary law suggested by the Court and managed to keep the foreign banks out after all.

Two years after the bank case, McKinley managed to depart from his brethren once more, in *Groves v. Slaughter* (1841). At issue in the case was a newly enacted amendment to the Mississippi state constitution that prohibited the importation of slaves from other states. The case posed the perplexing issue of whether a state could impose such a clear burden on interstate commerce in slaves and whether that imposition intruded on Congress's power to regulate commerce among the states. A majority of the Court was not prepared to undertake this issue and ruled instead on the technical ground that Mississippi's constitutional provision required state legislation to implement its terms and was not enforceable without such legislation. Alone on the Court, McKinley would have upheld Mississippi's choice to regulate slavery in the way it saw fit.

The immense territory included within the circuit assigned to McKinley assured that circuit riding would dominate his responsibilities as a justice on the Supreme Court. Even at the time of his appointment to the Court, McKinley seemed to realize the arduous task that would face him. He described the post he was undertaking as "certainly the most onerous and laborious of any in the United States. Should I perform all the duties of the office I shall have to hold eight circuit courts, and assist in holding the Supreme court, and travel upwards of five thousand miles every year." Even this sober estimation of his task failed to capture the true extent of McKinley's responsibilities. In 1839 the justices of the Court compiled a survey of their respective circuit-riding duties, as measured in annual miles traveled. The total miles traveled by each justice varied immensely:

Roger B. Taney	458
Henry Baldwin	2,000
James M. Wayne	2,370
Philip P. Barbour	1,498
Joseph Story	1,896
Smith Thompson	2,590
John McLean	2,500
John Catron	3,464
John McKinley	10,000

Congress declined to relieve the justices of the burden of circuit riding, but it did adjust McKinley's responsibilities in 1842 to eliminate Mississippi and Arkansas from his circuit. Later, however, it added Kentucky to McKinley's duties, because he was living in Louisville. But the 10,000-mile years inevitably took their toll on the Alabama justice. In the second half of his time on the Court, McKinley suffered regularly from illness, so much so that he became a virtually invisible member of the nation's highest judicial fraternity. He died in Louisville on July 19, 1852. Chief Justice Taney's eulogy on McKinley's death captured the limitations that illness had inflicted on the Alabama justice's latter career on the Court. He was, said Taney, "a sound lawyer, faithful and assiduous in the discharge of his duties while his health was sufficient to undergo the labor."

In a curious career characterized by abrupt transitions from one political post to another, John McKinley's service on the high court was more extended than any other public position he held during his lifetime. Nevertheless, even his career as a Supreme Court justice was relatively brief, at least if measured in the years McKinley was healthy enough to devote himself to his responsibilities. Even at his peak, though, McKinley failed to demonstrate any extraordinary measure of ability as a justice. Competent at best, and occasionally eccentric in his views, Alabama's first Supreme Court justice remains a relatively minor figure within the Court's history.

FURTHER READING

Gatell, Frank Otto. "John McKinley." In *The Justices of the United States Supreme Court 1789–1969: Their Lives and Major Opinions,* vol. 1. Edited by Leon Friedman and Fred L. Israel. New York: R. R. Bowker Co., 1969.

Hicks, Jimmie. "Associate Justice John McKinley: A Sketch." *Alabama Review* 18 (1965): 227–233.

Levin, H. "John McKinley." In *The Lawyers and Law Makers of Kentucky.* Chicago: Lewis Publishing Co., 1897.

Martin, John M. "John McKinley: Jacksonian Phase." *Alabama Historical Quarterly* 28 (1966): 7–31.

Whatley, George C. "Justice John McKinley." *North Alabama History Association Bulletin* 4 (1959): 15–18.

PETER VIVIAN DANIEL (1784–1860)

Associate Justice, 1841–1860

Appointed by President Martin Van Buren

PETER VIVIAN DANIEL
(United States Supreme Court)

Justice Peter V. Daniel was a conservative of conservatives. He sat on a court characterized by conservatism and made his fellow colleagues on the bench seem almost moderate in comparison to him. So extreme were his views that he was able to exert little influence on the course of constitutional development.

Peter Vivian Daniel was born in the wake of the Revolutionary War on April 24, 1784, on a farm in Stafford County, Virginia, the son of Travers Daniel and Frances Moncure Daniel. He grew up on a family estate called "Crow's Nest," was educated privately, and then attended the College of New Jersey (now Princeton University) in 1802. He left Princeton after a few months to return home. In 1805 he moved to Richmond to pursue legal studies in the law office of a famous Virginian, Edmund Randolph, who had played a principal role in the Constitutional Convention and later served as attorney general and secretary of state under President George Washington. By 1808 Daniel had completed his studies with Randolph and returned to Stafford County, where he was admitted to the bar. That same year he participated in a duel, for reasons now unknown, and mortally wounded his opponent, John Seddon.

Daniel followed in the steps of innumerable legal apprentices by marrying Lucy Randolph, the daughter of his mentor, on April 20, 1810. The marriage, which raised Daniel's social standing considerably, lasted until Lucy's death nearly four decades later in 1847. The couple had no children together.

Peter Daniel's political career began in 1809 with his election to the Virginia legislature. Within four years he had won an appointment to the Virginia Council of State, to which position he added concurrent service as lieutenant governor beginning in 1818. He would hold these two posts until 1835. These appointments secured Daniel's membership in the loose confederation of Virginia leaders, referred to as the Richmond Junta, who controlled the state's political affairs. From this political base Daniel participated in the alliance forged between Virginia and New York Republicans, known commonly as the Richmond-Albany axis, and cultivated a friendship with New York's rising political star, Governor Martin Van Buren.

At the time that Van Buren's political fortunes were on the ascendancy, Daniel's own reached something of a zenith and soon commenced a decline. He supported President Andrew Jackson vigorously, including his choice of Van Buren as a vice-presidential candidate in 1832, but Daniel was not able to convert his alliance with Jackson and Van Buren into tangible political attainments. He lost a bid for the Virginia governorship in 1830, and by the middle of the decade he had also lost his posts on the Virginia Council of State and as lieutenant governor. President Jackson made some attempt to reward Daniel's loyalty by offering him the post of attorney general of the United States after Roger Taney moved from this position to that of secretary of state in 1833, but Daniel declined the position for financial reasons. In 1836, however, Jackson found a new position for Daniel, this time as a federal district judge for the Eastern District of Virginia. Daniel happily accepted this position, in which he served for five years.

Even as a district judge, Daniel had continued to demonstrate his loyalty to Van Buren. He presided over the Democratic state convention in 1840 that proposed Van Buren's reelection. Although Van Buren lost this bid, he still found a way to reward Daniel when Justice Philip Barbour died suddenly on February 25, 1841. Two days later, before Barbour had been buried and scarcely a week before Van Buren left office, the president appointed Daniel to the vacant seat on the Court. The Senate confirmed the nomination on March 2, and Daniel took his seat the following January. The Whig party, now in control, retaliated against Van Buren's last-minute appointment by rearranging the federal circuits, assigning Daniel to the circuit that covered Arkansas and Mississippi. While all of the Supreme Court justices had to serve as a circuit-court judge as well as manage their responsibilities on the Court, Daniel's new circuit-riding responsibilities proved particularly onerous.

Daniel's previous political service and his tenure as a federal district judge imbued him with political principles that would dominate his work as a Supreme Court justice. He brought with him to the Court an ingrained suspicion of federal power, an unyielding devotion to the rights of states, and an abiding hostility to corporations. Daniel arrived on the Court at a time when Chief Justice Roger B. Taney had forged a new majority increasingly hospitable to state legislative power and more willing to limit federal power. But Daniel soon showed himself to be an arch-conservative and one of the Court's most vigorous advocates for states' rights. He so outdistanced his colleagues in his devotion to state power and his suspicion of all federal encroachments on it that the following decade and a half would find him dissenting alone far more often than any of his brethren. Fifty dissents would flow from his pen before death muzzled his uniquely dissident voice in 1860.

Influence is often a casualty of dissent, and Justice Daniel's eccentric views largely stripped him of the capacity to influence the Court's direction during his years of service as an associate justice. He championed agrarian policies in an age of rapid commercial expansion. Even justices who shared with him a significant regard for states' rights did not share this backward-looking devotion to policies that seemed increasingly out of place in the economic climate of the mid-19th century. Moreover, although the Court under Chief Justice Roger B. Taney took pains to reserve an important place for states at the national economic table, it also held in part a significant respect for Congress's constitutionally designated role in supervising commerce among the states. Justice Daniel, however, scarcely ever encountered a federal commercial law of which he approved; they invariably seemed to him pernicious encroachments on the prerogatives of states. For example, his rejection of federal power to build roads and other internal improvements within the states drove him to dissent in *Searight v. Stokes* (1845). It also fueled his dissent in the *Passenger Cases* (1849), when a majority of the Court held that a state tax on immigrants interfered with Congress's power under the Commerce Clause. In the latter case, Justice Daniel viewed with great alarm the majority's lack of respect for state authority over what he viewed as essentially internal affairs. The Court's decision had "trampled down some of the strongest defenses of the safety and independence of the states."

Daniel combined a fierce devotion to states' rights with an equally fervent distaste for corporations. Against a majority of the Court, he denied that corporations were "citizens" within the meaning of the Constitution and so denied that they could invoke the jurisdiction of federal courts to hear disputes between the "citizens" of different states. To similar effect in *Planters' Bank of Mississippi v. Sharp* (1848), and again in dissent, Justice Daniel denied that such protections as the Constitution provided to business arrangements under the clause forbidding impairments of contracts applied to corporate charters. These, he thought, could be freely regulated in service of state police power. Daniel matched his public distrust of corporations and banks with a similarly adamant private distrust, an antipathy so fixed in his mind that his will stipulated that none of his estate be invested in "stocks or bonds of banks, railroads, or corporation or joint stock companies of any kind."

As would be expected from a champion of states' rights, Justice Daniel settled comfortably within the majority of the Court that rejected Dred Scott's claim to freedom in *Dred Scott v. Sandford* (1857). He agreed emphatically with Chief Justice Taney that Scott, by reason of his race, could not be a citizen of the United States and thus could not invoke the Court's power to hear disputes between "citizens" of different states. He counted as settled the principles that

> The African negro race never have been acknowledged as belonging to the family of nations; that as amongst them there never has been known or recognized by the inhabitants of other countries anything partaking of the character of nationality, or civil or political polity; that this race has been by all the nations of Europe regarded as subjects of capture or purchase; as subjects of commerce or traffic; and that the introduction of that race into every section of this country was not as members of civil or political society, but as slaves, as property in the strictest sense of the term.

As a species of property, slaves could not—in Daniel's view—be citizens, not even if some act or event freed a slave. Once property, the Virginian declared, never a citizen—a point that he took pains to buttress with copious quotations from Roman legal authorities. As to the Missouri Compromise, Daniel saw a clear constitutional violation, stating that the Compromise purported to exact a forfeiture of "that equality of rights and immunities which are the birthright or the donative from the Constitution of every citizen of the United States within the length and breadth of the nation."

Justice Daniel served through the Court's 1858 term. After the Court recessed, he returned to his home in Richmond, Virginia, where he died on May 31, 1860, in time to see his state declare its secession from the Union.

Dissenters on the Court sometimes prophesy the future, and when that future arrives, their dissents earn them lasting recognition. For example, Justice John Marshall Harlan dissented from the decision in *Plessy v. Ferguson* (1896), which established the "separate but equal" doctrine that would legitimize racial segregation in the South for half a century and urged instead a "color-blind" construction of the Constitution. Eventually Harlan's view prevailed, and his *Plessy* dissent was acknowledged to be a harbinger of a more just future. Justice Peter V. Daniel's dissents, however, tended to cling to doctrines and principles of the past, championing the waning rather than the waxing judicial tide, and placing him at the rearguard of judicial advancement.

Further Reading

Burnette, Lawrence, Jr. "Peter V. Daniel: Agrarian Justice." *Virginia Magazine of History and Biography* 62 (1954): 289–305.

Frank, John Paul. *Justice Daniel Dissenting: A Biography of Peter V. Daniel, 1784–1860.* Cambridge: Harvard University Press, 1964.

Gatell, Frank Otto. "Peter V. Daniel." In *The Justices of the United States Supreme Court 1789–1969: Their Lives and Major Opinions,* vol. 1. Edited by Leon Friedman and Fred L. Israel. New York: R. R. Bowker Co., 1969.

Samuel Nelson (1784–1873)

Associate Justice, 1845–1872

Appointed by President John Tyler

Samuel Nelson
(United States Supreme Court)

The Court led by Chief Justice Roger B. Taney had more than its share of mediocre jurists, men who had enjoyed some measure of political or judicial respect prior to joining the Court but whose names history has mostly forgotten. Samuel Nelson must be numbered among these. Fifty years of judicial service, first at the state and subsequently at the national level, produced scarcely a ripple across the surface of American law. Though he authored nearly 350 opinions during his time on the Court, these mostly occupy dusty pages that few people ever find the need to consult. He is best known perhaps for the restrained position he took in the *Dred Scott* case, but since his restraint vindicated the rights of slaveholders, few observers today characterize it as a virtue.

The son of farmers, Samuel Nelson was born on November 11, 1792, in Hebron, New York. His parents, John Rodgers Nelson and Jean McArthur Nelson, entertained hopes of a ministerial career for their son and arranged for his education in private academies and ultimately at Middlebury College in Vermont. But Samuel chose to pursue a career in law after graduating from college in 1813. He apprenticed in a law office in Salem, New York, for two years before migrating to Madison County and entering into a law partnership with one of his former mentors. In 1818 he was admitted to the bar, and two years later he married his partner's daughter, Pamela Woods.

Nelson's wife died within three years after giving birth to a son. Nelson then left his law partnership to set up a practice of his own in Cortland, New York. He soon earned a measure of prominence as an attorney and also secured a position as the town postmaster. At the same time, he embarked on a brief political career, serving as a presidential elector in 1820 and as delegate from his county at the State Constitutional Convention in 1821. Two years later, in 1823, Nelson began what would eventually become a 50-year judicial career when he accepted an appointment to the Sixth Circuit Court of New York. He moved to Cooperstown and married again, this time to Catherine Ann Russell. Three children would be born to this union, and one of them—Rensselaer P. Nelson—would one day follow in his father's judicial footsteps by becoming a federal district court judge in Minnesota.

After eight years as a state circuit court judge, Nelson received an appointment in 1831 to the New York Supreme Court. Six years later he replaced John Savage, one of his original legal mentors, as chief justice of the court. Nelson's steady advance in his career as a judge seems to have owed a great deal to solid ability and a judicial temperament. "Nature intended him for a judge," one biographer wrote. "His opinions are pervaded by a humane and liberal spirit. They were read and admired for their terseness, directness, lucidity and practical comprehension of the cases under consideration. . . ."

After 20 years of distinguished service on the New York bench, Nelson found himself belatedly considered for a seat on the U.S. Supreme Court. When fellow New Yorker Smith Thompson died in 1843, however, Nelson was far from the first candidate to be considered for the vacancy Thompson's death created on the Court. President John Tyler proved remarkably incapable of finding a candidate willing to undertake an appointment to the Court and—more important—able to obtain confirmation from the U.S. Senate. The Senate rejected Tyler's first choice, Secretary of the Treasury John Spencer. A subsequent series of candidates declined to accept the appointment. When Chancellor Reuben H. Walworth of New York withdrew from consideration in the face of political opposition, Tyler turned at last to Samuel Nelson. The Senate easily confirmed his appointment, and the 52-year-old New Yorker took his seat on the Supreme Court on March 5, 1845.

After years of demonstrated competence on the New York bench, Associate Justice Nelson undertook what would be a long but wholly unexceptional career as a U.S. Supreme Court justice. Modesty, restraint, and precision characterized his service on the Court and cast him into a supporting role rather than a leading character on the Taney court. Thus, even though he was a prolific writer of opinions during his 27-year tenure on the Court, his impact on the course of American law was negligible.

History remembers Samuel Nelson most for his role in the Court's decision of *Dred Scott v. Sandford* (1857). When Dred Scott, a slave, argued before the Court that his travels with his master into free territory had made him free once he returned to Missouri, a slave state, a majority of the Court seemed initially poised to decide the case on technical grounds. Nelson took the position that Missouri law controlled the question of Scott's status as a slave and that the Court had no jurisdiction to override the state's determination in this matter—which was adverse to Scott's claim. In fact, Nelson prepared an initial draft of an opinion for the Court, resolving the case on this ground. But the other members of the Court eventually decided to address the core issues posed by the case: whether blacks were citizens of the United States and thus entitled to invoke the Court's jurisdiction; and whether the Missouri Compromise of 1820, which limited slavery in certain territories, violated the Constitution. At the suggestion of Justice James M. Wayne, a majority of the Court chose to decide these controversial questions, ultimately ruling that Dred Scott, because he was black, could not be a citizen of the United States and that the Missouri Compromise was unconstitutional. Nelson, however, persisted in his belief that the case should be resolved more circumspectly and submitted his original opinion for the Court as his own separate opinion in the case. Though his opinion did not earn him the same blistering attacks heaped on Chief Justice Taney and the other justices who followed the reasoning of Taney, many Northern observers chastised Nelson for ruling against Dred Scott. An editorial from the *New York Tribune* dismissed him as a timid jurist who had failed to stand up for the truth: ". . . a New York Democrat of the perishing school. . . . He hesitated to go with the Southern Judges in their revolutionary opinions, yet he had not sufficient virtue to boldy stand up against their heresies." History has not rescued Nelson from this judgment.

The national resolution of the slavery debate that Taney and his colleagues hoped to achieve through the *Dred Scott* decision never materialized. As the country stood on the precipice of war, Nelson again sought some intermediate resolution that would stave off conflict. He served for a time with Justice John Campbell of Alabama as an intermediary in discussions between President Abraham Lincoln's secretary of state, William Seward, and a confederate delegation concerning federal occupation of Fort Sumter in South Carolina. When Seward failed to keep a commitment to remove federal troops from the fort, Nelson abandoned his role as a mediator, and war soon followed.

In the face of Lincoln's vigorous attempts to subdue Southern rebellion, Nelson preferred strict adherence to constitutional principles even if this meant allowing Southern states to withdraw from the Union, which, he thought, could not be preserved by force. When Lincoln took the contrary view and blockaded Southern ports even before a congressional declaration of war, Nelson sided with the minority of the Court that thought the president had overstepped his constitutional bounds. In the *Prize Cases* (1863), he joined with justices Taney, Catron, and Clifford in a dissent from the majority holding that Lincoln's blockage was justified. Writing for the dissenters, Justice Nelson agreed that Congress alone had the constitutional power to declare war and that, in the absence of such a declaration, Lincoln's vigorous action was illegitimate.

After the war, President Ulysses S. Grant solicited Nelson to put his mediation skills to the service of his country once again by appointing the aged justice in 1871 to be a member of the Alabama Claims Commission. This commission sought reparations from England for damages caused by British-built ships, such as the *Alabama*, used by the Confederacy against the Union. Overtaxed by this final public service and plagued with insomnia and general ill health, Justice Nelson resigned from the Supreme Court in November 1872. He retired to Cooperstown, New York, and died there, just over a year later, on December 13, 1873.

Nelson's moderating influence on the Supreme Court failed to avert the crisis of war. In the fierce controversy over slavery and secession, he seemed always willing to perpetuate the South's "peculiar institution" and even the Union's disintegration before he would countenance the stern measures that eventually abolished the one and preserved the other. Whether labeled admirable restraint or cowardly timidity,

Nelson's temperament earned him only the prize of being mostly forgotten. If there was a back row on the Court over which Chief Justice Roger B. Taney presided, then Samuel Nelson surely occupied one of its seats. History has tended to judge him neither a hero nor a villain of his age, only a minor footnote to the events over which he failed to exert any significant influence.

FURTHER READING

"Biographical Sketch of Justice Samuel Nelson." *Central Law Journal* 1 (1874): 2–3.

Countryman, Edwin. "Samuel Nelson." *Green Bag* (1907): 329–334.

Gatell, Frank Otto. "Samuel Nelson." In *The Justices of the United States Supreme Court 1789–1969: Their Lives and Major Opinions,* vol. 2. Edited by Leon Friedman and Fred L. Israel. New York: R. R. Bowker Co., 1969.

Leach, Richard H. "Rediscovery of Samuel Nelson." *New York History* 34 (1953): 64–71.

"The Old Judge and the New." *Albany Law Journal* 6 (1872): 400–401.

LEVI WOODBURY (1789–1851)

Associate Justice, 1845–1851

Appointed by President James K. Polk

LEVI WOODBURY
(United States Supreme Court)

Justice Levi Woodbury sat on the U.S. Supreme Court for just over five years—long enough to earn mention in histories of the Court but not long enough to leave any significant mark on it. In fact, there is no reason to suspect that a lengthier judicial career would have significantly altered his place in the Court's history. Woodbury's tenure on the Court exhibited capable but undistinguished judicial talent. These were traits so common to the justices who served on Chief Justice Roger B. Taney's court that they earned for it the designation as the worst Court in history, at least according to some observers, though Taney himself generally earns higher marks. The most that can be said for Levi Woodbury is that he did not descend beneath the plane of judicial mediocrity common to the period, even if he did not soar above it.

Born on December 2, 1789, in Francetown, New Hampshire, Levi Woodbury might later read some significance into the fact that his birth occurred in the same year the Constitution of the United States was ratified. Woodbury's father provided a moderately prosperous living for his family as a farmer and a merchant and was able to see Levi educated first at a public school and eventually at Dartmouth College. After graduating from Dartmouth in 1809, Levi Woodbury pursued a legal education briefly at the Tapping Reeve Law School in Litchfield, Connecticut. He eventually determined to supplement this education with legal apprenticeships, first with Samuel Dana of Boston and later with Jeremiah Smith in Exeter, New Hampshire.

By 1812 Woodbury had been admitted to the bar and had set up a legal practice in his hometown. During these early years, the young lawyer also busied himself with political affairs, becoming an ardent supporter of President James Madison's administration and a rising Republican star. Beginning in 1816, Woodbury was appointed clerk of the New Hampshire senate. Soon thereafter, when New Hampshire Republicans decided to reorganize Dartmouth College as a public institution, he was appointed one of its new trustees. In 1817 Republican Governor William Plumer elevated the 27-year-old Woodbury to a seat on the New Hampshire Supreme Court. That same year a constitutional challenge to the state's reorganization of the college came before the court. Not surprisingly, Woodbury, a Dartmouth trustee, saw no constitutional offense in the state's treatment of the college and appears to have joined in the court's decision upholding the state's actions in *Dartmouth College v. Woodward* (N.H. 1817). When the case eventually arrived at the U.S. Supreme Court in 1819, Chief Justice John Marshall famously disagreed by holding that the attempted public takeover of Dartmouth violated the Constitution's Contracts Clause.

In 1819 Levi Woodbury married Elizabeth Williams Clapp, the daughter of Asa Clapp, a wealthy merchant in Portland, Maine, who supported his son-in-law's political aspirations. With Clapp's connections and his own political talents, Woodbury was poised four years later to become governor of New Hampshire when Republican infighting made him an attractive compromise candidate. He won, but gubernatorial elections occurred annually in New Hampshire at that time, and Woodbury was not able to hold onto the post past his initial term. In his reelection bid, when a close vote threw the governor's election into the state legislature, he lost to his opponent. His short-lived career as governor, and the political opposition that marked it, prompted Woodbury to comment wryly in a letter to his father-in-law that one must do his duty and create "some memorial to his children and friends, that his life was not that of a mere vegetable or an oyster."

On the heels of his gubernatorial loss, Woodbury landed quickly on his feet. He won a seat in the New Hampshire legislature in 1825 and was immediately chosen speaker of the House. That same year the legislature elected him to serve as U.S. senator. After Woodbury had served six years in the Senate, President Andrew Jackson tapped him for a position in the Cabinet as secretary of the Navy. Woodbury joined the Cabinet with Roger B. Taney, Jackson's attorney general, who would shortly be named chief justice of the Supreme Court that Woodbury himself would later join. The two men would both become embroiled in the war President Jackson waged against the Bank of the United States. After Jackson vetoed the bill rechartering the bank, he decided to strangle the Bank's remaining life by removing federal deposits from it. When two successive treasury secretaries declined to follow the president's orders on this point, Jackson finally appointed Taney to the post, and Taney promptly accomplished the president's controversial wishes. For this loyalty, Taney was assured that he would receive a permanent appointment as secretary of the treasury. Nevertheless, the Senate rejected Taney's appointment, upon which Jackson nominated Woodbury for the position. Woodbury would hold the post of treasury secretary from 1834 through 1841. His advance to this influential cabinet position during a controversial period owed a good deal to his ability to appear uncommitted on contested issues until circumstances forced his hand. This, at least, was the judgment of Roger Taney in connection with the controversy over the Bank of the United States. Woodbury, he observed, "was a singularly wary and cautious man, unwilling to commit himself upon any opinion which he was not obliged immediately to act and never further than that action acquired."

With the arrival of William Henry Harrison's presidential administration in 1841, Levi Woodbury returned home to New Hampshire, only to be chosen immediately by the state legislature to return to Washington as a U.S. senator. By now Woodbury's name was a fixture in national Democratic political circles. He was mentioned in 1844 as a possible Democratic presidential candidate and, after James K. Polk's nomination, as a possible candidate for vice president. Though neither nomination ultimately fell to Woodbury, his name remained prominent when President Polk began to fill positions in his administration. In 1845 Polk suggested Woodbury as minister to Great Britain. Woodbury declined this appointment, but when Associate Justice Joseph Story died in the fall of that year, the president nominated Woodbury to fill the vacant seat on the Supreme Court. He was appointed while the Senate was not in session and began service in 1845. The Senate confirmed the appointment on January 3, 1846.

Associate Justice Woodbury demonstrated a marked enthusiasm for state legislature power in his five years on the Court. In the ongoing controversy over the relative powers of Congress and the states to regulate commercial matters, Woodbury tended to side with the states. He joined with the majority in the *License Cases* (1847), upholding the power of states to regulate liquor traffic. Later, in the *Passenger Cases* (1849), he sided with Justices Roger Taney, Peter Daniel, and Samuel Nelson in dissenting from the Court's declaration that a state tax on immigrants usurped congressional authority under the Commerce Clause of the Constitution.

Woodbury's support for states' rights was congenial enough to traditional southern sensibilities to earn for him the characterization as a "dough face" in some quarters—that is, a northerner with the political views characteristic of southerners. Justice Woodbury's views on slavery certainly did nothing to counter this characterization, though they were generally consistent with the views of other conservative northern Democrats of the time. The abolitionist case against slavery was, he thought, simply inconsistent with the Constitution's treatment of the issue. In *Jones v. Van Zandt* (1847) Woodbury wrote the opinion for a unanimous Court upholding the constitutionality of the Fugitive Slave Act of 1793 and thus reaffirming the Court's previous ruling to the same effect in *Prigg v. Pennsylvania* (1842). The immorality of slavery held no place in Woodbury's constitutional scheme. The framers of the Constitution had wrestled with issues relating to slavery, he believed, and had negotiated an uneasy resolution of them. "Whatever may be the theoretical opinions of any as to the expediency of some of those compromises or of the right of property in persons which they recognize, this Court has no alternative while they exist, but to stand by the Constitution and laws with fidelity to their duties and their oaths. The path is a straight and narrow one." The Constitution had "flung its shield" over the institution of slavery, and the moral darts of the abolitionists could not pierce through its defense.

The year after the decision in *Jones v. Van Zandt,* Woodbury seemed a strong candidate for the Democratic presidential nomination. He lost, however, to Lewis Cass, who subsequently lost the presidential election to Zachary Taylor. Woodbury's close brush with the nation's highest office fueled his determination to win the Democratic nomination in 1852. Death intervened, though, and stilled Woodbury's political ambition: He died in Portsmouth, New Hampshire, on September 4, 1851.

—~—

In its history as an institution of American government, the Supreme Court has often provided occupations to men whose aspirations were more political than judicial. Though some of the Court's justices, such as John Jay, have moved from the high bench to other political pursuits, more often an appointment to the Court has spelled the end of further political advancement. Two justices from the Taney era flirted with higher political opportunities but ultimately failed to win them: John McLean and Levi Woodbury. Woodbury's brief term of service on the Court took place under the shadow of two national elections in which he enjoyed some serious possibility of winning a presidential or vice-presidential nomination. The first opportunity eluded him and death intruded before he had a chance to make a second attempt. In any event, Levi Woodbury's political aspirations dominated a judicial career that was middling at best.

FURTHER READING

Bader, William D., Henry J. Abraham, and James B. Staab. "The Jurisprudence of Levi Woodbury." *Vermont Law Review* (1994): 261–312.

Woodbury, Charles Levi. *Memoir of Honorable Levi Woodbury, LL.D.* Boston: David Clapp and Son, 1894.

Woodbury, Levi. *Writings of Levi Woodbury, LL.D., Political, Judicial and Literary.* Boston: Little, Brown, 1852.

ROBERT COOPER GRIER (1794–1870)

Associate Justice, 1846–1870

Appointed by President James K. Polk

ROBERT COOPER GRIER
(United States Supreme Court)

Associate Justice Robert C. Grier served on the Supreme Court for nearly a quarter of a century. The years of his tenure saw the nation plunge toward war and subsequently emerge deeply scarred but intact. Perched on his seat on the nation's highest court during these years, Grier played a mostly insignificant role in the great events of his age. He cast a vote in support of the court's infamous *Dred Scott* decision, approving the Court's result but declining to offer reasons in support of it. Though his opinion in the case supported the South's "peculiar institution" of slavery, he was not subsequently a friend of Southern efforts to secede from the Union. By the end of his lengthy tenure on the Court, ill health had sapped his mental and physical powers and his brethren finally had to persuade him to resign his seat.

Robert Cooper Grier was born on March 5, 1794, in Cumberland County, Pennsylvania, to Isaac Grier and Elizabeth Cooper Grier. From his family background, he might have been expected to become a clergyman, since both his father and his maternal grandfather were Presbyterian ministers. When Robert was 12 years old, his father moved the family to Northumberland, where he pastored three churches and ran a private school. Here Robert gained a solid classical education and demonstrated significant aptitude as a student of Latin and Greek. In 1811 Dickinson College recognized his academic promise by admitting him as a junior; he graduated the following year.

Grier remained at Dickinson for a year as an instructor, but eventually he returned home to Northumberland, where he assisted his father in running the school. When his father died in 1815, the 21-year-old son donned the mantle of administrator and teacher. His time still not sufficiently occupied, Grier also studied law with Charles Hall, a lawyer in a nearby town. By 1817 this study had yielded admission to the bar. Grier thereupon established a legal practice that helped him support the large family that his father's death had cast into precarious financial circumstances. He practiced first in Bloomsburg, then later in Danville. Toward the end of the next decade, he married Isabella Rose, the daughter of a wealthy Scottish immigrant.

After 15 years of legal practice, Grier became a judge through something of a political accident. The creation of a district court for Allegheny County had occasioned a good deal of wrangling over an appropriate candidate to fill the judicial seat. Through a series of backroom manipulations, the governor offered the post first to Grier, who was expected to decline the appointment. But Grier surprised everyone involved by accepting and then by moving to Pittsburgh to become district judge. Though he received a chilly welcome at first, solid—if not exceptional—judicial work eventually made him a respected member of the Allegheny County legal community.

Robert Grier had stumbled into his first judicial appointment. His advancement 13 years later to the nation's highest court had the same unexpected air, as though he had happened on a seat reserved for some other man, more qualified or at least more prominent than Grier. The series of events that would catapult Grier onto the Supreme Court began with the death of Associate Justice Henry Baldwin of Pennsylvania in 1844 during the last year of President John Tyler's administration. Tyler could not find a candidate suitable for the Senate's approval prior to his leaving office. President James Polk had similar difficulty finding a candidate both willing to accept the appointment and able to win Senate confirmation. Polk's first nominee, George Woodward, was rejected, and James Buchanan, whom President Tyler had unsuccessfully approached about an appointment to the Court, declined to serve when Polk made a similar overture. Finally, Polk nominated Robert Grier, and the Senate confirmed his appointment at once on August 4, 1846.

By the time Grier joined the court, Chief Justice Roger B. Taney had led his colleagues to a minor revision of the strong nationalism that had prevailed on the Supreme Court during the first three decades of the 19th century. In a trilogy of cases decided in 1837, the Court had granted increasing power to states to regulate matters affecting interstate commerce. Over several years after Grier's appointment, the Court continued to refine the balance between federal and state power. In this process, Grier occupied solid middle ground on the Court, joining first in the majority that upheld state power to regulate liquor traffic in the *Licence Cases* (1847), and then in the majority that found a state tax on immigrants an intrusion on Congress's commerce power in the *Passenger Cases* (1849). When the Taney court finally articulated the doctrine of "selective exclusiveness" in *Cooley v. Board of Wardens* (1852), which gave formal expression to the attempt to balance congressional power against the legitimate police power of states, Grier once again joined with the Court's majority.

In *Dred Scott v. Sandford* (1857), the most famous—or infamous—case decided by the Taney court, Justice Grier played a significant role. Initially, a majority of the Court appeared inclined to resolve the case narrowly against Dred Scott, deferring to the judgment of Missouri, where Scott resided, as to whether he was still a slave after having traveled into free territory. By this resolution the Court would avoid two more controversial questions: whether Scott was a U.S. citizen and thus entitled to bring a claim in federal court, and whether Congress had the power to prohibit slavery in U.S. territories, as it purported to do in the Missouri Compromise.

Behind the scenes, some of the justices wished to tackle the larger questions. Justice John Catron, for one, desired the Court to provide a more substantial resolution of the issues roiling the nation. To this end he wrote to President-elect James Buchanan in February 1857, suggesting that Buchanan gently encourage Justice Grier to join in a comprehensive resolution of the case and not simply to "take the smooth handle for the sake of repose." Buchanan accepted the mission, wrote to Grier, and shortly received Grier's assurance that he would follow Justices Taney and Wayne in seeking an authoritative declaration of the Court on the controversial issues presented. True to his word, Justice Grier ultimately wrote a brief opinion in the *Dred Scott* case agreeing with the core points in Chief Justice Taney's opinion for the Court—that blacks were disqualified from U.S. citizenship by reason of their subordinate race and that the Missouri Compromise's attempt to restrict slavery in the territories was unconstitutional.

The Court's Olympian pronouncements in the *Dred Scott* case failed to settle the growing sectional tension over slavery. And when war finally added its own perverse coda to the case, Justice Grier proved less of a friend to the South than his opinion in *Dred Scott* might have suggested. After the battle of Bull Run, the prospect of a lengthy war seemed likely to Grier, but the preservation of the Union was for him a prize worth the sacrifice. "We must conquer this rebellion," he informed Justice Nathan Clifford, "or declare our republican government a failure, if it should cost 100,000 men and 1,000 millions of money." Grier read the Constitution as granting great latitude to President Abraham Lincoln in his choice of strategies to quell the Southern rebellion. Thus, when the *Prize Cases* (1863) arrived before the Court, Grier spoke for a bare majority that upheld Lincoln's blockade of Southern ports even before Congress had declared war. "A civil war is never solemnly declared," he wrote for the Court, "it becomes such by its accidents." Faced with Southern insurrection, Grier said, Lincoln was entitled to respond aggressively: "The President was bound to meet it in the shape [Civil War] presented itself, without waiting for Congress to baptize it with a name; and no name given to it by him could change the fact."

Shortly after the decision in the *Prize Cases,* Grier suffered a sharp decline in his physical and mental condition. He ceased riding the judicial circuit assigned to him, and by the end of the decade he was the subject of veiled reference on the floor of Congress as a justice "who is not able today to reach the bench without being borne to it by the hands of others." Rumors of Grier's growing incompetence and increasing evidence of senility ultimately persuaded Grier's colleagues on the Court to press for his retirement. He finally agreed to this course in December 1869, with his resignation from the Court to be effective at the end of the following month. A little over seven months later, he died in Philadelphia, Pennsylvania, on September 25, 1870.

—~~—

After his death, Associate Justice Robert C. Grier faded into the historical obscurity common to many of the justices who served on the Supreme Court during the central years of the 19th century. The crisis that plunged the nation into war had scant patience for the solid but unexceptional judicial competence demonstrated by justices such as Grier. The Pennsylvania justice could not escape the conservatism that had produced the *Dred Scott* decision, and his historical reputation—when he is remembered at all—suffers from his performance in this most fateful case of his generation. Grier's subsequent vindication of Lincoln in the *Prize Cases* (1863) and his eloquent defense of the Union have served to rescue him only partially from the judgment heaped on him for his role in *Dred Scott*.

Further Reading

Gatell, Frank Ott. "Robert C. Brier." In *The Justices of the United States Supreme Court 1789–1969: Their Lives and Major Opinions,* vol. 2. Edited by Leon Friedman and Fred L. Israel. New York: R. R. Bowker, Co., 1969.

Jones, Francis R. "Robert Cooper Grier." *Green Bag* 16 (1904): 221–224.

Livingston, John. "Honorable Robert C. Grier." In *Portraits Of Eminent Americans Now Living.* New York: R. Craighead, Printer, 1854.

Benjamin Robbins Curtis (1809–1874)

Associate Justice, 1851–1857

Appointed by President Millard Fillmore

Benjamin Robbins Curtis
(United States Supreme Court)

The middle years of the 19th century saw more than their share of mediocre justices on the U.S. Supreme Court. In many cases these men had shown some political or judicial skills prior to their appointments, but they contributed little to the law's course once they arrived on the nation's highest bench. Associate Justice Benjamin Robbins Curtis was one of two justices who stand out during this period, even though he served only six years on the Court. Together with Chief Justice Roger B. Taney, Curtis would gain frequent mention in subsequent years as one of the Court's brightest stars of the time. Ironically, though, a clash between Taney and Curtis over the controversial case of *Dred Scott v. Sandford* (1857) ultimately caused Curtis to leave the Court before he had the chance to make a deeper impact.

Benjamin Robbins Curtis was born to Lois Curtis and Benjamin Curtis III on November 4, 1809, in Watertown, Massachusetts. His father, a ship's captain, died on a voyage to Chile when Benjamin was five years old, leaving his mother with the responsibility of earning a livelihood to care for herself and two sons. She managed to provide for her family by running a dry-goods store and a library. When her son gained admission to Harvard at the age of 15, she paid for his tuition by operating a boardinghouse for college students in Cambridge. With his mother's support, Curtis graduated from Harvard in 1829 with highest honors. He enrolled at once in Harvard Law School and was fortunate to be a student there after Associate Justice Joseph Story had been appointed to a newly created chair in law. Story was one of the finest legal minds of the 19th century and brought his prodigious intellectual talents to legal education at Harvard. From his law school lectures, he would ultimately pen some of the foremost legal commentaries of the century.

Curtis arrived at Harvard Law School the same year that Story commenced his professorship, but he did not initially complete his course of studies. In March 1831 he interrupted his legal education to begin practice in Northfield, Massachusetts. He returned to Harvard the following spring, however, to complete his law degree, and he was admitted to the bar that summer.

In 1833 the young lawyer embarked on a career as a husband and a father by marrying Eliza Maria Woodward, a cousin. This union produced five children before Eliza's death of tuberculosis in 1844. Within a year and a half, Curtis remarried, this time to another, more distant cousin, Ann Wroe, his law partner's daughter. This marriage lasted 14 years and produced three children before Ann also died. A year later Curtis married his third wife, Maria Malleville Allen; their union eventually added four more children to his large family.

While he steadily built a family, Curtis also built a thriving legal practice. In 1834 he moved to Boston to join the law firm of a distant cousin, Charles Pelham Curtis. Benjamin Curtis specialized in commercial matters and quickly established himself as a talented and hardworking lawyer. He argued numerous cases before the Supreme Judicial Court of Massachusetts and before the federal circuit court of appeals in Boston. In 1845, when he was 36 years old, he was appointed to replace Justice Joseph Story, his old law school professor, as a fellow of the Harvard Corporation; this appointment testified to the esteem he had earned through his decade of practice in Boston.

To his work as a lawyer, Benjamin Curtis eventually added a brief but significant term of service as a state legislator. He served in the legislature from 1849 through 1851 and further enhanced his growing legal reputation by sponsoring legislation to reform legal procedure in Massachusetts. Appointed to chair a commission to study judicial improvements that he had proposed, Curtis managed to produce a plan of reform and see it enacted as the Massachusetts Practice Act of 1851. This legislation placed Massachusetts, together with New York, at the forefront of national legal development in the area of procedural reform. Combined with Curtis's reputation as an outstanding Massachusetts lawyer and an outspoken Whig, it made him an attractive candidate for the federal bench.

When Justice Levi Woodbury died in 1851, Curtis figured immediately in President Millard Fillmore's search to identify Woodbury's successor. On September 10, 1851, Fillmore wrote to Daniel Webster, his secretary of state, indicating his interest in Curtis. He was, the president informed Webster, "desirous of obtaining as long a lease and as much moral and judicial power as possible from this appointment." With these goals in mind, the qualifications for a potential appointee to the Court were clear: "I would therefore like to combine a vigorous constitution with high moral and intellectual qualifications, a good judicial mind, and such age as gives a prospect of long service." Neither for the first or the last time, the Whig president sought a like-minded appointment to counter the hold Southern Democrats had on the Taney court. Curtis was a natural for the position, and Fillmore indicated as much to Webster: "I have formed a very high opinion of Mr. B. R. Curtis. What do you say of him? What is his age? Constitution? Legal attainments? Does he fill the measure of my wishes?" Webster had no information to blunt the president's initial enthusiasm for Curtis. Subsequently, Benjamin Curtis, then 41 years of age, found himself nominated to the Court and promptly confirmed as an associate justice on December 20, 1851.

Almost immediately, the junior justice made an ongoing mark on constitutional law by authoring the Court's decision in *Cooley v. Board of Wardens* (1851). At issue in the case was the enduring controversy over the intersection between federal and state power to regulate matters affecting interstate commerce. Curtis, newly arrived on the Court, managed to broker a consensus among the justices through his articulation of the doctrine of "selective exclusiveness." *Cooley* involved a challenge to a state law that levied a fine against vessels entering the Philadelphia harbor that chose not to employ a local pilot. The challenger of this law argued that it intruded on Congress's exclusive power to regulate pilots, given its Constitutional authority to regulate interstate commerce under the commerce clause. By this reading of the clause, only Congress had power to pass legislation affecting interstate commerce; even if Congress had no law on a particular subject matter affecting such commerce, states should be precluded from enacting legislation in the area. On the opposite extreme, it had sometimes been suggested that the commerce clause posed no limitation on state laws affecting interstate commerce unless such laws conflicted with a contrary federal law. Curtis's opinion for the majority in *Cooley* struck a middle ground between these two opposing views of the commerce clause. Under his formulation, certain national commercial matters dictated that only Congress may attempt legislative solutions in these areas and that states should be precluded from attempted regulation on these subjects, even if Congress had not yet passed contrary laws. On the other hand, Curtis reasoned for the majority, certain local matters were appropriate forums for state and local lawmaking, even if the laws crafted had some impact on interstate commerce, and so long as they did not conflict with federal laws in the area. By its balanced resolution of a controversial issue, Curtis's *Cooley* opinion became one of the most important Commerce Clause cases of the 19th century, ranked by some commentators as second only in importance to Chief Justice John Marshall's opinion in *Gibbons v. Ogden* (1824), decided a generation before.

Curtis's reputation on the Court was forged chiefly out of his participation in one case—*Cooley*—decided hard on the heels of his arrival, and one case—*Dred Scott v. Sandford* (1857)—whose decision would spark his resignation from the Supreme Court. The *Dred Scott* case plunged the Court into the fiercest controversy of its day: the national debate concerning slavery. Curtis was a key participant in the Court's own attempt to wrestle with the issues posed by slavery. When Dred Scott, a slave transported from Missouri—a slave state—into free territory and then back again, asserted in a suit brought in federal court that he was a free man, a majority of justices seemed initially inclined to rule against him on narrow grounds: Missouri had ruled that Scott was still a slave, and this ruling might have settled the matter conclusively. But certain justices at either pole on the Court were inclined to address the larger issues posed by the case. Two issues, especially, framed the debate. First, could a black—even a free black—qualify as a citizen under the Constitution and thus be entitled to sue a citizen from a different state in federal court? Second, did Congress have the power to abolish slavery in U.S. territories, such as it had purported to do in the Missouri Compromise of 1820? Justices Curtis and McLean were of a mind to answer these questions in the affirmative and declare Dred Scott a free man. Justices Catron and Vivian wished the Court to make a decisive declaration to the contrary on these two momentous issues. The remainder of the justices were initially inclined to resolve the case more narrowly. Eventually, though, a majority of the Court attempted to place the weight of its authority behind a comprehensive resolution of the case. Chief Justice Taney's opinion for the Court rejected Dred Scott's claim to freedom, concluding along the way that he was not a U.S. citizen because he was black and that the Missouri Compromise of 1820 was unconstitutional in its attempt to limit the introduction of slavery into the territories. Justice Curtis penned a lengthy dissent to the Court's ruling and specifically rejected the two principal declarations in Taney's opinion.

After the Court announced the decision in the *Dred Scott* case, Curtis delivered a copy of his dissent to the clerk of the Court and also forwarded a copy to a Boston newspaper. In the normal course of events, it takes some time for opinions to be officially printed and distributed. Curtis's action in sending his dissent to a newspaper meant that it would be widely disseminated prior to publication of the opinions of the other justices in the case. Chief Justice Taney was outraged by Curtis's action and appears to have revised his opinion in the case to respond to points made in Curtis's dissent. But when Curtis asked to receive a copy of the revised opinion, Taney sharply rebuffed his request. The antagonism between Curtis and Taney soon prompted Curtis to resign from the Court. On September 1, 1857, Curtis informed President James Buchanan by letter of his resignation.

Once he left the Supreme Court, Benjamin Curtis returned to a prosperous law practice. His reputation as a superior lawyer had only been enhanced by his six-year sojourn on the Court, and over the following years he would return frequently to argue cases before the same high bench on which he had sat as a justice of the Supreme Court. In 1868 he appeared before another tribunal, this time as one of the lawyers who successfully defended President Andrew Johnson in his impeachment trial before the U.S. Senate. Within a few years, though, the health of this great advocate had begun to decline, while near the end of his life, in 1874, he almost won election to the Senate. He died in Newport, Rhode Island, of a brain hemorrhage on September 15, 1874.

Benjamin Curtis earned a place as one of the 19th century's most able lawyers and jurists. He authored the pivotal opinion in *Cooley v. Board of Wardens* (1851), which cemented an important consensus on the constitutional balance to be struck between federal and state legislative power in the area of commerce. In the case he most decisively lost—*Dred Scott v. Sandford* (1857)—his dissent became a blueprint for the future. A majority of the Court, led by Chief Justice Roger B. Taney, tried to bind the Constitution to a discredited past in which blacks were viewed as too inferior to count as U.S. citizens and the rights of slaveholders to their property were treated as more substantial than the rights of slaves to freedom and human dignity. Curtis, however, repudiated the Court's twisted constitutional logic. In the end, a civil war and a series of constitutional amendments would assure that Curtis's constitutional vision prevailed over that of Chief Justice Taney's majority.

Further Reading

Curtis, Benjamin Robbins, ed. *A Memoir of Benjamin Robbins Curtis, LL.D., with Some of His Professional and Miscellaneous Writings*. 1879. Reprint. New York: Da Capo Press, 1970.

Gillette, William. "Benjamin R. Curtis." In *The Justices of the United States Supreme Court 1789–1969: Their Lives and Major Opinions*, vol. 2. Edited by Leon Friedman and Fred L. Israel. New York: R. R. Bowker Co., 1969.

Leach, Richard H. "Benjamin R. Curtis: Case Study of a Supreme Court Justice." Ph.D. diss., Princeton Univ., 1951.

Robbins, Chandler. "Memoir of the Hon. Benjamin Robbins Curtis, LL.D." *Proceedings of the Massachusetts Historical Society* 16 (1879): 16–35.

John Archibald Campbell (1811–1889)

Associate Justice, 1853–1861

Appointed by President Franklin Pierce

JOHN ARCHIBALD CAMPBELL
(United States Supreme Court)

John A. Campbell of Alabama served only briefly on the U.S. Supreme Court before civil war fractured the nation and forced him to choose between the Union or the Confederacy. Unlike Justice James M. Wayne of Georgia, who remained in his seat on the Court when war broke out, Campbell resigned to cast his lot with the Confederacy. But his anxiety to find the middle way through every crisis alienated him from both the North and the South. The war left Campbell bankrupt, though his impressive legal talents helped him achieve a significant measure of material and professional success in the last two decades of his life. His ultimate impact on the Court was minimal, however.

John Archibald Campbell was born on June 24, 1811, near Washington, Georgia, to Duncan G. Campbell and Mary Williamson Campbell. Law and politics surrounded his childhood and youth, for his father was a successful lawyer and politician. John Campbell himself proved to be quite precocious; he graduated at the age of 14 from Franklin College (which was to become the University of Georgia) and enrolled shortly thereafter at West Point Military Academy. His performance at West Point, though, was lackluster; before his father's sudden death in 1828 forced him to resign to find employment, he had ranked in the bottom third of his class at West Point. To pay debts left by his father, Campbell found work as a teacher in Florida for a year. Eventually, though, he returned to Georgia and studied law with two of his uncles. In 1829, when Campbell was only 18 years old, his precociousness surfaced again when the Georgia legislature admitted him to the practice of law. He moved shortly thereafter to Montgomery, Alabama, where he married Anna Esther Goldthwaite and established a successful law practice. This marriage produced one son and four daughters.

In 1837 Campbell moved his family to Mobile and soon became a prominent attorney there—so accomplished, in fact, that he was twice offered a seat on the Alabama Supreme Court, the first time when he was a mere 24 years old. Instead of a judicial career, however, Campbell elected initially to follow his father's footsteps into politics. He served twice in the Alabama legislature, winning a seat first in 1837 and then in 1843. In 1850 he ventured onto the national state when he was elected to serve as a delegate to the Southern convention that met in Nashville, Tennessee to discuss growing sectional differences. Campbell was a moderating force at this convention, proposing relatively conciliatory resolutions whose substance the convention ultimately adopted. Around the same time, his reputation as a skilled legal advocate grew rapidly. In 1851 he argued six cases before the U.S. Supreme Court, so impressing the justices that they would shortly move behind the scenes to acquire him as a colleague. The death of Justice John McKinley of Alabama in July 1852 soon created a vacancy on the Court. President Millard Fillmore proposed three different candidates to the Senate, but each was rejected. After the inauguration of President Franklin Pierce, the justices of the Supreme Court dispatched two of their members—John Catron and Benjamin R. Curtis—to urge the new president to appoint Campbell to fill the vacancy on the Court. President Pierce promptly complied with this extraordinary request, and the Senate readily confirmed Campbell's appointment on March 24, 1853.

Justice John Campbell left no significant mark on the law during his tenure of service on the Court—no well-known opinion or enduring legal formulation. Initially, such attention as he drew to himself stemmed from a series of dissents involving the rights of corporations. Campbell was an implacable foe of corporate power and of federal encroachment into state prerogatives to regulate this power. He had scarcely arrived on the Court before he declared himself opposed to the Court's already established finding that corporations amounted to "citizens" under the Constitution and were thus entitled to invoke the protection of federal courts. In his dissent to the Court's decision in *Marshall v. Baltimore and Ohio Railroad* (1853), he scoffed at the idea that corporations needed protection from state regulation. To the contrary, according to Campbell, growing corporate power mocked "the frugal and stinted conditions of state administrations." Corporations had targeted state administrations as prey, and used "corrupt and polluting appliances" to achieve their ends. Campbell's hostility to corporations found similar expression in his dissent to the holding of the Court in *Dodge v. Woolsey* (1856), in which the Court wielded the Constitution's contracts clause to bar a state from amending its constitution to revoke a tax exemption originally granted to banks under state law. Once again, Campbell railed at corporate arrogance and at the Court's intrusion into a matter of state sovereignty.

The most important case to appear before the Court during Campbell's years as an associate justice was *Dred Scott v. Sandford* (1857), in which Chief Justice Taney led a majority in rejecting the claim by Dred Scott that his sojourn with his master in free territory had permanently emancipated him. If anything, Campbell's views on slavery were more moderate than one might have expected from a Southern justice. He had freed his own slaves when he joined the Court and seems to have believed that slavery would eventually vanish from North America. In the *Dred Scott* case, though, he lined up as might be expected with the other Jacksonian Democrats who turned aside Scott's claim to freedom. The hope that these justices may have harbored of putting to rest the most turbulent political issues of the day by their Olympian pronouncement proved illusory, however. The *Dred Scott* decision exacerbated rather than healed the sectional strife that then threatened to dissolve the bonds of the Union.

As the nation tilted toward civil war, Campbell steadfastly exhorted his fellow Southerners to reject the counsel of secessionists. Southern rights had ample security within the Union, he urged: the Fugitive Slave Act of 1850 protected their slaveholding interests and the Supreme Court had shown itself a strong tower for the defense of slaveholding rights in the *Dred Scott* case. When President Lincoln's election in 1860 threatened this security, Campbell continued to advocate calm and restraint. In spring 1861 commissioners from the newly created Confederacy arrived in Washington to negotiate with the new presidential administration. Lincoln's secretary of state, William Seward, declined to meet personally with the delegation. Instead, Justice Campbell and Justice Samuel Nelson served as intermediaries between the Southern commissioners and Seward. For a time, it appeared that a crisis might be averted. In the middle of March 1861, Seward relayed through the justices that federal forces would not reinforce Fort Sumter but would, rather, surrender it immediately. But surrender did not occur and Justice Nelson soon abandoned his mediating role, leaving Campbell alone to attempt some resolution between the Southern commissioners and Seward. By early April, federal reinforcements were en route to Sumter, Campbell's efforts at mediation collapsed, and the Confederacy fired on Sumter.

Justice Campbell resigned from the Court on April 26, 1861. But when he arrived in Mobile, Alabama, the following month, he found a threatened lynching rather than a hero's welcome awaiting him. His previous counsels of restraint, his opposition to unilateral secession, and a resignation from the Court that seemed rather tardy to some Southerners made him persona non grata in his home state. He settled instead in New Orleans, where he practiced law for a year and a half. By the fall of 1862, though, he had cast his lot more deliberately with the Southern war effort, agreeing to serve as Confederate Assistant Secretary of War and, in this role, to supervise the draft. As the war dragged on, Campbell began to pursue prospects for some peaceful resolution to the conflict. As early as 1864, he communicated with Justice Samuel Nelson, his original partner in the failed negotiations of 1861 between Seward and the Southern commissioners, about possible terms for ending the war. In January 1865 Campbell served as one of three Confederate commissioners who met with President Lincoln in Hampton Roads, Virginia, to discuss options for peace. Nothing came of this discussion, however. Richmond fell to Union forces in the spring. When Lincoln came to visit the city at the beginning of April, Campbell, who was the highest ranking Confederate official to remain in the city, obtained an interview with the president. He proposed that Lincoln allow the Virginia legislature to meet for the purpose of considering a Confederate surrender, but when Lee surrendered shortly thereafter, Lincoln, who had originally agreed to Campbell's request, rescinded his authorization.

After Lincoln's assassination, federal officials ordered Campbell's arrest, and he was imprisoned in Fort Pulaski, Georgia. Justices Benjamin Curtis and Samuel Nelson interceded on his behalf with President Andrew Johnson, however, and the president ordered Campbell freed after four months. He left prison bankrupt. His property in Mobile was destroyed and his future prospects as a former Confederate official seemed bleak. He was also stripped of the right to hold public office or to vote. Moreover, Congress passed legislation in 1865 that barred lawyers from the states that had seceded from practicing in federal courts unless they swore an oath that they had not assisted in the Confederate war effort. Campbell, of course, was in no position to swear such an oath. Had the law been upheld, the former Supreme Court justice would have been permanently barred from appearing before his former colleagues as an advocate. The Supreme Court, however, invalidated the oath requirement in *Ex parte Garland* (1867).

After the war, John Campbell returned to New Orleans, where he set up a law practice with his son, Duncan, and former Louisiana judge Henry Spofford. Over the following years, the old foe of banks and corporations established a lucrative practice representing their interests in courts. He became a fixture before the Supreme Court, arguing cases regularly before the bench on which he had once sat. One of these, the *Slaughterhouse Cases* (1873), provided the Supreme Court with the opportunity to interpret the newly ratified Fourteenth Amendment to the Constitution. The case involved a Louisiana statute that attempted to regulate animal slaughter by requiring that all slaughtering in New Orleans be done at a single, newly chartered company. The grant of this monopoly inconvenienced many butchers and generated inevitable complaints of government favoritism and corruption. Campbell represented an association of butchers who challenged the Louisiana law, and he seized on the newly ratified Fourteenth Amendment as grounds for declaring the law unconstitutional. Chief among his arguments was the contention that the Fourteenth Amendment's privileges and immunities clause prevented state governments from abridging the "privileges or immunities" of U.S. citizens. By depriving his clients of a right to engage in the business of animal slaughter, Campbell argued, Louisiana had in fact denied them the "privilege" of practicing their trade. The Supreme Court narrowly turned aside this argument, holding in a decision that remains controversial to this day that the privileges and immunities clause protects only a limited category of rights.

Former Justice Campbell maintained an active legal practice until the early 1880s. His son Duncan died in 1882, and his wife died two years later. In 1884, the year of his wife's death, Campbell retired from active practice and moved to Baltimore, where two of his daughters lived. He still argued occasional cases before the Supreme Court, however. A reporter who witnessed Campbell's last argument before the Court described him in the following terms:

> He is a very old man. His form is thin and bent, his skin is in the parchment state, and his hair is as white as the driven snow; but a great mind looks out through his keen eye and a great soul controls his fragile body. He is a lawyer to the core—in some respects one of the wisest, broadest, deepest, and most learned in the United States. He has neither the presence, voice, nor tongue of the orator, but when he speaks in his thin, measured tones, never wasting a word, the Supreme Court of the United States listens as it listens to almost no other man.

Death finally claimed the aged advocate on March 12, 1889, when he died in Baltimore after a long illness.

John Archibald Campbell might have had a greater impact on the Court had he served on it longer. But his term as a Supreme Court justice became one of the Civil War's first casualties. A certain cautiousness of mind made him inclined to proceed more deliberately than the rush of events around him seemed to require. Looking always for some middle course between what he viewed as perilous extremes, Campbell found himself at odds with the temper of the times. He thus proved incapable of finding any significant following for the middle ground he sought, blunting his achievements both as a justice and as a public officer. His abilities found their greatest scope during his final years, when his service as an advocate gained him the respect he failed to obtain as a Supreme Court justice.

FURTHER READING

Connor, Henry Groves. *John Archibald Campbell, Associate Justice of the United States Supreme Court, 1853–1861.* Boston: Houghton Mifflin, 1920. Reprint. New York: Da Capo Press, 1971.

Jordan, Christine. "Last of the Jacksonians." *Supreme Court Historical Society Yearbook, 1980.* Washington, D.C.: Supreme Court Historical Society, 1980.

Holt, Thad, Jr. "The Resignation of Mr. Justice Campbell." *Alabama Law Review* 12 (1959): 105–18.

Mann, Justin S. "The Political Thought of John Archibald Campbell: The Formative Years, 1847–1851." *Alabama Law Review* 22 (1970): 275–302.

Saunders, Robert, Jr. *John Archibald Campbell: Southern Moderate, 1811–1889.* Tuscaloosa: University of Alabama Press, 1997.

Nathan Clifford (1803–1881)

Associate Justice, 1858–1881

Appointed by President James Buchanan

Nathan Clifford
(United States Supreme Court)

A hardworking man of modest intellectual ability, Nathan Clifford served for 23 years on the Court. He wrote no enduring opinions but managed nevertheless to clog the pages of the Supreme Court reports with legal writing characterized more by length than by light—attempting, perhaps, to secure by painstaking research and extended exposition what he could not obtain through judicial brilliance. His conservative Democratic sensibilities became increasingly out of step with the gradual Republican ascendancy on the Supreme Court. At the end of a lackluster judicial career, Clifford waited desperately for the election of a Democratic president who would replace him with a kindred spirit. None ever appeared, however, and death finally removed Nathan Clifford from the seat he had long occupied but never distinguished.

Nathan Clifford was born on August 18, 1803, in Rumney, New Hampshire, to an industrious farming family. As the oldest child and only son of the seven children born to Nathaniel Clifford and his wife, Lydia Simpson Clifford, Nathan discovered early that his parents valued manual toil more than education. He absorbed their devotion to work but aspired to more education than his parents thought necessary. His mother and father grudgingly permitted Nathan to attend a nearby academy, where he financed his education by part-time teaching and by providing singing lessons to young men. When his father died, however, college proved beyond his means, and he settled instead for a legal apprenticeship with Josiah Quincy, a prominent local attorney.

By 1827 Nathan Clifford had been admitted to the New Hampshire bar and soon established a legal practice in Newfield, Maine. He also married Hannah Ayer, the daughter of an influential family in the town. The match brought Clifford a good deal of business and, eventually, a sizable family. Within a few years of his marriage, Clifford entered politics, winning election to the state legislature as a Democrat in 1831. His political skills proved substantial enough to earn him the post of speaker of the House in 1833, when he was only 28 years old. He held that position until the following year, when he was appointed state attorney general.

While serving as attorney general from 1834 to 1838, Clifford campaigned for a seat in the U.S. Senate. Failing in this bid, he won election to the U.S. House of Representatives in 1838. He served in Congress for two terms until voter redistricting in Maine undercut his Democratic base and cost him his congressional seat in 1843. With only a dozen years of political service, Clifford was hardly a prominent figure on the national front by this time. He was, though, a loyal Democrat and a New Englander, and President James K. Polk eventually had need of both traits to fill the position of attorney general in his cabinet. Not for the last time, party loyalty and a reputation for competent, hard work secured the appointment for Clifford in 1846. Almost immediately, though, self-doubt besieged Clifford, afflicting him with uncertainty over whether he was qualified to appear on behalf of the U.S. government in the various federal courts. According to President Polk, who referred to Clifford's anxiousness in his diary, the latter "had some apprehensions that, having come into office but a short time before the meeting of the Court, he might be able to maintain himself reputably." Polk managed to reassure his worried appointee, and the Senate confirmed Clifford's nomination unanimously.

The new attorney general did, in fact, warm to his position and managed to acquit himself competently. Of most interest historically, Clifford participated as attorney general in the argument of *Luther v. Borden* (1849), a case that involved legal claims arising out of the Dorr Rebellion in Rhode Island. The rebellion occurred when disenfranchised Rhode Island citizens attempted to establish a new state constitution and elect officials under it. After officials under the existing state government refused to recognize the new constitution or the elections held under it, they declared martial law, and state judges convicted the reform governor of treason. The *Luther* case was brought by Rhode Island resident Martin Luther against a state militiaman, Luther Borden, who had entered his house and searched it pursuant to martial law. The case challenged the declaration of martial law and insisted that the existing Rhode Island government did not satisfy the requirement in Article IV of the Constitution that states be provided a "Republican Form of Government." Attorney General Clifford appeared in the case on behalf of Martin Luther to argue that states had no power to order martial law. The Supreme Court on which he would one day sit ruled, however, that the resolution of the issues presented in the cases were political questions that must be decided by the political process rather than by the courts.

While serving on Polk's cabinet, Clifford vigorously supported the president's pursuit of the war against Mexico. He acted as an informal mediator between the president and Secretary of State James Buchanan over the president's policy regarding the war, managing to remain on good terms with both. After Mexico surrendered, President Polk persuaded Clifford to resign his position as attorney general and undertake a mission to Mexico as a peace commissioner to ensure that the administration's preferred terms of peace were met. What Clifford may have lacked in political brilliance he supplied in loyalty, and he agreed to undertake the dangerous mission, seeing it through to a successful conclusion. He also agreed to delay his return to the United States for an additional year while he served as minister to Mexico during the remainder of Polk's term of office, again at great personal peril. Before he returned from Mexico he was twice attacked by bandits and once robbed. But his loyalty to the president and his friendship with James Buchanan had created a debt that would—after some delay—be amply rewarded.

When he returned from Mexico to private life in 1849, Clifford settled in Portland, Maine, and set up a legal practice with John Appleton. His three years of service in the Polk administration had made the private practice of law tedious, though, and he tried, without success, to return to public life by winning a seat in the U.S. Senate in 1850 and again 1853. The return of the Democrats to power with the election of Franklin Pierce as president in 1852 cast no political plums into Clifford's lap, nor did his old friend James Buchanan immediately find a place for Clifford in his administration upon his election as chief executive in 1856. Only after Justice Benjamin Curtis resigned from the Supreme Court in the wake of the controversial decision in *Dred Scott v. Sandford* (1857), and after Buchanan had cast about without initial success for a replacement for the retiring justice, did the president finally remember Clifford. But the Senate that had unanimously confirmed Clifford as attorney general more than a decade earlier was much less enthusiastic about his nomination as an associate justice of the Supreme Court on December 9, 1857. Now his political opponents characterized him variously as "dough-faced," a Northerner with Southern sentiments; incompetent; or, at best, a political hack being rewarded for nothing more than loyal party service. In the face of such stiff opposition, Clifford nevertheless won confirmation by a cliff-hanging vote of 26-23 in the Senate.

The man who had trembled 10 years before at the thought of appearing before the robed assemblage of justices on the nation's highest court now donned a judicial robe himself for the first time. Chief Justice John Marshall and Associate Justice Joseph Story were long dead, but their ghosts must have haunted Clifford's arrival on the Court. He brought with him no reputation for legal greatness, whether as an advocate or as a judge, only a dogged determination to work. And though he authored no significant constitutional opinion during his long tenure on the Court, he wrote copiously and meticulously, filling his opinions with long-winded accumulations of extensive legal research.

The general temper of Clifford's judicial mind lay out of step with his colleagues on the Court. His distrust of national government played increasingly poorly in a political environment that came to see state action as a great threat to liberty, greater perhaps even than federal activity. A fifth of the opinions Clifford authored in his long career were dissents. Furthermore, his mechanical interpretations of the Constitution's text seemed crabbed and uninspired. But Clifford steadfastly insisted that inspiration was precisely what interpreters of the Constitution had no need of. His conservative sensibilities bridled especially at the notion that judges should invalidate a law "on the vague ground that they think it opposed to a general latent spirit supposed to pervade or underlie the Constitution."

In terms of historical significance, Clifford's service as chairman of the commission appointed by Congress to resolve the disputed presidential election of 1876 surpassed his service as a justice. Samuel Tilden, the Democratic candidate, had won a majority of the popular vote, but Republicans disputed whether he had also secured a majority in the electoral college over his Republican opponent, Rutherford B. Hayes. The commission, consisting of eight Republicans and seven Democrats, ultimately approved by a straight party-line vote an electoral count that certified Hayes as the winner of the presidential contest by one electoral vote (185-184). Justice Clifford duly communicated the result to Congress on behalf of the commission but declined to attend Hayes's presidential inauguration. In fact, the disputed Republican victory apparently stiffened his resolve to hold onto his seat until a Democratic presidency assured him of a suitable replacement, even as the closing years of the decade saw his health fail. He had been eligible for full retirement since 1873, but he held his seat even after the election of Republican candidate James Garfield in 1880 ended Clifford's hope of a Democratic replacement and a stroke the same year incapacitated him. Mentally and physically unable to serve any longer, Justice Clifford refused to relinquish his seat until his death on July 25, 1881, in Cornish, Maine, rendered the issue moot.

Justice Nathan Clifford ranks among the bottom tier of the justices who have sat on the Supreme Court. Dedicated and hardworking, he nevertheless lacked the intellectual gifts necessary to leave an enduring mark on the Court. Instead, he practiced a rigid conservatism that was at odds with the judicial spirit of more famous justices such as John Marshall. Without the brilliance to offer a countering vision of the Constitution, his views appeared stinted and impoverished.

Further Reading

Chandler, Walter. "Nathan Clifford: A Triumph of Untiring Effort." *American Bar Association Journal* 11 (1925): 57–60.

Clifford, Philip Greely. *Nathan Clifford: Democrat, 1803–1881.* New York: Putnam's, 1922.

Clinton, Robert Lowry and Kevin Walsh. "Judicial Sobriety: Nathan P. Clifford." In *Sober as a Judge: The Supreme Court and Republican Liberty.* Edited by Richard G. Stevens and Matthew J. Franck. Lanham, Md.: Lexington Books, 1999.

Gillette, William. "Nathan Clifford." In *The Justices of the United States Supreme Court 1789–1969: Their Lives and Major Opinions,* vol. 2. Edited by Leon Friedman and Fred L. Israel. New York: R. R. Bowker Co., 1969.

Noah Haynes Swayne (1804–1884)

Associate Justice, 1862–1881

Appointed by President Abraham Lincoln

Noah Haynes Swayne
(United States Supreme Court)

Despite his best efforts, Noah H. Swayne never became chief justice of the U.S. Supreme Court. He did, however, serve almost 20 years as an associate justice on the Court, having pursued this post with the same measure of zeal and political resourcefulness as he would later apply to his attempt to capture the chief seat. This continued hankering after a higher seat became the most memorable aspect of a judicial record that was, by itself, no more than mediocre.

Noah Haynes Swayne was born on December 7, 1804, to devout Quaker parents who migrated from Pennsylvania to Frederick County, Virginia, the place of his birth. Noah was the last of nine children born to Joshua and Rebecca Smith

Swayne. The death of his father when he was four years old cast the care of a large family on his mother. Noah gained his education first from a local school and then at the Quaker academy operated by Jacob Mendenhall in Waterford, Virginia. Following two years at Mendenhall's school, the young Swayne embarked on the study of medicine with George A. Thornton in Alexandria. His prospects for a medical career were cut short by Thornton's death a year later, though, and Swayne turned next to preparing himself for college by studying classics at an academy in Alexandria. But news that his guardian would not be able to pay for the cost of a college education caused him to prepare instead for a career in the law. He therefore apprenticed himself to the law office of John Scott and Francis Brooks in Warrenton, Virginia, and gained admission to the bar in 1823.

Swayne, though, had in mind a future that Virginia could not provide him. Not yet 20 years of age, he possessed such a fierce hatred of slavery that he chose to leave his home state and strike out on horseback for Ohio. He settled first in Zanesville, then migrated north to Coshocton, where he established a successful law practice in 1825. Within a year he had been appointed prosecuting attorney for Coschocton County.

The next decade saw Swayne immerse himself in the legal and political affairs of his adopted state. In 1829 he won election to the Ohio legislature as a Jacksonian Democrat. When he contemplated accepting the nomination for a seat in the U.S. Congress the following year, President Andrew Jackson persuaded him to accept instead the post of U.S. attorney for Ohio, a position Swayne held until 1841. Service as U.S. attorney required Swayne to move to Columbus, Ohio, where he married Sarah Ann Wager of Virginia in 1832 and promptly freed the slaves his wife brought to their union. As if life were not already full enough for the young man, he served on the Columbus city council in 1834 and won election to another term in the Ohio legislature in 1836.

Noah Swayne also continued to practice law during this period, and in 1839 he formed a partnership with James Bates. After this partnership disbanded in 1852, Swayne formed another practice with Llewellyn Taber that lasted until the end of the 1850s. Throughout these years, Swayne earned a statewide reputation as an outstanding trial lawyer. He also contributed considerable time and energy to a variety of civic causes, serving as a delegate from Ohio sent to Washington to resolve a boundary dispute, as a member of a commission appointed to reduce Ohio's public debt, and as a member of another commission charged with surveying the condition of the blind in the state.

The 1850s saw the creation of the Republican party. Swayne, a Jacksonian Democrat until this time, soon joined the new party, whose views on slavery more closely paralleled his own. He supported Republican presidential candidate John C. Frémont in the election of 1856 and cheered with other Republicans when their candidate, Abraham Lincoln, won the presidential election of 1860. In April 1861 the death of Justice John McLean of Ohio, a friend of Noah Swayne, created a vacancy on the Supreme Court. Justice McLean had made it known that he hoped Swayne might succeed him. Following McLean's death, therefore, Swayne wasted no time in launching a vigorous campaign to have President Lincoln appoint him to the Court. He had the support of the entire Ohio congressional delegation and immediately solicited the aid of Salmon Chase, Lincoln's treasury secretary, also from Ohio, and Samuel J. Tilden of New York. Swayne even hurried to Washington himself to investigate his prospects. Lincoln ultimately nominated Swayne on January 21, 1862, and three days later the Senate confirmed the appointment with only a single dissent.

Noah Swayne was Lincoln's first appointment to the Supreme Court and generally considered to be his weakest. Lincoln's later choices included Samuel Miller, Stephen Field, Salmon Chase, and David Davis—jurists typically ranked above Swayne in ability and accomplishment. From Lincoln's perspective, though, Justice Swayne proved at least to be a loyal supporter of the administration's war effort. He joined a majority in the Court both in upholding Lincoln's blockade of Southern ports prior to a congressional declaration of war in the *Prize Cases* (1863) and in the issuance of greenbacks to finance the war in *Roosevelt v. Meyer* (1863). Even after the war ended and most of the Court became less receptive to the kind of extraordinary measures necessary, perhaps, to preserve the Union but not—in the minds of the justices—necessary to the postwar era, Swayne continued to support vigorous actions to suppress disloyalty. Thus, in *Cummings v. Missouri* (1867) and *Ex parte Garland* (1867), when a majority of the Court invalidated retroactive test oaths—which disqualified from political or civil offices ex-rebels who could not swear that they had not supported the rebellion—Swayne joined Justice Samuel Miller and two other Republican justices in dissent.

The years following the Civil War saw the Constitution amended to include the Reconstruction Amendments: the Thirteenth, which abolished slavery; the Fourteenth, which guaranteed the equal protection and due process of the law against infringement by state government; and the Fifteenth, which prohibited racial discrimination in connection with voting. Soon after ratification of these amendments, the Supreme Court was called on to interpret their sweeping terms. In the *Slaughterhouse Cases* (1873), for example, the Court considered the applicability of the newly ratified Fourteenth Amendment to a challenge brought against a monopoly granted by the state of Louisiana to a particular New Orleans slaughterhouse. Competitors of the favored company challenged the monopoly, arguing in part that it deprived them of rights guaranteed by the Fourteenth Amendment—in particular, the protection of their "privileges and immunities." Justice Swayne agreed that deprivation of the chance to engage in a business enterprise might well present a claim under the privileges and immunities clause. He found himself on the losing side of this constitutional issue, though. Justice Samuel Miller wrote the opinion for the majority of the Court, concluding that the Fifteenth Amendment had no application to the case. He interpreted the privileges and immunities clause narrowly and doubted whether any of the other provisions of the Fourteenth Amendment would have an expansive application. For Swayne, however, the amendment's guarantees were plain and not to be whittled away by the cleverness of Supreme Court justices. The future would at least partially vindicate Swayne's views. Although the privileges and immunities clause of the Fourteenth Amendment would never rebound from the cramped construction given it by the Court, the other provisions of the amendment—the equal protection and due process clauses in particular—would become important guarantors of civil rights and civil liberties in the 20th century.

Justice Swayne's most significant opportunity to speak on behalf of the Court came in *Springer v. United States* (1881). The case involved a challenge to the federal income tax that had been levied during the Civil War. Swayne concluded for the Court that the income tax did not amount to a "direct tax" and therefore did not have to be apportioned among the states according to population, as required by the Constitution, since it did not fall directly on individuals but on their profits and other income. Fourteen years later, a new majority on the Court would reopen the issue in *Pollock v. Farmers' Loan & Trust Co.* (1895) by invalidating the 1894 income tax as a direct tax not apportioned among the states. Ultimately the nation would have to adopt the Sixteenth Amendment to obtain the result that Swayne had originally approved.

In 1864, two years after Swayne joined the Supreme Court as an associate justice, Chief Justice Roger B. Taney died. Though President Lincoln's secretary of the treasury, Salmon P. Chase, was widely expected to replace Taney in the chief seat, Swayne lobbied vigorously to receive the appointment himself. But Lincoln proceeded as expected and appointed Chase chief justice in December 1864. Less than 10 years later, though, Chase himself was dead and the chief seat on the Court vacant again. Swayne was a little more than a year away from being 70 years old, but zeal to be chief justice once again inspired him to maneuver for the position. Swayne's old antagonist on the Court, Justice Samuel Miller, observed caustically that Swayne had "artfully beslobbered the President" for the nomination. But President Ulysses S. Grant chose Morrison Waite instead, thus ending for all practical purposes Swayne's long campaign to become chief justice. Within a few years it was abundantly clear that Grant had made the right decision. By 1877 Swayne's health and mental facilities had both slipped into a long twilight. Nevertheless, he clung doggedly to his seat until President Rutherford B. Hayes persuaded him to step down in 1881 in return for the president's commitment to replace him with his close friend Stanley Matthews. The year after Swayne retired from the Court, his wife died. He followed her on June 8, 1884, two years later.

Associate Justice Noah Swayne numbers among that great mass of Supreme Court justices distinguished neither as terribly bad nor terribly good. No doubt presidents and citizens wish the nine seats on the Court to be reserved for jurists of true brilliance; but, in fact, the Court has had more than its share of men who were only competent. Swayne was such a man. His nomination testified to the fact that even a great president can find it difficult to staff the nation's highest court with jurists of similar caliber.

Further Reading

Barnes, William Horatio. "Noah H. Swayne, Associate Justice." In *The Supreme Court of the United States.* Part 11 of Barnes's *Illustrated Cyclopedia of the American Government.* n.p.: 1875.

Gillette, William. "Noah H. Swayne." In *The Justices of the United States Supreme Court 1789–1969: Their Lives and Major Opinions,* Vol. 2. Edited by Leon Friedman and Fred L. Israel. New York: R. R. Bowker Co., 1969.

Silver, David Mayer. *Lincoln's Supreme Court.* Urbana: University of Illinois Press, 1956.

SAMUEL FREEMAN MILLER (1816–1890)

Associate Justice, 1862–1890

Appointed by President Abraham Lincoln

SAMUEL FREEMAN MILLER
(Photograph, United States Supreme Court)

The first Supreme Court justice born west of the Appalachians and the first appointed from west of the Mississippi River, Samuel Miller embodied the possibilities of the frontier. A large man, mostly self-taught, he came to the law as a second career and ultimately ascended to its pinnacle. By dint of hard work, a keen mind, and an energetic spirit, he dominated the Court to which he was appointed, even though he never served as its chief justice. With no significant judicial experience when he came to the Court, Miller nevertheless proved himself to be an excellent judge.

Samuel Freeman Miller was born on April 5, 1816, in the bluegrass country of Kentucky. His father, Frederick Miller, had only recently moved from Reading,

Pennsylvania, to Richmond, Kentucky, where Samuel Miller was born. His mother, Patsy Freeman Miller, came from a family that had settled in Kentucky a generation earlier. Samuel spent his early years on the family farm, with intermittent stints at a local academy, until he dropped out of school at the age of 14 to work in a pharmacy. Inspired by this work to study medicine, Miller read medical texts on his own and attended lectures at Transylvania University in Lexington, Kentucky (later to become the University of Kentucky). He received his M.D. from Transylvania in the spring of 1838.

At the age of 21, Miller embarked on the practice of medicine in Barbourville. He shared an office with a young lawyer, Silas Woodson, and dispensed medical advice and treatment to the people scattered around the small village he had chosen for a home. Over the next nine years, Samuel Miller gradually discovered that he desired something more than the toil and tedium provided by his career as a country doctor. Even before he had begun his medical practice he had helped organize the Barbourville Debating Society, and in the discussion of public issues sponsored by this society, Miller found an intellectual satisfaction not paralleled by his simple medical practice.

In November 1842 Miller married Lucy L. Ballinger; this union produced three children. With a growing family, Miller began to focus his energy on pursuits other than medical practice. By 1844 he had been appointed justice of the peace for Barbourville, and this public service focused his attention on the possibility of a legal career. He read law with his office mate and gained admission to the bar in 1847.

Miller was already a confirmed opponent of slavery. After a few years of practicing law in Kentucky, he began to cast about for another place to work. In 1850 he decided to relocate his family, his slaves (whom he freed on arrival), and his legal practice to the free state of Iowa. He settled in Keokuk, where a prominent local lawyer, Lewis Reeves, invited Miller to practice with him, and Miller's legal career immediately prospered. Four years later, though, both Miller's wife Lucy and his law partner died. He replaced his lost legal partnership by joining another Keokuk lawyer, John Rankin, in practice, and he formed a new marital partnership by marrying Eliza Reeves, the widow of his former partner. One contemporary source said of this union that "the old firm of Reeves and Miller was renewed under a different contract."

With the birth of the Republican party in the 1850s, Samuel Miller quickly joined its ranks. A growing legal prominence in the state of Iowa brought with it a growing political prominence, though Miller was initially unsuccessful in his quest for a significant political post. He served as chairman of the Keokuk Republican party organization in 1856 but lost a bid for the state senate, and in 1861 he lost to incumbent governor Samuel Kirkwood in his quest to obtain the Republican nomination for governor of Iowa. Miller's Republican credentials were nevertheless impeccable. He opposed slavery and secession, supported Abraham Lincoln in the election of 1860, and above all supported the Union, whose cause he contributed to financially when Civil War broke out.

All said, however, Samuel Miller lacked the significant political or judicial experience normally expected of potential Supreme Court appointees. He was a prominent Iowa lawyer by this time, but his practice had been confined mainly to Keokuk, a relatively small town. Congress eventually came to his rescue by creating a new federal circuit court to cover the area west of the Mississippi River. Supreme Court justices still served double duty by not only participating in cases brought before the Court but also by serving as federal circuit court judges, with each assigned to a particular circuit. With a newly created circuit in need of a Supreme Court justice, Miller's prospects for capturing one of the three seats on the Court then vacant improved markedly. His political supporters eventually besieged President Lincoln with an overwhelming display of support for Miller's appointment to the high court. Lincoln nominated the Iowa lawyer on July 16, 1862, the Senate immediately confirmed the appointment, and the American western frontier had its first Supreme Court justice.

Miller proved to be an energetic addition to the Court. During his 28 years as an associate justice, he authored more than 600 opinions for the Court, many of them on constitutional questions. Salmon P. Chase, who would join the Court as chief justice in 1864, described Miller as the Court's "dominant personality," a man "whose mental force and individuality are felt by the Court more than any other." This dominant personality arrived on a Court whose reputation had been severely weakened by the disastrous *Dred Scott* decision of 1857, in which Chief Justice Roger Taney led his Court to grant slaveowners a major constitutional victory. Miller's antislavery views initially prompted him to despise Taney, the principal author of *Dred Scott*'s constitutional mischief. Ironically, though, by the time Taney died in 1864, Miller's relationship with the chief justice was extremely cordial. Miller himself described the unexpected transformation:

> When I came to Washington, I had never looked upon the face of Judge Taney, but I knew of him. I remembered that he had attempted to throttle the Bank of the United States, and I hated him for it. I remembered that he took his seat upon the Bench, as I believed, as a reward for what he had done in that connection, and I hated him for that. He had been the chief spokesman of the Court in the *Dred Scott* case, and I hated him for that. But from my first acquaintance with him, I realized that these feelings toward him were but the suggestions of the worst elements of our nature; for before the first term of my service in the Court had passed, I more than liked him, I loved him. And after all that has been said of that great good man, I stand always ready to say that conscience was his guide and sense of duty his principle.

Samuel Miller arrived on the Court during the crisis of Civil War, and he generally supported the extraordinary measures employed by President Lincoln to preserve the Union, including the blockage of southern ports upheld in the *Prize Cases* (1863), the issuance of greenbacks to finance the war, and the operation of military trials to try persons suspected of disloyalty to the Union. After the war he would uphold the retroactive loyalty oaths that a majority of the Court invalidated in *Cummings v. Missouri* (1867) and *Ex parte Garland* (1867). The most important decision of his long judicial career, however, would be rendered in the *Slaughterhouse Cases* (1873).

The Reconstruction Congress proposed a great triumvirate of constitutional amendments to secure the civil rights and liberties of the newly freed slaves. The Thirteenth Amendment abolished slavery and other forms of involuntary servitude in the United States. The Fourteenth Amendment negated the effects of Chief Justice Taney's opinion in the *Dred Scott* case, which had disqualified blacks from U.S. citizenship. It also prohibited states from abridging the "privileges or immunities of citizens of the United States" or of depriving persons of due process of law or the equal protection of the laws. The Fifteenth Amendment barred states from discriminating along racial lines in connection with the right to vote. Though forged in the crucible of controversy over African-American slavery, the Reconstruction amendments, as ratified, set forth general protections of civil rights and civil liberties not restricted by their terms solely to the condition of the newly freed slave. In the *Slaughterhouse Cases* (1873), the Court confronted the issue of whether the Fourteenth Amendment, in particular, might create a new federal superintendence over the rights and liberties of citizens against state infringement. Associate Justice Samuel Miller, writing for a majority of the Court, declared that it did not.

This momentous question presented itself to the Court through a legal contest that was essentially commercial. Louisiana had given one enterprise a monopoly on the slaughterhouse business in and around New Orleans. Competing enterprises challenged this monopoly and, ably represented by former Supreme Court justice John A. Campbell, relied in part on the newly ratified Fourteenth Amendment to press their claims. The monopoly, they argued, deprived them of the privileges or immunities of U.S. citizens, as well as the due process and equal protection of law.

Justice Miller, for a bare majority of the Court, concluded otherwise. He summarily rejected the claim that the slaughterhouse monopoly deprived any person of due process of law. As to the assertion that Louisiana had failed to accord equal protection of the law to competitors of the monopoly, he suggested that discrimination not directed at blacks probably did not raise any Fourteenth Amendment claim. Finally, as to the claimed abridgment of "the privileges or immunities of U.S. citizens," he interpreted this clause narrowly to cover only a handful of rights uniquely applicable to the federal government, such as the right of petitioning the federal government for a redress of grievances. By this construction Miller made the privileges and immunities clause of the Fourteenth Amendment into a virtual dead letter. In the next century, new majorities of the Court would rescue the due process and equal protection clauses of the amendment from Miller's cramped reading in the *Slaughterhouse Cases.* But his construction of the privileges and immunities clause would survive to the present.

Unlike some justices who, on their appointment to the Supreme Court, receded into an august obscurity, Miller remained at the forefront of national affairs. He served on the commission appointed to settle the disputed presidential election of 1876 and voted with the Republican majority on the commission to certify Rutherford B. Hayes as the victor. Two presidents considered him for the position of chief justice: Ulysses S. Grant in 1873 and Grover Cleveland in 1888. He was even considered briefly as a possible presidential candidate in the 1880s. None of these advancements ever materialized, however, and Miller continued to serve as an associate justice until his death from a stroke on October 13, 1890, in Washington, D.C.

Samuel Miller served as an associate justice of the Supreme Court under four chief justices: Roger B. Taney, Salmon P. Chase, Morrison R. Waite, and Melvin W. Faller. He served during the crisis of the Civil War and its tumultuous aftermath, influencing the course of constitutional doctrine as much as or more than any man during the Reconstruction years. Though he is not generally thought of as one of the greatest justices to have sat on the Court, he must certainly be reckoned among those justices just outside the precincts of greatness: a jurist of significant ability who left an important mark on the Court and on the American constitutional tradition.

Further Reading

Fairman, Charles. *Mr. Justice Miller and the Supreme Court, 1862–1890.* Cambridge, Mass.: Harvard University Press, 1939.

Gillette, William. "Samuel Miller." In *The Justices of the United States Supreme Court 1789–1969: Their Lives and Major Opinions,* Vol. 2. Edited by Leon Friedman and Fred L. Israel. New York: R. R. Bowker Co., 1969.

Gregory, Charles Noble. *Samuel Freeman Miller.* Iowa City: State Historical Society of Iowa, 1907.

Miller, Samuel Freeman. *The Constitution and the Supreme Court of the United States of America: Addresses by the Hon. Samuel F. Miller.* New York. London, D. Appleton & Co., 1889.

———. *Lectures on the Constitution of the United States.* Littleton, Colo.: F. B. Rothman, 1980.

Palmer, Robert C. "The Parameters of Constitutional Reconstruction: *Slaughter-House, Cruikshank,* and the Fourteenth Amendment." *University of Illinois Law Review* (1984): 739–770.

David Davis (1815–1886)

Associate Justice, 1862–1877

Appointed by President Abraham Lincoln

David Davis
(United States Supreme Court)

The friend of one of America's greatest presidents, David Davis saw Abraham Lincoln advance from relative obscurity to become the Union's great captain. More than this, he—as much as any man—shepherded Lincoln into the presidency. After Lincoln had raised Davis himself to national prominence by elevating him to the Supreme Court, Davis fretted that he was not qualified to serve as a justice and chafed at his isolation from the rough and tumble of political affairs. Moreover, when an assassin's bullet felled Lincoln and lesser men succeeded him in the presidency, Davis hankered to be president himself. He eventually resigned from the Court to pursue this ambition. Though he came close to it, he never quite grasped the prize. Late in life he won election to the U.S. Senate, where he was named president *pro tem*. For a time, after Vice President Chester A. Arthur became president upon the assassination of James A. Garfield (so leaving the vice presidency temporarily vacant), this position placed Davis first in the line of succession for the presidency.

—❧—

David Davis was born on March 9, 1815, in Cecil County, Maryland, to Ann Mercer Davis. Davis's father died eight months before his birth. When he was five years old, his mother remarried a Baltimore bookseller named Franklin Betts, and the new couple shortly packed David off to live in Annapolis with his uncle Henry Lyon Davis, the rector of St. Anne's Episcopal Church and president of St. John's College. A nasty custody battle with accusations of financial mismanagement leveled by Henry Davis against Betts and of drunkenness leveled by Betts against Davis eventually landed David back with his stepfather. By age 12, though, he had been sent to New Ark Academy in Delaware, and two years later he matriculated at Kenyon College in Ohio. After graduating from Kenyon in 1832, Davis studied law for a time with Henry W. Bishop in Lenox, Massachusetts, and then attended the New Haven Law School for a little less than a year before gaining admission to the Illinois bar.

Davis decided to establish a legal practice in Peskin, Illinois. This decision almost killed the young attorney but also introduced him to a young legislator whose future would be inextricably bound with Davis's own. Davis met Abraham Lincoln after both were appointed to a delegation from Peskin formed to obtain a charter for a railroad line from Peskin to the Wabash River. The two young men would eventually become fast friends. First, though, Davis contracted malaria in 1836 and almost died. When the chance came to leave the town later that year and purchase a law practice in Bloomington, Davis leaped at the opportunity. He moved to Bloomington and called it home for the rest of his life. Two years later, in 1838, he married Sarah Walker. Their union would last for more than 40 years, though it would know significant tragedy. The couple's first child died at birth; and of three children subsequently born to Davis and his wife Sarah, only one, George Perrin Davis, survived infancy.

The man who would one day be a heartbeat away from the presidency began his political career rather timidly. He made a lackluster bid to win election as a district attorney in 1839. He lost, then mounted an equally unsuccessful campaign to win election to the Illinois Senate in 1840. Finally, in 1844 he won an election, this time to the Illinois legislature. Three years later he was selected to serve as a delegate to the state constitutional convention, where he distinguished himself by championing judicial reforms for the state, including the popular election of judges. Davis himself won election in 1848 as a circuit judge. Thus began a judicial career that would last almost 30 years.

The following decade saw the friendship between Davis and Abraham Lincoln grow. Lincoln appeared regularly before Davis as an advocate, though Davis appears to have been careful to avoid letting his friendship with Lincoln interfere with his judgment: In cases tried without a jury before Davis, Lincoln lost as regularly as he won. Both men migrated from the Whig party to the newly formed Republican one, though Davis remained in many ways a Whig at heart. On the issue of slavery, the views of Lincoln and Davis would never quite parallel, and later the men would disagree sharply over the wisdom of Lincoln's Emancipation Proclamation.

By the close of the 1850s, Davis had become his friend's principal campaign strategist, first in Lincoln's unsuccessful bid for the U.S. Senate and then, in 1860, in Lincoln's dark horse quest for the Republican party's presidential nomination. Chiefly due to a brilliant ploy authored and administered by his friend Davis, Lincoln won the Republican nomination against a field crowded with better-known candidates. Davis secured commitments from delegates to support Lincoln as a second choice and, when agreement on the more prominent candidates failed to be reached, Lincoln—the underdog—won the nomination. After Lincoln followed this surprising upset with a victory in the presidential election of 1860, Davis continued to play a key role as adviser, helping the president-elect form his cabinet and even undertaking to critique the first draft of Lincoln's inaugural address.

Davis's support of Lincoln did not immediately yield an appointment to any high-ranking federal post. At first, he seemed to hope merely for appointment to the federal district court in Illinois, since his sole judicial experience had been that of a trial judge. He had never served as an appellate court judge, nor even appeared as an advocate to argue a case on appeal. But Lincoln shortly had three vacancies to fill on the Supreme Court, and when Davis learned that Illinois lawyer and politician Orville H. Browning was poised to receive a nomination to fill the seat recently vacated by the resignation of Alabama Justice John Campbell at the outset of the Civil War, he sought the position for himself rather than see it go to Browning, whom he disliked.

Lincoln was far from swift in settling on Davis for a seat on the nation's highest court, but he eventually appointed his old friend in 1862. After receiving the appointment, though, Davis worried that he might not be well suited for a position as a Supreme Court justice. He explained to his wife: "I can't throw off the great dread that I have of going on the bench. Writing opinions will come hard to me. I don't write with facility. . . . What strikes everybody as the highest good fortune, has been to me like ashes. . . . I will try the judgeship & if it don't suit me, or if I don't suit it, I will resign." Davis was especially sensitive concerning the deficiencies in his formal education. "Some of the justices are learned men, others not," he wrote to his wife. "I feel my want of learning lamentably but I will try to get along by study."

In spite of his initial misgivings, Davis persevered in his post. He edited his opinions with more painstaking attention than other justices, so as not to display his intellectual shortcomings. But after Justice Catron informed him privately that the other members of the Court appreciated the style of his opinions, Davis settled into the work of the Court. During the upheaval of the Civil War, he could be counted on to support the measures adopted by Lincoln to preserve the Union. Nevertheless, he opposed Lincoln's Emancipation Proclamation, believing it jeopardized any hope of preserving the Union. He also opposed the use of military tribunals in areas where loyal civilian courts were still operating. This opposition would be reflected after the war's end and Lincoln's death in the opinion that is Davis's chief claim to judicial fame: the decision in *Ex parte Milligan* (1866).

In 1864 Union army officials in Indiana arrested Lambdin P. Milligan for conspiracy to steal munitions from federal arsenals and to release Confederate prisoners of war being held in Northern prisoner-of-war camps. Although civilian courts were available in which Milligan might have been tried for treason in Indiana, he and other coconspirators were tried instead before a military commission. The commission found Milligan guilty and sentenced him to hang. Milligan eventually challenged his conviction in federal court, and the case found its way to the Supreme Court. A unanimous Court found that the military tribunal had no authority to try Milligan and ordered his release, but the justices did not agree on the reasons for this decision.

Justice Davis, writing for the Court, announced the most sweeping grounds for the ruling in Milligan's favor; and his opinion for the Court has generally been viewed as a classic of American liberty. He acknowledged candidly that the question before the Court was one not well suited for consideration while war was being waged. "During the late wicked Rebellion, the temper of the times did not allow that calmness in deliberation and discussion so necessary to a correct conclusion of a purely judicial question." But with the war concluded, it was possible to consider the issue at hand calmly, and this issue was a most important one, implicating "the birthright of every American citizen when charged with crime, to be tried and punished according to law." Questions of asserted necessity were not sufficient to blunt the requirements of law, for "[b]y the protection of the law human rights are secured; withdraw that protection, and they are at the mercy of wicked rulers, or the clamor of an excited people." If, as Davis concluded for the majority, the Constitution did not permit military trials of civilians in areas in which loyal civilian courts were available, then not even the exigencies of war could justify curtailment of constitutional requirements.

> The Constitution of the United States is a law for rulers and people, equally in war and in peace, and covers with the shield of its protection all classes of men, at all times, and under all circumstances. No doctrine, involving more pernicious consequences, was ever invented by the wit of man than that any of its provisions can be suspended during any of the great exigencies of government. . . . This nation, as experience has proved, cannot always remain at peace, and has no right to expect that it will always have wise and humane rulers, sincerely attached to the principles of the Constitution. Wicked men, ambitious of power, with hatred of liberty and contempt of law, may fill the place once occupied by Washington and Lincoln; and if this right is conceded, and the calamities of war again befall us, the dangers to human liberty are frightful to contemplate.

Republicans who saw *Milligan* as a threat to Reconstruction efforts, especially their plans to impose military governments on the rebel states, quickly denounced the ruling, though Davis's opinion for the Court was ambiguous on the issue of whether the *Milligan* result would apply to insurrectionist areas, and he seems personally to have believed that it would not. One newspaper opined that "treason, vanquished upon the battlefield and hunted from every other retreat, has at last found a secure shelter in the bosom of the Supreme Court."

Davis remained on the Court for a little more than a decade after his *Milligan* opinion, but he grew increasingly restless with his absence from the political arena. He briefly considered a presidential candidacy in 1872; then in 1877 the Illinois legislature elected him to the U.S. Senate. He immediately resigned his seat on the Court to accept this position. In 1881 he became president *pro tem* of the Senate, and for a brief period he was first in line of succession to the presidency. It was as close as he would come to the prize he had helped Lincoln obtain but which always eluded him. He served a single term in the Senate, retiring in 1883. After leaving Washington he returned to Bloomington, where he died on June 26, 1886.

David Davis spent 15 years on the Supreme Court, and though he was unsure at first of his fitness for the job, in one instance, at least, he demonstrated significant judicial ability. His opinion in *Ex parte Milligan* (1866) remains a classic text of American constitutional liberty, securing his reputation as a better-than-average judge. But a continual hankering after the presidency, a virus that infected more than a few justices during the later half of the 19th century, robbed Davis of the focus necessary to produce a more impressive body of judicial work. In the end, he is remembered less for his accomplishments on either the state or the federal bench than for his role in securing the presidency for Abraham Lincoln and for his friendship with a great president.

FURTHER READING

Dent, Thomas. "David Davis of Illinois: A Sketch." *American Law Review* 53 (1919): 535–560.

King, Willard Leroy. *Lincoln's Manager: David Davis.* Cambridge: Harvard University Press, 1960.

Kutler, Stanley I. "David Davis." In *The Justices of the United States Supreme Court 1789–1969: Their Lives and Major Opinions,* Vol. 2. Edited by Leon Friedman and Fred L. Israel. New York: R. R. Bowker Co., 1969.

STEPHEN JOHNSON FIELD (1816–1899)

Associate Justice, 1863–1897

Appointed by President Abraham Lincoln

STEPHEN JOHNSON FIELD
(United States Supreme Court)

Only one justice, William O. Douglas, served on the Supreme Court longer than Stephen J. Field's nearly 35 years. The Californian came to the Court during the wartime administration of President Abraham Lincoln and served up to the threshold of the 20th century. He was a colorful and contumacious character, bold and self-assured as a prophet, dogmatic as the Puritans from whose lineage he sprang. He made abundant enemies in both his public and private lives, but he also—as much as any justice of the late 19th century—made law. He reasoned with, railed at, and badgered his colleagues on the bench to make the protection of private property a cornerstone of constitutional interpretation. Before he finished his long tenure as a justice of the Supreme Court, he had converted the Court to something close to his devotion to this cause.

Stephen Johnson Field was born on November 4, 1816, in Haddam, Connecticut, the sixth of nine children in the family of David Dudley Field, a Congregationalist minister, and his wife, Submit Dickinson Field. He grew up in Connecticut and later Massachusetts, where his family moved when he was three years old. At the age of 13, Field traveled to present-day Turkey, where he lived for two and a half years with his sister and brother-in-law, who were missionaries. After his return, he attended Williams College in Massachusetts, from which he graduated first in his class in 1837. He then began the study of law with his older brother David Dudley Field, Jr., who was a prominent lawyer in New York at this time and in the early stages of a campaign for legal and judicial reforms that would make him famous in his own right. Thereafter, Stephen continued his legal studies in the office of the state's attorney general, John Van Buren. He was admitted to the bar in 1841 and spent the first seven years of his practice in a partnership with his brother. In 1848, though, he left the partnership to travel with his family to Europe. When he returned, news of the gold rush in California tempted him to try his fortune there. Thus, in December 1849 he arrived in San Francisco with little money but a boundless ambition to forge a prosperous future for himself.

Choosing not to settle in San Francisco, Field traveled instead 100 miles inland to Marysville, a rude assortment of tents and shacks and the occasional adobe hut sufficient to shelter the settlement's 600 or so inhabitants. The transplanted New York lawyer and world traveler immediately convinced his new neighbors to appoint him town *alcalde,* a position of Spanish legal origin that combined the offices of mayor and judge. His tenure as *alcalde* proved short-lived, however. In 1850 the ratification of California's state constitution created a new set of local political offices, and Field returned to the practice of law. Almost immediately, he exhibited a facility he would possess throughout his life—that of making enemies. Under the new constitutional system, Field's judicial duties in Marysville had been assumed by district judge William R. Turner. The first time Field the lawyer appeared before Turner the judge, a fiery confrontation between the two men won for Field a fine, a two-day imprisonment, and the loss of his license to practice law in California. After persuading the California Supreme Court to reverse Turner's decision, Field launched an editorial tirade against the judge in a local newspaper, and Turner again stripped him of his license. But Field found relief from the order a second time with the California Supreme Court. Blood was bad enough between the two men for Turner to threaten to cut off Field's ears, causing the latter to arm himself with pistols and a Bowie knife. Finally, Field won a seat in the California legislature and had his revenge: He sponsored legislation that created a new judicial district in the California northwest and exiled Turner to the post. While in the legislature, Field was also instrumental in causing California to adopt a variety of legal reforms that had been championed by his brother in New York.

After an unsuccessful bid to win a seat in the California state senate in 1851, Field returned to the private practice of law. In 1857 he made an equally unsuccessful attempt to win the Democratic nomination for the U.S. Senate, but won election that same year to the California Supreme Court, thus launching a 40-year career as a judge. Field proved to be a talented judge, adept at navigating the intersection between arcane features of Mexican land law and the seven-year-old California constitution. During his early years on the bench, though, Field exhibited the first inclination toward being the guardian spirit for property rights and commercial industry. He wrote an opinion for the court holding that the right to the gold and silver on property did not belong to the state but to the property owner. He also developed lasting friendships with California businessmen such as Leland Stanford.

Two other important events marked the years Stephen Field spent on the California

Supreme Court. In 1859 he married Sue Virginia Swearingen, and though their union would produce no children, it lasted until Field's death 40 years later. Also in 1859, Field became chief justice of the California Supreme Court. David S. Terry, who had been chief justice, resigned from the court to engage in a duel with David C. Broderick, a close friend of Field. Broderick died as a result of a mortal wound he received in the duel and his death fueled bitterness between Field and Terry that would not be extinguished until Terry died violently 30 years later at Field's feet.

The outbreak of the Civil War encouraged Congress to create a 10th seat on the U.S. Supreme Court to be held by a justice from the Pacific states. In part, Congress hoped to secure the loyalty of California and Oregon to the Union by this move. Field, in spite of having cultivated more than his share of enemies during his years in California, was nevertheless the chief contender for the new position. He was a Democrat, but he was outspokenly loyal to the Union. With the unanimous support of the California congressional delegation, of his brother David, and of tycoon Leland Stanford, Field received President Abraham Lincoln's nomination to the Supreme Court on March 6, 1863. The Senate quickly confirmed the appointment, and on May 20, 1863, Field began what would become the longest tenure of service by any justice of the U.S. Supreme Court to that date.

Field exerted a profound influence on the course of American constitutional law by his dogged persistence in using the Constitution to protect property rights and to shield business from burdensome regulation. His years on the California Supreme Court had tutored him in the possibilities of applying a recently adopted state constitution to the practical exigencies of the day. Shortly after Field's arrival on the Court, the country ratified a cluster of new amendments to the U.S. Constitution. In the Fourteenth Amendment, in particular, Field found a constitutional harbor for his already well-developed probusiness sensibilities. The guarantees of protection for the privileges or immunities of U.S. citizens, as well as of equal protection and due process of law, seemed to him the constitutional charter for the judiciary to vigorously police federal and state lawmakers in their attempts to harry business enterprises with burdensome legal requirements. At first, Field proved unsuccessful in persuading a majority of the Court to a similar appreciation of the Fourteenth Amendment's property-protecting virtues. He could only dissent, for example, when a majority of the Court adopted a cramped reading of the Fourteenth Amendment in the *Slaughterhouse Cases* (1873) that cast grave doubt on whether it would have any significant application outside of the context of racial discrimination. But he doggedly besieged his brethren on the Court with opinions that urged the use of the due process clause of the Fourteenth Amendment to protect property rights from state interference.

The understanding of due process that Field championed is often referred to as the doctrine of "substantive due process," and reads the text of the Fourteenth Amendment to require that laws infringing on "life, liberty, or property" be reasonable. In *Munn v. Illinois* (1877), for example, he dissented from the Court's decision upholding a state's power to regulate grain elevator rates. He insisted that such regulations amount to a deprivation of property without due process of law. Field's persistence eventually paid off. By the 1890s the Court had finally come round to Field's appreciation of the due process clause as a barrier against unreasonable attempts by states to regulate businesses and property. More than any other justice, Field presided over the marriage of laissez-faire economic policy and the Constitution. Curiously, though, Field's expansive interpretation of the Fourteenth Amendment's due process clause to vindicate property rights was not paralleled by a similar expansiveness in the use of the amendment to protect the civil rights of African Americans. He refused to join in the majority's finding in *Ex parte Virginia* (1880) that the amendment guaranteed the rights of blacks to serve on juries. To the contrary, Field insisted that the Fourteenth Amendment does not assure the right of individuals to "participate in the administration of [the state's] laws" or "to discharge any duties of public trust."

Field's protection of property extended to a fierce opposition to the income tax. He joined in the Court's decision in *Pollock v. Farmers' Loan & Trust Co.* (1895), declaring the tax unconstitutional. The aged justice summoned the energy to write a concurrence, announcing in apocalyptic terms the damage to be done by failing to adhere to the Constitution's mandate:

> If the provisions of the Constitution can be set aside by an act of Congress, where is the course of usurpation to end? The present assault on capital is but the beginning. It will be but the stepping-stone to others, larger and more sweeping, till our political contests will become a war of the poor against the rich—a war constantly growing in intensity and bitterness.

Field managed to remain prominent in the public eye even when he was not sitting on the bench. He was one of the five justices who served on the commission appointed by Congress to decide the disputed presidential election of 1876. Field, like every other member of the commission, voted along strict party lines and saw his party's candidate, Samuel Tilden, who had received the greater popular vote, lose to Republican Rutherford B. Hayes. This result caused great consternation for Field, and he refused to attend Hayes's inauguration.

The following decade saw Field capture public attention again as the result of a long-running feud with his predecessor as chief justice of the California Supreme Court, David S. Terry. Terry was the attorney and eventually the husband of Sarah Hill, a woman whose case appeared before Field in his role as a circuit court judge. When Field announced a decision in the case that included unfriendly comments about Hill's character, she and her husband, Terry, created such a storm of protest in the courtroom that Field ordered them jailed. In the aftermath, word spread that Terry had threatened Field's life. The next time Field returned to California to perform his circuit-riding duties, a deputy marshal, David Neagle, was assigned to protect him. It happened that Field encountered Terry in a restaurant, and when Terry struck Field, the marshal—believing Terry to be reaching for a weapon—shot him dead. The matter finally landed before the U.S. Supreme Court. After a California officer arrested Neagle, the latter protested in federal court that he had been protecting Field at the order of the U.S. attorney general and therefore could not be prosecuted under state law. The Supreme Court (with Field recusing himself from the decision) agreed in *In re Neagle* (1890).

The 1880s were years of political disappointment for Field. Twice—in 1880 and 1884—his name was featured as a possible presidential candidate. Even more significant, in 1888 Chief Justice Morrison Waite died, and Field expected that President Grover Cleveland would elevate him to the Supreme Court's chief seat. But the president appointed Melville Fuller instead. Denied this advancement, Field remained on the Court as an associate justice. By the mid-1890s his health had begun to fail, but he continued to serve, though without the energy of his former days. He undoubtedly found some pleasure in sitting on the Court with his nephew, David Brewer, who was appointed in 1890.

Justice Field lingered on the Court to claim one final distinction: that of serving longer than any other justice to that date. By 1896 his colleagues on the Court had concluded that Field no longer possessed the mental powers necessary to do the work of a justice and appointed Justice John Marshall Harlan to ask Field to resign. Field himself had once undertaken just such a delicate mission to seek the resignation of Justice Robert Grier. When Harlan reminded him of this, Field is reported to have replied, "Yes, and a dirtier day's work I never did in my life!" He finally agreed to resign, effective December 1, 1897, thus managing to serve almost 35 years, longer than any justice before and second only to Justice William O. Douglas in the 20th century. He died on April 9, 1899.

If one measures greatness as a justice by his or her influence on the development of the law, then Stephen Field must be acknowledged one of the Supreme Court's greatest justices. He championed a constitutional vision that would ultimately prevail on the Court for nearly half a century. Long after his colorful feuds had been forgotten, his probusiness interpretation of the Constitution presided over the American economy.

Further Reading

Bergan, Philip J., Owen M. Fiss, and Charles W. McCurd. *The Fields and the Law: Essays.* San Francisco: United States District Court for the Northern District of California Historical Society, 1986.

Black, Chauncey Forward, and Samuel B. Smith, eds. *Some Account of the Work of Stephen J. Field, as Legislator, State Judge, and Justice of the Supreme Court of the United States.* New York: S. B. Smith, 1895.

Field, Stephen Johnson. *Personal Reminiscences of Early Days in California.* 1893. Reprint. New York: Da Capo Press, 1968.

Kens, Paul. *Justice Stephen Field: Shaping Liberty from the Gold Rush to the Gilded Age.* Lawrence: University Press of Kansas, 1997.

McCurdy, Charles W. "Justice Field and the Jurisprudence of Government-Business Relations: Some Parameters of Laissez-Faire Constitutionalism, 1863–1897." *Journal of American History* 61 (1975): 970–1005.

Swisher, Carl Brent. *Stephen J. Field: Craftsman of the Law.* 1930. Reprint. Chicago: University of Chicago Press, 1969.

SALMON PORTLAND CHASE (1808–1873)

Chief Justice, 1864–1873

Appointed by President Abraham Lincoln

SALMON PORTLAND CHASE
(United States Supreme Court)

Salmon P. Chase had an extraordinarily prominent political career before he became the sixth chief justice of the Supreme Court. The only political achievement denied him was that of being president of his country, and the ambition for this position filled his years on the Court with partisan calculation. President Abraham Lincoln, who nominated Chase to the Court, wryly observed that Chase "had the Presidential maggot on his brain, and he never knew anybody who once had it to get rid of it." The "presidential maggot" distracted Chase and, by at least some accounts, made him overly concerned with the political effects of his decisions. Morrison R. Waite, the man who succeeded Chase on the Court, observed that "my predecessor detracted from his fame by permitting himself to think he wanted the Presidency. Whether true or not it was said that he permitted his ambitions in that direction to influence his judicial opinions." The statesman-like abilities that had distinguished Chase in the other offices of public life failed to accompany him onto the Court. He proved incapable of exercising substantial leadership among his brethren and when he did lead them, it was to results now generally viewed as improvident. For this reason he often earns mention as one of the worst chief justices ever to have presided over the Court.

Salmon Portland Chase was born on January 13, 1808, in Cornish, New Hampshire, to Ithamar and Janette Chase. Salmon was just nine years old when his father died, and three years later he moved to the farm of Philander Chase, one of his uncles and the first Episcopalian bishop of Ohio. Philander Chase subsequently became the president of Cincinnati College and Salmon spent a year studying there. He showed significant academic promise, and his family sent him to Dartmouth College, from which he graduated in 1826. He eventually moved to Washington, D.C., where he studied law with Attorney General William Wirt.

After being admitted to the bar, Chase returned to Ohio and established a law practice in Cincinnati. He supplemented this legal occupation by lecturing and writing. He also married, though his career as a husband proved tragic. His first wife, Katherine Jane Garniss, died within two years of their marriage; his second, Eliza Ann Smith, died after six years of marriage, leaving him to raise their daughter, Kate, who would become her father's closest political confident. Finally, his third wife, Sarah, died of tuberculosis after having given birth to another daughter.

By the second half of the 1830s, Salmon Chase had put his legal skills to use in representing abolitionists. In 1837 he represented James G. Birney, who would become the Liberal Party candidate for president in 1840 and 1844, on the charge of harboring a fugitive slave. Several years later he defended John Van Zandt, a conductor of the Underground Railroad. With William Seward as co-counsel, Chase took the case to the Supreme Court, where he argued that the Fugitive Slave Act of 1793 was unconstitutional. In *Jones v. Van Zandt* (1847), however, a unanimous Court rejected Chase's argument. Nevertheless, his representation of clients such as Van Zandt earned for him the distinguished title of "Attorney General for the Runaway Negroes." Though intended as an insult, the label pleased Chase, who declared himself happy with the office "because there were neither fees nor salary connected with it."

During the 1840s, Chase migrated from the Whigs to the Liberty Party and then to the Free-Soil Party in 1848. The following year Chase's new party was able to have one of its own elected by the Ohio legislature as U.S. senator in return for supporting a Democratic reorganization of the state legislature. Chase became the new senator from Ohio as a result of this compromise. In Washington he quickly made a name for himself as a fierce opponent of slavery, voting against both the Compromise of 1850 for its implicit support of fugitive slave law and the Kansas-Nebraska bill of 1854. Chase helped to establish the Republican party in 1854 and the next year won election on the Republican ticket as governor of Ohio. He served as governor for two terms, from 1855 to 1859, and then was reelected to the U.S. Senate. At the Republican National Convention of 1860, Chase arrived as a front-runner along with William Seward, only to see the nomination and the presidential election itself go to the lesser-known Illinois politician, Abraham Lincoln.

After the election, President Lincoln appointed his chief Republican rivals to serve in his cabinet: Chase as secretary of the treasury and Seward as secretary of state, with Chase abandoning his new seat in the Senate to join Lincoln's administration. The Civil War dominated the attention of Lincoln's cabinet, and Chase played a significant role in policy decisions affecting the war because of the weakness of Lincoln's original secretary of war, Simon Cameron. To Chase's lot also fell the task of financing the war effort. Financial necessity eventually drove the administration to issue paper money not redeemable in species, currency commonly referred to as greenbacks. By the terms of the Legal Tender Act of 1862, creditors were forced to accept greenbacks in payment of any debt. Chase appears to have been reluctant to adopt this course, but he nevertheless administered the printing of $450 million in greenbacks. After the war was over, though, and Chase had become chief justice of the Supreme Court, he reverted to his original disapproval of government use of greenbacks and led a slim majority of the Court in declaring them unconstitutional in *Hepburn v. Griswold* (1870). This slender victory for Chase's views occurred, however, at a time when the Supreme Court had only seven members. President Ulysses S. Grant promptly appointed two new justices to the Court and pressed for reconsideration of the Legal Tender Act. His new appointees joined with the original three dissenters in the *Hepburn* case to produce a new 5–4 majority that overruled *Hepburn* and upheld the constitutionality of the Legal Tender Act.

Radical Republicans disapproved of Lincoln's moderate views on the question of slavery and proposed Salmon P. Chase as a possible Republican presidential candidate in 1864. When public news of this candidacy surfaced, Chase offered to resign, but Lincoln—who captured the party's nomination a second time—declined to accept his offer. The threat of resignation seems to have been one of Chase's preferred maneuvers while he served as treasury secretary. In the summer of 1864, however, he finally resorted to it once too often. After Chase used the threat following a disagreement with Lincoln concerning a political appointment, the president surprised Chase by accepting his resignation. After Lincoln's reelection in 1864, though, he turned to Chase once again, this time to fill the vacancy on the Supreme Court created by the death of Chief Justice Roger B. Taney in December of that year. On December 6, 1864, the president nominated Chase to be the Court's new chief justice; the Senate confirmed the appointment the same day. Lincoln seems to have realized early on that Chase might not prove effective as chief justice: "If he keeps on with the notion that he is destined to be President of the United States, and which in my judgment he will never be, he will never acquire . . . fame and usefulness as Chief Justice."

Such leadership as Salmon P. Chase was able to exercise on the Supreme Court expressed itself chiefly by avoiding the decision of controversial cases. The years after the war, especially, were politically perilous times for a Court whose institutional prestige had suffered grievously because of its decision in *Dred Scott v. Sandford* (1857). During President Andrew Johnson's administration, the executive branch and Congress battled one another over the reconstruction of the Southern states. In the cases that reached the Court concerning Reconstruction policy, Chase generally preferred to defer to congressional and state legislative decision-making rather than to risk the Court's institutional prestige in a clash with these legislative branches. Thus, he joined in the result of *Ex parte Milligan* (1866), which freed a Confederate sympathizer convicted of treason by a military court, but declined to join the majority opinion by Justice David Davis, which repudiated any power of Congress to allow military trials of civilians in areas where civilian courts were open. Chase also upheld the retroactive loyalty oaths struck down by a majority of the Court in *Cummings v. Missouri* (1867) and *Ex parte Garland* (1867). In these cases he could not marshal other justices to adopt his stance of deference toward legislation, but occasionally he proved successful in directing the Court down the path of least confrontation with other branches of government. Thus, when Congress attempted to limit the Court's power to hear cases brought by prisoners convicted before military tribunals, Chase led his brethren in deferring to this congressional judgment in the unanimous *Ex parte McCardle* (1868) decision. For some historical observers, Chase's willingness to avoid political confrontations with other branches of government was a sign of wisdom. For many others, though, these avoidances amounted to judicial timidness and an unseemly preoccupation with the impact of decisions on Chase's own political ambitions.

Chase generally earns high marks all around for his conduct during the impeachment trial of

President Andrew Johnson in 1868. Johnson's clashes with Congress, especially its Radical Republicans, were frequent and serious. But his attempt to remove Edwin Stanton from his cabinet and Congress's attempt to restore Stanton to his post ultimately precipitated a constitutional confrontation between the president and Congress. After the House of Representatives impeached Johnson, the Senate convened in March 1868 to try the president on the impeachment charges. Chase, as chief justice, presided over the impeachment trial. To the consternation of Radical Republicans eager to remove the president from office, Chase insisted on a fair process which, in the end, failed to approve the articles of impeachment by a single vote. Chase's bearing during the impeachment trial secured him a new measure of general public approval on which he immediately tried to capitalize by seeking the Democratic nomination for president in 1868. Once again, though, this final political prize eluded him. He died five years later, on May 7, 1873, on a visit to one of his daughters living in New York.

By all accounts, Justice Chase, a deeply religious man, was the soul of charity in his relations with individuals. Associate Justice Stephen Field, a frequent renegade from Chase's attempts to lead the Court, observed that he never heard Chase "utter an unkind word of a single human being, although his conversation was frequently of persons who at the time were assailing his conduct and maligning his motives." But this generosity toward his adversaries was also coupled with a relentless ambition to obtain the highest political office, an ambition that—then and now—poisoned his reputation as a judge. Samuel Miller, Chase's colleague and frequent adversary on the Court, may have exaggerated when he described Chase as "warped, perverted, shriveled by the selfishness generated by ambition." But his criticism of Chase, expressed with less venom, has echoed down history's corridor, leaving Chase's record as chief justice of the Supreme Court permanently tarnished.

Further Reading

Blue, Frederick J. *Salmon P. Chase: A Life in Politics.* Kent, Ohio: Kent State University Press, 1987.

Chase, Salmon Portland. *Inside Lincoln's Cabinet: The Civil War Diaries of Salmon P. Chase.* Edited by David Donald. New York: Longmans, Green, 1954.

Hart, Albert Bushnell. *Salmon P. Chase.* 1899. Reprint. New York: Chelsea House, 1980.

Middleton, Stephen. *Ohio and the Antislavery Activities of Attorney Salmon Portland Chase, 1830–1849.* New York: Garland Publishing, 1990.

Niven, John. *Salmon P. Chase: A Biography.* New York: Oxford University Press, 1995.

Smith, Donnal Vore. *Chase and Civil War-Politics.* 1930. Reprint. Freeport, N.Y.: Books for Libraries Press, 1972.

"A Symposium on Salmon P. Chase and the Chase Court: Perspectives in Law and History." *Northern Kentucky Law Review* 21 (1993): 1–252.

William Strong (1808–1895)

Associate Justice, 1870–1880

Appointed by President Ulysses S. Grant

William Strong
(United States Supreme Court)

Justice William Strong arrived on the Court under a cloud of undeserved controversy. Once on the Court, Strong tendered a decade of competent but generally unremarkable service. His best work as a justice lay in crafting opinions in the area of commercial matters, but the minutiae of these issues—though important at the time—excite little interest more than a century later. Strong wrote few significant constitutional opinions, and his participation in important constitutional cases tended to reflect the positions of judicial conservatives of the time. He placed a premium on the protection of property rights but seemed curiously insensitive to the plight of the newly freed slaves whose hope of finding protection for their civil rights and liberties gradually faded during the period when Justice Strong sat on the nation's highest judicial bench.

William Strong was the first child born to William Lighthouse Strong, a Presbyterian minister, and Harriet Deming Strong; 10 other brothers and sisters would be added to the family. He grew up on a small farm in Somers, Connecticut, where he was born on May 6, 1808. After his early schooling, Strong entered Yale at the age of 15 and graduated in 1828. The following few years he taught school while studying law in a local attorney's office. In 1832 he returned to Yale to study law briefly. He was admitted the same year to practice law in Connecticut and Pennsylvania.

William Strong moved to Reading, Pennsylvania, and opened a law office. Within a short time he was an important figure in the community. His legal practice flourished, bringing him clients such as the Philadelphia and Reading Railroad Company and positions as director of the Farmers' Bank and the Lebanon Valley Railroad. In addition, he took an active part in civic affairs, serving on the city council and the school board during his first decade in Reading. He married Priscilla Lee Mallery in 1836, and the couple had three children—two daughters and a son—before Priscilla died in 1844. Two years after her death, Strong successfully ran as a Democratic candidate for Congress, serving while he was there with two men who would subsequently play an important part in American history: Abraham Lincoln and Andrew Johnson. He served two terms in Congress before returning to the full-time practice of law and marrying again, this time to Rachel Davies Bull. Strong's second wife gave birth to another son and two more daughters.

In 1857 Strong was elected to sit on the Pennsylvania Supreme Court and thus began a 23-year career as a judge, first at the state level and later on the nation's highest court. He began his 15-year term of office as a Democrat, but his antislavery views and his staunch support for the Union ultimately caused him to migrate to the newly founded Republican party by the start of the Civil War. Strong did not complete his full term on the Pennsylvania Supreme Court but resigned instead to return to what immediately became a prosperous practice in Philadelphia. Through a tangled course of events, however, he soon became a judge again, although this time he was elevated to an even more illustrious bench.

The sequence of events that placed William Strong on the U.S. Supreme Court began with the resignation of Robert Grier from the Court, effective February 1, 1870. Grier's resignation left two seats unfilled on the Supreme Court, one created by Grier's resignation and the other after Congress increased the number of seats on the Court to nine in 1869. President Ulysses S. Grant wished to replace Grier with William Strong, but congressional sentiment vigorously favored Edwin M. Stanton, Lincoln's secretary of war. Grant capitulated to this pressure and on December 20, 1869, nominated Stanton, who was confirmed by the Senate the same day. (In mid-December, Grier had signaled his intent to resign.) But this expeditious action on the part of Senate proved not quick enough: Within four days, Stanton died before taking the oath of office and joining the Court. Grant subsequently moved to fill the two vacant seats on the Court by nominating William Strong and Joseph P. Bradley on February 7, 1870. As it happened, later that same day the Supreme Court announced its decision in *Hepburn v. Griswold* (1870), a case involving one of the most controversial matters of the day: the constitutionality of the Legal Tender Act. The justices had privately decided the outcome of the case the previous November, and Grant appears to have known the result some two weeks in advance of the announcement. But the timing of the Strong and Bradley nominations and the *Hepburn* opinion, which found the Legal Tender Act unconstitutional, immediately fueled suggestions that Grant was trying to pack the Court with justices who would uphold the Legal Tender Act. *Hepburn* had decided the issue by a vote of 4 to 3, and the addition of two new justices supportive of the Act would probably lead to a reversal of *Hepburn* in short order. Consequently, Democrats cried foul, and they castigated what they claimed to be the president's machinations in finding two supporters of the Act to fill his vacancies. Strong had voted in support of the Act's constitutionality when he was a justice on the Pennsylvania Supreme Court, and Bradley was accused of signing a written promise prior to his appointment, binding him to vote in favor of the Act.

The charge of "court packing" seems to have been wholly without foundation, though. Both Strong and Bradley did view the Legal Tender Act as constitutional, but it would have been difficult to find Republican nominees who did *not* approve of the Act. Moreover, the appointments of both men had been in the works for some time before the Court announced its *Hepburn* decision. In any event, the Senate eventually confirmed Strong's appointment to the Court in late February and Bradley's at the end of the following month. William Strong took the oath of office as an associate justice of the Supreme Court on March 14, 1870.

Though President Grant almost certainly did not appoint Strong and Bradley to the Court simply for their support of the Legal Tender Act, his administration did move at once to have the decision in *Hepburn* revisited by the Court. Grant's attorney general maneuvered to have two new cases on the issue come up before the Court, and a new majority of five justices—the original three dissenters in *Hepburn* plus Strong and Bradley—voted to hear the cases and then voted to overrule *Hepburn* by holding the Legal Tender Act constitutional.

On May 1, 1871, Associate Justice William Strong announced the judgment of the Court in *Knox v. Lee* (1871) and *Parker v. Davis* (1871). Strong's opinions for the Court in the two cases rejected the reasoning adopted by Chief Justice Salmon P. Chase in *Hepburn* and concluded that the federal government had had the power during the Civil War to issue paper money—or greenbacks—and to require creditors to accept this currency for the satisfaction of debts. Chase's original conclusion to the contrary had summoned the "spirit of the Constitution" as a witness against the Legal Tender Act. The Constitution prohibited states from impairing contractual obligations, and though this clause did not precisely apply to federal laws, Chase urged that the "spirit" though not perhaps the "letter" of the Constitution ought to infer a similar prohibition against federal actions that interfered with contractual obligations. Strong, for a new majority of the Court, rejected this inference and sustained the constitutionality of the federal act.

During his decade of service on the Court, Justice Strong developed a reputation as a talented jurist in commercial cases. He tended to distrust state commercial regulations and this predisposition sometimes placed him on the dissenting side of cases, together with the Court's other probusiness champion, Stephen Field. In the area of civil rights, Strong shared the inclination common to a majority of the Court during this period to construe the provisions of the Reconstruction Amendments (Thirteenth, Fourteenth, and Fifteenth Amendments) narrowly. This construction prohibited certain forms of discrimination against newly freed blacks but generally left them at the mercy of Southern officials and citizens intent on denying them basic civil rights and liberties. Justice Strong wrote the opinion for the Court in *Strauder v. West Virginia* (1880), overturning a state law that excluded blacks from jury service. But he also authored the twisted reasoning of *Blyew v. United States* (1872). The Civil Rights Act of 1866 made it a federal crime to engage in criminal conduct "affecting persons" denied their lawful rights. After the defendant in the case had been acquitted of charges in state court of murdering three African Americans, he was prosecuted in federal court. When the case arrived before the Supreme Court, Justice Strong concluded for a majority of the justices that the Civil Rights Act gave federal courts the power only to try cases affecting *living* persons. Since the murder victims were dead, there was no federal crime.

William Strong's tenure on the Court passed in relative obscurity. He was one of the least politically active of the justices. When the disputed presidential election of 1876 caused

Congress to name a special commission to resolve the controversy, Strong counted it a great misfortune when he was appointed as one of the five Supreme Court justices among the members of the commission. In the main, however, Strong attracted little notice during his years on the Court. Unlike several of his colleagues, Strong chose to resign from the Court in 1880 after ten years of service, at a time when his mental and physical faculties were still strong. He preferred, it was said, to have people greet his retirement with the question, "Why does he?" rather than to endure his lingering presence on the Court with the question, "Why doesn't he?" In fact, some indication exists that he resigned when he did precisely to serve as an example to three justices who had—by common understanding—outstayed their usefulness of the Court: Noah H. Swayne, Nathan Clifford, and Ward Hunt.

After Strong's resignation from the Supreme Court in 1880, he continued an active involvement in religious affairs. He had accepted the vice presidency of the American Bible Society in 1871 and continued in this position through 1895. He was also the president of the American Tract Society from 1873 to 1895 and of the American Sunday School Union from 1883 to 1895. These activities reflected an enduring Christian faith, exhibited most famously during the Civil War by Strong's leadership of an unsuccessful campaign to cure the Constitution's relative "godlessness" by amending it to acknowledge "the Lord Jesus Christ as the ruler of all nations, and his revealed will as the supreme law of the land."

After retiring from the Court, Strong's experience as a justice formed the basis for an article he published in the *North American Review* in 1881, and the reforms he suggested in the article were at least partially implemented by Congress in 1891. In 1895 Strong died at Lake Minnewaska, New York, in his 87th year.

Brought onto the Court in a period of great controversy, Associate Justice William Strong eventually proved himself to be an able judge, removed from the tangle of partisan politics except when his country drafted him to help resolve the presidential crisis of 1876. Conservative and probusiness, Strong participated in the Supreme Court's prolonged dismantling of Reconstruction efforts and joined Justice Stephen Field in championing constitutional protections for private property. In general, though, he labored in obscurity over the host of minor commercial matters decided by the Court during the 1870s but long since forgotten, a fate largely shared by the justice himself.

Further Reading

Kutler, Stanley I. "William Strong." In *The Justices of the United States Supreme Court 1789–1969: Their Lives and Major Opinions,* vol. 2. Edited by Leon Friedman and Fred L. Israel. New York: R. R. Bowker Co., 1969.

Barnes, William Horatio. "William Strong, Associate Justice." In *The Supreme Court of the United States.* Part 11 of Barnes's *Illustrated Cyclopedia of the American Government.* n.p.: 1875.

"Retirement of William J. Strong." *American Law Review* 15 (1881): 130–131.

Strong, William. "The Needs of the Supreme Court." *North American Review* 132 (1881): 437–450.

JOSEPH P. BRADLEY (1813–1892)

Associate Justice, 1870–1892

Appointed by President Ulysses S. Grant

JOSEPH P. BRADLEY
(United States Supreme Court)

Many historians consider Joseph P. Bradley one of the most brilliant justices on the Supreme Court during the last half of the 19th century. He has similarly been hailed as one of the Court's great judicial craftsmen, capable of assembling legal precedents into the form of elegant and straightforward opinions. With outstanding ability, he proved himself capable of transcending the view he had advocated as the lawyer of wealthy commercial interests and, independently of his previous loyalties, to train the formidable talents of his legal mind on the constitutional work of the Court.

Born in Berne, New York, on March 14, 1813, Joseph Bradley was the first child of Philo and Mercy Gardner Bradley. (He adopted the middle initial sometime in his youth, but it does not stand for anything further. His father's name may be the source of the choice.) He grew up on a farm and largely taught himself. He set out for New York City when he was 17 years old. By his own account, he missed the last boat available to take him to New York City and had to tarry instead in Albany, where he taught school and made contacts that ultimately directed him to Rutgers College in New Jersey in 1833. Bradley declared ever afterward that had he not missed the boat, he "would have become a grocer in New York." Instead, he graduated from Rutgers in 1836, was briefly a teacher and a journalist, and then turned to the study of law in the office of Archer Gifford, who served as collector for the port of Newark.

Bradley was admitted to the bar in 1839, and after practicing law a few years, he married Mary Hornblower, daughter of William Hornblower, the chief justice of New Jersey Supreme Court. For the next 25 years, Bradley practiced law in Newark, New Jersey, representing a variety of business clients, including the Camden and Amboy Railroad and the Mutual Benefit Life Insurance Company of Newark. During this time, Bradley argued a number of cases before the U.S. Supreme Court. He ran for Congress in 1862 as a Republican and, not surprisingly in view of the Democratic strength in his district, he lost. By the end of the decade, however, Joseph P. Bradley was a lawyer of national stature, well known by a number of important political figures, and considered a possible nominee for the Supreme Court.

During the administration of President Andrew Johnson, Congress had whittled the seats on the Court from 10 to seven, pending resignations of sitting justices, to prevent Johnson from making any appointments. In fact, only one justice resigned while the 1869 act was in effect, so the number of actual justices never slipped below eight. The Judiciary Act of 1869 increased the number of seats on the Court to nine. This increase, combined with Associate Justice Robert Grier's announcement in mid-December 1869 of his intention to resign effective February 1, 1870, presented President Ulysses S. Grant with the opportunity of making two appointments to the Court. Because the eventual timing of these two appointments coincided with the Supreme Court's announcement of *Hepburn v. Griswold* (1870), one of the most controversial cases in years, and because the appointments ultimately resulted in the reversal of the Court's original decision, many observers at the time complained that Grant had arranged to pack the Court with the votes necessary for him to have the Court to overrule its earlier decision.

Hepburn concerned legal tender, an issue over which Democrats and Republicans tended to split along party lines. During the Civil War, President Abraham Lincoln's secretary of the treasury, Salmon P. Chase, had (reluctantly) issued paper currency to help finance the Union cause. Congress had reciprocated by passing the Legal Tender Act of 1862, which required creditors to accept the currency—commonly called greenbacks—in payment of debts. After the war, Republicans tended overwhelmingly to approve the constitutionality of the Legal Tender Act, Democrats to decry it as unconstitutional. Unfortunately for the Republicans, however, when a challenge to the Legal Tender Act arrived before the Supreme Court toward the end of the 1860s, Salmon P. Chase now sat as chief justice, and he believed the Legal Tender Act to be unconstitutional. In November 1869 the Court privately decided the challenge to the Act in *Hepburn v. Griswold,* with the chief justice of a truncated Court commanding a majority in favor of striking the law down. The Court did not immediately announce its decision publicly, however, and in the meantime, Justice Robert C. Grier's resignation at the end of January 1870 left two seats vacant on the Court, which President Grant moved to fill. Congress pressured Grant to appoint Lincoln's secretary of war, Edwin M. Stanton, to one of the vacancies; and Grant himself nominated Attorney General E. Rockwood Hoar to the other vacant seat. The Senate declined to confirm Hoar, however, and Edwin Stanton died suddenly four days after his confirmation and before he could assume the office of justice. Consequently, on February 7,

1870, Grant nominated William Strong and Joseph P. Bradley to fill the two open seats on the Court. The day he announced these nominations, the Court announced the result in the *Hepburn* case, leading to the charge of court-packing—a charge that was almost surely unfair. Grant would have had to look outside his own Republican party for judicial nominees who would have opposed the Legal Tender Act. That he did not is scarcely noteworthy. He certainly benefited when Strong and Bradley soon had the opportunity with the rest of the Court to reconsider the legal tender issue in *Knox v. Lee* (1871) and *Parker v. Davis* (1871); and not surprisingly, Strong and Bradley joined together with the three dissenters in the original case to uphold the constitutionality of the Legal Tender Act.

Bradley, who thus arrived on the Court in controversial circumstances, found himself plunged into controversy again seven years later, when he was appointed to serve on the special commission selected by Congress to resolve the disputed presidential election of 1876. On a commission evenly balanced between Republicans and Democrats—including four other Supreme Court justices in addition to Bradley—Bradley, one of the Court's least partisan justices, was expected to be the swing vote. Yet although he professed at the time and thereafter that he had made his decision on legal and constitutional grounds rather than political ones, Bradley joined with the other Republicans on the commission in a party-line vote. Thus, Rutherford B. Hayes, the Republican candidate, was declared the winner over Samuel Tilden, the Democratic candidate who had received the greater popular vote in the election. Bradley endured harsh criticism for his decision, but he accepted it philosophically:

> [L]et it pass. If I have the ill-fortune to be unjustly judged, I am not the first who has been in that predicament. We must take the world as it is, and having done what we conceived to be our duty, trust the rest to a higher power than that rules the ordinary affairs of man in society.

In all, Bradley served almost 22 years on the Court, and during that period he earned a reputation as one of the Court's most vigorous intellects. The two great constitutional controversies of his day involved the issues of civil rights and property rights. On both issues Bradley's positions were complicated and not readily reduced to a predictable posture.

In the area of civil rights, Justice Bradley exhibited the conservative tendencies common to many public figures of his age: He opposed slavery and rejoiced in its abolition, but he seems not to have seen in the Reconstruction Amendments of the Constitution (Thirteenth, Fourteenth, and Fifteenth) any promise of an end to racial (or sexual) discrimination in society. He penned the Court's opinion in the *Civil Rights Cases* (1883), invalidating core provisions of the Civil Rights Act of 1875, which had attempted to prohibit racial discrimination in a variety of public contexts. For the Court, Bradley concluded that under the Fourteenth Amendment—which guarantees the equal protection of the law—Congress can do no more than pass laws to abolish official acts of discrimination as opposed to private acts. In a passage of his opinion remarkable for its lack of sympathy for the plight of newly freed slaves, Bradley observed:

> When a man has emerged from slavery, and by the aid of beneficent legislation has shaken off the inseparable concomitants of that state, there must be some stage in the progress of his elevation when he takes the rank of mere citizen and ceases to be the special favorite of the laws, and when his rights as a citizen, or a man, are to be protected in the ordinary modes by which other men's rights are protected.

Bradley turned a similarly blind eye to the possibility that the Fourteenth Amendment's equal protection clause might prevent governments from discriminating on the basis of gender. In *Bradwell v. Illinois* (1873), he concurred in the Court's decision upholding an Illinois law that prevented women from becoming lawyers. In Bradley's estimation, such career aspirations were inconsistent with the will of the Creator, who had destined women to occupy "the noble and benign offices of wife and mother."

On issues relating to property rights, Bradley proved surprisingly more independent in his views than one might have expected from a business and railroad lawyer. He regularly upheld the constitutionality of state business regulations—including regulations of railroads. In the 20th century, Felix Frankfurter, a Harvard law professor who eventually ascended to the Supreme Court himself, said of Bradley: "He who by his previous experience would supposedly reflect the bias of financial power, was as free from it as any judge, and indeed much more radical." In fact, Justice Bradley made crucial behind-the-scenes contributions to the Court's decision in *Munn v. Illinois* (1877). The case upheld the constitutionality of a state Granger law that regulated the prices charged by grain elevators. Though the majority opinion was crafted by Chief Justice Morrison Waite, Bradley provided the chief justice with relevant legal authorities and suggested language for what became one of the most important decisions of the last half of the 19th century.

Even though Bradley was a skilled and productive jurist, he found ample time to pursue a variety of other intellectual interests. His private library boasted 16,000 volumes, and he pursued not only his professional interest in the law but also significant inquiries into scientific and mathematical subjects. These prompted Bradley to write a history of the steam engine, for example, and to devise a perpetual calendar with which he could identify the day of the week on which significant historical events had occurred. He remained active throughout his life and finally died, near 80 years of age, on January 22, 1892.

Though Justice Joseph P. Bradley brought no judicial experience to the Supreme Court, he nevertheless proved to be a jurist of the first order. This does not mean that history judges his decisions to have been invariably correct or his opinions always agreeable. On issues relating to racial and sexual discrimination, for example, Bradley seems to have suffered the common captivity of his age to the view that the law, including the Constitution, could do no more than eliminate the formal bonds of slavery. It could, he believed, do little else to rescue blacks—or women, for that matter—from the variety of official and social inequalities with which they were burdened after the Civil War. Nevertheless, Bradley demonstrated great skill as a judicial craftsman and a marked ability to rise above the settled financial prejudices of the class to which he belonged. For these traits, history recognizes Justice Bradley as one of the finer jurists ever to have donned the robes of a Supreme Court justice.

Further Reading

Fairman, Charles. "Mr. Justice Bradley." In *Mr. Justice*. Edited by Allison Dunham and Philip B. Kurland. Chicago: University of Chicago Press, 1964.

Friedman, Leon. "Joseph P. Bradley." In *The Justices of the United States Supreme Court 1789–1969: Their Lives and Major Opinions,* Vol. 1. Edited by Leon Friedman and Fred L. Israel. New York: R. R. Bowker Co., 1969.

Lurie, Jonathan. "Mr. Justice Bradley: A Reassessment." *Seton Hall Law Review* 16 (1986): 343–375.

Parker, Cortland. "Joseph P. Bradley." *American Law Review* 28 (1984): 481–509.

Pope, Dennis H. "Personality and Judicial Performance: A Psychobiography of Justice Joseph P. Bradley." Ph.D. diss., Rutgers Univ., 1988.

WARD HUNT (1810–1886)

Associate Justice, 1873–1882

Appointed by President Ulysses S. Grant

WARD HUNT
(United States Supreme Court)

In 1873 Ward Hunt joined a Supreme Court crowded with judicial talent: Samuel F. Miller, Joseph P. Bradley, and Stephen Field dominated the intellectual life of the Court. Among this august assembly of jurists, Justice Hunt was clearly of lesser stature. Though an agreeable man, he lacked the mental power of the Court's more influential justices. Added to this deficiency was his short tenure on the Court: Hunt ultimately contributed barely five years of active service as a justice. Not surprisingly, lesser ability and truncated service deprived Justice Hunt of any significant place in the Supreme Court's history. History remembers him most for two dissenting opinions and for presiding over the trial of Susan B. Anthony for violating a federal voting law.

Ward Hunt was born on June 14, 1810, in Utica, New York, the son of Elizabeth Stringham Hunt and Montgomery Hunt, who worked as a cashier in a local bank. Hunt studied in local academies before attending Hamilton College briefly and then Union College in Schenectady, New York, from which he graduated with honors in 1828. The following year he moved to Litchfield, Connecticut, to study law with Judge James Gould at the Tapping Reeve School. After law school, Hunt returned to Utica, where he clerked with Judge Hiram Denio and was admitted to the bar in 1831. Within a short time Denio and Hunt established a partnership and Hunt rapidly gained a reputation as an outstanding lawyer.

Like many lawyers then and now, Ward Hunt gravitated to political affairs. Because of his opposition to the spread of slavery, he followed the well-trodden path from the ranks of Jacksonian Democrats to the Republican Party. In 1838 he won election to the New York legislature and served there one term. Thereafter, he was elected mayor of Utica in 1844. Later that decade, Hunt's antislavery views led him to support Martin Van Buren for president in 1848.

In the following years, Hunt tried unsuccessfully to obtain a judicial post. Twice he sought election to New York's Court of Appeals, losing on both occasions. After his failure to win a seat on this court as a Democrat in 1853, Hunt abandoned the Democratic Party for good. In 1856 he helped organize New York's fledgling Republican party. In the course of this political activity, he became acquainted with Roscoe Conkling, a New York politician whose political career would intersect with Hunt's life at several points in the future.

Hunt was prominent in the early years of New York's Republican Party. He was briefly considered as a possible Republican candidate for the U.S. Senate in 1857, and in 1863 he served temporarily as chairman of the Republican Union Convention in Syracuse, New York. But Hunt still longed to be a judge, and he finally won a seat on the New York Court of Appeals in 1865 under the Republican banner. Within three years he had been elevated to chief justice of the court. When constitutional amendments to the New York constitution reorganized the New York courts in 1869, Hunt was chosen to continue his judicial service to the state as commissioner of appeals.

Associate Justice Samuel Nelson of New York resigned from the Supreme Court in the fall of 1872. Ward Hunt's political ally, Roscoe Conkling, was a U.S. senator from New York at the time, and he pressed President Ulysses S. Grant to appoint Hunt to fill the vacancy left by Nelson's retirement. Though there were other potential candidates for the position, Grant was convinced that most New Yorkers preferred Hunt. Conkling's blessing clinched the appointment, and Grant forwarded Hunt's name to the Senate on December 3, 1872. The Senate confirmed the appointment eight days later without controversy, and Hunt took the oath of office as a justice of the U.S. Supreme Court on January 9, 1873.

Though he was an able and hardworking judge, from the beginning Justice Hunt occupied a seat far from the center of the Court's power and influence. His appointment to the Court was overshadowed within a few months of his arrival by the death of Chief Justice Salmon P. Chase. And in the company of luminous judicial minds and personalities such as Samuel Miller, Joseph Bradley, and Stephen Field, Hunt was a relatively dim light.

Justice Ward Hunt did not often dissent during his five years of active service on the Court. He wrote an average number of opinions—152—and dissented seven times. One of these dissents was in an important case concerning the extent to which state courts could exert jurisdiction over nonresidents of the state. The case—*Pennoyer v. Neff* (1877)—is still read by law-school students. More memorable than his dissent in *Pennoyer*, though, was Hunt's lone protest against the majority's decision in *United States v. Reese* (1876), an outcome that struck a crippling blow to black voting rights. *Reese* involved the Enforcement Act of 1870, by which Congress had attempted to enforce the Fifteenth Amendment's protection of voting rights against the emerging campaign in the South to strip African Americans of the right to vote. The case arose after two municipal inspectors in Kentucky were prosecuted for violating the Enforcement Act when they refused to count the vote of William Garner, a black man. Before the Supreme Court, the decision in

United States v. Reese turned on the technical wording of the Enforcement Act, which generally prohibited racial discrimination in connection with voting. The Act's punishment provisions did not refer explicitly to actions based on race, but only referred generally to punishment of conduct described "as aforesaid." According to Chief Justice Morrison Waite, who wrote for the majority of the Court, this was a crucial defect in the Act. Under the Fifteenth Amendment, Congress had no power to guarantee citizens a right to vote, only to protect that right from racial discrimination. Congress, said Waite, had not specifically linked punishments under the Enforcement Act to racial discrimination and therefore it had exceeded its power. Hunt, alone of all the justices, rejected this overtechnical reading of the statute and argued that the Court wield the Act precisely as Congress intended—to punish attempts then blossoming in the South to strip blacks of the right to vote.

Like the other members of the Court, Justice Hunt was required to serve as a judge in the Circuit Courts of Appeals. In this capacity he presided over the trial of Susan B. Anthony in the summer of 1873. Anthony was prosecuted under the Enforcement Act for "knowingly . . . voting without having a lawful right to vote." She had voted in an election in Rochester, New York, even though New York law allowed only men to vote. Hunt summarily concluded that Anthony had broken the federal law, instructed the jury to declare her guilty, and fined her $100.

Justice Ward Hunt's arrival on the Court received not nearly as much attention as the circumstances of his departure from it. Beginning in 1877, he missed sessions of the Court while suffering from gout. Then, in January 1879, Hunt suffered a stroke that left him permanently disabled on one side of this body. He returned to the bench only one more time, but he nevertheless refused to resign from the Court. In part, he clung to his seat on the Court because he had not served the 10 years required by law to obtain a pension. He also declined to resign out of deference to his old New York ally, Roscoe Conkling—still a U.S. senator—who was not willing to allow President Rutherford B. Hayes to make an appointment to the Court. Finally, Congress broke the impasse by passing a special law to provide Hunt with a pension; he submitted his resignation the day the law became effective. Once more, though, the paths of Hunt and Conkling crossed: After Hunt's retirement President Chester A. Arthur nominated Conkling to fill the seat on the Court vacated by Hunt. The Senate, in fact, confirmed Conkling, but he declined to accept the appointment in order to pursue his ambition to become president. Four years later, Hunt died in Washington, D.C., on March 24, 1886.

Ward Hunt lacked the intellectual brilliance and the extended tenure of service necessary to make any significant impact on the Supreme Court. Both factors were beyond his control, but they nevertheless combined to deprive him of a memorable place in the Court's history. It did not help his reputation as a justice that he refused to step down from his seat when he could no longer fulfill its responsibilities. This final act of determination, however necessitated by his personal financial circumstances, tarnished what would otherwise have been a brief but workmanlike career on the nation's highest court.

Further Reading

Barnes, William Horatio. "Ward Hunt, Associate Justice." In *The Supreme Court of the United States.* Part 11 of Barnes's *Illustrated Cyclopedia of the American Government.* n.p.: 1875.

Kutler, Stanley I. "Ward Hunt." In *The Justices of the United States Supreme Court 1789–1969: Their Lives and Major Opinions,* Vol. 2. Edited by Leon Friedman and Fred L. Israel. New York: R. R. Bowker Co., 1969.

Morrison Remick Waite (1816–1888)

Chief Justice, 1874–1878

Appointed by President Ulysses S. Grant

Morrison Remick Waite
(United States Supreme Court)

Scarcely any chief justice who ever presided over the U.S. Supreme Court had the honor and responsibility of the office offered to them more unexpectedly than Morrison Remick Waite. President Ulysses S. Grant first plucked the little-known Ohioan from obscurity to represent the claims of the United States against Great Britain that had arisen out of the Civil War. Then the president, weary of a failed series of attempts to replace the vacancy on the Court created by the death of Chief Justice Salmon P. Chase, reached out again to nominate Waite, even though he lacked judicial experience and had never so much as argued a case before the high court. In spite of Waite's surprising appointment to the Court, by dint of hard work and a congenial temper, he achieved a modest measure of success as chief justice.

The man who would become the seventh chief justice of the Supreme Court was born in Lyme, Connecticut, on November 27, 1816. His father, a judge who would eventually serve as chief justice of the Connecticut Supreme Court, steered his son down the path of the law. Morrison Waite graduated from Yale in 1837, studied law briefly in his father's office, and then escaped the elder Waite's long shadow by moving to Maumee City, Ohio, near Toledo, in 1838. There he studied law with Samuel D. Young, was eventually admitted to the bar, and formed a partnership with Young. Waite supplemented this partnership with another by his marriage to Amelia C. Warner, a second cousin from his hometown, in 1840.

Over the next three decades Waite practiced law and intermittently ran for political office. He earned a modest measure of material success as a lawyer, though his practice was far from lucrative, in spite of his earning a reputation as a railroad lawyer. Waite's political aspirations met with mixed success, however. He ran for Congress as a Whig in 1846 and as Republican nearly 20 years later, in 1862, but lost on both occasions. He did serve a single term in the Ohio legislature after winning election in 1849. The following year he moved his family to Toledo, where he established a law practice with his brother, Richard Waite. Although he had the chance to follow in his father's footsteps by serving on the Ohio Supreme Court in the early 1860s, Waite declined this appointment in favor of an advisery role to Ohio governor John Brough.

In the following decade, national prominence unexpectedly presented itself to Morrison Waite. When the United States prepared to arbitrate claims against Great Britain arising out of Britain's role in the outfitting of Confederate ships, President Ulysses S. Grant appointed Waite—in spite of his lack of national prominence—as one of three representatives for the United States sent to Geneva in 1871. Waite acquitted himself well in this service to his country, and the arbitration award of $15.5 million to the United States placed him on the national political map—at least for the moment. With his newfound prominence, Waite won a seat as a delegate to the Ohio Constitutional Convention of 1873 and, in fact, became the Convention's president.

While Waite presided over the Ohio Convention, a weightier drama was being played out in Washington. Earlier, in spring 1873, Chief Justice Salmon P. Chase died, leaving to President Grant the task of finding a suitable candidate to fill the chief justice's seat. Grant, though, had a peculiar talent for elevating incompetent or corrupt individuals to important federal posts. Thus, his initial attempts to replace Salmon Chase produced a string of political embarrassments as the president made one improvident choice after another to find a candidate suitable for Congress's approval. Finally, as Morrison Waite tended to his duties as president of the Ohio Constitutional Convention, Grant telegraphed him to announce that he had been nominated chief justice of the U.S. Supreme Court. Although Waite lacked judicial experience and had never even practiced before the Supreme Court as a lawyer, the Senate, recognizing that he was an improvement over normal Grant appointments, unanimously approved Waite's appointment on January 21, 1874.

Waite's colleagues on the Court were far less approving of the president's choice for chief justice. The other justices greeted Waite's arrival on the Court with coolness and seemed at first reluctant to accept his leadership. Another Ohioan in Grant's administration, Benjamin R. Cowan, encouraged Waite to "gather up the reins and drive," advice which Waite apparently took to heart. The next day he informed Cowan: "I got on the box as soon as I arrived there this morning, gathered up the lines and drove, and I am going to drive and these gentlemen know it."

Chief Justice Waite proved to be a congenial pilot of the Court's business, well-liked if not always deeply respected, a hardworking jurist who wrote opinions in almost a third of the cases decided by the Court during his tenure as chief justice. Two issues dominated the Court's business during the years that Waite presided over it: the extent to which the Constitution's newly ratified Reconstruction Amendments would protect the civil rights of African Americans, and the role that the Constitution would play in the conflicts between government and business in an increasingly industrialized economy. In part the Waite court simply carried on the course established the year before Waite was appointed in the decision of the *Slaughterhouse Cases* (1873). In this case, a majority of the justices adopted a view of the Fourteenth Amendment that limited its potential to secure both civil rights and civil liberties for newly freed African Americans and that severely diminished its potential to serve as a source of protection for commercial interests against state regulation. In both areas Waite's court continued to hew to the path announced in the *Slaughterhouse Cases.*

During the years that Chief Justice Waite presided over the Supreme Court, a majority of the justices adopted stunted interpretations of the Reconstruction Amendments that largely blunted their ability to protect the civil liberties of the African Americans. On occasion the Court recognized particular official action as trespassing on the Fourteenth Amendment's guarantee of the equal protection of law. Thus, in *Strauder v. West Virginia* (1879) the Court invalidated a state statute that limited jury duty to whites, and in *Ex parte Virginia* (1879), the Court also held unconstitutional a state judge's exclusion of blacks from jury service.

In other conspicuous cases the Court systematically dismantled the Reconstruction Amendments as a constitutional bulwark against the new civil war being waged against the civil rights and liberties of African Americans in the South. The Reconstruction Congress had attempted to use the power granted to it in the Fourteenth and Fifteenth Amendments to protect blacks, but the Court narrowly interpreted congressional power in this area. For example, in *United States v. Reese* (1876), a majority of the Court, in an opinion by Chief Justice Waite, concluded that the Fifteenth Amendment, which prohibits states from denying the right to vote on the grounds of race, color, or previous condition of servitude, did not actually guarantee to blacks the right to vote. In 1870 Congress had passed a law prohibiting interference with any person's federal rights. This law was used to prosecute two Louisiana election officials who had prevented blacks from voting. But, the chief justice declared for the Court, the Fifteenth Amendment had not actually guaranteed the right to vote, only the right to be free from official racial discrimination in voting. Since the 1870 law did not focus on racially discriminatory voting practices, it was unconstitutional and could not be used to prosecute the officials in question. Of similar effect was Waite's opinion for the Court in *United States v. Cruikshank* (1876). After three Louisiana men murdered more than a hundred blacks and three whites outside a Louisiana courthouse on Easter 1873, they were prosecuted under the federal law of 1870. The indictment, however, did not specify that the accused had undertaken their bloody rampage out of racial considerations and this, the Court held, was a fatal defect. "We may suspect that race was the cause of the hostility," Waite admitted from his high perch far away from the violence that had spawned the suit, "but it is not so averred."

In an even more significant decision for civil rights, Waite's court dealt a lethal blow to Reconstruction efforts to protect blacks from discrimination in the *Civil Rights Cases* (1883). At issue were provisions of the Civil Rights Act of 1875 that prohibited racial discrimination in inns, public conveyances, and places of public amusement. The Fourteenth Amendment, according to the Court, prohibited only government discrimination rather than private acts of racial discrimination. Thus, though Congress had power to enforce the provisions of this amendment, it had no power to pass legislation prohibiting discrimination by any but state officials or representatives. Furthermore, the Court rejected the contention that various acts of private discrimination violated the Thirteenth Amendment's prohibition against slavery. Combined together with the holdings of the *Slaugh-*

terhouse Cases and the voting rights cases decided by the Waite court, the decision in the *Civil Rights Cases* banished the federal government from the field of significant civil rights legislation for nearly a century. Not until the passage of the 1964 Civil Rights Act did federal law return to the work that the Reconstruction Congress had first begun but that Waite's court had interrupted.

On the other great issue of his day—the ability of states to restrict the growing power of business relationships—Waite led his Court to grant the states broad latitude in this area. In perhaps the most significant case of his judicial career, *Munn v. Illinois* (1877), Chief Justice Waite authored the Court's opinion approving state legislation that regulated grain elevator rates. To the argument that this regulation deprived elevator owners of an interest in property without due process of law, in violation of the Fourteenth Amendment, Waite declared that the due process clause did not shield property owners from state regulation when their private property touched on the public interest. When a property owner puts "property to a use in which the public has an interest, he, in effect, grants to the public an interest in that use, and must submit to be controlled by the public for the common good, to the extent of the interest he has created." Justice Stephen Field launched a vigorous dissent from Waite's reasoning and would eventually capture a majority of the Court for an interpretation of due process more protective of commercial interests. But for the time at least, Waite was able to muster a solid majority of the Court to his approval of judicial restraint in the review of state economic regulations.

Unlike several of his colleagues on the Court, Chief Justice Waite had no aspiration to use his position as a springboard to a higher government post. For a man who had been catapulted from obscurity into a place of national prominence, being chief justice was an honor worthy of an entire life's career. In 1876 several members of the Court were chosen by Congress to participate on a commission to decide the contested presidential election between Democrat Samuel J. Tilden and Republican Rutherford B. Hayes. Waite refused to serve on the commission, however, partially out of his personal acquaintance with both candidates but also because participation in the commission threatened, in Waite's mind, the separation between the Court and political disputes that was necessary to preserve the Court's institutional authority. The previous year Waite had written to his nephew, John Turner, a congressman for Connecticut, explaining his reticence to pursue a possible presidential candidacy:

> The office [of chief justice] has come down to me covered with honor. When I accepted it, my duty was not to make it a stepping-stone to something else, but to preserve its purity and make my own name as honorable, if possible, as that of my predecessors . . . Time and persevering patience, added to my habits of work, may give me honor where I am. The other field is altogether untried. If I should fail there, it would to a certain extent drag my office down with me. No man ought to accept this place unless he takes a vow to leave it as honorable as he found it.

So Waite remained on the Court, overseeing its affairs with diligence and competence, even though he brought no particular judicial brilliance to his post. "I can't make a great chief justice out of a small man," Justice Samuel Miller—who wished to be chief justice himself—once said of Waite.

Chief Justice Morrison Waite served 14 years on the Court before death plucked him out of his seat as suddenly as he had arrived on it. In March 1888 Waite contracted pneumonia. He attended Court in a weakened state because he feared that his wife—away on vacation—would read of his absence from Court and become unduly alarmed. But the pneumonia suddenly worsened, and Waite died on March 23, 1888, in Washington, D.C. The modest income he earned as chief justice and the expensive entertaining obligations thrust on him by his position left Waite nearly bankrupt at the time of his death. Friends had to create a fund to see that Waite's wife could live out her life comfortably.

—∞—

Morrison Waite was chief justice of the Supreme Court during turbulent times. He followed predecessors who had damaged the Court's reputation by the decision in *Dred Scott v. Sandford* (Roger B. Taney) and soiled it with political ambition (Salmon P. Chase). Waite's quiet devotion to acquitting the responsibilities of chief justice without an eye to political advancement served to partially restore the Court's institutional reputation. It is less clear whether the decisions reached by the Court under Waite's leadership contributed to restoring its reputation as an arbiter of the great questions of constitutional moment that came before it. His Court generally receives acceptable marks for its restraint in the battles that were waged between state regulation and commercial interests. But historians of the late 20th and early 21st centuries have less praise—and often outright criticism—of the judicial conservatism that Waite and a majority of his colleagues wielded, which dismantled the civil rights legislation crafted by the Reconstruction Congress to protect the rights of African Americans. Here, Waite's court consigned African Americans to a system of racial discrimination that would flourish until the second half of the 20th century.

Further Reading

Magrath, C. Peter. *Morrison K. Waite: The Triumph of Character.* New York: Macmillan, 1963.

Morris, Jeffrey Brandon. "Morrison Waite's Court." In *Supreme Court Historical Society Yearbook, 1980.* Washington, D.C.: Supreme Court Historical Society, 1980.

Stephenson, D. Grier, Jr. "The Chief Justice as Leader: The Case of Morrison Remick Waite." *William and Mary Law Review* 14 (1973): 899–927.

Trimble, Bruce Raymond. *Chief Justice Waite: Defender of the Public Interest.* 1938. Reprint. New York: Russell and Russell, 1970.

*J*OHN *M*ARSHALL *H*ARLAN (1833–1911)

Associate Justice, 1877–1911

Appointed by President Rutherford B. Hayes

JOHN MARSHALL HARLAN
(Engraving by Max Rosenthal, Library of Congress)

Chief Justice John Marshall, the Supreme Court's greatest captain, was two years from his death when a lawyer in rural Kentucky celebrated the birth of a son by naming him John Marshall Harlan. Seldom have a father's implicit hopes for a son been so thoroughly fulfilled as this father's were to be, as John Marshall Harlan would one day find a seat on the Court so brilliantly piloted by his namesake. And during his long career on the Court he would champion a nationalism worthy of the chief justice who had breathed life into the Constitution and made it a charter for a nation rather than simply a bargain among states.

John Marshall Harlan was born in Boyle County, Kentucky, on June 1, 1833, to James Harlan and Eliza Davenport Harlan. James Harlan had won distinction as a Whig politician, serving a term in Congress and several terms as attorney general of Kentucky. He named his two sons for the prophets of nationalism in the early 19th century: Henry Clay and John Marshall. John Marshall Harlan obtained his college education from Centre College in Danville, Kentucky, before studying law at Transylvania University (later the University of Kentucky), beginning in 1851. Two years later Harlan was admitted to practice law in Kentucky. After a few years as a lawyer, he married Melvina F. Shanklin from Evansville, Indiana; the couple had six children. (One of their sons, John Maynard Harlan, would become the father of the family's second Supreme Court justice, John Marshall Harlan II, who would serve on the Court from 1955 to 1971.)

For the next two decades, John Marshall Harlan pursued the life of a lawyer-statesman. He began as a Whig with a gift for delivering rousing stump speeches. In 1858 he was elected county court judge in Franklin County. When, a little less than 20 years later, Harlan was appointed to the U.S. Supreme Court, the year he spent as a county court judge was his only prior judicial experience.

In 1859 Harlan tried to leap from the local political stage to a national one by running for Congress, but he lost his election bid. With the outbreak of the Civil War in 1861, Harlan threw himself behind the Union cause. He fought politically to keep Kentucky from seceding and volunteered to bear arms for the Union, serving as colonel of the Tenth Kentucky Volunteer Infantry. But when his father died in 1863, Harlan returned home to take over the elder Harlan's legal practice and—as it happened—to try his hand again at politics. This time Harlan succeeded in winning election as attorney general of Kentucky, a position he held from 1863 to 1867.

By the late 1860s, Harlan had shifted his allegiance to the Republican party, but the party's strength in Kentucky was not sufficient for him to win the governorship when he ran for this post in 1871 and again in 1875. In spite of these defeats, however, Harlan had begun to gain some measure of national prominence. His conversion to the Republican fold also made him first acquainted with and later a law partner of Benjamin H. Bristow, who became secretary of the treasury during the administration of President Ulysses S. Grant.

Harlan's association with Benjamin Bristow proved to be the catalyst for his own advancement on the national scene. He led the Kentucky delegates to the 1876 Republican National Convention and worked hard on behalf of Bristow's bid for the presidential nomination. When Bristow's prospects to gain the nomination eventually dissipated, Harlan swung the Kentucky delegates to the support of Rutherford B. Hayes. After Hayes survived the contested presidential election that year and the special commission appointed to resolve the crisis it had produced, he did not forget Harlan's support—though neither did he immediately reward it lavishly. At first the president simply dispatched Harlan to serve on the 1877 Louisiana Commission charged with settling that state's own election crisis from the previous year. After this commission had completed its work, however, Harlan was poised to receive a far greater appointment. The resignation of Justice David Davis in March 1877 created a vacant seat on the Court that President Hayes—anxious to make peace with the South—wished to fill with a southerner. Harlan's abilities and his Republican loyalties—though doubted in the latter aspect by some of the more radical members of the party—sufficiently impressed Hayes that he nominated Harlan as an associate justice of the Supreme Court on October 16, 1877. The Senate confirmed Harlan's appointment the following month, and by the end of 1877 he had taken his seat on the Court.

John Marshall Harlan's tenure on the Supreme Court lasted almost 34 years. During that time he secured a prominent place in the Court's history, though he earned this place in spite of his failure to influence his colleagues on the bench in most of the key cases heard during his tenure. Surrounded by strong and able justices such as Samuel Miller, Joseph Bradley, and

Stephen Field, Harlan found himself unable to join these men in many of the important decisions of the day. So often did Harlan part ways in his thinking with the rest of the Court that he earned the title of the "Great Dissenter." Nevertheless, many of Justice Harlan's dissenting opinions ultimately became law in the 20th century, and subsequent observers of the Court have often seen Harlan as a kind of prophet in exile from his own time, proclaiming legal principles that would triumph only after his death.

John Marshall Harlan achieved a prominent place in the history of American constitutional law partially through his dissents in important civil rights cases decided in the second half of the 19th century. In the years after the Civil War, the Reconstruction Congress attempted to secure the civil rights and liberties of black Americans by proposing constitutional amendments and federal laws designed to achieve these aims. The Reconstruction Amendments were the most important expression of this effort. The Thirteenth Amendment abolished slavery, the Fourteenth guaranteed the equal protection and due process of law, and the Fifteenth prohibited voting discrimination along racial lines. These amendments authorized Congress to pass legislation implementing their various guarantees; and Congress did, in fact, pass a variety of laws intended to achieve their aims. But when these laws and other questions involving the interpretation of the Reconstruction Amendments arrived at the Supreme Court, most of the justices gave a cool welcome to the hopes of African Americans. Harlan, however, penned significant dissents in a series of civil rights cases.

Harlan's vigorous support of civil rights reflected a remarkable personal transformation. He had been born into a slaveholding family and had himself owned slaves until the ratification of the Thirteenth Amendment forced him to free them. Moreover, in the 1850s Harlan had joined the Know-Nothing Party and had cheered Kentucky audiences with rousing stump speeches full of racist and states' rights invective. The following decade found him no less friendly to the rights of blacks. He opposed Lincoln's Emancipation Proclamation and the president's reelection in 1864. After the war, Harlan similarly opposed ratification of the Reconstruction Amendments, which sought to guarantee civil rights for the newly freed slaves. But by the end of the 1870s, Harlan had moved sharply away from these earlier positions. Virtually alone on the Supreme Court, he championed vigorous interpretations of the Reconstruction Amendments that would have made them into a significant source of protection for civil rights.

The *Civil Rights Cases* (1883) reflected the dominant pattern of decisions handed down by the Court as it interpreted the Reconstruction Amendments. In 1875 Congress had passed the Civil Rights Act, which prohibited racial discrimination in public inns, transportation, and amusement facilities. An overwhelming majority of the Court held this law unconstitutional by finding that the Fourteenth Amendment, which guarantees equal protection of law, prohibits only racial discrimination involving "state action," that is, action by state officials or state representatives. The Court concluded that since the amendment only prohibited governmental acts of discrimination rather than private discrimination, Congress had no power under the amendment to ban private discrimination. Harlan penned a lone dissent from this ruling, finding the majority's distinction between official and private acts of discrimination "narrow and artificial." In his mind, the Thirteenth Amendment, which abolished slavery, was ample authorization for Congress to pass laws prohibiting the "badges of slavery," including even so-called private acts of discrimination. The holding in the *Civil Rights Cases* essentially stripped the federal government of any power to combat racial discrimination. It would be nearly a century before Congress moved again in a comprehensive fashion to attack racial discrimination through its passage of the Civil Rights Act of 1964.

Harlan dissented even more famously from the decision in *Plessy v. Ferguson* (1896), which upheld a Louisiana law that required railroads to provide "equal but separate accommodations for the white and colored races" and required passengers to adhere to this racially segregated scheme. Writing for a majority of the Court, Justice Henry Billings Brown concluded that the Fourteenth Amendment's equal protection clause did not prevent states from enforcing rules of segregation, since this did not imply any inferiority between the races. Harlan, again alone in his opinion, disagreed. The Constitution, he argued, prohibited racial discrimination, including the "separate but equal" variety embodied most famously in Jim Crow laws that enforced racial segregation. Under the Constitution,

> There is in this country no superior, dominant, ruling class of citizens. There is no caste here. Our Constitution is color-blind, and neither knows nor tolerates classes among citizens. In respect of civil rights, all citizens are equal before the law. The humblest is the peer of the most powerful. . . . The destinies of the two races, in this country, are indissolubly linked together, and the interests of both require that the common government of all shall not permit the seeds of race hate to be planted under the sanction of law. . . .

More than half a century would pass before a new majority on the Supreme Court finally pronounced Harlan's view correct and abolished public school segregation in *Brown v. Board of Education* (1954).

In another area of constitutional law, Harlan also dissented from positions taken by the majority of the Court that would ultimately be discarded in the 20th century in favor of Harlan's views. The issue had to do with the effect of the Fourteenth Amendment's due process clause on various rights protected by the Bill of Rights. Prior to the Civil War, the Supreme Court had ruled in *Barron v. Baltimore* (1833) that the protections offered by the provisions of the Bill of Rights, such as the freedom of speech guaranteed by the First Amendment and the freedom from unreasonable searches and seizures guaranteed by the Fourth, applied only to federal action. The Bill of Rights, according to the Court, did not restrain states from depriving citizens of freedom of speech, for example. With the ratification of the Fourteenth Amendment, however, it became possible to argue that the protection of life, liberty, and property from state deprivation without "due process of law" changed this. The due process clause, some argued, *incorporated* the various provisions of the Bill of Rights and made them applicable to states as well as to the federal government. Justice Harlan was an early proponent of this view. Thus, for example, in *Twining v. New Jersey* (1908) the Court considered whether the Fifth Amendment's privilege against self-incrimination applied to state criminal proceedings. Eight members of the Court concluded that it did not. Harlan, in lone dissent, argued to the contrary. In his view, the Fourteenth Amendment had nationalized the Bill of Rights and made them a bulwark against governmental action at every level. Though the Court has never adopted the view that *all* the provisions of the Bill of Rights are equally applicable to federal and state governments, it has generally vindicated Harlan's view by finding that most of the liberties protected in the Constitution's first 10 amendments do indeed apply with equal force to all levels of government.

John Marshall Harlan died suddenly of pneumonia on October 14, 1911. At the time of his death, he was generally thought of as a superior judge. But the passage of time quickly dimmed his prestige. Harlan was a devout Presbyterian who taught Sunday school most of his life. It was not hard for others to see in his steadfast constitutional principles a kind of religious faith. Justice David J. Brewer, who served with Harlan on the Court from 1890 to 1910, observed that Harlan "retires at eight with one hand on the Constitution and the other on the Bible, safe and happy in a perfect faith in justice and righteousness." Brewer's judgment reflected a common perception that Harlan tended to follow his heart rather than his head. In more recent years, however, his reputation has swelled again, as positions he championed have eventually gained acceptance by new majorities on the Court.

Further Reading

Baker, Liva. "John Marshall Harlan I and a Color Blind Constitution: The Frankfurter-Harlan II Conversations." *Journal of Supreme Court History* (1992): 27–37.

Beth, Loren P. "Justice Harlan and the Uses of Dissent," *American Political Science Review* 49 (Dec. 1955): 1085–1104.

———. *John Marshall Harlan: The Last Whig Justice.* Lexington: University Press of Kentucky, 1992.

Clark, Floyd B. *The Constitutional Doctrines of Justice Harlan.* Baltimore: The Johns Hopkins Press, 1915.

Przybyszewski, Linda. *The Republic According to John Marshall Harlan.* Chapel Hill: University of North Carolina Press, 1999.

Yarbrough, Tinsley E. *Judicial Enigma: The First Justice Harlan.* New York: Oxford University Press, 1995.

William Burnham Woods (1824–1887)

Associate Justice, 1881–1887

Appointed by President Rutherford B. Hayes

William Burnham Woods
(United States Supreme Court)

The Supreme Court of the United States has the capacity to absorb talented and successful jurists onto the bench and make them seem insignificant in comparison to the Court's greater lights. Not even diligent labor will invariably rescue a justice from the disinterest of history. This, at least, is the fate that befell William Woods and a good many other justices like him. Before his ascension to the Court he had been a highly regarded officer in the Union army and later a respected judge on the U.S. Fifth Circuit Court of Appeals. But the talents that had made him stand out in these lesser positions were too little to make him luminous on the Supreme Court. He arrived with little fanfare and died suddenly six years later, without having left a significant mark on the Court's history.

William Burnham Woods was born in Newark, Ohio, on August 3, 1824. His father, Ezekiel Woods, was a farmer-merchant married to Sarah Burnham Woods, from New England. Woods attended three years of college at Western Reserve College before transferring to Yale and graduating valedictorian of his class in 1845. Thereafter, he returned to Newark and studied law with S. D. King, eventually being admitted to the Ohio bar in 1847 and becoming King's partner. Toward the middle of the following decade he married and won his first political position. His union with Anne E. Warner in 1855 eventually produced two children, a boy and a girl. In 1856 he won the election for mayor of Newark. The following year his political experience moved to the state level when he was elected on the Democratic ticket to serve as a representative in the Ohio legislature. Almost immediately, he won the post of Speaker of the House and held it until elections in 1860 put the Republicans in the majority, upon which he became the minority leader.

William Woods did not welcome the onset of the Civil War, but he soon devoted himself to the Union cause, following his younger brother, Charles R. Woods, who would become a well-regarded field general in the Union army, into military service. He entered the war as a lieutenant colonel, serving with the 76th Ohio Volunteer Regiment in 1862, and saw significant action at Shiloh, Vicksburg, and on General William Sherman's long march through Georgia. He impressed virtually everyone with whom he served, earning the favorable regard of Generals Sherman and Ulysses S. Grant. By the end of the war he had been promoted to the rank of breveted major general.

After the war Woods was posted to Alabama, and when he left military service he chose to remain there. His brother-in-law had already achieved prominence as U.S. senator from Alabama and Woods decided to settle in Bentonville, where he planted cotton and practiced law. Now a Republican, Woods was elected to the Middle Chancery Court in 1868 and served two years before President Grant appointed him a judge on the U.S. Fifth Circuit Court of Appeals in 1869. Woods spent a little more than a decade traveling across the states covered by the Fifth Circuit, mastering the laws of these states, including the intricacies of Louisiana civil law, and generally earning the respect of southerners who found him to be a fair and hardworking judge. He eventually moved to Atlanta, Georgia, in 1877 and won a similar reputation there. The chief justice of the Georgia Supreme Court commented of Woods: "We are proud of him because he is identified with us, and while serving as a Judge in our midst has known nothing but the law, and been loyal to nothing but the law."

Federal courts of the time, including the Supreme Court itself, found their dockets crowded with mostly mundane legal matters. Occasionally, though, an issue of constitutional magnitude presented itself for decision. As a circuit judge, the most important cases to come before Woods were the cluster of cases that eventually became well known as the *Slaughterhouse Cases.* Supreme Court justices of the time handled not only the cases before the Court, but also served as circuit judges in the federal circuit courts of appeal. Associate Justice Joseph P. Bradley served for a time as a judge on the Fifth Circuit, and in this capacity he and William Woods presided over the *Slaughterhouse Cases.* The three suits underlying what would become the *Slaughterhouse Cases* involved a Louisiana law that had granted a monopoly in the slaughterhouse business in and around New Orleans to a favored enterprise. The competitors, represented ably by former Supreme Court justice John Archibald Campbell, challenged the legislative monopoly and wielded the newly ratified Fourteenth Amendment as their chief weapon against the monopoly. They argued that the government-backed monopoly deprived them of the "privileges and immunities" to which they were entitled as United States citizens, as well as due process and equal protection of law. Justice Bradley and Judge Woods agreed that the monopoly violated the Fourteenth Amendment, giving the text of the Constitution an expansive reading that would shortly be repudiated by the U.S. Supreme Court when deciding the *Slaughterhouse Cases* (1873).

Upon the resignation of Justice William Strong from the Supreme Court in 1880, President Rutherford B. Hayes was eager to find a southerner to replace him. He shortly found himself inundated with expressions of support for William Woods as a replacement. Former justice John Archibald Campbell and General William Sherman were among the prominent voices raised in support of Woods's candidacy for the Supreme Court. Inevitably, there were scattered suggestions that Woods was not a true southerner but rather a carpetbagger. Nevertheless, Hayes found Woods's experience as a Fifth Circuit judge and his service to the Union as a military officer ample reason to forward his nomination to the Senate on December 15, 1880, the day after Strong's resignation. The Senate confirmed the appointment before the close of the year.

Two factors combined to make Justice William B. Woods's tenure on the Supreme Court less than noteworthy. First, though a hard worker, he simply lacked the intellectual brilliance to influence a Court already crowded with more able jurists—men such as Samuel Miller, Joseph Bradley, Stephen Field, and John Marshall Harlan. Second, sudden illness and death removed him from the Court after he had served as a justice for only six years. Thus, while his colleagues respected his toil over the host of mundane legal problems that required the Court's attention, Woods failed to distinguish himself on the more difficult constitutional issues that came before the justices during this period. He was a man who seldom ventured far from the direction taken by the majority and seldom led that majority to its decision. He worked hard, writing more than his share of opinions, and only rarely dissented.

Two cases highlighted Woods's Supreme Court career. In *United States v. Harris* (1883), Woods penned the majority's decision declaring the Ku Klux Klan Act of 1871 unconstitutional. The act, adopted by Congress to protect the civil rights of African Americans from terrorist organizations such as the Klan, made it a crime for two or more people to conspire or use disguises to deprive another person of the equal privileges and immunities of the laws. The law was defended as an appropriate means of enforcing the protections provided by the Constitution's Reconstruction Amendments, particularly the Fourteenth Amendment, which prevents states from depriving persons of equal protection or due process of law. For the majority, however, Woods's opinion concluded that the Fourteenth Amendment prohibited only official acts of racial discrimination and not private conduct that might deprive a person of life, liberty, or property. If the Klan's campaign of violence against blacks was to be ended, then states—rather than the federal government—would have to end it; Congress had no power to intrude on the province of states in enforcing the law.

In *Presser v. Illinois* (1886), Woods again wrote for a majority of the Court in a case involving the Second Amendment's right to bear arms. An Illinois statute made it a crime to parade with arms except in an official state militia. When a citizen was prosecuted for leading an armed fraternal organization in a parade, he argued that the Illinois law violated the Second Amendment. Woods, writing for a unanimous Court, rejected this claim. The Second Amendment, he reasoned, prohibited only federal attempts to restrict the ability of citizens to bear arms. Since the *Presser* case involved a state gun control law, the Second Amendment had no application.

Woods's tenure on the Court proved to be quite brief. He became ill in the spring of 1886 and died in Washington, D.C., a year later, on May 14, 1887. Obituaries were modestly favorable, but they tended to focus less on Woods's career as a justice than on the question of who would replace him. As it turned out, one of Woods's key supporters for the appointment to the Court, L. Q. C. Lamar of Mississippi, was nominated to replace Woods.

—⁓—

The history of the Supreme Court has more than its share of brilliant justices; and those who occupy the second rank, no matter how diligent and competent their service, tend to be relegated to historical footnotes. William B. Woods was such a justice. It is hard to imagine him as a dominant force on any Supreme Court, least of all the one on which he actually served. More a follower than a leader, more an echo of the reverberating ideas of others than an original thinker in his own right, his brief years on the Court climaxed a life too far removed from the center of events to warrant more than passing historical mention.

FURTHER READING

Baynes, Thomas E. "A Search for Justice Woods: Yankee from Georgia." *Supreme Court Historical Society Yearbook, 1978*. Washington, D.C.: Supreme Court Historical Society, 1978.

Filler, Louis. "William B. Woods." In *The Justices of the United States Supreme Court 1789–1969: Their Lives and Major Opinions,* Vol. 2. Edited by Leon Friedman and Fred L. Israel. New York: R. R. Bowker Co., 1969.

STANLEY MATTHEWS (1824–1889)

Associate Justice, 1881–1889

Appointed by President James Garfield

STANLEY MATTHEWS
(United States Supreme Court)

Stanley Matthews secured more attention by the circumstances of his joining the Supreme Court than by anything he did after he became a justice. He brought to the nomination process a career's worth of opponents and came within a single vote of failing to receive confirmation as a justice by the U.S. Senate. Although the friendship of one president and the acquiescence of another secured for Matthews a place on the nation's highest court, they could not secure for him a prominent place in the Court's history.

Justice Matthews was born Thomas Stanley Matthews on July 21, 1824, in Cincinnati, Ohio. He eventually stopped using his first name and was known from adulthood on as Stanley Matthews. He grew up with his parents, Thomas

Johnson Matthews and Isabella Brown Matthews, in Lexington, Kentucky, and in Cincinnati. Matthews's father was a talented educator who taught mathematics in Cincinnati, then obtained the position of professor of Mathematics and Natural Philosophy at Transylvania University (later the University of Kentucky). In 1832 he returned with his family to Cincinnati, where he became president of Woodward High School.

After attending school in Cincinnati, Stanley Matthews enrolled in Kenyon College in Ohio in 1839. There he met a classmate—Rutherford B. Hayes—who would one day gain the presidency of the United States and deeply influence the course of Matthews's life. After Matthews graduated from Kenyon College, he returned to Cincinnati to study law and then set out for Tennessee, where—unlike Ohio, which required attorneys admitted to the bar to be at least 21 years of age—the 18-year-old Matthews could begin the practice of law. In Columbia, Tennessee, Matthews combined a legal career with the work of editing the *Tennessee Democrat.* He also found time to marry Mary Ann Black, known to her friends and family as Minnie. The couple had 10 children together. In the mid-1840s Matthews returned to Cincinnati and gained admission to the bar there, practicing law and soon becoming the editor of the *Cincinnati Herald.* By the end of the decade he had been appointed clerk of the Ohio House of Representatives.

In 1851 Matthews was elected to the Hamilton County Court of Common Pleas, serving for two years before the position's inadequate salary forced him back to the practice of law. But political ambition lured him again in 1855 when he won election to the Ohio state senate and served there three years. The decade would end with tragedy for Matthews and Minnie, however, when an epidemic of scarlet fever claimed the lives of four of their six children. Four more children would be added to the family over the coming years, but the loss redirected the course of their lives. Before the deaths of their children, Matthews and his wife had gravitated to theological free thinking, traveling with what Rutherford B. Hayes described as a "circle of fast men" in religious affairs. Tragedy rerouted their religious affections toward a devout, and conservative, Presbyterian faith.

In 1858 President James Buchanan appointed Matthews U.S. Attorney for the Southern District of Ohio. The post, which Matthews held until Abraham Lincoln was elected president in 1860, thrust on him the first of many public controversies. As U.S. attorney, Matthews prosecuted W. B. Connelly, a highly regarded Cincinnati reporter, for aiding the escape of two slaves in violation of the Fugitive Slave Act. Though no friend of slavery himself, Matthews secured Connelly's conviction.

With the outbreak of the Civil War, Stanley Matthews decided with his friend and fellow Cincinnati lawyer Rutherford B. Hayes to enlist in the 23rd Ohio Infantry. Matthews entered military service as a lieutenant-colonel and was later promoted to the rank of colonel in the 51st Ohio Volunteers. He resigned from military service in 1863, though, and successfully ran as a Republican for the Cincinnati Superior Court. After two years as a judge, he returned again to the private practice of law in 1865. The following years saw him develop a successful reputation as a railroad lawyer. In 1869 he courted controversy again when he represented the Cincinnati Board of Education in a volatile case that seemed to many observers inconsistent with his Presbyterian faith. The Board of Education passed a resolution, challenged in court, providing that "religious instruction, and the reading of religious books, including the Holy Bible, are prohibited in the common schools of Cincinnati, it being the true object and intent of this rule to allow the children of all sects and opinions, in matters of faith and worship, to enjoy alike the benefit of the Common School Fund." Losing initially, Matthews pursued the case to the Ohio Supreme Court, where he vindicated the board's position in *Board of Education of Cincinnati v. Minor* (1873).

In 1876 Matthews's longtime friend Rutherford B. Hayes was locked in what would become one of the most controversial election campaigns in presidential history. Matthews himself ran unsuccessfully for Congress during the same election season but soon became deeply embroiled in his most significant political controversy yet. The presidential election contest between the Republican Hayes and Democratic candidate Samuel J. Tilden erupted into crisis when Tilden received a majority of the popular vote, but contested electoral votes from four states cast the election into the House of Representatives for determination. Congress appointed a special commission, including five Supreme Court justices, to resolve the issue, and Hayes turned to his friend Matthews to represent his claim to the presidency before the commission. Matthews mounted an able case, and with a Republican majority on a commission that ultimately voted strictly on party lines, Hayes was declared the victor. Matthews continued to assist Hayes after this by helping to negotiate the Compromise of 1877, which assured that Hayes would be declared president by the House of Representatives in exchange for his commitment to withdraw federal troops from the South and end Reconstruction.

Stanley Matthews's initial prize for his service to Hayes and the Republican party was to be named U.S. senator from Ohio in the spring of 1877 to complete the term of John Sherman, who had joined Hayes's administration as secretary of the treasury. A more generous compensation lay before him, though. As Hayes's presidency drew to a close in the early part of 1881, he named Stanley Matthews to fill the vacancy on the Supreme Court created by Associate Justice Noah Swayne's resignation. Matthews, however, had found himself in too many political hot spots to hope for an easy confirmation. In fact, the Senate Judiciary Committee refused to act on his nomination until after Hayes had retired from office. Thereafter, though Hayes had secured a commitment from President James A. Garfield to resubmit Matthew's appointment, even the blessing of a second president did not assure Matthews of the post. The Senate did finally confirm him, in spite of a 7-1 vote to the contrary in the Judiciary Committee, but the final tally was close: 24-23 in favor of confirmation.

Justice Stanley Matthews proved to be an able though unspectacular justice, and the relative brevity of his tenure on the Court—eight years in all—deprived him of any opportunity to influence the course of the Court's decisions over an extended period. Three cases he authored during his years on the Court stand out, however. In *Poindexter v. Greenhow* (1885), Matthews spoke for the Court in concluding that the Eleventh Amendment, which bars suits against a state, does not prevent aggrieved persons from suing state officials who followed a state's illegal policy of refusing to pay its just debts. In *Yick Wo v. Hopkins* (1886), Matthews wrote the opinion for the Court holding that the Fourteenth Amendment's equal protection clause prohibited not only laws that discriminated on the basis of race but also the racially discriminatory administration of laws. "Though the law itself be fair on its face and impartial in appearance," he said for the Court, "yet, if it is applied and administered by public authority with an evil eye and an unequal hand, so as practically to make unjust and illegal discrimination between persons in similar circumstances, material to their rights, denial of equal justice is still within the prohibition of the Constitution." Finally, in *Hurtado v. California* (1884), Matthews's opinion for the Court held that the Fourteenth Amendment's due process clause did not mandate that state criminal proceedings be initiated by a grand jury indictment rather than, as California law provided, by information filed with a magistrate by a prosecuting attorney.

Justice Matthews's wife Minnie died in 1885, and he remarried two years later to Mary Theaker. This marriage, though, did not endure long. Matthews was caught in New York City in the great blizzard of 1888, and the illness he contracted from this experience led to his death the following spring. He died in Washington, D.C., on March 22, 1889.

—∾—

The man who gained a seat on the Supreme Court by a single vote would thereafter be remembered more for his nomination's close finish than for the substance of his work on the Court. This is not to say that some of his opinions do not have an enduring place within American constitutional law. Matthews's opinion in *Yick Wo v. Hopkins,* especially, was one of the few victories for civil rights during the later half of the 19th century, and its holding remains an important bulwark against covert forms of racial discrimination. But in the long sweep of the Court's history, Matthews remains one of its lesser figures.

Further Reading

Filler, Louis. "Stanley Matthews." In *The Justices of the United States Supreme Court 1789–1969: Their Lives and Major Opinions,* Vol. 2. Edited by Leon Friedman and Fred L. Israel. New York: R. R. Bowker Co., 1969.

Greve, Charles Theodore. "Stanley Matthews." In *Great American Lawyers,* Vol. 2. Edited by William Draper Lewis. Philadelphia: J. C. Winston Co., 1907–1909.

Helfman, Harold M. "The Contested Confirmation of Stanley Matthews to the United States Supreme Court." *Historical and Philosophical Society of Ohio* 8 (1958): 154–170.

Stevens, Richard G. "Due Process of Law: Stanley Matthews." In *Sober as a Judge: The Supreme Court and Republican Liberty.* Edited by Richard G. Stevens and Matthew J. Franck. Lanham, Md.: Lexington Books, 1999.

Horace Gray (1828–1902)

Associate Justice, 1882–1902

Appointed by President Chester A. Arthur

Horace Gray
(United States Supreme Court)

Horace Gray turned early to a judicial career and eventually spent nearly half a century close to or on the bench. Though he was born to wealth and influence, a sudden reversal in his family's fortunes forced him to make a living and directed him down the path of the law. It was a path that he proved abundantly gifted to follow. Gray brought to judicial work a sharp mind and an enthusiasm for legal research that made him an able judge, first on the Massachusetts Supreme Court and later as an associate justice of the U.S. Supreme Court.

Horace Gray was born on March 24, 1828, in Boston, Massachusetts, to Horace Gray, Sr., and Harriet Upham Gray. His grandfather had built a family fortune as a merchant and shipbuilder and had served two terms as lieutenant governor of Massachusetts. His uncle Francis Calley Gray was a legal historian famous for having discovered the original copy of Massachusetts's earliest legal code, "The Laws and Liberties of the Massachusetts Colony in New England," adopted in 1641. Gray's half brother John Chipman Gray, born of his father's remarriage after Gray's mother died, became a famous professor at Harvard Law School.

Educated at first in private schools, Horace Gray enrolled in Harvard at the age of 13, though his 6'6" frame assured that he would not look like a typical 13-year-old student. He gravitated to the study of natural history and graduated in 1845. After his graduation, Gray enjoyed the benefits of wealth in the form of a leisurely tour of Europe. While traveling, however, he received word that his family's fortune had collapsed as a result of improvident business dealings. Gray returned home and enrolled in Harvard Law School in 1848. He graduated the following year and continued to study law thereafter with John Lowell and as clerk with the firm of Sohier and Welsh, gaining admittance to the bar in 1851.

Shortly after Horace Gray began the practice of law, a fortuitous opportunity presented itself to him: He was asked to assist Luther S. Cushing, the official reporter of decisions for the Massachusetts Supreme Court, who had become ill. When Cushing himself died in 1854, Gray assumed the position of reporter at the age of 26. For the next 10 years Gray combined an active legal practice with his responsibilities as reporter for the court. This work had a crucial influence on Gray's legal thinking, making him forever afterward embued with a great respect for legal precedents and confident that answers to legal questions might invariably be located by close attention to precedent. During this time he argued as an attorney before the Massachusetts Supreme Court more than 30 times. To this full professional life Gray also added scholarly work concerning slavery. He published a history, entitled *Slavery in Massachusetts,* as well as a collaboration with another author on the famous *Dred Scott* case.

The office of reporter for the state Supreme Court had sometimes been a springboard for the men who held it to a seat on the court itself. This was the case with Horace Gray. In 1864, when Gray was only 36 years old, Governor John A. Andrew appointed him to the Massachusetts Supreme Court. Gray thus became the youngest man in the state's history to sit on one of the nation's most prestigious state courts. In 1873 he ascended to the court's chief seat and served as chief justice for the next nine years. As a state court judge, Gray presented a formidable demeanor—formal and aloof, a figure of austerity and cool reason. He also worked hard; opinions spilled from his pen in torrents over the years. Of these, only one opinion was a dissent. Gray believed that dissents weakened the institutional prestige of his state's highest court, and on most occasions he either persuaded fellow justices to his view of a case or else kept his opposing view silent. His opinions, moreover, were sturdy enough to stand the test of time: Not one decision he authored while on the Massachusetts Supreme Court was overruled during his lifetime. Gray's reputation as an outstanding state court jurist was sufficient to attract the services of a younger generation of legal talent. In 1879, for example, Gray hired a young Harvard Law School graduate as his legal clerk. The clerk, Louis D. Brandeis, worked for Gray from 1879 through 1881, before setting out on a distinguished legal career that would culminate in his becoming one of the 20th century's greatest Supreme Court justices. Horace Gray, Brandeis's early mentor, continued the practice of hiring recent law school graduates as temporary clerks once he was appointed himself to the Supreme Court. Other justices on the Court—as well as judges across the nation—eventually emulated Gray's practice. Today most appellate judges hire outstanding recent law school graduates for one or more years to assist them in legal research and opinion writing.

In summer 1881 Associate Justice Nathan Clifford of the U.S. Supreme Court died after suffering the prolonged disabling effects of a stroke that had felled him the previous year. Clifford's departure left a vacancy for which Horace Gray was immediately considered to be a strong contender. President James A. Garfield, in fact, solicited the assistance of Senator George Hoar, an old Harvard classmate of Gray's, to have Gray send the president copies of his opinions. Gray, however, thought that to do so might appear to be an unseemly attempt to capture the Supreme Court nomination by political machination; he therefore refused the president's request. Whether this rebuff might have influenced Garfield's choice of an appointee to the Supreme Court is moot, because his assassination soon thereafter placed the issue into the hands of President Chester A. Arthur. In the face of continued support in the Senate for Gray's appointment, led by Senator Hoar, Arthur nominated Gray to the Supreme Court on December 19, 1881, and the Senate confirmed the appointment on the following day.

Justice Horace Gray's 20-year tenure on the Supreme Court is difficult to summarize briefly, though historians of the Court tend to characterize him as a "nationalist." He frequently interpreted the Constitution in ways that gave substantial power to Congress. For example, in *Galleried v. Greenman* (1884), his opinion for the Court reiterated Congress's power to issue paper currency, even during peacetime. Civil libertarians probably remember Gray best for his opinion in *United States v. Wong Kim Ark* (1898). The case arose during the anti-Chinese exclusion fever of the late 19th century. Congress had barred persons of Chinese descent from becoming U.S. citizens in 1882, but an issue remained as to whether persons of Chinese descent actually born in the United States could be denied U.S. citizenship. Those who favored this denial argued that citizenship should be based on the nationality of one's parents rather than on the place of one's birth. When Wong Kim Ark, a man born of Chinese parents in San Francisco, briefly left the country for a visit to China and then attempted to return to the United States, he was barred from reentry on the grounds that he was not a U.S. citizen. When Wong Kim Ark's case eventually landed before the Supreme Court, Gray—for a majority of the Court—concluded to the contrary. The Fourteenth Amendment declares that "all persons born or naturalized in the United States, and subject to the jurisdiction thereof, are citizens of the United States." This language, Gray reasoned, settled the issue. Persons born in the United States were U.S. citizens notwithstanding the nationality of their parents.

Justice Gray remained a bachelor for most of his life, but his close friendship with another justice, Stanley Matthews, brought him into close contact with Matthews's daughter Jane. Justice Matthews died in the spring of 1889, but the relationship between Gray and Jane Matthews continued. They married a few months after her father's death: Gray, a 61-year-old man come to marriage in the twilight of his life, his bride, a woman 30 years younger than he. Their marriage lasted a little more than a decade, until Gray's own death.

By the mid-1890s, illness had begun to limit Justice Gray's work on the Court. He still brought a famed meticulousness to his labors, but ill health subtracted from the quantity of his work. He suffered a stroke in February 1902 and notified President Theodore Roosevelt in the summer of that year of his intention to resign once the president had decided on someone to replace him. Gray died, however, on September 15, 1902, before the president could appoint a successor. As it happened, Roosevelt nominated Oliver Wendell Holmes, Jr., to fill the seat vacated by Gray. Holmes was a Massachusetts judge who had succeeded Gray on the Massachusetts Supreme Court and who would, after Gray's death, become one of the most famous justices in the history of the Supreme Court.

History would remember Horace Gray as a distinguished member of the Court, even if not one who had managed to find a place among its greatest luminaries. He championed the authority of precedent, believing that the answers to cases of the present lay in the accumulated decisions of the past. This backward-looking judicial perspective may have been the decisive factor in denying Gray a place among the Court's most influential members, for whom the work of judging often represented acts of judicial creation and not just a sterile addition of one precedent to another.

Further Reading

Filler, Louis. "Horace Gray." In *The Justices of the United States Supreme Court 1789–1969: Their Lives and Major Opinions,* vol. 2. Edited by Leon Friedman and Fred L. Israel. New York: R. R. Bowker Co., 1969.

Hoar, George F. "Memoir of Horace Gray." *Massachusetts Historical Society Proceedings* 18 (1904): 155–187.

Spector, Robert M. "Legal Historian on the United States Supreme Court: Justice Horace Gray, Jr., and the Historical Method." *American Journal of Legal History* 12 (1968): 181–210.

Williston, Samuel. "Horace Gray." In *Great American Lawyers,* vol. 8. Edited by William D. Lewis. Philadelphia: J. C. Winston Company, 1907–1909.

SAMUEL BLATCHFORD (1820–1893)

Associate Justice, 1882–1893

Appointed by President Chester A. Arthur

SAMUEL BLATCHFORD
(United States Supreme Court)

Known during his time on the Supreme Court as one of its hardest workers, Samuel Blatchford labored in relative obscurity on the Court until his last years as a justice. In the end he was caught up in one of the great debates of the age and cast into the center of public attention. Struggling to find some middle way between the extremes of the day, Blatchford instead seemed to embrace inconsistent positions that satisfied no one. In spite of this controversy, however, Blatchford's most important work for the Court lay in the patient toil he devoted to admiralty and patent cases, cases that—though they received scant attention compared to the greater issues of constitutional law—were nevertheless an important and significant part of the Court's work at the end of the 19th century.

Samuel Blatchford was born on March 9, 1820, in New York City, the son of Richard Milford Blatchford—a New York lawyer and Whig politician—and Julia Ann Mumford Blatchford. After preparatory education, he entered Columbia College at the age of 13 and graduated at the top of his class in 1837. Thereafter he studied law for a year in his father's office and then accepted a position as private secretary of New York governor William H. Seward, a close friend of Samuel's father. Following two years of work for Seward, Samuel Blatchford was admitted to the bar in 1842 and began practice with his father. Two years later he married Caroline Appleton.

The following decade witnessed Samuel Blatchford's precocious rise among the ranks of New York lawyers. For a time, he was a law partner with William Seward in Auburn, New York, during one of the latter's temporary sabbaticals from public life. By 1854 Blatchford had returned to New York City, where he established the law firm of Blatchford, Seward, and Griswold—the Seward in this partnership being the nephew and adopted son of former governor William Seward. So prosperous was Blatchford's steadily expanding practice, focused especially on admiralty and international matters, that he turned down a seat on the New York Supreme Court when it was offered to him in 1855.

The 1850s also saw Blatchford begin the work of reporting decisions in federal cases, a work that would occupy him for many years to come and would greatly assist the legal profession. He initially reported the federal circuit court opinions decided in the second circuit by Associate Justice Samuel Nelson. Blatchford eventually published 24 volumes of second circuit opinions, continuing his reporting work even after he became a judge, and also added to these volumes a 1855 collection of admiralty decisions, *Blatchford's and Howland's Reports,* and a collection of decisions in prize cases published as *Blatchford's Prize Cases.*

Blatchford's own career as a jurist began with his appointment as a federal judge for the southern district of New York in the spring of 1867. After five years his ability and impressive work habits—as well as his political connections—were acknowledged by his appointment to the Second Circuit in 1872. Here, in 10 years of judicial service, he developed substantial expertise in admiralty and patent issues and demonstrated indefatigable energy in his handling of the court's business. When fellow New Yorker Ward Hunt resigned from the U.S. Supreme Court in 1882, Blatchford seemed to be in an excellent position to be appointed in Hunt's place. He was, after all, a New Yorker, and Hunt was the latest holder of what was commonly referred to as the Court's "New York seat." Blatchford was, moreover, an experienced federal judge of proven ability and moderate politics. But President Chester A. Arthur turned first to New York politician Roscoe Conkling for the appointment. After being confirmed by the Senate, though, Conkling—who had higher political aspirations—declined the appointment. Next, Arthur nominated George F. Edmunds of Vermont, but he declined as well. Finally, the president nominated Blatchford, and the Senate promptly confirmed this appointment on March 27, 1882. Associate Justice Samuel Blatchford took his seat on the Court in the first week of April 1882.

The work of the Supreme Court intrudes on the consciousness of the public most often in cases involving significant constitutional controversies. But in the closing decades of the 19th century, the great majority of cases before the Court did not present these sorts of issues but rather, more commonly, issues relating to commerce or admiralty or patents. News reporters took little interest in these cases, and they passed through the corridors of the Supreme Court without causing so much as ripple in the public consciousness. But such cases required a substantial amount of the Court's collective energy, and Justice Blatchford immediately proved himself invaluable in their resolution. He brought to the Court both an impressive measure of expertise in the areas of admiralty and patent law and a willingness to cast himself fully into the labor of resolving these and other cases. He wrote 435 of the 3,237 signed opinions delivered by the Court during his years as an associate justice, well more than his proportionate share. Nor was Blatchford's industry the mere short-lived enthusiasm of a novice on the Court. Chief Justice Melville Fuller, who joined the Court in 1888, eight years after Blatchford, would later observe of his New York colleague that "the discharge of duty was an impulse, and toil a habit."

Blatchford might have served out his tenure on the Court in relative obscurity, tending to the substantial docket of commonplace issues far from the limelight of constitutional controversy. But in the latter years of his service on the Court, he was assigned to write an opinion for the Court that would thrust him into the harsh glare of public attention. The case was *Chicago, Milwaukee & St. Paul Railway Co. v. Minnesota* (1890), and it proved to be the harbinger of a fundamental development in constitutional law. At issue in the case was a state law that created a commission to establish rates for railroad transportation. This kind of legislation—called a Granger law—represented a common victory for small farmers and businesses over their Goliath-like economic antagonists: the railroads and the operators of grain elevators. Granger laws typically established maximum rates for railway shipping or grain elevator storage, or—as in the *Chicago, Milwaukee* case—set up a commission to establish such rates. The railroads and associated interests retaliated by challenging the Granger laws on constitutional grounds, arguing that these laws deprived them of their property without due process of law, in violation of the Fourteenth Amendment. "Unreasonable" restrictions on one's property, the railroads argued, violated the due process clause, and the reasonableness of commercial regulations was, they urged, an issue properly determined by the courts.

This "substantive due process" claim, as it came to be called, had met with little success when presented to the Court in the years immediately after the ratification of the Fourteenth Amendment. Associate Justice Stephen Field famously championed the idea of substantive due process, but he was largely alone at first. In *Munn v. Illinois* (1877), for example, the Court's majority explicitly rejected a due process challenge to maximum grain elevator rates and held that the "reasonableness" of such rates was a matter for legislatures rather than courts to decide. Justices Stephen Field and William Strong dissented from this holding, but their views were clearly in a minority at the time.

Thirteen years later, though, in *Chicago, Milwaukee* a new majority asserted itself, and Samuel Blatchford, one of the Court's lesser-known members, wrote the opinion for the Court. This time the Court's majority held that the state law establishing the rate commission and leaving no route to challenge the commission's decisions in court violated the Fourteenth Amendment's due process clause. Blatchford's opinion for the Court, though hailed among commercial interests, nevertheless exposed him to blistering criticism from many legal observers, especially progressive ones. When, less than two years later, Blatchford again announced the Court's decision in *Budd v. New York* (1892), conservatives launched their own tirades against Blatchford. In *Budd,* Blatchford reiterated the Court's commitment to the principle of *Munn v. Illinois* and refused to review the reasonableness of a New York law that regulated the rates charged by grain elevators. The apparent inconsistency of Blatchford's opinions in *Chicago, Milwaukee* on the one hand and *Budd* on the other endeared him to neither conservative nor progressive observers; and legal scholars were far from complimentary about Blatchford's legal reasoning. But the controversy concerning both *Chicago, Milwaukee* and *Budd* occurred in the twilight of Blatchford's years on the Court. He died after a brief illness on July 7, 1893, in Newport, Rhode Island, at the age of 73.

A memorial service in Washington several months after Blatchford's death elicited warm appraisals of his judicial career. Attorney General

Richard Olney characterized Blatchford as "safe" rather than "brilliant." The attorney general continued by observing that if Blatchford "did not make large contributions to the science of jurisprudence, he won respect for the law and its administration by the uniform righteousness of the results reached in natural causes." There were, no doubt, many observers who questioned the "uniform righteousness" of the results in Blatchford's controversial substantive due process opinions. But the justice's seeming vacillation in these prominent cases may vindicate the attorney general's suggestion that Blatchford was more safe than brilliant. Faced with one of the great issues of his day, Blatchford tried—in vain, many would say—to find some middle way that would mediate between the commercial and progressive combatants before the Court. After his death, the principle of substantive due process that Blatchford wielded so hesitantly would find an ever more important place on an increasingly conservative Court. It is not likely that Blatchford would have been entirely happy with this development.

Further Reading

Hall, A. Oakey. "Justice Samuel Blatchford." *Green Bag* 5 (1893): 489–492.

"Honors to the Memory of Mr. Justice Blatchford." *Albany Law Journal* 48 (1893): 415–416.

Paul, Arnold. "Samuel Blatchford." In *The Justices of the United States Supreme Court 1789–1969: Their Lives and Major Opinions,* Vol. 2, edited by Leon Friedman and Fred L. Israel. New York: R. R. Bowker Co., 1969.

Lucius Quintus Cincinnatus Lamar (1825–1893)

Associate Justice, 1888–1893

Appointed by President Grover Cleveland

Lucius Quintus C. Lamar
(United States Supreme Court)

Known more as a politician than a jurist, L. Q. C. Lamar served only half a decade on the nation's highest court. These few years amounted to a brief coda to a prominent political career. An ardent secessionist and a Confederate officer, Lamar nevertheless enjoyed greater public success after the Civil War than before it. From the sectional narrowness that had characterized his political temper in the years leading up to war, Lamar remade himself into a statesman of national caliber. He remained a Southerner, of course, but one who served not only the interests of the South but those of the Union he had once been happy to depart. For this startling transformation Lamar was selected as one of John F. Kennedy's eight *Profiles in Courage.*

Lucius Quintus Cincinnatus (L. Q. C.) Lamar was born on September 17, 1825, in Eatonton, Georgia, to a prominent Southern family. The family was well-connected politically on both his father's and his mother's side. One of his mother's sisters was married to John Clarke, who served as governor of Georgia; another was the mother of John A. Campbell, associate justice of the U.S. Supreme Court from 1853 to 1861. Lamar's uncle on his father's side, Mirabeau B. Lamar, was the second president of the Republic of Texas.

Lamar's father, Lucius Q. C. Lamar, was a Georgia state judge whose career was cut short when he committed suicide when his eldest son, L. Q. C., was only nine years old. Thereafter, Lamar's mother—Sarah Bird Lamar—enrolled him in the Georgia Conference Manual Labor School, a Methodist educational institution committed to providing its students a combination of classical education and strenuous physical toil. In 1841 Lamar entered Emory College, another Methodist institution, and graduated four years later. During Lamar's years at Emory, Reverend Augustus B. Longstreet was the college's president. At one time a judge and a state lawmaker, Longstreet had become a Methodist minister in 1838. He continued to preach the doctrine of states' rights as though it were gospel, and his ardent advocacy of Southern sectionalism would profoundly influence the course of young L. Q. C. Lamar's life. The ties between Longstreet and Lamar were immeasurably strengthened when, two years after Lamar's graduation from Emory, he married Longstreet's daughter Virginia.

After college, Lamar turned at once to the study of law in the office of an uncle in Macon, Georgia. He practiced briefly with his uncle and then set up his own law office in Covington, Georgia. In 1849, though, Lamar's father-in-law was appointed president of the University of Mississippi. Lamar consequently moved with his family to Oxford, Mississippi, where he accepted a position as an assistant professor of mathematics at the university while practicing law on the side. He returned to Georgia in 1852, establishing a law practice in Covington with a close friend. He also plunged into the tempestuous political world of the time, winning election to the Georgia state legislature in 1853. The following year his Covington law partnership dissolved and he established a new practice on his own in Macon. He also ran for Congress and lost. By 1855 Lamar had returned to Mississippi, acquired a thousand-acre plantation with which to occupy the labors of more than 20 slaves, and practiced law in Holly Springs.

Lamar's political career in Mississippi proved immediately more successful than the one he had left in Georgia. He won a Democratic seat in Congress in 1857 and was reelected two years later. As a Mississippi congressman, Lamar established at once an extreme states' rights position. His maiden speech in the House made clear the narrow sectionalist tenor of his political mind-set. "Others may boast of their . . . comprehensive love of this Union," he declared. "With me, I confess that the promotion of Southern interests is second in importance only to the preservation of Southern honor."

During his congressional years, Lamar developed a close relationship with Jefferson Davis. When the Democratic National Convention met in Charleston in the spring of 1860, Davis urged Lamar to attend and to counsel moderation on the part of the Southern delegates. But Stephen Douglas's success in framing the party's platform incited the Mississippi and Alabama delegates to abandon the convention. Though Lamar did not initiate the walkout, he gave it an after-the-fact blessing; the Democratic party was fractured, he concluded, and "broken faith, like broken heads, cannot be mended." Lamar then returned home to Mississippi, where he attended the state's secession convention and drafted the secession ordinance overwhelmingly approved by the delegates. The same month, in the shadow of war, he resigned his congressional seat and—improbably—undertook an appointment as professor of mental and moral philosophy at the University of Mississippi. But the university's students soon departed Oxford to take up Confederate arms, and Lamar joined them shortly thereafter.

Lamar saw action at the Battle of Williamsburg in May 1862 as a lieutenant colonel in the 19th Mississippi Regiment. Bouts of paralysis and other disability stemming from an apparent nervous disorder limited his military service, however. Still eager to serve the Southern cause, Lamar accepted an appointment as Confederate envoy to Russia, though the reluctance of the European powers to recognize the Confederacy ultimately led the South to recall its foreign envoys before Lamar could arrive in Russia. After his return, he spent the remainder of the war assisting Jefferson Davis and briefly serving as a judge advocate, a responsibility that he later described as "the most unpleasant duty I ever had to perform in my life." Present when General Robert E. Lee surrendered at Appomattox, Lamar returned home to Mississippi after being paroled.

Like so many touched by the cold hand of war, Lamar suffered great personal loss. In particular, the war claimed the lives of both of his brothers. Lamar himself was disqualified from returning to the political life that had occupied him prior to war. He turned instead to the university post he had left at the outset of hostilities. For the fall of 1866, he held the position of professor of ethics and metaphysics. But with the new year, Lamar received an appointment as the only professor in the University of Mississippi Law School. Here he taught law while also practicing on the side until in 1870 Republicans took over the state board that oversaw the university. Lamar, ever the stalwart Democrat, resigned his professorship and concentrated on his legal practice.

Within two years Lamar had won a seat in Congress, where he obtained a pardon that allowed him to serve in this elected position. The fiery sectionalist of 15 years before was no longer in evidence, however. In this incarnation as a congressional representative, Lamar emphasized reconciliation. He stepped onto the platform of national prominence with his impassioned eulogy on the occasion of the death of abolitionist Charles Sumner, the Republican senator from Massachusetts. The sharp memory of national fratricide now spurred Lamar to plead for a new national fraternity between North and South: "Would that the spirit of the illustrious dead whom we lament today could speak from the grave to both parties to this deplorable discord in tones which should reach each and every heart throughout this broad territory: 'My countrymen! Know one another, and you will love one another!'" For this and other gestures of reconciliation, Lamar earned renown as "the Great Pacificator."

L. Q. C. Lamar's newfound political prominence won him election to the U.S. Senate in 1876 and reelection in 1881. With the election of Grover Cleveland as president in 1884, Lamar's already impressive political career took on a new dimension when Cleveland invited the Mississippi senator to join his administration as secretary of the interior. Lamar resigned from the Senate and accepted the cabinet position, earning an additional measure of political respect for his solid work in this post from 1885 to 1888. He oversaw an overhaul of land policy that reclaimed millions of acres of public lands, instituted humane Indian policies, and helped secure passage of the Interstate Commerce Act of 1887.

When Associate Justice William B. Woods from Georgia died in the spring of 1887, Lamar was an obvious candidate to fill the vacant seat on the Supreme Court. President Cleveland did, in fact, nominate Lamar to replace Justice Woods, but the proposed appointment of the first Democrat to the Court in a quarter of a century inevitably sparked controversy. Pointing to Lamar's advanced age and his lack of judicial experience, the Republican-dominated Senate Judiciary Committee voted against the nomination. Nevertheless, when Lamar's appointment came before the full Senate, the 62-year-old Mississippian received confirmation on January 16, 1888, by a vote of 32-28.

Prior to his appointment Lamar had expressed private doubts concerning his qualifications to be a Supreme Court justice to his wife—doubts that continued for some time after he joined the Court. He expressed these to a friend in the spring of 1889: "I would be an imposter . . . if I were to allow you to believe that I am doing anything useful or even with moderate ability." He warmed to his new position eventually, though, undertaking a proportionate share of opinion writing for his first four years before declining health largely disabled him in 1892. Generally conservative in outlook, Lamar tended to side with the majority during his years on the Court. His most notable dissents challenged results that expanded national power. He joined in Justice Joseph Bradley's dissent to *Chicago, Milwaukee & St. Paul Railway Co. v. Minnesota* (1890), in which the Court's majority held that the constitutional guarantee of due process of law authorized the Court to determine the reasonableness of railroad rates imposed by a state commission. More famously, Lamar dissented from the result in *In re Neagle* (1890), involving the much-publicized circumstances of his colleague on the bench, Justice Stephen Field. The case arose when a longtime antagonist of Field was shot dead by a federal marshal appointed by the U.S. attorney general to protect Field. When a California sheriff arrested Neagle, the marshal, for murder, Neagle applied for a writ of habeas corpus from a federal court to secure his release. He argued that federal law prevented his being held "for an act done or committed in pursuance of a law of the United States." When the case arrived before the Supreme Court, a majority of the justices agreed with Neagle and ordered his release. Lamar, however, dissented, arguing that there was no specific law that authorized Neagle to defend Justice Field with force and that the Court's order removing Neagle from the state criminal process was an unwarranted intrusion into that process.

L. Q. C. Lamar's marriage of 37 years to Virginia Lamar had ended with her death in 1884. Three years later, in the year that President Cleveland nominated Lamar to the Supreme Court, Lamar married Henrietta Dean Holt. This marriage was as brief as Lamar's tenure on the Court, for he died on January 23, 1893, in Macon, Georgia.

The middle years of L. Q. C. Lamar's life must have seemed at the time like its ending. As he witnessed General Robert E. Lee's surrender at Appomattox, he had every reason to surrender his own political ambitions. He had aggressively supported a losing cause and had to eat the bitter fruit of that loss. Ironically, though, Lamar's most significant successes lay in front of him. After the war he served in Congress—both the House and the Senate—on a president's cabinet, and as an associate justice of the U.S. Supreme Court. The "Great Pacificator," as he became known, by his own political career became an emblem of the gradual reconciliation of the North and the South.

Further Reading

Cate, Wirt Armistead. *Lucius Q. C. Lamar: Secession and Reunion*. Chapel Hill: The University of North Carolina Press, 1935.

Hoffheimer, Michael H. "L. Q. C. Lamar: 1825–1893." *Mississippi Law Journal* 63 (1993): 105–6.

Mayes, Edward. *Lucius Q. C. Lamar: His Life, Times, and Speeches. 1825–1893*. Nashville, Tenn.: Publishing House of the Methodist Episcopal Church, South, 1896.

Murphy, James B. *L. Q. C. Lamar: Pragmatic Patriot*. Baton Rouge: Louisiana State University Press, 1973.

Melville Weston Fuller (1833–1910)

Chief Justice, 1888–1910

Appointed by President Grover Cleveland

Melville Weston Fuller
(United States Supreme Court)

The eighth chief justice of the U.S. Supreme Court was an able administrator of the Court's affairs, though not a brilliant jurist. Chief Justice Melville W. Fuller occupied the nation's highest judicial post during a period of conservative ascendancy. His Court interpreted the U.S. Constitution as a charter for laissez-faire economic policy and, thus construed, wielded it as a sharp sword against a variety of state and federal attempts to regulate commercial affairs. Chief Justice Fuller, though by no means the architect of this conservative moment on the Court, was nevertheless a consistent ally of its constitutional vision.

Melville Weston Fuller was the second son born to Frederick Augustus Fuller and Catherine Martin Weston Fuller. The marriage of his parents did not, however, survive long after Fuller's birth on February 11, 1833, in Augusta, Maine. Three months after Fuller's birth, his mother filed suit for divorce from his father, alleging that he had committed adultery with certain unidentified persons beginning two months after their wedding date and continuing thereafter. The subsequent decree of divorce severed Fuller's relationship with his father. His mother returned home to live with her parents, taking her two sons with her. Thereafter, Melville Fuller grew up in the home of his maternal grandfather, Nathan Weston, the chief justice of the Supreme Court of Maine. When his mother remarried a little more than a decade after her divorce from his father, Melville Fuller continued to live with his grandparents.

At the age of 16, Fuller entered Bowdoin College in Brunswick, Maine. For a time, at least, it appeared that a college education might be beyond his financial reach. His father had made no provision for his education, his mother's second husband had suffered business failures that left no possibility of sending Fuller to college, and his grandfather refused to undertake the expense. In the end, Fuller's mother provided half of his educational expenses from her earnings as a piano teacher, and Fuller's grandmother provided the other half. He graduated in 1853, was elected a member of Phi Beta Kappa, and turned at once to the pursuit of a legal career. He studied law first with an uncle who practiced in Bangor, Maine, before attending Harvard Law School for six months. This time at Harvard Law School would eventually make Fuller the first chief justice to receive a law school education.

Fuller subsequently returned to Bangor, where he was admitted to the bar in 1855 and worked briefly in his uncle's law office before returning to Augusta and accepting an editorial position on *The Augusta Age,* a Democratic newspaper run by another uncle. The following year, the 22-year-old Fuller was elected as an alderman of Augusta and appointed city solicitor and president of the city's common council. He did not remain long in these positions, however. Like many New Englanders of his day, Melville Fuller found his attention directed westward. Two months after his success in the Augusta elections, Fuller, suffering the pangs of a broken marriage engagement, set out for Chicago. He arrived there in May 1856.

Fuller devoted his early years in Chicago to the practice of law, though a succession of law partnerships provided him with only modest financial and professional success. He made more of a mark in the tumultuous politics of the time, lending his energy to the Democratic cause in Illinois and campaigning successfully for Stephen Douglas against the Republican Abraham Lincoln for U.S. Senate in 1858 but less successfully in the presidential election of 1860, which Lincoln won. After the outbreak of the Civil War, Fuller supported the Union but castigated Lincoln's administration for its conduct of the war, heaping special blame on Lincoln's suspension of habeas corpus and his Emancipation Proclamation. He leveled these criticisms from the safety of civilian life, since he did not undertake military service on behalf of the Union. Instead, he played an increasingly prominent role in Illinois politics, winning election to the Illinois Constitutional Convention in 1861 and to the Illinois House of Representatives in 1863.

Fuller had married Calista Ophelia Reynolds two years after his arrival in Chicago. The couple had two daughters before their six-year marriage ended with Calista's death of tuberculosis in 1864. Fuller might have remained a minor Illinois politician and a lawyer of modest means had he not remarried in 1866 to Mary Ellen Coolbaugh. His second wife's father was the president of Chicago's largest bank, the Union National, and Fuller's marriage soon brought him legal work from his father-in-law and Union National Bank, as well as an increasingly prominent clientele. Within a few years Fuller had a prestigious legal practice that included regular appearances before the U.S. Supreme Court on behalf of his clients. By the 1880s Fuller was making close to $30,000 per year (an excellent income at the time), profiting from astute real estate dealings, and a member of the Chicago

Literary Club, an association that reflected his lifelong interest in poetry and other literature. This interest was also reflected in Fuller's impressive private library of more than 6,000 volumes.

During the 1880s, Melville Fuller formed a close relationship with Grover Cleveland, elected president in 1884. Cleveland looked to him for advice about various political appointments and received Fuller's complaints that the Seventh Circuit—the federal judicial district covering Illinois, Indiana, and Wisconsin—had lacked a representative on the U.S. Supreme Court since the resignation of Associate Justice David Davis of Illinois in 1877. Toward the end of the 1880s, Chief Justice Morrison Waite died, and Illinois Democrats renewed their case for an appointment from the Seventh Circuit to fill the vacancy on the Court. After President Cleveland's first choice, Illinois Supreme Court Judge John Sholfield, declined to accept the appointment, Cleveland turned to his friend Melville Fuller. Fuller had turned down earlier offers from President Cleveland to chair the Civil Service Commission and to serve as solicitor general of the United States, but he did not refuse the offer to become chief justice of the Supreme Court. After some protests by Republicans, who criticized Fuller's failure to serve in the military during the Civil War, the Senate confirmed his nomination as chief justice on July 20, 1888, by a vote of 41-20.

Chief Justice Melville Fuller presided over the Court for nearly 22 years and earned praise less for his intellectual leadership of the Court than for his administration of the Court's affairs. He cultivated collegiality on the Court, hosting conferences of the justices frequently at his home and inaugurating the practice of having the justices shake hands before they formally conferred about cases and before they entered the courtroom. He earned the abiding gratitude of his colleagues and of future justices by helping to convince Congress to pass the Circuit Court of Appeals Act of 1891, which finally relieved Supreme Court justices of the onerous circuit-riding responsibilities that had burdened the members of the Court for more than a century.

The years during which Fuller served as chief justice witnessed a strengthening conservativism on the Court, which used the Constitution to defend property and other commercial interests from government regulation. Fuller did not lead this conservative movement on the Court, but he was generally a loyal ally of those who did. Thus, Fuller joined in the majority's opinion in the famous decision of *Lochner v. New York* (1905), which held that the Fourteenth Amendment's due process clause authorized the Court to invalidate economic regulations that unreasonably pinched property interests. Over the next 30 years, *Lochner* would be the charter for the Court's vigorous protection of commercial interests and property rights.

Though Chief Justice Fuller routinely assigned the writing of important constitutional cases to other justices, he wrote the Court's opinion in two important cases that reflected the economic conservativism of the Court at the time. In *United States v. E. C. Knight Co.* (1895), Fuller declared for a majority of the Court that Congress's power under the Constitution to regulate interstate commerce did not authorize it to regulate manufacturing. Thus, he concluded, the Sherman Antitrust Act—intended by Congress to limit the power of monopolies—was unconstitutional as applied to prevent one company from acquiring a monopoly over the manufacture of sugar. This decision severely limited the effectiveness of the Sherman Antitrust Act, though Fuller's Court in later decisions affirmed other applications of the Act. Chief Justice Fuller also wrote for the closely divided Court in *Pollock v. Farmer's Loan & Trust Co.* (1895), which declared the federal income tax law of 1894 unconstitutional. Often regarded as a triumph for laissez-faire constitutionalism, the case ultimately prompted the nation to ratify the Sixteenth Amendment to the Constitution, which authorized the federal income tax and effectively overruled the Court's decision in *Pollock*.

During President Cleveland's second term of office, he offered Melville Fuller the post of secretary of state. But Fuller declined this appointment, explaining to the president that "The surrender of the highest judicial office in the world for a political position, even though so eminent, would tend to detract from the dignity and weight of the tribunal. . . . We cannot afford this." Fuller was, however, willing to accept two appointments that did not require him to abandon "the highest judicial office in the world." In 1897 he served on a commission to resolve a border dispute between Venezuela and British Guiana, and in 1898 he accepted a seat on the Permanent Court of Arbitration in The Hague, which he held for 10 years.

The first decade of the 20th century brought Melville Fuller personal loss and declining health. His second wife died suddenly of a heart attack in 1904 after nearly 40 years of marriage. Fuller confessed to Oliver Wendell Holmes, Jr., one of his colleagues on the bench, that he and Mary Ellen had shared "a love match." He took his wife's death hard, and his health began to decline, but a growing friendship with Justice Holmes partially supplied the companionship he had lost. Fuller himself died of a heart attack on July 4, 1910, at the summer home in Sorrento, Maine, where Mary Ellen had died six years earlier.

For Oliver Wendell Holmes, Jr., himself one of the most talented justices ever to serve on the Supreme Court, Melville Fuller was "the greatest Chief Justice I have ever known." This was high praise from a man who, as much as any, occupied one of the most elevated stations on the Court's Olympian heights and who served under four chief justices. Other chief justices before and after Fuller earned more prominent recognition as intellectual leaders, but Fuller deserves some measure of praise for his ability as an administrator of the nation's highest court. "He turned off the matters that daily called for action," said Holmes, "easily, swiftly, with the least possible friction, with inestimable good humor that relieved any tension with a laugh." There are worse epitaphs.

Further Reading

Ely, James W., Jr. *The Chief Justiceship of Melville W. Fuller, 1888–1910.* Columbia: University of South Carolina Press, 1995.

Furer, Howard B. *The Fuller Court.* Port Washington, N.Y.: Associated Faculty Press, 1986.

King, Willard Leroy. *Melville Weston Fuller: Chief Justice of the United States, 1888–1910.* New York: Macmillan, 1950.

Morris, Jeffrey B. "The Era of Melville Weston Fuller." *Supreme Court Historical Society Yearbook* (1981): 36–51.

Umbreit, Kenneth Bernard. *Our Eleven Chief Justices: A History of the Supreme Court in Terms of Their Personalities.* New York: Harper, 1938.

DAVID JOSIAH BREWER (1837–1910)

Associate Justice, 1889–1910

Appointed by President Benjamin Harrison

DAVID JOSIAH BREWER
(United States Supreme Court)

David Brewer joined the Supreme Court in the shadow of an illustrious uncle, Associate Justice Stephen Field. The two served together on the Court for eight years. Brewer was very much the intellectual successor of his uncle, though he lacked the same measure of legal brilliance that earned Field recognition as one of the greatest justices ever to have sat on the Supreme Court. Nevertheless, Brewer shared his uncle's conservativism, and both justices are remembered for their aggressive use of the Constitution as a sword against government regulations that affected the interests of property owners.

David Josiah Brewer was born in modern-day Turkey to missionary parents. His father, Josiah Brewer, was a Congregational minister serving in Smyrna, Asia

Minor, at the time of David's birth on June 20, 1837. His mother, Emilia Field Brewer, was the sister of two men who would enjoy considerable fame in the law: David Dudley Field, Jr., who would draft a pathbreaking and widely copied legal code to reform civil procedure in New York; and Stephen Field, a future Supreme Court justice. In fact, Emilia's brother Stephen accompanied David's mother and father while they were abroad. The family returned to the United States after about two and a half years, and David's father accepted a position as chaplain of St. Francis Prison in Wethersfield, Connecticut. When he was 15 years old, David entered Wesleyan College, where he studied for two years before transferring to Yale, his father's alma mater. After graduating from Yale in 1856, Brewer studied law with his prominent New York uncle, David Dudley Field, Jr., followed by a year's course of study at the Albany Law School. He graduated in 1858 and was thereafter admitted to the New York bar.

A decade before David Brewer graduated from law school, his uncle Stephen Field had been lured west by the California gold rush. Brewer chose a similar course, though unlike his uncle he actually spent some time prospecting for gold on Pikes Peak before finally settling in Leavenworth, Kansas. He was soon working as a notary public and serving on the school board. In 1861 Brewer married Louise R. Landen. That same year Brewer undertook the first in a long series of public offices that would occupy his life over the next half century. Initially he accepted an administrative position as commissioner for the federal circuit court in Leavenworth. After two years and a failed bid to obtain a seat in the state legislature, Brewer was first elected judge for the criminal and probate courts in his county and then, in 1864, elected judge of the First Judicial District Court of Kansas. He briefly left the bench in 1869, after being elected Leavenworth County Attorney. But by 1870 Brewer had resumed his judicial career, winning election that year to the Kansas Supreme Court and being reelected in 1876 and 1882.

Brewer's judicial temperament, moderately conservative to begin with, became increasingly conservative as he grew older. In his years as a state supreme court judge, he did not exhibit the same vigor in challenging laws that restricted the rights of property owners that he would demonstrate as a Supreme Court justice in the 1890s. His dissent in *State v. Mugler* (Kan. 1883), though, was suggestive of the future course his thinking would take when he argued that Kansas's Prohibition Amendment, barring most manufacture and sale of intoxicating beverages, amounted to an unconstitutional taking of a brewery without just compensation. Brewer phrased his conclusion in this case tentatively; future years would find him more confident in his defense of property rights. Brewer's years on the Kansas Supreme Court also demonstrated a sensitivity to women's issues that would exhibit itself when he joined the Supreme Court. In *Wright v Moell* (Kan. 1876), he held that a woman elected County Superintendent of Public Instruction could not be deprived of her office because of her sex.

In 1884 President Chester A. Arthur appointed Brewer to the Eighth Judicial Circuit Court; Brewer resigned his position on the Kansas Supreme Court to accept this federal appointment. When Associate Justice Stanley Matthews died five years later in the spring of 1889, Brewer was an early candidate to fill the vacant position on the Supreme Court. President Benjamin Harrison soon narrowed the field to two men: Brewer and Henry Billings Brown, a federal district judge from Michigan and Brewer's former Yale classmate. Harrison eventually learned that Brewer had written a letter suggesting that the appointment go to Brown. This apparently gracious act so impressed the president that he nominated David Brewer as associate justice of the Supreme Court. The Senate confirmed the appointment on December 18, 1889, by a vote of 53-11.

Shortly after David Brewer joined the Court, a majority of the justices charted a new constitutional course in the area of conflicts between property interests and laws regulating commercial affairs. The last part of the 19th century witnessed a rapid expansion of economic development and a parallel expansion of laws designed to regulate this development. Sometimes, as in the case of Granger law, antagonistic economic interests wrestled in state legislatures to secure passage of laws that would benefit their respective economic situations. Granger laws, for example, represented legislative victories for small farmers and businesses at odds with railroads and grain elevator operators over transportation and storage fees. These laws typically established maximum rates to be charged by railroads and grain elevators. The ratification of the Fourteenth Amendment after the Civil War, which included a clause prohibiting state deprivation of life, liberty, or property without "due process of law," provided the railroads and grain elevators with a possible constitutional weapon in their battles against the proliferation of Granger laws. But at first the Supreme Court gave a cool welcome to due process claims against these laws. In *Munn v. Illinois* (1877), seven justices joined in a majority holding that the reasonableness of state legislation establishing maximum rates for grain elevator storage was a matter for determination by the legislature, not the courts.

In the first few weeks of Justice Brewer's tenure on the Court, he and his colleagues heard arguments in a new case challenging a Granger law. This time, in *Chicago, Milwaukee, & St. Paul Railroad Co. v. Minnesota* (1890), a new majority of the Court—including Brewer—held that the due process clause required judicial review of rates set by a state's Railroad and Warehouse Commission. "Unreasonable" economic regulations offended the due process guarantee, and *Chicago, Milwaukee* suggested that federal courts were prepared to determine the reasonableness of state economic regulation.

With his colleague, Associate Justice Rufus W. Peckham, Brewer became a leader of the Court's conservative block. Over the following decades Brewer and the other conservatives guided the Court toward an expansive use of constitutional provisions—especially the due process clauses of the Fifth and Fourteenth Amendments—to defend property rights against a variety of state and federal regulations. He joined with a majority of the Court to reject the federal government's attempt to regulate manufacturing monopolies in *United States v. E. C. Knight Co.* (1895), concluding that congressional power to regulate interstate commerce did not include power to regulate manufacturing. Brewer also joined the majority that declared unconstitutional the federal income tax of 1894 in *Pollock v. Farmer's Loan & Trust Co.* (1895), a decision effectively overruled by ratification of the Sixteenth Amendment. In these and other cases, Brewer sided with an aggressive defense of property rights, making the Court a principal guarantor of laissez-faire capitalism. Brewer viewed himself as pitted in a great constitutional battle against socialists and other progressive elements who would trample the property rights of individuals. He characterized the Court's decision in the *Chicago, Milwaukee* case as "a strong and unconquerable fortress in the long struggle between individual rights and the public good." Of his own participation in the result announced in the case, he observed: "I rejoice to have been permitted to put one stone into that fortress."

History remembers Justice Brewer most for two opinions. One of these, *In re Debs* (1895), gave Brewer the opportunity to enhance federal power to secure essentially conservative economic results. *Debs* involved the 1894 Pullman strike in which Eugene Debs led a strike against railroads that used Pullman cars. The federal government eventually obtained injunctions that prohibited certain activities associated with the strike, but Debs and his associates refused to obey the injunctions. They were arrested, tried for contempt of court, fined, and sent to jail. Debs subsequently petitioned the Supreme Court for a writ of habeas corpus ordering his release. Among the lawyers who represented Debs was one of the most famous advocates of the 20th century: Clarence Darrow. Debs's lawyers argued that the injunctions he had violated were themselves illegal and that his trial without a jury for contempt violated his constitutional rights. Brewer, though, for a unanimous Supreme Court, rejected these arguments, leaving Debs locked in jail and organized labor dealt a significant defeat.

Even more important than Brewer's opinion in the *Debs* case was his opinion for the Court in *Mueller v. Oregon* (1908), decided 15 years later. In this case Brewer's economic conservativism clashed with his more progressive but nevertheless paternalistic—attitudes concerning women. *Mueller* involved a constitutional challenge to a state law limiting women in factories and laundries to a 10-hour workday. Three years previously, the Supreme Court had invalidated a 10-hour workday limit for bakers in *Lochner v. New York* (1905), finding no reasonable connection between the health and safety of bakers and the 10-hour workday limit. But in *Mueller,* Louis D. Brandeis—a future Supreme Court justice himself—defended the state law as necessary to protect the health of women. Brandeis filed with the Court a mass of documentary material—now famously referred to as a "Brandeis brief"—evidencing the connection between work hours and women's health. In an opinion by Justice Brewer, the Court unanimously upheld the state law. "[W]oman's physical structure and the performance of maternal functions place her at a disadvantage in the struggle for subsistence," he wrote. "[A]s healthy mothers are essential to vigorous offspring, the physical well-being of women becomes an object of public interest and care."

In addition to his work as a Supreme Court justice, David Brewer lectured and wrote copiously about the law. He taught at Yale and at what became George Washington University. He was a vigorous and friendly man, even as he advanced into old age. His wife Louise died in 1893, and a few years later Brewer remarried, to Emma Miner Mott. He died of a stroke on March 28, 1910, in Washington, D.C.

Justice David Brewer was an able judge who might have known greater prominence had he not occupied a seat on the Supreme Court at the same time as three men of extraordinary talent and influence: his uncle Stephen Field; John Marshall Harlan; and Oliver Wendell Holmes, Jr. As it was, Brewer still exerted a powerful influence on the Court for 20 years. He helped to engineer an economically conservative ascendancy that would endure for almost half a century. Ironically, his famous opinion in *Mueller v. Oregon* set the stage for the eventual dismantling of this ascendancy.

FURTHER READING

Brodhead, Michael J. *David J. Brewer: The Life of a Supreme Court Justice, 1837–1910.* Carbondale, Ill.: Southern Illinois University Press, 1994.

Bergan, Francis. "Mr. Justice Brewer: A Perspective of a Century." *Albany Law Review* 25 (1961): 191–202.

Eitzen, D. Stanley. *David J. Brewer, 1837–1910: A Kansan on the United States Supreme Court.* Emporia: Kansas State Teacher's College, 1964.

Gamer, Robert E. "Justice Brewer and Substantive Due Process: A Conservative Court Revisited." *Vanderbilt Law Review* 18 (1964–1965): 615–41.

Hylton, Joseph Gordon. "David Josiah Brewer: A Conservative Justice Reconsidered." *Journal of Supreme Court History* (1994): 45–64.

———. "The Judge Who Abstained in *Plessy v. Ferguson:* Justice David Brewer and the Problem of Race." *Mississippi Law Journal* 61 (1991): 315–64.*

*Justice David Brewer abstained in the famous *Plessy v. Ferguson* decision of 1896 because he missed the case due to his daughter's sudden death.

HENRY BILLINGS BROWN (1836–1913)

Associate Justice, 1891–1906

Appointed by President Benjamin Harrison

HENRY BILLINGS BROWN
(United States Supreme Court)

Henry Billings Brown owns the dubious distinction of having penned one of the worst opinions ever announced by the Supreme Court: *Plessy v. Ferguson* (1896). In *Plessy,* Brown enunciated for the Court the "separate but equal" doctrine, which granted constitutional harbor to laws officially segregating individuals on the basis of race. Ironically, though, Brown's opinion for the Court represented not the rantings of a reactionary conservative but the settled assumptions of a political moderate. So representative were his views on the subject of race that the nation scarcely blinked when Brown established the blueprint for the edifice of Jim Crow segregation that would tower over the South for half a century.

The future author of *Plessy* was born on March 2, 1836, in the village of South Lee, Massachusetts, to Billings Brown and Mary Tyler Brown. His father ran flour and lumber mills in South Lee before selling the mills and moving the family to Stockbridge in 1845 and later to Ellington, Connecticut, in 1849. Henry Brown attended private academies before entering Yale at the age of 16. One of Brown's classmates at Yale was a future colleague on the Supreme Court, David Brewer. Brown graduated in 1856 after four years, having attained no particular scholarly prominence, though his father rewarded him for his graduation with a trip to Europe for a year.

When Brown returned from Europe, he embarked on a course of study for the legal career his father had planned for him. Dissent from this paternal control did not occur to Brown. "I felt that my fate was settled," he later wrote, "and had no more idea of questioning it than I should have had in impeaching a decree of Divine Providence." In any event, Brown worked for a time as a law clerk in Ellington, Connecticut, until his refusal to participate in a local religious revival made life there unpleasant. He left Ellington to pursue legal studies, first at his alma mater and then at Harvard. He then migrated west to Detroit, Michigan, where he served a further legal apprenticeship before receiving an appointment as deputy U.S. marshal for Detroit in the summer of 1860.

Brown's new position as deputy marshal placed him in close contact with the thriving shipping industry located around Detroit harbor, and he began to acquire an expertise in admiralty law. In 1863 he was appointed an assistant U.S. attorney, a position he was to hold for five years. The following year he married Caroline Pitts, the daughter of a wealthy Detroit family. A few years after the marriage, Caroline's father died and she inherited a sizable estate that gave the young couple a measure of financial independence. Like other men of some means, Henry Brown was able to avoid military service during the Civil War by hiring a substitute to serve in his place for the sum of $850.

Brown's newfound financial independence also allowed him to pursue a judicial career rather than a more lucrative legal practice. But he was not immediately able to obtain a settled position as a judge. He was appointed by the Republican governor of Michigan to the Wayne County Circuit Court in 1868, but later that year, when he stood for election to this position, he lost to a Democratic opponent. This loss sent him back to the practice of law. He became a partner specializing in admiralty law in the firm of Newberry, Pond & Brown, and practiced there for seven years. During this period Brown made another bid to win a political office in 1872, but he failed in his attempt to win the Republican nomination for a congressional seat. Finally, in 1875, he obtained an appointment to the federal bench when President Ulysses S. Grant picked him to serve as U.S. district judge for the Eastern District of Michigan.

Life as a judge suited Henry Brown well. He preferred to "take refuge in the comparative repose of the bench" and "to exchange a position where one's main ambition is to *win* for one where one's sole ambition is to do justice." He served 14 years as a federal district judge, enjoying an excellent reputation, especially in the area of admiralty law, his specialty. He taught regularly at the University of Michigan Law School and was awarded honorary degrees from the University of Michigan and Yale University. Brown also consciously sought a more prestigious judicial appointment, ultimately casting his aspirations toward a seat on the U.S. Supreme Court itself. According to an early biographer, Brown "did not hesitate to use all honorable means to attain the object of his ambition." The exact means pursued by Brown in this ambition remain unclear, but they seem to have included his willingness to ride circuit, helping to decide cases in other districts in need of temporary judicial assistance and making important political contacts along the way.

When Justice Stanley Matthews died in the spring of 1889, Judge Brown was one of the two most promising candidates to fill the vacancy left on the Supreme Court. The other was one of Brown's classmates from Yale, David Brewer. President Benjamin Harrison eventually appointed Brewer to fill the seat left vacant by Matthews's death. The following year, though, Justice Samuel F. Miller also died, and the president promptly nominated Brown to assume the vacant seat on the Court. The Senate confirmed Brown's appointment in December 1890, and he took his seat on the Court at the beginning of the New Year. Justice Brown credited his appointment to the support of his friend Judge Howell Edmunds Jackson, a Tennessee judge on the U.S. Court of Appeals for the Sixth Circuit. Brown reciprocated the favor by urging President Harrison to appoint Jackson to the Court two years later, after Justice L. Q. C. Lamar died, and the president obliged by appointing Jackson in February 1893.

Justice Brown was moderately conservative in his judicial views, but on a Court with such archconservatives as Stephen Field, David Brewer, and Rufus Peckham, Brown often found himself in the center of the Court's political spectrum, anxious to secure compromise and to avoid dissent. In his years on the Court, he contributed most in the areas of admiralty and patent opinions, in which he had acquired considerable expertise in the course of his judicial career. But he could not avoid participating in the great constitutional conflict of his era between government regulation and property interests. On this issue he was an unpredictable pragmatic. He joined in the majority that invalidated a 10-hour workday limit for bakers in *Lochner v. New York* (1905) but wrote the opinion for the Court in *Holden v. Hardy* (1898), upholding the constitutionality of an eight-hour workday limit for miners. In both of the cases, Brown found himself aligned with a majority of the Court. But the conflict between government power and property rights could sometimes pierce even Brown's reluctance to disagree publicly with his colleagues. In *Pollock v. Farmer's Loan and Trust Co.* (1895), a narrow majority of the Court invalidated the federal income tax and forced the normally conciliatory Brown into sharp dissent. He believed that the majority's declaration that the income tax was unconstitutional amounted to "nothing less than a surrender of the taxing power to the moneyed class," and he denounced the Court's decision in measured but sober terms:

> I hope it may not prove the first step toward the submergence of the liberties of the people in a sordid despotism of wealth. As I cannot escape the conviction that the decision of the court in this great case is fraught with immeasurable danger to the future of the country, and that it approaches the proportions of a national calamity, I feel it a duty to enter my protest against it.

The nation managed to avoid the calamity Justice Brown foresaw by amending the Constitution to permit the federal income tax. But on another crucial issue of the day, Brown was blind to the calamity occasioned by the opinion he authored in a case that would do much harm to his judicial reputation. *Plessy v. Ferguson* (1896) presented the Court with the opportunity to consider whether state-sanctioned racial segregation violated the Fourteenth Amendment's equal protection clause. A Louisiana state law required railroads to provide segregated railway cars and required passengers to occupy only those cars designated for their race. Homer Plessy, an African American, defied this segregation scheme and was arrested and convicted for violating the state law. When the case arrived before the Supreme Court, a majority of the justices—with Henry Brown as spokesman—denied that "separate but equal" public facilities segregated according to race violated the equal protection clause.

In a startling but apparently commonly suffered form of cultural myopia, Brown declared that forced segregation of the races should not be understood to imply any inferiority on the part of blacks: "[T]he assumption that the enforced separation of the two races stamps the colored race with a badge of inferiority . . . is not by reason of anything found in the act, but solely because the colored race chooses to put that construction upon it." For a Court that had announced a generation earlier in the *Dred Scott* decision that blacks were so inherently inferior they could under no circumstances qualify as U.S. citizens, this was an astounding statement. That it was pronounced by a centrist on the Court rather than by an archconservative suggested how long and treacherous a path the nation would have to follow before Brown's opinion for the Court in *Plessy* would finally be repudiated more than half a century later.

From his childhood, Brown had suffered eye problems. By the time he joined the Court, he was blind in one eye, and his work as a justice gradually ruined his other eye. After 15 years of service, he could scarcely see; consequently, he resigned in 1906. His first wife had died while on a trip abroad in 1901, and two years before leaving the Court Brown had married again to Josephine E. Tyler, the widow of his cousin. Brown died in New York City on September 4, 1913.

But for his opinion in *Plessy v. Ferguson,* Justice Henry Brown might have faded into the historical obscurity normally reserved for middling Supreme Court justices. He served on a Court dominated by legal titans such as Stephen Field, John Marshall Harlan, and Oliver Wendell Holmes, Jr., and it was inevitable that these men would attract the most popular and historical attention. Yet Justice Brown, by voicing the racial views common to his age but repudiated in our own, captured for one enduring historical moment the harsh glare of unfavorable attention. He was a better justice than his opinion in *Plessy* suggested, but his judicial performance in this case has tended to overshadow his other modest accomplishments.

FURTHER READING

Brown, Henry Billings. *Memoir of Henry Billings Brown: Late Justice of the Supreme Court of the United States: Consisting of an Autobiographical Sketch With Additions to His Life by Charles A. Kent.* New York: Duffield and Company, 1915.

Glennon, Robert J., Jr. "Justice Henry Billings Brown: Values in Tension." *University of Colorado Law Review* 44 (1973): 553–604.

Goldfarb, Joel. "Henry Billings Brown." In *The Justices of the United States Supreme Court 1789–1969: Their Lives and Major Opinions,* Vol. 2. Edited by Leon Friedman and Fred L. Israel. New York: R. R. Bowker Co., 1969.

George Shiras, Jr. (1832–1924)

Associate Justice, 1892–1903

Appointed by President Benjamin Harrison

George Shiras, Jr.
(United States Supreme Court)

George Shiras, Jr., served on the Supreme Court for nearly 11 years. During this period he tendered capable, though generally undistinguished, support for the Court's reigning conservativism. Even when circumstances thrust him to the forefront of public attention in a controversial case, Shiras remained an enigma. In that case, his contemporaries widely believed he had changed his vote, dealing a temporary death blow to the federal income tax, but no real evidence supporting this suspicion could ever be marshaled. After suffering a brief period of national derision for this suspected treachery to democratic ideals, Shiras returned to the Court's shadows until he traded his seat on the Court for a long and equally undistinguished retirement.

George Shiras, Jr., was born on January 26, 1832, in Pittsburgh, Pennsylvania, to George Shiras and Eliza Herron Shiras. Shiras's father made enough money running a brewery to retire early and devote his energy to farming, especially to the cultivation of peach orchards. The man who would one day occupy a seat on the nation's highest court thus spent his early years working on the family farm, some 20 miles outside Pittsburgh. George Shiras, Jr., left the farm in 1849 to attend Ohio University in Athens, Ohio. In 1851 he transferred to Yale, where he obtained his B.A. in 1853.

Although Shiras remained briefly at Yale to study law at the university's law school, he soon chose to pursue a more practical curriculum. He returned to Pittsburgh, where he read law in the office of a former county district court judge, Hopewell Hepburn, and was admitted to the bar of Allegheny County in 1855. For a few years Shiras practiced with his brother Oliver, a recent Yale Law School graduate, in Dubuque, Iowa. During this period he married Lillie E. Kennedy in 1857; the couple would eventually have two sons, both lawyers, one a U.S. congressman.

After his marriage, Shiras exchanged the law partnership with his brother in Dubuque for one in Pittsburgh with his former mentor, Hopewell Hepburn, a partnership that lasted until Hepburn's death in 1862. For the next 30 years, George Shiras practiced law in Pittsburgh. He rode the tide of economic prosperity in Pittsburgh to his own personal prosperity by gradually coming to represent the titans of Pittsburgh's iron and steel industry, in addition to such prestigious clients as the Baltimore and Ohio Railroad. By the end of his third decade of practice in Pittsburgh, Shiras's income was estimated at $75,000 per year, an extraordinary sum for the times.

Shiras's prominence in the Pennsylvania legal community made it inevitable that he would be considered as a possible political candidate for some significant post. Nevertheless, the same independent spirit that had propelled Shiras to practice law by himself made him a poor ally for the dominant Pennsylvania Republican machine of his day. Though he was briefly considered as a possible U.S. senator, his refusal to accept this position ultimately alienated him from Pennsylvania Republican leaders such as James Donald Cameron and, later, Matthew Quay. But Shiras's independent Republicanism proved attractive to President Benjamin Harrison when Associate Justice Joseph P. Bradley's death in January 1892 created a vacancy on the Supreme Court. Harrison had strong political reasons for appointing someone from Pennsylvania to the vacant seat; but less than cordial relationships between the president and the state's two senators, James Cameron and Matthew Quay, also gave Harrison reason to find an independent candidate, not controlled by the Republican machine in Pennsylvania, for the post. Though lacking in both political and judicial experience, George Shiras, Jr., was amply supplied in independence of spirit. President Harrison, as if to emphasize Shiras's independence even further, defied the tradition of senatorial courtesy by failing to consult with Pennsylvania senators Cameron and Quay about Shiras's appointment. Thus, when the president sent Shiras's nomination to the Senate, Cameron and Quay initially launched an indignant campaign of opposition to the nomination. Nevertheless, widespread support for Shiras soon scuttled their efforts, and the Senate confirmed the new justice's appointment on July 26, 1892.

Sixty-year-old George Shiras moved with his wife to Washington, D.C., where he undertook a decade-long tenure of service on the Supreme Court. In spite of bringing no judicial experience with him to the bench, Shiras proved to be an able judge. He wrote his fair share of opinions, though his concern for the Court's institutional authority caused him to practice restraint in authoring dissents; he wrote only 14 dissenting opinions in nearly 11 years on the Court. In all, Shiras participated actively in the life of the Court, though he almost never took the center stage occupied by more influential justices of the times. More craftsman than artist, Shiras's opinions were generally well respected, even though they seldom touched on the great issues of the day.

On one occasion, however, George Shiras became the center of national attention in a controversial case. In the last years of the 19th century, the Supreme Court considered a constitutional challenge to the federal income tax law passed in 1894. The case, *Pollock v. Farmers' Loan & Trust Co.* (1895), stirred national passions and produced no little confusion on the Supreme Court itself. On the issue of whether a tax on private and corporate incomes was a "direct" tax, and thus required by the Constitution to be apportioned to the states according to their populations, the Court split badly. Only eight justices participated in the original decision of the case, and these divided evenly on the crucial question. At the time, Shiras was widely believed to have been one of the justices who voted to uphold the constitutionality of the income tax, though the positions of the justices in the original decision were not announced by the Court. Instead, the justices decided to reconsider the case. Justice Howell Edmunds Jackson, suffering from a terminal illness, had not participated in the original decision, but when the Court reconsidered the matter, he cast his vote in support of the constitutionality of the tax. The final vote in the case, though, was 5-4, invalidating the income tax. This meant that one of the justices who had originally approved the tax had switched his vote. At the time, Shiras was thought to be the guilty party, though subsequent Court historians have doubted this. In any event, Shiras suffered fierce attacks for his vote in the case, and he was momentarily cast into the harsh glare of attention from a nation that would ultimately vote the justices down by enacting the Sixteenth Amendment in 1913, authorizing the federal income tax.

Apart from the notoriety Shiras earned in the income tax case, he generally maintained a low profile on the Court. During his tenure as a justice, conservatives on the Court were able to revolutionize constitutional law by championing business and property interests against attempts by federal and state governments to regulate commercial matters. Shiras proved to be a regular, though not an invariable, ally of his conservative brethren. But at times, especially in the area of civil liberties, he charted a judicial course more progressive than conservative. Perhaps the most significant opinion to his credit was that of *Wong Wing v. United States* (1896), in which Shiras wrote for a unanimous Supreme Court no longer willing to tolerate the anti-Chinese fervor that gripped Congress toward the end of the 19th century. The Court had already blessed congressional attempts to prevent Chinese immigration and to deport illegal Chinese aliens. But Congress added a further law to these measures allowing illegal Chinese aliens to be sentenced to a year of hard labor and then deported, all without any jury trial. This the Court could not stomach. Writing for his brethren, Shiras declared that the law violated the due process and jury trial guarantees of the Fifth and Sixth Amendments.

During his years on the Court, George Shiras lived a relatively quiet life in Washington with his wife. The couple declined to engage in the rounds of social activities customary for his prominent post. After Shiras had been an associate justice for a little more than 10 years, he kept a longstanding commitment he had made to retire after a decade of service on the Court. Elderly, but still vigorous, he submitted his resignation on February 23, 1903, and he lived another 21 years in retirement before dying on August 2, 1924, in Pittsburgh, at the venerable age of 92.

George Shiras, Jr., brought to the Court the solid legal ability and generally conservative sensibilities one would expect from a prosperous corporate lawyer. He thus lent crucial conservative support to the probusiness revolution in constitutional law that occurred during the last years of the 19th century and the first years of the 20th. An independent temper, though, made him willing to depart occasionally from the course set by more conservative members of the Court. But even these miniature rebellions were accomplished quietly, little noticed either by Shiras's contemporaries or by later observers of the Court.

Further Reading

Paul, Arnold. "George Shiras, Jr." In *The Justices of the United States Supreme Court 1789–1969: Their Lives and Major Opinions,* vol. 2. Edited by Leon Friedman and Fred L. Israel. New York: R. R. Bowker Co., 1969.

Shiras, George III. *Justice George Shiras, Jr., of Pittsburgh, Associate Justice of the United States Supreme Court, 1892–1903: A Chronicle of His Family, Life, and Times.* Edited and completed by Winfield Shiras. Pittsburgh: University of Pittsburgh Press, 1953.

HOWELL EDMUNDS JACKSON (1832–1895)

Associate Justice, 1893–1895

Appointed by President Benjamin Harrison

HOWELL EDMUNDS JACKSON
(United States Supreme Court)

The Tennessean Howell E. Jackson served actively on the Supreme Court for only a little more than a year. He contracted tuberculosis after his appointment to the Court, and the disease tragically cut short his life. But history placed him on the nation's highest court at a time of great controversy and focused attention on him that he would not otherwise have experienced. In spite of his illness, Jackson summoned the energy to participate in a famous case challenging the constitutionality of the federal income tax, though this participation crushed the last vestiges of his health and sent him to his grave within a few months after the Court rendered its decision in the case.

Howell Edmunds Jackson was born on April 8, 1832, in Paris, Tennessee. His father, Alexander Jackson, was a physician, and his mother, Mary Hurt Jackson, was the daughter of a Baptist minister. The couple had migrated from Virginia to Tennessee shortly after their marriage in 1830, and Howell was the first of two sons born to them. Eight years after Howell's birth, his parents moved to Jackson, Tennessee, where his father served two terms in the state legislature and as mayor of the town from 1854 to 1856. After Howell's early education in a preparatory school, he attended Western Tennessee College, from which he graduated in 1850, and then completed two more years of academic study at the University of Virginia. Afterward he studied law for a year with Judge A. W. O. Totten, a relative on the Tennessee Supreme Court, and Milton Brown, a former congressman, before spending a year studying law at Cumberland Law School, from which he graduated in 1856.

After being admitted to the bar, Howell Jackson returned to Jackson, Tennessee, to practice law. In 1858, however, he moved to Memphis in search of more fertile opportunities for practice. Here he established a law partnership with David M. Currin. Through his legal work, Jackson soon came into contact with Sophia Malloy, the daughter of one of the firm's banking clients. Howell and Sophia formed their own marital partnership in 1859. Together the couple would have six children.

The Civil War that soon intruded on the nation's peace also intruded on Jackson's legal practice. Though he opposed secession, he remained loyal to the South after war broke out. He did not take up arms for the Confederacy, but he accepted a post that called on him to oversee the liquidation of property confiscated from Unionists in his area of Tennessee. Later during the war, he sought a position as a Confederate military judge. Although he did not obtain this position, his interest in it was the first inkling of judicial aspirations that would one day earn him a seat on the U.S. Supreme Court.

After the war, Jackson resumed legal practice in Memphis with Bedford M. Estes. Jackson specialized in corporate and banking matters, and his partnership with Estes flourished. Tragedy struck, however, in 1873 when an epidemic of contagious diseases descended on Memphis and claimed Sophia's life. Following the loss of his wife, Jackson returned to Jackson, Tennessee, where he formed a new law partnership with General Alexander Campbell. He soon remarried, to Mary E. Harding, whose father, General W. G. Harding, divided his 3,000-acre plantation and stock farm between his two daughters and their families. Jackson and his wife took over part of the plantation while his wife's sister—fortuitously married to Jackson's brother—assumed control of the remaining portion of the plantation.

At the end of the Civil War, Jackson had become a Democrat, and within a decade he was able to realize a long-held aspiration to become a judge. First, he obtained a position as a special judge to the Madison County chancery court, followed in 1875 by an appointment to the Court of Arbitration for West Tennessee. This temporary court assisted the Tennessee Supreme Court in resolving cases that had arisen from the Civil War. After it was dissolved, Jackson came within a single vote of gaining the Democratic nomination for a seat on the Tennessee Supreme Court in 1877.

The temporary frustration of Jackson's judicial aspirations did not spell the end of his political career. By 1880 he had won a seat in the Tennessee House of Representatives. Within a few months, however, a far more prestigious political prize fell into his lap. James E. Bailey, incumbent U.S. senator from Tennessee, had surrounded himself with sufficient political controversy to scuttle his reelection prospects. In the ensuing scramble to find a candidate, Jackson's political moderation eventually made him an attractive compromise candidate for both Democrats and Republicans and secured him a seat in the U.S. Senate. The five years Jackson spent in the Senate were less important for any legislative initiatives he sponsored than for the relationships he forged there. He sat beside Indiana Republican senator Benjamin Harrison, and the two men formed a relationship that would one day place Jackson on the Supreme Court. More immediately, however, he formed a cordial relationship with President Grover Cleveland. In 1887, toward the end of Jackson's term in the Senate, President Cleveland solicited from him names of possible candidates for an appointment to the Sixth Circuit Court of Appeals. Set on appointing a Tennessean to this position, the president eventually rejected the candidates Jackson suggested and persuaded Jackson himself to accept a seat on the federal appeals court.

In all, Jackson served seven years on the federal circuit court. He demonstrated a meticulous mind, adept at wading through the details of contracts and patent cases that formed a large part of his docket as an appellate judge, though not at crafting concise and interesting opinions in these cases. During his years on the circuit court, Jackson also cemented a friendship with a federal district judge in Michigan, Henry Billings Brown. This friendship proved fortuitous for both judges, since each assisted the other in obtaining a position on the U.S. Supreme Court.

When Justice Stanley Matthews died in 1889, Jackson pressed his old Senate colleague, Benjamin Harrison—now president of the United States—to appoint Henry Brown to the vacant position on the Supreme Court. Though Harrison appointed David Brewer to the Court instead, a year later another vacancy opened on the Court after the death of Associate Justice Samuel Miller. This time President Harrison heeded his old friend's recommendation and appointed Henry Brown to the Supreme Court. In 1893 the Court's Mississippian, L. Q. C. Lamar, died toward the end of Harrison's term in office. The Republican president was not enthusiastic about the appointment his Democratic successor—Grover Cleveland—was likely to make. But any appointment Harrison himself might make would have to be confirmed by a Democratic-controlled Senate. Under these circumstances, Associate Justice Henry Brown returned a favor to his Tennessean friend by urging Harrison to appoint Howell Jackson to the Court. The president saw the wisdom in this proposal and nominated Jackson in early February 1893. The Senate unanimously confirmed the appointment a little more than two weeks later.

Howell E. Jackson would probably never have been a great Supreme Court justice. Plodding and pedestrian in temperament, he was capable of solid work but not of judicial brilliance. But the onset of tuberculosis shortly after he began service deprived him even of the opportunity to tender as much as workmanlike toil to the Court. In the end he managed to pen only 46 opinions in his 15 months of active service on the Court. The only event that rescued him from complete obscurity in the annals of Supreme Court history was his participation in one of the most famous cases of his generation, *Pollock v. Farmers' Loan & Trust Co.* (1895).

Pollock involved a challenge to a federal income tax law passed in 1894 and presented the Court with the question of whether the income tax was a "direct" tax required by the Constitution to be apportioned among the states on the basis of their respective populations. When the case first appeared before the justices, the ailing Jackson did not participate in the Court's decision. But his brethren deadlocked in a 4-4 vote that failed to resolve the constitutional question. At this point Jackson indicated his willingness to join his fellow justices in a reconsideration of the case, even though his participation endangered his already fragile heath.

When Justice Jackson arrived in Washington to hear rearguments in the case, the nation's eyes were on the little-known Tennessean who was expected to cast a tie-breaking vote in the case. He was a southerner, and southerners on the whole favored the income tax, so his vote might be expected to sustain its constitutionality. But public attention focused on Jackson also because of the perilous condition of his health. As one paper at the time reported, "He interests the crowd more than all the rest of the bench; that his life can last but a short time and that it will probably be shortened by the effort which he has made to attend the hearing." In the end, Jackson voted to uphold the income tax against the constitutional challenge, but his vote proved not enough to rescue it. One of the justices who had originally voted in favor of the tax—never conclusively identified—switched his vote, and the Court declared the tax unconstitutional in a 5-4 decision. Jackson thus became a dissenter in the case. Prognostications about the dangers to his health presented by his participation in the case proved tragically accurate. Less than three months after the decision in *Pollock* was announced, Justice Howell E. Jackson died on August 8, 1895, in West Meade, Tennessee.

Few justices on the Supreme Court can be said to have risked their lives in the defense of some constitutional principle, but Howell Jackson seems to have earned this epitaph. He characterized the majority's decision in *Pollock* as "the most disastrous blow ever struck at the Constitutional power of Congress." His unsuccessful attempt to defend the federal income tax from this blow may well have shortened his life. He would, nevertheless, win a posthumous vindication when, 18 years later, the nation added the Sixteenth Amendment to the U.S. Constitution, restoring to Congress the power to enact a federal income tax.

FURTHER READING

Calvani, Terry. "The Early Career of Howell Jackson." *Vanderbilt Law Review* 30 (January 1977): 39–72.

Doak, Henry M. "Howell Edmunds Jackson." *Greenbag* (May 1893): 209–215.

Green, John W. "Judge Howell E. Jackson." In *Law and Lawyers: Sketches of the Federal Judges of Tennessee,* by John W. Green. Jackson, Tennessee: McCowat-Mercer Press, 1950.

Hardawy, Roger D. "Howell Edmunds Jackson: Tennessee Legislator and Jurist." *West Tennessee Historical Society Papers* 30 (1976): 104–119.

Phillips, Harry. "Tennessee Lawyers of National Prominence." *Tennessee Bar Journal* 17 (May 1981): 34–53.

Schiffman, Irving. "Howell E. Jackson." In *The Justices of the United States Supreme Court 1789–1969: Their Lives and Major Opinions,* Vol. 2. Edited by Leon Friedman and Fred L. Israel. New York: R. R. Bowker Co., 1969.

EDWARD DOUGLASS WHITE (1845–1921)

Associate Justice, 1894–1910

Appointed by President Grover Cleveland

Chief Justice, 1910–1921

Appointed by President William Howard Taft

EDWARD DOUGLASS WHITE
(United States Supreme Court)

A mountainous man, by all accounts kind and generous, Edward Douglass White served nearly three decades on the Supreme Court, first as an associate justice and subsequently as the ninth chief justice of the Court. He has the distinction of being the first associate justice promoted to the chief seat from within the Court. History adds to this distinction the circumstance that the man who appointed him chief justice became the man to succeed him in this position. Despite White's long service on the Court, however, and the high esteem he enjoyed at the time of his death, the passage of time has witnessed a decline in his reputation as a jurist. His influence on American law endures chiefly in a single area rather than broadly, as in the case of better-known justices. Thus, history places him securely in the middle ranks of the justices who have occupied seats on the nation's highest court.

—∞—

Sprung from a family of judges and politicians, Edward Douglass White was born on November 3, 1845, on a plantation of 1,600 acres six miles north of Thibodaux, Louisiana. His grandfather was a physician, lawyer, politician, and U.S. federal judge. His father, in turn, had been a judge for the New Orleans City Court, a congressman, and, eventually, governor of Louisiana. Edward White was thus born into a family securely fastened to the law—and as equally fastened to Roman Catholicism. This religious heritage would play a prominent role in the early educational experiences of the future Supreme Court justice. After attending a Jesuit school called the College of the Immaculate Conception in New Orleans and then prep school at Mount St. Mary's College in Maryland, White was admitted to Georgetown College in the fall of 1857.

The Civil War eventually intruded on White's educational career at Georgetown, sending him home to Louisiana, where he soon enlisted to fight on behalf of the South. The Rebel cause, though, frustrated whatever dreams of battle glory the young Louisianan may have secretly harbored. The 16-year-old White found himself assigned to the staff of General W. N. R. Beal, commander of the defense of Port Hudson, Louisiana. Thereafter, in the summer of 1863, White was trapped in Port Hudson along with thousands of other Rebel soldiers who endured the siege of General Nathaniel Banks. Eventually the Southern forces surrendered in July 1863, and Edward White found himself prematurely evicted from the war. After being detained as a prisoner of war for several months, he was paroled and made his way home, weakened and ill, to Thibodaux, where he watched the grim conclusion of the war from the sidelines.

After the war, White promptly resumed his life's course by undertaking to study law with Edward Bermudez, a noted New Orleans attorney. After three years he passed the Louisiana bar in 1868 and began to practice law. While White struggled to forge a legal career in New Orleans, he also plunged into the turbulent politics of the time, denouncing carpetbaggers and Reconstruction and working to restore the power of the Democratic party. He subsequently won election to the state senate in 1874. Three years later the Compromise of 1877, which secured the disputed U.S. presidency for the Republican Rutherford B. Hayes in exchange for the removal of federal troops from the South, spelled the end of Reconstruction. Democrats swept back into power in Louisiana, and newly elected Governor Francis R. T. Nichols rewarded White's previous vigorous support by appointing him to the Louisiana Supreme Court in 1878. At the age of 33, Edward White had become an associate justice on his state's highest court. But his judicial career there was soon truncated before it had scarcely begun. In 1880 Democrats hostile to the administration of Governor Nichols seized power in the state and promptly evicted White from his office by amending the Louisiana constitution to prevent men of White's youth from holding the position.

For most of the next decade, Edward White suffered exile from political life and busied himself instead with legal practice and a variety of civic endeavors, including the establishment of Tulane University in 1884. But toward the end of the 1880s, he returned to the aid of his old mentor, ex-governor Francis Nichols, and assisted Nichols in re-capturing the governorship of Louisiana. Nichols, for his part, rewarded White again, this time by persuading the Louisiana legislature to appoint White a U.S. senator in 1891.

In the Senate, White warned against federal attempts to regulate business and, not entirely consistently, championed high tariffs to protect Louisiana's sugar industry—of which his Thibodaux plantation was a part—and federal subsidies for that industry. Though generally on favorable terms with President Grover Cleveland, White opposed the president's attempt in 1893 to reduce tariffs. But Cleveland also had other matters to attend to, not the least of which was the appointment of someone to fill the seat on the U.S. Supreme Court left vacant by the death of Samuel Blatchford in the summer of 1893. The president's attempt to find a replacement for Blatchford encountered more than a little political turbulence, owing chiefly to his estrangement from New York's elder senator, David B. Hill. Cleveland tried to fill the vacancy on the Court with a New Yorker at first, since Blatchford had been from that state, but Hill and his fellow New York senator managed to block the nominations of the two New York lawyers nominated by the president: William Hornblower and Wheeler Peckham, brother of future Supreme Court Justice Rufus Wheeler Peckham, Jr. Frustrated with these two rebuffs, President Cleveland decided to look outside of New York for Blatchford's replacement. On February 19, 1894, the president summoned Senator Edward White to the White House. The Louisiana senator, expecting to be dressed down for his opposition to the president's proposed tariff reforms, found himself instead nominated as an associate justice to the Supreme Court.

The curious sequence of events that led to White's nomination to the Supreme Court had a further, unusual coda. Quite popular in the Senate, White easily won confirmation to the Court the day after the president nominated him. But he refused for a time to relinquish his Senate post and accept confirmation as an associate justice. He tarried in the Senate through February and into March 1984 to champion the interests of the sugar industry in the ongoing tariff debates. Only after the passage of the highly protectionist Wilson-Gorman Tariff Act did White the politician undertake his new vocation as a judge.

Edward Douglass White took the oath of office and assumed his position on the high court on March 12, 1894. In fall of the same year White also made a change in his marital circumstances. For years he had courted Virginia Leita Montgomery Kent and had been decisively rejected in his amorous overtures—so decisively, in fact, that she had married another man. But finally, after the death of her first husband, Virginia accepted Edward's marriage proposal, and their wedding took place in November 1894.

White arrived at the Supreme Court during a historic moment when the Court increasingly served as a conservative bulwark against a rising tide of political progressivism. White's career on the Court fit comfortably within its dominant conservativism, though this career was punctuated from time to time with somewhat erratic departures from the general mold. The Court during this period generally protected business and property interests from state and federal regulatory measures, most famously in *Pollock v. Farmers' Loan & Trust Co.* (1895), which declared the federal income tax unconstitutional, and *Lochner v. New York* (1905), which held unconstitutional a state law that set maximum work hours for bakers. Though generally aligned with the Court's direction in this area, White dissented in both these landmark cases, inaugurating a pattern of seemingly inconsistent decisions that would characterize his judicial career.

After serving on the Court as an associate justice for 17 years, White was elevated to the chief seat in 1910. Chief Justice Melville Fuller died in the summer of that year, leaving to President William Howard Taft the responsibility of choosing a successor for the position he coveted for himself. "It seems strange," the president complained, "that the one place in the government which I would like to fill myself I am forced to give to another." The "other" who seemed most poised to step into Fuller's vacant seat was Associate Justice Charles Evans Hughes, whom Taft had recently appointed to the Court with the implicit promise to make Hughes chief justice when Fuller died. But Fuller's unexpected death only a few months later put the president in a quandary. Hughes was a relatively young man at 48 years old. If Taft made Hughes chief justice, then when Taft left the presidency there was little chance that he would ever obtain an appointment to the chief seat himself. In light of these calculations, the 65-year-old Justice White seemed not likely to serve on the Court nearly as long as Hughes might be expected to serve. Thus, by elevating White to the chief justiceship of the Court, Taft increased the likelihood of there being a vacancy in this position at a later date, when he might be in a position to claim it. Whatever his reasoning, the president appointed Edward White chief justice on December 12, 1910, and the Senate confirmed the appointment the same day.

Although personable in his relations with the other members of the court, Chief Justice White did not earn recognition either as an exceptional administrator or as a brilliant jurist. He did, however, have at least one lasting impact on American law by grafting onto the Sherman Antitrust Act the so-called rule of reason. The Sherman Act prohibited business practices and arrangements that acted as restraints on trade, such as monopolies. But in the landmark antitrust case, *Standard Oil v United States* (1911), Chief Justice White greatly blunted the potential reach of the Act by limiting its prohibition to "unreasonable" business practices and arrangements. By this interpretation White and his colleagues on the Court assured that the 20th-century United States would be largely hospitable to the growth of massive corporations and other business enterprises.

White piloted the Supreme Court through the decade that ended with the First World War. By the close of that war he was in his mid-70s and suffering from cataracts that made it increasingly difficult for him to accomplish his work as chief justice. Former President William Howard Taft now hovered anxiously in the wings, hoping for an appointment to the Court's chief seat and campaigning for White to relinquish it. But the chief justice held on until the spring of 1921, when he underwent bladder surgery from which he failed to recover. He died on May 19, 1921, in Washington, D.C. The following month, Taft, the president who had appointed White to the Court, accepted an appointment to fill the position that White's death opened on the Court.

Edward Douglass White's primary distinction during his 27 years on the Supreme Court was that he was the first associate justice to advance to the seat of chief justice. Otherwise his long tenure on the Court produced little in the way of momentous accomplishments, except for his influence on developing antitrust law by virtue of the "rule of reason" he championed. He was a genial man and a competent administrator of the Court's affairs, but these traits were not sufficient to secure him a prominent place in the history of the Supreme Court.

FURTHER READING

Cassidy, Lews C. "An Evaluation of Chief Justice White." *Mississippi Law Journal* 10 (1938), 136–153.

Fegin, Hugh E. "Edward Douglass White, Jurist and Statesman." *Georgetown Law Journal* 14 (1925): 1–21; and 15 (1926): 148–168.

Highsaw, Robert B. *Edward Douglass White: Defender of the Conservative Faith.* Baton Rouge: Louisiana State University Press, 1981.

Stevens, Dennis G. "Constitutional Jurisprudence at the Crossroads: Edward Douglass White." In *Sober as a Judge: The Supreme Court and Republican Liberty.* Edited by Richard G. Stevens and Matthew J. Franck. Lanham, Md.: Lexington Books, 1999.

Rufus Wheeler Peckham, Jr. (1838–1909)

Associate Justice, 1896–1909

Appointed by President Grover Cleveland

Rufus Wheeler Peckham, Jr.
(United States Supreme Court)

History remembers Rufus Peckham as an archconservative on a conservative Court and as the author of the opinion in *Lochner v. New York* (1905), a decision commonly regarded as one of the worst ever rendered by the Supreme Court. Though Peckham arrived on the Court after the first salvos had been fired by its conservatives on a rising tide of progressivism, he immediately became one of the surest allies of the conservative revolution that came to dominate the Court at the end of the 19th century and the beginning of the 20th. He helped nurture the Court's growing commitment to the protection of economic liberty from state and federal interference. From the vantage of the early 21st century, however, when governmental regulation of commercial and economic affairs is commonplace, Peckham tends to be viewed as a conservative ideologue of the worst sort, willing to twist the Constitution into the shape of his own laissez-faire sensibilities.

—∾—

Rufus Wheeler Peckham, Jr., was born on November 8, 1838, in Albany, New York, the second son of Rufus Wheeler Peckham, Sr., and Isabella Lacey Peckham. His father—a prominent New York lawyer, politician, and eventually a judge—charted a professional career whose details Peckham, Jr., would emulate with startling similarity. Rufus senior served as district attorney of Albany County, as judge on the New York Supreme Court, and finally as a justice on the New York Court of Appeals, the state's highest judicial tribunal. Rufus junior would himself hold each of these positions in turn, until he eventually leapt past the high mark of his father's achievements to become an associate justice of the U.S. Supreme Court.

Peckham received his early education at the Albany Boys Academy, followed by private instruction in Philadelphia. He then read law in his father's law firm and gained admittance to the New York bar in 1859. By the time Peckham started practice, his father had taken a seat on the New York Supreme Court. Peckham spent a decade representing a variety of railroad and commercial interests before he followed in his father's political footsteps by winning election as district attorney for Albany County in 1869, a position he held for three years. This public service brought him into contact with a number of important New York politicians. Not the least important to his future was Grover Cleveland, whose own political career would follow a path from mayor of Buffalo to governor of New York and finally to the presidency of the United States. More than two decades later, this political friendship would yield a seat on the Supreme Court for Peckham.

After his stint as district attorney, Peckham resumed private practice for nearly a decade. In 1881, though, he returned to the political arena by becoming corporate counsel for the city of Albany, New York. He held this position until 1883, but his real ambition seems to have been to find a judicial career. He made an unsuccessful bid for the Democratic nomination for a seat on the New York Court of Appeals in 1882, but he followed this effort the next year with a successful campaign to gain a seat on the New York Supreme Court. Three years later he attempted again to win a seat on the more prestigious Court of Appeals. This time Peckham won election in 1886 to the very seat that his father had held 13 years earlier on the same court before being lost at sea while on a vacation voyage. Peckham's election to the New York Court of Appeals was alone an achievement worthy of crowning a legal career, since it was one of the most prestigious state courts in the nation. Here, for a decade, Peckham labored and revealed in his opinions the conservative bent that would characterize his later service on an even higher court.

Rufus Peckham eventually found himself nominated as an associate justice of the Supreme Court in 1896, but the sequence of events that placed him in this position comprised a tangle of political circumstances. In the summer of 1893, Justice Samuel Blatchford died, leaving a vacancy on the Supreme Court that President Grover Cleveland tried originally to fill with a New Yorker, since Blatchford himself had been from New York. But Cleveland immediately clashed with New York's senior senator, David B. Hill, who had long been politically at odds with the president and who invoked the principle of senatorial courtesy to defeat the president's first two nominations to fill the vacancy left by Blatchford's death. Thus, the Senate rejected William B. Hornblower and Wheeler Peckham, both prominent New York lawyers who were nevertheless unacceptable to Senator Hill because both had been involved in the investigation of one of Hill's political allies for election tampering. Wheeler Peckham was Rufus Peckham's older brother and a man whose standing in the New York legal community was reflected in his chairmanship of the New York State Bar Association. During the confirmation battles over Hornblower and Wheeler Peckham, Senator Hill was reported to have announced that he would have voted to confirm an appointment of "the other Peckham"—that is, Rufus

Peckham. But President Cleveland had wearied of confirmation fights, and he eventually settled on the nomination of Senator Edward White from Louisiana for associate justice of the Supreme Court. White, quite popular among his senatorial colleagues, easily won confirmation and the matter was settled.

In 1895, though, the death of Justice Howell E. Jackson created another vacancy on the high court, and once again President Cleveland attempted to fill this seat with a New Yorker. Cleveland was willing to defy Hill and consulted with William Hornblower about accepting a renewed nomination to the Court, but Hornblower declined, as did Frederic Coudért, another New York lawyer approached by the president. Finally, President Cleveland recalled Senator Hill's earlier comment about Rufus Peckham and inquired by letter whether the senator still viewed Peckham as an acceptable choice for the Court. Hill had no complaint, and the president therefore submitted Rufus Peckham's name to the Senate in December 1895. The Senate moved quickly to confirm the appointment, and Peckham took the oath of his new office in January 1896. He seems not to have originally viewed the appointment as an unmitigated blessing, apparently because he found life as an appellate judge somewhat too cloistered for his taste. He remarked of his appointment to a friend, "If I have got to be put away on the shelf I suppose I might as well be on the top shelf."

Peckham wasted no time before aligning himself squarely with the Court's most conservative members. The Supreme Court had already begun to construct constitutional doctrines that would shield economic interests from government interference. Peckham immediately showed himself to be an industrious workman in this cause. He wrote the opinion for the Court in *Allgeyer v. Louisiana* (1897), which, for the first time, ruled a state law unconstitutional for infringing on the right of the individual to make contracts, a right the Court found implicit in the Fourteenth Amendment's due process clause. Even more famously, Peckham authored the majority opinion in *Lochner v. New York* (1905), perhaps the most controversial of the Court's attempts to graft laissez-faire economics onto the Constitution.

At issue in *Lochner* was a New York law that limited the hours worked in bakeries to 10 per day or 60 per week. The law had been passed on the basis of concerns for the health of bakers—who often worked in poorly ventilated tenement cellars—as well as concern that bakers lacked the bargaining power to assure fair labor conditions for themselves. Opponents of the law, however, insisted that it unconstitutionally infringed on the contractual liberties of both bakers and their employers. Peckham's opinion for the Court in *Allgeyer* had first invalidated state legislation on the basis of this asserted right. Now, in a closely divided case, Justice Peckham again spoke for a bare majority of the Court and dealt a fatal constitutional blow to the New York law. He relied on the developing doctrine of "substantive due process" to invalidate the law. According to this doctrine, the due process clauses of the Fourteenth and Fifth Amendments—which protect against deprivations of life, liberty, or property without "due process of law"—guarantee not only that deprivations will be procedurally fair but that they will be substantively reasonable. Applying this doctrine to the New York law, Justice Peckham concluded that it unreasonably interfered with the liberty of contract. As a matter of common understanding, he insisted, baking was not thought of as an unhealthy occupation, and therefore the state of New York had no reasonable basis for limiting freedom of contract. As to the asserted purpose of equalizing the bargaining power between bakers and their employees, Peckham denied that this was a legitimate legislative purpose at all. Thus, the act was unconstitutional.

The opinion in *Lochner v. New York* would become the blueprint by which a conservative Court invalidated a host of laws over the next three decades. Not until the late 1930s would the Court finally extricate itself from the course on which Justice Rufus Peckham had helped to set it by rejecting its self-appointed role as overseer of the reasonableness of economic regulations. Peckham, though, would not live to see the flourishing of his conservative judicial philosophy. Four years after he wrote the opinion in *Lochner,* and while still serving on the Court, he died in Altamont, New York, on October 24, 1909.

—∞—

Even while he served on the Court, Justice Rufus Wheeler Peckham was not reckoned among its most preeminent justices. A law clerk once asked Justice Oliver Wendell Holmes, "What was Justice Peckham like, intellectually?" Holmes reportedly replied, "Intellectually? I never thought of him in that connection. His major premise was, 'God damn it!'" Few of the 315 opinions Peckham wrote while on the Court left any lasting mark on American law. His opinion in *Lochner* was a notable exception, but the mark it left came to be regarded as something of a constitutional scar, an unfortunate intrusion of judicial power into the democratic process, by which conservative justices shackled the law to their own biases. Eventually the Court would reject *Lochner*'s reasoning, and the case would become a byword for judicial overreaching. Not surprisingly, history has not viewed with any great affection the justice who authored one of the 20th century's most reviled opinions.

Further Reading

Duker, William F. "Mr. Justice Rufus W. Peckham and the Case of *Ex parte Young:* Lochnerizing *Munn v. Illinois.*" *Brigham Young University Law Review* (1980): 539–558.

———. "Mr. Justice Rufus W. Peckham: The Police Power and the Individual in a Changing World." *Brigham Young University Law Review* (1980): 47–67.

Hall, A. Oakey. "The New Supreme Court Justice." *Green Bag* 8 (January 1896): 1–4.

Procter, L. B. "Rufus W. Peckham." *Albany Law Journal* 55 (1897): 286–288.

Skolnik, Richard. "Rufus Peckham." In *The Justices of the United States Supreme Court 1789–1969: Their Lives and Major Opinions,* Vol. 3. Edited by Leon Friedman and Fred L. Israel. New York: R. R. Bowker Co., 1969.

JOSEPH MCKENNA (1843–1926)

Associate Justice, 1898–1925

Appointed by President William McKinley

JOSEPH MCKENNA
(United States Supreme Court)

The son of immigrant Catholic parents, Joseph McKenna's life encapsulated the promise of the American dream. McKenna, who delivered bakery goods in the street at the age of 15, eventually found himself seated on the nation's highest Court, though his passage from one social rank to the other partook of all the turbulence characteristic of the West where he grew up. Lacking any formal education beyond early parochial school, McKenna had to rely on native energy and common sense. He was the last justice to take a seat on the Supreme Court in the 19th century, and he arrived there without significant legal and judicial expertise, more a politician than a judge or even a lawyer. From his early 20s until he was appointed as a federal appellate judge in 1892, McKenna was either holding a political office or campaigning for one, spending only a short amount of time in the private practice of law. Once appointed to the Court, though, McKenna grew steadily, if slowly, in the role that eventually occupied 27 years of his life. He arrived on the Court with generally conservative principles but displayed over the years of his tenure an erratic pattern of thinking that found him often on the side of moderate or even progressive opinions, at least until the last years of his life, when his earlier conservativism reasserted itself.

—∞—

Joseph McKenna was born on August 10, 1845, or perhaps, according to a baptismal record, August 14. His father, John McKenna, an Irish baker, had migrated to Philadelphia three years earlier. There he met and married Joseph's mother, Mary Ann Johnson, who had herself emigrated from England only a few years previously. The young couple struggled to operate a bakery in the harsh economic circumstances in which they found themselves in mid-19th-century Philadelphia. They struggled even more to survive in the virulently anti-Catholic climate of the city. Members of the infant Know-Nothing movement routinely burnt Catholic churches and Catholic homes during this time, forcing the McKenna family to move their bakery frequently to find a place where they might practice the trade that barely kept them alive. By the mid-1850s a rate war among steamship companies finally gave the McKennas a chance to escape Philadelphia, and they booked passage to San Francisco, California. The family soon settled in the small town of Bencia, at the southern end of the Napa Valley. Though they found a measure of economic prosperity, tragedy soon tempered their gain with loss. John McKenna died three years after the family arrived in California, and two of the family's children would soon follow. By age 15, Joseph McKenna found himself the man of the family, and while the Civil War raged far away from California, he struggled with his mother to keep their bakery going. On the side he started to study law; he was eventually able to pass the California bar in 1865.

Within six months of being admitted to practice law in California, McKenna won election to the position of Solano County district attorney. It was the first step in a political career that would predominantly occupy McKenna's life over the next 25 years. At the threshold of that career, he cast his lot with the newly created Republican party. McKenna served as district attorney for four years altogether before returning to private life and the practice of law. After leaving his public post, he married Amanda Frances Bornemann. The union would last more than 50 years and produce four children who survived to adulthood.

In the mid-1870s McKenna returned to political life. He won a seat in the California legislature in 1875 and promptly set his sights on winning election to the U.S. Congress. But this political prize eluded him for a time. McKenna won the Republican nomination from California's third congressional district in 1876, but he lost in the general election to the Democratic incumbent, John King Luttrell. When Luttrell retired at the end of the term, McKenna garnered the Republican nomination again and this time lost the general election to the Democratic candidate C. P. Berry by a mere 189 votes in 1878. Six years later he renewed his quest for a seat in Congress. This time, after a spirited battle for the Republican nomination, McKenna emerged victorious from his party's primary and easily won the general election. In 1885 he took his seat as a Republican congressman from California. Once in Congress, McKenna had no difficulty remaining there. He became a fierce advocate for California's economic interests, especially its railroad interests. Along the way he cemented close relationships with Leland Stanford, one-time governor of California who would become a U.S. senator and—even more important—William McKinley of Ohio, with whom McKenna served on the House Ways and Means Committee.

The political connections McKenna forged during four congressional terms ultimately made him an attractive candidate for a more substantial political appointment. In 1892, when Republican President Benjamin Harrison had to fill a vacant seat on the U.S. Ninth Circuit Court of Appeals, which covered

California, Leland Stanford—now a U.S. senator from California—was quick to suggest that the president appoint Joseph McKenna to the court. When President Harrison accepted this advice, however, and named McKenna to the Ninth Circuit, not everyone was pleased. More than a few critics complained that McKenna was nothing more than a political hack, lacking in judicial or even significant legal experience and likely to show favoritism toward railroad interests.

In five years on the Court of Appeals, McKenna avoided the kind of overt favoritism for the railroads that others had prognosticated, but his generally weak educational background and lack of significant legal experience combined to make his service on the court quite lackluster. Nevertheless, when McKenna's old friend from congressional days, William McKinley, returned to Washington as president of the United States, McKenna's name was prominent among those expected to feature in the new administration. Though it was widely rumored that he might assume a seat in the president's cabinet as secretary of the interior, he and McKinley doubted whether McKenna's Catholicism would serve him well in a post with significant oversight of Native American education, generally in the hands of Protestant missionaries at that time. McKinley found a place for the Californian instead as attorney general of the United States, but this appointment proved to be the shortest in McKenna's political career. He took office as attorney general in March 1897, and the following December, Justice Stephen J. Field of California announced his retirement from the Supreme Court. President McKinley immediately nominated McKenna to fill this vacancy on the Court; in spite of renewed criticism of McKenna's aptitude as a jurist, he won confirmation from the Senate on January 21, 1898, and thus became the last justice to join the Court in the 19th century.

True to his detractors' criticisms, McKenna's 27 years on the Court never found him located among its most brilliant lights. McKenna himself was unsure enough of his judicial ability that he attended courses briefly at Columbia University Law School before taking his seat on the Court. But eventually he made a place for himself as a competent jurist with a plain and simple writing style. Curiously, in light of his previous political partisanship on behalf of railroad interests, McKenna carved a reputation as a moderate rather than a conservative ideologue.

Toward the end of his long career on the Court, McKenna reverted to the conservativism of his younger days, at least until advancing old age began to rob him of his mental faculties. By the time William Howard Taft became chief justice of the Court in 1921, McKenna's health had begun to fail and his mind and temperament soon followed a declining path. His wife of more than 50 years died in 1924, and that year Chief Justice Taft—despairing of McKenna's erratic behavior and decisions—secured the agreement of the other justices on the Court not to let McKenna's vote be decisive in any case. At the same time, Taft pressured McKenna to step down from the Court. Finally on January 5, 1925, the aged Californian did so. He died in Washington, D.C., almost two years later, on November 21, 1926.

—m—

History would remember Joseph McKenna more for the length of his service on the Supreme Court than for any significant contributions to the course of American law. But McKenna also illustrated that the opportunity to serve on the nation's highest court might make more of a man as a jurist than a previously political career would have indicated. Though he labored in the shadows cast by more luminous jurists—such as Oliver Wendell Holmes, Jr., and Louis Brandeis—he sided with their progressive position more than might have been expected, from his earlier political loyalties to railroads and other conservative interests.

Further Reading

McDevitt, Matthew. *Joseph McKenna: Associate Justice of the United States.* Washington, D.C.: The Catholic University of America Press, 1946.

Watts, James F., Jr. "Joseph McKenna." In *The Justices of the United States Supreme Court 1789–1969: Their Lives and Major Opinions,* Vol. 3. Edited by Leon Friedman and Fred L. Israel. New York: R. R. Bowker Co., 1969.

Oliver Wendell Holmes, Jr. (1841–1935)

Associate Justice, 1902–1932

Appointed by President Theodore Roosevelt

Oliver Wendell Holmes, Jr.
(Photograph, Library of Congress)

Though Oliver Wendell Holmes, Jr., died well before the first half of the 20th century had run its course, he towers over the legal history of that century. Only one other jurist in the Court's history, Chief Justice John Marshall, surpasses Holmes in brilliance and influence. Unlike Marshall, though, Holmes never sat in the Court's chief seat. Moreover, unlike Marshall, Holmes seldom dominated the Court in his own day. His most famous judicial opinions were often dissents. But these often became blueprints for the judicial architecture erected in later years.

Oliver Wendell Holmes, Jr., was born on March 8, 1841, in Boston, Massachusetts, into what his illustrious father once referred to as New England's aristocracy. Both his father, Dr. Oliver Wendell Holmes, and his mother, Amelia Lee Jackson Holmes, were numbered among the Boston Brahmins. Dr. Holmes was a famous physician and man of letters, the author of *The Autocrat at the Breakfast Table* and one of the founders of the *Atlantic Monthly.* Justice Holmes's maternal grandfather had been an associate justice of the Supreme Judicial Court of Massachusetts. The family into which the future Supreme Court justice was born was not wealthy by standards of the time. But it was eminently well-connected, and Holmes, Jr., enjoyed the benefits of his family's social status, which included preparatory education at Dixwell's Private Latin School. Later, Holmes attended Harvard College, from which he graduated in 1861, and where he was elected class poet after compiling a generally inauspicious record of academic achievement.

Holmes wrote in his college annual that he intended to embark on the study of law, but the summer of 1861, when he graduated, saw the Civil War intrude on these plans. Holmes accepted a first lieutenant's commission in the Massachusetts 20th Volunteer infantry shortly after the Battle of Bull Run. The following years found him in the thick of fighting and wounded repeatedly: shot in the chest at Bulls Bluff, in the neck at Antietam, and stricken by shrapnel at Fredericksburg. "Then will he strip his sleeve and show his scars," Shakespeare's King Henry V declared, and Holmes finally mustered out of the Union army in July 1864 with his share of the nation's scars.

He briefly contemplated a career as a philosopher and visited Ralph Waldo Emerson to explore this inclination. Ultimately, though, Holmes returned to his previous aspiration to find a vocation in the law and enrolled in Harvard Law School in the fall of 1864. For a year and a half he attended the various lectures of which formal legal education consisted in those days. He also—not surprisingly in light of the his own philosophical inclinations—struck up a friendship with William James, who would eventually number among the early 20th-century's most prominent American philosophers. Cutting short the normal two-year course of legal study by a semester, Holmes was nevertheless awarded a Bachelor of Laws degree in the summer of 1866 and promptly embarked on a European tour.

When he returned to Boston, Holmes found work with the law firm of Chandler, Shattuck, and Thayer while he studied for the Massachusetts bar examination. After he was admitted to the bar in March 1867, Holmes practiced law for a time with the firm before deciding to practice with his brother Ned. Alongside his work as an attorney, Holmes began writing articles for the newly founded *American Law Review* and, in 1870, became one of its editors. Around the same time, Holmes accepted a part-time position teaching constitutional law at Harvard Law School. To this professional activity Holmes added the personal event of marrying Fanny Bowdich Dixwell. The couple's marital union, though childless, would last for 57 years until Fanny's death in 1929.

In the years immediately after Holmes's marriage, he practiced law with new partners, in the firm of Shattuck, Holmes, and Monroe, which focused its energies on commercial and admiralty matters. Toward the end of the 1870s, Holmes began writing a series of essays about the common law, which he eventually used as a basis for the Lowell Lectures, which he was invited to deliver in November and December 1880. These lectures, in turn, he eventually published in 1881 as *The Common Law,* a work widely recognized as one of the most influential books of American legal scholarship. In *The Common Law,* Holmes announced his sharp departure from the philosophy of legal formalism, which envisioned the law as an intricate tapestry of principles brought to bear on individual cases, from which judges deduced results that reflected the logical application of those principles to particular contexts. Holmes, though, would have none of this. "The Life of the Law," he wrote, "has not been logic: it has been experience." Judges decided cases, he insisted, in accordance with the "felt necessities of the time" and devised principles after the fact to explain the results. *The Common Law* thus became an early manifesto for the philosophy of legal realism.

Harvard Law School recognized the now-secure legal stature of Oliver Wendell Holmes, Jr., by appointing him as a professor of law in 1882, but Holmes aspired to the more mentally vigorous life of a judge. This ambition was fulfilled almost immediately when Holmes, after teaching only a semester at Harvard Law School, accepted an appointment as an associate justice of the Supreme Judicial Court of Massachusetts.

Over the years on the Massachusetts court, Holmes wrote nearly 1,300 judicial opinions, grappling mostly with the common-law issues on which he had forged his scholarly reputation. When called on to decide constitutional matters, Holmes tended to practice deference toward legislatures. He remained on the Supreme Judicial Court for the next 20 years, becoming chief justice toward the end of his tenure, in 1899.

In fall 1902 Justice Horace Gray of Massachusetts died, leaving a vacant seat on the U.S. Supreme Court. Like Holmes, Gray had served as chief justice of Massachusetts's highest court before accepting an appointment to the Supreme Court. President Theodore Roosevelt shortly expanded the parallels between the two Massachusetts judges by nominating Holmes to fill the vacancy left by Gray's death. After his Senate confirmation, Holmes took his seat, on December 8, 1902, undertaking what would eventually become a 30-year career as an associate justice on the Supreme Court. He also became the first justice appointed to the Court in the 20th century. Before his long tenure on the Court ended, he served under four chief justices—Melville W. Fuller, Edward Douglass White, William Howard Taft, and Charles Evans Hughes. By the time he finally laid down his judicial pen, he had written 873 opinions for the Court, as well as influential dissenting opinions in the areas of substantive due process and free speech that later majorities on the Court would embrace.

Holmes found himself famously at odds with a majority of the Supreme Court only a few years after his appointment. In *Lochner v. New York* (1905), the Court's majority, led by Justice Rufus Peckham, flexed its judicial muscle to review the reasonableness of a state law regulating bakery work hours. Writing for the Court, Peckham insisted that the law amounted to a deprivation of liberty without due process of law, since, he concluded, it unreasonably interfered with the contractual rights of bakeries and their employees.

This application of the Fourteenth Amendment's due process clause—referred to as the doctrine of "substantive due process"—would, in the coming years, be wielded by the Court to invalidate a wide variety of legislative economic initiatives. Holmes, though, railed against the majority's reasoning and its result, charging that the Court had mistakenly imposed its own conservative economic philosophy on the state legislature in the name of constitutional principle. "The 14th Amendment," he insisted, "does not enact Mr. Herbert Spencer's *Social Statistics,*" a famous philosophical defense of laissez-faire economics. Though Holmes's dissent failed to move the majority in *Lochner,* three decades later a new majority on the Court adopted Holmes's position and decisively repudiated the reasoning of *Lochner.*

Later in his career on the Court, Justice Holmes established an equally important tradition of dissent against the Supreme Court's cramped reading of the free speech guarantee in the First Amendment. Holmes initially found himself in step with the Court's majority in *Schenck v. United States* (1919). *Schenck* raised the issue of whether Congress could punish speeches and publications that threatened to interfere with the draft. Holmes wrote for a unanimous Court that since the government could punish obstruction of the draft, it could also punish speech that posed a "clear and present danger" of such obstruction.

Though the First Amendment might be read to prohibit *any* restrictions on speech, Holmes rejected this possibility. Surely, he declared, the man who causes panic and injury by shouting "Fire!" in a crowded theater was not immune from punishment.

Later that same year, however, Justice Holmes departed from the Court's majority in *Abrams v. United States* (1919). He challenged the punishments assigned to men who had thrown from a building window leaflets that criticized the draft and the United States's involvement in World War I. No "clear and present danger" of interfering with the war effort could be assigned to the pamphlets, he argued. Even more broadly, he insisted that toleration was the wisest response to objectionable speech:

> Persecution for the expression of opinions seems to me perfectly logical. If you have no doubt of your premises or your power and want a certain result with all your heart you naturally express your wishes in law and sweep away all opposition. To allow opposition by speech seems to indicate that you think the speech impotent, as when a man says that he has squared the circle, or that you do not care whole-heartedly for the result, or that you doubt either your power or your premises. But when men have realized that time has upset many fighting faiths, they may come to believe even more than they believe the very foundations of their own conduct that the ultimate good desired is better reached by free trade in ideas—that the best test of truth is the power of the thought to get itself accepted in the competition of the market, and that truth is the only ground upon which their wishes safely can be carried out. That at any rate is the theory of our Constitution.

For the remainder of his tenure on the Court, Oliver Wendell Holmes, Jr., waged rhetorical war against the Court's crabbed readings of the First Amendment and was ultimately joined in his dissents by Justice Louis Brandeis. The two championed an expansive view of free speech that finally found a welcome climate on the Supreme Court in the last half of the 20th century.

By the end of his years on the Court, Justice Holmes had served longer than any previous justice. But old age eventually deprived him of his wife Fanny in 1929. He managed to continue his work on the Court past his 90th birthday, but declining health eventually robbed him of the strength and mental attention necessary to continue his judicial work. At the urging of his friend Justice Louis Brandeis Holmes agreed to resign from the Court on January 12, 1932. Three years later Holmes contracted pneumonia and died, a few days before turning 94, on March 6, 1935. Leaving neither wife nor children, Holmes bequeathed an estate of some quarter of a million dollars to the country he had served, first as a soldier and later as a judge.

Justice Oliver Wendell Holmes, Jr., once described "the secret isolated joy of the thinker," the one who knows that,

> a hundred years after he is dead and forgotten, men who never heard of him will be moving to the measure of his thought—the subtle rapture of a postponed power, which the world knows not because it has no external trappings, but which to his prophetic vision is more real than that which commands an army.

Holmes was an influential and highly respected judge in his day, but history has only increased his stature, awarding him, on subjects such as freedom of speech and substantive due process, the "subtle rapture of postponed power." Positions that he championed in dissent now reign in constitutional law, and his judicial pronouncements reach across nearly a century and still guide, in important respects, the course of American law.

FURTHER READINGS

Baker, Liva. *Justice from Beacon Hill: The Life and Times of Oliver Wendell Holmes.* New York: HarperCollins, 1991.

Gordon, Robert W., ed. *The Legacy of Oliver Wendell Holmes, Jr.* Stanford: Stanford University Press, 1992.

Holmes, Oliver Wendell. *The Collected Works of Justice Holmes: Complete Public Writings and Selected Judicial Opinions of Oliver Wendell Holmes.* Edited by Sheldon M. Novick. Chicago: University of Chicago Press, 1995.

Howe, Mark De Wolfe. *Justice Oliver Wendell Holmes.* 2 vols. Cambridge: Belknap Press of Harvard University Press, 1957.

Novick, Sheldon M. *Honorable Justice: The Life of Oliver Wendell Holmes.* Boston: Little, Brown, 1989.

White, G. Edward. *Justice Oliver Wendell Holmes: Law and the Inner Self.* New York: Oxford University Press, 1993.

William Rufus Day (1849–1923)

Associate Justice, 1903–1923

Appointed by President Theodore Roosevelt

William Rufus Day
(United States Supreme Court)

Close friend of a slain leader, William Rufus Day entered public life at the urging of President William McKinley and remained there after an assassin's bullet had accomplished its work. In the space of six years, Day's friendship with McKinley saw him transformed from a small-town lawyer to the nation's secretary of state and still later into a federal appellate judge. After McKinley's death a new president, Theodore Roosevelt, advanced Day to a seat on the U.S. Supreme Court. There, for nearly 20 years, Justice Day generally occupied a centrist position on a Court sharply divided between conservative and progressive jurists. Unlike more conservative members of the Court, Day supported state economic regulations even when they restricted property and contract rights. But unlike more progressive figures on the Court, Day frequently opposed attempts by Congress to regulate economic matters using its commerce power. These contrasting positions often distinguished Day from other justices who saw no constitutional infirmity with either federal or state regulation of the economy as well as those who saw constitutional defects in both.

—∞—

William Rufus Day was born in Ravenna, Ohio, on April 17, 1849, the son of Emily Spaulding Day and Luther Day. The reluctance that the future Supreme Court justice exhibited toward entering public life once he reached adulthood cannot be traced to his family background. Though Ravenna was a small town some 30 miles southeast of Cleveland, Ohio, Day's family connections were considerably more prestigious than the venue of his birth might have suggested. Both sides of his family boasted prominent judges: His mother's grandfather had served as chief justice of the Connecticut Supreme Court, and his father and maternal grandfather both served on the Ohio Supreme Court. William Day's choice of a vocation seems to have been early directed toward the path of the law. He graduated from high school in 1866 and pursued an undergraduate literature major from the University of Michigan in Ann Arbor the same year. Upon his graduation in 1870, he returned home to Ravenna, where he studied law for a year in the office of Judge George F. Robinson and then supplemented this study by returning to spend a year in Ann Arbor at the University of Michigan Law School.

After law school, William Day returned to Ohio but veered away from Ravenna in favor of settling in the nearby town of Canton, where he was admitted to practice law in the summer of 1872. For the next quarter-century he lived the life of a small-town lawyer in Canton. Upon being admitted to practice, Day immediately formed a partnership with William S. Lynch, who had been practicing law for seven years when he and Day formed the firm of Lynch and Day. William Day soon added a marital partnership to his legal one, by his marriage to Mary Elizabeth Schaefer in 1875. This union, which produced four sons, William, Luther, Stephen, and Rufus, and lasted until Mary's death in 1911.

Before Day arrived in Canton and began a law practice with William Lynch, his future partner had suffered political defeat at the hands of another young Canton lawyer named William McKinley, Jr., in races for the post of prosecuting attorney for Stark County. Once William Day began practice in Canton and became involved in the town's Republican politics, he and McKinley gradually formed a fast friendship. Over the following years, as McKinley, the Civil War hero, clambered up the political ladder—first as a U.S. congressman, then as governor of Ohio, and finally as president of the United States—Day acted as a behind-the-scenes adviser to his prominent friend. Day himself, though, preferred private life. In 1886, with bipartisan support from both Republicans and Democrats, Day obtained a seat on the Court of Common Pleas; but he served only six months as a judge before resigning, explaining at the time that the small salary attached to the position was not sufficient to meet his family needs. Three years later, in 1889, President Benjamin Harrison nominated Day to serve as a U.S. federal district judge. Nevertheless, even though the Senate confirmed the appointment, Day felt compelled to turn in down for reasons of poor health.

The following decade saw William McKinley win the presidential election of 1896, and he carried William Day into national public life in his wake. In April 1897 the president appointed Day as first assistant secretary of state. Though this position seemed at first less consequential than Day's ability and long friendship with the president might have warranted, it soon proved to be a critical placement. The position of secretary of state had been filled by John Sherman, who had resigned his seat as U.S. senator from Ohio to accept the cabinet appointment. But failing mental faculties besieged Sherman and made him unable to fulfill the responsibilities of his position, especially during the turbulent events that culminated with the Spanish-American War—known as "the splendid little war," a conflict with Spain over Cuba. In the weeks leading up to this conflict, Assistant Secretary of State Day, whose credentials as a lawyer were impeccable but whose qualifications as a diplomat were far more obscure, became de facto secretary of state. He generally favored a moderate course with Spain, but after the explosion of the USS *Maine* in Havana's harbor in February 1898, national sentiment resolutely marched toward war. Finally, when the United States declared war against Spain in April 1898, Sherman resigned his post and the president appointed Day to be secretary of state in title as well as fact. He did not remain in this cabinet position for long, though. After six months, Day resigned to head the United States delegation to the Paris peace conference that met in the fall and early winter of 1898. As the leader of this diplomatic mission, William Day eventually spearheaded the bargaining that acquired Puerto Rico, Guam, and the Philippine Islands for the United States.

When he completed the mission to Paris, Day attempted to return home to Canton, but President McKinley had other uses for his friend. In February 1899 the president appointed Day as a judge on the U.S. Sixth Circuit Court of Appeals. Here, Judge Day joined William Howard Taft and Howard H. Lurton, both of whom would eventually serve with him on the U.S. Supreme Court as well. But when Day did advance to a seat on the Court, it was not his presidential friend who placed him there; McKinley was killed by an assassin's bullet in the summer of 1901, ending the long friendship. A new president, however, Theodore Roosevelt, soon had occasion to consider Day for an appointment to the nation's highest court when Justice George Shiras, Jr., resigned in October 1902. Roosevelt turned first to William Howard Taft to fill the vacancy, but Taft, by this time U.S. civil governor of the Philippines, felt he could not abandon his post there. Thus, the president determined to shore up political support in Ohio by naming William Day to the Court instead. On March 2, 1903, William Rufus Day took his seat as an associate justice of the U.S. Supreme Court. He would hold this position for almost 20 years.

Day arrived on the Court at a time when it was wrestling with constitutional issues that pitted progressive influences on the Court against conservative justices who championed laissez-faire economics. In the early decades of the 20th century, business interests found support among a majority of the justices of the Supreme Court in their efforts to escape regulations imposed on them by federal and state government authorities. Congress attempted to regulate many of the growing economic problems of the century through use of its commerce power—that is, the power to pass laws to regulate commerce among the states. In their attempts to address similar economic problems, state and local governments relied, in turn, on their general powers to regulate matters affecting the health and welfare of citizens. Commercial interests were able to frustrate a good deal of lawmaking at both levels. They persuaded a majority of the Court to narrowly construe Congress's power to regulate interstate commerce, chiefly by defining "commerce" itself narrowly. They also persuaded a majority of the Court to safeguard contractual and property rights from unreasonable state and local regulations. The sharp distinction between progressives and conservatives did not capture Day's own thinking, however. In contrast with some conservatives on the Court, he tended to favor a wide latitude for state lawmaking, even when it affected the contractual and property interests of businesses, but, in contrast with liberal justices on the Court, Day tended to narrowly construe federal power to regulate interstate commerce.

William Day's most famous opinion, announcing the Court's decision in *Hammer v. Dagenhart* (1918), reflects his miserly view of the federal commerce power. The case involved a constitutional challenge to the federal Child Labor Act, passed in 1916, which prohibited the interstate transportation of goods produced by factories that employed child labor. In passing the act, Congress had relied on its power to regulate interstate commerce. Day, however, writing for a bare majority of the Supreme Court, rebuffed this attempt by Congress to use the commerce power to address social ills such as child labor. He insisted for the Court that the manufacturing process did not amount to "commerce" and that Congress therefore had no constitutional power to intrude its regulatory wishes on industries that used child labor.

In 1911 Day's wife Mary died, but he continued to enjoy the close companionship of his son Rufus, who served as his secretary. Day missed several months of work in 1915, after suffering a severe illness, but otherwise occupied his seat on the Court faithfully until he reached the age of 73. He announced his retirement from the Court on November 13, 1922. President Warren G. Harding tempted the elderly Day into a position on the Mixed Claims Commission, which was established to resolve claims arising out of World War I, but Day soon resigned from this post because of ill health. He died on July 9, 1923, while vacationing at his summer home on Mackinac Island, Michigan.

In an age roiled with conflicts between business and progressive influences, William Rufus Day clearly envisioned a role for government to address the ills spawned by the Industrial Revolution. But he generally believed that state rather than national government authorities should take the lead in tackling these ills. His suspicion of federal power over commerce ultimately proved to be unpalatable to a later generation of jurists. Less than two decades after his death, the Supreme Court abandoned its opposition to the New Deal legislation that President Franklin D. Roosevelt had prodded Congress into enacting to remedy a broad range of social and economic ills. The Court thus repudiated the cramped reading of federal commerce power to which Justice Day had partially contributed.

Further Reading

"Character of Mr. Justice Day." *American Law Review* 37 (1903): 402–403.

Duncan, George W. "The Diplomatic Career of William Rufus Day, 1897–1898." Ph.D. diss., Case Western Reserve Univ., 1976.

McLean, Joseph E. *William Rufus Day: Supreme Court Justice from Ohio.* Baltimore: The Johns Hopkins University Press, 1946.

Morris, Jeffrey B. "The Era of Melville Weston Fuller." *Supreme Court Historical Society Yearbook* (1981): 36–51.

Roelofs, Vernon R. "William R. Day and Federal Regulation." *Mississippi Valley Historical Review* 37 (1950): 39–60.

William Henry Moody (1853–1917)

Associate Justice, 1906–1910

Appointed by President Theodore Roosevelt

William Henry Moody
(United States Supreme Court)

More than one Supreme Court justice has found his way onto the Court because of a close friendship with a president. William Henry Moody was one of these. He is best known as a confidant of President Theodore Roosevelt, although history has mostly remembered the president and forgotten the friend. Perhaps if Moody had not been stricken with a debilitating illness soon after joining the Court, more notice might have been taken of him. But sadly, ill health forced him into a premature retirement and death. As it is, Moody enjoyed only a brief season in the public eye, though he crammed this period with energy and accomplishment.

William Henry Moody was born on December 23, 1853, in Newbury, Massachusetts, to Henry L. Moody and Melissa A. Emerson Moody. His New England roots stretched back to the earliest days of the Massachusetts Bay Colony, when his forebear, William Moody, migrated from Suffolk, England, and helped found the town of Newbury in 1635. William Henry Moody's family eventually moved to Danvers, Massachusetts, where his father ran a dairy farm. In these early years Moody developed a love of baseball that he carried with him the rest of his life. He attended public schools until 1869, when he entered Phillips Academy in Andover to prepare for an Ivy League college education. While at Phillips he captained the school's baseball team. He graduated in 1872 and proceeded on to Harvard, where at first he proved to be a better baseball player than a student. But toward the end of his college career he fell under the influence of Henry Adams and became fascinated with the study of history and literature. He eventually graduated *cum laude* in 1876, ranked third in his class. Moody followed college with a brief stint of formal legal education at Harvard Law School, but he abandoned his studies after a semester and chose instead to read law in the office of Richard Henry Dana, a nationally prominent attorney of the time and author of *Two Years Before the Mast,* a classic tale of life at sea. After 18 months, however, Dana died suddenly of pneumonia in 1878 while traveling in Europe, thus cutting short Moody's education. Moody proceeded to sit for the oral bar examination in Massachusetts in spite of his aborted studies. Although the bar authorities were initially of a mind to deny his application for lack of sufficient preparatory legal education, Moody persuaded them to examine him, and he performed so well that his accomplishment became something of a legend for excellence.

Admitted to practice in 1878, Moody established himself in Haverhill, Massachusetts. Over the next decade he practiced law and plunged himself into the affairs of the community, becoming, not least of all, president of the Haverhill Baseball Club, as well as city solicitor from 1888 to 1890. Beginning in 1890, he served two terms as district attorney for the eastern district of Massachusetts. The highlight of his tenure as district attorney was his appointment as one of two special prosecutors in the notorious Lizzie Borden murder case, tried in 1892 and memorialized in the children's rhyme:

Lizzie Borden took an axe,
And gave her mother forty whacks,
When she saw what she had done,
She gave her father forty-one.

Though a jury ultimately acquitted Borden, Moody gained a solid reputation for his performance as a prosecutor in the trial.

Moody stepped onto the national stage in November 1895, when he was elected as a Republican to fill a vacant seat in the U.S. House of Representatives. At about the same time, he made the acquaintance of New York City's police commissioner, a man who would subsequently exert a profound influence on the course of Moody's life: Theodore Roosevelt. Roosevelt had come to Boston to address a Republican group and returned home speaking highly of Moody. Moody himself soon traveled to Washington, D.C., to begin what would become six and a half years in Congress, where his reputation as a progressive young Republican increased steadily. Over these years, Moody's relationship with Roosevelt grew closer. Consequently, when Roosevelt became president in 1901, he promptly added William Moody to his cabinet as secretary of the Navy. In this position, working closely with the president, the 49-year-old Moody—the youngest member of the cabinet—initiated a number of progressive developments in the Navy and oversaw its expansion at a time when President Roosevelt was anxious to strengthen the naval power of the United States. Moody also spearheaded the acquisition by the United States of a 99-year lease on Guantanamo, Cuba, where a U.S. naval base was established.

In summer 1904 Attorney General Philander Knox resigned from his cabinet position to accept a seat in the U.S. Senate. Roosevelt promptly named Moody to this position. The appointment came at a propitious time for a man eager for activity. Roosevelt's enthusiasm for "trust-busting" meant that his new attorney general soon found himself plunged into legal battles with the likes of Standard Oil and the Beef Trust. In Moody, Roosevelt had clearly found a kindred spirit, for the attorney general pursued these battles vigorously, often appearing in person to argue cases and wielding the Sherman Antitrust Act as a cudgel against monopolistic abuses. Moody preferred, when possible, to prosecute antitrust cases as criminal, rather than merely civil, violations.

The work, though, was demanding, and after two years as the nation's chief lawyer, Moody informed President Roosevelt of his wish to retire. In June 1906, however, the retirement of Justice Henry B. Brown left a vacancy on the Supreme Court. Although Roosevelt initially leaned toward appointing southern Democrat Horace Lurton, a judge on the U.S. Sixth Circuit Court of Appeals, to fill the vacancy, he was ultimately convinced to appoint his friend William Moody to the position instead. After some protest that Moody's close relationship with the president might jeopardize his judicial independence, the Senate confirmed his nomination on December 12, 1906, and Moody took his seat as an associate justice on the nation's highest court before the end of the year. Moody's climb to the pinnacle of American law had been dizzying in its swiftness. Barely 11 years from the date he had entered national politics as a young man by winning election to the House of Representatives, he donned black robes and took his seat beside Justice Oliver Wendell Holmes, one the greatest legal minds ever to sit on the Supreme Court.

If Moody's rise to national prominence had occupied only a brief span of time, his tenure of service on the high Court was even more brief. Technically, he held his seat on the Court for four years, but in reality, illness had felled him within a mere two years, leaving him an invalid incapable of so much as lifting a book to read. Nevertheless, for his first two years on the Court, Moody seemed to exemplify the kind of liberal nationalism that Roosevelt wished to see dominate the Supreme Court. He moved to the spirit of Alexander Hamilton and John Marshall rather than Thomas Jefferson and John Calhoun, favoring broad interpretations of federal power that would equip the national government with tools to address the problems of the early 20th century. Thus, he dissented from the majority's decision in the *Employers' Liability Case* (1908), which invalidated Congress's attempt to make railroads liable for the injury and death of their employees. But Moody also believed that not every social or legal problem required a national resolution. Thus, in *Twining v. New Jersey* (1908), he wrote his most famous opinion for the Court, concluding that the Fifth Amendment's privilege against self-incrimination, though applicable to federal criminal proceedings, was not also applicable to states. Justice John Marshall Harlan argued in dissent that the Fourteenth Amendment's due process clause, which prohibited *state* deprivations of life, liberty, or property without "due process of law," had made the provisions of the Bill of Rights, including the Fifth Amendment, applicable to the states. Led by Moody, however, the rest of the Court disagreed. Eventually, Harlan's view would largely triumph, but Moody's opinion in *Twining* survived for more than 50 years before finally being overruled in *Mallory v. Hogan* (1964).

After two years on the Court, Moody contracted a severe case of rheumatism, which crippled him. By 1909 he had been forced to retire to his home in Haverhill and to depend on his sister—unmarried as he was—to care for him. Congress responded to his plight by passing special legislation to allow him to retire early; the financial support this legislation provided allowed him to resign from the Court officially on November 10, 1910. His sister cared for him another seven years before he finally died in Haverhill on July 2, 1917.

For a decade in the first part of the 20th century, William Henry Moody captured the nation's attention—as an energetic congressman, a progressive secretary of the Navy, a zealous attorney general, a justice on the U.S. Supreme Court, and a close friend and confident of a president. But the Supreme Court and its history is a spacious place, large enough to swallow notable and talented minds into obscurity. Next to a Marshall or a Holmes, who remembers Moody? Those who see past the Court's giants, though, to the lesser souls who occupied a seat on the highest court in the land for a time, sometimes ponder whether men like Moody might have made a greater mark had circumstances lent them a longer tenure on the Court. Moody, in particular, possessed the energy and talent that might have left a more permanent mark on American law, if only sickness had not felled him in his prime.

Further Reading

Heffron, Paul T. "Profile of a Public Man." *Supreme Court Historical Society Yearbook 1980.* Washington D.C.: Supreme Court Historical Society (1980): 30–31, 48.

———. "Theodore Roosevelt and the Appointment of Mr. Justice Moody." *Vanderbilt Law Review* 18 (1965): 545–568.

Moody, William Henry. "Constitutional Powers of the Senate: A Reply." *North American Review* 174 (1902): 386–94.

Watts, James F., Jr. "William Moody." In *The Justices of the United States Supreme Court 1789–1969: Their Lives and Major Opinions,* vol. 3. Edited by Leon Friedman and Fred L. Israel. New York: R. R. Bowker Co., 1969.

McDonough, Judith R. "William Henry Moody." Ph.D. diss., Auburn Univ., 1983.

Horace Harmon Lurton (1844–1914)

Associate Justice, 1910–1914

Appointed by President William Howard Taft

Horace Harmon Lurton
(United States Supreme Court)

A southerner, a Civil War veteran, and a lifelong Democrat, Horace Harmon Lurton served the better part of his adult life as a judge. He might have remained a widely regarded appellate judge and never have sat on the Supreme Court had circumstances not made him a friend of a Republican judge and later president of the United States, William Howard Taft. Taft himself eventually found his way onto the Supreme Court as chief justice, although his older friend had died some years earlier. For four years before his death, however, Lurton had helped preside briefly over the legal affairs of the nation that he had, in his youth, labored mightily to fracture. The years after the war saw him find a solid place within the legal affairs of that nation, culminating with his service on the U.S. Supreme Court, where he became, at the age of 65, the oldest justice ever to take a seat there.

—⁓—

Horace Harmon Lurton was born in Newport, Kentucky, on February 26, 1844, to Sarah Ann Harmon Lurton and Lycurgus Leonidas Lurton. His father practiced medicine and pharmacy before becoming an Episcopalian minister. Horace would not follow his father's path in either medicine or ministry, but he would become an Episcopalian vestryman himself. The elder Lurton eventually transported his family to Clarksville, Tennessee, where Horace received his early education in public schools. He traveled to Chicago at the age of 16 to enroll at Douglas University, which is no longer in existence. Within two years, however, the din of Civil War had distracted him from his academic career and drawn him into the ranks of the Confederate army. Lurton enlisted in the Fifth Tennessee Infantry in 1861, saw repeated action, and soon advanced to the rank of sergeant-major. By early February 1862, though, a sickness of the lungs had earned him a medical discharge and instructions to find rest at home. No sooner had he arrived in Clarksville than he heard word of General Ulysses S. Grant's nearby presence. He immediately reenlisted in the Second Kentucky Infantry, only to be taken prisoner when Grant subsequently took Fort Donnelson, where Lurton and 12,000 other Confederate soldiers were forced to surrender. Within a few weeks, he had escaped or, perhaps, was released. Lurton promptly celebrated his freedom by attaching himself to the irregular guerrilla force of General John Hunt Morgan, which spent better than a year making calvary raids against railroads, bridges, and Union communication centers. Finally, in summer 1863, Morgan's force was captured and Lurton, a prisoner of war for the second time, found himself consigned for 18 months to a prison camp on Johnson's Island in Lake Erie.

Stricken with tuberculosis, Lurton might have died there. But, according to his later account, his mother interceded on his behalf. After discovering his condition, she traveled to Washington and eventually obtained the ear of President Abraham Lincoln himself. Upon hearing her plea, the president ordered Lurton released. "Let the boy go home with his mother," he ordered, and Lurton managed to spend the last two months of the war in Clarksville, where he gradually recovered.

Once the Civil War was over, Horace Lurton set his sights on a career in the law and enrolled at Cumberland University Law School, near Nashville, Tennessee. He graduated in the summer of 1867, and a few months later married Mary Francis Owen. This union would last until Lurton's death 44 years later and would produce three sons and two daughters. Returning home to Clarksville, Lurton began his professional life by practicing first with Gustavus A. Henry and then with the firm of James E. Bailey. Bailey himself was a prominent Democratic politician appointed in 1875 to complete the term of former president and U.S. senator Andrew Johnson, who died in congressional office. The same year, Tennessee governor James G. Porter appointed 31-year-old Horace Lurton as presiding judge of the Sixth Chancery Division of Tennessee when the previous judge resigned. Already recognized as a solid attorney, Lurton's service as chancery judge so impressed his colleagues on the bench that they voted unanimously on his continuation as presiding judge once his initial term had expired. By 1878, though, the financial needs of Lurton's family proved more substantial that his judge's salary would accommodate, and he consequently returned to the private practice of law. The next eight years saw him well-established financially and socially. By the mid-1880s he had become president of Farmers' and Merchants' National Bank, a vestryman in the Trinity Episcopal Church, and a trustee of the University of the South.

In 1886 Horace Lurton's reputation in the state was sufficient to win him election to the Tennessee Supreme Court. There he established a reputation for courtesy, diligence, and fair-mindedness, qualities that would subsequently accompany him in steadily advancing judicial responsibilities. The departure of the chief justice of the Tennessee Supreme Court in January 1893 promptly resulted in Lurton's advancement to this position, but an even more prestigious opportunity presented itself when President Grover Cleveland appointed Lurton that same year to sit on the U.S. Court of Appeals for the Sixth Circuit, filling the seat left vacant after the president appointed Howell Jackson to the U.S. Supreme Court. Lurton joined a court presided over by 36-year-old Republican William Howard Taft, and the two, though divided by party lines, soon formed a fast friendship. Several years after Lurton arrived on the court, William Day, an Ohio Republican, was appointed to it. The friendship forged among Taft, Lurton, and Day would ultimately produce important dividends for Lurton. For the time being, as a federal appeals judge, Lurton reinforced the reputation for civility, fairness, and meticulousness that he had first established on the Tennessee Supreme Court. To his work as a federal judge, he added teaching and administrative responsibilities at Vanderbilt University, where he taught constitutional law from 1898 to 1905 and served as dean of the law school from 1905 until 1910. Lurton eventually became presiding judge of the Sixth Circuit Court of Appeals, after Taft departed to become governor of the Philippines.

While Horace Lurton remained on the federal Court of Appeals, his two friends, Taft and Day, each left the court for other public positions: Taft to become chair of the Philippine Commission and later civil governor of the Philippines, and then, in 1904, secretary of war under President Theodore Roosevelt; Day to become an associate justice of the Supreme Court in 1903. Both men interceded for Lurton with President Roosevelt when a seat on the Court became vacant in 1906 with the retirement of Henry Billings Brown. Roosevelt seriously considered appointing Lurton but eventually nominated his friend and attorney general, William Henry Moody, instead. Three years later, however, William Howard Taft was in a position to do more than intercede for Lurton. By the time Associate Justice Rufus Peckham died in October 1909, Taft had become president himself. He pondered over the appointment briefly, because although he wished to elevate his friend to the high Court, Lurton's 65 years of age seemed excessively venerable for such an appointment, at least to some observers. In a letter to Lurton in 1909, the president confided his dissatisfaction with the Court, especially the age and debilitation of its members:

> The condition of the Supreme Court is pitiable, and yet those old fools hold on with a tenacity that is most discouraging. Really the Chief Justice [Melville W. Fuller] is almost senile; Harlan does no work; Brewer is so deaf that he cannot hear and has got beyond the point of the commonest accuracy in writing his opinions; Brewer and Harlan sleep almost through all the arguments. I don't know what can be done. It is most discouraging to the active men on the Bench.

But the president nominated Lurton in spite of his age on December 13, 1909, and after he was confirmed and took his seat at the beginning of the new year, Lurton became—and remains—the oldest justice ever appointed to the Supreme Court. The president wired Lurton on announcing his nomination: "It is just the truth to tell you that the only pleasure of my administration, as I have contemplated it in the past, has been to commission you a justice of the Supreme Court."

It was perhaps too much to expect that Lurton might conclude an already notable judicial career with a long and illustrious career on the Supreme Court. Lurton was, both by age and judicial temperament, unlikely to find his way into the company of the Court's luminaries. His advanced age prognosticated a short term, and his general fondness for the status quo, paired with a conciliatory judicial temperament, made it likely that he would side with the modest progressive movement of the Court over the few years he sat on it. He authored 87 opinions during his four years on the high bench, none of great historical note. He supplemented his work on the Court by agreeing in

1911 to serve on the Committee to Revise the Equity Rules in Federal Court and devoted himself so energetically to this project that the culminating publication, the *New Federal Equity Rules,* when published in 1913, was dedicated to him. The following year illness forced Lurton to miss several weeks on the Court, though he recovered and finished out the term. In summer 1914 he traveled with his wife to Atlantic City for a vacation and died there unexpectedly of a heart attack on July 12, 1914.

The four years that Horace Harmon Lurton served on the Supreme Court crowned the accumulated achievements of a long career as a judge. During all of these years, Lurton demonstrated steady competence rather than judicial brilliance. He contributed to the work of the law without significantly altering its course, preferring order and precision, diligence and toil, to flights of jurisprudential creativity. In truth, the law's progress has more often than not rested more heavily in the hands of jurists such as Lurton than it has in those of legal geniuses such as Oliver Wendell Holmes or Benjamin Nathan Cardozo. These better-known jurists appear periodically to turn the course of the law down some previously unimagined causeway or guide it past some dangerous turbulence, but Lurton exemplifies the steady legal pilots who, without significant fanfare, steer the law when it passes through generally calm and familiar waters.

Further Reading

Green, John W. "Judge Horace H. Lurton." In *Law and Lawyers: Sketches of the Federal Judges of Tennessee, Sketches of the Attorneys General of Tennessee, Legal Miscellany, Reminiscences by John W. Green*. Jackson, Tenn.: McCowat-Mercer Press, 1950.

Phillips, Harry. "Tennessee Lawyers of National Prominence." *Tennessee Bar Journal* 17 (1981): 34–53.

Tucker, David M. "Justice Horace Harmon Lurton: The Shaping of a National Progressive." *American Journal of Legal History* 13 (1969): 223–232.

Watts, James F., Jr. "Horace H. Lurton." In *The Justices of the United States Supreme Court 1789–1969: Their Lives and Major Opinions,* Vol. 3. Edited by Leon Friedman and Fred L. Israel. New York: R. R. Bowker Co., 1969.

Williams, Samuel C. "Judge Horace H. Lurton." *Tennessee Law Review* 18 (1944): 242–250.

Charles Evans Hughes (1862–1948)

Associate Justice, 1910–1916

Appointed by President William Howard Taft

Chief Justice, 1930–1941

Appointed by President Herbert Hoover

Charles Evans Hughes
(Photograph, Library of Congress)

Few men in American history have rivaled the breadth of political achievements that Charles Evans Hughes accomplished in his lifetime. He served twice as a justice on the U.S. Supreme Court: first as an associate justice and then as its chief justice. He added to these accomplishments service as the governor of New York, as a nearly successful candidate for the presidency of the United States, and as secretary of state. The decade in which he occupied the Court's chief seat proved to be one of historic importance, surpassed only by the earlier period in the Court's history when Chief Justice John Marshall led the Court in translating the newly ratified Constitution of the United States into living political realities. Hughes fended off perhaps the most serious challenge to the Court's authority ever experienced by any chief justice, when President Franklin Delano Roosevelt proposed packing the Court with justices more open to his legislative agenda. Rather than suffer this result, Chief Justice Hughes partially capitulated to Roosevelt's political vision, preserving the Court's institutional authority for the challenges that yet awaited it in the 20th century.

Charles Evans Hughes was born on April 11, 1862, in Glen Falls, New York, as the nation in which he would later play a prominent part struggled to survive the Civil War. His parents, whose character would form the foundation of his own, were hardworking and religiously devout. His father, David Charles Hughes, was a Baptist minister, and his mother, Mary Catherine Connelly Hughes, was a former schoolteacher. "Whatever I do, wherever I go," he would later write, "when the question of right or wrong comes up, it is decided by what Pa or Ma will say if I did it."

Charles, an only child, was precocious from an early age, reading English by the time he was three, Greek and German beginning when he was eight. When his parents tried to send their six-year-old son off to school, he suffered boredom and persuaded them to teach him at home by presenting them with the "Charles E. Hughes Plan of Study." The appeal worked, and Charles's parents directed his early education until the family moved to New York City, where his father became secretary of the American Bible Union and Charles was enrolled in public school. By the time he was 14, Charles had been admitted to Madison College (later to become Colgate University). His parents had sent him to college, hoping that he would become a minister, but Charles's college years saw him fix his aspirations instead on a career in law. In 1878 he transferred to Brown University, where he excelled, gaining admittance to Phi Beta Kappa at the end of his junior year, winning election as an editor of the student newspaper, and graduating third in his class.

A lack of financial resources left Hughes unable to begin formal legal studies immediately. He settled instead for a teaching position with the Delaware Academy in Delhi, New York, where he supplemented his teaching responsibilities by reading law in the office of William M. Gleason. By the fall of 1882, however, his father was able to support his entrance into Columbia Law School, from which he graduated with highest honors in 1884. Thereafter, he passed the bar examination—with a score of $99\frac{1}{2}$—and began work with the prestigious New York firm of Chamberlin, Carter, and Hornblower. Five years later he became a partner in a reorganized version of the firm, and on December 5, 1888, he married one of his partner's daughters, Antoinette Carter, with whom he would have four children: a son, who would later serve as solicitor general of the United States, and three daughters. Within a few years of his marriage, however, Hughes left the practice of law to teach at Cornell University Law School after suffering from the effects of ill health and overwork. His firm managed to lure him back after two years, but even then, Hughes supplemented his legal practice by teaching at Cornell and at New York Law School.

In the years that followed, Hughes gradually acquired a reputation as one of New York's brightest lawyers. In 1905 he gained statewide prominence after being designated counsel for a legislative committee investigating utility rates. Hughes ferreted out systematic abuses that had resulted in utility overcharges. That same year, another legislative committee drafted him to lead its investigation of insurance companies. Again, Hughes sifted through the details and machinations of a complex industry to reveal the practices that padded the pockets of insurance executives and their cronies at the expense of the public. The following year, on the heels of these widely publicized and successful legislative crusades, Charles Evans Hughes was nominated as the Republican candidate for New York governor and won the general election handily. In this office he championed a host of progressive measures, including workers' compensation laws and public commissions to oversee utilities.

Hughes's reputation as a Republican reformer attracted the attention of President William Howard Taft, who appointed him on April 25, 1910, to fill the vacancy left on the Supreme Court when Justice David Brewer died. Hughes was easily confirmed by the Senate on May 2 and took his seat at the beginning of the Court's next term, on October 10, 1910. Taft had suggested to Hughes the possibility of his being advanced to the Court's chief seat should the position become open during the president's term of office. But Taft thought better of this when Chief Justice Melville Fuller died in the summer of 1910, for he aspired to sit in the seat of chief justice himself after leaving the presidency. "It seems strange," Taft declared, "that the one place in the government which I would have liked to fill myself I am forced to give to another." If he made the 48-year-old Hughes chief justice, then that seat on the Court might never become vacant during his own lifetime. Accordingly, Taft appointed Associate Justice Edward White—65 years old and likely to retire within a decade or so—to the position of chief justice.

Charles Evans Hughes served six years on the Court as an associate justice, carving a reputation for himself as a progressive justice in the area of civil rights and on the issue of whether federal and state governments should have power to regulate economic matters. Hughes left the Court, however, when on June 7, 1916, the Republican party nominated him as its candidate for president against the Democratic incumbent, President Woodrow Wilson. Hughes came close to the presidency, losing to Wilson by a narrow margin of 277 to 254 electoral votes and a popular vote of 9,126,300 to 8,546,789. With this defeat, Hughes returned to the private practice of law in New York City as the senior partner of Hughes, Rounds, Schurman, and Dwight, representing mainly corporate clients and appearing several times on their behalf before the Supreme Court on which he had previously sat.

In 1921 newly elected president Warren G. Harding immediately tapped Hughes to be his secretary of state; Hughes held this post for the next five years, into the administration of Calvin Coolidge. As secretary of state, Hughes spearheaded disarmament efforts after World War I and secured an international agreement guaranteeing Japan's security in the Western Pacific and recognizing the Open Door principle with respect to China. After five years of diplomatic service, however, Hughes returned once again to the private practice of law to shore up his personal finances.

During the years after Charles Evans Hughes had resigned from the Court, President William Howard Taft had managed to achieve his ambition of being named chief justice of the U.S. Supreme Court. In February 1930, though, after just nine years, ill health forced Taft to resign; he died barely a month later. Twenty years earlier, Taft had declined to appoint Hughes as chief justice, but now another president, Herbert Hoover, awarded Hughes with the appointment that Taft had denied him. On the day Taft resigned, President Hoover announced his appointment of Charles Evans Hughes to fill the now-vacant seat of chief justice. But the warm acclaim that had greeted Hughes's appointment as an associate justice of the Court in 1910 was absent in 1930. The New York lawyer's frequent professional service on behalf of American corporate interests had made him suspect to many Democrats, and the Senate debated his nomination at length before finally confirming him as chief justice by a vote of 52-26 on February 24, 1930.

The Court whose reins Hughes now grasped presided over the legal affairs of a nation in desperate economic straits. Very shortly a new chief executive, President Franklin Delano Roosevelt, attacked the nation's economic woes by securing the passage of expansive New Deal legislation in Congress. In so doing, Roosevelt collided squarely with a predominantly conservative court that had, for the last three and a half decades, regularly curtailed the power of Congress to legislate on economic matters and had also frequently championed property and contract rights over the attempts by state and local governments to regulate commercial matters. Hughes was an inconsistent ally of the conservatives. In *Home Building and Loan Association v. Blaisdell* (1934), for example, he joined with the Court's liberals and announced the opinion for a 5-4 majority that upheld a state law suspending mortgage foreclosures against the constitutional challenge that it impaired contract obligations. The right of contract, Hughes reasoned, was not absolute, and might have to give way in the face of an economic emergency.

In the main, however, the chief justice presided over a Court that soon dealt the Roosevelt administration crucial defeats. In particular, on what came to be known as "Black Monday"—May 27, 1935—a unanimous Court struck down three key pieces of New Deal legislation, including the National Recovery Act, which was invalidated in *Schechter Poultry Corp. v. United States* (1935) in an opinion written for the Court by Chief Justice Hughes. Although the entire Court joined in these cases, the Court's great triumvirate of liberals—Louis Brandeis, Benjamin Nathan Cardozo, and Harlan Fiske Stone—more often refused to join the Court's conservatives in striking down federal and state economic legislation. Chief Justice Hughes, however, though often a swing vote on the Court, joined many of the decisions that accomplished these results.

After President Roosevelt's landslide reelection in 1936, he moved to strike back against the Court by proposing his "court-packing" plan, according to which a new justice would be added to the Court for each justice who refused to retire at the age of 70. The president claimed that the elderly justices—there were six at the time—were not able to carry the Court's heavy workload and needed relief. In fact, his plan was clearly intended to wrest control of the Court away from its conservatives. The proposal, however, received a cool welcome in Congress. Moreover, shortly after the president announced his plan, the Court, led by Chief Justice Hughes, veered sharply away from its previous path and, beginning in *West Coast Hotel v. Parrish* (1937), upheld one key piece after another of New Deal legislation. Then and now, it appeared to some observers that the chief justice had sacrificed principle to pragmatism and had reversed positions he had made plain in earlier cases. In any event, with the crisis between Court and president averted, Congress declined to enact President Roosevelt's plan.

Hughes often voted with the Court's conservatives on issues relating to government regulation of the economy. But his record in the area of civil rights and civil liberties was generally more progressive. For example, he wrote the opinion for the Court in an early victory for free speech, *Stromberg v. California* (1931), which overturned a state law prohibiting the use of red flags. Hughes's stance in the case hearkened back to his days as an attorney a decade earlier, when he had championed the cause of five New York legislators who had been denied their seats because they belonged to the Socialist party. Later in his tenure, Hughes announced the decision for the Court in *DeJonge v. Oregon* (1937), which overturned a state conviction of a man for conducting a meeting of the Communist party. "[P]eaceable assembly for lawful discussion," he declared emphatically, "cannot be made a crime."

As the 1940s began, Chief Justice Hughes was nearly 80 years old. The nation had weathered its economic crisis and, through Hughes's leadership, the Court had weathered its showdown with a determined president. Above all, the chief justice was anxious to depart from the Court before his mental faculties departed him. Thus, on July 1, 1941, he resigned from the Court. He lived another seven years before dying on August 27, 1948, at his summer home on Cape Cod.

By most estimations, Charles Evans Hughes was an outstanding justice. Justice Felix Frankfurter, who joined the Court at the end of Hughes's tenure as chief justice, likened Hughes to a great conductor: "To see him preside was like witnessing Toscanini lead an orchestra." Hughes led the Court, according to Frankfurter, "with a mastery . . . unparalleled in the history of the Court, a mastery that derived from experience as diversified, as intense, as extensive, as any man ever brought to a seat on the Court." Nevertheless, Chief Justice Hughes's frequent alliance with the conservative justices who read the Constitution as a manifesto of laissez-faire economics and his seemingly unprincipled repudiation of this alliance in the face of Roosevelt's court-packing plan has led some to a less honorific judgment.

Further Reading

Friedman, Richard D. "Switching Time and Other Thought Experiments: The Hughes Court and Constitutional Transformation." *University of Pennsylvania Law Review* 142 (June 1994): 1891–1984.

Hendel, Samuel. *Charles Evans Hughes and the Supreme Court*. New York: King's Crown Press, 1951.

Hughes, Charles Evans. *The Supreme Court of the United States: Its Foundation, Methods and Achievements: An Interpretation*. New York: Columbia University Press, 1928.

Perkins, Dexter. *Charles Evans Hughes and American Democratic Statesmanship*. Boston: Little, Brown, 1956.

Pusey, Merlo John. *Charles Evans Hughes*. New York: Macmillan, 1951.

Willis Van Devanter (1859–1941)

Associate Justice, 1910–1937

Appointed by President William Howard Taft

Willis Van Devanter
(United States Supreme Court)

History remembers Willis Van Devanter as one of the Four Horsemen, the quartet of conservative justices on the Supreme Court who consistently defied the New Deal program of President Franklin Delano Roosevelt and his Democratic Congress in the 1930s. Court historians generally recognize Van Devanter as the intellectual leader of these conservatives. Although Van Devanter helped to precipitate what came to be known as the "Constitutional Crisis" of the 1930s, when President Roosevelt threatened to pack the Court with justices more amenable to his New Deal aspirations, especially in the earlier years of his tenure on the Court, Van Devanter was nevertheless highly regarded among his brethren as a valuable participant in the Court's deliberations. His contribution, though, took place mostly behind closed doors in the conferences held by the justices to discuss cases rather than in published opinions.

Willis Van Devanter was born in Marion, Indiana, on April 17, 1859, the first of eight children born to Isaac Van Devanter and Violetta Spencer Van Devanter. Isaac was a lawyer who encouraged his eldest son to pursue the same calling. After attending schools in Marion, Willis enrolled at Indiana Asbury University (later to become DePauw University) but had to interrupt his studies after two years to earn a livelihood when his father became ill. Upon his father's recovery, Willis Van Devanter was able to resume his academic career by enrolling in the University of Cincinnati Law School in 1879, from which he graduated second in his class in 1881. Two years later he married Delice Burhan, with whom he would have two sons.

After law school, Van Devanter joined his father's law practice in the firm of Lacey and Van Devanter; but when Isaac Van Devanter retired in 1884, his partner John W. Lacey moved to Wyoming, where he accepted an appointment as chief justice of the Wyoming Territorial Supreme Court. Willis followed Lacey to Wyoming and set up his own practice in Cheyenne. Twenty-five years old at the time, the rough and tumble of frontier life suited Willis more than the settled possibilities available to him in Indiana. He was the kind of man who would one day hunt grizzly bears with Buffalo Bill in the Bighorn Mountains. For the time being, though, he spent his first few years in Cheyenne finding clients among ranchers and others who feuded over cattle and land rights. In 1887 he formed a partnership with the influential Republican lawyer Charles N. Potter, and the two men's practice soon boasted a client list that included the Burlington Railroad.

Around the same time, Van Devanter threw himself into Republican politics, casting his lot in support of the territorial governor, Francis E. Warren, and winning election himself as Cheyenne city attorney in 1887 and to the Wyoming territorial legislature in 1888. During these years he worked on a commission to revise and codify the territorial statutes of Wyoming. The climax of this early period was his appointment in 1889—at the age of 30—by President Benjamin Harrison as chief justice of the Wyoming Territorial Supreme Court. The appointment, which paid only $3,000 a year, enhanced Van Devanter's reputation more than his bank account, and the young man returned to the more financially rewarding practice of law a year later, when Wyoming became a state. By this time John W. Lacey had also returned to the private practice of law, and the two men formed a new partnership whose core client was the Union Pacific Railroad. The newly formed state of Wyoming acknowledged the growing reputation of Van Devanter when it retained him to argue a case on its behalf before the U.S. Supreme Court. *Ward v. Race Horse* (1896) involved the question of whether Wyoming's statehood superseded an Indian treaty that was inconsistent with state law on the question of Indian hunting rights. Van Devanter prevailed for the state in his appeal to the Supreme Court.

Van Devanter's efforts on behalf of the Republican party bore fruit once President William P. McKinley took office. McKinley appointed Van Devanter an assistant attorney general in the Department of the Interior in 1897, where Van Devanter's knowledge of land law and his familiarity with Native American issues served him in good stead. This position was less than Van Devanter—who aspired to be solicitor general of the United States—might have hoped for, but it was followed in six years by a more prestigious appointment in 1903, when President Theodore Roosevelt nominated Van Devanter to a seat on the United States Court of Appeals for the Eighth Circuit. Here, over the course of seven years, Van Devanter reinforced his already substantial expertise in legal issues relating to land claims and railroads. He also proved adept at resolving complicated issues relating to jurisdiction.

The judge from Wyoming secured his final and most prestigious advancement in public service when President William Howard Taft appointed him an associate justice on the U.S. Supreme Court on December 12, 1910. Confirmed by the Senate a few days later, Van Devanter took his seat on the Court on January 3, 1911, inaugurating what would eventually be a term of service that stretched for more than a quarter of a century. Until the end of this period, Justice Van Devanter remained relatively unknown by the general public, finding a place for himself on the Court as its resident expert on questions relating to land and water rights, admiralty, jurisdictional disputes, and issues relating to Native Americans. His expertise concerning jurisdictional matters, in particular, was substantial, and resulted in his being appointed to the commission that drafted the Judiciary Act of 1925. For his length of service on the Court, however, Van Devanter wrote relatively few opinions: a mere 346 opinions for the Court over 26 years. But his fellow justices held him in higher esteem than this output might suggest. Especially in the private conferences in which the justices discussed their opinions about cases pending before the Court, Van Devanter played a significant role. William Howard Taft, who as president appointed Van Devanter to the Court and later joined the Court as its chief justice, declared that the justice from Wyoming was "far and away the most valuable man in our court." Justice Louis Brandeis, far removed from Van Devanter in terms of political orientation, nevertheless declared him to be the "master of formulas that decided cases without creating precedents."

By the 1930s, however, Justice Willis Van Devanter came to occupy a more visible place on the Court and one less characterized by superlatives. As President Roosevelt and the Congress labored to craft legislation to deal with the economic and social ills associated with the Great Depression, four conservative justices on the Court steadfastly opposed these legislative initiatives; Van Devanter was their intellectual leader. They were soon labeled by their critics as the "Four Horsemen," the image borrowed from the New Testament book of Revelation's description of four riders and their horses who plague the earth. These justices—Willis Van Devanter, James McReynolds, George Sutherland, and Pierce Butler—joined by Justice Owen Roberts, dealt the New Deal nearly mortal wounds. They overturned the Railway Pension Act in *Railroad Retirement Board v. Alton Railroad* (1935) on the grounds that it exceeded Congress's power under the commerce clause; declared unconstitutional an agricultural processing tax in *United States v. Butler* (1936) as an abuse of Congress's taxing power; and, finally, invalidated a state minimum wage law in *Morehead v. New York ex rel. Tipaldo* (1936), on the grounds that it violated the due process clause of the Fourteenth Amendment. Eventually these and other holdings prompted Roosevelt to propose legislation that would have seated additional justices on the Court, ostensibly to assist in carrying the workload on a Court dominated by men over the age of 70, but in reality to remake the Court into a friend of New Deal legislation. A majority of the Court finally came round to a view that found no constitutional defect in Roosevelt's legislation, and the so-called constitutional crisis was averted. But Van Devanter, until his retirement at the end of the Court's 1936 term, continued to pronounce constitutional malediction on what he viewed as the legislative excesses of the New Deal.

By the summer of 1937, President Roosevelt had signed into law bills that provided an attractive retirement package for justices over the age of 70 who had served at least 10 years on the Court. Justice Van Devanter promptly took advantage of this law and tendered his resignation from the Court on June 2, 1937, when he was 78 years old. He moved to New York and handled cases for the lower federal courts there. Finally, he died in Washington, D.C., on February 8, 1941.

The Four Horsemen have generally suffered severe criticism at the hands of historians, since their judicial vision so severely departed from the dominant constitutional tradition that would emerge in the last part of the 1930s and continues, in large measure, to the present. Their use of the Constitution to enforce the values of laissez-faire economics came to seem a form of vast judicial overreaching. Though Justice Willis Van Devanter provided the intellectual backbone for the plagues visited on the New Deal by the Four Horsemen, history's judgment of him has been more benevolent than for others of that group. Capable and diligent, even in the eyes of his opponents, Van Devanter's long service on the Court, not always so reactionary as in his later days, has helped to redeem what might otherwise have been viewed as a poor judicial career.

FURTHER READING

Burner, David. "Willis Van Devanter." In *The Justices of the United States Supreme Court 1789–1969: Their Lives and Major Opinions,* vol. 3. Edited by Leon Friedman and Fred L. Israel. New York: R. R. Bowker Co., 1969.

Cushman, Barry. "The Secret Lives of the Four Horsemen." *Virginia Law Review* 83 (1997): 559–645.

Holsinger, M. Paul. "The Appointment of Supreme Court Justice Van Devanter: A Study of Political Preferment." *American Journal of Legal History* 12 (1968): 324–335.

Holsinger, M. Paul. "Willis Van Devanter: Wyoming Leader, 1884–1897." *Annals of Wyoming* 37 (1965): 170–206.

Nelson, Daniel A. "The Supreme Court Appointment of Willis Van Devanter." *Annals of Wyoming* 53 (1981): 2–11.

Joseph Rucker Lamar (1857–1916)

Associate Justice, 1911–1916

Appointed by President William Howard Taft

Joseph Rucker Lamar
(United States Supreme Court)

The Supreme Court, often the center of great national controversy, sometimes passes through years of relative quiet, when more often than not the justices agree among themselves and with the nation. Joseph Rucker Lamar served on the Court during such a period. The character of the times very much accorded with his own steady temperament, the model of a southern gentleman. Unfortunately, he suffers the inevitable dividend of quiet times: obscurity. History dotes on crisis, calamity, and confusion. Never called on to encounter these, Lamar was forgotten almost as soon as death removed him from the Supreme Court.

Joseph Rucker Lamar was born on a plantation in Elbert County, Georgia, on October 14, 1857, three and a half years before the outbreak of Civil War. He was the child of an illustrious southern family, both on his mother's and his father's side, with near relatives including Mirabeau Lamar, who served as president of the Republic of Texas from 1838 to 1841, and L.Q.C. Lamar, congressman, secretary of the interior, and associate justice of the U.S. Supreme Court from 1888 to 1893. Joseph's father, James Lamar, studied law and was admitted to practice. But he ultimately became a convert to the Disciples of Christ and instead of practicing law, he became the pastor of the Disciples of Christ Church in Augusta, Georgia. Joseph's mother, Mary Rucker Lamar, died before he turned seven years old. Driven for a time from Augusta by General Sherman's siege, James Lamar eventually remarried and returned to his pastorate in Augusta in 1865. There, next door to the home of the Presbyterian pastor, the young Joseph Lamar became a boyhood friend of that pastor's son, Woodrow Wilson.

By 1870 the Wilsons had moved away from Georgia, and Joseph and his brother were sent to the first of a series of private schools, including the Richmond Academy in Augusta and the Penn Lucy Academy in Baltimore, Maryland. In 1874 Joseph began his college education at the University of Georgia but had to withdraw in his second year there because of illness. In the meantime his father accepted a new pastorate in Louisville, Kentucky, and eventually persuaded his two sons to complete their college educations at his alma mater, Bethany College in West Virginia, from which Joseph graduated in 1877. Following his graduation, Lamar set out to prepare himself for the career in law that his father had abandoned for the ministry. He attended Washington and Lee University in Virginia for a time but abandoned this study after a semester in order to read law with Henry Clay Foster, a prominent Augusta attorney. Lamar was admitted to practice law in Georgia in April 1878, at the age of 21. Shortly after the beginning of the next year he married Clarinda Huntington Pendelton. Their union, which survived until Lamar's death in 1916, produced two sons and a daughter.

Though admitted to practice law in Georgia, Lamar did not immediately take advantage of this privilege. Instead, he taught Latin for a year at Bethany College. But in 1880 his legal mentor, Henry Clay Foster, offered to form a partnership with him, and Lamar quickly accepted this opportunity. For the next decade until Foster's death in 1890, the two men practiced law together. During the later part of this decade Lamar won election to the Georgia legislature, where he served from 1886 to 1889 and where he made important contributions in the area of law reform. After Foster's death, Lamar continued to practice law and at the same time became even more involved in public affairs. In 1893, the governor of Georgia appointed him to a commission assigned the task of revising Georgia's legal codes. In 1898 he was appointed by the Georgia Supreme Court to begin what became a decade of service on the state board that examined the character and fitness of bar applicants. He served as chairman of this board from 1905 to 1910. During this period Lamar earned additional recognition for a series of legal articles he penned concerning the history of Georgia law.

By the beginning of the 20th century, Joseph Lamar numbered among Georgia's most prominent attorneys. When a vacancy on the Georgia Supreme Court occurred in 1902, it came as no surprise that Governor J. S. Terrell would turn to Lamar to fill it. Lamar served with distinction from 1903 to 1905 but ultimately resigned to return to the private practice of law. Establishing a new partnership with E.H. Callaway, also a former judge, Lamar threw himself into representing a variety of corporate and railroad clients.

A year after this case, Lamar, an avid golfer, played the most important series of games of his life. President-elect William Howard Taft had decided to recuperate from his arduous presidential campaign by vacationing in Augusta, where he played golf frequently with Joseph Lamar. He received a favorable impression of

Lamar, such that when he assumed office, he contemplated appointing the Georgian to the Commerce Court. Taft conferred with Georgia Senator Augustus O. Bacon, who suggested that the Supreme Court would be a better placement for Lamar. The president agreed and nominated Lamar to fill the seat that Edward D. White had vacated on being named chief justice of the Court. Lamar, a Democrat, feared that his nomination might not pass the Senate; but on December 15, 1910, the Senate unanimously confirmed the president's choice, and Joseph Rucker Lamar took his seat on the Supreme Court on January 3, 1911.

Lamar served five unremarkable years on the high court—unremarkable partly because of his own moderate temperament and partly because the Court itself decided few questions of great note during this period. Those it did decide produced broad consensus among the justices rather than sharp differences of opinion. The Court approved modest expansions in the areas of federal and state power over economic matters—reflecting, in so doing, the general tenor of the times. Essential conservativism dressed in a robe of modest progressivism characterized the Court during this period—and it characterized Justice Joseph Lamar as well. His most famous opinion combined both elements. In *Gompers v. Bucks Stove and Range Company* (1891), Lamar spoke for a unanimous Court in overturning on a technicality a contempt citation issued against certain labor organizers but supporting the use of injunctions against labor boycotts. The unanimity of the Court in *Gompers* reflected a harmony that generally prevailed during the years of Lamar's service. Only eight times during the course of his tenure did Lamar deem it necessary to pen a dissent from the decision announced by a majority of his brethren.

After Lamar's childhood friend Woodrow Wilson became president in 1912, he tapped Lamar to head a diplomatic mission to Mexico in 1914 to resolve a dispute there. But the effort required in this mission, compounded by Lamar's work on the Court, proved so stressful that it incapacitated the justice for a time during the Court's 1914 term. He would not serve another. In September 1915 he suffered a stroke that prevented him from beginning the Court's new term, and he died at the age of 58 in Washington, D.C., on January 2, 1916.

Both Joseph Lamar's own temperament and the circumstances of his few years on the Court contrived to make his impact as a justice minimal. Competent but not creative, patient but not pathbreaking, the justice from Georgia lacked the spark of judicial brilliance that history takes most note of. But even if he had possessed it, his short tenure on the Court and the lack of great legal controversies to resolve would have limited the uses even of brilliance. Ten years after Lamar's death, his widow published his biography in an attempt to preserve his memory. But even her devotion could not rescue Justice Lamar from the obscurity to which history shortly consigned him.

Further Reading

Dinnerstein, Leonard. "Joseph Rucker Lamar." In *The Justices of the United States Supreme Court 1789–1969: Their Lives and Major Opinions,* vol. 3. Edited by Leon Friedman and Fred L. Israel. New York: R.R. Bowker Co., 1969.

Lamar, Clarinda Pendleton. *The Life of Joseph Rucker Lamar, 1857–1916.* New York: Putnam, 1926.

O'Connor, Sandra Day. "Supreme Court Justices from Georgia." *Georgia Journal of Southern Legal History* 1 (Fall–Winter 1991): 395–405.

Sibley, Samuel Hale. *Georgia's Contribution to Law: The Lamars.* New York: Newcomen Society of England, American Branch, 1948.

Mahlon Pitney (1858–1924)

Associate Justice, 1912–1922

Appointed by President William Howard Taft

Mahlon Pitney
(United States Supreme Court)

A man with a promising political career, Mahlon Pitney switched course in his early middle years to become a respected judge, first at the state level and eventually on the U.S. Supreme Court. He became the 65th justice to serve on the Court and the last of the justices appointed by President William Howard Taft, who was able to choose a chief justice and appoint five new associate justices in the course of a single presidential term. Though Pitney's record of decisions makes it difficult to pigeonhole him neatly, history remembers him primarily as a determined foe of the labor movement.

Mahlon Pitney was born on February 5, 1858, on a farm near Morristown, New Jersey, the second son of Henry Cooper Pitney and Sarah Louisa Halsted Pitney. His father practiced law and encouraged his son to pursue the same vocation. The two would eventually serve together briefly in the New Jersey state judicial system. After an early education in private schools, Mahlon entered the College of New

Jersey (eventually to become Princeton University) in 1875, where he was a classmate of future president Woodrow Wilson. There, in addition to his studies, he proved to be a talented debater and also managed the college's baseball team. He graduated in 1879 and promptly turned to the study of law in his father's office, learning it, he later wrote, mostly by absorption from his father, who was "a walking encyclopedia of the law." Once he passed the bar in 1882, however, he escaped his father's shadow and set up practice in Dover, New Jersey. There he also found time to serve as director of an iron company and to help manage a department store.

When Henry Pitney was appointed to serve as vice chancellor of New Jersey in 1889, Mahlon moved back to Morristown and took charge of his father's law office. Soon after, in 1891, he married Florence T. Shelton, with whom he would have three children: Guy Shelton; Mahlon, Jr.; and Beatrice Louis. Pitney himself had sprung from a family of lawyers—in addition to his father, his two brothers practiced law—and he transmitted the vocation of law to his own children and grandchildren. Both his sons, as well as one grandson, became lawyers.

Back in Morristown, Mahlon Pitney rapidly plunged into the thick of Republican politics, winning election in 1894 to Congress and reelection in 1896. He resigned his seat, though, shortly before the end of his second congressional term, after being elected to serve in the New Jersey Senate, a political move calculated to place him in line for a gubernatorial run. In the state senate, he was first minority leader for the Republicans and then, after his party took control of the senate in 1900, senate president. Pitney seemed poised to capture the Republican nomination for New Jersey governor in 1901, but there was a significant problem: The incumbent Republican governor, Foster M. Voorhees, desired a different successor than Pitney. The governor derailed Pitney's political ambition by offering him an appointment to the New Jersey Supreme Court on February 5, 1901. Pitney accepted the appointment and for the next seven years served on New Jersey's highest court until he received an even more prestigious state court appointment. On Janaury 22, 1908, New Jersey governor J. Franklin Fort appointed Pitney to serve as chancellor of New Jersey, a judicial position—the highest in the state—that placed Pitney as the head of both the equity and law branches of New Jersey's appellate courts.

The next, and final, professional advancement Mahlon Pitney achieved came as a surprise to him, and began with the death of Associate Justice John Marshall Harlan on October 14, 1911. The choice of Harlan's successor fell to President William Howard Taft. At first, Judge William C. Hook of the U.S. Court of Appeals for the Eighth Circuit seemed likely to obtain the appointment to fill the vacancy, but controversy quickly surrounded Hook's candidacy and Taft ultimately abandoned it. In mid-February 1912, however, the president met Pitney at a dinner in Newark and was so impressed by their conversation together that he announced his nomination of Pitney for a seat on the Supreme Court a week later, on February 19. This, the last of Taft's appointments to the Court, did not receive a warm welcome in the Senate. As New Jersey chancellor, Pitney had written an anti-union opinion in *Jones Glass Co. v. Glass Bottle Blowers Association* (1908), and the views he revealed in that case promptly stirred Democrats and Progressive Republicans to oppose his nomination. One critic pronounced Pitney "irrevocably pledged to property rights as against human rights" and declared that he was "the consistent enemy of the working man." Taft, though, insisted in support of his nominee that Pitney was "of a great lawyer stock," and Pitney himself denied that he was "the enemy of labor." In the end, the Senate confirmed Pitney's nomination to the Court on March 13, 1912, by a vote of 50-26.

As it turned out, Pitney's opponents had measured the man at least partially correctly. Over the decade that he served on the Court, he regularly, if not invariably, demonstrated himself to be the legal foe of organized labor. In 1915 he wrote the Court's opinion in what would be his most famous case, *Coppage v. Kansas* (1915), involving the constitutionality of a state law prohibiting the use of so-called yellow-dog contracts, by which employees accepted employment on the condition that they not join a union. Pitney declared for the U.S. Supreme Court that the attempt to prohibit yellow-dog contracts was unconstitutional because it violated the freedom of contract protected by the Fourteenth Amendment's due process clause. Pitney's opinion in this and other cases amply supported the prognostication at the time of his nomination that he would be anti-union, but the corollary accusation that he would prove to be the enemy of the workingman finds less support in Pitney's judicial career. In fact, he regularly championed the legality of state workers' compensation laws in cases such as *New York Central Railroad Co. v. White* (1917). The great liberal justice Louis Brandeis announced that "[b]ut for Pitney we would have had no workmen's compensation laws." In truth, Pitney seems to have distrusted economic combinations whether on the corporate or the labor side. He was, for example, happy to apply the antitrust provisions of the Sherman Antitrust Act to both.

Pitney worked diligently—perhaps overworked—as a justice. He wrote 244 majority opinions while on the Court, together with 19 dissenting and five concurring opinions. He was rarely absent from Court, and he participated in nearly all of the decisions rendered by the Court during his years as a justice. In August 1922, however, he suffered a stroke that left him unable to continue his service, and so he resigned on December 31, 1922. He died in Washington, D.C., on December 9, 1924.

—∞—

In general, Justice Mahlon Pitney proved to be a solid conservative during his years on the Court, though even more progressive justices came to admire his competence and diligence. Justice Brandeis observed of him that he had "a great sense of justice affected by Presbyterianism, but no imagination whatever. And then he was much influenced by his experience, and he had mighty little." Nevertheless, Brandeis acknowledged Pitney's "absolute concentration" as a judge and admitted that he possessed "real character." Justice Oliver Wendell Holmes concurred in the latter judgment, especially. Holmes declared after Pitney's death that "[i]t is hard to get a man as good as he was, whatever reserve one may make in superlatives." The great Massachusetts jurist observed of Pitney:

> When he first came on the bench he used to get on my nerves, as he talked too much from the bench and in conference, but he improved in that and I came to appreciate his great faithfulness to duty, his industry and candor. He had not wings and was not a thunderbolt, but he was a very honest hard working judge and a useful critic.

This quiet praise from eminent colleagues was not sufficient to secure Mahlon Pitney a prominent place in the Court's history. He remains securely among the Court's lesser lights. But it offers a reminder that brilliance alone is not a secure footing on which to fasten an institution such as the Supreme Court. For every Holmes dispatching thunderous judicial pronouncements from Olympus, the Court requires jurists such as Pitney, who labor faithfully at the business of the law.

Further Reading

Belknap, Michael R. "Mr. Justice Pitney and Progressivism." *Seton Hall Law Review* 16 (1986): 380–423.

Breed, Alan Ryder. "Mahlon Pitney: His Life and Career—Political and Judicial." B.A. thesis, Princeton University, 1932.

Israel, Fred. "Mahlon Pitney." In *The Justices of the United States Supreme Court 1789–1969: Their Lives and Major Opinions,* vol. 3. Edited by Leon Friedman and Fred L. Israel. New York: R. R. Bowker Co., 1969.

Levitan, David Maurice. "Mahlon Pitney, Labor Judge." *Virginia Law Review* 40 (1954): 733–770.

James Clark McReynolds (1862–1946)

Associate Justice, 1914–1941

Appointed by President Woodrow Wilson

James Clark McReynolds
(United States Supreme Court)

President Woodrow Wilson elevated James C. McReynolds to the Supreme Court after the latter's abrasive manner mired his service as attorney general of the United States in controversy. But it proved impossible to promote McReynolds out of controversy. Over the course of his 27 years of service on the Court, he proved to be the most boorish man ever to hold a seat there. Intemperate, uncivil, and anti-Semitic to the core, he seemed to have declared himself emancipated from the normal demands of courtesy and forbearance. Those he disliked—and he disliked many—he showered with rudeness and abuse, and he seldom passed by the opportunity of expressing a personal attack against anyone opposed to him on an issue. In the 1930s he became numbered among the four adamantly conservative justices who opposed the economic and social policies of the New Deal era. But his allies eventually departed the Court, leaving him at the end a lone and bitter dissenter against many of the Court's decisions. He died in the mid-1940s, unwept-for and unloved.

James Clark McReynolds was born on February 3, 1862, in Elkton, Kentucky, the son of Dr. John O. McReynolds and Ellen Reeves McReynolds, members of the Disciples of Christ, a Christian denomination founded by Alexander Campbell. Stern, hardworking, and filled with righteous certainty about fundamental moral verities, James's father earned the nickname of "Pope," and the son inherited the dispositions of the father. McReynolds received his early education on his family's plantation, where his interests ran to botany and ornithology, until he enrolled at Vanderbilt University, in Nashville, Tennessee, at the age of 17. There he continued his focus on science and graduated first in his class in 1882. After a brief period of postgraduate study in science, McReynolds departed for the University of Virginia and the study of law, where his course work included study with the South's leading legal scholar, John B. Minor. While many other law teachers of the time had fallen under the spell of the Socratic method then popular at Harvard Law School, Minor continued to teach the law by lecture, dispensing it to his students as fixed and unyielding first principles.

After receiving his law degree from the University of Virginia in 1884, McReynolds served for a few months as secretary to Tennessee senator, Howell E. Jackson, who was soon appointed an associate justice of the Supreme Court. McReynolds then established a legal practice in Nashville. His skills as a trial lawyer were lackluster, but he soon forged a reputation as a solid adviser for business interests such as the Illinois Central Railroad. In fact, beginning in 1900, he was appointed a professor of commercial law at Vanderbilt University Law School.

Four years earlier, in 1896, McReynolds ran as a Democrat for Congress, but the temperament that would later earn legendary renown for its irascibility and sternness failed to appeal to voters, and he lost the election. His path into political life followed the route of appointment, however. It began by his gaining a post in 1903 as assistant attorney general under Philander C. Knox, acceptable to Republican President Theodore Roosevelt for his support of the gold monetary standard. McReynolds was given charge of prosecuting the tobacco trust, a task that he undertook with particular animation and ability as well as a diligence inspired by his conviction that monopolies were "essentially wicked," a species of moral as well as economic evil. In 1907 he resigned this office to pursue the practice of law in New York City with the Cravath firm but was soon recalled to service in the attorney general's office to conduct the case against American Tobacco. In December 1912 he resigned again in protest of Attorney General George Wickersham's approved terms of settlement for the case, and once again he departed for New York City, where he set up a law practice on his own.

McReynolds did not remain long in New York. After President Woodrow Wilson was inaugurated, he looked first to Louis Brandeis, later a Supreme Court justice, as a likely candidate to assume the position of attorney general. But Brandeis proved too controversial and Edward M. House, Wilson's adviser, pressed for McReynolds instead. After meeting McReynolds, the president appointed him attorney general in February 1913. The Tennessean served nearly a year and a half in this position, but his belligerent and unbendable temperament soon mired his office in controversy, not least over his decision to delay prosecution of the son-in-law of an administration official accused of violating the Mann Act, which prohibited transportation of women across state lines "for immoral purposes." In this and other controversies, history has generally acquitted McReynolds of any actual wrong doing except that of an intemperate response to his accusers. In any event, President Wilson soon cast about for a way to remove McReynolds from his position and seized on the presence of a vacancy on the Supreme Court owing to the death of Associate Justice Horace Lurton in 1912. Like Lurton, McReynolds was a Tennessean, and this geographic congruity prompted the president to nominate him to a seat on the Court on August 19, 1914. Ten days later the Senate confirmed the appointment by a vote of 44-6, and McReynolds took his seat on the Court at the beginning of the next term, on October 12, 1914.

McReynolds served on the Court for the next 27 years, compiling a record of staunch conservativism. Occasionally he bore the Court's standard for libertarian results, as in his opinions relating to the rights of parents in connection with education. In *Meyer v. Nebraska* (1923), for example, his opinion for the Court declared unconstitutional a state law that had prohibited foreign language instruction until after the eighth grade. Similarly, in *Pierce v. Society of Sisters* (1925), he delivered the Court's opinion declaring unconstitutional an Oregon law that attempted to force all children between the ages of eight and sixteen to attend public school. Generally, though, McReynolds could be counted on to reach conclusions less respectful of civil rights and liberties.

Especially in the area of racial discrimination, McReynolds dissented from even the modest efforts of the Court's majorities to give effect to the Constitution's requirements of equal protection and due process of law. Thus, for example, when the notorious Scottsboro cases arrived before the Court in *Powell v. Alabama* (1932), a majority of the Court found that the summary conviction of eight black defendants for the alleged rape of two white women violated the Fourteenth Amendment's guarantee of due process of law. After being summarily indicted, the defendants were immediately tried. The two counsel appointed to represent them were given no time to investigate the case and a mere 30 minutes to consult with their clients before defending them in a sensational trial in which the jury eventually found them guilty and sentenced them to death. McReynolds, along with Justice Pierce Butler, dissented from the majority's decision. In a similar case, *Aldridge v. United States* (1932), the allegation of possible racial prejudice on the part of a juror in a murder case raised no constitutional issue in McReynolds's mind. The need to maintain law and order could not be undermined by attention to such matters: "Unhappily, the enforcement of our criminal laws is dangerously ineffective; crimes of violence multiply; punishment walks lamely. Courts ought not to increase the difficulties by magnifying theoretical possibilities."

Justice McReynolds may have been unfeeling toward the racism that often infected criminal proceedings at the time because he himself was infected with racist views, in the form of a virulent anti-Semitism. Chief Justice William Howard Taft, who presided over the Court during part of the period in which McReynolds served, declared him to be "fuller of prejudice than any man I have known." McReynolds once declared privately to Justice Oliver Wendell Holmes, "that for four thousand years the Lord tried to make something out of the Hebrews, then gave it up as impossible and turned them out to prey on mankind in general—like fleas on the dog for example." McReynolds's behavior toward Justices Louis Brandeis and Benjamin Nathan Cardozo, both Jewish, was shocking. The justices met regularly during each term of the Court to discuss their respective views on the appropriate disposition of each case. For a time, at least, McReynolds refused to stay in the conference room when Brandeis spoke. He would leave the room, stand just outside the door, which he held slightly ajar in order to hear, and return only when Brandeis had finished speaking. When Justice Cardozo was sworn in, McReynolds made a point of reading a newspaper.

Justice McReynolds did not confine his rudeness to Jews, however, but rather liberally dispensed it to a variety of the souls about him at any particular time. Taft found him to be "selfish beyond everything, though full of the so-called Southern courtesy, but most inconsiderate of his colleagues and others and contemptuous of everybody." Justice Harlan Fiske Stone once commented to McReynolds on the dullness of a particular attorney's legal argument, to which McReynolds is said to have replied, "The only duller thing I can think of is to hear you read one of your opinions."

For most of his career on the Court, McReynolds played a rather minor role in the Court's affairs, writing relatively few opinions compared to other members of the Court, and these mostly in cases involving rather technical and obscure legal issues. In the 1930s, though, he earned fame as one of the "Four Horsemen," the four justices who consistently voted against New Deal legislation. Together with the other members of this quartet—Willis Van Devanter, Pierce Butler, and George Sutherland—and joined for a time by Justice Owen Roberts, McReynolds helped engineer a "constitutional crisis." Their steadfast opposition to President Franklin Delano Roosevelt's New Deal programs ultimately prompted the president to propose packing the Court with additional justices, intended to produce results more pleasing to the president's agenda. Beginning shortly after the announcement of this proposal, Chief Justice Charles Evans Hughes and Associate Justice Owen Roberts, sometime legal allies of the Four Horsemen, voted consistently to uphold the economic and social programs of the New Deal from constitutional challenge. The Four Horsemen suddenly found themselves consistently in dissent to a new majority. Justice Van Devanter retired soon afterward, followed by Justice Sutherland, who retired in 1938. Justice Butler died in 1939, leaving McReynolds the last of the Four Horsemen. When his great nemesis, President Roosevelt, won a third term of office in 1940, he finally conceded defeat and resigned on January 31, 1941. He died of pneumonia in Washington, D.C., five years later, on August 24, 1946, a confirmed bachelor to the end. His will left most of his estate to charities.

—ııı—

Even those of McReynolds's contemporaries who witnessed his foul and arrogant temper firsthand found themselves forced to soften what might otherwise have been a uniformly negative judgment of the man. Justice Felix Frankfurter, on the Court with McReynolds for two years at the end of the latter's term of service, wrote:

> He was rude. . . . He was handsome, able, and honest. I sort of respected him. . . . I respected that he refused to sign a letter when Brandeis left the Court. There was the usual letter of farewell to a colleague, and he wouldn't sign it. I respected that, because he did not remotely feel what the letter expressed, and I despise hypocrites even more than barbarians.

Justice Oliver Wendell Holmes, who served much longer with McReynolds, also found some cause to mitigate what might otherwise have been a harsh judgment against the Tennessean. "Poor McReynolds is a man of feeling and of more secret kindliness than he would get credit for. But as is so common with Southerners, his own personality governs him without much thought of others when an impulse comes, and I think without sufficient regard for the proprieties of the Court." Nevertheless, Justice James Clark McReynolds tends to be remembered as one of the worst Supreme Court justices ever to have sat on the nation's highest court. His role as one of the legendary Four Horsemen, whose conservative constitutionalism grew out of favor before the midpoint of the 20th century, accounts for some, but certainly not all, of this damning historical judgment. The other Horsemen managed to escape the sharp verdict generally pronounced against McReynolds. The boorishness of his character accounts, perhaps, for the persistently negative judgment reserved for McReynolds.

Further Reading

Bruner, David. "James Clark McReynolds." In *The Justices of the United States Supreme Court 1789–1969: Their Lives and Major Opinions,* vol. 3. Edited by Leon Friedman and Fred L. Israel. New York: R. R. Bowker Co., 1969.

Bond, James E. *I Dissent: The Legacy of Chief Justice James Clark McReynolds.* James E. Bond. Fairfax, Va.: George Mason University Press, 1992.

Cushman, Barry. "The Secret Lives of the Four Horsemen." *Virginia Law Review* 83 (April 1997): 559–645.

Fletcher, R. V. "Mr. Justice McReynolds: An Appreciation." *Vanderbilt Law Review* 2 (December 1948): 35–46.

Langram, Robert W. "Why Are Some Supreme Court Justices Rated as 'Failures'?" *Supreme Court Historical Society Yearbook* (1985): 8–14.

Louis Dembitz Brandeis (1856–1941)

Associate Justice, 1916–1939

Appointed by President Woodrow Wilson

Louis Dembitz Brandeis
(Photograph, Library of Congress)

Louis Dembitz Brandeis ranks among the greatest justices ever to have sat on the Supreme Court. Nevertheless, he influenced the course of American law and life as much before he won a seat on its highest court as he did afterward. As "the people's lawyer" he devoted impressive energy to the solution of the social and economic problems that traveled in the wake of the Industrial Revolution, establishing as much as any modern lawyer the tradition of *pro bono publico*—service by lawyers for the public good. As a legal scholar, he buttressed the analysis of legal principles with close attention to sociological fact and laid the groundwork for the recognition of a right of privacy that would flourish in the last half of the 20th century. As a nonobservant Jew nevertheless intimately concerned with the fate of his people, he lent his impressive leadership abilities to the cause of Zionism. Once on the Court, Brandeis found himself frequently in the minority on important questions of law, but his cogent dissents often became the basis for the law as it would be, if not always the law as it was.

—∾—

Louis David Brandeis was born on November 13, 1856, in the last turbulent years before the outbreak of Civil War, in Louisville, Kentucky. He changed his middle name to Dembitz in his teens, in honor of the influence of Lewis Naphtali Dembitz, a maternal uncle who was an abolitionist lawyer. His mother and father, Frederika Dembitz Brandeis and Adolph Brandeis, immigrated to America in the late 1840s. Here they married and settled finally in Louisville in 1851, where Louis's father established a prosperous business as a wholesale grain and produce dealer. Young Louis received his early education from the Louisville Male High School, before his father took his family to Europe in the early 1870s to escape the recession that followed the Civil War.

At the age of 16, Louis Brandeis gained entrance into the Annen-Realschule in Dresden, Germany, where he proved to be an excellent student. When his family returned to the United States in 1875, he enrolled in Harvard Law School, where, in the course of his two years of study, he earned the highest grades ever awarded by the school. The law school nearly declined to graduate Brandeis, though, since he was, at 20 years of age, a year younger than the normally required 21 years. But the school made an exception for Brandeis, and he stayed on another year for additional graduate work. Therafter, he returned to St. Louis to work for a law firm there, only to find himself restless for the legal environs of New England. Thus, when his classmate Samuel Warren suggested they form a partnership in Boston, Brandeis leaped at the opportunity. Beginning in 1879, the two soon established a prosperous practice, representing mostly small and medium-sized businesses.

The following years saw Brandeis develop a reputation as a lawyer who knew as much about his clients' businesses as he did about the law. This fact-centered legal practice would come to characterize much of his approach to the law. Not content to ponder abstract legal principles in a vacuum, Brandeis excelled at plunging into the thicket of factual detail and the sociological background of his clients' problems, often becoming a general adviser to them, not only about the law but about the needs of their businesses.

The last decade of the 19th century found Brandeis active on a variety of fronts, including the matrimonial one. On March 23, 1891, he married his second cousin, Alice Goldmark, with whom he had two daughters, Susan and Elizabeth. With his partner, Samuel Warren, he also wrote a seminal legal article titled "The Right to Privacy," published in the *Harvard Law Review* in 1890. This article, as much as any other scholarly work, formed the foundation for the recognition of a right to privacy in a wide variety of legal contexts. Throughout most of this decade, Brandeis also waged war against the monopolistic aspirations of the Boston Elevated Railway. His involvement in this public issue was one of the first of many occasions when he applied his legal talents for the public good, often without receiving compensation. In fact, Brandeis contributed so much of his professional time to such cases that he eventually believed it necessary to reimburse his law firm for the value of the time he dispensed free of charge on public matters, laboring, as he would become known, as "the people's lawyer."

By the turn of the century, Louis Brandeis had already achieved prominence as a progressive reformer. He supported unions as a necessary counterweight to the growing power of corporations. In 1908 he made a famous appearance before the U.S. Supreme Court on behalf of the National Consumers' League to defend an Oregon law setting maximum hours for female workers in *Mueller v. Oregon* (1908). Since the Court had held only three years previously in *Lochner v. New York* (1905) that a maximum-hours law for bakers unconstitutionally infringed on the right of contract, Brandeis faced formidable obstacles in persuading the Court to uphold the Oregon law. He eventually prevailed, however, partly on the strength of an innovative brief that devoted a mere two pages to discussion of the applicable legal precedents and the remainder to a detailed presentation of sociological data supporting his contention that excessive work hours were harmful to women. This kind of brief, later emulated by other lawyers, came to be known as a "Brandeis brief."

In 1914 Brandeis became the leader of the American Zionist movement, and he would remain active in this cause for the rest of his life. Brandeis supported the idea of a Palestinian home for his people, in part as a kind of laboratory in which his views about the value of participatory democracy might be given a concrete setting. The perfect state, he believed, should be small, democratic, and agrarian; and a Palestinian Jewish state offered the possibility of realizing this ideal. In Zionism, Brandeis's political faith in democracy found expression. Democracy, one person declared of Brandeis—who was not a practicing Jew—was for him "not a political program. It is a religion."

When President Woodrow Wilson nominated Louis Brandeis to the Supreme Court in 1916 to replace Justice Joseph R. Lamar, it was inevitable that corporate interests would rally to oppose the appointment of "the people's lawyer." The battle over his confirmation raged for four months, but the Senate eventually confirmed Brandeis as the Court's first Jewish justice on June 1, 1916, by a vote of 47-22. He took his seat on the Court four days later and began what would be a 22-year career of service on the Supreme Court.

Although 454 of the 528 opinions Justice Brandeis wrote were for the Court's majority, he often found himself dissenting in important cases, and many of his dissents would later become law. For example, he soon found himself at odds with conservatives on the Court who cast a suspicious constitutional eye on a variety of federal and state laws regulating economic matters. These conservatives, who often commanded a majority on the Court, viewed such laws as unwarranted intrusions upon sacrosanct individual contract or property rights. Brandeis, however, thought that the federal and state governments generally had to be free to experiment with new legal solutions for the problems created by 20th-century industrialism. He preferred, in the main, to see such experimentation come from the state level, since he distrusted the accumulation of excessive power by the federal government as much as he distrusted its accumulation by corporations. Nevertheless, he generally practiced judicial restraint in reviewing economic regulations, including those passed by the federal government.

Justice Brandeis was not similarly deferential, though, when federal and state laws affected individual rights, especially the rights of privacy and freedom of speech. Again, mainly in dissent, Brandeis became the Court's most vigorous defender of these rights. He dissented from the majority's decision in *Olmstead v. United States* (1928), which upheld the constitutionality of government wiretaps. Brandeis, in dissent, argued that wiretaps violated the Fourth and Fifth Amendments, which, he suggested, guaranteed a right of privacy. As applied to the wiretaps, this was "the right to be let alone—the most comprehensive of rights and the right most valued by civilized men." It did not matter to Brandeis that government agents who used the wiretaps were in pursuit of worthwhile causes. "The greatest dangers to liberty," he wrote, "lurk in insidious encroachment by men of zeal, well-meaning but without understanding." Nearly 40 years after Brandeis penned these words, the Supreme Court finally approved his view by overruling *Olmstead*.

Brandeis was similarly adamant in his defense of free speech, and here, too, his most important opinions tended to be dissents. In one case he did join with the majority decision sustaining the punishment of a Socialist speaker. But he explained his general views about freedom of speech in a separate concurring opinion that became an important milestone in the history of First Amendment law:

> Those who won our independence believed that the final end of the state was to make men free to develop their faculties, and that in its

> government the deliberative forces should prevail over the arbitrary. They valued liberty both as an end and as a means. They believed liberty to be the secret of happiness and courage to be the secret of liberty. They believed that freedom to think as you will and to speak as you think are means indispensable to the discovery and spread of political truth; that without free speech and assembly discussion would be futile; that with them, discussion affords ordinarily adequate protection against the dissemination of noxious doctrine; that the greatest menace to freedom is an inert people; that public discussion is a political duty; and that this should be a fundamental principle of the American government.

The "people's lawyer," though elevated to the Supreme Court, never quite retired as an advocate. Brandeis continued to act behind the scenes to achieve his progressive social and political aims. He did not hesitate to convey his ideas about appropriate policy to others, including Harvard Law professor and later Supreme Court justice Felix Frankfurter. More recent historical investigations have discovered that Brandeis even had contact with various New Deal government officials about how they should write laws. Though this practice is inconsistent with contemporary standards about appropriate judicial behavior, his otherwise sterling historical reputation has not been seriously diminished by it.

By the end of the 1930s, Brandeis was 83 years old and found the responsibilities of his position increasingly difficult to bear. He retired on February 13, 1939, and died of a heart attack two years later on October 5, 1941, in Washington, D.C.

By the end of his long tenure on the Supreme Court, Justice Brandeis seemed to colleagues and friends to possess the visage of an ancient Hebrew prophet. His law clerks, and even President Franklin Delano Roosevelt, referred to him as "Isaiah." And certainly there was something of the legal prophet in his character. In many cases where his impassioned pen had urged a different legal result than the one adopted by a majority of his colleagues on the Court, Brandeis seemed to have peered across the decades of the 20th century and seen the law as it would be rather than the law as it was in his own day. Even before he left the Court, his judicial deference toward economic legislation had found support among a majority of the Court beginning in 1937. His notions of privacy and free speech, though, would incubate longer and find their place in modern constitutional law beginning in the 1960s, more than two decades after the voice of "the people's lawyer" had finally been stilled by death.

Further Reading

Baker, Leonard. *Brandeis and Frankfurter: A Dual Biography.* New York: New York University Press, 1986.

Dawson, Nelson L., ed. *Brandeis and America.* Lexington: University Press of Kentucky, 1989.

Paper, Lewis J. *Brandeis.* Englewood Cliffs, N.J.: Prentice Hall, 1983.

Strum, Philippa. *Louis D. Brandeis: Justice for the People.* Cambridge: Harvard University Press, 1984.

Urofsky, Melvin I. *Louis D. Brandeis and the Progressive Tradition.* Boston: Little, Brown, 1981.

JOHN HESSIN CLARKE (1857–1945)

Associate Justice, 1916–1922

Appointed by President Woodrow Wilson

JOHN HESSIN CLARKE
(United States Supreme Court)

Justice John H. Clarke caused more of a stir when he resigned from the Supreme Court than when President Woodrow Wilson appointed him in the first place. Barely six years after he took the oath of office as an associate justice, he announced his retirement to the nation, citing as justification his desire to seek the admission of the United States into the League of Nations. Though this stated reason surely accounts for part of Clarke's impetus to leave the Court, closer examination would probably reveal that Justice Clarke was, by temperament, simply unsuited for the judicial work entailed in his office. He warned his successor on the Court, George Sutherland, to expect a "dog's life," and the desire to escape this life accounted perhaps as much as anything for Clarke's controversial exit from the Court.

John Hessin Clarke was born on September 18, 1857, in New Lisbon, Ohio, the son of John Clarke and Melissa Hessin Clarke. The elder John Clarke had emigrated from Ireland nearly three decades earlier, settled in New Lisbon, and established a prosperous career as a lawyer and later a county court judge. The younger Clarke attended high school in New Lisbon and later enrolled in Western Reserve College, from which he graduated in 1877, a member of Phi Delta Phi. He spent the following year studying law with his father, and he was admitted to the bar in the fall of 1878. He began his legal career practicing law with his father in New Lisbon but decided to relocate to Youngstown in 1880, where he set up his own legal practice and purchased an interest in a local Democratic newspaper, the *Youngstown Vindicator*. Through Clarke's influence the paper became a leading progressive voice. His legal practice, however, found its clientele chiefly among railroads and other corporate interests, for whom he proved himself to be an able advocate in court. This tension between Clarke's own political commitments and those of his generally conservative business clients became a feature of his professional life; it followed him when he moved to Cleveland in 1897 to join the firm of Williamson and Cushing where, once again, he represented a variety of business interests, including the Nickle Plate Railroad.

Active early in political affairs, John Clarke initially seemed to have no aspirations for a political office himself. As a "Gold Bug," though, Clarke vigorously campaigned against William Jennings Bryan's attempt to abolish the gold standard for currency. Finally, in 1904 he ran as a Democratic candidate for the U.S. Senate, but his progressive campaign suffered defeat at the hands of the incumbent, Mark Hanna. He made another bid for the Senate 10 years later but eventually dropped out of the race when President Woodrow Wilson appointed him as a judge on the federal district court for the northern district of Ohio. He served a rather undistinguished two years in this position, his tenure on the district court being chiefly remembered for the elaborate receptions he held for people being naturalized in his court.

When Associate Justice Charles Evans Hughes retired from the U.S. Supreme Court to pursue a presidential bid, President Wilson took the opportunity to nominate Clarke to fill the vacancy on July 14, 1916. Wilson had already placed one progressive on the high Court, Louis D. Brandeis, and he hoped that Clarke's additional liberal influence would help to blunt the Court's overall conservative stance. The Senate confirmed the nomination soon afterward, and Clarke took the oath of office on October 9, 1916.

Once on the Court, Clarke generally met Wilson's expectations in his voting patterns. For example, he joined Justices Holmes, McKenna, and Brandeis in dissent when a majority of the Court struck down a federal law that prohibited the interstate transportation of goods made with child labor in *Hammer v. Dagenhart* (1918). He also welcomed the use of antitrust laws against monopolies and supported labor rights. But his progressivism on economic matters did not always follow into the territory of individual rights. Perhaps his most famous majority opinion for the Court was one that cast Justice Oliver Wendell Holmes as a dissenter. In *Abrams v. United States* (1919), the Court upheld the conviction of certain Russian-born socialists for distributing leaflets that castigated President Wilson for sending U.S. troops to Russia and called for a general workers' strike to protest this action. A majority of the Court, in an opinion written by Clarke, sustained the conviction of the defendants under the Sedition Act of 1918 and rejected the defendants' argument that their right to freedom of speech had been violated. Holmes, joined by Brandeis in his dissent, scoffed at the supposed threat to the United States being engineered by "the surreptitious publishing of a silly leaflet by an unknown man."

In the main, Clarke did not create an altogether favorable impression on his colleagues while on the Court. Holmes complained that

Clarke frequently made up his mind about the outcome of cases in advance, though he admitted missing his "affectionate companionship" once Clarke had resigned from the Court. Chief Justice William Howard Taft thought that Clarke imagined—wrongly—that deciding cases was like voting on bills in Congress. Justice McReynolds, notorious for his rudeness, made Clarke the special object of his venom and went so far as to refuse to sign the Court's farewell letter to Clarke on his resignation.

In fact, history remembers Clarke more for his resignation from the Court than for anything he did while he was a justice. In September 1922 he announced his retirement and explained to Justice Brandeis his reason for doing so:

> I would die happier if I should do all that is possible to promote the entrance of our government into the League of Nations than if I continued to devote my time to determining whether a drunken Indian had been deprived of his land before he died or whether the digging of a ditch in Iowa was constitutional or not.

The latter part of his explanation suggests that Clarke lacked the temperament and patience necessary to continue the work of a Supreme Court justice, which involved not only celebrated cases raising issues of national importance but also a myriad of lesser disputes for which the Court was the final arbiter. Whatever his reasons, though, many observers found them insufficient. Former President Wilson, in particular, found no pleasure in Clarke's resignation, even though it was to pursue a cause dear to Wilson himself: U.S. membership in the League of Nations. He would have rather had Clarke remain as a progressive influence on the Court.

True to his word, though, John Clarke cast himself into the work of persuading the United States to join the League of Nations once he left the Court. Through articles and speeches he lobbied incessantly for this result, becoming the president of the League of Nations Non-Partisan Association in 1923 and a trustee of the World Peace Foundation. But the nation that had refused to follow President Wilson into the League of Nations was no more inclined to follow a former Supreme Court justice there, and so Clarke eventually retired from this campaign and moved to San Diego, where he lived out his life. He made one final prominent public appearance in March 1937, when he went on national radio on behalf of President Franklin Delano Roosevelt. Roosevelt's frustration at the Supreme Court for declaring unconstitutional many of the jewels of his New Deal agenda ultimately prompted the president to propose packing the Court with an additional justice for every existing justice over the age of 70 who refused to retire. Though framed as a relief for the Court's workload, in fact the president's proposal was a transparent attempt to stack the Court with new justices who would support his legislative programs. In any event, the 80-year-old Clarke took to the airwaves on March 22, 1937, to defend the constitutionality of the president's court-packing plan. He died eight years later to the day in San Diego, on March 22, 1945, on the eve of the formation of the United Nations. A bachelor all his life, Clarke left his estate to charities.

Of the more than 100 men and women who have sat on the Supreme Court, Justice John H. Clarke was certainly one of the less illustrious of this number. He seems to have lacked a talent for judging, and, to his credit, promptly vacated his seat on this discovery, unlike some men who have burdened the Court with their continued presence long after ceasing to make any significant contribution to its work. Clarke remains, though, a curious footnote in the Court's history: the man who left the highest court in the nation to pursue an elusive dream of world peace.

FURTHER READING

Burner, David. "John H. Clarke." In *The Justices of the United States Supreme Court 1789–1969: Their Lives and Major Opinions,* vol. 3. Edited by Leon Friedman and Fred L. Israel. New York: R. R. Bowker Co., 1969.

Levitan, David Maurice. "The Jurisprudence of Mr. Justice Clarke." *Miami Law Quarterly* 7 (December 1952): 44–72.

Warner, Hoyt Landon. *The Life of Mr. Justice Clarke: A Testament to the Power of Liberal Dissent in America.* Cleveland: Western Reserve University, 1959.

Wittke, Carl. "Mr. Justice Clarke in Retirement." *Western Reserve Law Review* 1 (June 1949): 28–48.

WILLIAM HOWARD TAFT (1857–1930)

Chief Justice, 1921–1930

Appointed by President Warren G. Harding

WILLIAM HOWARD TAFT
(Photograph, Library of Congress)

More than one Supreme Court justice has aspired to be president of the United States. Charles Evans Hughes resigned his seat on the Court to pursue a failed presidential bid against Woodrow Wilson. John McLean waited expectantly to see whether Republicans might choose him to bear their presidential standard in 1860, only to have his ambition frustrated when a dark horse candidate named Lincoln captured the Republican nomination and then the presidency itself. But for at least one man, ambition traveled in the opposite direction. William Howard Taft was president before he was chief justice, and he viewed this progression of offices as a decided advancement. In his mind, the chief justiceship and not the presidency crowned his life's achievement. Later historical observers have tended to concur in Taft's own judgment of himself: He was a better chief justice than chief executive. But he alone in American history offers the possibility of such a comparison, because no other individual has held both offices.

—⌇—

William Howard Taft was born on September 15, 1857, in Cincinnati, Ohio, the son of Alphonso Taft and Louisa Maria Torrey Taft, Alphonso's second wife. Both Taft's father and his grandfather had followed legal careers. Alphonso Taft, in particular, rose to national prominence, serving as a judge on the Ohio Superior Court; as attorney general and secretary of war under President Ulysses S. Grant; and as an ambassador, first to Austria-Hungary and then to Russia under the administration of President Chester A. Arthur. The younger Taft attended high school in Cincinnati; Yale University, from which he graduated second in his class in 1878; and Cincinnati Law School, graduating and passing the Ohio bar in 1880. Taft plunged immediately into Republican politics and served in his first public office as assistant prosecuting attorney for Hamilton County, Ohio, from 1881 to 1883, followed by service as assistant county solicitor for Hamilton County from 1885 to 1887. In 1886, while serving in the county solicitor's office, Taft married Helen Herron, a woman whose ambitions for her husband would play as prominent a role in his public career as his ambitions for himself. The couple had three children and remained married until Taft's death nearly half a century later. One of their children—Robert Alphonso Taft—was a U.S. senator from 1939 to his death in 1953.

Taft began what would become a mostly intermittent judicial career in 1887, when Ohio Governor Joseph B. Foraker appointed him to the Ohio Superior Court. He was 29 years old at the time, and within a few years he would begin to sound out the possibilities of a Supreme Court appointment from President Benjamin Harrison. Harrison, though, had different uses for the young man and appointed him solicitor general instead. Taft served in this position from 1890 to 1891 but continued to seek a judicial appointment. In 1892, much to Helen Taft's consternation, President Harrison appointed the 34-year-old Ohioan to the U.S. Court of Appeals for the Sixth Circuit. Within a few years, in addition to his service as a federal appellate judge, Taft took on teaching and administrative responsibilities at his law school alma mater, the University of Cincinnati Law School, where he became professor of law and dean in 1896.

Taft's eight years on the Sixth Circuit Court of Appeals were satisfying to him—though not to his wife, who had higher political aspirations for her husband. Those years ended when President William McKinley persuaded Taft in January 1900 to take charge of a commission appointed to bring civil rule to the Philippines in the wake of the Spanish-American War. The following year saw Taft named governor-general of the Philippines, a position whose responsibilities so consumed his attention that he turned down a proffered appointment from President Theodore Roosevelt to the Supreme Court. Finally, in 1904 Roosevelt persuaded Taft to join his administration as secretary of war, and the two formed so harmonious a relationship that Roosevelt threw his weight behind Taft to be his successor in the 1908 presidential election. Thus William Howard Taft, who longed for nothing so much as to be chief justice of the U.S. Supreme Court, found himself instead the president of the United States.

The presidency of William Howard Taft tends to draw low marks for its achievement, but in at least one respect, Taft contributed significantly to the very institution he longed to command—the U.S. Supreme Court. In a single term of office, he was able to remake the Court by appointing five new justices (Lurton, Hughes, Van Devanter, Lamar, and Pitney) and elevating Associate Justice Edward Douglas White to the Court's chief seat. His appointment of White as chief justice illustrated how his presidential responsibilities were influenced by his own yet-unsatisfied ambition to be chief justice himself. At the time, he rued having to make the appointment, since, as he phrased it, "the one place in the government which I would have liked to fill myself I am forced to give to another." Before the vacancy in the chief seat had appeared, Taft had intimated that he would place Charles Evans Hughes in that position. But on further reflection, he appears to have taken into account the respective ages of Edward White and Hughes. White was older than Taft by 12 years and older than Hughes by 17. White might be expected to occupy the position of chief justice for a relatively short time, as compared with the time Hughes might serve in that position. If Taft had any hopes of the chief justiceship becoming vacant after he left the presidency, they hinged on appointing the older man to the position. This, in fact, he did in 1910.

The other events of Taft's presidency were inauspicious. Through a series of circumstances, including his decision to replace several of former President Theodore Roosevelt's cabinet members, Taft and Roosevelt eventually became at odds. Roosevelt, stymied by Taft's grip on the Republican National Committee, bolted the party and turned the presidential election of 1912 into a three-way contest from which the Democratic candidate Woodrow Wilson emerged triumphant and Taft suffered resounding defeat. The former president retreated to Yale University Law School, which named him Kent Professor of Constitutional Law. At last, in 1920, Republican President Warren G. Harding assumed the presidency and Edward White, Taft's choice for chief justice a decade earlier, died only a few months after Harding's inauguration. In June 1921 President Harding nominated Taft to the position and the Senate, with only four dissenting votes, confirmed the appointment and made Taft the first—and only—individual in the history of the nation to hold both the offices of president and chief justice of the Supreme Court.

Taft's tenure at the helm of the nation's highest court combined the character of a conservative judge and a progressive administrator. On the great constitutional questions of his day, especially the degree to which the Court would defend property and contract rights from progressive federal and state legislation, Taft displayed a generally consistent conservativism. No sooner had he joined the Court than he led all but one of his colleagues to invalidate the first federal child labor law in *Bailey v. Drexel Furniture Company* (1922). The law attempted to restrict the use of child labor by prohibitively taxing the products of such labor. Chief Justice Taft, for the Court's majority, declared this attempted regulation an unconstitutional meddling in subjects appropriately reserved to the states for regulation. Taft's conservative judicial inclinations were, however, paired with a reformist's zeal when it came to the administration of the federal courts. Especially in the early years of his tenure as chief justice, while he was still in good health, Taft set on a program of streamlining federal judicial procedures and taking control of the caseload of federal courts—especially that of the Supreme Court—which did as much to mold the shape of the federal judiciary as anything since the establishment of that judiciary at the nation's beginning. Through the force of his own genial temperament and persistent labor, he was for a time able to bring an atmosphere of collegiality to a Court that had known more than its fair share of fractiousness. And he made an even more tangible and enduring contribution to the nation's highest court by obtaining congressional blessing and support for a new Supreme Court building, conceived and planned during Taft's tenure as chief justice but completed only after his death.

Eventually, Taft's health began to fail toward the end of the 1920s, and sharp fissures developed between the Court's conservatives, led by the ailing chief justice, and its more progressive members. These fissures would crack wide open in the following decade, but their beginnings dismayed the aging chief justice. Taft was able to assume his center seat on the Court at the beginning of the 1929 term in October of that year, but his health soon collapsed. Shortly after the first of the new year, illness made him unable to continue his duties, and he resigned from the Court on February 3, 1930. A little more than a month later, on March 8, 1930, the former president and chief justice died.

For his judicial ability, William Howard Taft enjoys only a modest reputation among historians of the Court. In the decade after his death, the conservative principles that he championed would for a time defy the will of a president and a nation. But by the end of the 1930s, those principles had been soundly repudiated. The New Deal agenda of President Franklin Delano Roosevelt triumphed as new majorities on the Court abandoned the constitutional conservativism that had threatened it for a time. As the chief administrator of the nation's federal courts, however, Taft crafted a legacy that has earned considerably more praise. He became in some ways the father of the modern Court, not in its doctrines but in its inner workings.

Further Reading

Anderson, Judith Icke. *William Howard Taft: An Intimate History.* New York: Norton, 1981.

Burton, David Henry. *Taft, Holmes, and the 1920s Court: An Appraisal.* Madison, N.J.: Fairleigh Dickinson University Press; Cranbury, N.J.: Associated University Presses, 1998.

Hicks, Frederick Charles. *William Howard Taft: Yale Professor of Law & New Haven Citizen.* New Haven: Yale University Press, 1945.

Mason, Alpheus Thomas. *William Howard Taft: Chief Justice.* New York: Simon and Schuster, 1965.

Pringle, Henry Fowles. *The Life and Times of William Howard Taft.* New York: Farrar and Rinehart, 1939.

GEORGE SUTHERLAND (1862–1942)

Associate Justice, 1922–1938

Appointed by President Warren G. Harding

GEORGE SUTHERLAND
(United States Supreme Court)

In the 1930s, George Sutherland became the intellectual spokesman for the Four Horsemen, an alliance of four justices on the Supreme Court who consistently opposed social and economic reforms of the New Deal era. Together with Justices Willis Van Devanter, Pierce Butler, and James Clark McReynolds, Sutherland formed the core of a conservative alliance that ultimately prompted President Franklin Delano Roosevelt to propose packing the Court with additional justices to "assist" the "Nine Old Men" in the exercise of their duties. This transparent attempt to seize political control of the Court eventually collapsed, but only after a new majority on the Court repudiated the constitutional philosophy of the Four Horsemen. In spite of this defeat, however, Sutherland commands historical note for surprisingly liberal opinions for the Court in other areas of constitutional law, including the rights to be accorded those accused of a crime and the breadth of freedom of speech.

—∞—

George Sutherland was born on March 25, 1862, in Buckinghamshire, England, across the Atlantic Ocean from the war then waging between the North and the South. His Scottish father, Alexander George Sutherland, and his English mother, Frances Slater Sutherland, became converts the same year to the Church of Jesus Christ of Latter-day Saints (the Mormons) and migrated from England to Utah Territory in the summer of 1863. Soon after arriving in Springville, Utah, however, Alexander renounced Mormonism and moved his family to Montana. By 1869, though, the family had moved back to Utah Territory and eventually settled in Provo. There Alexander Sutherland followed a vocational migration as varied as the geographic one on which he led his family: mining prospector and recorder, postmaster, justice of the peace, and eventually lawyer. Young George Sutherland experienced the harsh and arduous life of the frontier and in later years thought of himself as a pioneer or, at least, a "pio-nearly." He was forced to drop out of school by the age of 12 and subsequently earned a living in a succession of jobs. By 1879, however, when Sutherland was 17 years old, he had managed to save enough to enroll in Brigham Young Academy (later Brigham Young University) in Provo, where he came under the formative influence of Karl G. Maeser, the headmaster of the school. Maeser drilled his students in the social Darwinism of Herbert Spencer and in the proposition that God had divinely inspired the men who framed the Constitution a century before in Philadelphia.

Following this educational experience, Sutherland worked for 15 months for the contractors building the Rio Grande Western Railroad and then headed north to Michigan, where in 1882 he enrolled in the University of Michigan Law School. There he studied with Dean Thomas M. Cooley, one of the leading constitutional scholars of the time, whose influence readily supplemented that which Sutherland had already absorbed from Karl Maeser. Cooley defended the principles of natural rights and limited government, famously expressed in his 1868 work, *Treatise on the Constitutional Limitations Which Rest upon the Legislative Power of the State of the American Union*. This influence lasted less than a year, for Sutherland soon determined to return to Utah without obtaining a degree. He practiced law for a time with his father in Provo, and in 1883 he married Rosamund Lee. Their union would last almost 60 years and produce three children: two daughters, Edith and Emma, and a son, Philip, who died in childhood.

In 1886 Sutherland and his father dissolved their law partnership, and he formed a new partnership with Samuel R. Thurman, who would later become chief justice of the Utah Supreme Court. The two were eventually joined by William King, who in later years would become one of Sutherland's political opponents. Sutherland made an early foray into politics in 1890 by running as a member of the Liberal party—which opposed the Mormon practice of polygamy—for mayor of Provo. He lost handily but soon announced himself a member of the Republican party after the Mormon church abandoned the practice of polygamy that same year. In 1892 he suffered his second political defeat after running as a Republican for a seat in Congress representing Utah Territory.

By 1893 Sutherland had moved to Salt Lake City, joined a prominent firm there, and helped organize the Utah bar association. When Utah became a state in 1896, Sutherland won his first political contest by gaining a seat in the Utah state senate. After four years in this position, he made a successful bid for a congressional seat, defeating along the way his old law partner, William King. After his two-year term in the House of Representatives, however, Sutherland returned to the private practice of law and prepared to make a bid for a seat in the U.S. Senate. His bid was successful, returning him to Washington in 1905. There, somewhat surprisingly in light of his later judicial reputation, Sutherland proved to be a friend of at least some progressive causes, including women's suffrage and workmen's compensation laws. He opposed, though, a variety of federal laws designed to regulate businesses, including the Clayton Antitrust Act and the Federal Trade Commission Act, both passed in 1914.

After the ratification of the Seventeenth Amendment in 1913, which made U.S. senators subject to popular election, Sutherland ran again for the Senate but lost this time to William King. Instead of returning to Utah, however, he decided to remain in Washington, D.C., and to practice law there. Soon afterward, his prominence as an attorney won recognition when he was elected president of the American Bar Association. Though his senatorial loss had exiled him briefly from the political scene, the election of Warren G. Harding altered this. Sutherland and Harding had been colleagues in the Senate, and Sutherland had been one of Harding's advisers during his presidential campaign. These ties yielded a variety of minor appointments in the first year of Harding's administration, while the president and Sutherland bided their time for something infinitely more prestigious: a chance to place Sutherland on the Supreme Court. When Justice John Clarke resigned from the Court in September 1922, President Harding promptly nominated Sutherland to fill the vacant seat on September 5, and the Senate confirmed his appointment the same day. Thus began a 15-year career on the Court.

Justice Sutherland, who had known several of his colleagues prior to ascending to the high Court, proved to be an amiable and hardworking justice. Even Oliver Wendell Holmes, with whom Sutherland would regularly be at odds as to the outcome of cases, valued Sutherland for his abilities as a raconteur. Holmes, on arriving at the justices' conference room, would routinely approach Sutherland with the request: "Sutherland, J., tell me a story." The justice from Utah invariably complied, to the great entertainment of his colleagues. But this general personal harmony overlay sharp differences among the justices over a wide range of constitutional issues. Sutherland, especially in cases involving economic matters, proved to be a consistent conservative.

In one of his first and most important opinions, Sutherland wrote the Court's decision in *Adkins v. Children's Hospital* (1923), invalidating a District of Columbia law that set a minimum wage for women for unreasonably interfering with the right to contract. Sutherland refused to characterize the issue in the case as a choice between individual liberty and the common good: "To sustain the individual freedom of action contemplated by the Constitution, is not to strike down the common good but to exalt it; for surely the good of society as a whole cannot be better served than by preservation against arbitrary restraint of the liberties of its constituent members." His confidence in the constitutional rightness of laissez-faire economics earned Sutherland notoriety as one of the Four Horsemen who nearly stalled the progress of the New Deal, until President Franklin Delano Roosevelt's threat of packing the Court and the defection of sometime-allies Chief Justice Charles Evans Hughes and Justice Owen Roberts finally inspired a new majority of the Court to sustain the various federal and state economic reforms of the New Deal.

Though steadfastly conservative in economic matters, Sutherland's stance on other constitutional issues was not invariably so. For example, he wrote the opinion for the Court in *Powell v. Alabama* (1932), overturning the conviction of the young black men in the Scottsboro case because they had not been afforded adequate legal representation in their trial for capital rape. Moreover, in *Grosjean v. American Press Co.* (1936), Sutherland's opinion for the Court gave a liberal construction to the First Amendment by finding unconstitutional a state license tax on newspaper advertisements.

By 1937 the Four Horsemen had been cast into the role of dissenters. In March, less than two months after President Roosevelt announced his court-packing plan, a new majority on the Court, led by Chief Justice Hughes in *West Coast Hotel Co. v. Parrish* (1937), overruled

Sutherland's opinion in *Adkins v. Children's Hospital* (1923). Thereafter, the Court repeatedly sustained the constitutionality of federal and state economic legislation. The following year, on January 17, 1938, Sutherland retired from the Court. Four years later, at the age of 80, he died in Stockbridge, Massachusetts, on July 18, 1942.

—∾—

The apocalypse threatened by the Four Horsemen never occurred. Though President Roosevelt's court-packing plan eventually suffered defeat, his more immediate aim of coaxing the Supreme Court to support his legislative agenda ultimately prevailed. The laissez-faire philosophy that the young George Sutherland had learned in his student days thus fell out of constitutional fashion. Nevertheless, even though the core of Sutherland's judicial philosophy has generally been viewed as discredited, historians of the Court still accord him a measure of respect for the skill with which he articulated this philosophy in his great constitutional contest with a president. He is also respected for other more enduring aspects of his judicial legacy, such as his vigilance in protecting the Scottsboro boys' rights to a fair trial in *Powell v. Alabama* (1932) and the rights of the press in *Grosjean v. American Press Co.* (1936).

FURTHER READING

Arkes, Hadley. *The Return of George Sutherland: Restoring a Jurisprudence of Natural Rights.* Princeton: Princeton University Press, 1994.

Mason, Alpheus Thomas. "The Conservative World of Mr. Justice Sutherland, 1883–1910." *American Political Science Review* 32 (June 1938): 443–447.

Paschal, Joel Francis. *Mr. Justice Sutherland: A Man Against the State.* New York: Greenwood Press, 1951.

PIERCE BUTLER (1866–1939)

Associate Justice, 1922–1939

Appointed by President Warren G. Harding

PIERCE BUTLER
(United States Supreme Court)

Pierce Butler rose from humble origins to become one of the foremost railroad attorneys of his day and later an associate justice on the U.S. Supreme Court. The toil and self-determination that energized this steep climb forever afterward lent his mind an unswerving devotion to the principles of laissez-faire economics and a fierce patriotism toward the country that had permitted his rise to prominence. He eventually became one of the Court's staunchest conservatives, a member of the legendary Four Horsemen who for a time defied the will of a president during the New Deal era.

Pierce Butler was born in a log cabin on March 17, 1866, in Pine Bend, Minnesota. His parents, Patrick Butler and Mary Gaffney Butler, were devout

Roman Catholics who had immigrated to the United States from Ireland after the potato famine of 1848. Their son Pierce, the sixth of eight children, was born on St. Patrick's Day. Pierce's father—though at first a tavern keeper in Illinois and later a farmer in Minnesota—was an educated man who had studied at Trinity College in Dublin and had traveled widely. He and his wife, Mary, communicated to their son Pierce the value of work and a devotion to the Catholic faith, traits that would help define the future justice over the course of his life.

While helping to work on the farm, Pierce Butler received his early education from a local school, supplemented by instruction from his parents. In 1881 he enrolled in a college preparatory program connected with Carleton College in Northfield, Minnesota. After two years, he entered Carleton College itself, working part-time at a nearby dairy to support his education. In college, Butler developed the basic intellectual underpinnings for the conservative political and economic views that he would bring to the Supreme Court nearly 40 years later, though not always with accompanying academic success. Ironically, in light of his later career on the nation's highest Court, Butler failed a course in constitutional law. He nevertheless graduated in 1887 and moved to St. Paul, Minnesota, where he read law for a year in the firm of Pinch and Twohy before being admitted to the bar in 1888. He would eventually be the last Supreme Court justice appointed to the Court who had not attended law school. One evening at a dinner at John Twohy's home, Butler met Annie M. Cronin, a half sister of Twohy's wife, and Pierce and Annie were married in 1891. This union would eventually produce eight children.

Butler practiced law briefly with Stan Donnelly before working as an assistant county attorney for Ramsey County beginning in 1891. In 1892 he won election to the office of Ramsey county attorney, serving in the position for four years from 1893 through 1897. During the same period he became a partner in the firm of How, Butler, and Mitchell, where he became prominent as a railroad lawyer and an attorney for public utilities over the next 30 years. He forged expertise in the area of litigation valuing railroad and utility property, and was repeatedly successful at securing higher valuations for these properties and thus allowing his clients to charge higher rates. Butler displayed special talent as a trial lawyer and was famed for his vigorous cross-examinations of opposing witnesses. He was a man said by one contemporary to be "easy to meet, but dangerous to oppose." In 1908 Butler's reputation among his peers led to his election as president of the Minnesota State Bar Association. In 1906 Butler had narrowly lost election to the Minnesota state senate on the Democratic ticket; this political bid would be his last attempt to win an elected office. But three years later his adversarial skills came to the attention of George W. Wickersham, attorney general under President William Howard Taft. Wickersham persuaded the Minnesota lawyer to prosecute claims based on the Sherman Antitrust Act and the Pure Food and Drug Act, on behalf of the federal government against certain companies. The gifted Butler secured favorable verdicts at the trial level, but these were later reversed on appeal.

On November 23, 1922, ten days after the resignation of Associate Justice William Rufus Day, President Warren G. Harding appointed Pierce Butler to fill the vacant seat. Harding's decision to reach across party lines to nominate the Democratic Butler prompted substantial controversy. Butler's conservatism attracted the support of some influential Republicans, including Chief Justice William Howard Taft and Associate Justice Willis Van Devanter. Moreover, Butler's Catholicism was a point in his favor, since Taft himself had replaced Chief Justice Edward White, a Catholic, and many observers believed another Catholic appointment was in order, although the Ku Klux Klan opposed his nomination precisely because of his Catholic background. But substantial liberal opponents to Butler's nomination, including George Norris and Robert La Follette, soon emerged in the Senate. They argued, predictably, that Butler's three-decade career of legal efforts on behalf of railroad companies would make him biased toward their interests on the Court. They also challenged him on civil libertarian grounds, on the basis of his conduct as a member of the Board of Regents of the University of Minnesota, a position he held from 1907 to 1924. There was evidence that Butler had used this position to force the dismissal of several members of the faculty at the university whose views he disfavored. These and other criticisms of Butler managed to stall his confirmation until the end of the specially called congressional session, upon which President Harding renominated Butler. The Senate eventually confirmed his appointment by a vote of 61-8 on December 21, 1922. Butler took his seat on the Court at the beginning of the new year, inaugurating what would ultimately be a 17-year tenure of service on the high Court.

In general, Pierce Butler proved to be one of the most reactionary of the Court's conservatives, so resolute in his positions that Justice Oliver Wendell Holmes described him as a "monolith," having "no seams the frost can get through." Holmes concluded, "He is of one piece." Butler consistently adopted a narrow reading of First Amendment freedoms, especially when exercised in furtherance of "unpatriotic" causes. Thus, he joined Justice McReynolds in dissent from the Court's ruling in *Stromberg v. California* (1931), which overturned a woman's conviction for displaying a red flag, and announced the opinion for the Court in *United States v. Schwimmer* (1929), rejecting the naturalization petition of a woman with religiously-rooted conscientious objections to military service. His willingness to use the Fourteenth Amendment to eliminate officially sanctioned racial discrimination was equally stunted. Together with McReynolds again, he dissented from the Court's decision in the Scottsboro case, *Powell v. Alabama* (1932), which reversed the conviction of seven young black men accused of capital rape but denied adequate representation by counsel, and in *Missouri ex rel. Gaines v. Canada* (1938), in which a majority of the Court declared unconstitutional Missouri's refusal to allow a black student to attend the state's public law school.

In the area of economic regulation, Pierce proved to be implacably conservative, earning designation as one of the Four Horsemen, the quartet of justices—including McReynolds, Van Devanter, and Sutherland—who opposed New Deal programs. For a time, the Four Horsemen, sometimes joined by Chief Justice Charles Evans Hughes and by Associate Justice Owen Roberts, dealt critical blows to a variety of New Deal programs by declaring them unconstitutional. Eventually though, President Roosevelt threatened to pack the Court with justices more hospitable to his legislative agenda, and Chief Justice Hughes and Associate Justice Roberts parted company with the Four Horsemen in 1937. Thereafter, the Four Horsemen found themselves consistently in the minority position.

Justice Butler defied the conservative label so tightly stitched into his judicial character by consistently pressing for a vigorous concept of "due process of law" that would protect the rights of criminal defendants against official abuses. Thus, for example, he dissented from the Court's approval of wiretapping in *Olmstead v. United States* (1928). Moreover, his Roman Catholic faith, which led him to oppose artificial means of contraception, no doubt inspired his dissent for the notorious case of *Buck v. Bell* (1927), in which the rest of the Court upheld the compulsory sterilization of a young woman who was mentally infirm. Even great men may stumble badly, as Justice Oliver Wendell Holmes demonstrated by authoring the Court's majority opinion justifying this result:

> We have seen more than once that the public welfare may call upon the best citizens for their lives. It would be strange if it could not call upon those who already sap the strength of the State for these lesser sacrifices . . . in order to prevent our being swamped with incompetence. It is better for the world, if instead of waiting to execute degenerate offspring for crime, or to let them starve for their imbecility, society can prevent those who are manifestly

> unfit from continuing their kind. . . . Three generations of imbeciles is enough.

Butler alone dissented from this reasoning and its result.

By the end of the tumultuous decade of the 1930s, illness began to trouble Justice Butler. He could not join the Court as it began its 1939 session. Within a month of the October term's beginning, he died of a bladder illness on November 16, 1939, in Washington, D.C. He was 73 years old at the time.

History has little good to say about any of the legendary Four Horsemen, but two—James Clark McReynolds and Pierce Butler—normally find themselves prominently displayed in lists of the Court's worst justices. Implacably conservative on a wide range of issues, they normally earn damnation for their unwillingness to sacrifice absolute categories to changing legal and social conditions. Butler, in particular, deified the value of stable precedents at a time when other justices argued for the need to adapt the law, including constitutional law, to changing social conditions. Once, Butler reportedly chided Holmes after a lengthy discussion by the Court in conference, "I am glad we have finally arrived at a *just* decision." To this, Holmes retorted, "Hell is paved with *just* decisions." In the end, history has found little attractive in the "justice" that Pierce Butler championed.

Further Reading

Brown, Francis Joseph. *The Social and Economic Philosophy of Pierce Butler.* Washington, D.C.: Catholic University of America Press, 1945.

Cushman, Barry. "The Secret Lives of the Four Horsemen." *Virginia Law Review* 83 (April 1997): 559–645.

Danelski, David Joseph. *A Supreme Court Justice Is Appointed.* New York: Random House, 1964.

Langram, Robert W. "Why Are Some Supreme Court Justices Rated as 'Failures'?" *Supreme Court Historical Society Yearbook* (1985): 8–14.

Edward Terry Sanford (1865–1930)

Associate Justice, 1923–1930

Appointed by President Warren G. Harding

Edward Terry Sanford
(United States Supreme Court)

Edward T. Sanford was an urbane and genial southerner, "born to charm" according to Justice Oliver Wendell Holmes. He labored as a judge from 1908 until his death in 1930, first at the federal district court level and later on the U.S. Supreme Court. In these judicial roles Sanford earned a reputation as a gracious and diligent man. Ultimately seated on a Court among the likes of Holmes, Louis Brandeis, and former U.S. president William Howard Taft, however, Sanford's courtly presence tended to be overshadowed by better-known and more influential justices.

Edward Terry Sanford was born on July 23, 1865, in Knoxville, Tennessee, the eldest child of Edward J. Sanford and Emma Chavannes Sanford. His father, a transplanted Yankee, had become wealthy in the lumber and construction business. His mother, Swiss by birth, saw to it that her firstborn son acquired through education a cosmopolitan outlook, free of the narrow sectionalism that might otherwise have gripped him. After preparation in private schools, Sanford attended the University of Tennessee, where, at the age of 18, he graduated in 1883 first in his class. With a B.A. and a Ph.B. (a bachelor of philosophy) from Tennessee in hand, Sanford promptly enrolled in Harvard University, where he received his second bachelor's degree two years later. By 1886 he had been admitted to Harvard Law School, where he served as an editor for the newly founded *Harvard Law Review*. With a brief intermission from his studies to pass the Tennessee bar exam in 1888, Sanford remained at Harvard Law School for three years, earning his M.A. and LL.B. As if these educational accomplishments were not enough, Sanford then traveled to Europe, where he studied French and German for a year.

When he returned from Europe in 1890, Sanford joined the firm of Andrews and Thornburgh in Knoxville. The following year he married Lutie Mallory Woodruff, with whom he would have two daughters. Sanford practiced law in Knoxville for nearly 17 years, but he also devoted considerable time to civic activities, including service as a trustee of the University of Tennessee beginning in 1897. Over the years, the Tennessean would undertake an impressive array of civic responsibilities, which included work as chairman of the board of the George Peabody College of Teachers, alumni president for Harvard and the University of Tennessee, and vice president of the American Bar Association. His work in support of the American entrance into the League of Nations after World War I made a favorable impression on Chief Justice William Howard Taft and President Warren G. Harding's attorney general, Harry M. Daugherty. Both men would, in time, play a significant part in Sanford's appointment to the Supreme Court.

Edward Sanford's public career began in 1905, when he assumed the position of special assistant to the U.S. attorney general to help prosecute a business monopoly known as the fertilizer trust. Two years later he assumed the position of assistant attorney general in the administration of President Theodore Roosevelt and so impressed Roosevelt that the president appointed Sanford as a federal district judge for Tennessee in 1908. For the next 15 years, Sanford forged a reputation as an able, conscientious, and courteous judge, leaving his position as a district judge finally when President Warren G. Harding, with the encouragement of Chief Justice Taft and Attorney General Daugherty, appointed him to the Supreme Court on January 24, 1923. The Senate confirmed the nomination within the week and Sanford took his seat as an associate justice of the Supreme Court on February 5, 1923.

Though never a prominent figure on the Court, Justice Sanford nevertheless made several important contributions to modern constitutional law during his seven years as an associate justice. In particular, he spoke for the Court in two important First Amendment cases, *Gitlow v. New York* (1925) and *Whitney v. California* (1927), that established the applicability of the free speech guarantee to state laws that restricted speech. The First Amendment, by its terms, declares that "Congress" shall not make any laws abridging the freedom of speech; thus, as originally framed, it offered no protection from state laws that abridged the freedom of speech. But the Fourteenth Amendment, ratified in the wake of the Civil War, prohibits states from depriving persons of "life, liberty, or property" without "due process of law." Eventually the Court came to consider whether the protection of "liberty" in the Fourteenth Amendment's due process clause might be understood to make the First Amendment's free speech guarantee applicable to the states. In *Gitlow* and *Whitney,* Sanford delivered the Court's opinion declaring that the First Amendment's protection of speech was indeed applicable to state and local governments, that it had been "incorporated" by the terms of the Fourteenth Amendment's due process clause. The Court eventually applied the incorporation doctrine to find that most of the provisions of the Bill of Rights, though originally restrictions only on the federal government, were applicable to state and local governments as well.

Although the announcement of this incorporation principle would become a crucial feature in the modern constitutional protection of speech, the actual results reached by Sanford and a majority of the Court in *Gitlow* and *Whitney* permitted the punishment of speech. In *Gitlow,* the Court sustained the conviction of a member of the Socialist party who had been prosecuted under a state law that made it a crime to advocate the violent overthrow of government. Gitlow, the defendant in the case, published a leaflet that urged the establishment of socialism by "class action . . . in any form." Writing for a majority of the Court, Justice Sanford concluded that Gitlow's speech could be punished. "A single revolutionary spark may kindle a fire that, smoldering for a time, may burst into a sweeping and destructive conflagration." Sanford was no more solicitous of speech in *Whitney v. California* (1927). There he concluded for the Court that punishment of an individual for mere membership in an organization that promoted violence to effect industrial or political change did no violence to freedom of speech.

In the following decade, the Court would grapple with the constitutional limits on federal and state attempts to regulate economic affairs, especially in connection with the New Deal programs of President Franklin Delano Roosevelt. In cases that foreshadowed the coming battles that would pit the president against a majority of the Court, Sanford generally was to be found among a minority of justices who believed the Court should not interfere with such legislative initiatives. But he did not live to participate in the constitutional battles waged during the 1930s. He died suddenly on March 8, 1930, in Washington, D.C. A man who tended to be overshadowed by other men during his tenure on the Court, Sanford suffered a similar fate even in his death. Chief Justice William Howard Taft had been forced by illness to resign from the Court the previous month and he died the same day as Sanford, a few hours after Sanford's death. The nation's attention inevitably focused on the death of the former president and chief justice rather than on that of Associate Justice Sanford.

In terms of his overall impact on the Court and on the development of American law, Edward T. Sanford does not rank high among the pantheon of justices. He was a valuable colleague on the Court for the seven years of his tenure but was clearly overshadowed by the Court's more brilliant lights. His most important achievement was to announce the application of First Amendment protections to state and local governments—no mean achievement, since most of the cases from which the Court would eventually erect the modern vigorous protection of speech involved state, rather than federal, abridgements of speech. Even in this accomplishment, though, Sanford's obscurity displays itself. The application of the First Amendment to state and local laws has become such a constitutional commonplace that few remember it was a courtly Tennessean who first gave expression to the principle.

Further Reading

Burner, David. "Edward Terry Sanford." In *The Justices of the United States Supreme Court 1789–1969: Their Lives and Major Opinions,* vol. 3. Edited by Leon Friedman and Fred L. Israel. New York: R. R. Bowker Co., 1969.

Fowler, James A. "Mr. Justice Edward Terry Sanford." *American Bar Association Journal* 17 (1931): 229–233.

Green, John W. "Judge Edward T. Sanford." In *Law and Lawyers: Sketches of the Federal Judges of Tennessee, Sketches of the Attorneys General of Tennessee, Legal Miscellany, Reminiscences by John W. Green.* Jackson, Tenn.: McCowat-Mercer Press: 1950.

Phillips, Harry. "Tennessee Lawyers of National Prominence." *Tennessee Bar Journal* 17 (1981): 34–53.

HARLAN FISKE STONE (1872–1946)

Associate Justice, 1925–1941

Appointed by President Calvin Coolidge

Chief Justice, 1941–1946

Appointed by President Franklin D. Roosevelt

HARLAN FISKE STONE
(United States Supreme Court)

Commonly recognized to be among the Supreme Court's great or near-great justices, Harlan Fiske Stone stands astride a critical moment in contemporary constitutional law. In the late 1930s and early 1940s, he influenced the course of constitutional development as the Court retreated from its formerly vigorous protection of property and contract rights and focused attention on an increasing protection of civil rights and civil liberties such as freedom of speech and religion. Although President Franklin D. Roosevelt elevated him from the rank of associate justice to that of chief justice during this period, Stone's influence did not rest much on his ability to lead the Court from its center seat. In fact, he presided over a particularly fractious Court, often with little success in guiding his brethren to agreement on controversial issues. Nevertheless, he authored important opinions in this transition period and thus secured a lasting place within the Court's pantheon of notable justices.

Harlan Fiske Stone was born on October 11, 1872, in Chesterfield, New Hampshire, the son of Frederick Lauson Stone and Anne Butler Stone. His father and most of his forebears were farmers. Early in life, Stone moved with his family to Mill Valley, Massachusetts. After receiving his early education in the local school, amply supplemented with work on his family's farm, Stone enrolled in the Massachusetts Agricultural College in 1888, where he played quarterback on the football team for two seasons. But he was expelled in his sophomore year for his part in a brawl between freshmen and upperclassmen, in which Stone accidentally assaulted one of the college instructors. He moved in 1890 to Amherst College, where he played football again and from which he graduated Phi Beta Kappa in 1894.

After graduation, Stone taught high school and coached football for a time in Newburyport, Massachusetts, before deciding to enroll in Columbia Law School in 1895. He graduated in 1898, gained admittance to the New York bar, and worked as a law clerk for a year on Wall Street with the prestigious firm of Sullivan and Cromwell. At the same time, he accepted a position as instructor with the Columbia Law School. In fall 1899 he began an association with the Wilmer & Canfield firm, which gave him an office from which to practice part-time. That year Stone also married a childhood playmate from Chesterfield: Agnes Harvey, with whom he had two sons, Marshall and Lauson. Over the following six years, Stone juggled teaching responsibilities, a part-time legal practice, and his own scholarly efforts. Years later, when he became a justice on the Supreme Court, lawyers would mine the articles he wrote in these early years for citations in support of their arguments before him. "In younger and more innocent days," Stone later told the American Bar Association, "with no premonition of the future, I took the time from busy days at the bar to write occasional articles in the law journals of scientific and technical interest, only to experience, in a repentant old age, the unhappy fate of hearing them, on occasion, cited to me in court in support of both sides of the same question."

In 1905 Stone left Columbia to practice law full-time and accepted a partnership in the firm, now renamed Wilmer, Canfield & Stone. But Columbia Law School was finally able to tempt him back to legal academia in 1910, this time as professor of law and dean of the law school. For the next 13 years, Stone remained at Columbia, but the lure of a lucrative legal practice eventually prompted him to resign as dean in February 1923 and, after a summer's vacation in Europe, to accept a partnership in Sullivan and Cromwell, where he headed the firm's litigation section. No sooner had he made this transition, however, than President Calvin Coolidge persuaded him to accept the post of U.S. attorney general in the spring of 1924.

As attorney general, Stone's chief marching orders from the president were to restore the integrity lost to the Justice Department during the tenure of the previous attorney general, Harry M. Daugherty. Among Stone's most memorable acts in his position as attorney general was to appoint a young man named J. Edgar Hoover to direct the Federal Bureau of Investigation.

Shortly after Coolidge's reelection in 1924, Justice Joseph McKenna announced his retirement from the Court and the president promptly tendered Harlan Fiske Stone's name as McKenna's replacement. Initially there were minor objections to Stone's appointment, arising from claims that his days as a Wall Street attorney would make him unduly attentive to corporate America on the bench. After making an appearance before the Senate Judiciary Committee—the first of its kind by an appointee to the Court—Stone received confirmation from the Senate on February 5, 1924, by a vote of 71-6.

Once on the Court, Justice Stone soon parted company with a fellow Republican, Chief Justice William Howard Taft. Stone brought to his role as a Supreme Court justice a commitment to judicial restraint, and this restraint soon collided with the views of Taft and the Court's other conservatives, who were happy to exercise their judicial power in service of a laissez-faire approach to the Constitution. Majorities of the Court repeatedly invalidated federal and state laws regulating economic affairs, and Justice Stone—nominally a conservative—found himself dissenting in the company of the Court's more liberal justices, Louis Brandeis, Oliver Wendell Holmes, and later Benjamin Cardozo. Taft retired at the beginning of 1930, to be replaced by Chief Justice Charles Evans Hughes, but the divide between the Court's core conservatives—Justices Van Devanter, Sutherland, McReynolds, and Butler, called the Four Horsemen—and a trio of justices—including Stone, Brandeis, and soon Cardozo—continued to fracture the Court. Chief Justice Hughes and Associate Justice Owen Roberts frequently joined the Four Horsemen to invalidate economic regulations during the early New Deal period. Only after President Roosevelt threatened to pack the Court with additional justices more amenable to his legislative programs did Hughes and Roberts decisively break from the Four Horsemen and create a consistent new majority that upheld New Deal legislation. By 1937, when this new majority announced itself in *West Coast Hotel Co. v. Parrish* (1937), Stone's principle of judicial restraint had triumphed on the Court.

After the decision in *West Coast Hotel Co.*, the Court accorded a copious deference to economic legislation passed by federal and state governments. But it remained to be seen whether this deference would extend to all constitutional questions. On this crucial issue, Stone was to have important influence. In *United States v. Carolene Products* (1938), a case of little general significance decided the year after the Court's abrupt reorientation, Stone wrote the majority's opinion practicing the new deference toward a law regulating the sale of "filled" milk, that is, skim milk with vegetable oils added to substitute for butterfat. In perhaps the most famous footnote of American constitutional law, however—footnote four—Justice Stone considered whether such deference was inevitably required in all constitutional cases. He suggested that deference might not be appropriate in cases involving legislation that "restricts those political processes which can ordinarily be expected to bring about repeal of undesirable legislation" or that represents "prejudice against discrete and insular minorities." In the years after Stone penned these words, they would be quoted innumerable times by courts, lawyers, and legal scholars. Footnote four thus became a kind of blueprint for constitutional development over the next half century. Following the course established in 1937, the Court generally abandoned any vigorous review of federal and state attempts to regulate the economy. It broadly interpreted Congress's power to pass legislation regulating interstate commerce and generally rejected claims that economic regulations violated contract or property rights. Beginning around the same time, however, the Court became a more vigorous protector of specific liberties guaranteed in the Bill of Rights, such as freedom of speech. Eventually the Court took a far more active role in scrutinizing laws that distorted the voting process. Finally, in keeping with Stone's concern for laws that reflected prejudice against discrete and insular minorities, the Court breathed new life into the antidiscrimination norms inherent in the Fourteenth Amendment's equal protection clause.

Justice Harlan Fiske Stone played a central role in one of the early cases to test the Court's commitment to a vigorous protection of First Amendment rights. In the first of what became known as the "flag salute cases," *Minersville School District v. Gobitis* (1940), the Court faced the question of whether the First Amendment's protection of free speech and "free exercise of religion" applied to religious believers with conscientious scruples against saluting the American flag. Jehovah's Witnesses believed that saluting a flag amounted to offering homage to a "graven image," forbidden by God in the Old Testament. But many states, in the years leading to the Second World War, deemed the patriotic benefits of the salute as weightier than the unusual scruples of the Jehovah's Witnesses. These states passed laws that expelled from public school children who refused to pledge allegiance to the American flag and that often provided for the prosecution of their parents in criminal court. Faced with such a statute in *Gobitis,* eight members of the Court found that a state's flag-salute law did not offend the First Amendment. Only Justice Stone dissented from this result. Three years later, though, the Supreme Court announced an abrupt turnabout in the second flag-salute case, *West Virginia State Board of Education v. Barnette* (1943). Three of the justices who had originally joined in the majority in *Gobitis* now joined together with Justice Stone and two recently appointed justices to overrule the decision in *Gobitis.* This time the new majority insisted that compelling schoolchildren to swear allegiance to a flag in violation of their conscientious beliefs offended the free speech clause of the First Amendment. Although Stone did not write the Court's opinion in the new case, his eloquent dissent in *Gobitis* provided the anchor for what became one of the most celebrated free speech decisions of the 20th century.

Between the decision of the Court in *Gobitis* and its subsequent decision in *Barnette,* Harlan Fiske Stone had been appointed by President Roosevelt to replace retiring Chief Justice Charles Evans Hughes on June 12, 1941. The Democratic president's choice of a Republican chief justice was widely viewed as an attempt to emphasize bipartisan unity in the face of a rapidly advancing world war. Since each seat on the Court was occupied on the basis of seniority and Stone was senior associate justice at the time, his appointment to the chief seat made him the first justice to have sat in every seat on the Court. In many ways, though, Stone's advancement to the Court's center seat promoted him beyond his abilities. He possessed an academic's enthusiasm for intellectual debate but not the administrator's gift for "massing" the Court—that is, persuading justices to submerge their various differences to produce a united front for the Court on important issues. He also had to contend with a Court filled with fiercely independent thinkers—in particular, Justices Black, Douglas, and Frankfurter—often referred to as "wild horses." In the end, Stone's five years of service as chief justice were characterized by sharp differences among the Court's members, with Stone proving to be incapable of either cajoling or coercing unity among his colleagues.

Chief Justice Stone's career on the Court ended abruptly. On April 22, 1946, after announcing a dissent in one of the cases before the Court, the chief justice was suddenly incapacitated on the bench and had to be removed to his home. He died that evening of a massive cerebral hemorrhage.

Harlan Fiske Stone lacked the penetrating brilliance of a jurist like Oliver Wendell Holmes, and as a chief justice he lacked the leadership qualities that made Chief Justices William Howard Taft and Charles Evans Hughes more successful at "massing" the Court. For this reason, some observers place him just outside the precincts of the Court's great justices. But his importance to the development of constitutional law in the 20th century is well established. Stone stands clearly at the juncture of the Court's transition from a bastion of protection for property and contract rights to its role as a guardian of civil rights and civil liberties such as freedom of speech and religion. And in his famous *Carolene Products* footnote, he penned an enduring explanation of how this transition made sense.

Further Reading

Dowling, Noel T. "The Methods of Mr. Justice Stone in Constitutional Cases." *Columbia Law Review* 41 (1941): 1160–1189.

Konefsky, Samuel Joseph. *Chief Justice Stone and the Supreme Court.* New York: Macmillan, 1945.

Mason, Alpheus Thomas. *Harlan Fiske Stone: Pillar of the Law.* New York: Viking Press, 1956.

Urofsky, Melvin I. *Division and Discord: The Supreme Court under Stone and Vinson, 1941–1953.* Columbia: University of South Carolina Press, 1997.

Wechsler, Herbert. "Stone and the Constitution." *Columbia Law Review* 45 (1946): 764–800.

OWEN JOSEPHUS ROBERTS (1875–1955)

Associate Justice, 1930–1945

Appointed by President Herbert Hoover

OWEN JOSEPHUS ROBERTS
(United States Supreme Court)

Justice Owen J. Roberts is famous for having participated in the most important about-face in the history of the Supreme Court, the legendary "switch in time that saved nine." During the so-called constitutional crisis of 1937, the Supreme Court, which had previously dealt President Franklin Delano Roosevelt's New Deal programs a series of spectacular defeats, abruptly reversed course. Whether the president's threat to pack the Court with justices more hospitable to his agenda caused this reversal remains a matter of historical debate. But Justice Roberts, otherwise little known, lies at the heart of it.

—∞—

Owen Josephus Roberts was born on May 2, 1875, in Germantown, Pennsylvania, now a suburb of Philadelphia. His parents, Josephus and Emma Laferty

Roberts, saw to it that he obtained a private education at Germantown Academy before he enrolled in the University of Pennsylvania when he was 16 years old. He graduated Phi Beta Kappa in 1895 and then entered the University of Pennsylvania Law School, where he served as an associate editor of the *American Law Register* (later to become the *University of Pennsylvania Law Review*) and from which he graduated with honors in 1898. After graduation, the law school invited Roberts to teach part-time; he continued this association for the next 22 years, ultimately being granted the rank of full professor in 1907. In 1898 Roberts also began to practice law in Philadelphia. Over the course of the next 20 years, he forged a reputation as a gifted trial lawyer, acquiring along the way a number of professional honors, including election as president of the Law Academy of Philadelphia and secretary of the Law Association of Philadelphia. In 1904 he married Elizabeth Rogers, and the couple had one daughter.

In addition to representing a variety of business interests in court, Roberts periodically accepted appointments as a prosecutor. He was an assistant district attorney for Philadelphia County from 1903 to 1906, and then, a little more than a decade later, a special deputy U.S. attorney with responsibility for prosecuting cases under the Espionage Act. But the government service that cast him into the national spotlight came in 1924, when President Calvin Coolidge appointed him special U.S. attorney, together with Atlee Pomerene, to prosecute those involved in the infamous Teapot Dome Scandal, which had occurred during the administration of President Warren G. Harding. Roberts spearheaded the lengthy prosecution of cases arising out of the scandal, including one in which former Secretary of the Interior Albert B. Fall was convicted of bribery.

Six years after his appointment to this high-profile task, Robert's increased national stature made him a desirable candidate for the Supreme Court vacancy that occurred when Justice Edward T. Sanford died in March 1930. President Herbert Hoover initially tried to fill the seat with John J. Parker, a federal appellate judge from North Carolina. But Parker's nomination was defeated in the Senate by a vote of 39-41 on May 7, 1930, after he incurred the opposition of the NAACP and labor interests. A few months previously, President Hoover had fared better with his appointment of Charles Evans Hughes as chief justice of the Supreme Court, but Hughes's confirmation had prompted a bruising fight that, combined with the defeat of the Parker nomination, left the president and the Senate eager for a less controversial candidate. Roberts admirably satisfied this criterion and was promptly confirmed by the Senate after President Hoover nominated him to assume the vacant seat on the Court. Owen Roberts took the oath of office and began a 15-year career of judicial service—the first of his life—on June 2, 1930.

The first decade of Robert's tenure on the Court saw his colleagues split into two polarized camps. On the one side were four adamantly conservative justices known as the Four Horsemen (McReynolds, Sutherland, Butler, and Van Devanter), who stood united in their opposition to attempts by federal and state lawmakers to regulate the economy and its attendant social ills. On the other side were a triumvirate of liberal justices (Holmes, Brandeis, and Stone) who generally insisted on a policy of judicial restraint in economic matters and denied that the Constitution posed any barrier to the kind of New Deal legislation that soon commanded the attention of the Court. Together with Chief Justice Charles Evans Hughes, Justice Roberts occupied a midpoint between these two judicial camps. Joined with the votes of the Four Horsemen, the vote of either Hughes or Roberts was sufficient to ensure a conservative majority in a particular case; and, in fact, from his appointment until 1937, Roberts was a regular, although inconsistent, ally of the conservative quartet.

Upon his arrival on the Court, Roberts initially seemed to plot an orbit apart from his more conservative colleagues. He wrote, for example, the opinion for a majority of the Court in *Nebbia v. New York* (1934), upholding a state's power to regulate milk prices. But soon thereafter, Justice Roberts began to align himself with the Four Horsemen in a series of cases that dealt sharp defeats to President Roosevelt's New Deal agenda. He joined in declaring a portion of the National Industrial Recovery Act unconstitutional in *Panama Refining Co. v. Ryan* (1935), and then in holding the entire act unconstitutional in *Schechter Poultry Co. v. United States* (1935). He sided with the majority that invalidated the Bituminous Coal Act of 1935 in *Carter v. Carter Coal Co.* (1936), and he wrote the opinion for the Court that declared the Railroad Retirement Act unconstitutional in *Retirement Board v. Alton Railroad Co.* (1935). Most significantly, though, Justice Roberts wrote the majority opinion in *United States v. Butler* (1936), which overturned the first Agricultural Adjustment Act. The act had attempted to increase farm prices by discouraging production of certain farm products and reimbursed farmers for their lost production by paying them with proceeds from a tax levied on those who processed farm products. According to Roberts, this scheme invaded the prerogative of states to regulate what he deemed to be essentially a matter of local concern, in violation of the Constitution's 10th Amendment.

President Franklin D. Roosevelt did not quietly acquiesce in the constitutional destruction of his New Deal legislative agenda by the "nine old men." After his administration's repeated losses before the Court in 1935 and 1936, Roosevelt inaugurated the year of 1937 by announcing his "court-packing" plan in February. He proposed that Congress approve legislation that would allow him to appoint one additional justice for each current justice on the Supreme Court who was over the age of 70 and refused to retire. The president justified this plan as necessary to relieve the Court's work load, but in fact, it was evident to the nation—and certainly to the Court—that the president wished to seize political control of the Court by appointing justices disposed to sustain his policies. A month after Roosevelt announced this plan, Roberts joined with the chief justice and the Court's three liberal justices to uphold a state minimum wage law for women in *West Coast Hotel v. Parrish* (1937), thus reversing the Court's previous pattern and establishing a new policy of deference toward economic legislation. Contemporaries branded this abrupt reorientation the "switch in time that saved nine"—that is, from Roosevelt's court-packing plan. Roberts also wrote the majority opinion in *Mulford v. Smith* (1939), which upheld the second Agricultural Adjustment Act (the predecessor of which Roberts had declared unconstitutional in *United States v. Butler* (1936)) leaving historians ample grounds to question the consistency of his views.

On other constitutional subjects, Justice Roberts showed himself equally inconsistent. He could be a vigorous supporter of civil liberties at times, such as in his opinion in *Cantwell v. Connecticut* (1940), finding that the protection of religious liberty announced in the First Amendment was applicable to state governments through the due process clause of the Fourteenth Amendment; or his dissent in *Korematsu v. United States* (1944), protesting the unconstitutionality of the government's decision to relocate Japanese Americans to interment camps during World War II. But he could be found as often on the opposite end of the spectrum, as when he spoke for the Court in *Grovey v. Townsend* (1935), upholding the practice of all-white primaries.

Eventually Roosevelt was able to replace the Four Horsemen with more liberal justices, and Roberts's position in the middle of the Court became that of a conservative on an increasingly progressive Court. No longer able to play in the 1940s the crucial role that he had played in the 1930s, Roberts grew tired of his work on the Court and announced his resignation as of July 31, 1945. The years that followed saw him still active in legal affairs, though. Roberts served as dean of the Pennsylvania Law School from 1948 to 1951, and in 1953 he became chairman of the Fund for Advancement of Education. He died on May 17, 1955, in West Vincent Township, Pennsylvania.

Owen Roberts himself had "no illusions" about his judicial career: "Who am I to revile the good God that did not make me a Marshall, a Taney, a Bradley, a Holmes, a Brandeis, or a Cardozo?" History agrees with this candid self-assessment. Roberts certainly lacked the intellectual brilliance of the justices he named. But to this deficiency over which he surely had little control history has often added one for which he might be held more accountable—that of being unprincipled. The lack of a consistent pattern in Roberts's decisions has caused more than one historical observer to label him as simply confused. In fact, his career on the Court ended with just such an implicit criticism lingering after his departure. Upon Roberts's resignation, Chief Justice Harlan Fiske Stone drafted a farewell letter that praised the retiring justice for having made "fidelity to principle your guide to decision." Justice Hugo Black, though, objected to this phrase, and the resulting dispute among the Court's membership about the appropriate language for the farewell letter resulted in no letter being sent at all.

FURTHER READING

Fish, Peter G. "Spite Nominations to the United States Supreme Court: Herbert C. Hoover, Owen J. Roberts, and the Politics of Presidential Vengeance in Retrospect." *Kentucky Law Journal* 77 (1989): 545–576.

Frankfurter, Felix. "Mr. Justice Roberts." *University of Pennsylvania Law Review* 104 (1955–56): 311–317.

Friedman, Richard D. "Switching Time and Other Thought Experiments: The Hughes Court and Constitutional Transformation." *University of Pennsylvania Law Review* 142 (1994): 1891–1984.

Griswold, Erwin N. "Owen J. Roberts as a Judge." *University of Pennsylvania Law Review* 104 (1955–56): 322–331.

Leonard, Charles A. *A Search for a Judicial Philosophy: Mr. Justice Roberts and the Constitutional Revolution of 1937.* Port Washington, N.Y.: Kennikat Press, 1971.

Pusey, Merlo J. "Justice Roberts' 1937 Turnaround." *Supreme Court Historical Society Yearbook* (1983): 102–107.

Benjamin Nathan Cardozo (1870–1938)

Associate Justice, 1932–1938

Appointed by President Herbert Hoover

Benjamin Nathan Cardozo
(Photograph, Library Congress)

Benjamin Nathan Cardozo finished an illustrious judicial career by serving six years as an associate justice on the Supreme Court. His reputation as a preeminent judge was firmly settled even before he took the oath of office as a justice on the nation's highest court. Nevertheless, because death cut short his final career as a Supreme Court justice, he did not have the opportunity to forge as important a place in the Court's history as he might otherwise have possessed. Cardozo's impact on 20th-century American law was still significant, though, chiefly as a judge on one of the country's most prestigious state courts and to a lesser extent for contributions he made during tenure on the Supreme Court.

Benjamin Nathan Cardozo and his twin sister Emily were born on May 24, 1870, in New York City to Albert Cardozo and Rebecca Nathan Cardozo, members of the Sephardic Jewish community in New York, whose forebears had fled from Portugal during the Inquisition and had migrated to the New World prior to the American Revolution. Cardozo's father was a prominent New York judge, forced to resign from the New York Supreme Court in 1872 in the wake of corruption charges associated with Boss Tweed and Tammany Hall. He died when Benjamin was 15, leaving Cardozo, whose mother had died when he was nine, in the care of his older sister Ellen, or "Nellie," as he called her. The bond between the two siblings, thus cemented when Cardozo was a teenager, would form the chief personal attachment in Cardozo's life, since he never married.

Cardozo's early education included tutoring by the famous author of rags-to-riches stories for children, Horatio Alger, who came to the Cardozo home and taught the future justice and his siblings. Cardozo enrolled in Columbia University at the age of 15, graduating in 1889. Thereafter he continued work on a master's degree at Columbia, which he received in 1891, while also attending Columbia Law School. The law school had only recently expanded its curriculum from the traditional two years of study to three. However, Cardozo decided he was adequately equipped to practice law without attending the final year and receiving a degree. He was admitted to the New York bar in the fall of 1891, and at the age of 21 he joined the firm of Donohue, Newcombe, and Cardozo, where his brother Albert was a partner and where his father had once practiced. After the death of Richard Newcombe and the departure from the firm of Charles Donohue, the two brothers continued practicing together until Albert's death in 1909.

Benjamin Cardozo never served the role of apprentice so common for many lawyers. From the beginning of his practice he handled cases for clients on his own, gravitating early on to the more studious work of arguing cases on appeal rather than trying cases in court. Within a few years other lawyers began referring appellate cases to the young attorney, and Cardozo showed himself precociously gifted in preparing briefs and arguing cases before appellate judges. Quiet and reserved, he found that this work suited him more than the rough and tumble of trial law. After two decades of such labor, Cardozo had won a reputation as a lawyer's lawyer. His migration from the practice of law to the judicial bench therefore seemed natural when it occurred in 1913. That year he was elected by a thin margin on the Democratic ticket to the New York State Supreme Court—the court from which his father had resigned some 35 years previously. Almost immediately, though, New York governor Martin Glynn appointed Cardozo to fill a vacancy on the state's highest court, the New York Court of Appeals, in 1914. There for nearly 20 years he established a reputation as one of the country's leading judges, first as an associate judge on the state court and then, beginning in 1926, as its chief judge.

In his seat on the nation's preeminent state court, Cardozo had a profound influence on the development of 20th-century American law, especially in the area of common-law cases. The common law consists of those legal doctrines established not by legislatures but by the accumulation of judicial decisions. Cardozo earned nationwide fame as a judge able to shape the law to the needs of contemporary society without seeming to shatter its existing form. "Justice," he would write during this period, "is not to be taken by storm. She is to be wooed by slow advances." In this wooing Cardozo excelled. Progressive yet restrained, his opinions stretched legal doctrines to accommodate modernity without seeming to violate their spirit. Many of his decisions had an extraordinary impact on the development of the law and some continue to be the object of study by law students aspiring to grasp the elements of legal reasoning.

Soon after arriving on the New York court, for example, Cardozo wrote the opinion in *MacPherson v. Buick Motor Company* (1916), one of the most important cases in the history of product liability law. Prior to *MacPherson*, individuals injured by a defectively manufactured product often had no legal recourse against the manufacturer of that product because they had no contractual relationship, or no "privity," with the manufacturer. Consumers normally buy their products from dealers rather than from manufacturers, and the doctrine of "privity" shielded manufacturers from claims that they had built their products carelessly. In *MacPherson*, however, Cardozo argued that the manufacturer of a defective product should know that the product would eventually fall into the hands of a consumer who might be injured by it, and that this knowledge was sufficient cause for holding the manufacturer accountable for defective products. Courts and legislatures around the country soon followed Cardozo's reasoning. Generations of law students have also studied Cardozo's opinion in *Palsgraf v. Long Island Railroad Co.* (1928), which refused to hold a railroad liable for a passenger who was injured on a railway platform, because the nature of her injury had been too unusual for the railroad to have foreseen and taken steps to prevent.

To his growing reputation as a judge, Cardozo added that of legal scholar. Invited by the Yale Law School to deliver a series of lectures there, Cardozo eventually published them as *The Nature of the Judicial Process* (1921) and *The Growth of the Law* (1924). Toward the end of the 1920s, he lectured at Columbia University and published the results as *The Paradoxes of Legal Sciences* (1928). In these scholarly works, especially *The Nature of the Judicial Process,* Cardozo attempted to explain how judges decided cases. Many cases, he believed, had only one plausible result. But some involved situations where the case might reasonably be decided either of two conflicting ways and where the judicial resolution of the question might have substantial impact on the future course of the law. Cardozo was frank about the significance of this later circumstance: Judges did not simply find the law, they made the law. "Here," he declared, "come into play . . . balancing of judgment . . . testing and sorting of considerations of analogy and logic and utility and fairness. . . . Here it is that the judge assumes the function of a lawgiver. . . . I have grown to see that the process in its highest reaches is not discovery but creation. . . ."

When Justice Oliver Wendell Holmes, the Court's great liberal, announced his retirement at the beginning of 1932, Benjamin Cardozo was at the height of his professional power in the chief seat of the New York Court of Appeals. Many observers argued that President Herbert Hoover should appoint some progressive jurist of similar stature to replace Holmes, a legal titan in his own right, and that Cardozo was a logical successor for Holmes. There were, though, numerous considerations counting against such an appointment. Cardozo was a Democrat, while the president was Republican. Cardozo was a New Yorker, and the Court already had two other justices from New York (Stone and Hughes). Finally, Cardozo was Jewish, and another Jewish justice, Louis Brandeis, already sat on the high court. But support for Cardozo was overwhelming, and the president nominated him as an associate justice on February 15, 1932. Easily confirmed by the Senate, Benjamin Nathan Cardozo took his seat on the Supreme Court on March 14, 1932.

The Court that Cardozo joined in 1932 was badly split. Conservatives on the Court, who generally constituted a majority, would, over the next five years, deal blow after blow to the federal and state laws crafted during the early New Deal era to rescue the nation from economic depression. Three liberal justices (Brandeis, Stone, and Cardozo) would generally find no constitutional infirmity with such legislation and would argue that the Court should defer to federal and state legislatures on such matters. These three were forced into the role of dissenters until 1937, when President Franklin Delano Roosevelt threatened to pack the Court with new justices favorable to his legislative agenda. After Roosevelt announced his court-packing proposal, Chief Justice Charles Evans Hughes and Associate Justice Owen Roberts parted ways with the Court's adamant conservatives and joined the liberal justices in upholding federal and state economic regulations.

Cardozo remained on the Court long enough to see his position become a majority one, but his five-year exile in the territory of dissent meant that he seldom had an opportunity to write the Court's opinion in important cases. Outside of the economic area, though, Cardozo did speak occasionally for the Court. One case, especially, decided toward the end of his tenure, occasioned Cardozo's most important opinion as a Supreme Court justice. In *Palko v. Connecticut* (1937), his opinion for the Court's majority addressed the issue of which provisions of the Bill of Rights were applicable to state and local governments. Originally these provisions were thought to bind only the federal government, but after the ratification of the Fourteenth Amendment, whose due process clause prohibits state deprivations of "life, liberty, or property" without due process of law, the Court was called on to decide whether particular provisions from the Bill of Rights might be applicable to the states by virtue of the due process clause. Cardozo wrote for the Court's majority that only those provisions of the Bill of Rights that "represented the very essence of a scheme of ordered liberty . . . principles of justice so rooted in the traditions and conscience of our people as to be ranked fundamental" were applicable to state governments. In *Palko,* Cardozo applied this standard to find that the Fifth Amendment's prohibition against double jeopardy—that is, being tried twice for the same crime—did not bind the states. Although the Supreme Court would later overrule this particular result, Cardozo's standard for determining which rights are protected by the due process clause remains influential in modern constitutional law.

By fall 1937 Cardozo's health had taken a sharp turn downward. He had suffered a heart attack in the summer of 1935, from which he had gradually recovered. The second week in December 1937, though—the week that he announced the Court's decision in *Palko*—he had another heart attack, followed by shingles. Although he gradually seemed to pull out of danger, shortly after the new year began he had a stroke. In the spring he was encouraged to stay at a friend's home in Port Chester, New York. There he died, on July 9, 1938.

Like the man whom he succeeded on the Supreme Court, Justice Oliver Wendell Holmes, Benjamin Nathan Cardozo was a nationally respected judge before he ever donned the robes of a Supreme Court justice. Unlike Holmes, though, Cardozo arrived on the Court relatively late in life and died before he could make a contribution to it worthy of his abilities. History judges him, then, primarily on the basis of his monumental influence as a state court judge, where he made important contributions not simply to the law of his state, but to the laws developing elsewhere in the nation. His final years of service on the Supreme Court ornamented a judicial career among the most brilliant of the 20th century.

Further Reading

Hellman, George Sidney. *Benjamin N. Cardozo: American Judge.* New York: Whittlesey House, McGraw-Hill Book Company, 1940.

Kaufman, Andrew L. *Cardozo.* Cambridge, Mass.: Harvard University Press, 1998.

Polenberg, Richard. *The World of Benjamin Cardozo: Personal Values and the Judicial Process.* Cambridge, Mass.: Harvard University Press, 1997.

Posner, Richard A. *Cardozo: A Study in Reputation.* Chicago: University of Chicago Press, 1990.

*H*UGO *L*AFAYETTE *B*LACK (1886–1971)

Associate Justice, 1937–1971

Appointed by President Franklin D. Roosevelt

HUGO LAFAYETTE BLACK
(Photograph, Library of Congress)

From obscure and controversial beginnings, Hugo Lafayette Black earned a place as one of the 20th century's most influential Supreme Court justices. Raised on the Baptist piety of the South, Black became a kind of constitutional fundamentalist. He championed literal readings of the Constitution's text, and he generally employed this literalism to secure individual liberty from the encroachments of government power. In lectures to judges and at law schools after he became a justice, for example, Black never tired of arguing that the First Amendment's protection of free speech was absolute. The Constitution was not a murky text to be manipulated by clever judges but a precise command to be obeyed. "No law" abridging freedom of speech meant "no law," he insisted. And to emphasize the point, he would invariably pull a well-worn, 10-cent copy of the Constitution out of his coat pocket. He delighted in masquerading as a country simpleton but in truth brought to the Supreme Court a vigorous mind that would leave an indelible mark across the constitutional history of the 20th century.

Hugo Lafayette Black was born in rural Clay County, Alabama, on February 27, 1886, the eighth child of William Lafayette Black and Martha Ardella Toland Black. His father made a living as a farmer and a country storekeeper until the family moved, when Hugo was three years old, to the bustling metropolis of Ashland—population 350—where the elder Black opened a general store. Opposite the courthouse square, the store placed young Hugo Black in close proximity to open-air political speeches and lawyers arguing their cases before juries in the courthouse. These early rhetorical influences would eventually draw Hugo into the worlds of politics and law, although at age 17 he briefly embarked on training for a medical career. After a year at the Birmingham Medical School, though, he turned instead to the study of law and attended law school at the University of Alabama in Tuscaloosa.

By age 20 Black had graduated with honors from law school and had set up law practice in his hometown of Ashland. But fire destroyed his office and everything in it a year later, and he seized the occasion to strike out for more fertile opportunities in Birmingham, Alabama. There he set up a new practice, joined and was soon elected president of every civic group that would have him, and taught a popular Sunday School class at the First Baptist Church of Birmingham. When not engaged in these activities, Black proved to be an able attorney, representing unions and working-class citizens and undertaking a number of personal injury cases. He also included among his responsibilities part-time service as a police court judge. By 1914 he had managed to win office as county prosecutor, a position he would hold until he joined the military in 1917 to serve in World War I, although he was never called on to leave the United States.

Upon his return to private life, Black continued his law practice. In 1921 he married Josephine Foster, a union that would last until her death 30 years later. In 1923 he formed a less auspicious association—one that cast a long and unsavory shadow across an otherwise exemplary career—by joining the Ku Klux Klan. He withdrew from the organization within two years, on the eve of announcing his intent to seek election as a U.S. senator from Alabama. Emphasizing his own roots in relative poverty, Black earned the Democratic nomination as the poor man's candidate and was thereafter elected to the Senate in 1927.

During his first term as a senator, Black secured a basement room in the Capitol for study and regularly obtained books from the Library of Congress to supplement the education he had slighted in Alabama. His second term coincided with the election of President Franklin D. Roosevelt, and Black soon caught Roosevelt's attention by showing himself to be a New Deal liberal of the first order. He sponsored legislation that would become the Fair Labor Standards Act, and he supported Roosevelt's court-packing threat in the face of a conservative majority on the Supreme Court that had frustrated Roosevelt's New Deal legislative agenda by declaring its key elements unconstitutional. Black's harmony with Roosevelt's aims ultimately secured him a nomination to the first vacancy on the Supreme Court after the president took office. On August 17, 1937, at the age of 51, the Alabaman was confirmed by the Senate as an associate justice of the U.S. Supreme Court. The news media shortly discovered his former association with the Ku Klux Klan, requiring Black to begin his service on the Supreme Court with a radio address admitting his brief membership in the organization, calling attention to his withdrawal from it, and declining to comment further about the matter.

Once on the Court, Black forged a reputation for favoring straightforward constitutional rules not subject to exceptions. He was famously alone, for example, in his First Amendment absolutism. A majority of the Court viewed freedom of speech as a weighty constitutional principle, to be sure, but one subject to exception when necessary to serve grave public interests. Black railed against these exceptions and argued that they contradicted the plain language of the First Amendment's free speech clause. Although he never persuaded the Court to adopt his absolutist views, his relentless defense of free speech eventually contributed to a growing body of decisions increasingly protective of this principle.

Black adopted a similar stance concerning the issue of what provisions of the Bill of Rights were applicable to state and local laws, an issue often referred to as the incorporation controversy. By their terms the provisions of the first 10 amendments to the Constitution protect certain liberties from federal intrusions. The Fourteenth Amendment, though, prevents state and local governments from depriving individuals of life, liberty, or property without due process of law. Beginning in the 1940s, the Supreme Court considered whether this clause might be understood to make some or all of the provisions of the Bill of Rights applicable to state and local governments. In other words, did the Fourteenth Amendment *incorporate* the provisions of the Bill of Rights in its protection of "life, *liberty,* and property"? On this issue, Justice Black's position was a model of simplicity: The Fourteenth Amendment made every provision of the Bill of Rights applicable to state and local governments. Thus, for example, under his view the First Amendment's protection against federal laws prohibiting the free exercise of religion applied with equal force to state and local laws. Nevertheless, although a majority of the Supreme Court agreed with Black on this result, he was never able to convince his brethren to adopt his broader principle. Most of the justices on the Supreme Court were selective in their designation of which rights guaranteed by the Bill of Rights were sufficiently fundamental to warrant application to state and local laws. But, in part through Black's constant prodding, the Court eventually determined that most of the provisions in the Bill of Rights were indeed applicable to both federal and state laws.

Justice Black's contributions to this development were most notable in the area of rights in connection with the criminal process. As a county prosecutor in his early days of law practice during the 1920s, Black had investigated allegations of police brutality in obtaining confessions, demonstrating a serious regard for issues of fairness in the criminal process. On the Court, Black continued to champion constitutional principles of fairness in the treatment of those accused of crimes. He argued stridently that the protections of the Bill of Rights for criminal defendants were applicable to state and local criminal proceedings as well as to federal ones. Thus, in *Chambers v. Florida* (1940), Black authored the Court's opinion invalidating the convictions of four black defendants on the basis of coerced confessions; and in *Gideon v. Wainright* (1963), he penned the Court's opinion declaring that the Sixth Amendment required states to provide attorneys for criminal defendants who could not afford legal representation in state felony trials. Black's opinion in *Chambers* presented an early statement of the philosophy that would guide his approach to constitutional protections for criminal defendants over the next three decades:

> Under our constitutional system, courts stand against any winds that blow as havens of refuge for those who might otherwise suffer because they are helpless, weak, outnumbered, or because they are non-conforming victims of prejudice and public excitement. Due process of law, preserved for all by our Constitution, commands that no such practice as that disclosed by this record shall send any accused to his death. No higher duty, no more solemn responsibility, rests upon this Court, than that of translating into living law and maintaining this constitutional shield deliberately planned and inscribed for the benefit of every human being subject to our Constitution—of whatever race, creed or persuasion.

Justice Black also played a significant role in one of the 20th century's most important constitutional debates. Are there rights, not specifically named in the Constitution, which may nevertheless be protected by courts from government intrusion through the due process clauses of the Fifth and Fourteenth Amendments when these intrusions are not reasonable?

This question, commonly referred to as the issue of *substantive* due process, was a lively source of controversy for most of the 20th century. In the first part of the century, a conservative Supreme Court answered "yes" to this question and insisted that it had the power to protect freedom of contract—a right not specifically protected by the text of the Constitution—from unreasonable interference by state and local governments. Applying this doctrine, the Court for a time invalidated a wide variety of state laws, such as the law regulating the working hours of bakers in *Lochner v. New York* (1905). As a U.S. senator, Black had warred against this kind of judicial conservativism and its anti–New Deal leanings, and he waged the same war once he became a justice of the Supreme Court. There he argued that due process should not be read to protect such unnamed rights as freedom of contract. As to this particular right, Black's perspective eventually triumphed. The Court repudiated its readiness to overturn social and economic regulations that restricted contractual freedoms, and the opinion in *Lochner v. New York* became a byword for judicial tyranny. But on the broader principle of whether *any* unnamed rights should be protected from unreasonable interferences, Black was in a minority.

Beginning in the 1960s, the Court returned to the issue of whether the Constitution protected rights it did not specifically name. This time the Court determined that the Constitution protected a right of privacy, even though no specific mention of this right can be located within the constitutional text. A majority of the justices found this right of privacy implicit in the word "liberty" contained in the due process clause of the Fourteenth Amendment. In *Griswold v. Connecticut* (1963), over a vigorous dissent by Black, the Court concluded that the right of privacy prevented a state from prohibiting the use of contraceptives by married couples. Black insisted, however, that the Constitution authorized judicial protection of privacy rights no more than it had authorized protection of the right of contract. Neither were named in the Constitution, and for Black, the constitutional literalist, that settled the matter.

Black's service on the Supreme Court would consume the major part of his adult life. On September 17, 1971, he suffered a stroke that forced him to retire from his position on the Court, and he died eight days later.

Though President Richard Nixon appointed Louis F. Powell, Jr., to fill the seat that Black had vacated, the Alabaman's influence on the Court could not readily be replaced. His enthusiasm for close attention to the text of the Constitution and for simple constitutional rules was combined with the social sensibilities of a New Deal liberal. Both those who preceded and those who followed him tended to emphasize one but not the other of these characteristics. Black's form of constitutional literalism has generally been more at home on the conservative wing of the Court. His concern for the weak, the helpless, and the outnumbered has manifested itself most visibly in the opinions of justices more willing to see the Constitution's text in fluid terms and to view that text as the beginning point, perhaps, but seldom the ending of constitutional analysis.

Further Reading

Ball, Howard. *Hugo L. Black: Cold Steel Warrior.* New York: Oxford University Press, 1996.

Black, Hugo Lafayette. *A Constitutional Faith.* New York: Alfred A. Knopf, 1968.

Black, Hugo, Jr. *My Father, A Remembrance.* New York: Random House, 1975.

Newman, Roger K. *Hugo Black: A Biography.* New York: Pantheon Books, 1994.

Stanley Forman Reed (1884–1980)

Associate Justice, 1938–1957

Appointed by President Franklin D. Roosevelt

Stanley Forman Reed
(United States Supreme Court)

Justice Stanley Reed replaced George Sutherland, one of the legendary Four Horsemen, on the Supreme Court. Sutherland and the other Horsemen had defied President Franklin D. Roosevelt's New Deal agenda in the 1930s, and their suspicion of government power, especially as exercised over economic matters, was boundless. Reed, however, was a New Deal lawyer before he became a Supreme Court justice. He brought with him to the Court the New Deal's basic confidence in government to act wisely and benevolently. This confidence was no fixed principle, of course, and it overlay social convictions that were often conservative. As a result, Reed generally occupied a middle ground on the Court.

Stanley Forman Reed was born on December 31, 1884, in Minerva, Kentucky, the son of John R. Reed, a physician, and Frances Forman Reed. He received his early education in private schools and attended Kentucky Wesleyan College, from which he graduated in 1902. Thereafter, he enrolled in Yale University, receiving an additional bachelor's degree four years later. After his undergraduate education, Reed embarked on a law school career that would eventually take him to three universities across two continents. He began by studying for a year at the University of Virginia Law School. He did not complete the curricula at Virginia, though, and returned instead to Kentucky, where he married Winifred Elgin in May 1908. The couple would later have two sons, Stanley and John. In fall 1908 Reed and his wife moved to New York, where he enrolled in Columbia Law School. Here again, he decided not to remain for a degree but chose instead to travel to Paris with his wife, where they lived for a year while he studied law at the Sorbonne.

Upon returning to Kentucky, Reed was admitted to the bar in 1910 after a brief apprenticeship with a Maysville lawyer, and he set up his own practice, supplemented in its early years with political activities. Reed served as a representative to the Kentucky General Assembly from 1912 to 1916. With the entrance of the United States into World War I, Reed obtained a commission in 1918 as a lieutenant in the army, working for army intelligence. After the war, he returned to practice with the firm of Worthington, Cochran, Browning, and Reed in Maysville. Over the next decade, his firm represented clients including the Chesapeake and Ohio Railroad and—most important for Reed's future—the Burley Tobacco Growers Cooperative Association. His work for this association ultimately led to his appointment in 1929 as general counsel to the Federal Farm Board created during President Herbert Hoover's administration. Three years later Stanley Reed became general counsel to the Reconstruction Finance Corporation, created by Congress that year to combat the depression by providing financial aid to railroads, financial institutions, and agricultural operations.

With the election of President Franklin D. Roosevelt in 1933, Reed continued in his post at the Reconstruction Finance Corporation. That same year Congress passed legislation overriding clauses in private and public contracts that stipulated payment in gold. This act, intended to conserve the country's gold reserves, soon fell under legal attack. When the challenges made their way to the Supreme Court, the Roosevelt administration appointed Stanley Reed as a special assistant to the attorney general of the United States to argue the government's position in the trilogy of cases that became known as the *Gold Clause Cases* (1935). Within a month after the Court announced a victory for the government in these cases, Reed was appointed solicitor general of the United States on March 18, 1935, which placed him in charge of the federal government's important cases before the Court. Over the next three years, Reed pressed the cause of the New Deal before the "nine old men" who dealt the Roosevelt administration such vexing defeats that the president eventually proposed packing the Court with new justices who would treat his New Deal agenda more kindly. A near majority of conservative justices known as the Four Horsemen—George Sutherland, Pierce Butler, James McReynolds, and Willis Van Devanter—managed to attract the votes of Owen Roberts and Chief Justice Charles Evans Hughes and thus declare unconstitutional some of the most lustrous gems of the New Deal. In March 1937, however, Roberts and Hughes parted ways with the Four Horsemen in *West Coast Hotel Co. v. Parrish* (1937), a case in which a new majority of the Court upheld a state minimum wage law for women. In view of Roosevelt's threatened court-packing plan, this case earned a reputation as the "switch in time that saved nine." With the "constitutional crisis" thus resolved, Roosevelt's plan suffered defeat in Congress. In any event, the president had had his way.

The Four Horsemen, who had caused the president so much frustration, soon began to exit the Court by death or retirement. Willis Van Devanter retired in June 1937, and President Roosevelt chose to fill the vacancy with Hugo Black, who had been one of the fiercest allies of the New Deal as a senator from Alabama. At the beginning of 1938, Justice George Sutherland joined Van Devanter in retirement, and this time the president turned to Stanley Reed to fill the new vacancy on the Court. The Senate quickly confirmed the appointment, and Justice Reed, 53 years old at the time, took his seat on the Court on January 31, 1938.

By the time Reed joined the Court, the great "constitutional crisis" of 1937 had passed and the Court had adopted a posture of deference toward federal and state economic legislation. Reed, not surprisingly, reflected the same agreement with this posture in his role as a justice on the Supreme Court as he had urged in his arguments before the Court as solicitor general. But his generally "liberal" stance on economic issues did not reflect his decisions in other areas of constitutional law, where he tended to embrace relatively conservative positions. For example, in *Adamson v. California* (1947). Reed delivered the Court's opinion holding that a state court prosecutor's calling attention to a criminal defendant's refusal to testify did not violate the due process clause of the Fourteenth Amendment. At issue in the case was whether the Fifth Amendment's privilege against self-incrimination, which would normally bar such comments by a prosecutor, applied to state criminal proceedings. Reed, for a majority of the Court, held that it did not.

Justice Reed's conservative inclinations almost prompted him to dissent from the Court's monumental decision in *Brown v. Board of Education* (1954), which declared racial segregation in public schools unconstitutional. Even though Reed had written the opinion in *Smith v. Allwright* (1944), invalidating Texas's whites-only Democratic primary, he doubted whether the practice of segregation offended the Fourteenth Amendment's equal protection clause. Eventually, though, Reed was persuaded to overcome his misgivings about the legitimacy of the result in *Brown,* and he joined with the unanimous decision announced by the Court's new chief justice, Earl Warren.

Three years after the decision in *Brown,* Reed, 72 years old at the time, announced his retirement from the Court, effective February 25, 1957. But he was by no means retiring from public life. After leaving the Court, Reed continued to hear cases on the Court of Claims and the Court of Appeals for the District of Columbia. The year he resigned, President Dwight D. Eisenhower appointed him as chairman of the U.S. Civil Rights Commission, but since Reed was still active as a judge, he eventually decided this position might be inconsistent with his judicial responsibilities and he resigned from it. Reed continued to maintain an office at the Supreme Court until about 1967, when declining health forced him to forgo further work. He retired to Huntington, New York, where he died at the age of 95 on April 2, 1980.

Stanley Reed brought to the Supreme Court the values and perspectives of the New Deal and of the socially conservative South. Early in his legal career he gained an appreciation for collective action to solve economic problems, including action by government. This appreciation made him an economic liberal on the Court, happy to defer to legislative attempts to regulate the economy. But he never completely laid aside the abiding values of the small-town South, and these would influence his career as a Supreme Court justice, casting him most often into a middle position on the Court. Yet, on the one issue most fundamental to the South—that of racial segregation—Reed, after much internal struggle, eventually joined the Court's historic decision in *Brown v. Board of Education* (1954), sacrificing the instincts of a lifetime in order to allow the Court to speak with a single voice in one of the most important decisions it ever rendered.

Further Reading

Boskey, Bennet. "Justice Reed and His Family of Law Clerks." *Kentucky Law Journal* 69 (1981): 869–876.

Canon, Bradley C., Kimberly Greenfield, and Jason S. Fleming. "Justice Frankfurter and Justice Reed: Friendship and Lobbying on the Court." *Judicature* 78 (1995): 224–231.

Fasset, John D. "Mr. Justice Reed and Brown v. Board of Education." *Supreme Court Historical Society Yearbook* (1986): 48–63.

———. *New Deal Justice: The Life of Stanley Reed of Kentucky.* New York: Vantage Press, 1994.

O'Brien, William F. *Justice Reed and the First Amendment: The Religion Clauses.* Washington: Georgetown University Press, 1958.

Prickett, Morgan D. S. "Stanley Forman Reed: Perspectives on a Judicial Epitaph." *Hastings Constitutional Law Quarterly* 8 (1981): 343–69.

Felix Frankfurter (1882–1965)

Associate Justice, 1939–1962

Appointed by President Franklin D. Roosevelt

Felix Frankfurter
(Photograph, Library of Congress)

The third in the triumvirate of Jewish justices appointed to the Supreme Court in the first half of the 20th century, Felix Frankfurter defied many of the expectations that accompanied his elevation to the nation's highest court. Political liberals were confident that his record as a progressive professor at Harvard Law School would make him their ally on the Court. Conservatives predicted apocalyptically that he would insinuate communism into the high temple of American constitutionalism. Both predictions proved to be spectacularly mistaken. Far from linking hands in fraternity with liberal justices such as Hugo Black and William O. Douglas, Frankfurter became their most determined foe on the Court, waging a battle across two decades against a judicial activism he abhorred. Because he generally lost this battle against the constitutional revolution of the 1950s and 1960s, its victors tend to judge him harshly as a man who might have been a great justice but whose conservative impulses placed him at odds with the current of the times.

Felix Frankfurter was born in Vienna, Austria, on November 15, 1882, to Leopold and Emma Winter Frankfurter. He immigrated to New York City with his parents when he was 12 years old and became, later in life, a naturalized citizen. Frankfurter obtained his early education from the public schools of New York City and later graduated from the College of the City of New York in 1902. After working for a year, he enrolled in Harvard Law School, graduating with an outstanding academic record in 1906. While he was in law school he was challenged by Louis Brandeis, whose devotion to a variety of public causes had earned him renown as "the people's lawyer," to devote himself to public service. Similarly, he was chastised by the philosopher William James when the latter discovered that Frankfurter intended to work for a New York firm after graduation. "Yes, I see you are like all the rest," James accused him, "you are going to New York to make money!" Both encounters appear to have made a deep impact on the young lawyer, for though he initially took a job with the firm of Hornblower, Byrne, Miller and Potter, he soon accepted the invitation to became an assistant to Henry Lewis Stimson, then U.S. attorney for the Southern District of New York. With Stimson, Frankfurter worked on cases involving customs and immigration fraud, and when Stimson ran for governor of New York in 1910, Frankfurter ran his campaign. Stimson lost the race but soon was picked by President William Howard Taft to serve as secretary of war, and Frankfurter followed his boss to Washington as an assistant.

In 1914 Harvard offered Felix Frankfurter a position as a professor of law. He had by this time become acquainted with Justice Oliver Wendell Holmes, who urged him not to accept the professorship. "Academic life is but half life—it is withdrawal from the fight in order to utter smart things that cost you nothing except the thinking them from a cloister." Over the following years, Frankfurter would refute this dire prediction by using his position as a professor at Harvard to influence a generation of elite lawyers and to serve as a base for his own encounters with the public issues of the day. During these years he forged a solid reputation as a progressive, beginning with a short tenure of public service that took him away from Harvard during World War I. He served for a time as counsel to the Mediation Commission and in this capacity investigated several cases involving violence in connection with labor disputes, including the Bisbee, Arizona, case in which the management of a company, together with local law-enforcement personnel, broke a strike by forcing workers at gunpoint to a desert location and leaving them stranded there without food or water. Frankfurter's condemnation of these actions earned him cheers among American labor but opprobrium from conservative business interests.

After the war, Frankfurter married Marion A. Denman on December 20, 1919. Benjamin Nathan Cardozo, then a judge on the New York Court of Appeals, performed the ceremony. Cardozo would become a Supreme Court justice in 1932, and six years later Frankfurter himself would assume the seat on the Court left vacant by Cardozo's death. Frankfurter and his wife never had children, and in later years Marion would suffer recurring illness that kept her bedridden during much of her husband's tenure on the Court. With the end of the war, Frankfurter also returned to his teaching responsibilities at Harvard Law School, and there he proved himself a mentor of the first rank. He dispatched his students to clerk for eminent judges, and they soon began to occupy influential government positions.

During the war Frankfurter had met Assistant Secretary of the Navy Franklin D. Roosevelt, and the bond between the two men grew steadily over the years. After Roosevelt was elected president in 1933 and inaugurated his New Deal, Frankfurter contributed to the president's program by funneling his students into important positions within the Roosevelt administration. He also advised the president privately on a host of matters, becoming one of Roosevelt's closest confidants. The president initially proposed that Frankfurter accept the post of solicitor general of the United States as a steppingstone to a seat on the Supreme Court, but Frankfurter insisted that he could help the president more off the Court than on it. He seems to have been correct in this estimation as he helped draft crucial New Deal legislation such as the Securities Act of 1933 and the Securities Exchange Act of 1934. In all, Frankfurter made his professorship at Harvard Law School less the cloister that Holmes had predicated and more a legal citadel from which he made constant forays into public affairs. On the basis of these endeavors Justice Louis Brandeis named Frankfurter "the most useful lawyer in America."

When Justice Benjamin Nathan Cardozo died in 1938, President Roosevelt announced the nomination of Felix Frankfurter to Cardozo's seat on the Supreme Court. Friends of the New Deal were ecstatic with the appointment. Frankfurter had proved himself a progressive a hundred times over, as a New Deal adviser, a founding member of the American Civil Liberties Union, and a public-spirited law professor. The same credentials, of course, alarmed conservatives. Nevertheless, the Senate unanimously confirmed his appointment to the Supreme Court on January 17, 1939. Two weeks later he began what would ultimately be nearly a quarter-century career as a Supreme Court justice, serving from the brink of World War II until the beginning of the turbulent 1960s.

Supreme Court justices sometimes disappoint the expectations that secure their appointments, and Felix Frankfurter is one of the 20th century's most prominent examples of this reality. He arrived on the Court at an important junction in constitutional history. The early decades of the century had witnessed the Court's evolution into an active protector of property and contract rights by its interpretation of the Constitution in ways that restrained federal and state governments from attempting to regulate economic affairs. What was essentially a conservative form of judicial activism reached its high water mark in the 1930s, when the Court essentially waged war against the New Deal, declaring unconstitutional many of its key components. But this activism finally collapsed toward the end of the 1930s, before Frankfurter became a justice. Thereafter, the Court abandoned its partisanship in favor of property and contract rights. At the same time, though, new majorities on the Court became increasingly protective of the rights of racial and other minorities unfairly discriminated against in the political process and more vigilant in the protection of rights such as freedom of speech and religion. But Frankfurter, the New Deal foe of conservative judicial activism, soon demonstrated himself to be the foe as well of liberal judicial activism, as he classified it.

Frankfurter's frustration of the expectations that had accompanied his appointment to the Court came almost at once. A little more than a year after he joined the Court, he announced the decision for the majority in *Minersville School District v. Gobitis* (1940), which held that a state law compelling children to pledge allegiance to the flag could be enforced against Jehovah's Witness children, even though their faith viewed this act as idolatry. At the time, only a single justice—Harlan Fiske Stone—refused to join Frankfurter's opinion; but within three years, a new majority on the Court confessed its error in *Gobitis* and ruled unconstitutional a similar flag-salute statute in *West Virginia State Board of Education v. Barnette* (1943), a decision that became one of the foundation stones for the modern protection of free speech. In an impassioned dissent, joined by only two other justices, Frankfurter did not discount the irony of a Jewish justice proposing to tread harshly on the consciences of another religious minority, but he held fast to his insistence on judicial restraint:

> One who belongs to the most vilified and persecuted minority in history is not likely to be insensible to the freedoms guaranteed by our Constitution. Were my purely personal attitude relevant I should whole-heartedly associate myself with the general libertarian views in the Court's opinion, representing as they do the thought and action of a lifetime. But as judges we are neither Jew nor Gentile, neither Catholic nor agnostic. We owe equal attachment to the Constitution and are equally bound by our judicial obligations whether we derive our citizenship from the earliest or the latest immigrants to these shores. As a member

> of this Court I am not justified in writing my private notions of policy into the Constitution, no matter how deeply I may cherish them or how mischievous I may deem their disregard.

Frankfurter's position in the flag-salute cases dismayed those who had so wildly cheered his appointment to the Court only a few years before. And over the course of his career he would demonstrate that these cases were of a piece with his overall philosophy of judicial restraint. Just as he had warred against the conservative activism that imposed its vision on the Constitution during the early New Deal, he soon found himself at odds with what he viewed as an equally pernicious liberal activism. He clashed with Justice Hugo Black over the issue of whether the due process guarantee of the Fourteenth Amendment, applicable to states, "incorporated" the various protections of the Bill of Rights, including the protections for criminal defendants. Black's position was progressive and absolute: *All* the provisions of the Bill of Rights were applicable to the states through the Fourteenth Amendment. Frankfurter, however, resisted Black's absolutism, preferring a more nuanced consideration of society's developing norms—one which was, incidentally, more deferential to the criminal procedures of the states. Though the Court never quite adopted Black's position, it eventually abandoned Frankfurter's cautiousness by finding most of the provisions of the Bill of Rights applicable to states.

Felix Frankfurter served under four chief justices: Charles Evans Hughes, Harlan Fiske Stone, Fred Vinson, and Earl Warren. Toward the end of his tenure on the Court, he found himself often at odds with a liberal majority, insisting all the while that the Court had too great a confidence in its own ability to remake American society along progressive lines. "In a democratic society like ours," he insisted in *Baker v. Carr* (1962), "relief must come through an aroused popular conscience that sears the conscience of the people's representatives." That year a stroke followed by a heart attack forced the indefatigable champion of judicial restraint to retire on August 28, 1962. He died in Washington, D.C. on February 22, 1965.

—∾—

History is written by those who triumph in its great controversies, and Felix Frankfurter was a loser in one of constitutional history's great wars of the 20th century. His calls for judicial restraint fell on the deaf ears of his colleagues on the bench, who increasingly viewed their responsibility as enforcing the Constitution's guarantee of equality before the law, of due process of law, and of important rights such as freedom of speech and religion. He remains something of an enigma, in that his early progressivism did not place him on the side of judicial thought that eventually prevailed during the 1950s and 1960s. As it is, modern historians tend to praise him for his career as an activist law professor and to lament the failed opportunities they see in his career as a justice on the Supreme Court.

Further Reading

Baker, Leonard. *Brandeis and Frankfurter: A Dual Biography.* New York: New York University Press, 1986.

Burt, Robert. *Two Jewish Justices: Outcasts in the Promised Land.* Berkeley: University of California Press, 1988.

Hockett, Jeffrey D. *New Deal Justice: The Constitutional Jurisprudence of Hugo L. Black, Felix Frankfurter, and Robert H. Jackson.* Lanham, Md.: Rowman & Littlefield Publishers, 1996.

Murphy, Bruce Allen. *The Brandeis/Frankfurter Connection: The Secret Political Activities of Two Supreme Court Justices.* New York: Oxford University Press, 1982.

*W*ILLIAM *O*RVILLE *D*OUGLAS (1898–1980)

Associate Justice, 1939–1975

Appointed by President Franklin D. Roosevelt

WILLIAM ORVILLE DOUGLAS
(United States Supreme Court)

William O. Douglas was one of the youngest individuals ever appointed to the Supreme Court, and he served longer on it than any justice in history. He brought to the nation's highest bench a fierce individualism and a maverick's temperament, traits that endeared him to those whose causes he upheld and infuriated his opponents. He cared less about explaining his decisions than about getting them right. As a result, his influence on constitutional law is less than that of justices such as Hugo Black—Douglas's ally for many years on the Court—who paid more attention to developing a legal framework for their decisions. Across more than three decades, though, Douglas earned a reputation as one of the Court's most preeminent—and eccentric—libertarians.

William Orville Douglas was born on October 16, 1898, in Maine, Minnesota, the son of William Douglas, a Presbyterian minister, and Julia Bickford Fisk Douglas. He grew up in Yakima, Washington, where his father moved the family after William's birth and where the Reverend Douglas's death in 1904 left them penniless. Added to grinding poverty, William Douglas grew up battling the effects of the polio he had contracted when he was three years old, which had almost killed him. But his homegrown rehabilitation program included hiking in the foothills of the Cascade Mountains, and his encounters with the wilderness in these excursions would inspire in him a lifelong devotion to the outdoors that would fuel his commitment to environmental causes decades later.

After graduating first in his class from Yakima High School in 1916, Douglas obtained a scholarship to attend Whitman College in Walla Walla, Washington, from which he graduated Phi Beta Kappa in 1920. He followed college with two years of work as a high school teacher in his hometown before he finally headed east and enrolled in Columbia Law School. There he plunged into the study of law—and a variety of part-time jobs to finance that study—and graduated second in his class in 1925. Meanwhile, in 1924 he married Mildred Riddle, whom he had met while teaching in Yakima. This marriage produced two children and lasted until the couple divorced in 1953. The following years would see Douglas remarried three times: first to Mercedes Davidson from 1954 to 1963; then to Joan Martin, roughly 40 years his junior, from 1963 to 1966; and finally, in 1966, when he was 66, to the 22-year-old Cathleen Hefferman.

After law school Douglas practiced corporate law for two years with the Cravath firm in New York City before briefly attempting to establish his own small-town practice in Yakima. In 1927 Columbia Law School invited him to join its faculty and he returned to New York. The following year an internal dispute over the choice of a new dean for the law school saw many faculty leave, including Douglas, who migrated to Yale Law School. Within a short time, Douglas had been appointed to a prestigious endowed chair at Yale, where he taught corporate and bankruptcy law. In 1934 Douglas took a temporary leave of absence from Yale to work for the Securities and Exchange Commission (SEC), one of the New Deal's creations. As it turned out, the talented young professor never returned to academia. What he had expected to be a semester away from Yale stretched into two years, at the end of which, Joseph P. Kennedy, then SEC chairman, secured Douglas's appointment as a commissioner of the SEC in 1936. A year and a half later, President Franklin Delano Roosevelt made Douglas the SEC chairman. The former law professor soon became a regular at the president's poker parties and an informal adviser to Roosevelt on economic matters.

William Douglas's growing prominence had not escaped the notice of Yale, and at the beginning of 1939 he was offered the post of dean of the law school. Justice Louis Brandeis retired, however, in February 1939, and the president immediately announced his intention to appoint a justice from the West Coast. Douglas, in spite of his more recent career as an Ivy League scholar, lobbied aggressively for the position, and on March 19 President Roosevelt appointed him to Brandeis's seat. The Senate confirmed his nomination by a vote of 62-4, with the dissenters suggesting ludicrously that Douglas was a Wall Street lackey. On April 17, 1939, at the age of 41 Douglas became one of the youngest justices ever to sit on the Court, beginning a career as an associate justice that would eventually be the longest ever served.

When William O. Douglas joined the Court, he brought with him the typical New Deal support for government attempts to regulate the economy and general enthusiasm for civil rights and civil liberties, as long as these were balanced with a due respect for the needs of society. Like Hugo Black, Douglas had been appointed by a president he respected deeply, and loyalty to that president cast him in a role of support for the government—a role that he would later abandon. For example, both he and Black voted initially with the majority of the Court in

Minersville School District v. Gobitis (1940), which refused to exempt Jehovah's Witness children from a compulsory flag-salute statute, even though the Witnesses believed the salute to be idolatrous. Both justices eventually regretted this decision and joined a new majority that overruled *Gobitis* in *West Virginia Board of Education v. Barnette* (1943). The following year, though, in *Korematsu v. United States* (1944), the exigencies of war persuaded them to uphold the removal of Japanese Americans from the West Coast and their forced relocation to internment camps. That same year, Douglas was named as a possible running mate for Roosevelt's final presidential campaign, but Harry Truman won the second spot on the Democratic ticket—and eventually the presidency after Roosevelt's death in 1945.

With the end of the world war and the death of Roosevelt, Douglas steadily gravitated toward the aggressive civil libertarian stance that would characterize his remaining judicial career. Even before this period, when conditions of war did not present themselves, Douglas had shown himself prepared to defend the rights of minorities and outcasts. Thus, for example, in *Skinner v. Oklahoma* (1942), he had written the Court's opinion declaring unconstitutional a forced sterilization program for repeat criminal offenders. By the cold war era, his defense of civil rights and liberties began to take on an absolutist character. In *Terminiello v. Chicago* (1949), he defended the right of a speaker to prod a mob with angry words, suggesting that speech was often most valuable when it made people most angry. With Justice Black, he dissented from the majority decision in *Dennis v. United States* (1951), upholding the convictions of Communist speakers for advocating the violent overthrow of the United States.

Eventually Douglas's absolutism led him down constitutional paths that even Hugo Black was not prepared to follow, especially when Douglas began to speak for the majority in cases protecting rights not specially safeguarded by the Constitution. In the most famous of these, *Griswold v. Connecticut* (1963), Douglas found a right of privacy implicit within the "penumbras" of various provisions of the Bill of Rights. He determined that this right had been abridged by a state law that prohibited the use of contraceptives. Three years later, in *Harper v. Virginia State Board of Elections* (1966), Douglas again declared the existence of a fundamental right to vote in state elections that was unconstitutionally infringed on by a poll tax. Black, quite willing to pursue absolutism with respect to rights specifically named by the Constitution, was unwilling to join Douglas in these decisions protecting unenumerated rights.

In *Papachristou v. City of Jacksonville* (1972), Douglas wrote the Court's opinion overturning a vagrancy law, and his paean to the virtues of loitering expressed something of the heart of his own character. Of wandering and strolling about, he declared:

> These unwritten amenities have been in part responsible for giving our people the feeling of independence and self-confidence, the feeling of creativity. These amenities have dignified the right of dissent and have honored the right to be nonconformists and the right to defy submissiveness. They have encouraged lives of high spirits rather than hushed, suffocating silence.

Off the Court, Douglas was an inveterate wanderer of wildernesses. His frequent hiking vacations imbued him with a near-fanatical enthusiasm for protecting the environment, made famous especially by his campaign to preserve the Chesapeake and Ohio Canal towpath, today managed by the National Park Service and dedicated to Douglas. The high-spirited justice also supplemented his work on the Court with a torrent of books (more than 30) and countless speeches and articles. In fact, some of his colleagues faulted him for a failure to devote himself sufficiently to his official duties on the Court. He was accused by some observers of laziness and for producing slipshod opinions. He also offended notions of propriety by his public advocacy on issues he deemed important, such as the environment, and, late in life, by his marriages to women a third his age.

For conservatives, especially, Douglas's activism both on and off the Court became a lightning rod for those opposed to the general activism of the Court under Chief Justice Earl Warren. In the end, it also earned him the privilege of defending himself against an impeachment attempt launched in 1970 by House Republican leader Gerald Ford. By the end of the year, the House Judiciary Committee had ruled against impeachment. Nevertheless, four years after surviving this political assault Douglas was felled by a different adversary. On the last day of 1974, he suffered a stroke from which he never fully recovered and which finally forced his retirement on November 12, 1975. He died in Washington, D.C. on January 19, 1980.

Justice William O. Douglas's long service on the Court left him ample opportunity to leave a significant mark on it. And, to be sure, he did fashion an indelible place in the history of the Supreme Court. But his contributions to the Court did not take the form of elaborate doctrinal edifices or magisterial commentaries on the law. He tended to view each case on its own terms and pressed to a conclusion he believed right, even sometimes at the expense of offering a solid justification for it. But the very fervency of his dedication to the cause of civil rights and liberties and the lasting results to which it led him in cases such as *Griswold v. Connecticut* (1963) is its own kind of memorial.

FURTHER READING

Ball, Howard. *Of Power and Right: Hugo Black, William O. Douglas, and America's Constitutional Revolution.* New York: Oxford University Press, 1992.

Cooper, Phillip J. "Justice William O. Douglas: Conscience of the Court." In *The Burger Court: Political and Judicial Profiles.* Edited by Charles M. Lamb and Stephen C. Halpern. Urbana, Ill.: University of Illinois Press, 1991.

Douglas, William O. *The Court Years, 1939–1975: The Autobiography of William O. Douglas.* New York: Random House, 1980.

———. *Go East, Young Man: The Early Years—The Autobiography of William O. Douglas.* New York: Random House, 1974.

Duram, James C. *Justice William O. Douglas.* Boston: Twayne Publishers, 1981.

Simon, James F. *Independent Journey: The Life of William O. Douglas.* New York: Harper & Row, 1980.

Frank Murphy (1890–1949)

Associate Justice, 1940–1949

Appointed by President Franklin D. Roosevelt

Frank Murphy
(United States Supreme Court)

Scarcely any justice in the history of the Supreme Court has voted more consistently to uphold civil rights and liberties than Frank Murphy, who was perhaps the most result-oriented liberal the Court has ever known. He was a New Deal mayor of Detroit before the New Deal was born, governor general of the Philippines, governor of Michigan, attorney general of the United States, and finally, before heart disease prematurely ended his life, an associate justice on the U.S. Supreme Court for almost 10 years. In this last of his public positions, Murphy was a herald of the "rights revolution" that would begin under the leadership of Chief Justice Earl Warren, appointed to the Court four years after Murphy's untimely death. But because he favored achieving the right result more than explaining it, he left only a minor legacy in the development of American law.

—~—

Frank Murphy, christened William Francis Murphy, was born on April 13, 1890, in what is today Harbor Beach, Michigan, the son of John F. Murphy and Mary Brennan Murphy. His father was a small-town lawyer active in Democratic politics and his mother was a devout Catholic who communicated to her son a lifelong commitment to Catholicism. Throughout a distinguished public career, Murphy would champion the underdog and the radical. The impetus to do so may have risen out of his family background. His great-grandfather had been hanged by the British for insurrection. His father, born and raised in Canada, had been jailed at one time there for his association with Fenianism, a secret society of Irish nationalists that flourished for a time in the second half of the 19th century. Frank Murphy himself grew up Catholic in a predominantly Protestant state. The blood of the outcast and the rebel ran in his veins.

After receiving a public education, Murphy attended the University of Michigan, from which he graduated with an LL.B. in the 1914. He then began the practice of law with a Detroit firm, supplementing his work as an attorney by teaching night courses at the University of Detroit. With the declaration of war by the United States against Germany in 1917, Murphy—who coveted opportunities for military service during each of the country's world wars—received a commission as a first lieutenant. He served a tour of duty with the American Expeditionary Forces without seeing combat and then later in occupied Germany. After the war, and before he returned to the United States, he studied law briefly at Lincoln's Inn in London and Trinity College in Dublin. When he returned to the United States, he immediately accepted the position of assistant U.S. attorney for the eastern district of Michigan. Murphy's first bid for a political office suffered defeat when he ran for Congress on the Democratic ticket in 1920. Two years later he left public service briefly to practice law privately, but he returned to public life in 1923 when he became a judge for the Recorder's Court in Detroit, the city's principal criminal court.

After his six years of work as a judge, Murphy successfully ran for mayor of Detroit in 1930, assuming political control of the city just at is slipped into the grip of the depression. He won reelection in 1931. The key achievement of Murphy's career as mayor was his work in forming and serving as the first president of the U.S. Conference of Mayors. In 1932 he vigorously supported Franklin D. Roosevelt's first presidential campaign. When Roosevelt assumed the executive office, he dispatched Murphy to serve as governor-general of the Philippines, and then, when the Philippines became a commonwealth, high commissioner. Murphy proved to be a benevolent administrator, devoted to the cause of Philippine independence, and his years of service as governor general and high commissioner instilled a lifelong affection in him for the Philippines. When he joined the Supreme Court some years later, he decorated his office with the flags of the United States and of the Philippines.

When Roosevelt ran for re-election in 1936, he persuaded Murphy to return home and run for governor of Michigan, hoping that Murphy's campaign for governor would assist his own campaign for president. Both men won their election campaigns. As governor, Murphy attempted to infuse his state with the kind of New Deal programs that Roosevelt was bringing to the nation. He took office at the beginning of 1937, after a General Motors sit-down strike had already begun. His tenure as Michigan governor was marked by his refusal to use the Michigan National Guard to break up the strike and his contribution to the eventual settlement of the strike. His general prolabor stance, though, did not endear him to Republicans in Michigan, who defeated his reelection bid in 1938.

President Roosevelt did not forget Murphy's loyalty and promptly appointed him attorney general of the United States in 1939. Murphy served a short but distinguished tenure in this office, making his most significant mark by creating a civil rights division within the Justice Department. Possibly Murphy's work as an attorney general exhibited more reformist zeal than the president's political aspirations could tolerate. In any event, despite Murphy's apparent desire to receive an appointment as secretary of war, Roosevelt nominated him to the Supreme Court instead, after Associate Justice Pierce Butler died in November 1939. The Senate unanimously confirmed the appointment on January 16, 1940, and Murphy took the oath of office as a Supreme Court justice two days later.

Unlike President Roosevelt's other appointments to the high court, Murphy brought some measure of judicial experience with him. Nevertheless, he thought of himself more as a man of action than of contemplation and privately expressed some trepidation at the prospect of joining the Court. He wrote a former parish priest: "I am not too happy about going on the Court. A better choice could have been made. I fear that my work will be mediocre there while on the firing line where I have been trained to action I could do much better."

In some ways, Murphy's self-reflection proved quite accurate. He had "been trained to action," and the inclination to *do* the right thing in each particular case became his most abiding characteristic as a judge. For him, precedent and established doctrine took a secondary position to his blunt quest to find the right result in each case. If being right meant jettisoning previous decisions, then he was happy to do so. He would crash through a thicket of law to find space for individual rights and for freedom from discrimination. As he summed up in one dissenting opinion: "The law knows no finer hour than when it cuts through formal concepts and transitory emotions to protect unpopular citizens against discrimination and persecution." Murphy's dedication to this principle would express itself most vividly in his dissent to the Court decision in *Korematsu v. United States* (1944), which upheld the forced relocation of Japanese Americans from the West Coast to internment camps during World War II. Joining with Justices Owen Roberts and Robert Jackson to oppose this result, Murphy branded it nothing more than "legalized racism." Murphy's abiding sympathy for social outcasts also made him a powerful advocate for the rights of Jehovah's Witnesses to free speech and freedom of religion. During his first year on the Court he joined the nearly unanimous decision in *Minersville v. Gobitis* (1940), which found no constitutional infirmity in a state law that forced Jehovah's Witness children to salute the American flag in school, an act that Jehovah's Witnesses considered to be a form of idolatry; however, he soon reversed course on this issue. Three years later he joined with a new majority of the Court in *West Virginia Board of Education v. Barnette* (1943) to reverse the decision in *Gobitis,* and he emphasized in a separate opinion the value of religious freedom and his concept that he had "no loftier duty or responsibility than to uphold that spiritual freedom to its farthest reaches." In spite of the anti-Catholicism of the Jehovah's Witnesses, the Catholic justice became so regular a defender of the sect that one observer suggested that "If Frank Murphy is ever sainted, it will be by the Jehovah's Witnesses."

While World War II took its bloody course, Justice Murphy repeatedly sought to exchange his judicial robes for a military uniform. When the Court took its annual summer recess after the term in which Murphy became a justice, he pled with President Roosevelt to let him spend his vacation time doing something to further the war effort. Two summers later, in 1942, he actually persuaded the army to put him to use as a lieutenant colonel during training at Fort Benning, Georgia. This was as close to the war as he ever got. He had to content himself with the work of the Court, where he wrote, in the main, mostly forgettable cases in tax and labor matters. Occasionally, though, he was able to speak for the Court on important civil liberties issues, as in *Thornhill v. Alabama* (1940), his very first opinion, which applied the First Amendment's free speech guarantee to protect peaceful picketing. Had he lived longer, he might have played a more predominant role once the appointment of Earl Warren as chief justice in 1953 began to steer the Court down paths already well trodden by Murphy. But heart disease beset Murphy soon after he had joined the Court and ultimately caused his death of a coronary thrombosis in Detroit, Michigan, on July 19, 1949. He was 59 years old at the time of his death.

Frank Murphy always remained more a man who preferred to do rather than think, plunging forward in each case to the desired result; and he was accused of leaving the work of writing opinions mostly to his law clerks. One observer suggested that Murphy "looked upon hallowed juridical traditions as a drunk views a lamppost—as a means of support rather than a source of light." His unswerving devotion to the causes of civil liberty and civil rights, though, sustains a warm reputation among historians of the Supreme Court that his judicial craftsmanship alone would not have earned. It was, for example, no small feat to defy a nation, the president who appointed him, and a majority of the Court—including such famous liberals as Justices Hugo Black and William O. Douglas—over the lawfulness of the forced relocation of Japanese Americans in *Korematsu v. United States* (1944). When justice is interpreted to allow the internment of Americans solely because of their race, then perhaps the jibe that circulated in Washington during the 1940s—that the "Supreme Court tempers justice with Murphy"—is not wholly unflattering.

Further Reading

Fine, Sidney. *Frank Murphy.* Vol. 1, *The Detroit Years.* Vol. 2, *The New Deal Years.* Chicago: University of Chicago Press, 1979. Vol. 3, *The Washington Years.* Ann Arbor: University of Michigan Press, 1975—1984.

Howard, J. Woodford, Jr. *Mr. Justice Murphy: A Political Biography.* Princeton, N.J.: Princeton University Press, 1968.

Lunt, Richard D. *The High Ministry of Government: The Political Career of Frank Murphy.* Detroit: Wayne State University Press, 1965.

JAMES FRANCIS BYRNES (1882–1972)

Associate Justice, 1941–1942

Appointed by President Franklin D. Roosevelt

JAMES FRANCIS BYRNES
(United States Supreme Court)

Only two other men—and those from the earliest days of the republic—can rival James Byrnes's brevity of tenure on the Supreme Court. Byrnes retired from the Court just 15 months after he took the oath of office as a Supreme Court justice. He departed from the Court not to obscurity, however, but to a series of prominent political posts: as "assistant president" to Franklin Delano Roosevelt, secretary of state under the administration of President Harry Truman, and governor of the state of South Carolina. Since he had served as a U.S. congressman and then senator before taking his seat on the Court, he titled his autobiography, appropriately enough, *All in One Lifetime.*

James Francis Byrnes was born in Charleston, South Carolina, on May 2, 1879, the son of James F. Byrnes—who died of tuberculosis six weeks before his birth—and Elizabeth McSweeney Byrnes. Jimmy Byrnes's grandparents were Irish Catholic immigrants. Financial hardship forced Byrnes from school by the time he was 14, and he went to work in the office of Benjamin H. Rutledge, Jr., who traced his lineage back to one of the Supreme Court's first justices, John Rutledge. Rutledge guided Byrnes's attempt to further his education by after-hours reading and also aided him in obtaining a position as a court reporter. Byrnes supplemented his work in this position by reading law with Judge James A. Aldrich, eventually earning admission to the South Carolina bar in 1903. Three years later he married Maude Perkins Busch and migrated from Catholicism to his wife's Episcopalianism, a religious transition that would repeatedly affect his political prospects in the future. The couple had no children.

Byrnes began his political career in 1908 when he was elected as a solicitor (district attorney). After a two-year term of service in this position, he made the leap to national politics by winning election to Congress, where he served as a South Carolina representative for the next 14 years. In the course of committee work in the House of Representatives, Byrnes made the acquaintance of the young assistant secretary of the navy, Franklin Delano Roosevelt. In 1924 Byrnes made a run for the U.S. Senate and narrowly lost to Coleman L. Blease. Thereafter he returned to South Carolina and practiced law with the firm of Nichols, Wyche, and Byrnes in Spartanburg. Six years later he threw himself into a rematch against Blease for a seat in the Senate, and this time it was Byrnes who was sent to Washington as a senator from South Carolina by a narrow margin.

In 1932 Senator Byrnes supported the presidential candidacy of Franklin D. Roosevelt, serving as an informal adviser to the future president. After Roosevelt's election, the relationship between the two men deepened, and Byrnes established a reputation as the senator closest to the president. In the early years of Roosevelt's New Deal, Byrnes was a dependable ally for the president's programs, but his enthusiasm for the president's domestic agenda diminished during Roosevelt's second term of office. Toward the end of the 1930s, however, Roosevelt's attention began to turn toward foreign affairs and the rising threat of Nazism. On this issue, Byrnes's moderate conservativism and its harmony with the president's foreign policy cast him again into the role of presidential ally. By the end of the decade, Byrnes's service to the Roosevelt administration had earned him regular mention as a possible Supreme Court appointee. Finally, in February 1941, Justice James Clark McReynolds retired, and on June 12 the president named Byrnes to fill the resulting vacancy on the Court. The Senate confirmed the appointment the same day. A little less than a month later, Byrnes resigned his seat in the Senate and took the oath of office as an associate justice of the Supreme Court. He spent one fruitful term in this august judicial seat.

Justice Byrnes took advantage of a Supreme Court tradition giving new members to the Court the right to choose the first case for which they write an opinion, and for his own he chose the case of *Edwards v. California* (1941). The case involved a California law–often referred to as an "anti-Okie" law–that prohibited anyone from bringing indigents into the state. Though the justices were united in their belief that the law was unconstitutional, they splintered into two camps when called on to explain this result. Byrnes represented the clear majority of justices, who found the law an unconstitutional burden on interstate commerce. Justices Robert Jackson and William O. Douglas, however, would have recognized a right to travel as among those "privileges and immunities" guaranteed to U.S. citizens by the Fourteenth Amendment.

President Roosevelt had no sooner appointed James Byrnes to the Supreme Court than he returned to his old political ally for advice and assistance on a variety of political matters. Along the way Byrnes managed to write 16 opinions for the Court during his one term, but a significant portion of his time was consumed with president's business. Finally, on October 3, 1942, Byrnes relinquished his seat on the Court to serve the president full-time. He labored under the title of Director of Economic Stabilization for a time, and later as Director of War Mobilization, though Washington insiders dubbed him the "assistant president."

For a time, Byrnes seemed poised to earn a place on the 1944 Democratic ticket as President Roosevelt's vice-presidential running mate, but the president eventually supported Harry S. Truman for this spot. Byrnes labored on as "assistant president" until the spring of 1945, when he resigned shortly before Roosevelt's death. Upon Truman's inauguration as president, he quickly offered Byrnes a seat in his cabinet as secretary of state, which Byrnes accepted. He served in this capacity from 1945 to 1947, when he retired from public life and—nearing the age of 70—resumed a long-dormant law practice. His political energy had not yet been depleted, however. In 1950 he ran for governor of South Carolina and was elected to his last political post. He served as governor until 1955, presiding over that state during the turbulent years that saw the Court on which he had formerly sat declare segregation unconstitutional. Though generally moderate on racial issues for a southern politician of his time, Byrnes was no friend of the Court's desegregation decisions. In 1956 he published an article in *U.S. News and World Report* titled "The Supreme Court Must Be Curbed." He receded from national prominence after this, but lived on until April 9, 1972, when he died of a heart attack in Columbia, South Carolina.

James Francis Byrnes's tenure as a Supreme Court justice was but a brief interlude in a remarkably accomplished career as a politician. In view of the brevity of his service as a Supreme Court justice, it is not surprising that he accomplished little of historical note while on the Court. He was an active man who lacked the temperament for judicial activism. As a consequence, the role of Supreme Court justice simply failed to harness his immense energy and his boundless thirst for political engagement. He left the Court little changed by his brief presence there, choosing instead to pursue a political career as impressive as any engaged in by a former member of the nation's highest Court.

Further Reading

Burns, Ronald D. *James F. Byrnes.* New York: McGraw-Hill, 1961.

Byrnes, James F. *All in One Lifetime.* New York: Harper, 1958.

Clements, Kendrick A., ed. *James F. Byrnes and the Origins of the Cold War.* Durham, N.C.: Carolina Academic Press, 1982.

Langram, Robert W. "Why Are Some Supreme Court Justices Rated as 'Failures'?" *Supreme Court Historical Society Yearbook* (1985): 8–14.

Messer, Robert L. *The End of an Alliance: James F. Byrnes, Roosevelt, Truman, and the Origins of the Cold War.* Chapel Hill: University of North Carolina Press, 1982.

Robertson, David. *Sly and Able: A Political Biography of James F. Byrnes.* New York: Norton, 1994.

ROBERT HOUGHWOUT JACKSON (1892–1954)

Associate Justice, 1941–1954

Appointed by President Franklin D. Roosevelt

ROBERT HOUGHWOUT JACKSON
(United States Supreme Court)

With only a modest educational background, Robert H. Jackson became one of the country's greatest lawyers and one of the Supreme Court's most talented writers. Passages from his opinions as a Supreme Court justice continue to find prominent places in the texts from which modern-day law students study constitutional law. His influence on American law, while not as broad as better-known justices, has proved to be enduring. Added to this influence was that which he exerted on international law in his role as chief American prosecutor for the Nuremberg trials at the conclusion of World War II, which firmly settled the power of civilized countries to sanction war criminals. It is the rare individual whose legal talents enrich not only the law of the land but also the law of the world. Jackson was such an individual.

Robert Houghwout Jackson was born in Spring Creek, Pennsylvania, on February 13, 1892, the son of William Eldred Jackson and Angelina Houghwout Jackson. During his early childhood, Jackson's family moved to western New York, near Jamestown, where his father ran a livery stable and a hotel. Jackson's formal education ended, for the most part, on his graduation from Jamestown High School in 1911. He spent a year at Albany Law School, but he gained his legal education chiefly by "reading law" with his cousin, Frank H. Mott. Though a common form of preparation for a legal career in the 19th century, these informal apprenticeships were gradually replaced by law schools. Jackson was the last Supreme Court justice whose legal education followed the older pattern. He was admitted to the New York bar in 1913. Three years later he married Irene Gerhardt, and this marriage ultimately produced two children—a son and a daughter. The son, William Eldred Jackson, became a lawyer himself, and served as a personal aide to his father when Robert Jackson led the American legal delegation at the Nuremberg trials.

Jackson tried for a time to establish a legal practice in Buffalo, New York, but after a couple of years he returned to Jamestown, where he developed a thriving legal business over the next two decades. To this work he added active participation in Democratic politics, which brought him into contact with then Assistant Secretary of the Navy Franklin D. Roosevelt, for whom he became a personal adviser after Roosevelt was elected governor of New York in 1928. When Jackson left the private practice of law in 1934, he was regularly earning $30,000 a year, even during the depression. According to his later recollection, the income from these years "laid the foundation of financial independence which is an important asset in public office, relieving one of fear of loss of office and contributing a general sense of security."

In 1934 President Franklin D. Roosevelt persuaded Jackson to come to Washington as a general counsel to the Bureau of Internal Affairs. Jackson expected this appointment to be only a brief interlude in his lucrative private practice; in fact, he left this practice behind forever when he began to clear out the backlog of tax cases at the bureau. As general counsel for the bureau, Jackson's most notable accomplishment was obtaining a judgment in court against former treasury secretary Andrew Mellon for the payment of nearly a half-million dollars in back taxes. Jackson's success here earned him a transfer to the Justice Department in 1936, where he served as an assistant attorney general with oversight of the tax division and later the antitrust division.

Jackson's skill as an advocate in cases before the Supreme Court prompted President Roosevelt to elevate him to the post of solicitor general in 1938, when Stanley Reed left this position to become an associate justice of the Supreme Court. As solicitor general, Jackson appeared even more regularly before the Court on behalf of the federal government, performing so admirably in this position that Justice Louis D. Brandeis, one of the Court's most famous justices, suggested that Jackson should be named solicitor general for life. Roosevelt, though, had different plans, and in spite of Jackson's increasing legal stature, these did not immediately include an appointment to the Supreme Court. Instead, Roosevelt made him attorney general in 1940, when the president created a vacancy in that office by moving Frank Murphy to a seat on the Court. Finally, the resignation of Chief Justice Charles Evans Hughes in 1941 created another opportunity for Roosevelt to make a seventh appointment to the Court. Although the president considered placing Jackson in the chief justice's seat, he determined instead to elevate associate justice Harlan Fiske Stone to this position and to appoint Jackson to fill Stone's former seat; he did so on June 12, 1941. The senate confirmed the nomination within a few weeks and Robert H. Jackson took the oath of office on July 11, 1941, beginning a 13-year career as a justice.

On the Court, Justice Jackson established a reputation as a strong proponent of national power and of judicial restraint. Writing for a majority of the Court in *Wickard v. Filburn* (1942), Jackson validated an expansive view of Congressional power over interstate commerce. In *Wickard,* his opinion for the Court held that Congress had the power to regulate even private use and consumption of wheat by a farmer insofar as—considered in the aggregate with many other farmers—one farmer's use of his crop had a substantial effect on interstate commerce. Thus, Congress was empowered to regulate the use of wheat even if it was not intended to be marketed. As he later famously explained the breadth of Congress's power under the Constitution's commerce clause, if it is "interstate commerce that feels the pinch, it does not matter how local the operation which applies the squeeze."

In the area of civil liberties, Jackson tended to join Justice Felix Frankfurter in cautioning the Court against aggressive uses of its power, as justices such as William O. Douglas and Hugo Black favored. In *Terminiello v. Chicago* (1949), for example, he parted ways with a majority of the Court by dissenting from the decision overturning the conviction of a man for breach of the peace, after he delivered a speech that threatened to spark a riot. The majority, he thought, paid too little attention to the value of public order; and he warned that "if the Court does not temper its doctrinaire logic with a little practical wisdom, it will convert the constitutional Bill of Rights into a suicide pact."

Jackson, however, was hardly an enemy of the emerging dedication of the Court to the protection of civil rights and liberties. His most famous opinion protected the rights of Jehovah's Witness children to refrain from pledging allegiance to the flag in *West Virginia Board of Education v. Barnette* (1943), reversing the Court's decision to the contrary just three years earlier in *Minersville School District v. Gobitis* (1940). In the shadow of world war, Jackson warned the nation that even patriotic solidarity in the face of a vicious enemy could not justify the suppression of dissent, since "those who begin coercive elimination of dissent soon find themselves exterminating dissenters" and since coerced uniformity "achieves only the unanimity of the graveyard." In a justification of free speech that still adorns constitutional textbooks today, Jackson reasoned:

> If there is any fixed star in our constitutional constellation, it is that no official, high or petty, can prescribe what shall be orthodox in politics, nationalism, religion, or other matters of opinion or force citizens to confess by word or act their faith therein.

Justice Jackson found himself restless on the Court while the world waged war about him. He later rued that the day after the attack on Pearl Harbor, the Court convened to hear arguments in cases that included a controversy over whether green fees at country clubs could be taxed. It was not surprising, then, when Jackson readily accepted President Harry Truman's offer to take a sabbatical from the Court beginning in April 1945 to assume the role of chief counsel for the American prosecutors who joined with those from other Allied nations to try senior Nazi officials for war crimes at Nuremberg. His opening and closing arguments at Nuremberg are commonly recognized as among the greatest examples of legal advocacy. His opening statement emphasized the important step being taken by Allied powers in subjecting Nazi leaders to the judgment of law rather than the bare vengeance of angry victors.

> The wrongs which we seek to condemn and punish have been so calculated, so malignant, and so devastating, that civilization cannot tolerate their being ignored because it cannot survive their being repeated. That four great nations, flushed with victory and stung with injury, stay the hands of vengeance and voluntarily submit their captive enemies to the judgment of law is one of the most significant tributes that Power ever has paid to Reason.

When Jackson returned to the Court after the Nuremberg trials, he discovered that he had once again been passed over for appointment to the Court's chief seat. After Chief Justice Stone's death in April 1946, President Truman appointed Fred M. Vinson to this position instead of Jackson. Embittered, perhaps, by this slight, Jackson aired a long-festering feud between himself and Justice Hugo Black when he publicly stated his belief that Black had acted improperly in failing to recuse himself from an important case. The event cast an unseemly shadow across Jackson's otherwise notable career on the Court. He continued to serve as an associate justice until a heart attack toward the end of the Court's 1953 term interrupted his career. Advised to restrict his activities, Jackson nevertheless returned to Court to appear when Chief Justice Earl Warren announced the historic decision in *Brown v. Board of Education* (1954), which declared segregation in public schools unconstitutional. Jackson died five months later of a second heart attack on October 9, 1954, in Washington, D.C.

Robert Jackson began his legal career as a small-town lawyer and ended it as a justice on the U.S. Supreme Court. He is not generally acknowledged among the greatest of Supreme Court justices, but he nevertheless commands a respected position within the pantheon of American judges. He owes his place less to his ability to formulate important legal doctrines or to master subtle legal distinctions than to his rare gift of being able to translate questions of great constitutional moment into memorable opinions. He ranks among the Court's preeminent wordsmiths and is among the justices most often quoted. Added to this, his opinion for the Court in *West Virginia Board of Education v. Barnette* (1943) ranks among the most important declarations of civil liberties in the 20th century or, for that matter, in the history of the Court itself.

Further Reading

Gerhart, Eugene C. *America's Advocate: Robert H. Jackson*. Indianapolis: Bobbs-Merrill, 1958.

Hockett, Jeffrey D. *New Deal Justice: The Constitutional Jurisprudence of Hugo L. Black, Felix Frankfurter, and Robert H. Jackson*. Lanham, Md.: Rowman & Littlefield Publishers, 1996.

Kurland, Philip. "Justice Robert H. Jackson: Impact on Civil Rights and Civil Liberties." In *Six Justices on Civil Rights*. Edited by Ronald D. Rotunda. London: New York: Oceana Publications, Inc., 1983.

Jackson, Robert Houghwout. *The Struggle for Judicial Supremacy: A Study of a Crisis in American Power Politics*. New York: A.A. Knopf, 1941.

———. *The Supreme Court in the American System of Government*. Cambridge: Harvard University Press, 1955.

Prettyman, E. Barrett, Jr. "Robert H. Jackson: 'Solicitor General for Life.'" *Journal of Supreme Court History* (1992): 75–85.

WILEY BLOUNT RUTLEDGE (1894–1949)

Associate Justice, 1943–1949

Appointed by President Franklin D. Roosevelt

WILEY BLOUNT RUTLEDGE
(United States Supreme Court)

Sudden death robbed Wiley B. Rutledge of an influence on the history of the Supreme Court that would have undoubtedly have been greater had he served longer than six years as an associate justice. The outpouring of law review tributes after his death testified to a sense that he had scarcely been permitted to begin his work on the Court and that it would have been among the more lasting edifices of 20th-century American law, if only he had had more time to complete it. He was President Franklin D. Roosevelt's last appointment to the Court, and as it was, his steady outpouring of opinions over the course of six years yielded only a tantalizing glimpse of what might have been.

Wiley Blount Rutledge was born in Cloverport, Kentucky, on July 20, 1894, the son of Wiley B. Rutledge, Sr., and Mary Louise Wigginton Rutledge. His father was a fundamentalist Baptist preacher. His mother contracted tuberculosis in 1901, and—in spite of migrations by the family to Texas, and then Louisiana, and finally North Carolina in search of a climate that would restore her health—she died three years later, when Wiley was only nine years old. After her death, Wiley's father eventually moved again, first to Kentucky and later to Tennessee, where Wiley completed a college preparatory curricula at Marysville College in Marysville, Tennessee. There he majored in classical languages and met his future wife, Annabel Person, who taught Greek at the college. He eventually transferred to the University of Wisconsin, from which he graduated in 1914 with a B.A.

Rutledge was determined to study law, but he lacked the financial resources to continue on at the University of Wisconsin. Instead, he found work as a high school teacher in Bloomington, Indiana, and attempted to attend Indiana Law School at the same time. The same disease that had killed his mother soon destroyed his health as well, however, and he was forced to retire to a sanatorium, where he began the slow process of recovery from tuberculosis—and where he married Annabel in August 1917. This marriage would produce two daughters and a son. That same year, the couple moved to Albuquerque, New Mexico, in search of a climate that would further Rutledge's recovery, and the future justice obtained a position as a high school teacher. He still longed for a legal career, though, and by 1920 he made a second attempt to study law at the University of Colorado, again teaching high school while he pursued his legal degree. He graduated from the University of Colorado Law School in 1922.

Though he worked for a law firm in Boulder, Colorado, for two years after his graduation, he soon settled on a vocation as a law teacher rather than as a lawyer. He joined the faculty of the University of Colorado Law School in 1924, and over the next 15 years he held academic appointments at Colorado; as professor and later dean of the law school at Washington University, St. Louis; and as dean of the University of Iowa College of Law. His career as a law school administrator coincided with the New Deal era of President Franklin D. Roosevelt, and he proved to be one of Roosevelt's staunchest supporters and one of the fiercest critics of the justices on the Supreme Court who opposed Roosevelt's legislative agenda. When the president proposed his "court-packing" plan in 1937—a plan to stack the Supreme Court with justices more hospitable to his agenda—Rutledge supported it, much to the consternation of Iowa legislators, who threatened to cut faculty salaries at the University of Iowa in retaliation for the law school dean's obvious heresy. Officials in Roosevelt's administration went so far as to arrange for Rutledge to testify in Congress in support of the court-packing plan, and although Rutledge agreed to do so, he planned to resign from his post at the university so as not to jeopardize the livelihood of his colleagues there. The Court, though, soon reversed its opposition to Roosevelt's New Deal agenda and the court-packing plan was dropped before Rutledge could plant himself more formally under its banner before Congress. Rutledge's display of support, however, did not go unnoticed by Roosevelt, and it brought the western dean into national prominence.

Though Wiley Rutledge's name began to appear as a possible appointment to the Supreme Court in the late 1930s, President Roosevelt instead seated him first on the prestigious U.S. Court of Appeals for the District of Columbia. Rutledge served on this court from the spring of 1939 through the winter of 1943, and while there, he established his bona fides as a New Deal progressive. When Justice James Byrnes resigned from the Court to become Roosevelt's "assistant president" in October 1942, Roosevelt determined that it was time to advance Rutledge to the nation's highest court. Roosevelt had shown some inclination to favor academics, and Rutledge clearly possessed this qualification. But most decisive in the president's consideration was Rutledge's identity as a westerner. Western states had been clamoring to have one of their own on the Supreme Court, and Rutledge's western background tipped consideration firmly in his favor. As the president informed him, "Wiley, we had a number of candidates for the Court who were highly qualified, but they didn't have geography—you have that."

Wiley B. Rutledge was overwhelmingly confirmed by the Senate as President Roosevelt's last appointment to the Supreme Court on February 8, 1943, and he took the oath of office a week later. As was expected, he joined the Court's liberal wing, voting regularly with Justices William O. Douglas, Hugo Black, and Frank Murphy. In fact, together with Justice Murphy, Rutledge became one of the most aggressive defenders of civil rights and liberties on the Court during his six-year tenure there. Together with Murphy, he famously dissented in the *Application of Yamashita* (1946), when a majority of the justices on the Court refused to consider the fairness of the military proceeding in which Yamashita, the Japanese governor of the Philippines during World War II, had been charged with responsibility for atrocities committed by Japanese soldiers. Rutledge's dissenting opinion made an impassioned plea for the application of fundamental rules of fairness, even to those alleged to have engaged in horrendous behavior:

> More is at stake than General Yamashita's fate. There could be no possible sympathy for him if he is guilty of the atrocities for which his death is sought. But there can be and should be justice administered according to law. In this stage of war's aftermath it is too early for Lincoln's great spirit, best lighted in the Second Inaugural, to have wide hold for the treatment of foes. It is not too early, it is never too early, for the nation steadfastly to follow its great constitutional traditions, none older or more universally protective against unbridled power than due process of law in the trial and punishment of men, that is, of all men, whether citizens, aliens, alien enemies or enemy belligerents. It can become too late.
>
> This long-held attachment marks the great divide between our enemies and ourselves. Theirs was a philosophy of universal force. Ours is one of universal law, albeit imperfectly made flesh of our system and so dwelling among us. Every departure weakens the tradition, whether it touches the high or the low, the powerful or the weak, the triumphant or the conquered. If we need not or cannot be magnanimous, we can keep our own law on the plane from which it has not descended hitherto and to which the defeated foes' never rose.

Rutledge also penned a memorable dissent in one of the 20th century's most famous church-state cases. In *Everson v. Board of Education* (1947), a bare majority of the Court insisted that the First Amendment's establishment clause had erected a "wall of separation between church and state," but nevertheless approved a state statute that reimbursed the parents of private school children, including parochial school children, of transportation costs incurred in sending their children to school. Justice Rutledge, who was raised a Baptist and later became a Unitarian, wrote a dissenting opinion for the minority of four justices who disagreed with this result. For those who advocate a strict separation between church and state, Justice Rutledge's opinion remains one of the most important statements of this view ever set forth in a Supreme Court opinion. He wrote this dissent just two years before he died suddenly of a stroke on September 10, 1949, in York, Maine. He was only 55 years old at the time.

—∞—

It is difficult to gauge the historical significance of a judicial career as short as the one Wiley B. Rutledge completed. His was like the unfinished first symphony of a composer who might have gone on to create great masterpieces but who died before they could ever flow from his pen. He left no great expositions of constitutional doctrine and charted no seminal course for particular areas of law. Nevertheless, the eloquence of his opinions in a handful of cases suggests that time may have made of him a more august figure in the Court's history had his service on the nation's highest court not been cut short.

Further Reading

Brant, Irving. "Mr. Justice Rutledge—The Man." *Iowa Law Review* 35 (1950): 544–565.

Harper, Fowler V. *Justice Rutledge and the Bright Constellation*. Indianapolis: Bobbs-Merrill, 1965.

Mann, W. Howard. "Rutledge and Civil Liberties." *Indiana Law Journal* 25 (1950): 532–559.

Pollak, Louis H. "Wiley Blount Rutledge: Profile of a Judge." In *Six Justices on Civil Rights*. Edited by Ronald D. Rotunda. London: New York: Oceana Publications, Inc., 1983.

Rockwell, Landon G. "Justice Rutledge on Civil Liberties." *Yale Law Journal* 59 (1949): 27–59.

Rutledge, Wiley. *A Declaration of Legal Faith*. Lawrence, Kan.: University of Kansas Press, 1947.

HAROLD HITZ BURTON (1888–1964)

Associate Justice, 1945–1958

Appointed by President Harry S. Truman

HAROLD HITZ BURTON
(United States Supreme Court)

Harold H. Burton tendered 13 years of service on the Supreme Court but left no enduring legacy to it. Pleasant and hardworking, he was nevertheless not a gifted craftsman either of words or of ideas. Burton wrote no immortal opinions; he failed to build any lasting legal edifice from the timber of constitutional precedents. He preferred to focus on the details of particular cases and to decide them on the narrowest grounds. This trait, combined with the temper of a pragmatist rather than an ideologue, made him something of a conciliatory figure on a Court frequently fractured by jurisprudential warfare. He nurtured harmony in a climate frequently inhospitable to it. This, perhaps, was his most important contribution to the Court, but it is one largely invisible to outsiders, including historians. Thus, finding few more visible contributions, chroniclers of the Court generally rank Burton low among the pantheon of Supreme Court justices.

Harold Hitz Burton was born in Jamaica Plain, Massachusetts, on June 22, 1888, to Alfred Edgar Burton and Gertrude Hitz Burton. His father was a civil engineering professor and the dean of the faculty at the Massachusetts Institute of Technology. During his early childhood, Harold lived with his mother in Switzerland, but she died when he was seven years old, upon which he returned to the United States to live with his father. After his early education, Burton attended Bowdoin College in Maine, where he was captain of the football team and elected Phi Beta Kappa. He graduated from Bowdin in 1909, and thereafter enrolled in Harvard Law School, receiving his LL.B. in 1912. In the summer of that year he married Selma Florence Smith; this union eventually produced two girls and two boys.

In spite of Burton's roots in the East, he decided after graduating from law school that professional opportunities for him would be more plentiful in the West, and so he moved with his wife to Cleveland, Ohio. There he practiced law for two years with an uncle of his wife, and when the uncle migrated to Salt Lake City, Utah, Burton followed with his family. In Salt Lake and later in Boise, Idaho, he worked for public utilities, until World War I found him enlisting in the army and receiving a commission as a first lieutenant. After the war, during which he was awarded the Purple Heart and the Belgian Croix de Guerre, Burton resigned with the rank of captain in 1919 and returned to Cleveland, Ohio, where he practiced law with a firm there. In 1925 he became a partner in the firm of Cull, Burton & Laughlin, representing business and commercial interests and teaching corporation law part-time at Western Reserve University Law School. In addition, he was active in the affairs of the American Legion and in the First Unitarian Church of Cleveland.

By the end of the 1920s, Harold Burton had made his first foray into politics, winning election to the Ohio legislature as a Republican in 1928. The following year he began a three-year term of service as the director of law for Cleveland. During part of this period he was acting mayor of Cleveland. After briefly returning to practice with the firm of Andrews, Hadden, and Burton from 1932 to 1935, he was elected mayor of Cleveland in 1935 and enthusiastically reelected twice more. In 1940 he entered the national stage by winning election to the U.S. Senate. There he worked closely with Senator Harry S. Truman, the future president, on the Truman Committee, which investigated wartime claims against the government. Though the two men were divided by party affiliations, they were both pragmatists rather than ideologues and found that they shared a common approach to many issues.

After Truman's inauguration as president in 1945, Burton's relationship with the former senator bore important fruit. Justice Owen J. Roberts retired in the summer of 1945, and one of Truman's ambitions in appointing a successor was to satisfy the complaints of Republicans—with whom the president was anxious to work cordially—that the Court lacked a bipartisan complexion. No Republican had received an appointment since the Hoover administration, and Chief Justice Harlan Fiske Stone was the only remaining Republican on a Court dominated by the Democratic appointees of President Franklin D. Roosevelt. Burton was a Republican the president trusted. Moreover, elevating him to the Supreme Court was likely to yield the appointment of a Democratic replacement in the Senate by Ohio's Democratic governor. Thus, Truman nominated Harold Burton as associate justice of the Supreme Court on September 18, 1945, and the Senate promptly confirmed the appointment the next day. On October 1, 1945, Burton took the oath of office and launched a 13-year career as an associate justice.

Truman generally had cause to be satisfied with his appointee's performance on the Court. Although Burton joined in the majority decision that delivered a constitutional rebuke to President Truman's attempt to seize steel mills during the Korean War in *Youngstown Sheet & Tube Co. v. Sawyer* (1952), he generally followed the kind of moderately conservative course that might have been expected from his appointment. He allied himself in the main with justices who favored judicial restraint and against those—such as Hugo L. Black, William O. Douglas, Frank Murphy, and Wiley B. Rutledge—who practiced greater judicial activism. He tended to uphold exercises of power by federal and state governments, in, for example, areas such as criminal law and national security, including government treatment of individuals who belonged to Communist organizations.

On the racial questions that became prominent during his tenure, Justice Burton was generally a solid opponent of segregation. The exception was his lone dissent in *Morgan v. Virginia* (1946), which struck down a Virginia law requiring blacks to sit in the back of buses traveling across state lines. By the beginning of the next decade, however, Burton sided with majorities that waged increasing war against racially discriminatory laws. In 1950 he joined the Court's decisions striking down attempts to consign African Americans to allegedly "separate but equal"—but obviously inferior—higher education opportunities in *Sweatt v. Painter* (1950) and *McLaurin v. Oklahoma State Regents for Higher Education* (1950). That same year he wrote the Court's opinion in *Henderson v. United States* (1950), declaring that a state law requiring a partition between blacks and whites in railroad dining facilities violated Congress's power to regulate interstate commerce under the Constitution's commerce clause. Four years later Burton joined the Court's unanimous decision in *Brown v. Board of Education* (1954), declaring segregation in public schools a violation of the Fourteenth Amendment's equal protection clause.

For a time, Justice Burton joined with a dominant group of justices who led the Court down a centrist path somewhat more conservative than that preferred by more liberal justices such as Hugo Black and William O. Douglas. But with the appointment of Earl Warren as chief justice in 1953 and of William J. Brennan, Jr., in 1956, Burton's conservativism found him more regularly in dissent from the Court's new majority. By the summer of 1957, Burton had begun to suffer the effects of Parkinson's disease. His doctor recommended that he resign, which he did on October 13, 1958. He continued to work, hearing cases on the U.S. Court of Appeals for the District of Columbia for several years, but the disease finally took his life on October 28, 1964, in Washington, D.C.

Harold H. Burton brought no judicial experience with him to the Court, and unlike some justices who arrived on the nation's highest court with similar deficiencies, he never grew into a great judge. For several years his moderate vote contributed to judicial conclusions that represented a modest retreat from the more libertarian decisions of the Court toward the end of the Roosevelt era. But judicial architects tend to earn a higher ranking by Court historians than justices such as Burton, whose opinions neither sparkled with elegant prose nor framed important new legal understandings. For that reason he is remembered as one of the lesser lights of the Court at the middle of the 20th century.

Further Reading

Atkinson, David N. "American Constitutionalism Under Stress: Mr. Justice Burton's Response to National Security Issues." *Houston Law Review* 9 (1971): 271–288.

———. "Justice Harold H. Burton and the work of the Supreme Court." *Cleveland State Law Review* 27 (1978): 69–83.

Burton, Harold H. *The Occasional Papers of Mr. Justice Burton.* Edited by Edward G. Hudon. Brunswick, Me.: Bowdoin College, 1969.

Berry, Mary Frances. *Stability, Security, and Continuity: Mr. Justice Burton and Decision-Making in the Supreme Court, 1945–1958.* Westport, Conn.: Greenwood Press, 1978.

Langram, Robert W. "Why Are Some Supreme Court Justices Rated as 'Failures'?" *Supreme Court Historical Society Yearbook* (1985): 8–14.

Fred Moore Vinson (1890–1953)

Chief Justice, 1946–1953

Appointed by President Harry S. Truman

Fred Moore Vinson
(United States Supreme Court)

Had Chief Justice Fred M. Vinson been a brilliant jurist, he would have been taxed to create an enduring impact on the Supreme Court during the brief seven years during which he presided over it. His predecessors in the Court's chief seat had served on average twice as long as he did. But he was not a brilliant jurist, and this deficiency, combined with the brevity of his tenure on the Court, combined to yield a poor historical reputation. In his own mind, though, Vinson would have counted his seven years at the helm of the Court a success. He believed the Court should defer, in the main, to the elected branches of government, and his Court overwhelming carved for itself a limited place in American public life. He led the Court to restrict the number of cases it decided each year and—joined by other conservatives—produced decisions that generally deferred to the other political branches.

Frederick Moore Vinson was born on January 22, 1890, in Louisa, Kentucky, the second son of James Vinson and Virginia Ferguson Vinson. His father was a jailer in the small town of Louisa, located in Lawrence County. Vinson graduated from Kentucky Normal College in 1908 and earned a B.A. the following year from Centre College in Danville. He then earned his law degree from Centre College in 1911. Being a talented baseball player, he almost surrendered his prospective legal career to the hope of becoming a major-league ballplayer. Although he played baseball semiprofessionally, he never managed to win a spot in the majors, and so he returned home to Louisa and took up legal practice. By 1913 he had become city attorney.

Drafted during World War I, Vinson never made it overseas and was in officer training school in Arkansas when the war ended. After leaving the armed services he returned to Louisa, and within a few years he won his first political office as commonwealth attorney for the 32nd Judicial District of Kentucky in 1921. Two years later he married Roberta Dixson. This union eventually produced two sons: Fred, Jr., and James Robert.

In 1924 local voters sent Vinson to Congress. He served from 1924 through 1929 before losing in a landslide year for Republicans. He was back in Congress by 1931, however, and he remained there until 1939. Vinson's later congressional career coincided with President Franklin D. Roosevelt's New Deal era, and during these years the Kentucky congressman became nationally known as a leading member of the House Ways and Means Committee and as a tax expert. Though conservative by nature, Vinson generally supported Roosevelt, including the president's failed "court-packing" plan of 1937. In December of that year, Roosevelt appointed Vinson to the prestigious U.S. Court of Appeals for the District of Columbia, and in the spring of 1938 he began a five-year term of service on the court. Toward the end of this period, the chief justice of the Supreme Court, Harlan Fiske Stone, appointed Vinson to serve as chief judge on the Emergency Court of Appeals, created during World War II to deal with war-related cases. By 1943, though, President Roosevelt had devised other uses for Fred Vinson's political talents. He appointed Vinson director of the Office of Economic Stabilization in May 1943, followed by a brief assignment as head of the Federal Loan Agency in March 1945, and then director of the Office of War Mobilization.

After Harry S. Truman's inauguration in 1945, the new president found a prominent place for Fred Vinson in his own administration by appointing him secretary of the treasury in July of that year. But Truman became so impressed with his secretary's management and personal skills that he soon designated Vinson for an even more prestigious post. The Supreme Court in the mid-1940s was a fractious collection of superior intellects and strong personalities deeply divided on fundamental issues of constitutional law. A decisive shift had occurred at the end of the previous decade, when conservative judicial opposition to President Roosevelt's New Deal–era economic legislation finally collapsed and the Court abandoned any attempt to scrutinize regulations of the economy. But the Court almost immediately began to wrestle with its role in the area of civil liberties. Prominent liberals on the Court, such as Justices William O. Douglas and Hugo Black, were anxious to flex the Court's constitutional muscles to protect individual liberties from the intrusion of government. More conservative justices, however, such as Felix Frankfurter and Robert H. Jackson, believed that the lesson of judicial restraint learned by the Court in the late 1930s should be applied to issues relating to civil liberties as well. Two justices from these opposing camps, Black and Jackson, were especially at odds over Jackson's belief that Black had improperly participated in a case from which he should have—in Jackson's opinion—recused himself.

When Chief Justice Stone died suddenly in the spring of 1946, there was widespread speculation that Jackson might be appointed to replace him. Jackson was on temporary leave from the Court at the time, serving as the chief American prosecutor at the Nazi war crimes tribunal in Nuremberg. President Roosevelt had apparently held out to Jackson the promise of being chief justice after Stone, and many observers speculated that Truman would honor Roosevelt's promise to Jackson. But Jackson was already at odds with Black, and promotion of a candidate from within the Court to the chief's seat threatened further feuding and, perhaps, resignations from justices already on the Court. Fred Vinson had judicial experience, not to mention his experience in the legislative and executive branches; but more important, he seemed to possess the kind of temperament and management skills that might succeed in piloting the Court into less turbulent waters. Thus, on June 6, 1946, President Truman nominated Vinson to become the Court's new chief justice.

The announcement triggered one further unseemly episode, when Robert Jackson, still in Nuremberg, seized the moment to attack Justice Black publicly in the press. But this event seemed to embarrass both justices and for a time yielded if not the reality of peace on the Court, at least its appearance. Tensions seemed to subside some when Vinson took the oath of office on June 24, 1946, and the Court continued its work under new leadership. Vinson, though, proved unable to mend the Court's fractures. To be sure, death intervened suddenly before he had a lengthy opportunity to accomplish this mission, but in truth he probably would not have come closer to Truman's expectations in this regard even if he had served longer. Perhaps no one could have united the Court during this period, but Vinson seemed less successful than his predecessors in fostering a united face for the Court.

Chief Justice Vinson did not come to the Court with a settled philosophy that he sought to impose on the structure of the law. He was more pragmatic than this, focusing more on each individual case than its place within some overarching pattern of results, and he had settled predispositions that displayed themselves unerringly in these decisions. More important, his long service in public life—especially his career as a legislator and as a member of the executive branch—inspired him with a copious trust in the capacities of these branches to do good. The judiciary, he thought, must exercise restraint so that federal and state governments could set about wrestling with the problems of post–World War II America. In the area of the First Amendment, Vinson was prepared to practice the same kind of defense toward laws restricting speech as the Court had learned to exercise with respect to laws that restricted or regulated economic activities in the late 1930s. Thus, he authored the Court's opinion in *Dennis v. United States* (1951), which upheld the conviction of twelve Communist Party members under the Smith Act, which made it illegal to advocate the violent overthrow of the government. Similarly, deference toward executive authority pressed Vinson into dissent in the *Youngstown Sheet & Tube Co. v. Sawyer* (1952), in which the Court's majority held unconstitutional President Truman's attempt to seize steel mills during the Korean War to assure the steady production of steel. For Vinson, Truman's extraordinary assertion of power was justified by the "extraordinary times." He believed that the framers feared "executive weakness" as much as executive over-reaching.

In one area, though, Chief Justice Vinson led his colleagues to challenge the power of government to discriminate on the grounds of race between its citizens. During his tenure as chief justice, the Court began its assault on the citadel of segregation that would finally reach its climax just after Vinson's death. Vinson himself wrote the opinion for the Court in *Shelley v. Kraemer* (1948), which declared unconstitutional a state's enforcement of racially restrictive covenants—that is, private real estate agreements that prevented owners of property from selling to members of a racial minority. He also spoke for the Court in two important cases that rejected segregated arrangements in higher education alleged to be "separate but equal" but which were, in fact, anything but this. In *McLaurin v. Oklahoma State Regents* (1950), the Court held that segregation in classrooms, libraries, and university cafeterias violated the equal protection clause because they did not provide African-American students with an equal educational opportunity. Similarly, in *Sweatt v. Painter* (1950), the Court held that a black student prevented from attending the University of Texas Law School in favor of an obviously inferior substitute had not been accorded equal protection of the law.

President Truman never lost confidence in Fred Vinson's abilities and, in fact, wished the Kentuckian to succeed him as president. But Vinson himself declined to make a presidential bid in 1952. It was just as well. Chief Justice Vinson died suddenly of a heart attack on September 8, 1953, in Washington, D.C., after just seven years on the Court.

The Supreme Court under Chief Justice Fred M. Vinson generally exercised its office as the final arbiter of the Constitution with a restrained hand. At Vinson's direction, the Court reduced its caseload, avoiding decisions when possible and thus angering observers who believed the Constitution called for a more aggressive role from the Court. Vinson's patient and genial temperament helped to soften some of the sharp edges of disagreement that plagued the Court during this period. But on most questions he failed to lead the Court to enduring results. His lack of influence over the course of constitutional law during the later half of the 20th century was owing partially to his brief tenure at the head of the Court and partially to his modest judicial ability as well.

FURTHER READING

Franck, Matthew J. "The Last Justice Without a Theory: Fred M. Vinson." In *Sober as a Judge: The Supreme Court and Republican Liberty*. Edited by Richard G. Stevens and Matthew J. Franck. Lanham, Md.: Lexington Books, 1999.

Frank, John P. "Fred M. Vinson and the Chief Justiceship." *University of Chicago Law Review* 21 (1954): 212–46.

Lefberg, Irving F. "Chief Justice Vinson and the Politics of Desegregation." *Emory Law Journal* 24 (1975): 243–312.

Palmer, Jan S. *The Vinson Court Era: The Supreme Court's Conference Votes: Data and Analysis*. New York: AMS Press, 1990.

Pritchett, C. Herman. *Civil Liberties and the Vinson Court*. Chicago: University of Chicago Press, 1954.

Urofsky, Melvin I. *Division and Discord: The Supreme Court under Stone and Vinson, 1941–1953*. Columbia: University of South Carolina Press, 1997.

THOMAS CAMPBELL CLARK (1899–1977)

Associate Justice, 1949–1967

Appointed by President Harry S. Truman

THOMAS CAMPBELL CLARK
(United States Supreme Court)

Tom C. Clark left a prosperous legal practice in Texas to become a government lawyer in 1937. Once arrived in Washington, he began at the bottom and rapidly climbed to the top. In 1945 President Harry S. Truman appointed the Texan attorney general of the United States and, four years later, placed him on the Supreme Court. In his public career Clark was generally moderate, except on questions involving the collision between First Amendment expressive rights and issues of national security, posed most prominently during the Red Scare of the 1950s. On this issue Clark, with few exceptions, championed the government's power to protect itself from the threat of communism. History remembers him most for his zealousness on this issue—a zealousness now generally out of fashion—and for his equal dedication to the cause of reform in judicial administration, to which he devoted substantial energy during the later part of his career.

Thomas Campbell Clark was born on September 23, 1899, in Dallas, Texas, to William Clark and Virginia Falls Clark. In later years he preferred the more simple "Tom C. Clark." His father was a prominent Texas lawyer who served at one time as president of the Texas Bar Association but whose alcoholism ultimately devastated his legal practice and forced his son Tom to work part-time through most of his high school, college, and law school years. After Clark graduated from Bryan Street High School in 1917, he attended Virginia Military Institute for a year until forced to drop out for lack of finances. Thereafter, he joined the Texas National Guard and spent the last several months of World War I as a sergeant in the 153rd Infantry Division. With the war's end, he resumed his education by enrolling in the University of Texas, from which he earned a B.A. in 1921 and a law school degree the following year. In 1924 he married Mary Jane Ramsey, whom he had met while at the University of Texas. The couple had three children: a son Thomas Campbell, Jr., who died at the age of six from meningitis; a daughter, Mildred; and another son, William Ramsey, who eventually became attorney general of the United States.

Tom Clark began legal practice with his father's firm in Dallas, where his brother Bill also practiced. Five years later, in 1927, Clark became an assistant district attorney for Dallas County and was able to combine responsibility for the county's civil litigation with a private practice of his own. In 1932, he resigned from this position and formed a legal partnership with the former district attorney, William McCraw, for whom he had originally worked in the district attorney's office. Two years later McCraw ran for Texas attorney general, and with Clark as his campaign manager, he won the election.

In 1937 the prospect of being a government lawyer and an invitation from Texas Senator Tom Connally lured Clark to Washington, where he took a position in the Justice Department as special assistant in the War Risk Insurance Office. Within a year he had been transferred to the Antitrust Division of the Justice Department, where he began to develop an expertise in this complex area of law that he would one day carry with him to the Supreme Court. Posted for a time in New Orleans and later in San Francisco, Clark was working on the West Coast when the Japanese attacked Pearl Harbor. He soon found himself in charge of the relocation of Japanese civilians from the West Coast to internment camps, a nasty business that he supported at the time but later counted among the biggest mistakes of his life.

By 1942 Clark was back in Washington, in charge of the War Frauds Unit of the Justice Department's Antitrust Division. This was a fortuitous legal assignment, for it brought the Texan into contact with Senator Harry S. Truman, then chairman of the Senate War Investigating Committee, which itself was probing fraudulent claims made against the government. Their common battle against wartime fraud taught the two men to respect each other's ability.

In the years immediately following this assignment, Clark continued his steady rise in the Justice Department. In 1943 he became assistant attorney general over the Antitrust Division, and the next year he was given charge of the department's criminal division. In 1944 he also picked an important winner when—unlike his superior, Attorney General Francis Biddle—he cast his support behind Harry Truman as the Democratic vice-presidential candidate. Truman subsequently won the spot on his party's ticket. With President Franklin D. Roosevelt's election in 1944 and his death the following year, Clark's former associate in the prosecution of wartime fraud had become himself the president of the United States. Truman wasted little time in rewarding Clark's loyalty and proven ability: In 1945 the president made Tom Clark attorney general.

Clark's four-year tenure as the nation's highest-ranking lawyer proved to be an energetic one. His administration of the Justice Department continued to focus—not surprisingly—on antitrust matters, including several cases that Clark argued successfully before the Supreme Court. He also revealed a sturdy measure of support for civil rights, even though he was not as aggressive in this area as some observers wished him to be, by inaugurating the practice of having the Justice Department file *amicus curiae* briefs in important civil rights cases. By filing these "friend of the court" briefs in cases such as *Shelley v. Kraemer* (1948), even when the U.S. government was not formally a party, Clark was able to lend the impressive abilities of the Justice Department to the advocacy of civil rights. In *Shelly v. Kraemer,* for example, the department's amicus brief helped convince the Supreme Court to find that the enforcement of racially restrictive real estate covenants by state courts violated the equal protection clause of the Fourteenth Amendment. As attorney general Clark also threw the weight of his office behind domestic anticommunist policies during the early years of the cold war. Though not quite in the camp of Wisconsin Senator Joseph McCarthy in terms of zealous attempts to ferret out domestic communists, Clark was quite vigilant in his use of the Justice Department to develop legal strategies to curtail the spread of communism in the United States. After he became a justice on the Supreme Court, this vigilance would reassert itself.

When Associate Justice Frank Murphy died in the summer of 1949, President Truman promptly nominated Clark to assume Murphy's seat on the Court. This nomination displeased some observers because Murphy had been the only Catholic on the Court and they believed another Catholic—rather than a Presbyterian like Clark—should replace Murphy. Many liberal observers opposed Clark's nomination, believing him far to the right of Murphy, who had been one of the Court's most prominent liberal justices. But Clark won confirmation in the Senate by a vote of 73-8 and took the oath of office as a Supreme Court justice on August 24, 1949. By the time he retired from the Court 18 years later, he had served longer than any other justice appointed by Truman.

Truman had hoped that Clark would fortify the position of Fred Vinson, whom Truman had made chief justice in 1946, and during their four years on the Court together, Clark generally sided with Vinson. On one significant occasion, though, he parted ways both with the chief justice and with the president who had appointed him, when he joined the majority of the Court that declared Truman's seizure of steel mills during the Korean war unconstitutional in *Youngstown Sheet & Tube Co. v. Sawyer* (1952). He also proved to be less predictably conservative than Vinson. Although Clark carried his anticommunist zeal with him onto the Court and thus routinely supported government attempts to ferret out and frustrate the cause of the Communist Party in the United States, he also authored important decisions in the areas of civil rights and civil liberties. He wrote the Court's opinions in *Heart of Atlanta Motel v. United States* (1964) and *Katzenbach v. McClung* (1964), upholding the power of Congress to prohibit racial discrimination in hotels and restaurants that affected interstate commerce. Moreover, he spoke for the Court in *Mapp v. Ohio* (1961), which held that state courts could not consider evidence in criminal proceedings that had been obtained in an illegal search or seizure. Finally, and perhaps most significantly, the Presbyterian Clark announced the Court's decision in *Abington School District v. Schempp* (1963), which held that Bible readings in public schools violated the establishment clause of the First Amendment.

Justice Clark's son, William Ramsey Clark, decided to follow his father's footsteps in the Justice Department. In February 1967 William Clark's steady progress up the ranks of the Justice Department reached its zenith when President Lyndon B. Johnson nominated him to be attorney general of the United States. Justice Clark, fearing that he would inevitably be placed in positions of conflict once his son became attorney general, therefore resigned from the Court on June 12, 1967. He continued to accept assignments on the various federal courts of appeals over the next 10 years and also worked tirelessly to secure improvements in the area of federal judicial administration. He died of heart failure in New York City on June 13, 1977, a decade after he had stepped down from the Supreme Court.

—∾—

Justice Tom C. Clark generally earns ratings as an average justice, numbered neither among the Supreme Court's brightest luminaries nor its disappointing failures. But a long tenure on the Court, combined with significant ability and professional charm, made him generally well-respected while he was on the Court and not likely to be forgotten once he stepped down from it. His decisions regarding communism and free speech rights ultimately came to appear overly anxious of national security and not significantly protective of expressive rights. But he also contributed important opinions to the history of American constitutional law in the areas of civil rights and religious disestablishment that continue to be highly regarded.

Further Reading

Dorin, Dennis D. "Tom C. Clark: The Justice as Administrator." *Judicature* 61 (Dec.–Jan. 1978): 271–277.

Frank, John P. "Justice Tom Clark and Judicial Administration." *Texas Law Review* 46 (1967): 5–56.

Gazell, James A. "Justice Tom C. Clark as Judicial Reformer." *Houston Law Review* 15 (1978): 307–329.

Kirkendall, Richard. "Tom C. Clark." In *The Justices of the United States Supreme Court 1789–1969: Their Lives and Major Opinions,* Vol. 4. Edited by Leon Friedman and Fred L. Israel. New York: R. R. Bowker Co., 1969.

Mengler, Thomas M. "Public Relations in the Supreme Court: Justice Tom Clark's Opinion in the School Prayer Case." *Constitutional Commentary* 6 (Summer 1989): 331–349.

Srere, Mark. "Justice Tom C. Clark's Unconditional Approach to Individual Rights in the Courtroom." *Texas Law Review* 64 (1985): 421–442.

Sherman Minton (1890–1965)

Associate Justice, 1949–1956

Appointed by President Harry S. Truman

Sherman Minton
(United States Supreme Court)

Although Sherman Minton was expected at the time of his appointment to the Supreme Court to join its liberal wing, he became, in fact, one of its staunchest conservatives. Together with other Truman justices, Minton briefly participated in a mild counterrevolution of sorts against the more activist decisions of the 1940s. He virtually always supported the exercise of governmental power, except when he lent solid support to the constitutional war against segregation that climaxed with the Supreme Court's decision in *Brown v. Board of Education* (1954), unanimously declaring segregation in public schools unconstitutional. In the main, he trusted the executive and legislative branches to shepherd the country through the early years of the cold war and believed that the Supreme Court should defer to these branches.

Sherman Minton, known by his friends as "Shay," was born on October 20, 1890, on a farm near Georgetown, Indiana, the son of John Evans Minton and Emma Livers Minton. He graduated from New Albany High School in 1910 and then attended Indiana University, first as an undergraduate in a class that included Wendell L. Wilkie, Republican presidential candidate in 1940, and then as a law student. He graduated first in his class from Indiana School of Law in 1915 and then studied law for an additional year at Yale, where he obtained a master's degree. While at Yale, he took a class from former president and future chief justice of the Supreme Court William Howard Taft. After Minton challenged Taft over a particular legal question, the former president reportedly declared, "I'm afraid, Mr. Minton, that if you don't like the way this law has been interpreted, you will have to get on the Supreme Court and change it." After Yale, Minton returned to New Albany in the fall of 1916 and began a legal practice. The following year he married Gertrude Burtz on August 11, 1917; the two would eventually have two sons and a daughter. The United States entered World War I the same year, and Minton served as an infantry captain in Europe. When the war ended, he remained with the Army of Occupation, finding time to study law at the Sorbonne in Paris in the spring of 1919 and being finally discharged from the army in August of that year.

Upon returning to New Albany after the war, Minton resumed his legal practice. Over the following years he tried to win a seat in Congress but lost the Democratic primary in 1920 and then again in 1930. In the interim he practiced law, first in New Albany and then briefly in Miami, Florida. By 1928 he had returned to New Albany. One of his classmates from Indiana University, Paul McNutt—a man Minton also knew from work together in American Legion activities—was elected governor of Indiana in 1932. Minton's prospects brightened considerably that year, when McNutt appointed him as public counselor to Indiana's Public Service Commission. The following year, Minton's success in lowering utility rates formed the basis for a successful campaign for the U.S. Senate. Running as a New Dealer in 1934, Minton had no patience for arguments that the programs launched by President Franklin D. Roosevelt violated the Constitution. "You can't walk up to a hungry man today and say, 'Here have a Constitution,'" he insisted. "You can't hand to the farmer who has been ground into the soil a Constitution and tell him to dig himself out."

Minton arrived in Washington along with other freshmen senators such as Harry S. Truman, and these two men formed a lasting friendship during their Senate days. Minton used his political influence to rail against the conservative justices on the Supreme Court who had declared key aspects of President Franklin D. Roosevelt's New Deal programs unconstitutional. "The blight of the cold, dead hand of the Court must not be permitted to contaminate the blood stream of the Nation and destroy the right of the people to live and prosper," he argued. Minton proposed requiring the concurrence of seven justices on the Court to invalidate a federal law. Shortly thereafter, when President Roosevelt proposed his "court-packing plan" in 1937, Minton, now assistant Democratic whip, was an ardent supporter. Although the president's plan eventually collapsed and the Court veered away from its conservative activism, Minton's experiences during these years made a lasting impression on him. Ever afterward he would be a proponent of judicial restraint.

In 1940 he lost a bid for reelection when Wendell L. Wilkie and other Republicans dominated the political contests of that year in Indiana. But President Roosevelt rewarded Minton's loyalty in the Senate by making him a presidential assistant. His brief service in this capacity included urging the president to support Senator Harry Truman's plan to investigate wartime fraud. As a result, the Truman Committee, as it became known, conducted high-profile investigations into fraud that made Truman a prominent national figure and paved the way for his place as Roosevelt's running mate in 1944. In the meantime, Roosevelt appointed Minton a federal appellate judge in 1941 on the U.S. Court of Appeals for the Seventh Circuit.

Truman's ascension to the presidency on Roosevelt's death in 1945 made Minton's appointment to the nation's highest court unsurprising when it was announced in 1949. Justice Wiley B. Rutledge died on September 10, and five days later Truman nominated Minton to fill the vacancy on the Court. Ironically, in light of his future career on the Court, opposition to the nomination came chiefly from the conservative end of the political spectrum, which feared that Minton would bring his New Deal political activism to the Court. The Senate Judiciary Committee requested the nominee to appear before it for questioning, but Minton declined. He was nevertheless confirmed by a vote of 48-16 on October 4, 1949, and he took the oath of office as a Supreme Court justice eight days later.

Those who had prognosticated liberal activism from the Hoosier justice, with either fond anticipation or fearful foreboding, soon discovered that Minton the justice was an entirely different creature than Minton the politician. The new justice drew a sharp distinction between the work of a judge and the work of a legislator. The judge, he believed, had to resist the impulse to approach social problems with the same creative zeal as the legislator. The judge existed only to correct the patent abuses of the other branches, which, by constitutional charge, were given more immediate responsibility for lawmaking.

This mind-set immediately propelled Minton into the conservative orbit of Chief Justice Fred Vinson, generally occupied as well by Justices Tom Clark, Harold Burton, and Stanley Reed, and placed him at odds with liberal justices such as his former Senate colleague, Hugo Black, and William O. Douglas. In particular, and to the great consternation of liberal observers of the Court, Minton joined the Court's cold warriors, who regularly sided with government efforts to restrain the perceived threat of domestic communism at the expense of free-speech interests. He also routinely supported government interests over the constitutional claims of criminal defendants. Only in the area of racial segregation did Minton depart steadfastly from the conservative mold of the time. He enthusiastically joined in the Court's decisions dismantling segregation, culminating in the decision of *Brown v. Board of Education* (1954), which declared segregation in public schools unconstitutional.

Ill health finally forced Minton to retire from the Court on October 15, 1956. Neither he nor the nation had any illusions about the grandeur of his contribution to the Court during his seven years of service. "There will be more interest in who will succeed me than in my passing," he announced on the day of his resignation. "I'm an echo." He had already drifted to the periphery of the Court's power during the later days of his tenure. Earl Warren, who became chief justice in 1954, soon joined with the Court's liberal wing and Minton's conservative influence consequently suffered a sharp decline. After leaving the Court, Minton returned to New Albany, where he died on April 9, 1965.

Though well-liked by his colleagues on the Court, Sherman Minton was never recognized among its more prominent intellectual lights. His conservative dedication to the principle of judicial restraint lacked the philosophical underpinnings of other justices, such as Felix Frankfurter, another of the Court's opponents of judicial activism. His opinions garnered no praise for their erudition or their prose and generally expressed results that fell out of favor during the subsequent years of the Warren court, famous for its protection of civil rights and civil liberties. He remains one of the least respected justices of the 20th century.

Further Reading

Atkinson, David N. "From New Deal Liberal to Supreme Court Conservative." *Washington University Law Quarterly* (1975): 361–394.

———. "Justice Sherman Minton and the Protection of Minority Rights." *Washington and Lee Law Review* 34 (1977): 97–117.

Gugin Linda C. and James E. St. Clair. *Sherman Minton: New Deal Senator, Cold War Justice.* Indianapolis: Indiana Historical Society, 1997.

Kirkendall, Richard. "Sherman Minton." In *The Justices of the United States Supreme Court 1789–1969: Their Lives and Major Opinions,* vol. 4. Edited by Leon Friedman and Fred L. Israel. New York: R. R. Bowker Co., 1969.

Radcliff, William Franklin. *Sherman Minton: Indiana's Supreme Court Justice.* Indianapolis, Ind.: Guild Press of Indiana, 1996.

Wallace, Harry L. "Mr. Justice Minton: Hoosier Justice on the Supreme Court." *Indiana Law Journal* 34 (1959): 145–205, 377–424.

EARL WARREN (1891–1974)

Chief Justice, 1953–1969

Appointed by President Dwight D. Eisenhower

EARL WARREN
(Photograph, Library of Congress)

Earl Warren presided over the Court that remade the face of modern constitutional law. Not since the earliest days of the Republic, when Chief Justice John Marshall breathed life into the Constitution, has a Court so profoundly affected the structure of the American constitutional order. Less by judicial brilliance than by masterful leadership, Earl Warren led the Supreme Court to an aggressive protection of individual rights. In particular, he orchestrated the Court's united assault on the citadel of racial segregation and wrote perhaps the most important opinion in the 20th century, *Brown v. Board of Education* (1954), which declared segregation in public schools unconstitutional.

Earl Warren was born in Los Angeles, California, on March 19, 1891, the son of Methias Warren and Chrystal Warren, both of whom had immigrated to the United States when they were children. Methias or "Matt" Warren worked for a railroad, earning so little for his toil at first that he later joked with his son that when Earl was born, Matt was too poor to give him a middle name. But by dint of hard work and saving, Earl's father eventually bought a number of properties whose rents gradually became the family's chief livelihood. Earl, meanwhile, grew up in Bakersfield, California, graduating from Kern County High School in 1908. With money he had saved from a steady career of odd jobs and with the financial support of his family, he enrolled that fall in the University of California at Berkeley, where he earned his B.A. in 1912 and his law degree from Boalt Hall two years later. His law school career was without distinction.

After graduation, Warren spent an unhappy year working in the legal department of Associated Oil in San Francisco and 18 months clerking for the Oakland firm of Robinson and Robinson. Then, as he was on the verge of establishing his own practice with some friends, the United States entered World War I, and Warren entered the army. He arrived as a private and left, one month after the war was over and without serving overseas, as a first lieutenant.

After Warren returned to civilian life, he worked briefly for the California Assembly and then took a position as a deputy city attorney in Oakland. In 1920 he undertook work as a deputy district attorney for Alameda County. Five years later, when the district attorney advanced to a more prestigious political office, Warren was chosen to take his place. In 1925 he also married Nina Palmquist Meyers, a widow with a young son, after a two-year engagement. Warren adopted Nina's son, and over the following years the couple had five more children together. As district attorney, Warren was reelected in 1926, 1930, and 1934, steadily establishing through these years a reputation as an incorruptible foe of political corruption.

In 1938 Earl Warren, then one of the best-known district attorneys in the country, ran for attorney general of California, winning the general election after he had gained the nominations of the Republicans, the Democrats, and the Progressives. This victory came on the heels of learning that his father, who had become a miserly and disagreeable landlord in his later years, had been beaten to death with a lead pipe at home. The murder was never solved.

The most memorable aspect of Warren's four-year tenure as attorney general of California was his vigorous support of the internment of Japanese Americans on the West Coast in camps, following the attack on Pearl Harbor. In later years Warren came to deeply regret his participation in this affair. At the time, though, he was convinced that the military had authority during war "to tell me to get back 200 miles if it wants to do it, and as a good American citizen I have no right to complain. . . . Now," he concluded, "if a good American citizen cannot complain, I don't see why the Japanese should complain."

Warren used his political experience as attorney general of California to launch a successful campaign in 1942 for governor of the state and he proved as popular in this office as he had been as state attorney general. He won reelection in 1946 and again in 1950, in the later election defeating James Roosevelt, son of former President Franklin D. Roosevelt. Earl Warren was a progressive Republican, and his political success in California seemed to portend success on the national stage as well. He ran, in fact, as vice president with Thomas E. Dewey on the Republican ticket in 1948 and was a serious contender for the Republican nomination for president in 1952. But Dwight Eisenhower's capture of the Republican nomination and his election as president that year laid the ground for Earl Warren's ascension to the national stage in a different way than he had, perhaps, expected. Eisenhower eventually informed Warren that he planned to appoint the California governor to the Supreme Court as soon as there was a vacancy. The vacancy came sooner than expected when Chief Justice Fred Vinson died suddenly in September 1953. President Eisenhower gave Warren an interim appointment as chief justice on October 2, 1953, and then, when Congress reconvened, nominated him permanently for the position. The Senate confirmed the appointment on March 1, 1954, and the next day Earl Warren was sworn in as the Fourteenth chief justice of the U.S. Supreme Court.

The most famous case of Warren's career was already pending before the Court when he began his interim appointment as chief justice in October 1953. *Brown v. Board of Education*, which challenged the constitutionality of public school segregation, had been argued before the Court the previous term, but the justices had not reached a decision. When initially considered by the Court while Fred Vinson was alive and still chief justice, it appeared that the Court—by a divided vote—would declare segregation in public schools unlawful. When Warren arrived on the Court, however, he made it a priority to achieve a unanimous agreement among the justices regarding the case, and, in a first display of the leadership that would characterize his tenure as chief justice, he succeeded.

On May 17, 1954, two months after being officially confirmed for the post he had occupied since the previous fall, Warren announced the opinion of a unanimous Court in *Brown*. The opinion was brief, to the point, and addressed more to the American public than to legal scholars. Earlier, in conference with the other justices about the case, Warren had argued that no justification could exist for segregation except a mistaken idea that blacks were inferior as a race. This idea he firmly rejected, and his opinion for the Court centered on the devastating effects on African-American children of being branded inferior by the pernicious system of segregation. "To separate them from others of similar age and qualifications solely because of their race generates a feeling of inferiority as to their status in the community, that may affect their hearts and minds in a way unlikely ever to be undone." The argument, which aimed straight at the human element—the basic issue of fairness—was one that would become commonplace on the Warren Court. "But was it fair?" would be the chief justice's invariable question to lawyers trying to defend some result by piling precedent on precedent. Precedent, he believed, should not stand in the way of principle. He was result-oriented to the core, better known, as it has been observed, for his *decisions* than for his *opinions*—that is, better known for the conclusions he reached than for the arguments he marshaled to explain those conclusions.

In the name of right, *Brown v. Board of Education* (1954) launched a social revolution in southern states that had practiced Jim Crow segregation for generations. And in the name of right, Warren led his Court to revolutionize the face of American law in other areas as well. Criminal defendants gained from the Warren Court extensive new protections in the criminal process: *Mapp v. Ohio* (1961) held that states could not use evidence illegally seized to prosecute criminal defendants; *Gideon v. Wainwright* (1963) required states to provide attorneys for defendants who could not afford them; *Miranda v. Arizona* (1966) established guidelines for police treatment of those arrested of crimes. Under Earl Warren's leadership, the Court also upset the customary practices of many public school districts when it held in *Engel v. Vitale* (1963) that state-sponsored prayers in schools violated the First Amendment's establishment clause, and a year later made the same finding with respect to Bible readings in *Abington School District v. Schempp* (1964). Warren's court revolutionized voting law when it declared that the Constitution embodied the principle of "one person, one vote" in a series of voting rights cases beginning with *Baker v. Carr* (1962). And as if these landmark cases were not enough, the Warren court laid the foundation for the modern-day right to abortion when it recognized a fundamental right of privacy in *Griswold v. Connecticut* (1963), which prohibited states from outlawing the use of contraceptives by married couples.

Unlike his great constitutional predecessor, Chief Justice John Marshall, Earl Warren did not control the Court by assigning himself to write all or even most of its important decisions during his tenure. Instead, he routinely assigned others to craft the explanations for the Court's results in particular cases. But Warren was a master of the art of "massing the Court," as Chief Justice William Howard Taft had described in his own day the important work of corralling the fiercely independent spirits who sit on the Supreme Court at any particular time to achieve institutional consensus.

On November 22, 1963, an assassin's bullet felled President John F. Kennedy. A week later, President Lyndon B. Johnson appointed the President's Commission on the Assassination of President John F. Kennedy; he then persuaded Warren to chair the commission. The "Warren Commission," as it came to be known, worked feverishly over the next 10 months. Finally it issued a report to President Johnson in September 1964 concluding that Lee Harvey Oswald had acted alone in killing Kennedy and denying that the assassination had been the work of a conspiracy. The report, and Warren's participation in its preparation, earned a good deal of criticism from all sides—those who insisted in believing that the commission had covered up the truth and others who simply questioned the chief justice's decision to accept such a politically controversial appointment.

As the 1960s neared a close, Chief Justice Warren prepared to retire. When President Johnson announced that he would not seek reelection in 1968, Warren, worried about the possibility that Richard M. Nixon, whom he deeply distrusted and disliked, would be elected, tried to give the president a chance to appoint the next chief justice. Johnson proposed that Associate Justice Abe Fortas advance to the chief's seat. In the confirmation hearings that followed this nomination, however, accusations surfaced that Fortas had engaged in financial improprieties while on the Court, and in the ensuing controversy he requested that his nomination be withdrawn. By that time Nixon was president and the choice of appointing Warren's successor fell to him. Though Nixon chose a man opposite in name and judicial temper to Earl Warren—Warren Earl Burger—this appointment and others to follow failed to undo the revolution accomplished by the Warren court. The decisions of the Warren years became, in the main, enduring aspects of American constitutional law.

—m—

President Dwight Eisenhower, who appointed Earl Warren as chief justice, was said to have been greatly disappointed by the activism to which his appointee led the Court during the 1950s and 1960s. Though Warren was a progressive Republican during most of his career in California state politics, the dedication with which he pursued the protection of individual rights against the powers of federal and state governments once he joined the Court was a surprise that pleased some but was bitterly opposed then and now by others. But however one evaluates the results unswervingly pursued by Warren, it is impossible to deny his skill at leading the Court to those results. It is also impossible to deny the enduring character of those results. The chief justices who followed him were decidedly more conservative than Warren, but they proved unable to reverse the course established by the man who would always be known thereafter by at least some observers as the "super chief."

FURTHER READING

Cray, Ed. *Chief Justice: A Biography of Earl Warren.* New York: Simon & Schuster, 1997.

Horwitz, Morton J. *The Warren Court and the Pursuit of Justice.* New York: Hill and Wang, 1998.

Pollack, Jack Harrison. *Earl Warren: The Judge Who Changed America.* Englewood Cliffs, N.J.: Prentice-Hall, 1979.

Schwartz, Bernard. *Super Chief: Earl Warren and His Supreme Court.* New York: New York University Press, 1983.

Schwartz, Bernard, ed. *The Warren Court: A Retrospective.* New York: Oxford University Press, 1996.

White, G. Edward. *Earl Warren: A Public Life.* New York: Oxford University Press, 1982.

JOHN MARSHALL HARLAN II (1899–1971)

Associate Justice, 1955–1971

Appointed by President Dwight D. Eisenhower

JOHN MARSHALL HARLAN II
(United States Supreme Court)

John Marshall Harlan sprang from a line of lawyers and judges, including a grandfather for whom he was named—the first John Marshall Harlan—who was a justice on the Supreme Court when his grandson was born. The younger Harlan became first a gifted lawyer and later a Supreme Court justice like his grandfather. On the Court he generally favored a policy of judicial restraint and frequently occupied a dissenting position during the years when the Court, under Chief Justice Earl Warren, pursued a decidedly activist course. Nevertheless, Harlan himself contributed significant opinions to the "rights revolution" of the Warren years and helped to shape the course of modern constitutional law.

The second John Marshall Harlan was born in Chicago, Illinois, on May 20, 1899, the son of John Maynard Harlan and Elizabeth Palmer Harlan. His father was a distinguished Chicago attorney, active as a Republican in the city's politics, who served as an alderman and made two unsuccessful bids to become city mayor. The grandfather whose name he bore served as an associate justice on the Supreme Court from 1877 to 1911 and was famous for having dissented from the Court's approval of segregation in *Plessy v. Ferguson* (1896) and for insisting that the Constitution required the law to be "color-blind." Young Harlan received his early education at a boarding school in Oakville, Ontario, and then at the Lake Placid School in New York. He subsequently matriculated at Princeton University in 1916 and graduated in 1920 after compiling an outstanding university career and winning a Rhodes scholarship that allowed him to study law at Balliol College in Oxford, England, for the next three years.

After Harlan's return to the United States in 1923, he found a position with the Wall Street firm of Root, Clark, Buckner & Howland. One of the firm's partners, Emory R. Buckner, advised Harlan to obtain a law degree from an American law school. Harlan complied by earning an LL.B. from New York Law School over the course of a year while he continued to work for the firm. Thereafter, Buckner was appointed U.S. attorney for the Southern District of New York, and Harlan left the firm to become Buckner's assistant, assuming responsibility for the prosecution of Prohibition violations. By 1927 both Buckner and Harlan had returned to the Root, Clark, Buckner & Howland firm, but late in the year the two men undertook another political charge—this time to investigate graft involving municipal sewer construction.

Harlan worked as a special assistant attorney general with Buckner for the next two years. During this period he married Ethel Andrews, and this marriage eventually produced a daughter, Eve. In 1930 Harlan returned to his former law firm and was made a partner the following year. Over the next decade he grew to be one of the city's premier trial lawyers.

When the surprise attack on Pearl Harbor intruded on the nation's peace in December 1941 and the United States entered World War II, Harlan sought a military position. He obtained a post in England as chief of the Operational Analysis section of the Eighth Air Force. There, with a team of other civilians, Harlan advised the air force concerning bombing missions, helping to improve the accuracy of bombing raids. For this and other service, Harlan was awarded the United States Legion of Merit and the Croix de Guerre of Belgium and France.

The 46-year-old Harlan returned home in 1945 and resumed a litigation practice that became nationally prominent. To his work for important clients such as Du Pont Corporation, Harlan added a substantial range of professional activities. He served as director of the Legal Aid Society and was deeply involved in the activities of the New York City Bar Association. A new opportunity for public service presented itself to Harlan in 1951, when he was appointed chief counsel for the New York State Crime Commission, which was immersed in an investigation concerning the inroads of organized crime on state government. This post, which Harlan held from 1951 through 1953, brought Harlan into contact with Herbert Brownell, an associate of New York Governor Thomas E. Dewey. Soon thereafter, Brownell became the attorney general for President Dwight D. Eisenhower, and he offered Harlan a seat on the prestigious U.S. Court of Appeals for the Second Circuit.

Harlan accepted the appointment and took his seat in March 1954, but his career on this appellate court proved to be extraordinarily brief. In October that year, Associate Justice Robert Jackson died of a heart attack, and President Eisenhower promptly nominated Harlan to assume the vacant seat on the Court. Harlan's nomination, though, collided with the anger of southern senators over the Court's decision the previous spring in *Brown v. Board of*

Education (1954), which declared public school segregation unconstitutional. They were able to hold Harlan's nomination hostage for a short period while they railed against the Court. But President Eisenhower resubmitted Harlan's nomination on January 10, 1955, and two months later the Senate finally confirmed Harlan by a vote of 71-11. He took his seat on the Court on March 28, 1955.

John Marshall Harlan joined the Court during a historic period. The decision in *Brown,* handed down the previous year, inaugurated a period of revolutionary change in constitutional law, as a majority of the Court began to make the protection of civil rights and civil liberties a matter of increasing priority. Especially in the 1960s, this new resolve would undergird sweeping transformations in a wide range of areas. Harlan, though, proved to be an adversary of many of these developments. Together with Associate Justice Felix Frankfurter, he came to champion the value of judicial restraint and thus placed himself at odds with the increasing activism of the Warren court. Throughout the years of Warren's tenure as chief justice, Harlan was the most eloquent and precisely reasoned advocate of judicial conservativism. He believed that individual liberty was best protected by ensuring appropriate legal procedures and vigilantly policing the separate boundaries between political powers, rather than by rushing to defend particular liberties directly with the strong arm of the Constitution. He denied that every problem had a constitutional "fix." Thus, in dissenting from the Court's use of the equal protection clause to guarantee the "one person, one vote" principle in cases such as *Reynolds v. Sims* (1964), Harlan challenged his colleagues' belief that "every major social ill in this country can find its cure in some constitutional 'principle,' and that this Court should 'take the lead' in promoting reform when other branches of government fail to act." He believed firmly in a federalism that respected the role of states in the nation's life and often dissented from Court decisions that imposed a single constitutional standard on both federal and state governments. Thus, he dissented from the Court's landmark case of *Miranda v. Arizona* (1966), which required state law enforcement personnel to inform criminal suspects of their right to remain silent and to have counsel appointed or else be precluded from using any confessions obtained from the suspects.

Nevertheless, in spite of Harlan's insistence on judicial restraint, he both wrote and joined in opinions that defied a traditional "conservative" label. For example, he announced the opinion for the Court in *NAACP v. Alabama* (1958), which upheld the right of individuals to join civil rights organizations without having their identities disclosed, and thus acknowledged a right of association within the broader rights protected by the First Amendment's free speech clause. Toward the end of his judicial career, Harlan wrote the opinion for the Court in *Cohen v. California* (1971), which found that the First Amendment protected the right of a critic of the Vietnam War to wear in a public place a jacket with an offensive slogan on the back that criticized the draft. Similarly, Harlan firmly supported the Court's recognition of a right to privacy in *Griswold v. Connecticut* (1963), on the basis of which the Court declared unconstitutional a state law prohibiting the use of contraceptives. He had, in fact, been prepared to acknowledge this right two years earlier in *Poe v. Ulman* (1961), when a majority of the Court initially declined to hear a challenge against the Connecticut law prohibiting the use of contraceptive devices.

Harlan's vision began to fail during the 1960s. He continued to labor at the work of the Court, however, until persistent back pain caused by cancer of the spine eventually disabled him toward the beginning of the following decade. Harlan retired from the Court on September 23, 1971. He died in Washington, D.C., a little more than two months later, on December 29, 1971.

Through his years as a critic of Warren court activism, John Marshall Harlan II earned the respect of his colleagues and of Court observers for his judicial ability. His chief justice, Earl Warren, was the archetypal result-oriented judge, who decided what was right and then produced a judicial explanation to fit the result chosen. Harlan, on the other hand, insisted on the importance of identifying appropriate legal principles and applying them to particular cases. Otherwise, he thought, a result-oriented Court risked favoring one group or segment of American society unfairly. Harlan's opinions were a model of clarity and reason for which even his opponents on a particular issue could generally find some grudging respect. Moreover, his predominantly conservative criticism of the "rights revolution" during the 1960s was not reactionary, for Harlan himself supported at least some of the key elements of this revolution. He remained convinced, however, that the Constitution had not made the Court a final cure for the ills of American society. Some of these had constitutional solutions. But others, he thought, depended on the will and energy of the legislative and exexcutive branches for their cure.

Further Reading

Dorsen, Norman. "John Marshall Harlan, Civil Liberties, and the Warren Court." *New York Law School Law Reviews* 36 (1991): 81–107.

Fried, Charles. "The Conservatism of Justice Harlan." *New York Law School Law Review* 36 (1991): 33–52.

Mendelson, Wallace. "Justice John Marshall Harlan: Non sub Homine . . ." In *The Burger Court: Political and Judicial Profiles.* Edited by Charles M. Lamb and Stephen C. Halpern. Urbana: University of Illinois Press, 1991.

Shapiro, David L., ed. *The Evolution of a Judicial Philosophy: Selected Opinions and Papers of Justice John M. Harlan.* Cambridge, Mass.: Harvard University Press, 1969.

Yarbrough, Tinsley E. *John Marshall Harlan: Great Dissenter of the Warren Court.* New York: Oxford University Press, 1992.

William J. Brennan, Jr. (1906–1997)

Associate Justice, 1956–1990

Appointed by President Dwight D. Eisenhower

William J. Brennan, Jr.
(Photograph, Library of Congress)

The 20th century knew more brilliant justices on the Supreme Court than William J. Brennan, as well as more elegant writers and more careful craftsmen of precedents. But it knew no justice with more influence on the development of modern constitutional law than Brennan. Working behind the scenes, lobbying his fellow justices relentlessly, Brennan cobbled together majorities that produced a constitutional revolution in which the protection of individual civil rights and liberties took center stage on the Court for nearly three decades. Because epochs of Supreme Court history normally bear the name of the chief justice who presided over the period, Justice Brennan served on the Warren court, the Burger court, and finally, the Rehnquist court. But there is a real sense in which the first period especially, presided over by Chief Justice Earl Warren, could as readily be referred to as the Brennan court. The years from 1962 until 1969, in particular, saw the formation on the Court of a solid liberal majority of which Brennan was the indisputable intellectual leader. In these seven years, he and his colleagues rewrote constitutional law in a fashion so enduring that even a steady stream of generally conservative appointments beginning in 1969 did not unravel the work of those years.

—∞—

William Joseph Brennan, Jr., was born on April 25, 1906, in Newark, New Jersey, the second child of William Joseph Brennan and Agnes McDermott Brennan. His father had immigrated to the United States in 1892 from Ireland. He worked as a coal stoker at the Ballantine Brewery in Newark at the time of his son's birth and soon became a union leader and, still later, a member of the Newark Board of Commissioners with oversight of the city's police and fire departments. The younger Bill Brennan attended a Catholic elementary school and then public schools until he enrolled at the University of Pennsylvania in 1924, where he obtained a degree in economics from the university's Wharton School of Finance in 1928. Thereafter, he attended Harvard Law School, where he compiled a solid but not spectacular academic record. The editor-in-chief of the *Harvard Law Review* from his class, Paul Freund, would go on to be a prominent Harvard Law School professor, but the class's only future Supreme Court justice did not manage to make the law review. In fact, few of his classmates at Harvard remembered him 25 years later when he was appointed to the Supreme Court.

The spring before he started law school, Brennan married Marjorie Leanord, with whom he had three children: William III, Hugh, and Nancy. A year before he finished law school, Brennan's father died, leaving the family with no support and Brennan himself in peril of being unable to finish his law school career. But with a scholarship from Harvard and work waiting on tables at a fraternity house, he was able to graduate from Harvard Law School in the spring of 1931.

After law school, Brennan took a job with a prominent Newark law firm where he rapidly became an expert in the area of labor law. By 1938 he had been made a partner in the firm, and later the firm made him a named partner. World War II intervened, though, and in July 1942 Brennan began service in the army, first as a major and then as a lieutenant colonel with responsibility for manpower issues in the Ordnance Division. He ended his army career at the Pentagon, as chief of the Industrial Personnel Division, Labor Branch, upon which he returned to private practice with his old firm in September 1945. Four years later, though, New Jersey revamped its court system and the state governor, in an effort to staff the new courts with high-caliber judges, offered Brennan a position on the newly formed Superior Court, a trial court. Brennan was reluctant to give up the financial security of private practice and the sizable income he earned from his firm, but he finally agreed to become a Superior Court judge. He did not remain long in this post, however. By 1950 he had been elevated to the court's appellate division and, two years later, to the New Jersey Supreme Court.

Brennan's new career as a judge brought him new opportunities for public speaking, and he sometimes used these to express his opposition to the McCarthyism of the early 1950s. In two speeches he made during 1954, Brennan made clear his distaste for the investigations that had blossomed in the nation's capital and in many of its states seeking to identity communist infiltrators of important public positions. His sentences were a tangle of clauses, but their meaning was nevertheless clear enough. To the Charitable Irish Society meeting in Boston on Saint Patrick's Day, Brennan declared that "[t]he enemy deludes himself if he thinks he detects in some particles in the contemporary scene, reminiscent of the Salem witch hunts, any sign that our courage has failed us and that fear has palsied our hard-won concept of justice and fair play." Later that year he returned to this theme in an address to Rotarians: "A system of inquisition on mere suspicion or gossip without independent proofs tending to show guilt is innately abhorrent to us."

On October 15, 1956, Associate Justice Sherman Minton resigned from the Supreme Court. President Eisenhower had already listened to complaints about the composition of the Court and had determined that his next appointment to the Court would be a Catholic and a person with state court judicial experience. Brennan had recently given a speech about judicial administration in Washington that had impressed Eisenhower's attorney general, Herbert Brownell. This impression, combined with Brennan's Catholic background and his substantial experience on the New Jersey courts, won him the nomination to fill the vacant seat on the Supreme Court. He first served an interim appointment beginning on October 16, 1956. After Congress convened, the president sent forward Brennan's nomination on January 14, 1957. Had the Senate been able to foresee the future course of Brennan's judicial temperament, it might have tarried longer over his confirmation. As it was, Senator Joseph R. McCarthy, troubled by Brennan's veiled criticisms of his anticommunist investigations, cast the only dissenting vote against Brennan's confirmation on March 19, 1957.

In the course of his 33-year career on the Court, Justice William Brennan first contributed to and then helped to sustain a fundamental revolution in constitutional law. Two decades before he arrived on the Court, it had finally abandoned close scrutiny of federal and state laws regulating the economy. In the decades that followed, however, it had wrestled with the question of whether the same deferential attitude should be practiced toward laws that affected important rights and interests. The Court tilted back and forth between proponents of judicial restraint on the one hand and those of activism in the protection of civil rights and liberties on the other hand. By the early 1960s, though, a firm majority of justices committed to the more activist view finally dominated the Court, and Justice Brennan would play a central role as this majority—across a wide spectrum of doctrinal areas—repeatedly supported individual rights and liberties against the power of federal and state governments.

Baker v. Carr (1962), one of Brennan's most important opinions, would be emblematic of developments to come. The case involved the question of whether federal courts could be used as a forum to attack the constitutionality of voting districts. At the time, urban voters complained that voting districts at both the federal and the state level were designed in such a way that sparsely populated rural areas had substantially more power within the political process than more heavily populated urban areas. This, they urged, denied urban voters the equal protection of the laws guaranteed by the Constitution. But in early challenges to voter districting patterns, the Supreme Court refused to be drawn into this fierce conflict, insisting that the manner in which voter districts were drawn up was essentially a political question in which the Court should take no part. Brennan's opinion for the Court in *Baker v. Carr* revisited the issue and concluded that the Court, indeed, had the authority to determine whether particular groups of voters were denied equal protection of the law by the way voting districts were drawn. The case became a watershed as the Court found in subsequent cases such as *Reynolds v. Sims* (1964) that the constitutional principle of equality required that one person's vote have roughly the same weight as another's: the "one person, one vote" principle.

The willingness to use the Court's power to address fundamental questions of right and fairness became a core feature of Justice Brennan's judicial philosophy. Another was his conviction that the Constitution could not be measured simply in terms of the specific expectations of its framers, but that it must be given life within contemporary contexts frequently unforeseen by its original architects. Thus he was prepared to revisit the intersection of libel laws and free speech in *New York Times v. Sullivan* (1964), during the civil rights era, by limiting the ability of public officials to sue the press for statements critical of their conduct. And he was willing to use the Fourteenth Amendment's equal protection clause to challenge discrimination on the basis of gender in *Frontiero v. Richardson* (1973), even though 19th-century framers of the amendment may have been quite comfortable with laws that discriminated between men and women. Finally, in *Goldberg v. Kelly* (1970), Brennan contemplated the modern welfare state, in which individuals regularly rely on various forms of welfare payments from governments and found that these payments were a kind of "property" to which the procedural protections of due process should apply.

Brennan enjoyed the greatest influence on the Court while Earl Warren was its chief justice. But even after more conservative chief justices assumed their seats on the Court—first Warren E. Burger and then William H. Rehnquist—Brennan continued to play an important part in the Court's decisions and to see the revolution accomplished by the Warren court sustained and even expanded in some areas. He finally convinced a majority of the Court to accord greater suspicion of laws that discriminated on the basis of gender in *Craig v. Boren* (1976), and he helped secure at least a limited constitutional blessing for affirmative action programs in cases such as *Regents of the University of California v. Bakke* (1978) and *Metro Broadcasting v. Federal Communications Commission* (1990). Even at the very end of his tenure on the Court, he was able to lead a majority of the justices to overturn flag desecration laws in *Texas v. Johnson* (1989) and *United States v. Eichman* (1990) because, he explained for the Court, they violated the First Amendment right to free speech. Soon after these final victories, Brennan suffered a stroke that forced him to resign from the Court on July 20, 1990. Eight years previously, his first wife, Marjorie, had died, and Brennan had married Mary Fowler in 1983. He himself died seven years after stepping down from the Court, on July 27, 1997.

Upon his retirement from the Court, Justice Brennan announced: "It is my hope that the Court during my years of service has built a legacy of interpreting the Constitution and federal laws to make them responsive to the needs of people whom they were intended to benefit and protect. This legacy can and will withstand the test of time." Justice Brennan's Constitution was indeed a "responsive" one. To the great dismay of political and constitutional conservatives, his Constitution was a living, breathing, thing—always prepared to be transformed by a new context, waiting only for the hand of justices willing to accomplish the transformation. For his talent at doing so, Brennan became the idol of generations of progressive law students, lawyers, scholars, and judges. He also became the personification of abuse for those who opposed his willingness to remake the Constitution. But even his critics could never deny his influence. More than any other man of the 20th century, he directed the course of constitutional interpretation down new channels. Since the law, like a mighty river, does not readily alter its course, it is likely that the success of his constitutional vision will continue long after his departure from the Court.

Further Reading

Eisler, Kim Isaac. *A Justice for All: William J. Brennan, Jr., and the Decisions That Transformed America*. New York: Simon & Schuster, 1993

Friedelbaum, Stanley H. "Justice William J. Brennan, Jr.: Policy-Making in the Judicial Thicket." In *The Burger Court: Political and Judicial Profiles*. Edited by Charles M. Lamb and Stephen C. Halpern. Urbana: University of Illinois Press, 1991.

Marion, David E. *The Jurisprudence of Justice William J. Brennan, Jr.: The Law and Politics of "Libertarian Dignity."* Lanham, Md.: Rowman & Littlefield Publishers, 1997.

Mello, Michael. *Against the Death Penalty: The Relentless Dissents of Justices Brennan and Marshall.* Boston, Mass.: Northeastern University Press, 1996.

Michelman, Frank I. *Brennan and Democracy.* Princeton, N.J.: Princeton University Press, 1999.

Rosenkranz, E. Joshua & Bernard Schwartz, eds. *Reason and Passion: Justice Brennan's Enduring Influence*. New York: W. W. Norton & Company, 1997.

CHARLES EVANS WHITTAKER (1901–1973)

Associate Justice, 1957–1962

Appointed by President Dwight D. Eisenhower

CHARLES EVANS WHITTAKER
(United States Supreme Court)

Charles Evans Whittaker is a testimony to what dedicated toil may accomplish, and also to what it may not. A night-school law graduate who achieved prominence as a midwestern lawyer and then a federal trial and appellate judge, Whittaker's life was a rags-to-riches story such as he read in Horatio Alger as a young boy. But mere dedication, even when coupled with prodigious effort, could not supply the lack of intellectual gifts that became apparent once President Dwight D. Eisenhower placed Whittaker on the nation's highest court. Torn by indecision and conscious of his own inadequacies, Whittaker eventually collapsed under the weight of his responsibilities as a justice and had to retire from the Court.

Charles Evans Whittaker was born on February 22, 1901, on a farm near Troy, Kansas, the son of Charles Whittaker and Ida Miller Whittaker. Young Charles attended a nearby school for his first nine years, and then he spent a year and a half riding to and from Troy High School, some six miles away from the family farm. His mother died on his 16th birthday, a loss that prompted Whittaker to drop out of high school to work with his father on the farm and earn extra money hunting game and selling the pelts. Three years later, with the modest sum of money he had saved, he set out for Kansas City, Missouri, where he intended to study law. There he persuaded the Kansas City Law School, which offered courses at night, to accept him as a law student even though he lacked both a high school and a college degree. The law school insisted that he make up the high school courses he had missed but allowed him to begin his study of the law. At the same time, Whittaker had taken a position as an office boy with Watson, Gage & Ess, a Kansas City law firm. From 1920, when he started law school, until 1924, when he completed his studies, Whittaker worked full-time for Watson, Gage, attended law school classes at night, and studied after his classes concluded. Along the way, he managed to pass the Missouri bar exam in 1923, the year before he graduated from law school. The same year he took a job at Watson, Gage as a lawyer.

Over the next decade, Whittaker climbed the ranks of seniority in the firm: In 1930 he became a partner and in 1932 he had his name added to the firm's name. Meanwhile, he married Winifred R. Pugh in 1928; this union would eventually produce three sons. For the first part of his legal career, Whittaker was a trial lawyer, but by the third decade of law practice he had drifted away from litigation and had become instead a general legal adviser for a variety of corporate clients such as Union Pacific and Montgomery Ward. To this legal work he added participation in bar activities, including a term of service as the president of the Missouri State Bar Association, and in the affairs of the Methodist church of which he was a member. In all these activities Whittaker worked diligently, perhaps even compulsively, attending single-mindedly to his responsibilities; yet he never fully overcame the educational deficits that he had brought with him to adulthood.

When a position as a federal judge became vacant in March 1954, Whittaker let it be known that he wanted it. One of his clients was a friend of President Dwight D. Eisenhower and was able to recommend Whittaker for the position; thus, Whittaker became a judge on the federal district court for Missouri's western district in July 1954. He brought with him to the federal bench the same work ethic that had served him well in private practice and won praise for clearing out a docket of cases that had backlogged the court prior to his appointment. Two years later, a vacancy appeared on the U.S. Court of Appeals for the Eighth Circuit when that court's only Missouri judge died. Eisenhower nominated Whittaker to that position, and after the Senate confirmed the appointment, Whittaker undertook a career of less than a year on the federal court of appeals. A further opportunity for promotion presented itself when Justice Stanley Reed retired from the Supreme Court in February 1957. Previous presidential administrations had placed men on the Court with no judicial experience. Eisenhower had made one such appointment himself to the Court—former California attorney general and governor Earl Warren. But the president subsequently determined to make judicial experience a necessary prerequisite for his further nominations to the Court. He therefore nominated Whittaker, with three years of federal judicial experience, to assume the vacancy on the Court left by Stanley Reed's retirement. The Senate confirmed Whittaker's appointment unanimously, and he took the oath of office as an associate justice on the Supreme Court on March 25, 1957.

Charles Evans Whittaker brought essentially conservative values to the Court, but he liked to think of himself—a nominal Republican—as having no real political leanings. He was therefore prepared to take on the cases that came before him as a Supreme Court justice one by one, without established predilections. He lacked a firm judicial philosophy, however, and his decisions on the Court seemed somewhat erratic to most observers. He tended to vote conservatively, joining with Justices Felix Frankfurter, Harold Burton, Tom C. Clark, and John Marshall Harlan more often than with the Court's liberal justices: Earl Warren, Hugo L. Black, William O. Douglas, and William J. Brennan, Jr. But in particular cases he might supply the crucial fifth vote necessary to achieve some liberal result. Since these varying results were not accompanied by solid opinions explaining the grounds for Whittaker's decisions, they earned the justice no praise either from his colleagues on the Court or from the Court's observers. He seemed to be, rather, a man who could not make up his mind. His indecision crippled such contribution as he might otherwise have made to the Court. On one occasion, for example, Whittaker had been assigned to write the majority opinion in *Meyer v. United States* (1960). Unable to make any headway on it, he eventually admitted to Justice William O. Douglas, who had already written a dissenting opinion in the case, that he had not been able to complete the majority opinion. Douglas then offered to write it for Whittaker and, when Whittaker acquiesced, Douglas ended up preparing both opinions—one supporting the Court's decision and one opposing it.

Such problems as Whittaker had in accomplishing his responsibilities as a Supreme Court justice had nothing to do with his willingness to work hard. Diligent work was his lifelong habit, and he robed himself with it on the Court just has he had throughout his life. But mere toil proved to be insufficient to carry the day. By 1962 the stress of his position and of overwork trying to live up to it finally broke Whittaker's health. Toward the beginning of March 1962, he entered Walter Reed Army Medical Center. There he was advised to retire for the sake of his health. Thus, on April 1, 1962, Charles Whittaker retired from the Court.

It took the former justice more than a year to regain his health. Even after he left the Court, though, Whittaker seemed—by the choice of his activities—to be something less than a typical retired Supreme Court justice. He worked for a time for General Motors and then helped to draft a code of ethics for U.S. senators. But he also found time for speaking engagements, which he used to criticize a Court that had become increasingly activist in the protection of civil rights and liberties after his retirement from it. For this criticism, he earned the observation from Chief Justice Earl Warren that he "could never make up his mind about decisions until he left the Court." Charles Evans Whittaker died in Kansas City, Missouri, on November 26, 1973.

Well-intentioned, polite, and gracious by all accounts, Charles Whittaker nevertheless earned low marks for his service on the U.S. Supreme Court. He left no enduring opinions of significant note. His vote made a difference in some of the Court's close opinions for a time, but few of these were of great constitutional importance. Though he served diligently in the high place to which President Eisenhower promoted him, toil alone proved insufficient to accomplish the great weight of his judicial responsibility, and history generally names him as one of the worst justices ever to have sat on the Court.

Further Reading

Berman, D. M. "Mr. Justice Whittaker: A Preliminary Appraisal." *Missouri Law Review* 24 (1959): 1–15.

Friedman, Leon. "Charles Whittaker." In *The Justices of the United States Supreme Court 1789–1969: Their Lives and Major Opinions,* vol. 4. Edited by Leon Friedman and Fred L. Israel. New York: R. R. Bowker Co., 1969.

Potter Stewart (1915–1985)

Associate Justice, 1958–1981

Appointed by President Dwight D. Eisenhower

Potter Stewart
(United States Supreme Court)

Potter Stewart was the middle man during most of his career as a justice on the Supreme Court. He struggled to extricate himself from accusations of being either conservative or liberal and preferred instead to see himself as just a lawyer. In practice, this mind-set cast Stewart into a generally unpredictable role on the Court, causing him to join sometimes in results favored by its conservative wing and sometimes in results pressed for by more liberal members of the Court. For a time, Stewart's middle position made him the swing vote in important cases, but as the Court became more emphatically liberal in the early years of the 1960s, Stewart's influence waned. He nevertheless compiled a solid record of performance as a Supreme Court justice, earning consistent praise for the clarity and memorableness of his opinions.

Potter Stewart was born on January 23, 1915, in Jackson, Michigan, the eldest son of James Garfield Stewart and Harriet Loomis Potter Stewart. His father was a lawyer, a local politician, and, eventually, a justice on the Ohio Supreme Court from 1947 until his death in 1959, a year after his son had taken a seat on the U.S. Supreme Court. In his youth Potter enjoyed the privileges of modest wealth, including an education first at Cincinnati's University School and then later at the Hotchkiss School in Connecticut. To these opportunities he added an undergraduate degree at Yale in 1937 and, after a one-year fellowship at Cambridge University, a degree from the Yale Law School in 1941. While in law school, he served as an editor of the *Yale Law Journal.* This honor was characteristic of the outstanding academic ability Stewart demonstrated throughout his undergraduate and law school days.

After law school, Stewart worked briefly for a New York City law firm, but World War II found him serving in the Navy as an officer aboard fuel tankers, "floating around in a sea of 100 octane gas," as he later described it, "bored to death ninety-nine per cent of the time and scared to death one per cent." While still serving in the armed forces, Stewart met and, on April 24, 1943, married Mary Ann Bertles, with whom he had three children: Harriet, Potter, Jr., and David. In 1945, after the war was over, Stewart returned for a short time to New York but soon chose instead to pursue a legal career with a firm in Cincinnati. There he followed in his father's footsteps by participating in local politics, winning election to the Cincinnati City Council in 1949 and 1951 and serving a term as vice-mayor from 1952 to 1953.

In 1954, when Stewart was only 39 years old, President Dwight D. Eisenhower appointed him a judge on the U.S. Court of Appeals for the Sixth Circuit. Here, in spite of his Republican background, Stewart generally held to a moderate course. Four years after this appointment to the federal bench, Eisenhower appointed Stewart on an interim basis to fill the vacancy left by Associate Justice Harold Burton's retirement. Potter Stewart began service on the Court on October 14, 1958, and was formally confirmed by the Senate on May 5, 1959, after it had returned from recess, by a vote of 70-17.

Potter Stewart joined a Court fairly evenly divided between jurists of a conservative bent, who generally advocated a restrained use of the Court's power, and those of a more liberal inclination, willing to wield the Court's authority more aggressively to protect civil rights and civil liberties. Stewart labored to escape categorization in either of these camps and became, by consequence, a swing vote on the Court. He tended to side with conservatives in his respect for state power, thus joining in the decision of *National League of Cities v. Usery* (1976), which denied that Congress had the power to regulate the wages and hours of state and municipal employees. Moreover, in a series of criminal procedure cases, including *Miranda v. Arizona* (1966), Stewart dissented against the Court's subjection of state criminal practices to various regulations and restrictions of the Bill of Rights. He also dissented from the Court's decision in *Griswold v. Connecticut* (1965) recognizing a constitutional right of privacy that was violated by a state law prohibiting the use of contraceptive devices. Though Stewart characterized the law as "uncommonly silly," he denied that silliness was a constitutional defect.

Stewart could be found equally often in the camp of the Court's more liberal justices. For example, he joined in the Court's pronouncement of a moratorium on the use of the death penalty in *Furman v. Georgia* (1972), because its application in state criminal law proceedings seemed to be completely haphazard and thus violated the Eighth Amendment's cruel and unusual punishments clause. "These death sentences," he explained in a concurring opinion, "are cruel and unusual in the same way that being struck by lightning is cruel and unusual." Stewart also wrote the opinion for the Court's majority in *Jones v. Alfred H. Mayer Co.* (1968), which upheld the authority of Congress to prohibit private racial discrimination in housing through its power under the 13th Amendment to abolish both slavery itself and the "badges and incidences" of slavery.

Justice Stewart preferred to resolve constitutional issues as narrowly as possible, and thus he purposefully declined to elaborate the kind of doctrinal overviews that sometimes permit a justice to influence the broad course of constitutional development. He preferred instead to focus primarily on the case at hand. Though this focus often made his vote important in particular cases, it tended to deny him a lasting influence on constitutional doctrine. He is generally regarded, however, to have been better than average at the work of crafting judicial opinions. He also had the gift of aphorism, and some of his constitutional one-liners became widely quoted, none more so than a quip from his opinion for the Court in *Jacobellis v. Ohio* (1962), an obscenity case. At the time, the Court was wrestling with the task of defining obscenity or "hard-core" pornography, a category of speech recognized by the Court then and now to fall generally outside the protections of the First Amendment. In a separate opinion, Justice Stewart explained his own reasons for finding that the film at issue in the case was protected by the First Amendment. "I shall not today attempt further to define the kinds of material I understand to be embraced within [the category of "hard-core" pornography]," he wrote, "and perhaps I could never succeed in intelligibly doing so. But I know it when I see it, and the motion picture involved in this case is not that."

For a time, when Chief Justice Earl Warren announced his retirement from the Court in 1968, word circulated that President Richard Nixon might appoint Stewart the new chief justice. But Stewart privately communicated to Nixon his wish not to be considered for this position. He served more than a dozen more years on the Court, writing, in all, more than 600 opinions. Fearful of outstaying his usefulness on the Court, Justice Stewart resigned on July 3, 1981. He remained active for a time hearing cases by designation on the federal courts of appeals. In addition, he provided commentary for a television series titled "The Constitution: That Delicate Balance." He died on December 7, 1985, in Hanover, New Hampshire, after suffering a stroke.

As an undergraduate, the Republican Potter Stewart had surprised his college classmates by using his position as head of Yale's student newspaper to endorse President Franklin D. Roosevelt's New Deal agenda. The episode would be repeated once Stewart found himself on the Supreme Court, where he regularly defied easy attempts to categorize him as either conservative or liberal. For some observers, Stewart's apparent lack of a judicial philosophy was a sign of intellectual weakness. But for others, his steadfast commitment to a practice of judging that attempted to stand apart from conventional ideological commitments was a welcome addition to a Court that has frequently endured sharp splits between liberals and conservatives.

Further Reading

Binion, Gayle. "Justice Potter Stewart: The Unpredictable Vote." *Journal of Supreme Court History* (1992): 99–108.

"In Tribute of Honorable Potter Stewart." *Yale Law Journal* 95 (1986): 1321–1333.

Marsel, Robert S. "Mr. Justice Potter Stewart: The Constitutional Jurisprudence of Justice Potter Stewart—Reflections on a Life of Public Service." *Tennessee Law Review* 55 (1987): 1–39.

Monsma, Stephen V. "Justice Potter Stewart on Church and State." *Journal of Church and State* 36 (1994): 557–576.

Yarbrough, Tinsley E. "Justice Potter Stewart: Decisional Patterns in Search of Doctrinal Moorings." In *The Burger Court: Political and Judicial Profiles.* Edited by Charles M. Lamb and Stephen C. Halpern. Urbana: University of Illinois Press, 1991.

Byron Raymond White (1917–)

Associate Justice, 1962–1993

Appointed by President John F. Kennedy

Byron Raymond White
(United States Supreme Court)

Byron R. White was President John F. Kennedy's first appointment to the Supreme Court. Kennedy himself did not live long enough to take the measure of White's career, but the justice proved to be something of a disappointment for admirers of the slain president. White regularly opposed the activism of the Warren court, which produced a constitutional revolution in its zeal for the protection of individual rights against the power of government. Though not a typical conservative, White was not a typical liberal either. He joined in the Court's constitutional war against racial discrimination but consistently resisted its expansion of individual rights. To the end, he remained something of an intellectual loner on the Court, dismissive of brands such as conservative or liberal, preferring simply to decide cases without attempting to elaborate a judicial philosophy.

Byron Raymond White was born on June 8, 1917, in Fort Collins, Colorado, the second son born to Alpha Albert White and Maude Burger White. In 1920 the family moved to the nearby town of Wellington, Colorado, where Albert White became the manager of a lumber company. The town's chief economic livelihood centered on the sugar beet crop, and, as White would later recall, "Everybody worked for a living. Everybody. Everybody." The typical school year included a two-week holiday in October when children, including White, participated in the beet harvest.

Whatever disadvantages White experienced growing up in a small Colorado town during the depression did not hamper his educational attainments. He graduated first in his high school class in 1934 and earned a scholarship to the University of Colorado, where he demonstrated himself both an outstanding athlete and an extraordinary student. "Whizzer" White, as he came to be known at the university, became a star football player, was class president his senior year, graduated again number one in his class in 1938, and was awarded a Rhodes scholarship to study in Oxford, England. He did not set out immediately for Oxford on graduation, however. Instead, he agreed to play football for the Pittsburgh Pirates (now the Steelers) for one season for $15,000, the highest salary paid to a professional football player up to that time. Leading the NFL in rushing that season, White compiled a record that would make him better known among the public as a football player than as a Supreme Court justice. But by January 1939 he had left football behind to begin his study of law at Oxford. During a vacation on the French Riviera, he met John F. Kennedy, son of the American ambassador to Great Britain, Joseph P. Kennedy.

The outbreak of World War II interrupted White's Oxford career and sent him back to the United States in September 1939, where he enrolled in Yale Law School. Expecting to be drafted at any minute, White eventually put his law school plans on hold and accepted a contract to play football for the Detroit Lions in the 1940–41 season. After attempting to join the Marines in the summer of 1941 and being rejected because of his color-blindness, White started another season with the Lions. During the season, which was to be his last, he applied for and was accepted by Naval Intelligence into the naval reserve. The attack on Pearl Harbor in December of that year soon launched White into the South Pacific, where he spent nearly four years as a Naval Intelligence officer. While serving in the navy, White again encountered John F. Kennedy, recently returned after his P.T. boat had been sunk by a Japanese destroyer.

After the war was over, Byron White married Marion Lloyd Stearns on June 15, 1946; their family would eventually include a son, Charles, and a daughter, Nancy. He also finished his LL.B. degree at Yale Law School in November of that year, *magna cum laude,* the first student to have graduated with such honors from the law school in a decade. He then immediately went to work for a year as a judicial clerk for the newly appointed chief justice of the Supreme Court, Fred M. Vinson. Afterward, he returned to Colorado and took a job with the law firm of Newton, Davis & Henry in Denver. For the next 14 years, White developed a business practice while he tried to avoid the notoriety of having been a star football player.

Along with his law practice, White was active in Democratic politics at the local level, though he shunned elective office himself. When Senator John F. Kennedy began to lay the groundwork for his 1960 presidential campaign, White, who had had contact with Kennedy occasionally for two decades, helped to organize support for the Massachusetts senator, first in Colorado and later at the national level. After Kennedy's election, White was given a position as deputy attorney general under Robert Kennedy. He held this position from January 24, 1961, to April 12, 1962. During this period he helped recruit lawyers for the Justice Department, made recommendations concerning federal judicial appointments, and helped supervise the federal marshals dispatched to Alabama in May 1961 to protect the busloads of black and white "freedom riders" who were challenging continued segregation by riding buses across the South. He did not remain long at the Justice Department, though. Associate Justice Charles E. Whittaker retired from the Supreme Court on April 1, 1962, and President Kennedy used his first opportunity to make an appointment to the Court by nominating Byron White two days later. The Senate quickly confirmed the nomination, and White took his seat on the Court on April 16, 1962.

Many Court observers expected that Byron "Whizzer" White would promptly align himself with the Court's liberal bloc, consisting of Chief Justice Earl Warren, Hugo Black, William O. Douglas, and William Brennan, Jr. But within a few months of joining the Court, White spoiled these expectations. In late June 1962, the Court announced its decision in *Robinson v. California* (1962), holding that a state law making it a crime to be a drug addict violated the Eighth Amendment's prohibition against cruel and unusual punishment. White announced his first dissent as a justice, and in it he chastised the majority's reading of the Constitution:

> I deem this application of "cruel and unusual punishment" so novel that I suspect the Court was hard put to find a way to ascribe to the Framers of the Constitution the result reached today rather than to its own notions of ordered liberty. If this case involved economic regulation, the present Court's allergy to substantive due process would surely save the statute and prevent the Court from imposing its own philosophical predilections upon state legislatures or Congress. I fail to see why the Court deems it more appropriate to write into the Constitution its own abstract notions of how best to handle the narcotics problem, for it obviously cannot match either the States or Congress in expert understanding.

In *Robinson,* the junior justice placed the nation on notice of his distaste for "imposing [the Court's] own philosophical predilections on state legislature or Congress." White's reiteration of this theme over the next 31 years would dismay Kennedy admirers. He would, in fact, dissent from key liberal triumphs of the coming years such as *Miranda v. Arizona* (1966), which required law enforcement personnel to advise criminal suspects of their rights to remain silent and to have counsel appointed for them; and *Roe v. Wade* (1973), in which the Court held that women have a right to an abortion. In *Miranda,* White refused to characterize the majority's result as an advance for human dignity. The decision would inevitably return some killers and rapists to the streets, where they would repeat their crimes. The majority's result, then, was "not a gain, but a loss in human dignity." In *Roe,* he complained that "[a]s an exercise of raw judicial power, the Court perhaps has authority to do what it does today; but, in my view, its judgment is an improvident and extravagant exercise of the power of judicial review that the Constitution extends to this Court." In the 1980s White added to these dissents an opinion for the Court in *Bowers v. Hardwick* (1986), which rejected an attempt to overturn a state law on the grounds that its prohibition of consensual, homosexual acts violated a constitutional right to privacy.

Those observers who wished to characterize White in stereotypically conservative terms had to confront his voting record in cases involving racial discrimination and voting rights, though. Here he was a vigorous supporter of civil rights laws from various constitutional challenges and an equally resolute supporter of the Court's use of the equal protection clause to enforce a "one person, one vote" requirement.

On March 19, 1993, Justice White informed President Bill Clinton that he would retire from the Court at the end of that term. Having been appointed by a Democratic administration, White apparently believed it fitting that his replacement be secured by one. When he resigned from the Court on June 28, 1993, Democrats had their first opportunity to make a Supreme Court appointment since 1967. After retirement, White continued to hear cases on the federal courts of appeals.

—~—

More than one president has been disappointed by the course taken by a justice after appointment. President Dwight D. Eisenhower, for example, is said to have deeply regretted his appointment of Chief Justice Earl Warren, who led the Court to a burst of liberal activism in the 1960s. Debate continues as to whether President John F. Kennedy would have looked on his appointment of Byron White as a mistake. Calvin Trillin celebrated White's retirement with a poem in *The Nation* that began, "We'll bid adieu to Justice Whizzer White, a running back who moved well to his right. . . ." Popular wisdom among observers of the Court has generally been that Justice White's move to the right would have disappointed Kennedy. It surely disappointed many. Nevertheless, others have seen in White an admirable judicial modesty that believed the Constitution provided less of a blueprint for the Warren court's revolution in the area of individual liberties than its majorities imagined, and that controversial social and moral questions were best left to the judgment of elected officials.

Further Reading

Hutchinson, Dennis J. *The Man Who Once Was Whizzer White: A Portrait of Justice Byron R. White.* New York: Free Press, 1998.

Ides, Allan. "The Jurisprudence of Justice Byron White." *Yale Law Journal* 103 (1993): 419–461.

Kramer, Daniel C. "Justice Byron R. White: Good Friend to Polity and Solon." In *The Burger Court: Political and Judicial Profiles.* Edited by Charles M. Lamb and Stephen C. Halpern. Urbana: University of Illinois Press, 1991.

Lee, Rex E. "On Greatness and Constitutional Vision: Justice Byron R. White." *Journal of Supreme Court History* (1993): 5–10.

Nelson, William E. "Justice Byron R. White: A Modern Federalist and a New Deal Liberal." *Brigham Young University Law Review* (1994): 313–348.

"A Tribute to Justice Byron R. White." *Harvard Law Review* 107 (1993): xii–26.

"A Tribute to Justice Byron R. White." *Yale Law Journal* 103 (1993): 1–56.

ARTHUR JOSEPH GOLDBERG (1908–1990)

Associate Justice, 1962–1965

Appointed by President John F. Kennedy

ARTHUR JOSEPH GOLDBERG
(United States Supreme Court)

The Supreme Court has numbered among its members justices with patrician backgrounds, born to privilege and expected to hold places of high esteem in the life of their country. But the Court has also known the presence of justices who climbed much further to find themselves in that august place—justices born to poverty and weaned on manual toil. Arthur J. Goldberg belonged to the latter group of justices. He was the son of immigrant parents whose financial circumstances hovered near poverty. Goldberg managed to escape this life, though, and enjoy a career as a lawyer that eventually led to a cabinet post in the administration of John F. Kennedy, a seat on the U.S. Supreme Court, and, finally, a term of service as the U.S. ambassador to the United Nations.

Arthur Joseph Goldberg was born on August 8, 1908, in Chicago, Illinois, the last surviving child born to Joseph and Rebecca Goldberg, both Russian Jews who had immigrated to the United States. His father peddled produce to Chicago hotels before dying when his youngest son was eight years old. Although Arthur regularly worked at odd jobs as he grew up, he demonstrated precocious intellectual ability. He graduated from public high school at the age of 15 and continued his education at Crane Junior College by day and De Paul University by night until he was able to transfer to Northwestern University. There he obtained a B.S.L. degree in 1928 and, the following year, his J.D. degree from the Northwestern University Law School, graduating with an academic record better than any the school had produced up to that time. In 1931 he married Dorothy Kurgans, and the couple eventually had two children, Barbara and Robert.

After Goldberg finished law school and was admitted to the Illinois bar at the age of 20, he practiced briefly for the Chicago firm of Pritzer and Pritzer. Nevertheless, he ultimately found that the depression-era foreclosure work he did there was not palatable to him. Thus, he set up his own practice in 1933. Within five years he had made the first of a series of contacts with labor organizations that would eventually direct the course of his future career. He represented the Chicago Newspaper Guild in its 1938 strike, and this work led to further referrals from the Congress of Industrial Organizations (CIO). Within a short period, however, the entrance of the United States into World War II prompted Goldberg to volunteer for military service. He worked in the Office of Strategic Services, coordinating intelligence operations involving labor organizations in Europe. By 1944, though, he had resumed his legal practice.

In 1948 Goldberg's growing reputation as a labor lawyer earned him an appointment as the general counsel for the CIO and the United Steelworkers of America. Seven years later he played a major role in the merger of the American Federation of Labor (AFL) and the CIO. Toward the end of the 1950s, Goldberg's efforts to fight corruption in the AFL-CIO brought him into contact with Robert Kennedy and his brother, U.S. Senator John F. Kennedy. By the time of Senator Kennedy's 1960 presidential bid, Goldberg had become one of Kennedy's advisers, and he played a key role in securing labor support for the senator's candidacy.

After President Kennedy's inauguration, he appointed Goldberg to fill the post of labor secretary in his cabinet. In this position Goldberg spent roughly a year and a half representing the interests of labor within the Kennedy administration and acting as mediator in a variety of labor disputes. On August 28, 1962, however, Justice Felix Frankfurter resigned after suffering a stroke followed by a heart attack. To fill what had come to be thought of as the Court's Jewish seat, President Kennedy nominated Goldberg. The Senate confirmed the appointment on September 25, 1962, and Arthur Goldberg took his seat on the Supreme Court on the first day of October 1962.

Although Justice Goldberg served only three terms on the Court, his contribution during that brief period was significant. Most important, perhaps, Goldberg's presence on the Court finally gave Chief Justice Earl Warren a consistent and crucial fifth vote in support of the Court's liberal bloc, consisting previously of the chief justice, Hugo Black, William O. Douglas, and William Brennan, Jr. Replacing the great advocate of judicial restraint, Felix Frankfurter, Justice Goldberg tipped the balance of power on the Court toward Warren and his liberal allies and secured the majority necessary to accomplish what would become known as the Warren court's rights revolution. Five votes now routinely favored the claims of individual rights over competing government interests, and in short order this restructuring of the balance of power on the Court revolutionized the face of constitutional law. As secretary of labor, Goldberg had been charged with protecting the interests of American workers. As a Supreme Court justice, he perceived himself to have been given a different but related task. As Goldberg described it, "The Secretary left his post having tried, to the best of his ability, to fulfill the statutory mandate of advancing the interests of the wage earners and the industry of the country; the Justice enters on his judicial office conscious that he has been called on to do his part in the "sacred stir toward justice" and with the trembling hope "that the flame will burn bright while the torch is in [his] keeping."

Goldberg's presence on the Court made itself felt most significantly in the area of cases involving the rights of criminal defendants. His most important opinion for the Court on this subject was *Escobedo v. Illinois* (1964). Escobedo had been questioned by police in connection with their investigation of his brother-in-law's murder. Early in the interrogation, Escobedo had requested the opportunity to talk with his lawyer, who had actually come to see him in jail but had been denied the chance to talk with his client. The police thus prevented their consultation and failed to warn Escobedo of his right to remain silent. Ultimately Escobedo made incriminating statements to the police that were instrumental in securing his conviction for murder. Writing for a majority of the Court, Goldberg held that Escobedo's confession under these circumstances was inadmissible because the suspect had been denied his right to counsel as guaranteed by the Sixth Amendment of the Constitution. To the argument that police officers would be handcuffed in their efforts to investigate crimes if suspects were permitted to consult with their lawyers at an early point in the investigation, Goldberg responded sharply:

> [N]o system of criminal justice can, or should, survive if it comes to depend for its continued effectiveness on the citizens' abdication through unawareness of their constitutional rights. No system worth preserving should have to fear that, if an accused is permitted to consult with a lawyer, he will become aware of, and exercise, these rights. If the exercise of constitutional rights will thwart the effectiveness of a system of law enforcement, then there is something very wrong with that system.

The Court's decision in *Escobedo* laid the foundation for its decision two years later in *Miranda v. Arizona* (1966), requiring police to advise suspects taken into custody of their right to remain silent and to consult with an attorney.

After Arthur Goldberg had been on the Court for three years, President Lyndon B. Johnson persuaded him to resign from the Court to become the U.S. ambassador to the United Nations. Though Goldberg was reluctant to leave his seat on the Court, Johnson insisted that he would be more valuable to his country at the United Nations, where he might help negotiate some peaceful resolution to the Vietnam conflict. Historians have subsequently suggested that Johnson may have been trying to create a vacancy on the Court in order to appoint his friend Abe Fortas to it, and Johnson did in fact nominate Fortas to succeed Goldberg. In any event, Goldberg resigned from the Court on July 25, 1965, and agreed to accept the appointment as ambassador to the U.N., but he soon found himself at odds with Johnson concerning the president's continued escalation of the war in Vietnam.

In June 1968 Goldberg resigned as U.S. ambassador and returned to the private practice of law. He remained in New York City, where he ran for governor of the state in 1970 and lost. A year later he decided to return to Washington, D.C., where he continued to practice law. For a brief time toward the end of the 1970s, Goldberg served as an ambassador-at-large for President Jimmy Carter. He died on January 19, 1990, in Washington, D.C.

When Arthur Goldberg left the Supreme Court to undertake his role as U.N. ambassador, he informed President Johnson that he departed the Court with a great deal of pain, since it had provided him with some of the best years of his life. As it happened, President Johnson seemed to have lured Goldberg off the Court only to make room for a friend. Goldberg spent three frustrating years trying to halt the escalation of the Vietnam War, a conflict that poisoned his career as it had poisoned others'. Goldberg left the Supreme Court—and an influential role in the great constitutional revolution of the 1960s—only to have his public career sidetracked and eventually stalled by his conflict with Johnson over the prosecution of the Vietnam War.

FURTHER READING

Goldberg, Arthur J. *The Defenses of Freedom: The Public Papers of Arthur J. Goldberg.* Edited by Daniel Patrick Moynihan. New York: Harper & Row, 1966.

———. *Equal Justice: The Warren Era of the Supreme Court.* Evanston, Ill.: Northwestern University Press, 1971.

Goldberg, Dorothy. *A Private View of a Public Life.* New York: Charterhouse, 1975.

Lasky, Victor. *Arthur J. Goldberg: The Old and the New.* New Rochelle, N.Y.: Arlington House, 1970.

Van Tassel, Emily Field. "Justice Arthur J. Goldberg." In *The Jewish Justices of the Supreme Court Revisited: Brandeis to Fortas.* Edited by Jennifer M. Lowe. Washington, D.C.: Supreme Court Historical Society, 1994.

Stebenne, David L. *Arthur J. Goldberg: New Deal Liberal.* New York: Oxford University Press, 1996.

ABE FORTAS (1910–1982)

Associate Justice, 1965–1969

Appointed by President Lyndon B. Johnson

ABE FORTAS
(United States Supreme Court)

Born to poverty in Memphis, Tennessee, Abe Fortas became a justice on the Supreme Court, and very nearly its chief justice. He is known chiefly for his friendship with President Lyndon B. Johnson, whose desire to advance Fortas to the chief seat on the Court became his friend's undoing. In the confirmation battle that followed, details of alleged financial improprieties emerged that ultimately forced Johnson to withdraw his nomination of Fortas as chief justice and, still later, forced Fortas himself to resign under a cloud as an associate justice on the Court. Although an able, if not exceptional, judge, Fortas made his mark on the history of the Court chiefly by his embarrassing departure from it.

Abe Fortas was born on June 19, 1910, in Memphis, Tennessee, the last of five children born to William Fortas and Ray Berson Fortas. Fortas's parents were Jews who had immigrated to the United States from England. His father earned a living chiefly as a cabinetmaker, and from him Abe inherited a deep love for music. Abe became a talented violin player and formed a jazz band called the Blue Melody Boys Band while in high school. He was even more precocious as a student than he was as a musician. He graduated second in his class from South Side High School when he was 15 years old.

In fall 1926 Fortas was able to enter Southwestern College in Memphis on a scholarship. Four years later he graduated first in his class and set out to pursue a legal career by winning admission to Yale Law School. There he demonstrated his academic ability at one of the most prestigious law schools of the nation by serving as the editor of the *Yale Law Journal* and graduating second in his class in June 1933.

Yale recognized Fortas's ability by offering him a teaching fellowship, but before he undertook this opportunity, one of the law school's most brilliant young professors, William O. Douglas, helped to find Fortas a temporary assignment working in President Franklin D. Roosevelt's New Deal administration. The following years would see Fortas combine teaching responsibilities at Yale with a steady series of assignments in Washington, first working for the Agricultural Adjustment Administration and then later at the Securities and Exchange Commission (SEC). On July 9, 1935, he married Carolyn Eugenia Agger, an economist who had worked at the Department of Agriculture while he was there and whom he persuaded to attend law school at his own alma mater. The couple never had children.

By 1937, with Douglas's support, Fortas had been appointed assistant director of the public utilities division of the SEC. Two years later, leaving behind the career of a legal scholar at Yale for good, he became general counsel of the Public Works Administration and, soon thereafter, general counsel of the Bituminous Coal Division. These positions were short stops on the way to being named director of the Power division at the Department of Interior in 1941 and undersecretary of the department under Harold Ickes the following year, when the young bureaucrat was only 31 years old. He served as undersecretary until 1946, except for a brief stay in the navy in 1943, which was terminated by the confirmation that he had tuberculosis of the retina. So influential a role did Fortas play in the management of the Department of Interior during these years that he was dubbed "Ickes's Field Marshal" by the press.

At the beginning of 1946, Abe Fortas left the Department of the Interior and, first with Thurman Arnold and, later, Paul Porter, helped form what would become one of the most prestigious Washington law firms: Arnold, Fortas & Porter. The firm handled primarily corporate legal work, but Fortas found time to handle several high-profile civil liberties and criminal defense matters. These included his representation of Owen Lattimore, a scholarly adviser to the State Department concerning Asian affairs during the 1940s, who was accused by Senator Joseph McCarthy of being a "top Russian spy" in the U.S. government. In 1954 Fortas represented Monte Durham, a young man of questionable mental capacity convicted of breaking into and entering a house. Fortas was able to convince an appellate court to adopt a broad statement of the traditional insanity defense. Finally, in 1962, the United State Supreme Court appointed Fortas to represent Clarence Earl Gideon, who had filed a handwritten appeal to the Court challenging his conviction for robbery. Gideon had requested that the state provide him with an attorney at his original trial, but this had been denied him. In the case of *Gideon v. Wainwright* (1963), Fortas argued—and the Supreme Court agreed—that the Constitution's Sixth Amendment was applicable to the states and guaranteed that defendants charged with serious state crimes have counsel appointed for them if they cannot afford one.

During the years that Fortas practiced law in Washington, his relationship with Lyndon

B. Johnson grew steadily closer. The two men had been introduced in 1939, and Johnson, then a young congressman from Texas, had repeatedly turned to Fortas for assistance during the latter's years at the Interior Department. When Johnson's bid to became a U.S. senator was almost derailed by accusations in 1948 that he had stuffed the ballots in one Texas precinct, Fortas came to Johnson's legal aid by getting his friend's name back on the ballot for the general election. In the years that followed, as Johnson rose to power in the Senate, then became vice president and finally president, Fortas became one of his closest advisers. After Johnson became president, he began looking for a spot for Fortas in his administration but was unsuccessful in persuading his friend to take the job of attorney general in 1964. Johnson also had trouble convincing Fortas to accept a seat on the Supreme Court after he persuaded Associate Justice Arthur Goldberg to resign to become U.S. ambassador to the U.N. This time, though, Johnson refused to take no for an answer and nominated Fortas as a justice of the Supreme Court even after Fortas had privately declined the seat. After the Senate confirmed Fortas's appointment on August 11, 1965, he took his seat on the Court on October 4 of that year.

Fortas immediately allied himself with the Court's liberal wing, thus allowing Chief Justice Earl Warren to continue a revolutionary expansion in the area of individual rights. Fortas secured a lasting place in constitutional history by writing some of this period's most famous cases. *In re Gault* (1967) extended to juvenile criminal proceedings many of the constitutional protections available to adult criminal defendants and made applicable to state proceedings by the due process clause of the Fourteenth Amendment. *Tinker v. Des Moines Independent Community School District* (1969) protected the right of students to protest the Vietnam War by wearing black armbands to school. And *Epperson v. Arkansas* (1968), held that the First Amendment's establishment clause prevented states from barring the teaching of evolution in schools.

A little less than three years after Abe Fortas joined the Supreme Court, Earl Warren announced his intention of resigning as chief justice. On June 26, 1968, President Johnson nominated Fortas to replace Warren. Johnson's attempt to advance his friend, though, proved to be Fortas's undoing. In the confirmation hearing that followed, opponents of the nomination used the occasion to rail against Warren court activism and against Fortas's continuing close relationship with a sitting president. Soon it was discovered that Fortas's former law partner, Paul Porter, had raised $15,000—more than a third of the amount of Fortas's annual $39,500 salary as an associate justice—to pay Fortas to teach a seminar on law at American University Law School. In the face of a filibuster in the Senate, Johnson withdrew Fortas's nomination on October 4, 1968. But this was not the end of the matter. Seven months later, *Life* magazine published an article revealing that Fortas had accepted $20,000 from the Wolfson Family Foundation for legal advice and direction in the foundation's planning at a time when Louis Wolfson was under investigation for allegedly manipulating the stock market. The revelation prompted calls for Fortas's impeachment and led the justice to tender his resignation from the Court on May 14, 1969. When his former law firm refused to welcome him back, Fortas set up a practice in Washington, D.C. with another lawyer. He remained mostly out of public view until he appeared before the Supreme Court to argue a case on behalf of Puerto Rico in 1982. He died of a burst aortic valve on April 5, 1982, in Washington, D.C., before learning the outcome of the case.

From impoverished beginnings in Memphis, Tennessee, Abe Fortas rose to become a powerful federal bureaucrat, then a Washington lawyer, and finally a Supreme Court justice. But the swiftness of his rise to prominence was paralleled by his humiliating descent. In the long history of the Supreme Court, only one justice has been forced to resign from the Court because of accusations of wrongdoing. That justice was Abe Fortas. The stain of his departure from the Court has generally deprived him of the accolades often awarded the other members of the Warren court who contributed to the revolutionary constitutional changes in individual rights during the 1960s.

FURTHER READING

Brennan, William J., Jr. "Abe Fortas." *Yale Law Journal* 91 (1982): 1049–1051.

Goldberg, Arthur J. "A Tribute to Justice Abe Fortas." *Hastings Constitutional Law Quarterly* 9 (1982): 458–461.

Handberg, Roger. "After the Fall: Justice Fortas' Judicial Values and Behavior after the Failure of His Nomination as Chief Justice." *Capital University Law Review* 15 (1986): 205–222.

Kalman, Laura. *Abe Fortas: A Biography.* New Haven: Yale University Press, 1990.

Lee, Rex. "In Memoriam: Abe Fortas." *Supreme Court Historical Society Yearbook* (1983): 6–9.

Murphy, Bruce Allen. *Fortas: The Rise and Ruin of a Supreme Court Justice.* New York: William Morrow, 1988.

Shogan, Robert. *A Question of Judgment: The Fortas Case and the Struggle for the Supreme Court.* Indianapolis: Bobbs-Merrill, 1972.

THURGOOD MARSHALL (1908–1991)

Associate Justice, 1967–1991

Appointed by President Lyndon B. Johnson

THURGOOD MARSHALL
(Photograph, United States Supreme Court)

Thurgood Marshall had already earned a prominent place in history when President Lyndon B. Johnson nominated him to be the first African-American justice on the Supreme Court. Marshall had directed the campaign in the courts to dismantle segregation, culminating in the Supreme Court's decision in *Brown v. Board of Education* (1954), which declared segregation in public schools unconstitutional. At the time of his appointment to the federal court of appeals seven years later, Marshall was one of the foremost lawyers of his day. Thus, for President Johnson, his nomination of Marshall to the Supreme Court was "the right thing to do, the right time to do it, the right man and the right place." In his near quarter-century of service on the high court, Marshall showed himself to be a relentless champion of equal justice and individual rights.

Thurgood Marshall was born on July 2, 1908, in Baltimore, Maryland, the second son of William Canfield Marshall and Norma Arica Marshall. He graduated from Frederick Douglass High School in Baltimore in 1925 and then enrolled in Lincoln University in Chester, Pennsylvania, which had been chartered in 1854 as the nation's first institution of higher learning for blacks. He graduated cum laude in 1930, and shortly before he did, he married Vivian Burey, known as "Buster." Prevented by his race from attending the University of Maryland School of Law, Marshall pursued a legal education at Howard University instead. He graduated first in his class in 1933, was admitted to the Maryland bar, and began a law practice on his own in Baltimore.

Within a short time, Marshall was handling cases in association with the National Association for the Advancement of Colored People (NAACP). Perhaps most notable, in 1935 he assisted in pressing legal claims before the Maryland Court of Appeals that forced the University of Maryland School of Law to admit its first African-American student. The following year, Charles Hamilton Houston, who had been vice-dean of the Howard Law School while Marshall had been a student, invited Marshall to join him in New York as special assistant legal counsel to the NAACP. In 1938 Houston resigned as special counsel to the NAACP, and Marshall took his place. He was 30 years old at the time. A year later, the NAACP created the Legal Defense and Educational Fund to wage war against racial segregation and Marshall was chosen to be its director. In this position, he coordinated the litigation strategies that challenged segregation in a series of cases. By 1943 he had begun to press the cause of equal rights before the Supreme Court itself, and in the years that followed, he would serve as an advocate in cases whose holdings inched steadily closer to the dismantling of segregation. In *Smith v. Allwright* (1944), for example, he helped persuade the Court to declare unconstitutional the "whites-only" Democratic primary in Texas. Six years later he was back before the Court, winning a declaration in *Sweatt v. Painter* (1950) that Texas's refusal to admit a black applicant to the University of Texas Law School and its attempt to establish a parallel law school for blacks violated the equal protection clause.

With these and many other constitutional triumphs, for which Marshall earned renown as "Mr. Civil Rights," he eventually pursued the lion of segregation into the den of public education. Finally, in *Brown v. Board of Education* (1954), Marshall coordinated the litigation strategy that insisted on naming segregated public schools inherently unequal. On May 17, 1954, the Supreme Court announced its agreement in the case: that segregation in public schools violated the Constitution's equal protection guarantee. This ground-breaking ruling eventually spelled the end of government-sanctioned racial segregation not only in public schools but in all public facilities. The following year, however, disappointment followed fast on the heels of this victory. The Supreme Court declined to order immediate integration of previously segregated public school districts, declaring instead that schools had to integrate "with all deliberate speed." And on a personal level, Marshall's wife, Vivian, died of cancer in February 1955. At the end of that year, Marshall remarried, and with his new wife, Cecilia Suyat, he had two sons: Thurgood, Jr., and John William.

On September 23, 1961, after Marshall had devoted nearly a quarter-century to civil rights litigation, President John F. Kennedy appointed him to sit on the U.S. Court of Appeals for the Second Circuit. Resistance to the appointment from southern senators delayed Marshall's confirmation almost a year. But finally, on September 11, 1962, the Senate confirmed his nomination by a vote of 54-16. After Marshall had spent four years on the federal appeals court, President Lyndon B. Johnson appointed him solicitor general of the U.S. in July 1965. The solicitor general represents the U.S. government in cases before the Supreme Court, and Marshall's appointment made him the first African American to hold this prestigious post, often a stepping stone to a seat on the Supreme Court itself. In fact, on June 13, 1967, President Johnson nominated Marshall to become an associate justice, replacing Tom C. Clark of Texas, who had retired from the Court after Johnson had made Clark's son, Ramsey, attorney general. After the Senate confirmed the appointment by a vote of 69-11 on August 30, Marshall became the first African-American justice on the Court.

During the first part of his 24-year career on the Court, Marshall joined the solid liberal majority led by Chief Justice Earl Warren. He thus participated in the later part of the Warren court's constitutional revolution, which aggressively championed individual rights and liberties. He wrote, for example, the opinion in *Stanley v. Georgia* (1969), decided in Warren's last term as chief justice, which held that states could not punish the private possession of obscene materials in a home. After Earl Warren's departure, however, and his replacement by Chief Justice Warren E. Burger, the Court tilted to a more conservative perspective, and consequently Marshall often found himself in a dissenter's position in the years that followed. For example, he was part of the majority that temporarily halted capital punishment in the United States in *Furman v. Georgia* (1972) on the grounds that the death penalty, as then executed by the states, was cruel and unusual. But after states revised their capital punishment schemes and the Supreme Court approved these revisions beginning in *Gregg v. Georgia* (1976), Marshall joined with William Brennan, Jr., to dissent in every case that upheld the death penalty.

In contrast with some conservative justices on the Court, Marshall denied that the Constitution had to be strictly construed according to the understanding of its original 18th-century framers. In fact, during the country's celebration of the Constitution's bicentennial, Marshall had pointed words about the virtue of the founding document, as originally framed:

> I do not believe that the meaning of the Constitution was forever "fixed" at the Philadelphia Convention. Nor do I find the wisdom, foresight, and sense of justice exhibited by the framers particularly profound. To the contrary, the government they devised was defective from the start, requiring several amendments, a civil war, and momentous social transformation to attain the system of constitutional government, and its respect for the individual freedoms and human rights, that we hold as fundamental today. . . . If we seek . . . a sensitive understanding of the Constitution's inherent defects, and its promising evolution through 200 years of history, the celebration of the "Miracle at Philadelphia" will, in my view, be a far more meaningful and humbling experience.

Those who celebrated the Constitution's birth were off the mark, according to Marshall. The "true miracle," he declared, "was not the birth of the Constitution, but its life." For Justice Marshall, the amendments to the Constitution made after the Civil War—especially the Fourteenth Amendment, which guaranteed due process of law and the equal protection of the laws—had inaugurated a new era of constitutional history by finally giving legal expression to Jefferson's declaration that "all men are created equal."

Marshall retired from the Court on June 27, 1991. He was 82 years old at the time, with more than a half-century behind him as the champion of equal rights and civil liberties, first as a lawyer and later as a judge. He lived for another year and a half before dying of heart failure on January 24, 1993, in Washington, D.C., at the age of 84.

Across more than half a century, Marshall championed the cause of civil rights and civil liberties. The first 25 years of his labor were perhaps the most productive, when he served as field marshal for the battle against racial discrimination and laid a formidable ax to the root of segregation. *Brown v. Board of Education*

(1954) was his greatest triumph in his life as a lawyer, a constitutional victory sufficient to honor him in perpetuity even had he never sat on the nation's highest court. But he added to a brilliant career as a civil rights lawyer more than two and a half decades of service on the Supreme Court, where he continued to wage war for the rights and liberties of Americans.

Further Reading

Ball, Howard. *A Defiant Life: Thurgood Marshall and the Persistence of Racism in America*. New York: Crown Publishers, 1998.

Fenderson, Lewis H. *Thurgood Marshall: Fighter for Justice*. New York: McGraw-Hill, 1969.

Goldman, Roger L. *Thurgood Marshall: Justice for All*. New York: Carroll & Graf Publishers, Inc., 1992.

Rowan, Carl Thomas. *Dream Makers, Dream Breakers: The World of Justice Thurgood Marshall*. Boston: Little, Brown & Company, 1993.

Tushnet, Mark. *Making Civil Rights Law: Thurgood Marshall and the Supreme Court, 1936–1961*. New York: Oxford University Press, 1994.

———. *Making Civil Rights Law: Thurgood Marshall and the Supreme Court, 1961–1991*. New York: Oxford University Press, 1997.

Williams, Juan. *Thurgood Marshall: American Revolutionary*. New York: Times Books, 1998.

Warren Earl Burger (1907–1995)

Chief Justice, 1969–1986

Appointed by President Richard M. Nixon

Warren Earl Burger
(United States Supreme Court)

Warren Earl Burger, the 15th chief justice of the U.S. Supreme Court, tends to fare poorly in comparisons with his predecessor, Earl Warren. Burger was the reverse of Earl Warren not only in name but in judicial philosophy: conservative where Warren was liberal, devoted to law and order where Warren was devoted to the protection of the rights of criminal defendants. Earl Warren led his colleagues in a constitutional revolution that made the Court an aggressive ally of individual rights and liberties against countervailing governmental interests. President Richard M. Nixon appointed Warren Burger to undo Earl Warren's revolution, but Burger proved incapable of doing so. In some cases Burger's court managed to limit the further expansion of Warren court doctrines, but in others it actually expanded on beginnings made during the Warren court years. This was the great irony of the Burger years: He eventually aided and reaffirmed the revolution that many had hoped he would reverse.

—∞—

Warren Earl Burger was born on September 17, 1907, in St. Paul, Minnesota, to Charles Joseph Burger and Katharine Schnittger Burger. Burger's father worked as a rail cargo inspector and, occasionally, as a salesman. After graduating from John A. Johnson High School in St. Paul, Burger won a scholarship to Princeton University, but not one sufficient to cover his financial needs. Instead of Princeton, Burger enrolled in night classes at the University of Minnesota in 1925, supporting himself by selling insurance during the day. He continued his insurance job when he began taking night courses at St. Paul College of Law (later to become the William Mitchell College of Law) in 1927. Four years later he graduated magna cum laude and was admitted to the Minnesota bar.

After law school Burger joined the firm of Boyesen, Otis & Farley in St. Paul while continuing his relationship with the St. Paul College of Law by teaching contract law as an adjunct professor. In 1933 he married Elvera Stromberg, and the couple eventually had two children. Burger applied the same work ethic that had seen him through college and law school to his legal practice, focusing on corporate, real estate, and probate work with energy and success sufficient to see him soon made a partner in his firm. He plunged into civic and political affairs with equal zeal, serving as president of St. Paul's Junior Chamber of Commerce and helping to organize St. Paul's Council on Human Relations, which sought to combat racial discrimination. Burger also supported the political aspirations of Harold E. Stassen, who was elected the Republican governor of Minnesota in 1938 at the age of 31. Burger followed Stassen onto the national political stage, serving as Stassen's floor manager during the Republican national convention of 1952 and helping to orchestrate the decision of Minnesota Republicans to eventually cast their lot with Dwight D. Eisenhower as the Republican candidate for president.

After Eisenhower won the general election, he rewarded Burger's support by naming him assistant attorney general for the Claims Division of the Department of Justice (later to become the Civil Division) in 1953. In this position, Burger found himself in charge of the federal government's civil cases. But Eisenhower soon found another place for Burger when a vacancy appeared on the prestigious U.S. Court of Appeals for the District of Columbia in 1956. In his 13 years on the federal appeals court, Burger established a reputation as a moderately conservative judge, hostile to the revolutionary changes then being accomplished on behalf of the rights of criminal defendants by the Supreme Court, led by Chief Justice Earl Warren, the man whose seat Burger would one day occupy.

Toward the end of the 1960s, Earl Warren privately disclosed his intent to resign from the Court to President Lyndon B. Johnson, as he wanted to give Johnson the opportunity of naming his replacement. Johnson promptly attempted to elevate his friend, Associate Justice Abe Fortas, to the Court's chief seat. But the plan backfired when Republican opposition, fueled by the discovery that Fortas had engaged in a questionable financial arrangement after joining the Court, ultimately forced Johnson to withdraw Fortas's nomination without enough time remaining in his presidency to find a replacement. The chance to appoint Warren's successor thus fell to President Richard M. Nixon. Nixon, like Burger, opposed the Warren court's activism in the protection of the rights of criminal defendants. Burger's moderate conservativism, his harmony with the president on the issue of criminal procedure, and his 13 years of experience on the federal bench therefore combined to make him Nixon's choice for chief justice. Nixon announced his nomination of Burger as chief justice on May 21, 1969, and the Senate confirmed the appointment two weeks later by a vote of 74-3.

Whatever counterrevolution Nixon may have imagined that Burger would launch against the activism of the Warren years never appeared. In the area of constitutional protections for criminal defendants, for example, the high-water mark of the Warren court's constitutional revolution was represented by a trilogy of cases: *Mapp v. Ohio* (1961), which prohibited states from using evidence from illegal searches or seizures in the prosecution of criminal defendants; *Gideon v. Wainwright* (1963), which guaranteed a state criminal defendant an attorney at the state's expense in serious criminal cases; and *Miranda v. Arizona* (1963), which required police to advise suspects of their right to remain silent and to have counsel appointed for them. Burger's court never overruled these precedents, and they remain valid into the 21st century.

In other areas of constitutional law, the Burger court actually expanded on key elements of the Warren court revolution. Where the Warren court had applied the constitutional requirement of equal protection to begin the eradication of racial discrimination from American society, the Burger court extended the protection of the equal protection clause to other forms of discrimination. Burger, for example, wrote the opinion for the Court in *Reed v. Reed* (1971), which was the first decision in the Court's history to declare discrimination on the grounds of gender unconstitutional under the Fourteenth Amendment's equal protection clause. The Burger court also reinforced the principle of church-state separation that had been made emphatic by the Warren court's decisions in *Engel v. Vitale* (1962) and *Abington School District v. Schempp* (1963), declaring state-sponsored prayers and Bible readings in public schools unconstitutional. Burger, again, wrote the Court's opinion in *Lemon v. Kurtzman* (1974), which found unconstitutional a variety of state aid to parochial schools. Most controversially, the Burger court expanded the right of privacy recognized by the Warren court in *Griswold v. Connecticut* (1965) as protecting the right of married couples to use contraceptives to include the right of women to have an abortion in *Roe v. Wade* (1973).

The increasing conservativism of the Burger court, though it proved unable to repudiate wholesale the legacy of the Warren court, nevertheless managed to limit the force of this legacy in some cases. While not abandoning *Mapp v. Ohio*'s rule requiring the exclusion of illegally obtained evidence in criminal proceedings, for example, the Burger court made it easier for law enforcement personnel to search for and seize evidence. Similarly, Burger created an important exception to previously established principles of church-state separation when he declared for the Court in *Marsh v. Chambers* (1984) that the First Amendment's establishment clause did not forbid a state from opening legislative sessions with prayer.

Perhaps the greatest irony of President Nixon's hoped-for constitutional counterrevolution was Burger's opinion for the Court in *United States v. Nixon* (1974). In this case, Nixon found himself personally the subject of a historic constitutional dispute when he attempted to resist a subpoena directing him to produce secretly recorded White House tapes that eventually implicated him in the Watergate controversy. Nixon's claim that he should not have to turn over the tapes fell on the stony ears of the Burger court, and Burger himself announced the Court's opinion requiring Nixon to produce the tapes. Three weeks after this court order, Nixon resigned the presidency.

The chief justice of the Supreme Court not only manages the work of the Court but also serves as the administrative head of the entire federal judicial system. In the latter capacity, Burger proved to be an energetic administrator, and he used his position to encourage reforms in the administration of state as well as federal courts. He helped to establish the Institute for Court Management and the National Center for State Courts. With a sometimes critical eye, Burger also focused his attention on the legal profession at large, and he encouraged the creation of the American Inns of Court, an organization of local chapters dedicated to encouraging standards of professionalism and excellence among lawyers.

After 17 years as chief justice, Warren Burger resigned from the Court on September 26, 1986. For the next six years he served as chairman of the Commission on the Bicentennial of the U.S. Constitution and as chancellor of the College of William and Mary from 1986 to 1993. He died in Washington, D.C. of congestive heart failure on June 25, 1995, at the age of 87.

The Burger court has been dubbed "the counterrevolution that wasn't." It inherited sweeping changes accomplished by the Warren court in areas as diverse as criminal procedure and privacy rights and proved either unwilling or unable to reverse them. On some issues, such as the rights of criminal defendants, Burger led his Court to contain the constitutional protections established by the Warren court without overruling the cases that had established those protections. On other issues, such as the right to privacy, the Court under Warren Burger took emphatic strides forward by expanding it to include the right of women to obtain an abortion. Overall, however, Burger tends to be rated poorly as a leader of the Court.

FURTHER READING

Blasi, Vincent. *The Burger Court: The Counter-Revolution that Wasn't*. New Haven: Yale University Press, 1983.

Burger, Warren E. *It Is So Ordered: A Constitution Unfolds*. New York: William Morrow and Company, 1995.

Lamb, Charles M. "Chief Justice Warren E. Burger: A Conservative Chief for Conservative Times." In *The Burger Court: Political and Judicial Profiles*. Edited by Charles M. Lamb and Stephen C. Halpern. Urbana: University of Illinois Press, 1991.

Schwartz, Bernard, ed. *The Burger Court: Counter-Revolution or Confirmation?* New York: Oxford University Press, 1998.

Schwartz, Herman. *The Burger Years: Rights and Wrongs in the Supreme Court, 1969–1986*. New York: Viking, 1987.

"A Tribute to Chief Justice Warren E. Burger." *Harvard Law Review* 100 (1987): 969–1001.

HARRY ANDREW BLACKMUN (1908–1999)

Associate Justice, 1970–1990

Appointed by President Richard M. Nixon

HARRY A. BLACKMUN
(United States Supreme Court)

Harry A. Blackmun arrived on the Supreme Court slightly less than a year after his friend, Warren E. Burger, became chief justice. The two men had known each other since their childhood days in St. Paul, Minnesota, and Blackmun had served as Burger's best man in his wedding. The president who appointed them to the Court had every confidence that the two men, dubbed the "Minnesota twins" by the press, would serve in the vanguard of a counterrevolution against the judicial activism of the Court under its former chief justice, Earl Warren. But this confidence proved to be misplaced. The "Minnesota twins" remained friends but found themselves more and more on opposite spectrums of the Court, as Blackmun increasingly championed the cause of individual rights and thus drifted into a constitutional orbit separate from that of the chief justice.

Harry Andrew Blackmun was born on November 12, 1908, in Nashville, Illinois, the son of Corwin Blackmun and Theo Reuter Blackmun. While he was still a child his family moved to St. Paul, Minnesota, where Harry grew up. Upon graduation from high school, he received a scholarship from the Harvard Club of Minnesota that sent him to Harvard University in Cambridge, Massachusetts. At Harvard, while working a variety of jobs to meet expenses, Blackmun majored in mathematics. He graduated summa cum laude and Phi Beta Kappa in 1929. He considered studying medicine but determined instead to pursue a legal career, attending Harvard Law School and graduating in 1932.

Once out of law school, Blackmun was admitted to the bar in Minnesota and then worked briefly as a judicial clerk for Judge John B. Sanborn on the U.S. Court of Appeals for the Eighth Circuit. Thereafter Blackmun joined the Minneapolis firm of Dorsey, Colman, Barker, Scott, and Barber, where he practiced for 16 years in the areas of tax, estates, and general civil litigation. In addition to this practice, Blackmun taught courses at the St. Paul College of Law and the University of Minnesota Law School. He married Dorothy E. Clark in 1941, and together the couple had three daughters: Nancy, Sally, and Susan. Blackmun's abiding interest in medicine found an outlet in 1950 when he became counsel for the Mayo Clinic, a position he held until 1959.

After nearly a decade at the Mayo Clinic, Blackmun was appointed to the U.S. Court of Appeals for the Eighth Circuit by President Dwight D. Eisenhower in 1959, replacing the judge for whom he had clerked some 17 years before, John Sanborn. On the Eighth Circuit, Blackmun earned a reputation as a hardworking and studious judge of moderate, conservative leanings.

In 1970 Blackmun became President Richard M. Nixon's third choice to fill the seat on the Supreme Court recently vacated by Abe Fortas, who had resigned after being accused of engaging in financial improprieties while on the Court. Nixon had originally attempted to place Clement F. Haynsworth, Jr., in Fortas's seat. Haynsworth was a judge on the U.S. Fourth Circuit Court of Appeals whose nomination failed to win confirmation in the Senate by a vote of 55-45 in November 1969. Nixon subsequently nominated G. Harrold Carswell, a judge on the U.S. Fifth Circuit Court of Appeals. The Senate rejected Carswell by a vote of 51-45 in April 1970, after his abilities had been questioned; Republican senator Roman Hruska of Nebraska won Carswell a footnote in Supreme Court history by insisting to the Senate that even those who are mediocre are "entitled to a little representation." Finally, Nixon nominated Harry Blackmun on April 15, 1970. A month later the Senate, impressed with his competence and moderate conservativism and perhaps weary of confirmation battles, unanimously confirmed Harry Blackmun as an associate justice of the Supreme Court on May 12, 1970. Thereafter, Blackmun would jokingly refer to himself as "Old Number Three."

Nixon's second appointment to the Supreme Court seemed at first destined to make good the press's reference to him and Chief Justice Burger as the "Minnesota twins," as Blackmun voted regularly with Burger during his first year on the Court. But he gradually veered away from the chief to the left—or, as he described it, the Court veered away from Blackmun to the right. Whatever the truth is, Justice Blackmun often began to find himself in the judicial company of more liberal justices such as William Brennan, Jr., and Thurgood Marshall. A key to this transition was Blackmun's opinion for the Court in the controversial abortion case, *Roe v. Wade* (1973).

The decade before the *Roe* decision, in *Griswold v. Connecticut* (1965), the Court had recognized a constitutional right of privacy that prohibited a state from making it a crime to use contraceptives. In *Roe v. Wade* (1973), the Court was urged to take the controversial step of extending this right of privacy to include the right of women to obtain an abortion. The

Court, speaking through Blackmun, made precisely this step. "The Court has recognized," Blackmun wrote, "that a right of personal privacy or a guarantee of certain areas or zone of privacy, does exist under the Constitution. . . . This right of privacy . . . is broad enough to encompass a woman's decision whether or not to terminate her pregnancy." Blackmun reasoned that the right to an abortion was a "fundamental" right, thus requiring that government demonstrate an overwhelmingly persuasive justification for any limits imposed on this right. He then considered two interests offered to justify the restrictions on abortion before the Court: first, the interest of a state in protecting the health of pregnant women; and second, the interest of a state in preserving the life of the unborn child. The essence of Blackmun's opinion for the Court was to contemplate a typical nine-month pregnancy as consisting of three periods, or "trimesters." He concluded that during the first trimester, the state's interest neither in the health of a pregnant woman nor in the life of the fetus was sufficient to justify any restriction on the woman's right to an abortion. During the second trimester, he found, a state might properly impose such restrictions as were necessary to preserve the health of pregnant women seeking an abortion. Finally, Blackmun reasoned that during the third trimester, a state had a sufficient interest in both the health of the mother and the life of the fetus to ban abortions altogether, as long as the ban did not adversely affect the life or the health of the mother.

In the years that followed, Blackmun became a symbol of odium for pro-life forces outraged at the Court's decision in *Roe* and determined to unsettle it. But he remained a resolute supporter of abortion rights and publicly lamented the Court's direction at the end of the 1980s, when it began to approve some restrictions on the abortion right. In *Webster v. Reproductive Health Services* (1989), he dissented from the Court's decision to approve some restrictions on abortions, prognosticating that a new majority on the Court was but a step away from overruling *Roe v. Wade* altogether and lamenting that "the signs are evident and very ominous, and a chill wind blows." Three years later, in *Planned Parenthood v. Casey* (1992), the Court approved new limits on abortions while still preserving the basic right recognized in *Roe*. "[N]ow, just when so many expected the darkness to fall, the flame has grown bright," Blackmun wrote of the Court's reaffirmation of the abortion right. But four justices were prepared to overrule *Roe* altogether, and the aging Blackmun found this reality profoundly disturbing. "I fear for the darkness," he wrote, "as four Justices anxiously await the single vote necessary to extinguish the light."

Over nearly a quarter of a century, Justice Harry Blackmun made a remarkable odyssey from being a conservative centrist to a staunch liberal. His decision in *Roe v. Wade* (1973) was surely the most pronounced landmark in this journey but certainly not its only prominent feature. By the end of his tenure on the Court, Blackmun was, by some accounts, its most emphatically liberal justice. The man appointed to carry out the constitutional vision of a law-and-order president found himself at the end dissenting—alone—against the very idea of capital punishment, that jewel in the crown of law and order. In the winter of his final term on the Court, he penned a lone dissent when the Court declined to hear the appeal of a man condemned to be executed in Texas.

> From this day forward, I no longer shall tinker with the machinery of death. For more than 20 years I have endeavored—indeed, I have struggled—along with a majority of this Court, to develop procedural and substantive rules that would lend more than the mere appearance of fairness to the death penalty endeavor. Rather than continue to coddle the Court's delusion that the desired level of fairness has been achieved and the need for regulation eviscerated, I feel morally and intellectually obligated simply to concede that the death penalty experiment has failed. It is virtually self-evident to me now that no combination of procedural rules or substantive reg-

> ulations ever can save the death penalty from its inherent constitutional deficiencies. The basic question—does the system accurately and consistently determine which defendants "deserve" to die?—cannot be answered in the affirmative. . . . The problem is that the inevitability of factual, legal, and moral error gives us a system that we know must wrongly kill some defendants, a system that fails to deliver the fair, consistent, and reliable sentences of death required by the Constitution.

Within a few months of this opinion, Justice Blackmun retired on July 29, 1994. Nearly five years later he died on March 4, 1999, of complications suffered after hip-replacement surgery.

—∾—

In his dealings with others, Harry Blackmun was invariably generous and modest, so much so that fellow Minnesotan Garrison Keillor once called him "the shy person's justice." But in spite of his mild and gentle temperament, Blackmun never escaped the furor of those who considered his *Roe* opinion an abomination. "Murderer," "butcher of Dachau," and "Pontius Pilate" they called him in outpourings of hate mail that exceeded any received in response to other opinions of the 20th century. "I'll carry this one to my grave," Blackmun said of his opinion in *Roe*. Of course, the same opinion that earned Blackmun infamy in some quarters of American society earned him the lasting admiration of others. For many, Blackmun's transition from a Nixon law-and-order appointee to a liberal stalwart was a pilgrimage from darkness into light, from a sterile preoccupation with law to a sympathetic focus on the law's effects on people. As one of his former judicial clerks described Blackmun's ultimate judicial philosophy, "He never started with the law. He started with the people and how the law might affect them."

FURTHER READING

Coyne, Randall. "Making the Progress of a Humane Justice: Harry Blackmun's Death Penalty Epiphany." *University of Kansas Law Review* 43 (1995): 367–416.

"In Memoriam: Harry A. Blackmun." *Harvard Law Review* 113 (1999): 1–25.

"In Memoriam: Justice Harry A. Blackmun, Principle and Compassion." *Columbia Law Review* 99 (1999): x–1412.

King, Jeffrey B. "Now Turn to the Left: The Changing Ideology of Justice Harry A. Blackmun." *Houston Law Review* 33 (1996): 277–297.

"Symposium: The Jurisprudence of Justice Harry A. Blackmun." *Hastings Constitutional Law Quarterly* 26 (1998): 1–305.

Wasby, Stephen L. "Justice Harry A. Blackmun: Transformation from 'Minnesota Twin' to Independent Voice." In *The Burger Court: Political and Judicial Profiles.* Edited by Charles M. Lamb and Stephen C. Halpern. Urbana: University of Illinois Press, 1991.

Lewis Franklin Powell, Jr. (1907–1998)

Associate Justice, 1972–1987

Appointed by President Richard M. Nixon

Lewis F. Powell, Jr.
(United States Supreme Court)

Lewis Powell came to the Supreme Court reluctantly, at the age of 64, when he might have retired from an already illustrious legal career. But his family, his friends, and his president urged him to undertake further service as a Supreme Court justice, and to his previous legal career Powell eventually added 15 years as an associate justice on the nation's highest court. A gentlemanly Virginian, he brought with him to the Court a civility and courtesy that made him universally well-liked. He was also the centrist on the Burger court, and his moderate political temper made him the swing vote in a series of important cases.

—ɱ—

Lewis Franklin Powell, Jr., was born on September 19, 1907, in Suffolk, Virginia, the eldest child of Lewis F. Powell (who changed the spelling of his first name to "Louis" shortly before his son was born) and Mary Lewis Gwathmey Powell. He was related to Captain Nathaniel Powell, one of the original Jamestown settlers and an acting governor of the colony in the 17th century. Lewis grew up in Richmond, Virginia, where his father ran a successful business making a variety of wooden and corrugated boxes. His early education was in public schools, but he entered McGuire's University School in Richmond when he was 14 years old.

When the time came for Powell to attend college, he chose to enroll in Washington and Lee rather than, as his father wished, the University of Virginia. In 1929 he obtained his B.S. magna cum laude and Phi Beta Kappa, from the School of Commerce and Administration, and two years later he graduated first in his class from the Washington and Lee Law School. At the insistence of his father, who wanted the best educational opportunities for his son, Powell followed his career at Washington and Lee with a year at Harvard Law School, where he received his master's degree in law in June 1932.

After Harvard, Powell returned home to Richmond, where he took a position with the law firm of Christian, Barton, and Parker. By 1934 he had left this firm to join Hunton, Williams, Anderson, Gay, and Moore, Richmond's largest law firm. Two years later, on May 2, 1926, he married Josephine ("Jo") M. Rucker, with whom he had four children: Josephine McRae, Ann Pendleton, Mary Lewis Gwathmey, and Lewis F. Powell, III. Powell was a trial lawyer in the early days of his legal practice, but over the years he gradually spent more time advising and assisting corporations in the conduct of their businesses. In 1938 his firm made him a partner in less than half the time normally required for this advancement. Three years later, the Japanese attack on Pearl Harbor plunged the nation into World War II, and Powell wasted no time in trying to find a place in the military. He attempted to join the navy but was turned down when he failed to pass the eye exam. After enlisting in the army, Powell was eventually assigned to the Military Intelligence Service of the War Department, where he worked on the Ultra project, which involved the deciphering and use of German radio communications encrypted by the Enigma machine. After three and a half years of military service, Powell finally returned home to Richmond and his law firm in November 1945.

After the war, Powell combined an increasingly prominent corporate legal practice with a wide variety of civic activities. He was appointed to the Richmond School Board in 1950, elected in his own right in 1951, and made chairman from 1952 to 1961. From 1961 to 1969, he was a member of the Virginia State Board of Education, serving as its president from 1968 to 1969. These were turbulent years, as the state of Virginia first pledged massive resistance against desegregation and then reluctantly and slowly began to dismantle its segregated systems of public schools. Although Powell privately opposed Virginia's policy of resistance to the Supreme Court decision in *Brown v. Board of Education* (1954) that declared segregation illegal, he would later be criticized for having done little publicly to further desegregation efforts, either while on the Richmond School Board or while on the State Board of Education. During the 1960s, Powell also served as president of two prestigious legal organizations: the American Bar Association and the American College of Trial Lawyers. By the end of the decade he clearly was numbered among the most prominent lawyers in the nation.

By the beginning of the 1970s, Lewis Powell was nearing his mid-60s and had already compiled an impressive record as a lawyer and a citizen. But a further calling still lay in front of him. In September 1971 Justice Hugo Black retired from the Court, enabling President Richard M. Nixon to make his third appointment to the Court. The previous year, after Justice Abe Fortas had resigned, the president had suffered two embarrassing political defeats when he attempted to appoint first one and then another southerner to fill Fortas's seat—Clement Haynsworth, Jr., and G. Harrold

Carswell. Though Powell was a Democrat, he was nevertheless moderately conservative and seemed to share some of Nixon's law-and-order priorities. Moreover, his stature within the American bar made it unlikely that his appointment would receive the same rough senatorial treatment as Haysworth's and Carswell's had. Thus, on October 22, 1971, Nixon nominated Powell as an associate justice; on December 6, by a vote of 89-1, the Senate confirmed the nomination. Powell took the oath of office as an associate justice on the Supreme Court on January 7, 1972, beginning a 16-year career of service on the Court.

In cases involving the rights of criminal suspects and defendants, Powell's decisions on the Court generally vindicated Nixon's expectations. He tended to side with conservative colleagues who, while not overruling those cases decided the previous decade that had greatly expanded the constitutional protections in the criminal process, nevertheless managed to construe these protections narrowly in many cases. He also dissented vehemently when a bare majority of the Court pronounced a national moratorium on the death penalty in *Furman v. Georgia* (1972). Four years later, in *Gregg v. Georgia* (1976), Powell joined two other centrist justices on the Court in a controlling opinion that upheld the constitutionality of the death penalty as long as certain requirements were met.

During the decade of the 1970s, the Court wrestled with the question of whether and to what extent the Constitution protected certain unnamed or unenumerated rights. Powell hovered at the Court's center on these questions. He joined in the majority opinion in *Roe v. Wade* (1973), which found that the Constitution protected a woman's right to an abortion as fundamental. But that same year, he wrote the opinion for the Court in *San Antonio v. Rodriguez* (1973), which denied that there was a fundamental right to a public education. In *Rodriguez*, children in poorer Texas school districts had complained that the state's reliance on local property taxes to fund a significant portion of public education denied them an equal educational opportunity, since their districts contained less property wealth and therefore generated less revenue from property taxes. Powell, though—long experienced in public school affairs himself—declared for the Court that the interest in maintaining local control over public schools was sufficient to justify the inequalities inevitably produced by reliance on property taxes to finance public education. The following decade, Powell cast the decisive vote—one he later believed to have been wrong—in the Supreme Court's decision upholding a state antisodomy statute in *Bowers v. Hardwick* (1986).

Powell's position at the center of the Court was nowhere more apparent than in his opinion in *Regents of the University of California v. Bakke* (1978). The case posed the issue of whether a medical school's affirmative action program violated the equal protection clause of the Fourteenth Amendment. The Court split sharply over the issue, with four justices prepared to uphold both a fixed quota for racial minorities and a more informal use of minority status as a "plus" factor in the admissions determination, and four justices adamant that both forms of affirmative action violated federal civil rights laws. Powell lay squarely in the middle of these polar positions. He concluded in an opinion that controlled the case that the use of a fixed racial quota violated the equal protection clause but that universities might use an applicant's status as a racial minority as one "plus" factor among others designed to increase the educational diversity of an institution. Powell's middle position became the law of the land.

On June 26, 1987, the man who had reluctantly accepted an appointment to the Court retired from it with equal reluctance. Powell hesitated to give up the work in which he found great reward, but his strength had begun to diminish. After retirement, he continued to hear cases on the federal court of appeals and taught courses at the University of Virginia Law School and Washington and Lee

University School of Law. He died of pneumonia in his sleep in Richmond, Virginia, on August 25, 1998. He was 90 years old.

—⁂—

The high Court has had its share of irascible personalities who brought no courtliness with them to their responsibilities. Powell, though, is remembered as having graced the Court with more than the usual measure of kindliness and civility. Like other justices who brought no clearly articulated ideology with them to their work on the Court, Justice Powell left a judicial record that has seemed to some observers unpredictable. Defying labels such as conservative or liberal, he brought a sympathetic attentiveness to each case at hand. Although this temperament denied him a first place among the ranks of the Court's great intellects, it made him an influential justice in his own day.

Further Reading

Freeman, George Clemon, Jr. "Justice Powell's Constitutional Opinions." *Washington and Lee Law Review* 45 (1988): 411–465.

Jeffries, John Calvin, Jr. *Justice Lewis F. Powell, Jr.* New York: Charles Scribner's Sons, 1994.

"In Memoriam: Lewis F. Powell, Jr." *Harvard Law Review* 112 (1999): x–610.

"In Memoriam: Writing for Justice Powell." *Columbia Law Review* 99 (1999): viii–551.

Landynski, Jacob W. "Justice Lewis F. Powell, Jr.: Balance Wheel of the Court." In *The Burger Court: Political and Judicial Profiles.* Edited by Charles M. Lamb and Stephen C. Halpern. Urbana: University of Illinois Press, 1991.

"Symposium in Honor of Justice Lewis F. Powell, Jr." *Virginia Law Review* 68 (1982): 161–458.

"A Tribute to Justice Lewis F. Powell, Jr." *Harvard Law Review* 101 (1987): 395–420.

William Hubbs Rehnquist (1924–)

Associate Justice, 1972–1986

Appointed by President Richard M. Nixon

Chief Justice, 1986–

Appointed by President Ronald Reagan

William H. Rehnquist
(United States Supreme Court)

Not a few presidents have been disappointed by their nominees to the Supreme Court. Presumed liberals have drifted to the right, law-and-order conservatives to the left. But William H. Rehnquist, the 20th century's last chief justice, almost surely disappointed neither Richard M. Nixon—the president who made him an associate justice on the Court—nor Ronald Reagan—the president who advanced him to the Court's chief seat. Rehnquist has been predictably conservative throughout a long public career, including nearly 30 years on the Supreme Court. He was the Burger court's most conservative member, and as chief justice he has helped to steer the Court toward a renewed respect for state power in the federal system and for a more hospitable regard for government interests over those of individuals.

—∞—

William Hubbs Rehnquist was born in Milwaukee, Wisconsin, on October 1, 1924, the son of William B. Rehnquist, a wholesale paper salesman, and Margery Peck Rehnquist. In the suburban household in which William grew up, conservativism and Republicanism saturated the atmosphere of his childhood and youth. After graduating from high school in Shorewood, Wisconsin, he attended Keynon College in Ohio for a year before joining the Army Air Corp in 1943 and spending the next three years as a weather observer in North Africa.

After World War II, Rehnquist used the G.I. Bill and a willingness to hold a steady stream of part-time jobs to attend Stanford University, where he earned a bachelor's and a master's degree in political science. He added to this a master's degree from Harvard in government before returning to Stanford for law school. The man who would one day be chief justice graduated first in his class of 1952. The class's third position that year went to a woman who would one day join Rehnquist on the Supreme Court: Sandra Day O'Connor. Upon graduating from law school, Rehnquist accepted a judicial clerkship with Associate Justice Robert H. Jackson on the Supreme Court. As a clerk, Rehnquist wrote a memorandum for Justice Jackson as the Court was preparing to consider *Brown v. Board of Education* (1954), the case that eventually held racial segregation in public schools unconstitutional. The memorandum argued that *Plessy v. Ferguson* (1896), which had approved segregation under the "separate but equal" doctrine, was rightly decided and should be followed in *Brown*.

In 1953 Rehnquist married Natalie Cornell. This marriage lasted until Natalie's death in 1991 and produced three children: James, Janet, and Nancy. Rehnquist and his wife moved to Phoenix, Arizona, where he practiced law from 1953 until 1969. He became active in Republican party politics in Phoenix and campaigned for Barry Goldwater, the Republican candidate in the 1964 elections. His political activity brought him into contact with another Phoenix lawyer, Richard Kleindienst, who eventually became deputy attorney general under President Richard Nixon. Once Kleindienst was in this position, he found a place for Rehnquist in the Nixon administration as deputy attorney general in the Office of Legal Counsel of the Justice Department in 1969. Two years later, in September 1971, Justice John Marshall Harlan retired from the Court, giving Nixon the chance to make his fourth and last appointment to the Supreme Court. He chose William Rehnquist. Although the nomination met stiff resistance in the Senate, Rehnquist was confirmed by a vote of 68-26 on December 10, 1971. He thus began a career on the Court that would extend into the 21st century.

Rehnquist's conservative credentials were solidly in place before he advanced to the Court, and they did not waver after he arrived. In his early years on the Court, although he was the fourth Nixon appointee, he sometimes found himself the only justice of this group to carry the conservative vanguard in dissent. Most conspicuously, he alone of the Nixon appointees dissented from the Court's decision in *Roe v. Wade* (1973), recognizing a constitutional right of abortion. He was joined in that dissent by Justice Byron White, who had been appointed, curiously enough, by President John F. Kennedy. The same year, when the Court in *Frontiero v. Richardson* (1973) found that a federal law discriminated on the basis of gender by providing extra benefits to male members of the armed forces, Rehnquist dissented as well, this time alone.

Sometimes the other Nixon appointees joined Rehnquist in dissents, such as when Chief Justice Burger and Associate Justices Harry Blackmun and Lewis Powell dissented together with Rehnquist in *Furman v. Georgia* (1972), which temporarily invalidated the use of the death penalty as so arbitrary as to violate the Eighth Amendment's prohibition against "cruel and unusual punishment." But overall, Rehnquist outstripped the other Nixon appointees in his willingness to challenge what he viewed as overly broad readings of constitutional protections. Nixon, forced from office himself as a result of his role in the Watergate scandal, left no surer legacy on the Court than William Rehnquist.

As the 1970s progressed, Justice Rehnquist proved more successful in marshaling the Court's other nominally conservative justices in his campaign to revisit the relationship between states and the national government in the federal system. Prior to 1937, the Supreme Court had regularly rebuffed congressional attempts to regulate matters deemed by the Court to be properly within the province of states. But beginning in 1937, with the threat of President Franklin D. Roosevelt's "court-packing" plan, the Supreme Court abandoned this constitutional posture and gave a free rein to federal laws seeking to regulate a variety of economic and social matters. Rehnquist authored the Court's opinion in *National League of Cities v. Usery* (1976), which briefly reinvigorated the constitutional boundaries between states and the national government by holding that Congress had no authority to make certain minimum wage and maximum hour requirements of federal law applicable to state and municipal employees. Slightly less than a decade later, a new majority on the Court overruled *National League of Cities*. But in the 1990s, after Rehnquist became chief justice, he led the Court to other challenges of federal power over states.

In summer 1986 Chief Justice Warren E. Burger announced his intent to retire from the Court after 17 years of service. President Ronald Reagan promptly nominated Associate Justice William Rehnquist to become the Court's 16th chief justice. Confirmation debates in the Senate reprised those that had occurred 15 years earlier, on Rehnquist's original nomination to the Court. Finally, he was confirmed as chief justice by a vote of 65-13. He assumed his new office on September 26, 1986, the date Warren Burger formally retired from the Court.

Rehnquist was soon joined on the Court by two justices arguably even more conservative than he: Antonin Scalia, appointed by President Reagan to fill the position of associate justice that Rehnquist had vacated to become chief; and Clarence Thomas, appointed by President George H. W. Bush in 1991. No longer the principal conservative spokesman on the Court, Chief Justice Rehnquist seems to have paid more attention to the work of developing widespread agreement on important cases. Before he assumed the Court's chief seat, he had praised one of his predecessors, Charles Evans Hughes, for his efforts to build public confidence in the Court by seeking to present a uniform voice whenever possible, even when it meant resisting the urge to write dissenting opinions.

Nevertheless, the agreements to which Rehnquist led the Court were, in the main, conservative in nature. For example, in cases decided during the 1990s, the Rehnquist court sharply restricted the use of race-conscious affirmative action programs by requiring that they be justified by overwhelmingly persuasive reasons. Even more significant, the Court revisited the relationship between the national government and the states by imposing new limits on the power of Congress to pass legislation intended to regulate matters affecting interstate commerce and to protect various civil rights. In *Lopez v. United States* (1995), Rehnquist authored the Court's opinion holding that Congress lacked power under the commerce clause to criminalize the possession of guns near schools. The opinion in *Lopez* was the first occasion in more than half a century in which the Court had rebuffed a federal law passed under Congress's commerce power as regulating a subject not sufficiently connected with interstate commerce. The Court soon followed this decision with *United States v. Morrison* (2000), which declared that Congress lacked power under the commerce clause to make gender-related violence a federal crime.

Toward the end of the 1990s, the Rehnquist Court also restricted Congress's power to pass civil rights legislation that it believed necessary to guarantee the equal protection and due process of the laws. In *City of Boerne v. Flores* (1997), the Court declared unconstitutional an attempt by Congress to grant more protection for religious freedom than the Court itself had found warranted by the First Amendment's free exercise clause. This decision cast a shadow across a wide variety of civil rights legislation that Congress passed in the last three decades of the 20th century.

Chief Justice William Rehnquist arrived on the Supreme Court initially with a president's expectation that he would help to lead a counterrevolution against the liberal activism of the Court under Earl Warren in the 1950s and 1960s. But neither as an associate justice nor as chief justice has Rehnquist been able to accomplish the counterrevolution wished for by President Richard M. Nixon. By the end of the 20th century, most of Warren's legacy lay undisturbed, solidly entrenched within the fabric of contemporary constitutional doctrine. Nevertheless, Rehnquist participated in and later presided over an undoubtable shift by the Court toward more conservative stands on a wide range of constitutional questions. His Court has been especially vigilant in revisiting the appropriate constitutional boundaries between national and state legislative authority and has renewed a long-dormant debate about the values of federalism. This may be his most lasting contribution to the history of constitutional law.

Further Reading

Boles, Donald E. *Mr. Justice Rehnquist, Judicial Activist: The Early Years.* Ames: Iowa State University Press, 1987.

Davis, Sue. *Justice Rehnquist and the Constitution.* Princeton, N.J.: Princeton University Press, 1989.

———. "Justice William H. Rehnquist: Right-Wing Ideologue or Majoritarian Democrat?" In *The Burger Court: Political and Judicial Profiles.* Edited by Charles M. Lamb and Stephen C. Halpern. Urbana: University of Illinois Press, 1991.

Rehnquist, William H. *The Supreme Court: How it Was, How it Is.* New York: Morrow, 1987.

Savage, David G. *Turning Right: The Making of the Rehnquist Supreme Court.* New York: John Wiley and Sons, Inc., 1992.

Tucker, David F.B. *The Rehnquist Court and Civil Rights.* Brookfield, Vt.: Dartmouth, 1995.

*J*OHN PAUL STEVENS (1920–)

Associate Justice, 1975–

Appointed by President Gerald R. Ford

JOHN PAUL STEVENS
(United States Supreme Court)

Justice John Paul Stevens has spent more than a quarter of century on a Court sharply divided between conservative and liberal justices. For most of this period, he found a place at the Court's center and defied attempts to label him as being firmly allied with either of these two divisions. Toward the end of the 20th century, though, as the Court itself grew more conservative, Stevens found himself more often in the company of the Court's few remaining liberal justices. Overall, his judicial work has been characterized by a willingness to strike a course independent from his colleagues on the Court. Rather than join in opinions prepared by other justices to explain their reasoning in a case, Stevens, more than any other justice in recent times, has preferred to write his own opinions. His independent and uncompromising temperament has made him more a critic than a leader on the Court.

John Paul Stevens was born on April 20, 1920, in Chicago, Illinois, the son of Ernest J. Stevens and Elizabeth Street Stevens. His father was the wealthy owner of the Stevens Hotel, later to become the Chicago Hilton. John Paul grew up near the University of Chicago and attended the university's laboratory school for his preparatory education and then the university itself for his bachelor's degree with an English major. He graduated Phi Beta Kappa from the University of Chicago in 1941. The following year he married Elizabeth Jane Sheeren, and the couple had four children: John Joseph, Kathryn, Elizabeth Jane, and Susan Roberta. Stevens and his wife eventually divorced in 1979, and in 1980 he married Maryan Mulholland Simon.

The year of Stevens's marriage to Elizabeth Sheeren saw the United States plunge into World War II after the attack on Pearl Harbor. From 1942 to 1945, Stevens served in the navy, working on code-breaking and winning the bronze star. After the war, he enrolled in Northwestern University School of Law, where his father had studied. He was co-editor of the law review and graduated magna cum laude and first in his class in 1947, after compiling the highest academic average ever earned in the school. During the Supreme Court's 1947 term, Stevens was a judicial clerk for Justice Wiley Rutledge.

After his clerkship with Rutledge, Stevens returned to Chicago to practice law as an associate in Poppenhusen, Johnston and Raymond from 1950 to 1952, and then as a partner in his own firm, Rothschild, Stevens, Barry, and Myers, from 1952 to 1970. He soon developed a specialty in antitrust matters and supplemented his law practice during these years by teaching antitrust law at Northwestern University Law School from 1950 to 1954 and at University of Chicago Law School from 1955 to 1958. During the same period he also served as associate counsel to the Subcommittee on the Study of Monopoly Power of the House Judiciary Committee from 1951 to 1952 and as a member of the Attorney General's National Committee to Study Antitrust Law from 1953 to 1955.

John Paul Stevens's transition from lawyer to judge occurred in 1970, when President Richard M. Nixon appointed him to the U.S. Court of Appeals for the Seventh Circuit. In his five years on the federal court of appeals, Stevens earned a reputation as a hardworking, meticulous, and talented judge. This reputation stood him in good stead in 1975, when Associate Justice William O. Douglas retired from the Supreme Court, giving President Gerald R. Ford the opportunity to make his first, and what would be his only, appointment to the Supreme Court. Ford's attorney general, Edward Levi, took the lead in developing a list of potential nominees and also took the then-unusual step of asking the American Bar Association for its evaluation of the candidates on the list. The American Bar Association ranked Stevens as "highly qualified;" President Ford subsequently nominated him as an associate justice of the Supreme Court on November 28, 1975. A few weeks later the Senate confirmed his appointment by a vote of 98-0, and Stevens took the oath of office on December 19, 1975.

John Paul Stevens arrived on a Court divided between conservative and liberal poles with a broad center of moderate justices. On the conservative end lay Chief Justice Warren Burger and Justice Rehnquist. At the opposing extreme were Justices Thurgood Marshall and William J. Brennan, Jr. Making up the Court's center were Justices Potter Stewart, Byron R. White, Harry A. Blackmun, and Lewis F. Powell, Jr., and John Paul Stevens was soon numbered as well among these centrists. Stevens, though, in the ever-shifting balance among conservatives, liberals, and moderates, proved to be the Court's chief maverick. No other justice could name him as a consistent ally. Few escaped his razor-sharp rhetoric when they were on an opposing side from Stevens, who was more ready than any other justice to explain in a separate opinion why the course followed by other members of the Court in a particular case was erroneous.

After Associate Justice William Rehnquist became chief justice in 1986, the Court drifted toward a more conservative position on many issues, and Stevens found himself more often allied with the Court's liberal justices. Under Rehnquist, a conservative majority on the Court revisited long-dormant questions concerning the appropriate balance between national and state legislative power in the federal system. Since President Franklin Roosevelt's New Deal era, the Court had given Congress virtually free rein to legislate concerning a wide variety of subjects using its power under the Constitution's commerce clause to regulate interstate commerce. But in cases such as *United States v. Lopez* (1995) and *United States v. Morrison* (2000), the Court declared two federal laws unconstitutional as exceeding Congress's commerce power: the Gun Free Schools Zones Act in *Lopez* and the Violence Against Women Act in *Morrison*. Similarly, in *Printz v. United States* (1997), a majority of the Court found that a portion of the Brady Handgun Violence Prevention Act, which required local law enforcement personnel to perform background checks on gun purchasers, exceeded Congress's power insofar as it attempted to commandeer state agents. Stevens persistently dissented against this new conservative form of judicial activism.

In the area of church-state relations, Justice Stevens found himself consistently at odds with more conservative justices. He displayed unrelenting hostility to any interaction between government and religion, a hostility so implacable that some critics accused him of being hostile to religion and religious liberty. His insistence of separation between government and religious affairs placed him in the Court's majority when the issue involved religious exercises in public school contexts. He authored, for example, the Court's opinion in *Santa Fe Independent School District v. Doe* (2000), which found that a school's arrangement to let students vote on whether to have an invocation before football games violated the First Amendment establishment clause. But as the Rehnquist court gradually eased the previously vigorous constitutional barriers to the receipt of government funds by religious organizations, Stevens found himself in dissent.

Justice Stevens also demonstrated himself to be an ardent defender of abortion rights when, beginning in the late 1980s, the conservative momentum of the Rehnquist court entertained new restrictions on abortion. In *Planned Parenthood v. Casey* (1992), a fractured Court reconsidered the fundamental framework for abortion rights first established in *Roe v. Wade* (1973), when the Court first recognized a constitutional right to an abortion. Four justices in *Casey* were prepared to overrule *Roe v. Wade:* Chief Justice Rehnquist and Associate Justices White, Scalia, and Thomas. Three justices adopted a constitutional standard that made it easier for states to pass some restrictions on abortions, such as a 24-hour waiting period, but that reiterated the basic abortion right. Only two justices—Blackmun, who authored the original *Roe* opinion, and Stevens—argued against any diminution in the strength of the abortion right.

If there was a principal theme to Justice Stevens's work on the Court, it was his reluctance to let sterile formulas dictate the outcomes of cases. Stevens devoted close attention to the facts of each case and was unwilling to let doctrinal principles foreclose this kind of attention. Thus, for example, when deciding whether particular kinds of discrimination offend the equal protection clause of the Fourteenth Amendment, a majority of the Court has settled into a rigid framework of analysis. If a discrimination involves a so-called suspect classification such as race or a fundamental right, the Court requires on overwhelmingly persuasive justification for a law to pass constitutional scrutiny. If it involves a quasi-suspect classification—such as gender—the Court applies a slightly less vigorous scrutiny. And finally, if a discrimination involves neither suspect nor quasi-suspect classifications nor a fundamental right, the Court applies a very lenient scrutiny that generally results in the discrimination being upheld. Stevens would have none of this rigid categorization and preferred for the Court to consider any number of factors in deciding whether a particular discrimination was supported by a public interest that outweighed any harm it imposed on the people being discriminated against.

Early in his tenure as a judge of the U.S. Seventh Circuit Court of Appeals, John Paul Stevens seized the opportunity to express his disagreement with the result reached by a majority of his colleagues in a case. "Since I find myself out of step not only with respected colleagues but also with a whole parade of recent decisions," he wrote, "I shall explain at some length why I am convinced the parade is marching in the wrong direction." This became a kind of inaugural statement of judicial purpose for Stevens. When he became a justice of the Supreme Court a few years after writing these words, Stevens brought their spirit with him to his work on the Court. Of all the justices who have served on the Court during the last quarter of the 20th century and the beginnings of the 21st, he was most ready to declare how his colleagues and the precedents on which they relied were "marching in the wrong direction." Less a coalition builder than a critic, Justice Stevens authored a steady stream of concurring and dissenting opinions that landed not a few sharp barbs on his colleagues. This willingness to chart an independent judicial path and to prick his brethren with the sometimes harsh language of his opinions has deprived Stevens of any clear leadership role on the Court. He remains, then, an energetic and sometimes unpredictable maverick there.

Further Reading

Canon, Bradley C. "Justice John Paul Stevens: The Lone Ranger in a Black Robe." In *The Burger Court: Political and Judicial Profiles.* Edited by Charles M. Lamb and Stephen C. Halpern. Urbana: University of Illinois Press, 1991.

"Perspectives on Justice John Paul Stevens." *Rutgers Law Journal* 27 (1996): 521–661.

Sickels, Robert J. *John Paul Stevens and the Constitution: The Search for Balance.* University Park: Pennsylvania State University Press, 1988.

———. "The Bill of Rights: A Century of Progress." *University of Chicago Law Review* 59 (1992): 13–38.

———. "The Freedom of Speech." *Yale Law Journal* 102 (1993): 1293–1313.

———. "Is Justice Irrelevant?" *Northwestern University Law Review* 87 (1993): 1121–1130.

SANDRA DAY O'CONNOR (1930–)

Associate Justice, 1981–

Appointed by President Ronald Reagan

SANDRA DAY O'CONNOR
(United States Supreme Court)

In 1981 Sandra Day O'Connor became the first woman justice on the Supreme Court. On the court of Chief Justice Warren Burger and later that of William H. Rehnquist, O'Connor has generally occupied the center. Since Rehnquist's appointment as chief justice in 1986, which inaugurated more conservative trends in the Court's decision-making, O'Connor has partially contributed to and partially frustrated these trends. She has participated in the Rehnquist court's renewed attention to state power within the federal system and its increasing hostility to affirmative action programs, for example, but she was a crucial swing vote in upholding the right to abortion in the 1990s. In all, she has exemplified a moderate conservatism on a Court often polarized by more aggressive conservatives on the one hand and liberal justices on the other. As often happens in the case of centrist judges, O'Connor's place in the Court's ideological center has made her a powerful force in the Court's deliberations.

Sandra Day O'Connor was born in El Paso, Texas, on March 26, 1930, the daughter of Harry A. Day and Ada Mae Wilkey Day. Her parents owned and operated the Lazy B Ranch, a cattle ranch of nearly 200,000 acres located near the Arizona–New Mexico border that had been established by her grandfather, Henry Clay Day, in the 1880s, three decades before Arizona became a state. After Sandra was born in an El Paso hospital, she and her mother returned to a home that still lacked electricity and running water. There she spent her early childhood years. When it came time for her to begin school, Sandra's parents sent her to live with her grandmother, Mamie Wilkey, in El Paso, where she attended Radford School for Girls, a private institution, and then later Austin High School. She graduated at the age of 16 and then enrolled in Stanford University, earning a B.A. in economics, summa cum laude in 1950, and then her law degree from Stanford University Law School in 1952. She was an editor of the *Stanford Law Review* and graduated third in a class that included future Chief Justice of the Supreme Court William H. Rehnquist, who graduated first. Six months after her law school graduation, she married John Jay O'Connor III, a fellow graduate of Stanford Law School. The couple subsequently had three sons: Scott, Brian, and Jay.

The third-ranking student in Stanford Law's class of 1952 applied for jobs with a variety of San Francisco and Los Angeles law firms but received only one offer: as a legal secretary for the Los Angeles firm of Gibson, Dunn, and Crutcher. She settled instead for a position as deputy county attorney for San Mateo County, Arizona, from 1952 to 1953. Afterward, her husband, who had joined the U.S. Army's Judge Advocate General's Corps, was posted to Frankfurt, Germany; Sandra Day O'Connor thereupon worked as a civilian attorney for Quartermaster Market Center in Frankfurt from 1954 to 1957. When the couple returned to the United States and settled in Phoenix, Arizona, O'Connor gave birth to their first son. She preferred to practice part-time; to facilitate this, she opened her own firm in Maryvale, Arizona, with a friend. O'Connor's second son was born in 1960 and a third in 1962, and beginning in 1960 she left the practice to tend to her children. During this period she engaged in a steady stream of service to civic organizations, including periods as president of the Phoenix Junior League and as a board member of the Salvation Army.

In 1965 O'Connor resumed the practice of law as an assistant attorney general of Arizona, a position she held until 1969. That year she was appointed to fill a vacant seat in the Arizona State Senate. She was reelected as a Republican in her own right for two additional terms in the senate and served as majority leader from 1973 to 1974. She was the first woman in the nation to occupy this position in a state legislature. In 1974 O'Connor won a seat as a trial judge on the Maricopa County Superior Court and held it for five years until Arizona's Democratic governor, Bruce Babbitt, appointed her to fill a vacancy on the Arizona Court of Appeals in 1979. Since Arizona Republican leaders had unsuccessfully urged O'Connor to run against Babbitt in the 1978 gubernatorial race, some observers speculated at the time that Babbitt's appointment was designed to forestall a possible future challenge from Sandra Day O'Connor.

In the 1980 presidential campaign, Ronald Reagan had promised that he would, if elected, appoint a woman to the Supreme Court if he had the opportunity. The summer after his election, Associate Justice Potter Stewart retired from the Supreme Court, giving President Reagan the chance to fulfill his campaign promise. When he ultimately decided to submit Sandra Day O'Connor's name to the Senate, it fell to Attorney General William French Smith to contact O'Connor with the news. Ironically, Smith had been a partner in the Los Angeles law firm of Gibson, Dunn, and Crutcher, which had offered O'Connor a job as a legal secretary when she graduated from law school nearly 30 years before. In 1990 the firm invited her to speak at its centennial celebration, and she good-naturedly joked about the irony:

> I want to thank Bill Smith. I can remember as if it were yesterday when he telephoned me on June 26, 1981, to ask if I could go to Washington, D.C. to talk about a position there. Knowing his former association with your firm, I immediately guessed he was planning to offer me a secretarial position—but would it be as Secretary of Labor or Secretary of Commerce?

In hearings on the confirmation, senators spent a good deal of time trying to fix her position on abortion, but she remained noncommittal. In the end, the Senate confirmed her appointment on September 21, 1981, by a vote of 99-0. Four days later, Sandra Day O'Connor took the oath of office to become the first woman on the Supreme Court.

Justice O'Connor came to the Court with the credentials of a moderate conservative, and afterward she generally steered a course consistent with his background. Although at first she was dubbed the "Arizona twin" of associate justice and later chief justice William Rehnquist, she soon demonstrated a willingness to chart a course sometimes divergent from more conservative justices such as Rehnquist, Burger, and later, Antonin Scalia and Clarence Thomas. For example, when O'Connor joined the Court, many observers had concluded that the Court's decisions in the area of church-state relations were in disarray. Justice Rehnquist, later joined by Justices Scalia and Thomas, pressed hard during the 1980s and 1990s to reinterpret the First Amendment's establishment clause to pose less of a barrier to civic religious exercises such as moments of silence in schools and graduation invocations. Justice O'Connor resisted this reinterpretation while leading the Court to adopt a reformulation of its establishment clause doctrine that focused on whether government in any particular case had acted with the intent or the effect of endorsing a particular religion or religion generally. Applying this test, for example, O'Connor joined with a majority of the Court in *Lee v. Weisman* (1992) to declare that prayers offered at a public school graduation ceremony by a rabbi violated the establishment clause.

As many observers had predicted, Justice O'Connor's views on the subject of abortion eventually proved crucial to the Court's reexamination of this issues. President Reagan had made the reversal of *Roe v. Wade* (1973), which originally recognized the abortion right, a central ambition of his presidency. By the end of the 1980s, a series of Republican appointments had in fact seemed to lay the foundation for an imminent reconsideration of *Roe* in which Justice O'Connor was expected to be a swing vote. The issue came before the Court in *Planned Parenthood v. Casey* (1992). There, four justices were prepared to overrule *Roe:* Chief Justice Rehnquist and Justices Byron White, Antonin Scalia, and Clarence Thomas. Two justices, Harry A. Blackmun—the original author of the *Roe* opinion—and John Paul Stevens, favored affirming *Roe* in all respects. But Justice O'Connor joined with two other moderate conservatives—Anthony M. Kennedy and David H. Souter—to chart a middle position. Their opinion affirmed a constitutional right to an abortion while revising the standard for reviewing state abortion regulations in such a way as to permit states to impose some restrictions, such as a 24-hour waiting period, on the woman's right to an abortion.

On other issues Justice O'Connor has joined the Rehnquist court's more vigorous conservatives to produce significant changes in constitutional doctrine. She has, for example, aligned herself with Chief Justice Rehnquist and the Court's other conservatives to restrict though not quite abolish affirmative action programs in cases such as *Richmond v. J. A. Croson Co.* (1989) and *Adarand Constructors, Inc. v. Pena* (1995). Perhaps even more significant, she has joined in a series of revolutionary opinions dealing with the limits of congressional legislative authority. From the midpoint of

Franklin D. Roosevelt's New Deal era until the early 1990s, the Court had routinely approved federal laws passed by Congress using its power under the Constitution to regulate interstate commerce. It was widely assumed during this period that Congress could address virtually any social or economic problem it desired using the commerce power. Beginning in 1995, O'Connor joined a bare majority of the Court to question this assumption by holding in *United States v. Lopez* (1995) that Congress lacked the power under the commerce clause to criminalize the mere possession of guns near schools. Again, in *United States v. Morrison* (2000), decided five years later, O'Connor sided with a majority of the Court to hold the Congress's power to regulate interstate commerce could not be used to justify a federal law that made gender-based acts of violence federal crimes. Justice O'Connor has thus played a crucial role in what critics claim is an unwarranted form of conservative judicial activism.

When Sandra Day O'Connor took her place on the Supreme Court, many observers wondered what feminine ways of thinking she might introduce in a traditionally male enclave. She herself has protested against attempts to define her judicial role in terms of her sex. "Ironically," O'Connor has argued, "the move to ask again the question whether women are different merely by virtue of being women recalls the old myths we have struggled to put behind us." The Court's first woman justice does, however, play a unique and important role in its deliberations. Unlike her more conservative colleagues, Justice O'Connor prefers to focus on the facts of each particular case presented to her for decision rather than to elaborate hard and fast legal rules. A close eye to context and circumstances defines her method as a judge, and the pursuit of excellence in the calling of judging ranks at the top of her ambition. When asked at her confirmation hearings what epitaph she would wish to see engraved on her tombstone, Justice Sandra Day O'Connor responded simply, "Here lies a good judge."

Further Reading

Brown, Judith Olans, Wendy E. Parmet, and Mary E. O'Connell. "The Rugged Feminism of Sandra Day O'Connor." *Indiana Law Review* 32 (1999): 1219–1246.

Bruckmann, Barbara Olson. "Justice Sandra Day O'Connor: Trends Toward Judicial Restraint." *Washington and Lee Law Review* 42 (1985): 1185–1231.

Cook, Beverly B. "Justice Sandra Day O'Connor: Transition to a Republican Court Agenda." In *The Burger Court: Political and Judicial Profiles.* Edited by Charles M. Lamb and Stephen C. Halpern. Urbana: University of Illinois Press, 1991.

Maveety, Nancy. *Justice Sandra Day O'Connor: Strategist on the Supreme Court.* London: Rowman & Littlefield, 1996.

Van Sickel, Robert W. *Not a Particularly Different Voice: The Jurisprudence of Sandra Day O'Connor.* New York: P. Lang, 1998.

ANTONIN SCALIA (1936–)

Associate Justice, 1986–

Appointed by President Ronald Reagan

ANTONIN SCALIA
(United States Supreme Court)

Arguably the most conservative member of the Court, Justice Antonin Scalia is probably the Court's most talented writer and most entertaining wit. He delights in the colorful phrase and succinct repartee, especially when wielded to prick colleagues he believes to have erred in their judicial reasoning. He dismays liberal thinkers by his willingness to revisit victories they thought settled and by his success in contributing to a revitalized conservative activism on the nation's highest court. But he remains something of a loner on the Court. Except for Justice Clarence Thomas, who regularly joins him in particular cases, Scalia's rather rambunctious style and his willingness to be openly and sometimes sharply critical of his colleagues have tended to distance him even from fellow conservatives on the Court. Yet, though his temperament may hamper his ability to work behind the scenes on the Court to build support for results he favors, he nevertheless remains one of its most interesting public characters.

—∞—

Antonin Scalia (known as "Nino" by family and friends) was born on March 11, 1936, in Trenton, New Jersey, the only child of S. Eugene Scalia, a professor of Romance languages, and Catherine Panaro Scalia, a schoolteacher. Scalia's father was an immigrant to the United States from Sicily and his mother the child of Italian immigrants. After the senior Scalia joined the faculty of Brooklyn College, Antonin received his early education in the public schools of Queens, New York, and later at Xavier High School, a Jesuit military prep school in Manhattan from which he graduated first in his class. Afterward he attended Georgetown University and the University of Fribourg, Switzerland, continuing the academic success of his prep school days by graduating with his A.B. in history from Georgetown, summa cum laude and first in his class. He attended Harvard Law School next, where he served as note editor of the *Harvard Law Review* and graduated magna cum laude. He then followed this legal education with a year in Europe as one of Harvard's Sheldon Fellows. In 1960 he married Maureen McCarthy, and the couple eventually had nine children: Ann Forest, Eugene, John Francis, Catherine Elisabeth, Mary Clare, Paul David, Matthew, Christopher James, and Margaret Jane.

From 1961 to 1967, Antonin Scalia practiced law in Cleveland, Ohio, with the firm of Jones, Day, Cockley, and Reavis, where he handled a variety of commercial matters, including labor and antitrust issues. In 1967, however, he exchanged the life of a practicing lawyer for that of a law teacher by joining the faculty of the University of Virginia. He left the academic setting four years later to join the administration of President Richard M. Nixon, serving first in the Office of Telecommunication Policy as general counsel. Soon afterward, he assumed a position as chairman of the Administrative Conference of the United States, a role in which he served from 1972 to 1974. Shortly before President Nixon resigned in the wake of the Watergate scandal, he appointed Scalia as assistant attorney general for the Justice Department's Office of Legal Counsel. Scalia continued in that post after President Gerald Ford assumed the presidency, leaving only in 1977 after Jimmy Carter was elected president. Following a brief stint at the American Enterprise Institute, a conservative think tank in Washington D.C., and at Georgetown University Law Center, Scalia accepted a teaching position at the University of Chicago Law School. He taught there from 1977 to 1982, with a brief interlude as a visiting professor at Stanford University in California. Toward the end of this period Scalia served as the chairman of the American Bar Association's section on administrative law and its Conference of Section Chairs.

The return of a Republican administration to Washington under President Ronald Reagan soon ended Scalia's academic career. In 1982 Reagan appointed Scalia to the prestigious U.S. Court of Appeals for the D.C. Circuit, where he earned a reputation for his keen intellect, his pleasure in vigorous legal arguments, and his gregarious temperament. This appointment proved to be a step toward an even loftier position. In September 1986 Chief Justice Warren E. Burger retired from the Supreme Court, and President Reagan responded to the vacancy by nominating Associate Justice William H. Rehnquist to fill the post of chief justice and Antonin Scalia to step into the position of associate justice left open by Rehnquist's promotion. Rehnquist's nomination provoked the most controversy; he was eventually confirmed by the Senate by a vote of 65-33 on September 17, 1986. Scalia's nomination, by contrast, sailed through the Senate the same day unanimously, with virtually no comment from the floor. He took the oath of office as a justice on the Supreme Court nine days later, becoming its youngest member and its first Roman Catholic since the appointment of William J. Brennan, Jr., in 1957.

Justice Antonin Scalia soon became the darling of conservatives and the justice that liberals loved to hate. His conservativism was bullish rather than sedate, clothed in wit and memorable phrases rather than ponderous legal prose. But his readiness to launch pointed barbs at his colleagues in dissenting and concurring opinions soon appeared to leave him outside the private coalition-building that influential justices use to advance their legal visions. Though one of the Court's sharpest intellects, he has not become a leader among the justices. He appears content, however, with his role as conservative gadfly.

Unlike some justices, who seem to approach cases without any well-established judicial philosophy, Justice Scalia has been frank about his guiding principles. In the first place, he lays claim to being an "originalist," arguing that the Constitution should be interpreted in light of the understanding of its text at the time it was written. He has publicly mocked the idea of a "living Constitution," influential in the judicial decision-making of such famous liberal justices as William Brennan, Jr., and Thurgood Marshall. According to Scalia, a "living Constitution" can contain anything that five justices (a majority on the Supreme Court) are willing to find in it and is inconsistent with the notion of democratic rule. Scalia, for example, has explicitly denied that the Constitution should be interpreted to protect rights not specifically mentioned in it, such as a right to an abortion or a right to die.

Justice Scalia has also expressed a steadfast preference for clear constitutional rules rather than for vague standards that allow the justices to impose their own political preferences in controversial cases. Since modern constitutional law contains few categorical rules, this preference has placed him at odds with many of the Court's precedents. But it has also occasionally aligned him temporarily with liberal justices on the Court against other conservatives. For example, Justice Scalia favors a hard-and-fast rule preventing governments from restricting speech because of the viewpoint it expresses. This position placed him in the Court's majority in two important cases in which the Court held unconstitutional laws that attempted to prevent flag burning: *Texas v. Johnson* (1989) and *United States v. Eichman* (1990).

The opinion for which Justice Scalia is perhaps best known is *Employment Division v. Smith* (1990), and his reasoning in the case reveals again his preference for clear constitutional rules. The case involved two Native Americans who had been fired from their jobs at a drug rehabilitation clinic for using peyote, a controlled substance whose use violated state law. The two men argued that their use of peyote had been part of a ritual conducted by the Native American Church and that the free exercise clause of the First Amendment should exempt them from having to comply with the state controlled-substance law. In fact, some of the Supreme Court's precedents had previously suggested that the free exercise clause did protect religious believers from the effects of laws that inadvertently burdened their religious exercise. In these cases, the Court had sometimes applied a balancing test that weighed the interest in religious exercise against the governmental interest furthered by a law, with the scale being tilted strongly in favor of protecting the right of religious exercise. Scalia, though, led the Court to abandon this balancing test in favor of a straightforward rule with only limited exceptions. When government does not intentionally target religious practice for unfavorable treatment, he declared for a majority of the Court, then the free exercise clause does not ordinarily grant religious believers any protection from the unintended effects of laws on their religious exercise.

—∾—

The late 1980s and 1990s witnessed a resurgence of conservative activism on the Supreme Court and Justice Antonin Scalia has clearly played an important part in this conservative revival. He has contributed its most colorful phrases in judicial opinions and lectures to legal audiences. When displeased, for example, with the majority's reference to an establishment clause precedent—*Lemon v. Kurtzman* (1971)—he believed to have been abandoned, Scalia turned to metaphor to chide the majority: "Like some ghoul in a late-night horror movie that repeatedly sits up in its grave and shuffles abroad, after being repeatedly killed and buried, *Lemon* stalks our Establishment Clause jurisprudence . . . frightening the little children and school attorneys. . . ." Some observers have compared Scalia, for the sheer memorableness of his prose, to another of the Court's foremost writers, Justice Oliver Wendell Holmes, Jr. Like Holmes, one of the Court's great dissenters, Scalia's influence on the present Court may be less than his influence on future courts that will turn to his dissenting and concurring opinions for guidance in navigating the thickets of constitutional law. In particular, Scalia has demonstrated little respect for the traditional principle of *stare decisis*—that is, of respecting established precedents unless overwhelming justification exists for overruling them. Especially with respect to constitutional questions, Scalia tends to take the position that questions have not been decided until they have been decided right. On the present Court, Scalia clearly has the intellectual gifts that would allow him to be a leader. But he has deployed these gifts instead in service of a prophetic role in which he has been as quick to chasten the reasoning of his allies as his enemies. Scalia has also been willing to stake out extreme positions often not likely to gain adherence by even his fellow conservatives on the Court. It remains to be seen whether this role will secure him an important place in the history of the late 20th and the early 21st century Court.

FURTHER READING

Brisbin, Richard A. *Justice Antonin Scalia and the Conservative Revival.* Baltimore: Johns Hopkins University Press, 1997.

"The Jurisprudence of Justice Antonin Scalia." *Cardozo Law Review* 12 (1991): 1593–1867.

Kannar, George. "The Constitutional Catechism of Antonin Scalia." *Yale Law Journal* 99 (1990): 1297–1357.

Scalia, Antonin. *A Matter of Interpretation: Federal Courts and the Law.* Princeton, N.J.: Princeton University Press, 1997.

Schultz, David Andrew and Christopher E. Smith. *The Jurisprudential Vision of Justice Antonin Scalia.* Lanham, Md.: Rowman & Littlefield Publishers, 1996.

Smith, Christopher E. *Justice Antonin Scalia and the Supreme Court's Conservative Moment.* Westport, Conn.: Praeger, 1994.

Sunderland, Lane V. "Steady, Upright, and Impartial Administration of Laws: Antonin Scalia." In *Sober as a Judge: The Supreme Court and Republican Liberty.* Edited by Richard G. Stevens and Matthew J. Franck. Lanham, Md.: Lexington Books, 1999.

ANTHONY MCLEOD KENNEDY (1936–)

Associate Justice, 1988–

Appointed by President Ronald Reagan

ANTHONY M. KENNEDY
(United States Supreme Court)

Anthony McLeod Kennedy was President Ronald Reagan's last appointment to the Supreme Court. Reagan turned to Kennedy only after two men he might have seen as more reliably faithful to his conservative vision—Robert Bork and Douglas Ginsburg—failed to win confirmation in the Senate. Bork's nomination, in particular, had sparked a fierce ideological struggle in the Senate as a result of his staunch conservativism. The Senate refused to confirm his appointment by a vote of 58-42 and Reagan subsequently had to withdraw Ginsburg's nomination after news surfaced that he had smoked marijuana in the 1960s and 1970s. After these political defeats, Kennedy's more modest conservativism found quick confirmation in the Senate. On the Court, Justice Kennedy has exhibited precisely the kind of moderate conservativism that the history of his confirmation might have predicted.

Anthony McLeod Kennedy was born on July 23, 1936, in Sacramento, California, the second of three children born to Anthony J. Kennedy and Gladys McLeod Kennedy. His father was a lawyer and a lobbyist who practiced in Sacramento. After high school in Sacramento, Kennedy attended Stanford University, where he received his A.B. in 1958, Phi Beta Kappa. In the course of his undergraduate career, Kennedy attended the London School of Economics from 1957 to 1958. After graduating from Stanford, Kennedy proceeded to Harvard Law School, where he received his J.D. in 1961 cum laude. After being admitted to the California bar that year, Anthony Kennedy began his legal career as an associate with the San Francisco law firm of Thelen, Marrin, Johnson, and Bridges, though he took time off from his practice briefly in 1961 to serve as a private, first class, in the National Guard. In 1963 two important events occurred in Kennedy's life. First, his father died unexpectedly, causing Kennedy to return to Sacramento to take over his father's law practice. Second, he married Mary Davis. The couple eventually had three children: Justin, Gregory, and Kristin.

With the client base inherited from his father's practice, Kennedy developed a thriving practice in Sacramento. He also taught a constitutional law course at McGeorge School of Law of the University of the Pacific on a part-time basis beginning in 1965. Like his father, Kennedy combined the practice of law with lobbying activities for clients, and he soon established important California political contacts. Not the least of these was the friendship he formed with Ed Meese, who would soon play an important part in the administration of California governor Ronald Reagan and would eventually serve as President Reagan's attorney general. In 1973 Kennedy helped draft an ad campaign for the passage of California Proposition One, a ballot initiative designed to limit government spending. Although the initiative failed, Reagan rewarded Kennedy by recommending him for appointment to the U.S. Court of Appeals for the Ninth Circuit.

When Kennedy joined the Ninth Circuit in 1975, he was the youngest judge then serving on the federal bench. He was Republican, conservative, and Roman Catholic on a predominantly liberal court of appeals. But even when Kennedy found himself a frequent dissenter on the court of appeals, he earned a reputation for solid judicial craftsmanship and a conservativism more modest than strident. When Justice Lewis Powell retired in 1987, Kennedy's 12 years of solid service on the Ninth Circuit and his previous relationship with Reagan placed him on the list of possible nominees to replace Powell. Reagan, though, seems to have aspired to appoint someone more aggressively conservative than Kennedy. Consequently, he first nominated Robert H. Bork, a former Yale Law School professor, solicitor general, and a judge on the U.S. Court of Appeals for the D.C. circuit. The Iran-contra scandal had weakened Reagan's political strength, and he proved unable to muster sufficient support in the Senate for his nominee once the vigor of Bork's conservativism on issues such as the right to abortion became known. The measure of opposition to Bork is well illustrated by the speech that Senator Edward Kennedy made on the Senate floor:

> Robert Bork's America is a land in which women would be forced into back-alley abortions, blacks would sit at segregated lunch counters, rogue police could break down citizens' doors in midnight raids, schoolchildren could not be taught about evolution, writers and artists could be censored at the whim of government, and the doors of the federal courts would be shut on the fingers of millions of citizens for whom the judiciary is—and is often the only—protector of the individual rights that are the heart of our democracy.

The Senate eventually rejected the nomination by a vote of 58-42 on October 23, 1987. Reagan followed this defeat a week later by nominating Douglas H. Ginsburg, a 41-year-old former Harvard Law School professor who had worked in the Reagan administration and whom Reagan had appointed to the U.S. Court of Appeals for the D.C. Circuit in 1986. Accused of being a Bork clone, Ginsburg's nomination attracted swift opposition and ultimately floundered on the revelation that he had smoked marijuana as a college student and a law professor. On November 7, 1987, nine days after the announcement of his nomination to the Court, Ginsburg asked President Reagan to withdraw his nomination. Kennedy, Reagan's third choice, had now moved to the top. And although his nomination attracted token opposition, the Senate finally settled on an appointment that did not entirely please either its conservatives or its liberals but seemed like the best that either ideological camp could expect. The Senate unanimously confirmed Kennedy on February 3, 1988, and he took the oath of office as a Supreme Court justice on February 18, 1988.

Soon after he took his seat on the Court, Kennedy demonstrated a willingness to chart a judicial path separate from his more conservative colleagues, Chief Justice William H. Rehnquist and Associate Justice Antonin Scalia. A little more than a year after his appointment, Kennedy parted ranks with Rehnquist by voting with a majority of the Court in *Texas v. Johnson* (1989) to strike down a state law that prohibited flag burning. But his real declaration of independence from the conservative hard-liners on the Court came in *Planned Parenthood v. Casey* (1992), where Justices Sandra Day O'Connor, David H. Souter, and Anthony Kennedy co-authored the controlling opinion. Taking a centrist position on the long-controversial right to an abortion, first established in *Roe v. Wade* (1973), the opinion of Kennedy and his two other colleagues refused to overrule *Roe* but nevertheless reframed the structure of the right to abortion to allow states more power to regulate abortions.

In the years since Kennedy placed himself securely in the Court's center, he has remained in that position, sometimes siding with more liberal justices on particular questions, sometimes supplying the swing vote need by Chief Justice Rehnquist to achieve conservative results. Kennedy has tended to join the Court's liberals on social questions such as the rights of women and gays and on the constitutionality of public religious exercises. Thus, he wrote the Court's opinion in *Romer v. Evans* (1996), which declared unconstitutional a Colorado constitutional amendment that prohibited state and local laws from protecting gays from discrimination. He also authored the majority opinion in *Lee v. Weisman* (1992), which held that graduation prayers offered by a Jewish rabbi at a middle school ceremony violated the First Amendment's establishment clause.

On other issues, though, Justice Kennedy has supported important conservative decisions. He has, for example, sided with an emerging majority on the Court to cast increasing constitutional questions on affirmative action programs. In two decisions decided in 1989 and 1995, Kennedy joined a majority of the Court in questioning the constitutionality of minority set-aside programs that allocated a particular portion of public works contracts for minority-owned businesses. *Richmond v. J. A. Croson Company* (1989) and *Adarand Constructors, Inc. v. Pena* (1995) made it more difficult for both states and the federal government to award preferential treatment to minority groups on account of their race. Kennedy has also participated in the Rehnquist court's decisions raising new questions concerning the reach of Congress's power under the Constitution to regulate interstate commerce. From 1937 until the last decade of the 20th century, the Court had permitted Congress to regulate virtually any social or economic problem, using its commerce power. But in *United States v. Lopez* (1995) and *United States v. Morrison* (2000), the Court dealt constitutional rebukes to Congress, finding that attempts to regulate the possession of guns near school in *Lopez* and to make domestic violence a federal crime in *Morrison* exceeded its commerce power. These cases have reallocated the relative balance of legislative power between states and the federal government, and Kennedy has been a key ally of the Court's more conservative wing in bringing about significant constitutional change in this area. In this he joins regularly with Justice Sandra Day O'Connor, another of the Court's moderately conservative swing votes.

—∞—

The decade of the 1980s saw concentrated conservative efforts to place justices on the Supreme Court who would overturn the Court's decision in *Roe v. Wade* (1973), which had recognized a constitutional right to an abortion. The fierce political contests over the failed nominations of Robert Bork and Douglas Ginsburg partially reflected the widespread belief that the justice who replaced Lewis Powell, himself one of the swing votes on the Court, might well play a key role in the future of the abortion debate. On this controversial subject, Justice Anthony Kennedy proved to be a bitter disappointment to conservatives when, in *Planned Parenthood v. Casey* (1992), he joined in the decision that reaffirmed the abortion right originally announced in *Roe.* But against this defeat, conservatives have been heartened by the Rehnquist court on other points, such as its disapproval of affirmative action programs and its reassertion of the prerogatives of states in the federal scheme of government. In these areas, Kennedy has been a predictable ally of Chief Justice Rehnquist. All in all, Kennedy remains where he began, a moderately conservative centrist on a Court generally characterized by its conservativism.

FURTHER READING

Amar, Akhil Reed. "Justice Kennedy and the Idea of Equality." *Pacific Law Journal* 28 (1997): 515–532.

Friedman, Lawrence M. "The Limitations of Labeling: Justice Anthony M. Kennedy and the First Amendment." *Ohio Northern University Law Review* 20 (1993): 225–262.

Golden, Sue. "Justice Anthony M. Kennedy: A Trojan Horse Conservative," *Maryland Journal of Contemporary Legal Issues* 1 (1990): 229–246.

McArtor, Keith O. "A Conservative Struggles with *Lemon:* Justice Anthony M. Kennedy's Dissent in *Allegheny.*" *Tulsa Law Journal* 26 (1990): 107–133.

Smith, Christopher E. "Supreme Court Surprise: Justice Anthony Kennedy's Move Toward Moderation." *Oklahoma Law Review* 45 (1992): 459–476.

David Hackett Souter (1939–)

Associate Justice, 1990–

Appointed by President George Bush

David H. Souter
(United States Supreme Court)

The first of two Supreme Court appointments by President George Bush, David H. Souter arrived on the Court with little public record that would predict the positions he might take as an associate justice. Political commentators dubbed him the "stealth candidate" and regularly referred to him as "enigmatic." His prior political contacts seemed to prognosticate that Souter would exhibit a moderate conservativism. And, in fact, within a few terms on the Court, Souter had planted himself firmly at the Court's center, where it seemed he would remain. But by the middle of the 1990s, Souter was to be found regularly in dissent against decisions by a conservative majority of the Rehnquist court. After the arrival of Justice Ruth Bader Ginsburg, Souter regularly voted in tandem with her liberal positions. At the end of his first decade as an associate justice, Souter seemed to have remade himself as a fit successor for the justice whose seat he assumed, one of the Court's famous liberals, Justice William J. Brennan, Jr.

—w—

David Hackett Souter was born on September 17, 1939, in Melrose, Massachusetts, the son of Joseph A. Souter, a banker, and Helen Hackett Souter. He spent the years of his childhood on a farm in Weare, New Hampshire, first with his maternal grandparents, who owned the farm, and later with his parents, who moved there after his grandparents died, when David was 11 years old. He attended public school in Weare and later high school in Concord, the capital of New Hampshire, located some 20 miles from Weare, where his father worked for the New Hampshire Savings Bank. After finishing high school in 1957, where he was voted by his classmates "most likely to succeed," Souter attended Harvard University, majoring in philosophy and graduating magna cum laude and Phi Beta Kappa in 1961. From Harvard, he traveled to Oxford, England, on a Rhodes scholarship and studied jurisprudence there for two years. In 1963 he returned to the United States and studied at Harvard Law School. After receiving his law degree from Harvard, Souter moved back to New Hampshire and took a position as an associate with the Concord firm of Orr and Reno, where he engaged in a general legal practice. He did not remain long with this firm, however. By 1968 he had taken a job in the New Hampshire's attorney general's office as an assistant attorney general in the criminal division.

Three years later Warren B. Rudman became attorney general of New Hampshire and recognized Souter's ability by making the young lawyer his assistant. Rudman was not the only political figure to take notice of David Souter. When Rudman left the post of attorney general in 1976, Governor Meldrin Thompson appointed Souter to become the new attorney general. After two years in this position, though, Souter received his first judicial appointment, as an associate justice on the New Hampshire Superior Court. Souter and the other judges on the Superior Court, a general trial court, traveled across the state hearing cases in the state's various counties. As a trial judge, Souter established a reputation as a solid jurist, perhaps tougher than most on criminals, but nevertheless generally respected. After Souter had spent five years as a trial judge, New Hampshire Governor John Sununu, later President George Bush's chief of staff, appointed him to the state's supreme court in 1983. He served on the New Hampshire's highest court for seven years until President George Bush appointed him to the federal judiciary in April 1990 as a judge on the U.S. Court of Appeals for the First Circuit.

Three months after David Souter had stepped onto the federal bench, one of the Supreme Court's leading liberal justices, William J. Brennan, Jr., retired from the Court. President George Bush's predecessor in office, Ronald Reagan, had twice attempted to place strong conservatives on the high court toward the end of his term in office, only to have these nominations fail in the Senate. Robert Bork, after a fierce partisan debate in the Senate, had failed to secure confirmation. Subsequently, Douglas Ginsburg had also encountered stiff opposition in the Senate and had to request that his nomination be withdrawn after news surfaced that he had smoked marijuana as a law student and a law professor. President Reagan had to settle on a moderate conservative, Anthony Kennedy, for his final appointment to the Court. President Bush seemed to have learned from Reagan's experiences, and for his first appointment to the Court, he turned to the quiet, unknown bachelor and judge from New Hampshire, David Souter.

Many observers believed at the time that the justice who replaced William Brennan on the Court might play a decisive role in the decision of key constitutional issues, not the least of which was the question of whether the Court would overrule the controversial 1970s decision that had recognized a right to abortion, *Roe v. Wade* (1973). Souter, though, refused to tip his hand on how he would decide abortion cases, or other cases, either to President Bush or to the Senate. Without an extensive public record on constitutional cases, either as a scholar or a judge, he was a nominee whose future performance was difficult to predict; the press therefore dubbed him the "stealth justice". Though the Senate voted to confirm his nomination to the Supreme Court by a solid margin of 90-9, the nation waited expectantly to see what positions he would take on the Court.

Like many freshman justices, David Souter maintained a low profile during his first term on the Court, and his initial voting record seemed to place him firmly in alliance with the conservative chief justice, William H. Rehnquist. But soon afterward, Justice Souter carved out a place at the Court's center with Justices Sandra Day O'Connor and Anthony Kennedy. He did so most notably in *Planned Parenthood v. Casey* (1992), a case that squarely presented the Court with the opportunity of revisiting its decision 20 years previously in *Roe v. Wade* (1973). To the dismay of both abortion proponents and opponents, the Court, led by a controlling opinion announced jointly by O'Connor, Kennedy, and Souter, reaffirmed the basic right to abortion announced in *Roe* but created a new framework for evaluating abortion laws that made it easier for states to regulate abortion. With this declaration of independence from the Court's conservative pole, represented by Chief Justice Rehnquist and Justice Antonin Scalia, Souter seemed to have charted a solidly moderate course.

In succeeding terms, however, Souter has drifted more emphatically toward the Court's more liberal pole. Chief Justice Rehnquist, whose conservative attempt to overrule *Roe v. Wade* crashed against the independence of the Court's more moderate conservatives, proved more successful at leading the Court to resolutely conservative results on other issues. But Justice Souter dissented with respect to these results. For example, in 1995 he declined to join the majority's skeptical treatment of a federal affirmative action program in *Adarand Constructors v. Pena* (1995) and its introduction of new limits on Congress's power to pass social and economic legislation in *United States v. Lopez* (1995). By the Court's 1999 term, Souter had become a regular member of the liberal dissenting bloc that protested against new victories by the conservative majority, joined by Justices John Paul Stevens, Ruth Bader Ginsburg, and Stephen Breyer. This quartet of justices dissented from the majority's holding in *Boy Scouts of America v. Dale* (2000) that a state law prohibiting discrimination against gays was unconstitutional insofar as it prevented the Boy Scouts from dismissing an avowed gay rights advocate from a position as an assistant scoutmaster. The same justices dissented again when the majority in *United States v. Morrison* (2000) held that Congress lacked the power to make domestic violence and other forms of gender-based violence a federal crime, and in *FDA v. Brown Williamson Tobacco Corporation* (2000), when it held that the Food and Drug Administration was not authorized to regulate tobacco. Souter's divergence from the Court's more conservative majority also exhibited itself in establishment clause cases. During the 1999 term, in *Mitchell v. Helms* (2000), he joined two other dissenters in his disagreement with the majority's revision of establishment clause doctrine to permit financial aid to private schools—including private religious schools—to purchase equipment and materials.

Justice David Souter was appointed by President Bush to fill the seat vacated by William J. Brennan, Jr., an appointee of Republican president Dwight D. Eisenhower, as well as one of the most influential justices of the 20th century. Brennan's career as a leading liberal justice on the Court is ample evidence that presidents cannot control the careers of their appointees and sometimes cannot even correctly predict them. In this regard, Souter may well prove to be like Justice Brennan. It is too early to say whether Souter will become one of the Court's leading liberal lights or whether his rebellion against the Court's ascendant conservativism is merely temporary, waiting only for new appointments to restore both the Court's ideological balance and Souter to his position in the Court's center. But Souter has expressed a view of judging that focuses on the human consequences of each decision. Judges, he has suggested, must be aware that "at the end of our task some human being is going to be affected, some human life is going to be changed in some way by what we do." This sympathetic reading of the judicial role sounds a note not often heard by conservative jurists, and it may well stand as evidence that the modest conservativism expected of Souter at the time of his appointment has transformed itself into a nascent liberalism of which Justice Brennan, his esteemed predecessor, might be proud.

FURTHER READING

Fliter, John A. "Keeping the Faith: Justice David Souter and the First Amendment Religion Clauses." *Journal of Church & State* 40 (1998): 387–409.

Gomperts, John S. and Elliot M. Mincberg. "A Review of Justice David Souter's Public Record: Questions about His Views on Constitutional Issues." *Maryland Journal of Contemporary Legal Issues* 1 (1990): 195–228.

Kan, Liang. "A Theory of Justice Souter." *Emory Law Journal* 45 (1996): 1373–1427.

Meese, Alan. "Will, Judgment, and Economic Liberty: Mr. Justice Souter and the Mistranslation of the Due Process Clause." *William and Mary Law Review* 41 (1999): 3–61.

Smith, Christopher E. and Scott P. Johnson. "Newcomer on the High Court: Justice David Souter and the Supreme Court's 1990 Term." *South Dakota Law Review* 37 (1992): 21–43.

Smith, Robert H. "Justice Souter Joins the Rehnquist Court: An Empirical Study of Supreme Court Voting Patterns." *University of Kansas Law Review* 41 (1992): 11–95.

CLARENCE THOMAS (1948–)

Associate Justice, 1991–

Appointed by President George Bush

CLARENCE THOMAS
(United States Supreme Court)

The career of Clarence Thomas as a Supreme Court justice began as tumultuously as any in the Court's long history. When President George Bush nominated him to fill the vacancy left by the Court's legendary first African-American justice, Thurgood Marshall, Thomas's conservative views—especially on the subject of civil rights—assured that his nomination would be controversial. But his confirmation hearings turned into a tawdry national spectacle when accusations surfaced that Thomas, in a previous executive position, had sexually harassed a subordinate, Anita Hill, who was a professor of law at the University of Oklahoma Law School at the time of the confirmation hearings. The Senate Judiciary Committee conducted a televised hearing on the allegations, and Thomas, adamantly denying the charges, characterized the inquiry as a "high-tech lynching for uppity blacks." In the end, he was confirmed by the narrowest margin of any justice of the 20th century. Since joining the Court, he has consistently aligned himself with the most conservative end of the Court's ideological spectrum, voting frequently with Chief Justice William Rehnquist and Associate Justice Antonin Scalia.

Clarence Thomas was born on June 23, 1948, in Pinpoint, Georgia, the second child of M. C. Thomas and Leola Anderson. His father abandoned the family when Clarence was two years old. When Clarence was six years old, his mother remarried, and he and his brother went to live with his grandfather, Myers Anderson, in nearby Savannah, Georgia. This marked a distinct improvement in their material conditions, from the dirt-poor community of Pinpoint, which lacked even sewer facilities, to the comfortable home of his grandfather, where Clarence and his brother now enjoyed regular meals and indoor plumbing. The move also placed him in the home of the man who would influence his life more than any other person. Myers Anderson made an independent living selling wood, coal, ice, and heating oil from the back of his pickup truck. He was a member of the National Association for the Advancement of Colored People (NAACP) and a devout Catholic who worked hard and insisted that his grandsons do the same. He saw to it that Clarence and his brother attended St. Benedict the Moor, an all-black parochial school. Later Clarence, with an eye to becoming a Catholic priest in keeping with his grandfather's wishes, transferred to St. John Vianney Minor Seminary, a Catholic high school outside of Savannah.

After graduating from high school in 1967, Clarence Thomas briefly attended Immaculate Conception Seminary in Missouri, still planning to become a priest. But a series of racist encounters, including hearing a classmate celebrate on receiving news that Martin Luther King, Jr., had been assassinated, soon caused Thomas to leave the seminary. In 1968 he enrolled instead at the College of the Holy Cross, located in Worcester, Massachusetts, where he helped found the Black Student Union at the school and graduated cum laude in 1971 with an English major. Immediately after graduation, he married Kathy Grace Ambush, with whom he had one son, Jamal. The couple divorced in 1984. That fall he took advantage of an affirmative action program at Yale Law School to enroll there, although as a recipient of the law school's affirmative-action policies, Thomas later observed that "You had to prove yourself every day because the presumption was that you were dumb and didn't deserve to be there on merit." During law school, he tried to frustrate typical stereotypes about the subjects to which black students might expect to be drawn by focusing on business courses rather than those involving constitutional law or civil rights.

Upon his graduation from law school in 1974, Thomas took a job in Missouri as an assistant attorney general in the tax division, working for the state's attorney general, John Danforth. Within a few years, Danforth had won a seat in the U.S. Senate, and he would eventually champion Thomas's nomination to the Supreme Court. But when Danforth headed to Washington as a senator in 1977, Thomas found a job in the private sector as an in-house lawyer for Monsanto in St. Louis. He remained with Monsanto for only a short time, however. In 1979 he followed Danforth to Washington and became a legislative aide for the Missouri senator, focusing on environmental and energy matters. By this time Thomas's political views had assumed a solidly conservative cast that soon brought him to the attention of Ronald Reagan, elected president in 1980. Reagan appointed Thomas assistant secretary for civil rights in the Department of Education in 1981, thus planting him at the center of the subject he had studiously avoided from law school on. The following year, President Reagan made Thomas chairman of the Equal Employment Opportunity Commission (EEOC), the federal agency charged with enforcing civil rights laws in the workplace. In this position, Thomas attracted the ire of traditional civil rights organizations by refocusing the agency's antidiscrimination efforts away from its use of numerical timetables and goals to ensure minority representation in businesses and from its use of statistics to demonstrate that minorities were underrepresented in particular workplaces. Thomas headed the EEOC for nearly eight years. During this period he and his first wife divorced, and he met and married Virginia Lamp, who worked for the U.S. Chamber of Commerce.

President George Bush nominated Thomas to the U.S. Court of Appeals for the D.C. Circuit in 1989, and he was easily confirmed by the Senate in spring 1990 to replace Judge Robert Bork, who had himself resigned from the court of appeals after being rejected by the Senate for a seat on the Supreme Court. In June 1991 Justice Thurgood Marshall retired from the Supreme Court, and President Bush was placed under intense political pressure to appoint another African American to fill Marshall's vacant seat. Bush nominated Clarence Thomas for the position. Traditional civil rights organizations were torn by their desire to see another black fill the seat that Marshall, the Court's first African American, had long held on the Court and their opposition to Thomas's conservative record on civil rights. Ultimately, organizations such as the NAACP and the People for the American Way opposed his nomination. During initial confirmation hearings before the Democratic-controlled Senate Judiciary Committee, Thomas avoided expressing any indication of his stance on controversial constitutional issues, claiming, for example, that he could not remember having discussed with anyone the Court's decision in *Roe v. Wade* (1973), which had recognized a constitutional right to abortion and had been decided while he was in law school.

Shortly before the Senate Judiciary Committee was scheduled to vote concerning Thomas's nomination to the Court, news emerged that the FBI's background investigation of Thomas had uncovered an allegation that Thomas had sexually harassed a female subordinate 10 years earlier when he had worked at the Department of Education. His accuser was Anita Hill, who had worked for Thomas at the Education Department and at the EEOC, and who was, at the time of Thomas's confirmation hearings, a law school professor at the University of Oklahoma School of Law. After the allegation surfaced, the Senate Judiciary Committee reconvened to hold televised hearings concerning the charge in which Hill, Thomas, and a cast of other witnesses appeared. Thomas categorically denied the charges and declared indignantly that the proceedings were a "high-tech lynching for uppity blacks." In the end, after failing to discover conclusive evidence either to confirm or to refute Anita Hill's allegations, the Senate Judiciary Committee reported Thomas's nomination to the full Senate without a vote. There Clarence Thomas was confirmed as an associate justice on October 15, 1991, by the 20th century's narrowest margin, a vote of 52-48. He took his seat on the Court at the beginning of the following month.

On the Supreme Court, Justice Clarence Thomas became a regular ally of the Court's most prominent conservative, Associate Justice Antonin Scalia. Like Scalia, Thomas was willing to reconsider a host of long-settled constitutional doctrines, such as the 20th-century Court's willingness to permit Congress to engage in almost limitless lawmaking under the guise of its power under the Constitution to regulate interstate commerce. So closely allied was he with Scalia that early in his tenure on the Court some observers dubbed Thomas a Scalia-clone. More recent appraisals, though, have recognized that Justice Thomas's conservativism—though quite vigorous—is also quite his own. He regularly pens concurrences and dissents proposing radical revisions of constitutional precedents with which even Justice Scalia declines to join.

Thomas has angered liberal observers of the Court especially in the area of affirmative action, which he has treated with implacable judicial hostility. He has joined with other conservatives on the Court to visit renewed constitutional suspicion on government programs designed to benefit racial minorities and, in a concurrence to one important affirmative action case, *Adarand Constructors v. Pena* (1995), explained the basis of his own disagreement with such programs.

> These programs not only raise grave constitutional questions, they also undermine the moral basis of the equal protection principle. Purchased at the price of immeasurable human suffering, the equal protection principle reflects our Nation's understanding that such classifications ultimately have a destructive impact on the individual and our society. . . . [T]here can be no doubt that racial paternalism and its unintended consequences can be as poisonous and pernicious as any other form of discrimination. So-called "benign" discrimination teaches many that because of chronic and apparently immutable handicaps, minorities cannot compete with them without their patronizing indulgence. Inevitably, such programs engender attitudes of superiority or, alternatively, provoke resentment among those who believe that they have been wronged by the government's use of race. These programs stamp minorities with a badge of inferiority and may cause them to develop dependencies or to adopt an attitude that they are "entitled" to preferences.

His critics, as might be expected, charge that Thomas now hypocritically disfavors precisely those kinds of programs that paved his way to becoming a Supreme Court justice. The most vigorous of these have charged him with having forgotten his roots and being consumed with racial self-hatred. The latter charges Thomas has dismissed as being nothing more than "psycho-silliness."

Justice Clarence Thomas joined the Court at the age of 43, thus becoming its youngest member. He appears poised to continue in his position as an associate justice for many years to come and has therefore added a vigorous conservative vote to most of the issues presented to the Court. Continuing the course he charted in law school, Thomas defies those who insist on support of traditional liberal positions such as affirmative action as the sine qua non of black intellectualism. Predictably, his repudiation of such positions has branded him a constitutional reprobate in some circles and won him rave reviews in others. For the moment, he remains one of the most controversial members of the current Court.

Further Reading

Danforth, John C. *Resurrection: The Confirmation of Clarence Thomas*. New York: Viking, 1994.

Flax, Jane. *The American Dream in Black & White: The Clarence Thomas Hearings*. Ithaca, N.Y.: Cornell University Press, 1998.

Gerber, Scott Douglas. *First Principles: The Jurisprudence of Clarence Thomas*. New York: New York University Press, 1999.

Mayer, Jane and Jill Abramson. *Strange Justice: The Selling of Clarence Thomas*. New York: Plume, 1995.

Phelps, Timothy M. *Capitol Games: Clarence Thomas, Anita Hill, and the Story of a Supreme Court Nomination*. New York: Hyperion, 1992.

Simon, Paul. *Advice & Consent: Clarence Thomas, Robert Bork, and the Intriguing History of the Supreme Court's Nomination Battles*. Washington, D.C.: National Press Books, 1992.

RUTH BADER GINSBURG (1933–)

Associate Justice, 1993–

Appointed by President William Jefferson Clinton

RUTH BADER GINSBURG
(Photograph, United States Supreme Court)

A leading advocate for the cause of women's rights prior to her appointment as a federal judge, Ruth Bader Ginsburg became President William Jefferson Clinton's first appointment to the Supreme Court in 1993. She was the first appointment by a Democratic president since 1967, when Lyndon B. Johnson appointed legendary civil rights attorney Thurgood Marshall to the Court. In fact, Ginsburg's pioneering efforts to unravel legal distinctions based on gender have sometimes been compared to Marshall's own career as a civil rights lawyer who waged war against racial discrimination. Justice Ginsburg was the second woman to join the Court, but she has often found herself opposed in cases to Justice Sandra Day O'Connor, appointed by President Reagan in the 1980s and generally more conservative than Justice Ginsburg.

Ruth Bader Ginsburg was born Joan Ruth Bader on March 15, 1933, in Brooklyn, New York, the second child of Nathan Bader, a merchant, and Celia Amster Bader, both of whose families had immigrated to the United States. Ruth had an older sister, Marilyn, but she died in childhood, leaving Ruth to be raised as an only child. Celia Bader was a crucial influence on her surviving daughter's life until she died of cancer the day before Ruth graduated from Brooklyn's James Madison High School. After high school, Ruth Bader attended Cornell University, where she majored in government and graduated Phi Beta Kappa. While at Cornell, she met fellow student Martin D. Ginsburg, whom she married in 1954, after her graduation. Martin had already completed a year at Harvard Law School, but the young couple's educational ambitions were delayed briefly while he completed two years in the army. They lived at Fort Sill in Lawton, Oklahoma, where Ruth Bader Ginsburg gave birth to their first child, Jane Carol, in 1955. Afterward, the couple returned to Harvard Law School.

Ginsburg spent two years at Harvard, one of fewer than 10 women in a class of several hundred. Even this marginal feminine presence at the law school irritated its dean, Erwin Griswold, whom Ginsburg recalls asking how the women felt about occupying seats that could have been taken by deserving men. Ginsburg excelled in spite of the chilly welcome she and the other female students received, and earned a place as a member of the prestigious *Harvard Law Review*. But crisis struck in her second year: Her husband was diagnosed with cancer and had to undergo surgery and radiation therapy that prevented him from attending law school for a time. Ginsburg shouldered the labor of both caring for her husband and attending his classes and taking notes for him. Ultimately, Martin Ginsburg recovered and was able to graduate at the end of Ruth's second year at Harvard. He also accepted a position as an attorney at Weil, Gotshal & Managers, a New York law firm. Meanwhile, Ruth Bader Ginsburg transferred to Columbia for her final year of law school, winning a place on the *Columbia Law Review* and tying for first place in her graduating class.

The job offers that Ruth Bader Ginsburg might have expected did not materialize after her graduation from law school. The New York firms that would have eagerly courted a man with similar academic credentials declined to do so for Ginsburg, a woman and a Jew and, most significant in the eyes of firms, a mother. Eventually she took a position as a judicial clerk for Judge Edmund L. Palmieri, a federal district court judge for the Southern District of New York, from 1959 to 1961. After her judicial clerkship, Ginsburg worked for two years at the Columbia Law School Project on International Procedure, first as a research associate and subsequently as associate director of the project.

In 1963 Ginsburg took a teaching position on the faculty of the Rutgers University Law School. By 1969 she was a tenured professor at Rutgers. During this period, Ginsburg combined her responsibilities as a law teacher and scholar with regular legal work for the American Civil Liberties Union (ACLU) in sex discrimination cases, and in 1971 she was instrumental in helping to establish the ACLU's Women's Rights Project. That year the Supreme Court decided a case in which she helped write the brief, *Reed v. Reed* (1971). In *Reed*, the Court struck down a state law that displayed a preference for men over women as the administrators of estates. The case represented the first time that the Court had invalidated a statute under the Constitution's equal protection clause for engaging in gender discrimination, but the justices of the Court could not agree on the appropriate legal standard to be applied in cases of gender discrimination. This meant that the issue of sex discrimination would continue to be presented to the Court during the coming years. Ginsburg took a leading part in this presentation, eventually arguing six sex discrimination cases before the Court. These included *Frontiero v. Richardson* (1973), in which the Court struck down a policy of the U.S. Air

Force that granted various housing and insurance benefits to spouses of married male officers but not to the spouses of their female counterparts; *Craig v. Boren* (1976), which invalidated a state statute that prohibited the sale of 3.2% beer to males under age 21 and to women under 18; and *Weinberger v. Weisenfeld* (1975), which held unconstitutional a Social Security policy under which only women could collect their spouse's Social Security benefits.

In 1971 Ginsburg became a tenured professor on the faculty of Columbia Law School and taught on the faculty at Columbia until 1980, with only a brief interlude as a fellow at the Center for Advanced Study in the Behavioral Sciences at Stanford from 1977 to 1978. She served as the ACLU's general counsel from 1973 to 1980 and on its National Board of Directors from 1974 to 1980.

In 1980 President Jimmy Carter appointed Ruth Bader Ginsburg to the prestigious U.S. Court of Appeals for the District of Columbia Circuit. In her 13-year career as a federal appeals judge, Ginsburg became known for favoring what she described as "measured motions" in the development of the law. She publicly criticized the Court's controversial decision in *Roe v. Wade* (1973), which recognized a constitutional right to abortion, for not acting with appropriate restraint. She would have invalidated some abortion restrictions as varieties of gender discrimination that violated the Fourteenth Amendment's equal protection clause, but she would not have gone so far as the Court did in *Roe,* when it struck down virtually all abortion regulations that affected the first two trimesters of pregnancy. Ginsburg's public commitment to a measure of judicial restraint earned her a record as a moderate on the D.C. Court of Appeals.

In June 1993 Associate Justice Byron R. White retired from the Supreme Court, presenting President William Jefferson Clinton with his first opportunity to appoint a justice to the high court. Clinton responded to the opportunity by nominating Ruth Bader Ginsburg to fill the vacancy left by White's departure. Ginsburg's moderate record on the court of appeals made her pleasing to the members of both parties, and she was confirmed by the Senate by a vote of 96-3 on August 3, 1993. A week later, Ruth Bader Ginsburg took the oath of office to become the second female justice on the Supreme Court.

On the Court, Justice Ginsburg has continued to champion the cause of gender equity, most prominently by declaring the Court's decision in *United States v. Virginia* (1996), which declared unconstitutional the male-only admissions policy of the Virginia Military Institution (VMI). The state of Virginia had argued that the male-only policy was necessary because the school's combative educational practices—deemed by the state as crucial in the development of military officers—were better suited to men than to women. The state attempted to satisfy the demands of gender equality by creating a parallel institution for women seeking a military education in the form of the Virginia Women's Institute for Leadership, located at Mary Baldwin College. Nevertheless, Justice Ginsburg declared for the Court that this educational opportunity was not truly the equal of that provided by VMI and that the state's stereotypical views about the differences between men and women could not pass constitutional muster.

Although Justice Ginsburg's record on the court of appeals suggested that she might gravitate to the center of the Rehnquist court, recent years have seen a vigorous conservative majority on crucial constitutional issues, and Ginsburg has found herself regularly in dissent against this majority. On the issue of affirmative action programs, for example, she dissented from the majority opinion in *Adarand Constructors v. Pena* (1995), which cast new constitutional suspicion on the continued vitality of minority set-aside programs. And as a conservative majority on the Court has retreated from the so-called wall of separation in church-state cases in favor of a view of the establishment clause that allows religious groups to share in various forms of public support on terms equal to those enjoyed by nonreligious groups, Ginsburg has regularly dissented. Finally, the closing years of the 20th century and the opening years of the 21st have witnessed a renewed willingness by the Court to scrutinize the lengths to which Congress might legislate under the guise of its constitutional power to regulate interstate commerce. Justice Ginsburg has protested against this new, conservative form of activism by the Supreme Court, which resulted, for example, in the Court's striking down key provisions of the Violence Against Women Act in *United States v. Morrison* (2000).

It remains to be seen what role Justice Ginsburg will play on the Supreme Court in the future. News that Justice Ginsburg had been diagnosed with colon cancer shortly before the beginning of the 1999–2000 term prompted some observers to wonder whether she might be forced to step down from the bench. But the cancer was successfully treated, and Ginsburg seemed poised to remain on the bench a number of years. Her expressed willingness to display some measure of deference toward legislatures combined with a vigorous respect for civil rights might ordinarily place her in the Court's center. But the Rehnquist court at the turn of the century has embarked on a conservative course in which it frequently overturns laws in the area of affirmative action or examines the relative balance envisioned by the Constitution for federal and state lawmaking. The Court's critics have complained that this course exemplifies an activism as vigorous as any practiced by previous courts on behalf of traditional liberal causes, such as civil rights. In any event, Justice Ginsburg has been and will doubtlessly continue to be a judicial enemy of this activism.

Further Reading

Baugh, Joyce Ann, Christopher E. Smith, Thomas R. Hensley, and Scott Patrick Johnson. "Justice Ruth Bader Ginsburg: A Preliminary Assessment." *University of Toledo Law Review* 26 (1994): 1–34.

Confusione, Michael James. "Justice Ruth Bader Ginsburg and Justice Thurgood Marshall: A Misleading Comparison." *Rutgers Law Journal* 26 (1995): 887–907.

Elington, Toni J., Sylvia K. Higashi, Jayna K. Kim, and Mark Murakami. "Justice Ruth Bader Ginsburg and Gender Discrimination." *University of Hawaii Law Review* 20 (1998): 699–796.

Gillman, Elizabeth E. and Joseph M. Micheletti. "Justice Ruth Bader Ginsburg." *Seton Hall Constitutional Law Journal* 3 (1993): 657–663.

Halberstam, Malvina. "Ruth Bader Ginsburg: The First Jewish Woman on the U.S. Supreme Court." *Cardozo Law Review* 19 (1998): 1441–1454.

Walsh, Amy. "Ruth Bader Ginsburg: Extending the Constitution." *John Marshall Law Review* 32 (1998): 197–225.

Stephen Gerald Breyer (1938–)

Associate Justice, 1994–

Appointed by President William Jefferson Clinton

Stephen G. Breyer
(United States Supreme Court)

Stephen G. Breyer was the second and last appointment made by President Bill Clinton to the Supreme Court and the last justice to join the Court in the 20th century. Before assuming his seat on the Court, Breyer had earned a reputation as a consensus builder, and he was widely expected to play a moderating role on a Court that had often been split down partisan lines. Breyer also brought to the Court an unusual range of views: the social conscience of a moderate liberal but a suspicion of excessive governmental regulation more commonly exhibited by conservatives. These traits combined to win him ready confirmation by the Senate and to place him generally at the Court's center.

Stephen Gerald Breyer was born on August 15, 1938, in San Francisco, California, the son of Irving Breyer and Anne Breyer. His father was a lawyer who worked for the San Francisco Board of Education. His mother was active in the Democratic party and in a variety of civic affairs. Although as an adult Breyer's marriage to the daughter of British gentry would land him in affluent circumstances, he experienced a childhood in more commonplace surroundings and would later recall to members of the Senate who inquired into his background that he had been a Boy Scout, a delivery boy, and a ditch digger for the Pacific Gas and Electric Company.

Stephen Breyer attended a prestigious magnet school in the San Francisco area, Lowell High School, where he participated on the debate team and was voted by his graduating classmates "most likely to succeed." After high school, he attended Stanford University and graduated summa cum laude in 1959. Over the next two years, he studied at Magdalen College of Oxford University in England on a Marshall Scholarship and received his B.A. there in 1961. Upon his return to the United States, Breyer attended Harvard Law School, where he served as an articles editor on the *Harvard Law Review* and graduated magna cum laude in 1964. His record at Harvard paved the way for Breyer to obtain a coveted clerkship with Associate Justice Arthur Goldberg on the Supreme Court during the Court's 1964 term. His work for Justice Goldberg included preparing the first draft of Justice Goldberg's highly regarded concurring opinion in one of the most important cases of the 1960s, *Griswold v. Connecticut* (1965), which recognized a constitutional right of privacy for married couples to use contraceptive devices.

After Breyer's clerkship with Justice Goldberg, he accepted a job in the U.S. Justice Department as a special assistant to Assistant Attorney General Donald F. Turner in the antitrust division. Breyer worked for the Justice Department from 1965 to 1967. In the year he left this federal post, Breyer married Joanna Freda Hare, the daughter of a wealthy English family. The couple eventually had three children: Chloe, Nell, and Michael. That same year Breyer joined the faculty at the Harvard Law School, where he taught regularly from 1967 to 1994, focusing his scholarly and teaching work mainly in the area of subjects involving government regulation, such as antitrust law. His wife Joanna took a position as a psychologist at Boston's Dana Farber Clinic. Over the next 13 years, Breyer combined a career as a legal academic with frequent forays into the arena of public service. He briefly worked for Archibald Cox in 1973 as an assistant special prosecutor during the Watergate investigation. From 1974 to 1975 he was a special counsel to the Administrative Practices Subcommittee of the Senate Judiciary Committee and worked closely with the subcommittee chair, Senator Edward Kennedy, to sponsor legislation that eventually lowered airline fares by deregulating the airline industry. From 1979 to 1980 he was chief counsel to the Senate Judiciary Committee.

Breyer demonstrated repeated ability to forge alliances across partisan lines, and his excellent reputation among both Democrats and Republicans eventually earned him a place on the federal bench. Toward the end of President Jimmy Carter's term in office, he nominated Stephen Breyer to a seat on the U.S. Court of Appeals for the First Circuit. This nomination, made in November 1980, might easily have been stalled by Republicans until after Ronald Reagan was inaugurated in 1981. Nevertheless, Breyer enjoyed bipartisan respect that prompted the Republicans to support his appointment to the federal appeals court. He served on the court from 1980 until 1994 and as its chief judge from 1990 until 1994. In addition to his normal responsibilities as an appeals judge, Breyer, who had worked for the Senate Judiciary Committee at a time when the issue of sentencing reform was before Congress, served as a member of the Sentencing Commission from 1985 to 1989. This commission established guidelines for federal judges for the imposition of criminal sentences.

In 1993, when Justice Byron R. White retired from the Supreme Court, President Bill Clinton considered appointing Stephen Breyer to fill the vacancy on the Court, before ultimately nominating Ruth Bader Ginsburg. The following year, though, Associate Justice Harry A. Blackmun retired after 24 years of service, and this time President Clinton nominated Breyer to replace the retiring justice. Though Breyer was a lifelong Democrat and was championed by one of the Senate's most ardent liberals, Ted Kennedy, his reputation as a moderate won him easy approval in the Senate. In fact, he faced tougher questioning from Democrats anxious about his probusiness decisions as a federal appeals judge and about his work on the Sentencing Commission than from Republicans. Consumer advocate and frequent presidential candidate Ralph Nader testified against Breyer and chastised him for an overly solicitous regard for big business. Nevertheless, the pointed questions on issues such as abortion and capital punishment with which senators sometimes prick Supreme Court nominees did not trouble Breyer. Asked for his views on the death penalty, Breyer noted that its constitutionality in some circumstances was clearly established. "It seems to me that the Supreme Court has considered that matter for quite a long time in a large number of cases," Breyer said. "At this point it is settled." Similarly, he acknowledged the settled nature of the Court's abortion decisions. "The case of *Roe v. Wade* has been the law for 21 years, or more, and it was recently affirmed by the Supreme Court of the United States," he said. "That is the law." The Senate Judiciary Committee unanimously recommended that his appointment to the Court be approved, and in the end, Breyer was confirmed by a vote of 87-9 on July 29, 1994. He took his seat on the Court the following month.

By all indications, Breyer might have been expected to take a position in the middle of the Court's ideological range, and in his brief tenure on the Court to date he has tended to confirm this expectation. The labels "conservative" and "liberal," often misleading when applied to Supreme Court justices, do not sit easily on Justice Breyer. For example, in *United States v. Playboy* (2000), he dissented from the majority's decision to strike down a federal law that required cable television operators to block sexually oriented channels or to limit their transmission to hours when children are unlikely to be viewing as violating freedom of speech. Perhaps most significant, two of the Court's most conservative members, Chief Justice William Rehnquist and Associate Justice Antonin Scalia, joined in Breyer's dissent.

On many issues, though, Justice Breyer has found himself at odds with the Court's more conservative justices, who have formed a narrow majority on a variety of issues during the closing years of the 20th century and the beginning years of the 21st. A majority of the Rehnquist Court, for example, has been the midwife for a renewed concern for the prerogatives of states within the federal system, especially under the Constitution's Eleventh Amendment, which immunizes states from suits by citizens of other states and by aliens. In controversial decisions such as *Alden v. Maine* (1999) and *Kimel v. Florida Board of Regents* (2000), a conservative majority on the Court applied the Eleventh Amendment to bar claims against states brought under federal labor and antidiscrimination laws. Justice Breyer joined three other justices—John Paul Stevens, David Souter, and Ruth Bader Ginsburg—to protest this constitutional interpretation. Similarly, the same conservative justices have revisited the limits of Congress's power to regulate matters affecting interstate commerce and have invalidated federal laws such as the Gun Free Schools Zones Act, held unconstitutional in *United States v. Lopez* (1995), and the Violence Against Women Act in *United States v. Morrison* (2000). Again, Breyer—joined by Justices Stevens, Souter, and Ginsburg—has voiced his opposition to this constitutional development.

Justice Stephen G. Breyer came to the Court with a distinguished career as a legal scholar and a federal appeals judge but nevertheless confessed that his early terms on the Court left him with the nervousness typical of a freshman justice. "I keep thinking of a *New Yorker* cartoon," he said shortly after joining the Court. "A circus dog is about to set out, very gingerly, on a tightrope while a clown below unfolds a scroll. It says: 'All Rex could think about when he stepped out upon the high wire was that he was a very old dog and this was a brand-new trick.'" But with whatever trepidation Justice Breyer undertook his work as a Supreme Court justice, he has become comfortable with a judicial voice that is neither stridently liberal nor conservative. The last justice appointed in the 20th century is more a pragmatist than a prophet, more interested in solutions than in semantics. He has been accused of being a technocrat, but it is perhaps fitting that the appointment of such a justice should conclude the long and turbulent history of the 20th-century Supreme Court.

Further Reading

Breyer, Stephen G. *Breaking the Vicious Circle: Toward Effective Risk Regulation*. Cambridge: Harvard University Press, 1993.

———. "Does Federalism Make a Difference?" *Public Law* (1999): 651–662.

———. "Judicial Review: A Practicing Judge's Perspective." *Texas Law Review* 78 (2000): 761–775.

Fallone, Edward A. "The Clinton Court Is Now Open for Business: The Business Law Jurisprudence of Justice Stephen Breyer." *Missouri Law Review* 59 (1995): 857–893.

Joyce, Walter E. "The Early Constitutional Jurisprudence of Justice Stephen G. Breyer: A Study of the Justice's First Year on the United States Supreme Court." *Seton Hall Constitutional Law Journal* 7 (1996): 149–163.

Glossary

abstention The refusal by one court to hear a matter properly heard before another court.

accessory A person who, in a secondary role, assists in the commission of a crime.

accused A person who is charged with having committed a crime.

acquittal A judicial declaration that a criminal defendant has not been proven guilty.

actionable Events or conduct that provide a basis for a civil suit.

affidavit A sworn, written statement.

affirmative action Policies that use a person's status as a racial minority or as a woman as a basis for beneficial treatment.

aggravation Particular circumstances of a crime that cause the law to treat the crime more seriously.

ACLU American Civil Liberties Union.

***amicus curiae* brief** A brief filed with a court by parties who are not officially involved in a case but who are interested in its outcome.

antitrust law Laws that regulate monopolies and other business arrangements or practices that interfere with commercial competition.

appeal A request to a higher court to review the decision of a lower court.

appellant A person who appeals a decision from a lower court to a higher court.

appellee A person who attempts to defend the decision of a lower court when it is appealed to a higher court

arbitration A method for resolving legal disputes in which the parties to the dispute present their case to a third party for resolution.

arraignment The point in a criminal proceeding when a criminal defendant is brought before a court to be informed of the charges against the defendant and enters a plea to the charges.

arrest The taking of a person suspected of having committed a crime into custody.

assignment of error Points made by party appealing a case that specify the errors allegedly made in a lower court.

attempt Effort to commit a crime that may be punished even if the crime is not completed.

bail Money or other property given by a criminal defendant to obtain release from jail and to guarantee that the defendant will subsequently appear in court to answer criminal charges.

bankruptcy A legal procedure that allows a debtor to obtain a release from debts.

beyond a reasonable doubt Degree of certainty required in a criminal trial to convict a person accused of a crime.

bill of attainder Legislation, prohibited by the Constitution, that imposes punishment on a person without affording that person a trial.

Bill of Rights The first 10 amendments to the United States Constitution, which secure various individual rights and liberties.

blue laws Laws that restrict certain business and entertainment activities on Sundays.

boycott The refusal of a group of people to do business with someone.

breach of the peace A public disturbance punishable as a crime.

brief A written presentation to a court of a party's arguments concerning the issues in a case.

capital crime A crime punishable by death.

capital punishment Punishment by death.

case method of legal instruction A form of legal education that became predominant in the last part of the 19th century that taught students how to analyze legal problems by focusing on the published decisions of judges.

case law Law created by the decisions of courts, as opposed to laws enacted by legislative bodies.

cause of action The legal grounds for bringing a civil suit against another party.

certiorari, writ of An application to a higher court, especially the United States Supreme Court, seeking to overturn the result in a lower court.

chambers A judge's private office.

circuit riding The travel of a judge from one place to another to hear cases.

circumstantial evidence Evidence that does not directly prove a particular factual assertion but from which the truth of that assertion may be inferred.

citation A reference to a legal authority.

civil action As opposed to a criminal proceeding, a suit to obtain a remedy for a wrong committed against a person.

civil service Nonelected government employment other than military service.

class action suit Lawsuit brought on behalf of many individuals with a common interest by one or more representatives.

court clerk Official of a court who maintains the court's records.

common law Law created by the decisions of courts, as opposed to laws enacted by legislative bodies.

compensatory damages A monetary award that provides a remedy for an injury suffered.

concurring opinion A judicial opinion that sets forth other or additional reasons for a result reached in the opinion of a court.

confession An admission of guilt.

consent decree A court order resolving a case based upon the agreement of the parties.

conviction The final determination of guilt in a criminal proceeding.

court reporter Individual who makes a verbatim record of court proceedings.

creditor Party owed a debt.

cross-examination The questioning of a witness called on behalf of an opponent in court proceedings.

cruel and unusual punishments Punishments prohibited by the Constitution's Eighth Amendment because they are disproportionate, excessive, or otherwise outside normal bounds of punishment.

declaratory judgment An order of a court stating the rights and liabilities of parties to a civil suit.

defamation The making public of a statement, either orally or in writing, that injures the reputation of another.

default judgment A judgment entered against a person who has been sued in a civil lawsuit and who fails to respond in a timely fashion to the suit.

defendant A person sued in a civil case or charged with having committed a crime in a criminal case.

de minimus Matters that are trivial or unimportant.

deportation The removal of a person from a country.

deposition A legal procedure in which a witness is questioned under oath before a trial, normally to discover what the witness knows about the matters at issue in the trial.

derivative action A lawsuit brought by a shareholder to enforce a claim or right of the corporation.

dictum As opposed to the holding in a case, language in a court's opinion that is not necessary to the decision.

direct examination The questioning of a witness in a legal proceeding by the party who called the witness.

discovery, pretrial Procedures for allowing parties to a legal action to discover information concerning a case prior to the trial.

discrimination Treating persons or matters differently without adequate grounds for doing so.

dismissal The termination of a case.

disorderly conduct Conduct that disturbs the peace.

dissenting opinion An opinion written by a judge who disagrees with the result reached by a majority of judges in a case.

district attorney A prosecuting attorney who pursues criminal convictions for a particular judicial district.

domicile A permanent home or residence.

double jeopardy The prosecution by a government body of the same offence for which a criminal defendant has previously been prosecuted by the body.

due process The requirement of fair and orderly treatment by the government protected in the Fifth and Fourteenth Amendments.

duress Forcing one to act against his will through threats or other exercises of power.

eminent domain The power of government to take property for public purposes as long as just compensation is provided for the property.

en banc The determination of a case by all of the judges of a particular court rather than by a smaller panel of judges from the court.

enjoin A court order commanding certain action or inaction.

equal protection of the law The requirement of equal treatment protected by the Fifth and Fourteenth Amendments to the Constitution.

equity Legal principles and procedures that provide for the resolution of civil cases according to principles of fairness.

exclusionary rule A constitutional rule that prevents the government from offering evidence in a criminal trial when the evidence was obtained illegally.

exemplary damages Punitive damages; damages in excess of those needed to compensate a wrong or injury.

ex post facto law A law passed after some act or event has occurred that changes the legal consequences of the act or event.

extradition The surrender by one country of a person accused or convicted of a crime in another country.

felony A serious crime, as distinguished from lesser crimes referred to as misdemeanors.

fiduciary A person with special obligations to faithfully serve another's interest.

foreclosure The termination of property rights, often through a forced sale.

forum non conveniens Judicial doctrine that permits a court to decline to hear a case if another court more conveniently located can do so.

fraud The intentional misrepresentation of significant facts.

gag order A court order preventing persons before the court from discussing matters relating to a case.

garnishment A legal procedure used to seize money or wages of a party owing a debt or against whom a claim has been made.

grand jury A group of citizens appointed to hear evidence of alleged crimes and to determine whether criminal indictments should be brought on the basis of this evidence.

habeas corpus, writ of An application to a court seeking the release of a person in custody on the grounds that the person is being held unlawfully.

hate crime statutes Laws that impose or increase penalties for crimes committed on the basis of racial, gender-related, or other forms of prejudice.

hearing A legal proceeding, supplementary to a trial, in which evidence is taken or legal arguments are presented for a court to make some determination.

hearsay Statements made out of court and offered in court to prove some issue of fact.

holding The legal principle announced by a court's opinion.

homicide A killing of another person.

immunity Freedom from having to fulfill some legal duty or from being prosecuted for a crime.

impanelment The selection of a jury.

impeach To discredit a witness or to formally accuse a judge or other public official of wrongdoing.

in forma pauperis To bring a legal proceeding without having to pay normal legal costs.

inalienable Incapable of being transferred or given away, as in "inalienable rights."

incriminate To implicate someone in having committed a crime.

indictment The formal accusation made by a grand jury that an individual has committed a crime.

indigent Poor.

information An accusation by a public official that an individual has committed a crime, used in many states as a counterpart to a grand jury indictment.

injunction A court order commanding or prohibiting some action.

innocence, presumption of The requirement that government affirmatively prove that an individual has committed a crime in order to inflict punishment for that crime.

inquest An official investigation into whether a crime has occurred, especially in connection with a death.

INS Immigration and Naturalization Service.

IRS Internal Revenue Service.

insolvency The inability of a person or entity to pay debts as they become due.

judicial review The authority of courts to determine the constitutionality of legislative and executive actions.

jurisdiction The legal authority of a particular court to hear and decide a case.

jurisprudence Legal philosophy.

jurist A judge.

juvenile delinquent A person defined by the law as a minor who has committed a crime.

legal tender Currency that may be used to satisfy one's debts.

lesser included offense A crime, the elements of which are necessarily proven by evidence that a more serious crime has been committed.

libel A written defamation of one's character or reputation.

long arm statute A law that allows a court in one state to determine the legal rights and liabilities of a person presently located in another state.

magistrate A judicial official who decides preliminary matters or minor cases.

malice aforethought The predetermined intention to commit a criminal or otherwise wrongful act.

mandamus A court order commanding some public official to undertake certain action.

maritime law Law relating to the sea or to shipping.

martial law The control of civilians by a military authority.

mens rea A criminal intent.

minor A person who is not legally an adult.

Miranda rights Rights of which criminal defendants are required to be informed at the time of their arrest.

misdemeanor A minor crime punishable by a fine or less than one year of imprisonment, as distinguished from a more serious crime, referred to as a felony.

mistrial The termination of a trial because of some misconduct or other unusual occurrence.

motion A request to a court to take some action.

murder The killing of another person with malice aforethought.

naturalization The process by which a foreigner becomes a citizen.

natural law Legal principles derived from general moral principles rather than laws enacted by legislatures or otherwise created by some authority with power to make law.

negligence An unintentional failure to act with an appropriate measure of carefulness.

nominal damages A small monetary amount awarded to a party who has been wronged but has suffered no actual damages.

objection A protest directed to evidence offered in court or to some other event in court.

obscenity Patently offensive sexual material that lacks serious literary, artistic, political, or scientific value.

obstruction of justice A criminal interference with the administration of justice such as the destruction of evidence in a case.

opinion A written statement by a judge or court explaining the reasons for a judicial decision.

ordinance A local law.

original jurisdiction Authority of a court to make the initial determination of a particular issue in a trial setting, in contrast with appellate jurisdiction, the authority to determine whether a lower court's decision is correct.

overrule To disavow the legal authority of a prior case, or to deny an objection in a case.

patent The exclusive right granted by government to an inventor to produce or sell an invention for a designated period of time.

peremptory challenge An objection made to the seating of a potential jury member that needs to be justified, as opposed to a challenge for cause.

perjury A false statement made under oath.

personal property Property other than real estate.

plain error rule A rule allowing a higher court to reverse the result reached in a trial court even if the person appealing the trial court decision did not object to the error at trial.

plaintiff The party who brings a civil suit.

plain view doctrine A rule that permits law enforcement personnel to seize items in plain view even if they lack a search warrant.

plea The response made by a criminal defendant to an indictment, such as "not guilty."

plea bargain An agreement between a prosecutor and a criminal defendant that disposes of a criminal matter without further trial proceedings.

pleadings Official court documents filed by parties to a legal action containing their claims and/or defenses regarding the action.

precedent Past court decisions that amount to legal authority for the resolution of a present legal issue.

preemption A constitutional doctrine derived from the supremacy clause that allows federal laws on a subject to override inconsistent state laws.

preliminary hearing A hearing to determine whether there is probable cause to believe that an accused has committed a crime, used in situations in which there has been no grand jury indictment.

preponderance of the evidence The standard of proof in most civil cases, which requires evidence sufficient to suggest that it is more likely than not that an asserted claim is true.

prima facie case Evidence sufficient to prove the elements of a claim, in the absence of contrary proof by an opposing party.

privileged communication Communications protected from disclosure in a judicial proceeding without the consent of the parties to the communication.

probable cause Reasonable grounds for believing that a person alleged to have committed a crime has in fact done so.

probate Legal proceedings related to the administration of wills.

process The legal mechanism used by a court to obtain jurisdiction over a particular person or property, such as a summons to appear in court.

pro se To represent oneself in a legal proceeding.

prosecutor A lawyer who represents the government in cases against criminal defendants.

punitive damages Damages used to punish a wrongdoer in a civil proceeding as opposed to those intended to compensate an injured party; also known as exemplary damages.

real property Land and the structures or other items permanently attached to it.

recess A temporary adjournment of legal or legislative proceedings.

recusal A judge's determination not to participate in the decision of a case in which the judge has some personal interest.

remand An order by a higher court returning a proceeding to a lower court for some further legal action.

removal The transfer of a case from one court to another, as from a state court to a federal court.

repossession The process whereby a creditor takes possession of collateral for a loan upon the debtor's failure to pay the loan.

res judicata A judicial doctrine that makes the resolution of a legal issue in one court binding as to attempts to relitigate the same issue in another court.

restrictive covenant A provision in a real estate deed that limits the permissible uses of the property.

reversible error A legal error committed by a trial court sufficiently serious to justify an appellate court in overruling the trial court's decision.

ruling The result announced by a court either as to its decision on the outcome of a case or its decision of same issue raised in connection with case proceedings.

search warrant A judicial order permitting law enforcement personnel to enter and search a location.

self-incrimination Testimony by a person that tends to implicate the person in the commission of some unlawful conduct.

senatorial courtesy The practice by presidents of conferring with the senators of the state involved in a judicial appointment and seeking their approval of or at least acquiescence to that appointment.

sentencing The pronouncing of punishment on a criminal defendant convicted of having committed a crime.

seriatim opinions On courts with more than one judge, a series of opinions by each individual judge explaining the reasons for a decision as opposed to an opinion written for the entire court.

service of process The delivery to a defendant of a complaint or other documents representing the filing of a lawsuit against the defendant and summoning the defendant to appear in court and answer the lawsuit.

slander Verbal statements that injure another party's reputation.

Socratic method Form of legal instruction in which a law teacher engages students with a series of questions about the application of legal rules to particular problems; contrasted with lecture methods of instruction.

solicitor general A government lawyer appointed by the president of the United States to represent the United States in cases before the Supreme Court.

sovereign immunity A doctrine that bars suits against a government, such as a state or local government, unless the government has previously authorized such suits.

speedy trial requirement The constitutional right of criminal defendants to be tried without undue delay.

standing A judicial doctrine that prevents parties without some personal stake in a case from asserting a legal claim in court.

stare decisis The principle that courts should generally follow the decisions of previous cases dealing with the same legal issue.

statute Laws enacted by the legislative branch of government, such as the Congress or a state legislature.

statutory rape The crime of having sexual intercourse with an underage female.

subpoena An order for a witness to appear in court to testify or to produce certain documents or other tangible items in court.

summary judgment A judgment rendered by a court without a trial when the significant facts of a case are not disputed.

summons A notice to a defendant in a civil suit that a lawsuit has been filed against the defendant, specifying the time at which the defendant must appear in court to answer the claim.

test case A legal action pursued to clarify or challenge some legal principle.

testimony The statement made by a witness under oath in a legal proceeding.

tort A civil wrong done by one party against another, other than failures to abide by contractual agreements.

transcript The official record of a legal proceeding.

treason Rebellious conduct toward one's government, especially that attempting to overthrow government or kill a sovereign.

vacate To set aside a court order or decision.

venire A list of those summoned for jury duty.

venue, change of The transfer of the location of a legal proceeding.

verdict The decision of a jury in a trial.

visa Official permission to enter another country.

voir dire The examination of potential jurors to determine whether they are qualified to serve on a jury free of bias.

warrant An order permitting a public official to take some action, including an order permitting law enforcement personnel to arrest someone or search property.

witness A person who offers testimony in a legal proceeding.

writ A court's written order requiring or prohibiting some action.

Chronology

1760 Thomas Jefferson enters the College of William and Mary.

George III becomes King of England.

1762 Jean-Jacques Rousseau publishes *The Social Contract.*

1763 The Treaty of Paris ends the French and Indian War.

Patrick Henry argues the Parsons' Cause before the Hanover County Court, in which he challenges the Crown's right to nullify colonial laws.

1765 Parliament passes the Stamp Act, the first direct tax of the colonies.

The Stamp Act Congress meets in New York and passes a "Declaration of Rights and Grievances" calling for repeal of the Act.

Sons of Liberty, a secret organization of colonials opposed to the Stamp Act, is formed.

1766 Parliament repeals the Stamp Act.

Mason-Dixon Line established between Pennsylvania and Maryland, later to become the boundary between free and slave states.

1767 Parliament passes the Townshend Acts, which levy taxes on glass, lead, paint, paper, and tea in the colonies.

1770 Clash between British troops and colonists, known as the Boston Massacre, occurs in March.

1773 In December, American patriots disguised as Mohawk Indians throw chests of tea belonging to the British East India Company into Boston Harbor.

1774 Britain passes Intolerable Acts in the spring, which include provision for the closure of Boston harbor.

First Continental Congress convenes in Philadelphia in September, including delegates from all colonies except Georgia.

1775 American revolution begins.

Second Continental Congress convenes.

1776 Declaration of Independence signed on July 4.

1781 British capitulate to Americans at Yorktown in October.

1783 Treaty of Paris ends Revolutionary War.

1787 The members of the Philadelphia Constitutional Convention sign and submit the proposed Constitution to the states for ratification.

1788 The requisite number of states ratify the Constitution, making it effective.

1789 First Congress meets in New York. President George Washington inaugurated.

Judiciary Act of 1789 establishes the Supreme Court with six justices.

First six justices appointed by President Washington on September 24, 1789, and confirmed by the Senate two days later.

James Wilson becomes the first Supreme Court to take the oath of office on October 5.

John Jay becomes first chief justice of the Court. French Revolution takes place.

1791 The first 10 amendments to the Constitution (the "Bill of Rights") are ratified.

1793 President George Washington inaugurated for a second term. In *Chisholm v. Georgia,* Supreme Court holds that a state may be sued by the citizens of another state.

1794 Eleventh Amendment to the Constitution is ratified, restricting the ability of federal courts to hear suits against the states brought by aliens or citizens of other states.

Whiskey Rebellion occurs in Pennsylvania.

1796 Oliver Ellsworth becomes chief justice.

1797 President John Adams inaugurated.

1798 *July 14:* Congress passes the Alien and Sedition Act, designed by the administration of President John Adams to combat subversion and dissent thought to be caused chiefly by various European immigrants.

1800 Federal government moves to new capital in Washington, D.C.

1801 President Thomas Jefferson inaugurated. John Marshall becomes chief justice.

1803 United States makes the Louisiana Purchase.

In *Marbury v. Madison,* Supreme Court holds that it has the authority to declare federal laws unconstitutional.

1804 Twelfth Amendment to the Constitution is ratified and provides that presidential electors vote separately for president and vice president.

Alexander Hamilton is killed in a duel with Aaron Burr.

1805 President Thomas Jefferson inaugurated for a second term.

1808 United States prohibits further imports of slaves from Africa.

1809 President James Madison inaugurated.

1810 In *Fletcher v. Peck,* Supreme Court holds that it has authority to review the constitutionality of state laws.

1812 United States declares war on Great Britain.

1813 President James Madison inaugurated for a second term.

1814 Washington, D.C. burnt by British forces.

War between United States and Britain ends with the Treaty of Ghent.

1817 President James Monroe inaugurated.

1819 In *McColloch v. Maryland,* Supreme Court holds that Congress has power to create a Bank of the United States.

In *Dartmouth College v. Woodward,* Court holds that state's attempt to seize control of private university violated the contracts clause.

1820 Missouri Compromise allows Maine to enter the Union as a free state and Missouri as a slave state.

1821 President James Monroe inaugurated for a second term.

1823 President Monroe announces the "Monroe Doctrine," according to which the Western hemisphere is closed to further European colonization.

1824 John Quincy Adams elected president by the House of Representatives after none of the presidential candidates obtain a majority of the vote in the general election.

1825 President John Quincy Adams inaugurated.

1829 President Andrew Jackson inaugurated.

1831 In *Cherokee Nation v. Georgia,* Supreme Court refuses to hear claim brought by Cherokee.

1833 President Andrew Jackson inaugurated for a second term.

Jackson opposes Bank of the United States by withdrawing federal funds from it.

In *Barron v. Baltimore,* Supreme Court holds that provisions of the Bill of Rights limit only actions of the federal government, not state governments.

1836 Roger B. Taney becomes chief justice.

Texas obtains independence from Mexico.

1837 President Martin Van Buren inaugurated.

1841 President William H. Harrison inaugurated.

1841 President John Tyler inaugurated.

1845 President James K. Polk inaugurated.

1849 President Zachary Taylor inaugurated.

1850 President Millard Fillmore inaugurated.

1853 President Franklin Pierce inaugurated.

1854 Republican party formed.

1857 President James Buchanan inaugurated.

In *Dred Scott v. Sandford,* Supreme Court holds that blacks are not U.S. citizens and that Missouri Compromise is unconstitutional.

1861 President Abraham Lincoln inaugurated.

Civil War begins with firing by Confederate troops on Fort Sumter.

1863 President Lincoln issues Emancipation Proclamation, declaring slaves in rebel states free.

Lincoln delivers Gettysburg Address.

1864 Salmon P. Chase becomes chief justice.

1865 President Abraham Lincoln inaugurated for a second term.

Confederates States of America surrender at Appomattox.

President Lincoln is assassinated.

President Andrew Johnson inaugurated.

Thirteenth Amendment to the Constitution is ratified, abolishing slavery.

Southern states begin to enact Black Codes, which curtail the rights of newly freed slaves.

1868 Fourteenth Amendment to the Constitution is ratified, providing that persons born or naturalized in the United States are citizens of the United States, and prohibiting states from denying the privileges and immunities of U.S. citizens, equal protection of the law, or due process of law.

President Andrew Johnson is impeached by the United States House of Representatives but acquitted by the Senate.

1869 President Ulysses S. Grant inaugurated.

1870 Fifteenth Amendment to the Constitution is ratified, prohibiting voting discrimination on the grounds of race, color, or previous condition of servitude.

1873 President Ulysses S. Grant inaugurated for a second term.

In *Slaughterhouse Cases,* Supreme Court holds that a slaughterhouse monopoly did not violate the Fourteenth Amendment.

1874 Morrison R. Waite becomes chief justice.

1877 President Rutherford B. Hayes inaugurated after special commission decides in his favor.

1879 In *Reynolds v. United States,* Supreme Court upholds a federal law prohibiting bigamy in the territories against challenge that it violated the religious liberty of Mormons.

1881 President James Garfield inaugurated.

1881 President James Garfield is assassinated.

President Chester A. Arthur inaugurated.

1883 In the *Civil Rights Cases,* Supreme Court holds that Congress has no authority to prohibit racial discrimination in inns and public conveyances.

1885 President Grover Cleveland inaugurated.

1888 Melville W. Fuller becomes chief justice.

1889 President Benjamin Harrison inaugurated.

1893 President Grover Cleveland inaugurated.

1896 In *Plessy v. Ferguson,* Supreme Court upholds the practice of segregation under the "separate but equal" doctrine.

1897 President William McKinley inaugurated.

1898 United States goes to war with Spain over Cuba.

Treaty of Paris between Spain and U.S. cedes Cuba, Puerto Rico, Guam, and the Philippines to the U.S. for $20 million.

1901 President William McKinley inaugurated for a second term.

Cuba becomes U.S. protectorate.

President McKinley assassinated.

President Theodore Roosevelt inaugurated.

1902 U.S. gains control over Panama Canal.

1903 In *Champion v. Ames,* Supreme Court finds that Congress has authority to prohibit the interstate sale of lottery tickets.

1905 President Theodore Roosevelt inaugurated for an additional term.

In *Lochner v. New York,* Supreme Court holds that a state law restricting the working hours for bakers violated the due process clause of the Fourteenth Amendment.

1908 In *Muller v. Oregon,* Supreme Court upholds a law limiting work hours for women.

1909 President William Howard Taft inaugurated.

1910 Edward Douglass White becomes chief justice.

Mann Act passed by Congress, prohibiting transportation of women across state lines for immoral purposes.

1913 President Woodrow Wilson inaugurated.

Sixteenth Amendment to the Constitution ratified, allowing federal income tax.

Seventeenth Amendment to the Constitution ratified, providing for direct popular election of United States senators.

1914 World War I begins.

1917 President Woodrow Wilson inaugurated for a second term.

United States enters World War I.

1918 Eugene Debs, socialist, convicted of espionage and sentenced to 10 years in prison.

In *Hammer v. Dagenhart,* Supreme Court holds that Congress has no power to prohibit interstate commerce in goods made with child labor.

1919 Eighteenth Amendment to the Constitution is ratified, establishing the era of Prohibition.

1920 The U.S. Senate votes against joining the League of Nations.

Nineteenth Amendment to the Constitution is ratified, guaranteeing women the right to vote.

1921 President Warren G. Harding inaugurated.

William Howard Taft becomes chief justice.

1923 President Calvin Coolidge inaugurated.

1924 J. Edgar Hoover becomes director of Federal Bureau of Investigations (FBI).

1925 President Calvin Coolidge inaugurated for an additional term.

1925 President Herbert Hoover inaugurated.

1930 Charles Evans Hughes becomes chief justice.

1933 President Franklin D. Roosevelt inaugurated.

Twenty-first Amendment to the Constitution is ratified, repealing Prohibition.

1934 In *Home Building and Loan Association v. Blaisdell,* Supreme Court holds that moratorium on the repayment of mortgage loans did not violate the contracts clause.

1937 President Franklin D. Roosevelt inaugurated for a second term.

Roosevelt proposes "court-packing" plan.

Supreme Court retreats from opposition to Roosevelt's New Deal programs.

1939 World War II begins.

1941 President Franklin D. Roosevelt inaugurated for a third term.

Harlan Fiske Stone becomes chief justice.

Japanese attack Pearl Harbor.

1942 In *Wickard v. Filburn,* Supreme Court holds that Congress has power to regulate farmer's production of wheat for personal use.

1943 In *West Virginia State Board of Education v. Barnette,* Supreme Court holds that a compulsory flag-salute requirement in schools violates the First Amendment.

1944 Allied Forces invade Normandy on D-Day.

In *Korematsu v. U.S.,* Supreme Court upholds the constitutionality of the forced internment of Japanese Americans during World War II.

1945 President Franklin D. Roosevelt inaugurated for a fourth term.

United Nations succeeds the League of Nations.

President Harry S. Truman inaugurated.

War in Europe ends on V.E. Day.

President Truman orders atomic bombs dropped on Hiroshima and Nagasaki.

Japan surrenders, ending World War II.

Trial of Nazi leaders for war crimes commences at Nuremberg.

1946 Fred M. Vinson becomes chief justice.

1948 Congress passes Marshall Plan to provide economic aid to Europe.

1949 President Harry S. Truman inaugurated for an additional term.

1950 Senator Joseph McCarthy advises President Harry Truman that State Department has been infiltrated by Communists.

Korean War begins.

1951 Twenty-second Amendment to the Constitution is ratified, limiting presidents to two elected terms.

Julius and Ethel Rosenberg sentenced to death for espionage.

1952 In *Youngstown Sheet & Tube Co. v. Sawyer,* Supreme Court holds that President Harry Truman's attempt to seize the steel mills during the Korean War was unconstitutional.

1953 President Dwight D. Eisenhower inaugurated.

Earl Warren becomes chief justice.

1954 Supreme Court declares public school segregation unconstitutional in *Brown v. Board of Education.*

Senator Joseph R. McCarthy conducts televised investigation of alleged infiltration of the army by Communists; is censured by the Senate.

1957 President Dwight D. Eisenhower inaugurated for a second term.

1961 President John F. Kennedy inaugurated.

Twenty-third Amendment to the Constitution is ratified, creating the District of Columbia and granting its residents the right to elect representatives to the electoral college.

U.S.-backed Cuban exiles attempt Bay of Pigs invasion of Cuba.

In *Mapp v. Ohio,* Supreme Court holds that illegally seized evidence may not be used in state criminal prosecutions.

1962 Cuban missile crisis occurs. United States establishes military counsel in Vietnam.

In *Baker v. Carr,* Supreme Court holds that inequalities in legislative voting districts can be challenged in federal court.

In *Engel v. Vitale,* Court declares state-sponsored prayer in public schools unconstitutional.

1963 March on Washington by 200,000 "Freedom Marchers" who demonstrate for civil rights.

President John F. Kennedy assassinated by Lee Harvey Oswald.

President Lyndon B. Johnson inaugurated.

President Johnson forms a commission to investigate Kennedy's assassination and persuades Chief Justice Earl Warren to serve as its chairman.

In *Abington School District v. Schempp,* Court declares Bible readings in public schools unconstitutional.

In *Gideon v. Wainright,* Court holds that states must provide counsel to criminal defendants charged with serious crimes who cannot afford an attorney.

1964 Twenty-fourth Amendment to the Constitution is ratified, abolishing the poll tax in federal elections.

Congress, in Gulf of Tonkin Resolution, authorizes President Lyndon B. Johnson to resist North Vietnamese aggression.

Martin Luther King, Jr., wins Nobel Peace Prize.

In *Heart of Atlanta Motel v. United States,* Supreme Court holds that Congress has power to prohibit private racial discrimination by hotels involved in interstate commerce.

In *New York Times v. Sullivan,* Supreme Court makes it more difficult for libel suits to be brought against public officials.

In *Reynolds v. Sims,* Supreme Court requires "one person, one vote" principle in voter districting.

1965 President Lyndon B. Johnson inaugurated for an additional term.

In *Griswold v. Connecticut,* Supreme Court holds that right of privacy prevents states from prohibiting the use of contraceptives.

1966 In *Miranda v. Arizona,* Supreme Court holds that criminal suspects must be informed of their right to remain silent and to have an attorney appointed to represent them.

1967 Twenty-fifth Amendment to the Constitution is ratified, providing for presidential succession in the event of the president's death, resignation, or disability.

1968 Martin Luther King, Jr., is assassinated in Memphis by James Earl Ray.

Senator Robert F. Kennedy is assassinated in Los Angeles by Sirhan Sirhan.

1969 President Richard M. Nixon inaugurated.

Trial of the "Chicago Eight" results in finding of not guilty for violating the Civil Rights Act's antiriot provisions.

Nixon begins withdrawal of U.S. troops from Vietnam.

In *Brandenburg v. Ohio,* Supreme Court holds that mere advocacy of violence or illegal conduct is protected by freedom of speech.

Justice Abe Fortas resigns after being accused of financial improprieties while on the Court.

Warren E. Burger becomes chief justice.

1970 Student protestors against Vietnam War killed at Kent State University by National Guard.

1971 Twenty-sixth Amendment to the Constitution is ratified, giving 18-year-olds the right to vote.

In *Lemon v. Kurtzman,* Supreme Court holds that financial aid to parochial schools violates the establishment clause.

In *Swann v. Charlotte-Mecklenburg Board of Education,* Supreme Court approves busing as a remedy in desegregation cases.

1972 Watergate burglary occurs.

In *Furman v. Georgia,* Supreme Court declares moratorium on capital punishment.

1973 President Richard M. Nixon inaugurated for a second term.

Senate Watergate investigation begins.

Vice President Spiro T. Agnew resigns and Gerald Ford replaces him.

In *Miller v. California,* Supreme Court establishes definition of obscenity.

In *Roe v. Wade,* Court holds that the Constitution protects the right to abortion.

1974 House Judiciary Committee recommends three articles of impeachment against President Nixon.

Nixon resigns.

President Gerald R. Ford inaugurated.

1975 North Vietnamese overrun South Vietnam and U.S. withdraws its remaining forces.

1976 In *Buckley v. Valeo,* Supreme Court upholds the constitutionality of limits on campaign contributions but not on campaign spending.

In *Craig v. Boren,* Court requires more vigorous justification for gender discrimination than for most kinds of legislative classifications.

1977 President Jimmy Carter inaugurated.

1978 In *Regents of the University of California v. Bakke,* Supreme Court upholds affirmative action program that uses race as a factor in medical school admissions programs.

1981 President Ronald Reagan inaugurated.

1985 President Ronald Reagan inaugurated for a second term.

1986 William H. Rehnquist becomes chief justice.

In *Bowers v. Hardwick* Supreme Court upholds the constitutionality of a state law prohibiting private, consensual homosexual conduct.

1989 President George Bush inaugurated.

In *Richmond v. J. A. Croson Co.,* Supreme Court holds that a municipal set-aside program for racial minorities in the award of public contracts violated the equal protection clause.

In *Texas v. Johnson,* Court holds that a state statute providing for punishment of flag desecration infringed on the freedom of speech.

1992 Twenty-seventh Amendment to the Constitution is ratified, prohibiting Congress from altering its pay without an intervening election between the time the alteration takes effect.

1993 President William J. Clinton inaugurated.

1995 In *United States v. Lopez,* Supreme Court holds that Congress lacked authority under the commerce clause to regulate possession of firearms in the vicinity of schools.

1996 In *United States v. Virginia,* Supreme Court holds that exclusion of women from the Virginia Military Institute violates the equal protection clause.

1997 President William J. Clinton inaugurated for a second term.

In *Printz v. United States,* Supreme Court holds that Congress lacked power to require state law enforcement personnel to perform background checks on gun purchasers.

1998 President Clinton becomes second president in U.S. history to be impeached by the House of Representatives.

In *Clinton v. New York,* Supreme Court declares the Line Item Veto Act unconstitutional.

1999 President Clinton acquitted of impeachment charges by the U.S. Senate.

In *Alden v. Maine,* Supreme Court invalidates federal law that allowed state employee to sue state in a state court.

2000 In *Bush v. Gore,* Supreme Court halts manual recounts in Florida for president, thus effectively awarding the presidency to George W. Bush who wins a majority of the electoral college vote while losing the popular vote.

2001 President George W. Bush inaugurated.

Appendix 1
Justices

Name	State	President	Nominated	Confirmed (Rejected)	Oath Taken	Service Ended	Years of Service
Rutledge, J.	S.C.	Washington	9/24/1789	9/26/1789	2/15/1790	3/5/1791	1
Wilson	Pa.	Washington	9/24/1789	9/26/1789	10/5 /1789	8/21/1798	9
Jay	N.Y.	Washington	9/24/1789	9/26/1789	10/19/ 1789	6/29/1795	6
Cushing	Mass.	Washington	9/24/1789	9/26/1789	2 /2/1790	9/13/1810	21
Blair	Va.	Washington	9/24/1789	9/26/1789	2/2/1 790	10/25/1795	6
Iredell	N.C.	Washington	2/8/1790	2/10/1790	5/1 2/1790	10/20/1799	9
Johnson, T.	Md.	Washington	8/5/1791 R 10/31/1791	11/7/1791	8/6/1792	1/16/1793	1
Paterson	N.J.	Washington	3/4/1793	3/4/1793	3/1 1/1793	9/9/1806	13
Rutledge, J.	S.C.	Washington	7/1/1795	12/15/1795 Rej.	8/12/1795	12/15/1795	1
Chase, S.	Md.	Washington	1/26/1796	1/27/1796	2/4/1796	6/19/1811	15
Ellsworth	Conn.	Washington	3/3/1796	3/4/1796	3/8/1796	12/15/1800	4
Washington	Va.	Adams, J.	9/29/1798 R 12/19/1798	12/20/1798	2/4/1799	11/26/1829	31
Moore	N.C.	Adams, J.	12/4/1799	12/10/1799	4/21/1800	1/26/1804	4
Marshall, J.	Va.	Adams, J.	1/20/1801	1/27/1801	2/4/1801	7/6/1835	34
Johnson, W.	S.C.	Jefferson	3/22/1804	3/24/1804	5/8/1804	8/4/1834	30
Livingston	N.Y.	Jefferson	11/10/1806 R 12/13/1806	12/17/1806	1/20/1807	3/18/1823	16

Note: R=Recess appointment
Note: Two dates in "Nominated Column" for recess appointments

Name	State	President	Nominated	Confirmed (Rejected)	Oath Taken	Service Ended	Years of Service
Todd	Ky.	Jefferson	2/28/1807	3/3/1807	5/4/1807	2/7/1826	19
Duvall	Md.	Madison	11/15/1811	11/18/1811	11/23 /1811	1/14/1835	23
Story	Md.	Madison	11/15/1811	11/18/1811	2/3/18 12	9/10/1845	34
Thompson	N.Y.	Monroe	9/1/1823 R				
			12/8/1823	12/19/1823	2/10/1824	12/18/1843	20
Trimble	Ky.	Adams, J. Q.	4/11/1826	5/9/1826	6/16/1826	8/25/1828	2
McLean	Ohio	Jackson	3/6/1829	3/7/1829	1/11/1830	4/4/1861	32
Baldwin	Pa.	Jackson	1/4/1830	1/6/1830	1/18/1830	4/21/1844	14
Wayne	Ga.	Jackson	1/6/1835	1/9/1835	1/14/1835	7/5/1867	32
Taney	Md.	Jackson	12/28/1835	3/15/1836	3/28/1836	10/12/1864	28
Barbour	Va.	Jackson	12/28/1835	3/15/1836	5/12/ 1836	2/25/1841	5
Catron	Tenn.	Van Buren	3/3/1837	3/8/1837	5/1/1837	5/30/1865	28
McKinley	Ala.	Van Buren	4/22/1837 R				
			9/18/1837	9/25/1837	1/9/1838	7/19/ 1852	15
Daniel	Va.	Van Buren	2/26/1841	3/2/1841	1/10/1842	5/31/1860	19
Nelson	N.Y.	Tyler	2/4/1845	2/14/1845	2/27/1845	11/28/1872	27
Woodbury	N.H.	Polk	9/20/1845 R				
			12/23/1845	1/3/1846	9/23/1845	9/4/1851	5
Grier	Pa.	Polk	8/3/1846	8/4/1846	8/10/1846	1/31/1870	23
Curtis	Mass.	Fillmore	9/22/1851 R				
			12/11/1851	12/20/1851	10/10/1851	9/30/1857	5
Campbell	Ala.	Pierce	3/22/1853	3/25/1853	4/11/ 1853	4/30/1861	8
Clifford	Maine	Buchanan	12/9/1857	1/12/1858	1/ 21/1858	7/25/1881	23
Swayne	Ohio	Lincoln	1/22/1862	1/24/1862	1/27/1 862	1/24/1881	19

Name	State	President	Nominated	Confirmed (Rejected)	Oath Taken	Service Ended	Years of Service
Miller	Iowa	Lincoln	7/16/1862	7/16/1862	7/21/1 862	10/13/1890	28
Davis	Ill.	Lincoln	10/17/1862 R				
			12/1/1862	12/8/1862	12/10/1862	3/4/1877	14
Field	Calif.	Lincoln	3/6/1863	3/10/1863	5/20/1863	12/1/1897	34
Chase, S. P.	Ohio	Lincoln	12/6/1864	12/6/1864	12/15/1864	5/7/1873	8
Strong	Pa.	Grant	2/7/1870	2/18/1870	3/14/1870	12/14/1880	10
Bradley	N.J.	Grant	2/7/1870	3/21/1870	3/23/1870	1/22/1892	21
Hunt	N.Y.	Grant	12/3/1872	12/11/1872	1/9/1873	1/27/1882	9
Waite	Ohio	Grant	1/19/1874	1/21/1874	3/4/1874	3/23/1888	14
Harlan (I)	Ky.	Hayes	10/16/1877	11/29/1877	12/10/1877	10/14/1911	34
Woods	Ga.	Hayes	12/15/1880	12/21/1880	1/5/1881	5/14/1887	6
Matthews	Ohio	Garfield	1/26/1881 R				
			3/14/1881	5/12/1881	5/17/1881	3/22/1889	7
Gray	Mass.	Arthur	12/19/1881	12/20/1881	1/9/1882	9/15/1902	20
Blatchford	N.Y.	Arthur	3/13/1882	3/27/1882	4/3/1882	7/7/1893	11
Lamar, L.	Miss.	Cleveland	12/6/1887	1/16/1888	1/18/1888	1/23/1893	5
Fuller	Ill.	Cleveland	4/30/1888	7/20/1888	10/8 /1888	7/4/1910	22
Brewer	Kan.	Harrison, B.	12/4/1889	12/18/1889	1/6/1890	3/28/1910	20
Brown	Mich.	Harrison, B.	12/23/1890	12/29/1890	1/5/1891	5/28/1906	15
Shiras	Pa.	Harrison, B.	7/19/1892	7/26/1892	10/10/1892	2/23/1903	10
Jackson, H.	Tenn.	Harrison, B.	2/2/1893	2/18/1893	3/4/1893	8/8/1895	2
White, E.	La.	Cleveland	2/19/1894	2/19/1894	3/12/1894	12/18/1910	17
Peckham	N.Y.	Cleveland	12/3/1895	12/9/1895	1/6/1896	10/24/1909	13
McKenna	Calif.	McKinley	12/16/1897	1/21/1898	1/26/1898	1/5/1925	26

Name	State	President	Nominated	Confirmed (Rejected)	Oath Taken	Service Ended	Years of Service
Holmes	Mass.	Roosevelt, T.	8/11/1902 R				
			12/2/1902	12/2/1902	12/8/1902	1/12/1932	29
Day	Ohio	Roosevelt, T.	1/29/1903	2/23/1903	3/2/1903	11/13/1922	19
Moody	Mass.	Roosevelt, T.	12/3/1906	12/12/1906	12/17/1906	11/20/1910	3
Lurton	Tenn.	Taft	12/13/1909	12/20/1909	1/3/19 10	7/12/1914	4
Hughes	N.Y.	Taft	4/25/1910	5/2/1910	10/10/1910	6/10/1916	6
White, E.	La.	Taft	12/12/1910	12/12/1910	12/19/1910	5/ 19/1921	10
Van Devanter	Wyo.	Taft	12/12/1910	12/15/1910	1/3/1911	6/2/1937	26
Lamar, J.	Ga.	Taft	12/12/1910	12/15/1910	1/3/1911	1/2/ 1916	5
Pitney	N.J.	Taft	2/19/1912	3/13/1912	3/18/1912	12/31/1922	10
McReynolds	Tenn.	Wilson	8/19/1914	8/29/1914	9/ 5/1914	2/1/1941	26
Brandeis	Mass.	Wilson	1/28/1916	6/1/1916	6/5/1 916	2/13/1939	22
Clarke	Ohio	Wilson	7/14/1916	7/24/1916	8/1/1916	9/18/1922	6
Taft	Conn.	Harding	6/21/1921	6/30/1921	7/11/1921	2/3/1930	8
Sutherland	Utah	Harding	9/5/1922	9/5/1922	10/2/1922	1/17/1938	15
Butler	Minn.	Harding	11/23/1922 R				
			12/5/1922	12/21/1922	1/2/1923	11/16/1939	17
Sanford	Tenn.	Harding	1/24/1923	1/29/1923	2/19/1923	3/8/1930	7
Stone	N.Y.	Coolidge	1/5/1925	2/5/1925	3/2/1925	7/2/1941	16
Hughes	N.Y.	Hoover	2/3/1930	3/13/1930	2/24/1930	7/1/1941	11
Roberts	Pa.	Hoover	5/9/1930	5/20/1930	6/2/1930	7/31/1945	15
Cardozo	N.Y.	Hoover	2/15/1932	2/24/1932	3/14/1932	7/9/1938	6
Black	Ala.	Roosevelt, F.	8/12/1937	8/17/1937	8/19/1937	9/17/1971	34
Reed	Ky.	Roosevelt, F.	1/15/1938	1/25/1938	1/31/1938	2/25/1957	19
Frankfurter	Mass.	Roosevelt, F.	1/5/1939	1/17/1939	1/30/1939	8/28/1962	23
Douglas	Conn.	Roosevelt, F.	3/20/1939	4/4/1939	4/17/1939	11/12/1975	36

Name	State	President	Nominated	Confirmed (Rejected)	Oath Taken	Service Ended	Years of Service
Murphy	Mich.	Roosevelt, F.	1/4/1940	1/16/1940	1/18/1940	7/19/1949	9
Stone	N.Y.	Roosevelt, F.	6/12/1941	6/27/1941	7/3/1941	4/22/1946	5
Byrnes	S.C.	Roosevelt, F.	6/12/1941	6/12/1941	7/8/1941	10/3/1942	1
Jackson, R.	N.Y.	Roosevelt, F.	6/12/1941	7/7/1941	7/11/1941	10/9/1954	13
Rutledge, W.	Iowa	Roosevelt, F.	1/11/1943	2/8/1943	2/15/1943	9/10/1949	6
Burton	Ohio	Truman	9/18/1945	9/19/1945	10/1/1945	10/13/1958	13
Vinson	Ky.	Truman	6/6/1946	6/20/1946	6/24/1946	9/8/1953	7
Clark	Texas	Truman	8/2/1949	8/18/1949	8/24/1949	6/12/1967	18
Minton	Ind.	Truman	9/15/1949	10/4/1949	10/12/1949	10/15/1956	7
Warren	Calif.	Eisenhower	10/2/1953 R				
			1/11/1954	3/1/1954	10/5/1953	6/23/1969	15
Harlan (II)	N.Y.	Eisenhower	1/10/1955	3/16/1955	3/28/1955	9/23/1971	16
Brennan	N.J.	Eisenhower	10/15/1956 R				
			1/14/1957	3/19/1957	10/16/1956	7/20/1990	34
Whittaker	Mo.	Eisenhower	3/2/1957	3/19/1957	3/ 25/1957	3/31/1962	5
Stewart	Ohio	Eisenhower	10/14/1958 R				
			1/17/1959	5/5/1959	10/14/1958	7/3/1981	22
White, B.	Colo.	Kennedy	4/3/1962	4/11/1962	4/16/1962	3 /19/1993	30
Goldberg	Ill.	Kennedy	8/31/1962	9/25/1962	10/1/1962	7/25/1965	3
Fortas	Tenn.	Johnson, L.	7/28/1965	8/11/1965	10/4/1965	5/14/1969	4
Marshall, T.	N.Y.	Johnson, L.	6/13/1967	8/30/1967	10/2/1967	6/27/1991	24
Burger	Va.	Nixon	5/21/1969	6/9/1969	6/23/1969	9/26/1986	17
Blackmun	Minn.	Nixon	4/15/1970	5/12/1970	6/9/1970	7/29/1994	24
Powell	Va.	Nixon	10/22/1971	12/6/1971	1/7/1972	6/26/1987	16
Rehnquist	Ariz.	Nixon	10/21/1971	12/10/1971	1/ 7/1972	9/26/1986	14

Name	State	President	Nominated	Confirmed (Rejected)	Oath Taken	Service Ended	Years of Service
Stevens	Ill.	Ford	11/28/1975	12/17/1975	12/19/1975		
O'Connor	Ariz.	Reagan	5/7/1981	9/21/1981	9/26/1981		
Rehnquist	Va.	Reagan	6/17/1986	9/17/1986	9/26/ 1986		
Scalia	Va.	Reagan	6/17/1986	9/17/1986	9/26/1986		
Kennedy	Calif.	Reagan	11/24/1987	2/3/1988	2/18/1988		
Souter	N.H.	Bush	7/25/1990	10/2/1990	10/9/1990		
Thomas	Va.	Bush	7/1/1991	10/15/1991	11/1/1991		
Ginsburg	N.Y.	Clinton	6/14/1993	8/3/1993	8/10/1993		
Breyer	Mass.	Clinton	5/13/1994	7/29/1994	8/3/1994		

Appendix 2
Presidents and Their Appointments to the Supreme Court

Presidents	Justices
George Washington	James Wilson Associate Justice
	John Jay Chief Justice
	William Cushing Associate Justice
	John Blair, Jr. Associate Justice
	John Rutledge Associate Justice
	James Iredell Associate Justice
	Thomas Johnson Associate Justice
	William Paterson Associate Justice
	John Rutledge Chief Justice
	Samuel Chase Associate Justice
	Oliver Ellsworth Chief Justice
John Adams	Bushrod Washington Associate Justice
	Alfred Moore Associate Justice
	John Marshall Chief Justice
Thomas Jefferson	William Johnson Associate Justice
	Henry Brockholst Livingston Associate Justice
	Thomas Todd Associate Justice
James Madison	Gabriel Duvall Associate Justice
	Joseph Story Associate Justice
James Monroe	Smith Thompson Associate Justice
John Quincy Adams	Robert Trimble Associate Justice
Andrew Jackson	John McLean Associate Justice
	Henry Baldwin Associate Justice
	James Moore Wayne Associate Justice
	Roger Brooke Taney Chief Justice
	Philip Pendleton Barbour Associate Justice
Martin Van Buren	John Catron Associate Justice
	John McKinley Associate Justice
	Peter Vivian Daniel Associate Justice
William H. Harrison	. . .
John Tyler	Samuel Nelson Associate Justice
James K. Polk	Levi Woodbury Associate Justice
	Robert Cooper Grier Associate Justice
Zachary Taylor	. . .

Presidents	Justices
Millard Fillmore	Benjamin Robbins Curtis Associate Justice
Franklin Pierce	John Archibald Campbell Associate Justice
James Buchanan	Nathan Clifford Associate Justice
Abraham Lincoln	Noah Haynes Swayne Associate Justice
	Samuel Freeman Miller Associate Justice
	David Davis Associate Justice
	Stephen Johnson Field Associate Justice
	Salmon Portland Chase Chief Justice
Andrew Johnson	. . .
Ulysses S. Grant	William Strong Associate Justice
	Joseph P. Bradley Associate Justice
	Ward Hunt Associate Justice
	Morrison Remick Waite Chief Justice
Rutherford B. Hayes	John Marshall Harlan Associate Justice
	William Burnham Woods Associate Justice
James A. Garfield	Stanley Matthews Associate Justice
Chester A. Arthur	Horace Gray Associate Justice
	Samuel Blatchford Associate Justice
Grover Cleveland	Lucius Quintus C. Lamar Associate Justice
	Melville Weston Fuller Chief Justice
Benjamin Harrison	David Josiah Brewer Associate Justice

Presidents	Justices
Benjamin Harrison (cont.)	Henry Billings Brown Associate Justice
	George Shiras, Jr. Associate Justice
	Howell Edmunds Jackson Associate Justice
Grover Cleveland	Edward Douglass White Associate Justice
	Rufus Wheeler Peckham, Jr. Associate Justice
William McKinley	Joseph McKenna Associate Justice
Theodore Roosevelt	Oliver Wendell Holmes, Jr. Associate Justice
	William Rufus Day Associate Justice
	William Henry Moody Associate Justice
William Howard Taft	Horace Harmon Lurton Associate Justice
	Charles Evans Hughes Associate Justice
	Edward Douglass White Chief Justice
	Willis Van Devanter Associate Justice
	Joseph Rucker Lamar Associate Justice
	Mahlon Pitney Associate Justice
Woodrow Wilson	James Clark McReynolds Associate Justice
	Louis Dembitz Brandeis Associate Justice
	John Hessin Clarke Associate Justice
Warren G. Harding	William Howard Taft Chief Justice

Presidents	Justices
Warren G. Harding (cont.)	George Sutherland Associate Justice
	Pierce Butler Associate Justice
	Edward Terry Sanford Associate Justice
Calvin Coolidge	Harlan Fiske Stone Associate Justice
Herbert Hoover	Owen Josephus Roberts Associate Justice
	Charles Evans Hughes Chief Justice
	Benjamin Nathan Cardozo Associate Justice
Franklin D. Roosevelt	Hugo Lafayette Black Associate Justice
	Stanley Forman Reed Associate Justice
	Felix Frankfurter Associate Justice
	William Orville Douglas Associate Justice
	Frank Murphy Associate Justice
	James Francis Byrnes Associate Justice
	Harlan Fiske Stone Chief Justice
	Robert Houghwout Jackson Associate Justice
	Wiley Blount Rutledge Associate Justice
Harry S. Truman	Harold Hitz Burton Associate Justice
	Fred Moore Vinson Chief Justice
	Thomas Campbell Clark Associate Justice
	Sherman Minton Associate Justice
Dwight D. Eisenhower	Earl Warren Chief Justice
	John Marshall Harlan II Associate Justice

Presidents	Justices
Dwight D. Eisenhower (cont.)	William J. Brennan, Jr. Associate Justice
	Charles Evans Whittaker Associate Justice
	Potter Stewart Associate Justice
John F. Kennedy	Byron Raymond White Associate Justice
	Arthur Joseph Goldberg Associate Justice
Lyndon B. Johnson	Abe Fortas Associate Justice
	Thurgood Marshall Associate Justice
Richard M. Nixon	Warren Earl Burger Chief Justice
	Harry A. Blackmun Associate Justice
	Lewis Franklin Powell, Jr. Associate Justice
	William Hubbs Rehnquist Associate Justice
Gerald R. Ford	John Paul Stevens Associate Justice
James Earl Carter	. . .
Ronald Reagan	Sandra Day O'Connor Associate Justice
	William Hubbs Rehnquist Chief Justice
	Antonin Scalia Associate Justice
	Anthony M. Kennedy Associate Justice
George Bush	David H. Souter Associate Justice
	Clarence Thomas Associate Justice
William Jefferson Clinton	Ruth Bader Ginsburg Associate Justice
	Stephen G. Breyer Associate Justice

APPENDIX 3
IMPORTANT SUPREME COURT CASES

Case Name	Case Citation and Date	Author of Court's Opinion	Case Summary
Abington School District v. Schempp	374 U.S. 203 (1963)	Clark	Recitations of the Lord's prayer and Bible readings in public schools violated the establishment clause.
Abrams v. United States	250 U.S. 616 (1919)	Clarke	The First Amendment did not protect protests relating to policies involving Soviet Russia.
Adair v. United States	208 U.S. 161 (1908)	Harlan	A federal law prohibiting the firing of employees for union activity violated the Fifth Amendment's due process clause.
Adamson v. California	332 U.S. 46 (1947)	Reed	A state criminal prosecutor who called the jury's attention to a defendant's failure to testify did not violate the due process guarantee.
Adarand Constructors, Inc. v. Pena	515 U.S. 200 (1995)	O'Connor	Federal affirmative action programs required an overwhelmingly persuasive justification.
Adkins v. Children's Hospital	261 U.S. 525 (1923)	Sutherland	Federal minimum wage law for women violated liberty of contract.
Agostini v. Felton	521 U.S. 203 (1997)	O'Connor	Federal law that provided on-site remedial educational services to children in private schools did not violate the establishment clause.
Akron v. Akron Center for Reproductive Health, Inc.	462 U.S. 416 (1983)	Powell	State law requiring that physicians perform abortions in hospitals rather than clinics, that they provide women with detailed information about abortions before obtaining their consent, and that 24 hours elapse between such consent and an abortion, violated the right to abortion.

Case Name	Case Citation and Date	Author of Court's Opinion	Case Summary
Albertson v. Subversive Activities Control Board	382 U.S. 70 (1965)	Brennan	The McCarran Act, which required communist organizations to register with the attorney general, violated the Fifth Amendment's privilege against self-incrimination.
Alden v. Maine	527 U.S. 706 (1999)	Kennedy	Federal law that allowed state employee to sue state in a state court violated the state's sovereign immunity from such suits guaranteed by the Eleventh Amendment.
Alexander v. Holmes County Board of Education	396 U.S. 19 (1969)	Per curiam	The obligation of a public school district to desegregate schools had to be accomplished without further delay.
Allegheny County v. ACLU Greater Pittsburgh Chapter	492 U.S. 573 (1989)	Blackmun	Public nativity scene display violated the establishment clause, though display that included a menorah and other symbols did not.
Allgeyer v. Louisiana	165 U.S. 578 (1897)	Peckham	A state law that prohibited inhabitants of the state from entering into insurance contracts by mail with out-of-state insurance companies violated the freedom of contract implicit in the Fourteenth Amendment's due process clause.
American Communications Association v. Douds	339 U.S. 382 (1950)	Vinson	Congress had power under the commerce clause to pass the Taft-Hartley Act, which required labor union officers to swear that they were not members of the Communist party and did not support the violent overthrow of the U.S. government.
Amistad	40 U.S. 518 (1841)	Story	Certain African slaves who had mutinied on board the *Amistad* had been kidnapped and were therefore entitled to their freedom.
Apodaca v. Oregon	406 U.S. 404 (1972)	White for plurality	The Sixth Amendment's guarantee of a jury trial does not re-

Case Name	Case Citation and Date	Author of Court's Opinion	Case Summary
			quire a unanimous verdict in noncapital state criminal cases.
Apprendi v. New Jersey	530 U.S. 466 (2000)	Stevens	Statute allowing judge to lengthen the prison sentences of defendants found by judge to have committed a hate crime violated the due process clause.
Aptheker v. Secretary of State	378 U.S. 500 (1964)	Goldberg	Federal policy of denying passports to Americans who were communists violated the liberty of travel protected by the Fifth Amendment's due process clause.
Argersinger v. Hamlin	407 U.S. 25 (1972)	Douglas	The right to counsel guaranteed by the Constitution's Sixth Amendment applies to misdemeanor criminal cases as well as to felonies.
Arizona v. Fulminante	499 U.S. 279 (1991)	Rehnquist, White	The admission of an involuntary confession does not require the reversal of a criminal conviction when additional evidence supports the conviction.
Arlington Heights v. Metropolitan Housing Development Corp.	429 U.S. 252 (1977)	Powell	No proof of a violation of the equal protection clause was shown merely on the basis of the racially disproportionate impact of a zoning decision that prevented the building of a racially integrated housing development.
Ashwander v. Tennessee Valley Authority	297 U.S. 288 (1936)	Hughes	Congress had power to pass the Tennessee Valley Authority Act, which provided for the construction of dams and the sale of electricity.
Austin v. United States	509 U.S. 602 (1993)	Blackmun	Federal law that provided for the civil forfeiture of property used in illegal drug trafficking could be challenged under the Eighth Amendment.
Bailey v. Drexel Furniture Co.	259 U.S. 20 (1922)	Taft	Federal child labor law that sought to restrain the use of child labor by prohibitively

Case Name	Case Citation and Date	Author of Court's Opinion	Case Summary
			taxing the manufacturing products of such labor was unconstitutional.
Baker v. Carr	369 U.S. 186 (1962)	Brennan	The equal protection clause authorized a federal court to consider a challenge to the apportionment of voters in a state's legislative districts.
Ballard v. United States	329 U.S. 187 (1946)	Douglas	Systematic exclusion of women from juries in the federal courts of California violated federal law.
Ballew v. Georgia	435 U.S. 223 (1978)	Blackmun	Five-person jury in a state criminal misdemeanor trial violated the Sixth Amendment's right to a jury trial.
Bank of Augusta v. Earle	38 U.S. 519 (1839)	Taney	A state could only exclude an out-of-state corporation from doing business in the state if the exclusion was clearly stated in law.
Bank of the United States v. Deveaux	9 U.S. 61 (1809)	Marshall	A corporation could be a citizen for purposes of invoking the federal court's diversity jurisdiction, and its citizenship was measured by the citizenship of its shareholders.
Barenblatt v. United States	360 U.S. 109 (1959)	Harlan	The First Amendment did not bar holding a congressional witness in contempt for refusing to testify concerning his beliefs about communism and his membership in a communist organization.
Barker v. Wingo	407 U.S. 514 (1972)	Powell	A delay of five years between the arrest of a criminal defendant and that defendant's trial did not violate the right to a speedy trial, since the defendant did not desire an immediate trial.
Barnes v. Glen Theatre	501 U.S. 560 (1991)	Rehnquist	A state public indecency law used to prohibit nude dancing did not infringe upon freedom of speech.

Case Name	Case Citation and Date	Author of Court's Opinion	Case Summary
Barron v. Baltimore	32 U.S. 243 (1833)	Marshall	The protections provided by the Bill of Rights applied to federal rather than state actions.
Bates v. State Bar of Arizona	433 U.S. 350 (1977)	Blackmun	State ethics rules preventing lawyer advertising violated freedom of speech.
Batson v. Kentucky	476 U.S. 79 (1986)	Powell	The equal protection clause barred a prosecutor from using peremptory challenges to exclude blacks from a jury on account of their race.
Belle Terre v. Boraas	416 U.S. 1 (1974)	Douglas	A local zoning ordinance that limited occupancy of single-family dwelling places to traditional families or to no more than two unrelated people did not violate a constitutional right of privacy.
Bennis v. Michigan	516 U.S. 442 (1996)	Rehnquist	A state law allowing law enforcement officers to seize possession of property used in connection with a crime was not unconstitutional, even as applied to the forfeiture of a wife's interest in a car in which, without her knowledge, her husband had engaged in illegal sexual activity.
Benton v. Maryland	395 U.S. 784 (1969)	Marshall	Fifth Amendment's double jeopardy provision was applicable to the states through the Fourteenth Amendment's due process clause.
Berman v. Parker	348 U.S. 26 (1954)	Douglas	Urban renewal statute that allowed city to take private property and sell it to private developer to remove slums and provide beautification projects did not violate the takings clause.
Betts v. Brady	316 U.S. 455 (1942)	Roberts	State did not have to provide an attorney for criminal defendant charged with robbery; decision overruled by *Gideon v. Wainwright* (1963).

Case Name	Case Citation and Date	Author of Court's Opinion	Case Summary
Bigelow v. Virginia	421 U.S. 809 (1975)	Blackmun	State law prohibiting abortion advertisements violated freedom of speech.
Bivens v. Six Unknown Named Agents	403 U.S. 388 (1971)	Brennan	Federal officers who conduct an illegal search could be sued in a civil action.
BMW of North America, Inc. v. Gore	517 U.S. 559 (1996)	Stevens	A punitive damages award grossly out of proportion to the actual damages awarded in a case violated due process.
Board of Education of Kiryas Joel Village School District v. Grumet	512 U.S. 687 (1994)	Souter	A state law creating a school district to serve the needs of a religious community violated the establishment clause.
Board of Regents of University of Wisconsin System v. Southworth	529 U.S. 217 (2000)	Kennedy	Mandatory student activity fee that was used to fund activities opposed by some students did not violate their right to freedom of speech.
Bolling v. Sharpe	347 U.S. 497 (1954)	Warren	The District of Columbia's segregated public schools violated the Fifth Amendment's due process clause.
Bowers v. Hardwick	478 U.S. 186 (1986)	White	A state law making it a crime to engage in private, consensual homosexual conduct did not violate the due process clause.
Bowsher v. Synar	478 U.S. 714 (1986)	Burger	Provision of the Balanced Budget and Emergency Deficit Control Act of 1985 that permitted comptroller general to specify budget cuts if Congress could not agree on them amount to the delegation of an executive function to a legislative officer in violation of the Constitution's separation of power principle.
Boy Scouts of America v. Dale	530 U.S. 640 (2000)	Rehnquist	State law that would have forced Boy Scouts to accept avowed homosexual and gay rights activist as scout leader violated the organization's right to freedom of expressive association.
Bradwell v. Illinois	83 U.S. 130 (1873)	Miller	Refusal of a state supreme court

Case Name	Case Citation and Date	Author of Court's Opinion	Case Summary
			to admit a woman to the practice of law did not violate the privileges and immunities clause of the Fourteenth Amendment.
Brady v. United States	397 U.S. 742 (1970)	White	The choice of a defendant to plead guilty for fear of receiving the death penalty does not make the plea involuntary.
Brandenburg v. Ohio	395 U.S. 444 (1969)	Per curiam	The free speech clause prevents a state from punishing mere advocacy of illegal action so long as the advocacy is not directed toward inciting imminent lawless action and likely to produce such action.
Branzburg v. Hayes	408 U.S. 665 (1972)	White	The Constitution's First Amendment did not create a special privilege for reporters to shield their sources from discovery when subpoenaed to disclose them to a grand jury.
Brecht v. Abrahamson	507 U.S. 619 (1993)	Rehnquist	Failure of a criminal trial judge to declare a mistrial after the prosecutor improperly called jury's attention to a defendant's refusal to talk to police did not have a "substantial and injurious effect or influence in determining" the jury's finding that the defendant was guilty, and therefore a federal court should not overturn the conviction in an application for habeas corpus.
Breedlove v. Suttles	302 U.S. 277 (1937)	Butler	State law that required males but not females to pay a poll tax violated neither the Fourteenth Amendment's equal protection clause nor the Nineteenth Amendment's prohibition against gender discrimination in voting.
Bronson v. Kinzie	42 U.S. 311 (1843)	Taney	State law that retroactively gave debtors greater protections against mortgage foreclosures and greater rights to redeem

Case Name	Case Citation and Date	Author of Court's Opinion	Case Summary
			property after foreclosure violated the Constitution's prohibition against laws impairing the obligations of contracts.
Brown v. Board of Education	347 U.S. 483 (1954)	Warren	The equal protection clause prohibits official racial segregation of public schools.
Brown v. Maryland	25 U.S. 419 (1827)	Marshall	State law that required foreign importers to purchase a license violated the Constitution's ban on import taxes.
Brown v. Mississippi	297 U.S. 278 (1936)	Hughes	The due process clause prohibits use of coerced confessions in state criminal proceedings.
Browning-Ferris Industries v. Kelco Disposal, Inc.	492 U.S. 257 (1989)	Blackmun	The prohibition against excessive fines in the Eighth Amendment does not apply to punitive damage awards in suits between private parties.
Buchanan v. Warley	245 U.S. 60 (1917)	Day	Municipal ordinance that enforced residential segregation violated the Fourteenth Amendment.
Buck v. Bell	274 U.S. 200 (1927)	Holmes	The due process clause did not prohibit a state from sterilizing a woman who suffered from a mental impairment.
Buckley v. Valeo	424 U.S. 1 (1976)	Opinion unsigned	The free speech clause does not permit limits on the amounts candidates for office can spend on their campaigns but it does permit limits on campaign contributions.
Budd v. New York	143 U.S. 517 (1892)	Blatchford	State regulation of grain elevator rates did not violate the Fourteenth Amendment's due process clause.
Bunting v. Oregon	243 U.S. 426 (1917)	McKenna	A state law establishing a 10-hour workday and requiring pay for overtime in certain businesses did not violate the due process clause.
Burlington Industries, Inc. v. Ellerth	524 U.S. 742 (1998)	Kennedy	An employee who experiences improper sexual advances by a superior need not have suffered a

Case Name	Case Citation and Date	Author of Court's Opinion	Case Summary
			tangible job detriment to be able to sue an employer for sexual harassment; but the employee must take advantage of an employer's antiharassment policy to be entitled to a recovery.
Burton v. Wilmington Parking Authority	365 U.S. 715 (1961)	Clark	The refusal of a private restaurant to serve an African-American customer constituted a violation of the equal protection clause when the restaurant leased space in a public parking garage.
Bush v. Gore	121 S.Ct. 525 (2000)	Per curiam	State supreme court's order of manual recounts in presidential elections without standards for determining voter intent violated Fourteenth Amendment's equal protection clause.
Bush v. Vera	517 U.S. 952 (1996)	O'Conner for the plurality	A redistricting plan in which a desire to enhance minority voting strength predominated at the expense of other, traditional criteria for establishing such a plan violated the equal protection clause.
Butz v. Economou	438 U.S. 478 (1978)	White	Federal officials were not immune from suit by an individual for violating his constitutional rights when officials knew or should have known that they were acting unconstitutionally.
C & A Carbone, Inc. v. Clarkstown	511 U.S. 383 (1994)	Kennedy	A municipal ordinance that required all waste produced within the municipality be processed at a particular waste facility unconstitutionally intruded upon Congress's power to regulate interstate commerce.
Calder v. Bull	3 U.S. 386 (1798)	seriatim opinions	The Constitution's prohibition against ex post facto laws did not apply to civil disputes, but only to criminal proceedings.

Case Name	Case Citation and Date	Author of Court's Opinion	Case Summary
Cantwell v. Connecticut	310 U.S. 296 (1940)	Roberts	Prosecution of Jehovah's Witness for breach of the peace for playing a phonograph record critical of the Catholic Church violated the First Amendment.
Carmel v. Texas	529 U.S. 513 (2000)	Stevens	Conviction of alleged sex offender on the basis of the victim's testimony alone violated the ex post facto clause when, at the time the alleged crime was committed, the law required corroborating evidence.
Carroll v. United States	267 U.S. 132 (1925)	Taft	A car search conducted by federal officers who suspected that a vehicle was being used to carry liquor, against the law during the Prohibition era, did not require a warrant and did not violate the Fourth Amendment's prohibition against unreasonable searches and seizures.
Carter v. Carter Coal Co.	298 U.S. 238 (1936)	Sutherland	The commerce clause did not grant Congress power to regulate labor conditions in the coal mining industry.
Chambers v. Florida	309 U.S. 227 (1940)	Black	The due process clause prohibited a state from using improperly obtained confessions in criminal prosecutions.
Champion v. Ames	188 U.S. 321 (1903)	Harlan	Congress had power under the commerce clause to regulate interstate traffic in lottery tickets.
Chaplinsky v. New Hampshire	315 U.S. 568 (1942)	Murphy	Prosecution of speaker for using "fighting words" did not violate freedom of speech.
Charles River Bridge Co. v. Warren Bridge Co.	36 U.S. 420 (1837)	Taney	The contracts clause did not prevent a state from granting the right to build and collect tolls from a bridge to one party and then granting a similar right to build a different bridge to another party.

Case Name	Case Citation and Date	Author of Court's Opinion	Case Summary
Cherokee Nation v. Georgia	30 U.S. 1 (1831)	Marshall	Article III of the Constitution did not authorize the Supreme Court to hear a case brought by Cherokee because they were not a foreign nation.
Chicago v. Morales	527 U.S. 41 (1999)	Stevens	Municipal ordinance that prohibited "criminal street gang members" from loitering in public places was unconstitutional.
Chicago, Burlington & Quincy Railroad Company v. Chicago	166 U.S. 226 (1897)	Harlan	The Fourteenth Amendment's due process clause required the city to pay just compensation when it took private property for public use.
Chicago, Milwaukee & St. Paul Railway Co. v. Minnesota	134 U.S. 418 (1890)	Blatchford	The Supreme Court had authority to review the reasonableness of railroad rates established by a state commission.
Chimel v. California	395 U.S. 752 (1969)	Stewart	The Fourth Amendment does not prevent police from performing a warrantless search of an arrestee's person and the immediate vicinity in connection with an arrest to prevent the person arrested from gaining possession of a weapon or destroying evidence.
Chisholm v. Georgia	2 U.S. 419 (1793)	seriatim opinions	A state may be sued in federal court by the citizen of another state. (Decision overturned by ratification of the Eleventh Amendment).
Church of the Lukumi Babalu Aye v. Hialeah	508 U.S. 520 (1993)	Kennedy	Local ordinances targeted to prevent animal sacrifice by Santerians violated the free exercise clause.
City of Boerne v. Flores	521 U.S. 507 (1997)	Kennedy	Congress lacked authority to pass a law protecting religious believers from the incidental effects of generally applicable state laws.
City of Ladue v. Gilleo	512 U.S. 43 (1994)	Stevens	A local law banning residential signs infringed upon freedom of speech.

Case Name	Case Citation and Date	Author of Court's Opinion	Case Summary
Civil Rights Cases	109 U.S. 3 (1883)	Bradley	Neither the Thirteenth nor the Fourteenth Amendment authorized Congress to prohibit racial discrimination in inns and public conveyances.
Clinton v. City of New York	524 U.S. 417 (1998)	Stevens	The line-item veto is unconstitutional because it violates the Constitution's presentment clause.
Clinton v. Jones	520 U.S. 681 (1997)	Stevens	The president of the United States is not immune from civil law suits during the tenure of his office.
Cohen v. California	403 U.S. 15 (1971)	Harlan	The First Amendment's free speech protected the right of an individual to wear a jacket with the words "F – – – the Draft" on the back in a courthouse.
Cohens v. Virginia	19 U.S. 264 (1821)	Marshall	The Eleventh Amendment did not prevent the Supreme Court from hearing the appeal of men convicted for violating a state law that was arguably inconsistent with a federal law.
Coker v. Georgia	433 U.S. 584 (1977)	White for plurality	A death sentence for rape violated the cruel and unusual punishments clause.
Colegrove v. Green	328 U.S. 549 (1946)	Frankfurter	Federal courts lacked jurisdiction to entertain an action seeking to compel congressional redistricting since it was a political question.
Coleman v. Miller	307 U.S. 433 (1939)	Hughes	Issues of whether a state could ratify a constitutional amendment it had previously rejected and whether it could do so 13 years after Congress proposed the amendment were political questions reserved to Congress for decision.
Collector v. Day	78 U.S. 112 (1871)	Nelson	Federal government could not tax the income of a state judge. Decision subsequently overruled by *Graves v. New York ex rel. O'Keefe* (1939).

Case Name	Case Citation and Date	Author of Court's Opinion	Case Summary
Columbus Board of Education v. Penick	443 U.S. 449 (1979)	White	Proof of segregation in a substantial portion of an urban school district created a presumption that school officials had engaged in segregation throughout the district and thus authorized a federal court to fashion a district-wide desegregation plan.
Communist Party v. Subversive Activities Control Board	367 U.S. 1 (1961)	Frankfurter	Provisions of the McCarran Act, a federal law that required subversive organizations to register with the Justice Department, were not unconstitutional when used to force the registration of the American Communist Party.
Cooley v. Board of Wardens of the Port of Philadelphia	53 U.S. 299 (1852)	Curtis	A state law requiring vessels entering or leaving a port to pay a pilotage fee if they did not use a local pilot did not intrude upon Congress's power to regulate interstate commerce.
Cooper v. Aaron	358 U.S. 1 (1958)	Warren	The equal protection clause would not permit a school district to delay desegregation of to avoid racial unrest.
Cox v. New Hampshire	312 U.S. 569 (1941)	Hughes	Municipal ordinance that required persons wishing to conduct a parade to obtain a license and pay a fee did not violate the First Amendment rights of Jehovah's Witnesses.
Coyle v. Smith	221 U.S. 559 (1911)	Lurton	Condition that Congress placed on the admission of Oklahoma to the Union—of maintaining its state capitol in a certain city for a time—was invalid.
Craig v. Boren	429 U.S. 190 (1976)	Brennan	Gender classifications require greater justifications than ordinary legislative classification, and law that discriminated against men as to age when they could purchase 3.2% beer violated the equal protection clause.

Case Name	Case Citation and Date	Author of Court's Opinion	Case Summary
Cruzan v. Director, Missouri Dept. Of Health	497 U.S. 261 (1990)	Rehnquist	State law that required clear and convincing evidence of a person's wish to be removed from artificial life support systems did not violate due process.
Cumming v. Richmond County Board of Education	175 U.S. 528 (1899)	Harlan	School district's decision to close its only public high school for black students did not violate the equal protection clause unless it was proved that the decision was made solely because of "hostility to the colored population because of their race."
Cummings v. Missouri	71 U.S. 277 (1867)	Field	State law requiring individuals in certain occupations to swear that they had not aided or sympathized with the cause of rebellion during the Civil War was an unconstitutional bill of attainder and an ex post facto law.
Dandridge v. Williams	397 U.S. 471 (1970)	Stewart	Welfare legislation that imposed a maximum benefit per family without considering family size did not violate the equal protection clause.
Dartmouth College v. Woodward	17 U.S. 518 (1819)	Marshall	A state's attempt to seize control of a private college by revising its charter violated the contracts clause.
Daubert v. Merrell Dow	509 U.S. 579 (1993)	Blackmun	Expert scientific evidence in a products liability case was admissible even if not generally accepted by most scientists, as long as the evidence was relevant and reliable.
Davis v. Bandemer	478 U.S. 109 (1986)	White for the plurality	Manipulation of voting district boundaries to serve the ends of a controlling political party only violates the equal protection clause when the manipulation continually frustrates the political will of a majority of citizens or denies to minority voters "a fair chance to influence the political process."

Case Name	Case Citation and Date	Author of Court's Opinion	Case Summary
Davis v. Beason	133 U.S. 333 (1890)	Field	The First Amendment right to free exercise of religion by Mormons was not violated by a territorial law that denied the right to vote to those who advocated or practiced polygamy or belonged to an organization that did.
DeJonge v. Oregon	299 U.S. 353 (1937)	Hughes	The First Amendment's free speech clause prevented government from making peaceful attendance at a meeting organized by members of the Communist Party a crime.
Dennis v. United States	341 U.S. 494 (1951)	Vinson	The First Amendment's free speech clause was not violated by the conviction of Communist Party members for teaching or advocating the violate overthrow of the U.S. government, since the "gravity of the 'evil,' discounted by its improbability" justified this infringement of free speech.
Dickerson v. United States	530 U.S. 428 (2000)	Rehnquist	Congress had no power to override the Court's decision in *Miranda v. Arizona* (1996), which required that persons arrested be advised of their right to remain silent and to have counsel appointed for them.
Dillon v. Gloss	256 U.S. 368 (1921)	Van Devanter	Congress had authority to require that the Eighteenth Amendment, establishing Prohibition, be ratified within seven years.
Doe v. Bolton	410 U.S. 179 (1973)	Blackmun	State laws requiring that abortions be performed only in hospitals, that abortion decisions be reviewed by other physicians, and that prevented nonresidents of the state from obtaining an abortion in the state violated the right to an abortion.

Case Name	Case Citation and Date	Author of Court's Opinion	Case Summary
Dolan v. City of Tigard	512 U.S. 374 (1994)	Rehnquist	When city conditioned grant of a building permit on the property owner conveying part of the property to the city, the takings clause of the Fourth Amendment required the city to demonstrate that these conditions substantially advanced legitimate government objectives.
Dombrowski v. Pfister	380 U.S. 499 (1965)	Brennan	It was appropriate for a federal court to order state officials to cease harassment of civil rights organization.
Dred Scott v. Sandford	60 U.S. 393 (1857)	Taney	Blacks were not citizens of the United States and Congress lacked authority to enact the Missouri Compromise.
Duncan v. Louisiana	391 U.S. 145 (1968)	White	The Sixth Amendment right to a jury trial in criminal cases involving non-petty offences was applicable to state criminal prosecutions.
Dunn v. Blumstein	405 U.S. 330 (1972)	Marshall	The equal protection clause prevented a state from imposing a durational residency requirement as a condition of voter eligibility.
E. C. Knight Co. v. United States	156 U.S. 1 (1895)	Fuller	Congress did not have power under the commerce clause to prohibit a monopoly in the manufacture of a product.
Edmonson v. Leesville Concrete Co.	500 U.S. 614 (1991)	Kennedy	Attorneys for private parties in civil cases cannot peremptorily exclude jurors from a case on the basis of their race.
Edwards v. Aguillard	482 U.S. 578 (1987)	Brennan	The establishment clause prohibited a state law that required the balanced treatment of evolution and "creation science" in public schools.
Edwards v. California	314 U.S. 160 (1941)	Byrnes	"Okie" law that prohibited bringing indigent nonresidents into state violated a constitutional right to travel.

Case Name	Case Citation and Date	Author of Court's Opinion	Case Summary
Edwards v. South Carolina	372 U.S. 229 (1963)	Stewart	Conviction of peaceful demonstrators on public property for breach of the peace after being ordered to disperse by the police violated freedom of speech.
Eisenstadt v. Baird	405 U.S. 438 (1972)	Brennan	The equal protection clause prevented a state from limiting purchases of contraceptives to married couples.
Elfbrandt v. Russell	384 U.S. 11 (1966)	Douglas	Freedom of speech prohibits states from punishing employees for belonging to organizations with illegal purposes unless employees both know of and intend to join in the furtherance of such purposes.
Elrod v. Burns	427 U.S. 347 (1976)	Brennan	The right to freedom of speech is violated when public officials of one party discharge noncivil service employees who are not party members when the employees are not in policy-making positions.
Employment Division v. Smith	494 U.S. 872 (1990)	Scalia	The free exercise clause did not entitle Native Americans who wished to use peyote in religious ceremonies to an exemption from drug laws.
Engel v. Vitale	370 U.S. 421 (1962)	Black	The establishment clause prohibited a state from composing and requiring the recitation of a nondenominational prayer in public schools.
Erie Railroad Co.v. Tompkins	304 U.S. 64 (1938)	Brandeis	Federal courts deciding cases between citizens of different states must apply state law rather than general federal common law.
Escobedo v. Illinois	378 U.S. 478 (1964)	Goldberg	A criminal defendant's right to counsel was violated by use of a confession obtained when he was a suspect and had been prevented from speaking with his attorney as he requested.

Case Name	Case Citation and Date	Author of Court's Opinion	Case Summary
Euclid v. Ambler Realty Co.	272 U.S. 365 (1926)	Sutherland	Zoning ordinances do not generally offend either the equal protection, due process, or takings clauses.
Evans v. Abney	396 U.S. 435 (1970)	Black	When state returned park to its donor because it could not comply with the donor's "whites only" condition for donating the park, the state did not violate the equal protection clause, since both whites and blacks lost the ability to use the park.
Everson v. Board of Education	330 U.S. 1 (1947)	Black	A state's reimbursement of parents for costs of transportation to parochial schools did not violate establishment clause.
Ex parte Crow Dog	109 U.S. 557 (1883)	Matthews	Tribal, and not federal, law applied to the charge of one Sioux of murdering another, since Congress had not explicitly legislated a contrary result.
Ex parte McCardle	74 U.S. 506 (1869)	Chase	Recognizing that Congress may, at least in some circumstances, deprive the Supreme Court of power to hear cases by altering the contours of the Court's appellate jurisdiction.
Ex parte Milligan	71 U.S. 2 (1866)	Davis	The trial of civilians before a military tribunal was unconstitutional.
Ex parte Yarbrough	110 U.S. 651 (1884)	Miller	Federal government had power to punish members of the KKK who assaulted a black man to keep him from voting in a federal election.
Fay v. Noia	372 U.S. 391 (1963)	Brennan	Failure of a state prisoner to make a timely state court appeal did not bar his application for a writ of habeas corpus in federal court.
FDA v. Brown Williamson Tobacco Corporation	529 U.S. 120 (2000)	O'Connor	The Food and Drug Administration's power under the Food, Drug, and Cosmetic Act to

Case Name	Case Citation and Date	Author of Court's Opinion	Case Summary
			regulate drugs and devices does not include the power to regulate tobacco.
Feiner v. New York	340 U.S. 315 (1951)	Vinson	Conviction of speaker for breach of the peace—after heckler threatened violence, police requested speaker to end speech, and speaker continued notwithstanding this request—did not violate speaker's free speech rights.
First English Evangelical Lutheran Church of Glendale v. County of Los Angeles	482 U.S. 304 (1987)	Rehnquist	When a land-use regulation amounts to an unconstitutional taking of property without just compensation, even if government abandons its regulation, it may be required to compensate a landowner for interference with property rights prior to such abandonment.
First National Bank of Boston v. Bellotti	435 U.S. 765 (1978)	Powell	State law that banned corporations from spending money to influence ballot referendum violated freedom of speech.
Flast v. Cohen	392 U.S. 83 (1968)	Warren	Taxpayers were entitled to bring suit in federal court to prevent the expenditure of federal funds to parochial schools in violation of the establishment clause.
Fletcher v. Peck	10 U.S. 87 (1810)	Marshall	The Supreme Court had authority to determine the constitutionality of state laws.
Ford v. Wainwright	477 U.S. 399 (1986)	Marshall	The Constitution prohibited a state from executing an insane prisoner.
Frontiero v. Richardson	411 U.S. 677 (1973)	Brennan for the plurality	A federal law that discriminated between males and females in the provision of dependent benefits amounted to an unconstitutional gender discrimination.
Fullilove v. Klutznick	448 U.S. 448 (1980)	Burger	A federal affirmative action program for public works projects did not violate the equal protection clause.

Case Name	Case Citation and Date	Author of Court's Opinion	Case Summary
Furman v. Georgia	408 U.S. 238 (1972)	per curiam	In the sentencing phase of a death penalty case, the jury cannot be given complete discretion in the decision of whether to impose capital punishment.
Garcia v. San Antonio Metropolitan Transit Authority	469 U.S. 528 (1985)	Blackmun	Congress has authority to establish minimum wage and hour requirements for municipal employees, reversing the decision in *National League of Cities v. Usery* (1976).
Geduldig v. Aiello	417 U.S. 484 (1974)	Stewart	State disability benefits system that did not cover hospitalizations for normal pregnancy did not amount to unconstitutional sex discrimination.
Georgia v. McCollum	505 U.S. 42 (1992)	Blackmun	The equal protection clause barred a criminal defendant from using peremptory challenges to exclude potential jurors on racial grounds.
Gibbons v. Ogden	22 U.S. 1 (1824)	Marshall	A federal license granted to a steamboat owner under Congress's power to regulate interstate commerce took precedence over a conflicting state-granted monopoly.
Gideon v. Wainright	372 U.S. 335 (1963)	Black	Due process required a state to provide an attorney to represent a defendant charged with a serious offense.
Gitlow v. New York	268 U.S. 652 (1925)	Sanford	The First Amendment did not prevent a state from punishing advocacy of the violent overthrow of government even if such advocacy did not immediately incite criminal action.
Gold Clause Cases: Norman v. Baltimore & Ohio Railroad Co., Nortz v. United States, Perry v. United States	294 U.S. 240 (1935); 294 U.S. 317 (1935); 294 U.S. 330 (1935)	Hughes	Congress had authority to regulate the U.S. monetary system, including abrogating clauses in contracts that stipulated payment had to be made in gold.

Case Name	Case Citation and Date	Author of Court's Opinion	Case Summary
Goldberg v. Kelly	397 U.S. 254 (1970)	Brennan	The due process clause of the Fourteenth Amendment required that recipients of welfare benefits be afforded a hearing before having those benefits cut off.
Goldfarb v. Virginia State Bar	421 U.S. 773 (1975)	Burger	Minimum fee schedules established by bar association for lawyers amounted to a price-fixing arrangement in violation of the Sherman Antitrust Act.
Gomillion v. Lightfoot	364 U.S. 339 (1960)	Frankfurter	A state law that manipulated municipal boundaries to exclude black voters violated the Fifteenth Amendment Amendment.
Graham v. Richardson	403 U.S. 365 (1971)	Blackmun	The equal protection clause prevented a state from discriminating against aliens regarding eligibility for welfare benefits.
Graves v. New York ex rel. O'Keefe	306 U.S. 466 (1939)	Stone	The Constitution did not prevent states from taxing the salaries of federal employees, overruling *Collector v. Day* (1871).
Greater New Orleans Broadcast Association v. United States	527 U.S. 173 (1999)	Stevens	Federal law that prohibits advertisements concerning casinos in states where casino gambling is legal violated First Amendment's free speech clause.
Green v. County School Board of New Kent County	391 U.S. 430 (1968)	Brennan	A school district could not satisfy its obligation to eliminate racial segregation by adopting a plan that allowed students to choose the school they would attend.
Gregg v. Georgia	428 U.S. 153 (1976)	Stewart for the plurality	In death penalty cases, juries must be given the ability to consider the individual character of a defendant and the specific circumstances of the crime in deciding whether to impose capital punishment.
Griffin v. Breckenridge	403 U.S. 88 (1971)	Stewart	Congress had power to punish racially motivated assaults on public highways.

Case Name	Case Citation and Date	Author of Court's Opinion	Case Summary
Griffin v. County School Board of Prince Edward County	377 U.S. 218 (1964)	Black	Federal courts had power to prevent public school districts from closing and tax monies from being used to support private schools to avoid desegregation efforts.
Griffin v. California	380 U.S. 609 (1965)	Douglas	Fifth Amendment's privilege against self-incrimination prevents prosecutors and judges from commenting adversely on a defendant's failure to testify in a criminal proceeding.
Griggs v. Duke Power Co.	401 U.S. 424 (1971)	Burger	Congress could prohibit racial discrimination in employment and could require that job tests be related to job skills.
Griswold v. Connecticut	381 U.S. 479 (1965)	Douglas	A state law preventing married couples from using contraceptives violated the right of privacy.
Grosjean v. American Press Co.	297 U.S. 233 (1936)	Sutherland	State's attempt to limit circulation of certain newspapers by levying a license tax on advertisements sold in the particular newspapers violated freedom of the press.
Grove City College v. Bell	465 U.S. 555 (1984)	White	Federal law prevented gender discrimination in universities and colleges that received federal funds.
Groves v. Slaughter	40 U.S. 449 (1841)	Thompson for plurality	Purchaser of slaves could not avoid payment of notes given for imported slaves on the basis of state constitutional provision prohibiting importation of slaves when state had not passed legislation to enforce the constitutional provision.
Grovey v. Townsend	295 U.S. 45 (1935)	Roberts	Limitation of state Democratic party membership to whites violated the equal protection clause.
Guinn v. United States	238 U.S. 347 (1915)	White	A voter literacy requirement intended by a state to prevent blacks from voting violated the Fifteenth Amendment.

Case Name	Case Citation and Date	Author of Court's Opinion	Case Summary
Hague v. Congress of Industrial Organizations	307 U.S. 496 (1939)	Roberts	City's attempt to limit public meetings and expressive activities in streets, parks, and other public places by requiring speakers to obtain permits violated freedom of speech.
Hall v. Decuir	95 U.S. 485 (1878)	Waite	State law that required carriers involved in interstate commerce to offer integrated facilities unconstitutionally intruded on congressional authority to regulate interstate commerce.
Hammer v. Dagenhart	247 U.S. 251 (1918)	Day	Congress lacked power under the commerce clause to prohibit interstate shipment of goods produced with child labor.
Harmelin v. Michigan	501 U.S. 957 (1991)	Scalia	A mandatory life sentence without the possibility of parole did not violate the cruel and unusual punishments clause.
Harper v. Virginia State Board of Elections	383 U.S. 663 (1966)	Douglas	State poll taxes violate the equal protection clause of the Fourteenth Amendment.
Harris v. McRae	448 U.S. 297 (1980)	Stewart	The right to abortion was not violated by a federal restriction on the funding of medically necessary abortions.
Harris v. New York	401 U.S. 222 (1971)	Burger	Statements made by a defendant who had not been given constitutionally required warnings of the right to counsel and the right to remain silent may not generally be used against defendant at trial, but may be used to impeach defendants who choose to testify.
Harris v. Forklift Systems, Inc.	510 U.S. 17 (1993)	O'Connor	Woman claiming that she had been sexually harassed by a hostile work environment did not have to prove that she had suffered any psychological injury on the job or that her job performance had suffered as a result of the harassment.

Case Name	Case Citation and Date	Author of Court's Opinion	Case Summary
Harris v. United States	390 U.S. 234 (1968)	per curiam	Law enforcement personnel conducting an otherwise legal warrantless search were entitled to seize objects in plain sight.
Hawaii Housing Authority v. Midkiff	467 U.S. 229 (1984)	O'Connor	Government may take private property for a public use even if property is then placed in private hands immediately so long as the purpose of the taking is a public one.
Hayburn's Case	2 U.S. 409 (1792)	seriatim opinions	Justices of the Supreme Court refused to accept nonjudicial duties required by a federal law.
Heart of Atlanta Motel v. United States	379 U.S. 241 (1964)	Clark	Congress had power under the commerce clause to prohibit racial discrimination in privately owned places of public accommodation.
Helvering v. Davis	301 U.S. 619 (1937)	Cardozo	Congress had power under its taxing and spending authority to pass the old-age benefits provisions of the Social Security Act of 1937.
Herndon v. Lowry	301 U.S. 242 (1937)	Roberts	Attempts to incite insurrection were not protected by the First Amendment.
Hill v. Colorado	530 U.S. 703 (2000)	Stevens	State statute making it unlawful for a person to knowingly approach another person without that person's consent in order to pass a leaflet, display a sign, orally protest, etc. within 100 feet of a health care facility did not violate the First Amendment.
Hirabayashi v. United States	320 U.S. 81 (1943)	Stone	The equal protection clause did not prohibit a curfew law applicable to Japanese Americans during World War II.
Hodgson v. Minnesota	497 U.S. 417 (1990)	Stevens	State statute unconstitutionally limited right to abortion when it required minors seeking an abortion either to notify both parents or else to obtain a judi-

Case Name	Case Citation and Date	Author of Court's Opinion	Case Summary
			cial determination that she was mature or that an abortion without parental notice was in her best interests.
Holden v. Hardy	169 U.S. 366 (1898)	Brown	State law limiting work hours for miners was a reasonable regulation of contract rights.
Home Building and Loan Association v. Blaisdell	290 U.S. 398 (1934)	Hughes	A state law declaring a moratorium on the repayment of mortgages did not violate the contracts clause.
Hoyt v. Florida	368 U.S. 57 (1961)	Harlan	State law that did not allow women to serve on juries unless they specifically requested such service was not unconstitutional. Decision overruled by *Taylor v. Louisiana* (1975).
Hudson v. Palmer	468 U.S. 517 (1984)	Burger	Prisoners have no expectation of privacy in their prison cells that would prevent a search of their cells.
Hudson & Goodwin v. United States	11 U.S. 32 (1812)	Johnson	Federal courts have no authority to enforce a federal common law of crimes.
Hurtado v. California	110 U.S. 516 (1884)	Matthews	The Fourteenth Amendment's due process clause did not require a grand jury indictment in a state murder prosecution.
Hustler Magazine v. Falwell	485 U.S. 46 (1988)	Rehnquist	A public figure or official cannot recover damages for intentional infliction of emotional distress from a publication unless the publication contains a false statement of fact made with knowledge of its falseness or with reckless disregard for its truth or falsity.
Hutchison v. Proxmire	443 U.S. 111 (1979)	Burger	Senator accused of defaming an individual on the Senate floor who was not a public figure, where statements concerning the individual were not essential to Senate deliberations, was not immune from a defamation suit

Case Name	Case Citation and Date	Author of Court's Opinion	Case Summary
			under the speech and debate clause of the Constitution.
Hutto v. Davis	454 U.S. 370 (1982)	per curiam	A sentence that was excessive in relation to the seriousness of the crime was not unconstitutional.
Hylton v. United States	3 U.S. 171 (1796)	seriatim opinions	Federal carriage tax on passenger vehicles was not unconstitutional.
Illinois ex. rel. McCollum v. Board of Education	333 U.S. 203 (1948)	Black	Establishment clause prevented public schools from allowing religious teachers to provide religious instruction in public schools.
Illinois v. Krull	480 U.S. 340 (1987)	Blackmun	Evidence did not have to be excluded in a criminal trial when a search was made in reasonable reliance on a law authorizing warrantless administrative searches of vehicles, even though the search was later determined to be illegal.
Immigration and Naturalization Service v. Chadha	462 U.S. 919 (1983)	Burger	The legislative veto is an unconstitutional violation of separation of powers.
In re Debs	158 U.S. 564 (1895)	Brewer	Court was authorized to issue injunction against striking labor unions to remove obstructions to commerce and it had authority to punish violations of the injunction by holding violators in contempt of court.
In re Gault	387 U.S. 1 (1967)	Fortas	The privilege against self-incrimination and the right to counsel were applicable to criminal proceedings involving juveniles.
In re Neagle	135 U.S. 1 (1890)	Miller	Federal courts had power to grant a writ of habeas corpus compelling the release of a federal officer charged with homicide under state law for a killing that occurred in the line of the officer's duties.
In re Winship	397 U.S. 358 (1970)	Brennan	Standard of proof that government must meet in juvenile

Case Name	Case Citation and Date	Author of Court's Opinion	Case Summary
			delinquency proceedings is proof beyond a reasonable doubt.
International Society for Krishna Consciousness, Inc. v. Lee	505 U.S. 672 (1992)	Rehnquist	Ban in an airport on soliciting and leafleting did not abridge freedom of speech.
International Union v. Johnson Controls, Inc.	499 U.S. 187 (1991)	Blackmun	Company's policy of barring fertile women from working in positions that exposed them to lead amounted to unlawful discrimination.
J.E.B. v. Alabama Ex Rel. T.B.	511 U.S. 127 (1994)	Blackmun	Prosecutor's use of preemptory challenges to dismiss potential women jurors amounted to gender discrimination made unconstitutional by the equal protection clause.
Jackson v. Metropolitan Edison Co.	419 U.S. 345 (1974)	Rehnquist	Since a privately owned utility was not a public actor, its termination of a customer's utility service without due process was not unconstitutional.
Johnson v. Louisiana	400 U.S. 356 (1972)	White	The Constitution does not require unanimous verdicts in all state criminal trials.
Johnson v. Santa Clara County	480 U.S. 616 (1987)	Brennan	Affirmative action program for women did not violate federal civil rights law.
Johnson v. Zerbst	304 U.S. 458 (1938)	Black	Indigent defendants in federal criminal trials are constitutionally entitled to have attorneys appointed to represent them.
Joint Anti-Fascist Refugee Committee v. McGrath	341 U.S. 123 (1951)	Burton	Listing groups among subversive organizations without a hearing violated their constitutional rights.
Jones v. Alfred H. Mayer Co.	392 U.S. 409 (1968)	Stewart	Congress had authority under the Thirteenth Amendment to prohibit private acts of discrimination in housing sales.
Jones v. Van Zandt	46 U.S. 215 (1847)	Woodbury	Fugitive Slave Act of 1793 was not unconstitutional.
Kansas v. Hendricks	521 U.S. 346 (1997)	Thomas	Provision of the Sexually Violent Predator Act of that required sex offenders to be confined to

Case Name	Case Citation and Date	Author of Court's Opinion	Case Summary
			mental hospitals for an indeterminate time were not unconstitutional, even if offenders did not suffer from a mental illness.
Katz v. United States	389 U.S. 347 (1967)	Stewart	A wiretap on a telephone booth violated the Fourth Amendment's prohibition against unreasonable searches and seizures.
Katzenbach v. McClung	379 U.S. 294 (1964)	Clark	Congress had power under the commerce clause to prohibit racial discrimination in a local restaurant whose food was obtained out of state.
Katzenbach v. Morgan	384 U.S. 641 (1966)	Brennan	Congress had power under the Fourteenth Amendment to prohibit voter literacy tests, even though the Court had determined that such tests do not violate the equal protection clause of the Fourteenth Amendment.
Ker v. California	374 U.S. 23 (1963)	Clark	State law enforcement officials are subject to the same requirements regarding unreasonable searches and seizures as federal law enforcement officials.
Keyes v. Denver School District No. 1	413 U.S. 189 (1973)	Brennan	Racial segregation in one portion of a school district authorizes a federal court to impose districtwide desegregation remedies.
Keyishian v. Board of Regents	385 U.S. 589 (1967)	Brennan	State law that prevented individuals who were members of subversive organizations from being teachers or professors in state educational institutions was unconstitutional.
Kidd v. Pearson	128 U.S. 1 (1888)	Lamar	State law that prohibited the manufacture of liquor for sale out of state did not unconstitutionally intrude on congressional power to regulate interstate commerce.

Case Name	Case Citation and Date	Author of Court's Opinion	Case Summary
Kimel v. Florida Board of Regents	528 U.S. 62 (2000)	O'Connor	The Eleventh Amendment prevented the application of the Age Discrimination in Employment Act insofar as it allowed individuals to sue states for damages.
Korematsu v. United States	323 U.S. 214 (1944)	Black	The confinement of Japanese Americans in internment camps during World War II did not violate the equal protection clause.
Kunz v. New York	340 U.S. 290 (1951)	Vinson	State law requiring those desiring to hold religious services on the streets to obtain a permit from the police commissioner violated freedom of speech, where the law established no standards to be used in deciding whether to grant such a permit.
Lassiter v. Northampton County Board of Elections	360 U.S. 45 (1959)	Douglas	State voter literacy requirement did not amount to unconstitutional racial discrimination.
Lee v. Weisman	505 U.S. 577 (1992)	Kennedy	The establishment clause prohibited a public school from inviting a Jewish rabbi to deliver an invocation and benediction at graduation ceremonies.
Lemon v. Kurtzman	403 U.S. 602 (1971)	Burger	The establishment clause prohibited aid to parochial schools.
Lindsey v. Normet	405 U.S. 56 (1972)	White	The due process clause of the Fourteenth Amendment did not prohibit summary eviction proceedings for tenants.
Lochner v. New York	198 U.S. 45 (1905)	Peckham	A state law that restricted the number of hours bakers could work interfered with freedom to contract and thus violated due process.
Loewe v. Lawlor	208 U.S. 274 (1908)	Fuller	Union activities that amount to restraints of trade could be prosecuted under the Sherman Antitrust Act.
Louisiana ex rel. Francis v. Resweber	329 U.S. 459 (1947)	Reed	Second attempt to execute death row inmate after first attempt failed did not amount to double

Case Name	Case Citation and Date	Author of Court's Opinion	Case Summary
			jeopardy or cruel and unusual punishment.
Loving v. Virginia	388 U.S. 1 (1967)	Warren	State law that prohibited interracial marriages violated the equal protection clause.
Lucas v. South Carolina Coastal Council	505 U.S. 1003 (1992)	Scalia	A zoning ordinance that prevented any economic use of property violated the takings clause.
Luther v. Borden	48 U.S. 1 (1849)	Taney	Dispute over which of two opposing factions represented the legitimate government of a state was a political question that the Court had no power to decide.
Lynch v. Donnelly	465 U.S. 668 (1984)	Burger	A city's inclusion of a nativity scene in a holiday display did not violate the establishment clause.
Maher v. Roe	432 U.S. 464 (1977)	Powell	The right to abortion did not require a state to pay for an indigent woman's nontherapeutic abortion.
Malloy v. Hogan	378 U.S. 1 (1964)	Brennan	The privilege against self-incrimination was applicable to state criminal proceedings.
Mapp v. Ohio	367 U.S. 643 (1961)	Clark	The Fourth Amendment's prohibition against use of evidence obtained as a result of an illegal search was applicable in state criminal proceedings.
Marbury v. Madison	5 U.S. 137 (1803)	Marshall	The Supreme Court had the power of judicial review—that is, to determine the constitutionality of federal laws.
Martin v. Hunter's Lessee	14 U.S. 304 (1816)	Story	Federal courts had power to review state court decisions involving constitutional issues or other questions of federal law.
Maryland v. Craig	497 U.S. 836 (1990)	O'Connor	A defendant's right to confront witnesses is not inevitably violated by the testimony of a child witness in sexual abuse case via closed circuit television.

Case Name	Case Citation and Date	Author of Court's Opinion	Case Summary
Maryland v. Wilson	519 U.S. 408 (1997)	Rehnquist	A law enforcement officer making a traffic stop may order passengers out of the car.
Massachusetts v. Sheppard	468 U.S. 981 (1984)	White	Even if a search warrant is later determined to be defective, the exclusionary rule did not apply to a search conducted by police officers who reasonably relied on the warrant.
Massachusetts Board of Retirement v. Murgia	427 U.S. 307 (1976)	per curiam	Mandatory retirement for state police officers did not violate the equal protection clause.
Massiah v. United States	377 U.S. 201 (1964)	Stewart	Once government initiates criminal proceedings against a defendant, it must communicate with defendant through his or her attorney.
Maxwell v. Dow	176 U.S. 581 (1990)	Peckham	The Constitution does not require that state criminal procedures use a grand jury indictment nor that jury verdicts be unanimous.
McCleskey v. Kemp	481 U.S. 279 (1987)	Powell	Statistics revealing racial disparities in the imposition of the death penalty did not automatically establish an equal protection violation
McCulloch v. Maryland	17 U.S. 316 (1819)	Marshall	Congress had power to establish a Bank of the United States.
McLaurin v. Oklahoma State Regents for Higher Education	339 U.S. 637 (1950)	Vinson	The equal protection clause did not permit a state university to require that a black student sit in a separate row in class, eat at a separate table, and study at a separate desk in the library.
Metro Broadcasting v. Federal Communications Commission	497 U.S. 547 (1990)	Brennan	Affirmative action programs designed to increase participation of racial minorities in broadcast programming were not unconstitutional.
Meyer v. Nebraska	262 U.S. 390 (1923)	McReynolds	State law prohibiting instruction in foreign languages at schools violated parental right to control the education of their children.

Case Name	Case Citation and Date	Author of Court's Opinion	Case Summary
Miami Herald Publishing Co. v. Tornillo	418 U.S. 241 (1974)	Burger	State law that gave political candidates right to equal space to reply to newspaper attacks on candidate violated freedom of the press.
Michael M. v. Superior Court of Sonoma County	450 U.S. 464 (1981)	Rehnquist for plurality	Statutory rape law, which made males but not females criminally liable for underage sexual intercourse, did not violate the equal protection clause.
Miller v. California	413 U.S. 15 (1973)	Burger	Obscene materials are not protected by the First Amendment.
Milliken v. Bradley	418 U.S. 717 (1974)	Burger	A federal court's power to order multidistrict desegregation plans does not arise unless each district involved is shown to have engaged in segregation practices.
Minersville School District v. Gobitis	310 U.S. 586 (1940)	Frankfurter	Compulsory flag salute requirement in public schools did not violate First Amendment rights of children with religious objections to saluting the flag. Decision overruled by *West Virginia State Board of Education v. Barnette* (1943).
Minnick v. Mississippi	498 U.S. 146 (1990)	Kennedy	A confession obtained by interrogating an individual against his or her will after he or she had consulted with an attorney was inadmissible.
Minor v. Happersett	88 U.S. 162 (1875)	Waite	State could deny the right to vote to women.
Miranda v. Arizona	384 U.S. 436 (1966)	Warren	State law enforcement personnel were constitutionally required to inform suspects in police custody of their right to remain silent and to have counsel appointed.
Mississippi University for Women v. Hogan	458 U.S. 718 (1982)	O'Connor	Women's-only admissions policy at state university violated the equal protection clause.
Missouri v. Jenkins	495 U.S. 33 (1990)	White	Federal district court was without authority to levy a property

Case Name	Case Citation and Date	Author of Court's Opinion	Case Summary
			tax to support desegregation remedies.
Missouri ex rel. Gaines v. Canada	305 U.S. 337 (1938)	Hughes	State's refusal to admit black applicant to the state's law school and its offer to pay tuition for the student to attend an out-of-state law school violated the equal protection clause.
Mistretta v. United States	488 U.S. 361 (1989)	Blackmun	Federal law that created a commission to establish sentencing guidelines in criminal cases was constitutional.
Mitchell v. Helms	530 U.S. 793 (2000)	Thomas	Distribution of aid to a variety of public and private schools, including private religious schools, for the purchase of equipment and materials did not violate the establishment clause.
Mobile v. Bolden	446 U.S. 55 (1980)	Stewart	At-large voting scheme for municipal elections would not violate the equal protection clause, even if it resulted in diluted minority voting strength, unless at-large system was adopted for the purpose of diluting minority voting strength.
Monell v. Department of Social Services	436 U.S. 658 (1978)	Brennan	Pregnant women forced by municipality to take medically unnecessary maternity leave were entitled to sue the municipality.
Moose Lodge No. 107 v. Irvis	407 U.S. 163 (1972)	Rehnquist	The equal protection clause did not prevent a state from granting a liquor license to a private club that discriminated on the basis of race.
Morrison v. Olson	487 U.S. 654 (1988)	Rehnquist	Federal law providing for the appointment of independent counsel to investigate possible criminal violations by senior executive officials was constitutional and did not violate separation of powers principle.

Case Name	Case Citation and Date	Author of Court's Opinion	Case Summary
Mueller v. Allen	463 U.S. 388 (1983)	Rehnquist	A state income tax deduction for certain educational expenses did not violate the establishment clause even when used by the parents of parochial school children.
Muller v. Oregon	208 U.S. 412 (1908)	Brewer	A state law that established maximum work hours for women was not unconstitutional.
Munn v. Illinois	94 U.S. 113 (1877)	Waite	State law setting rates for grain elevator storage was constitutional.
National Association for the Advancement of Colored People v. Button	371 U.S. 415 (1963)	Brennan	Actions of the NAACP in providing attorneys to represent civil rights plaintiffs was protected by the First Amendment.
National Labor Relations Board v. Jones & Laughlin Steel Corp.	301 U.S. 1 (1937)	Hughes	Federal law granting workers right to organize union was a valid exercise of Congress's power under the commerce clause to regulate interstate commerce.
National League of Cities v. Usery	426 U.S. 833 (1976)	Rehnquist	Federal law that established minimum wage and maximum hour requirements was unconstitutional insofar as it applied to state and municipal workers. Decision overruled by *Garcia v. San Antonio Metropolitan Transit Authority* (1985).
National Organization of Women v. Scheidler	510 U.S. 249 (1994)	Rehnquist	Abortion protestors who engaged in violent and intimidating activities may be liable under the Racketeer Influence and Corrupt Organization Act (RICO).
National Treasury Employees Union v. Raab	489 U.S. 656 (1989)	Kennedy	Suspicionless drug testing of employees applying for positions relating to drug enforcement was not unconstitutional.
Near v. Minnesota	283 U.S. 697 (1931)	Hughes	A state law prohibiting the publication of a newspaper that had printed defamatory articles violated the First Amendment.

Case Name	Case Citation and Date	Author of Court's Opinion	Case Summary
Nebbia v. New York	291 U.S. 502 (1934)	Roberts	The Constitution did not prevent a state from regulating milk prices.
Nebraska Press Association v. Stuart	427 U.S. 539 (1976)	Burger	Gag order on the press during a criminal trial was a violation of the First Amendment.
Newberry v. United States	256 U.S. 232 (1921)	McReynolds	Congress did not have power to limit campaign expenditures in primary elections.
New Jersey v. T.L.O.	469 U.S. 325 (1985)	White	Fourth Amendment's protection against unreasonable searches and seizures applied to public school students.
New York State Club Association v. City of New York	487 U.S. 1 (1988)	White	State law prohibiting race and sex discrimination could be applied to certain private clubs.
New York Times v. Sullivan	376 U.S. 254 (1964)	Brennan	The First Amendment required that a defamation claim against the press could only succeed in a case involving a public official if the press acted with actual malice.
New York Times v. United States	403 U.S. 713 (1971)	Seriatim opinions	An injunction to prevent newspapers from publishing the Pentagon Papers would violate the First Amendment.
New York v. Ferber	458 U.S. 747 (1982)	White	Pornographic depictions of children could be prohibited even if they were not obscene.
New York v. Miln	36 U.S. 102 (1837)	Barbour	Local ordinance regulating ships' passengers did not intrude upon Congress's power to regulate interstate commerce.
Nixon v. Herndon	273 U.S. 536 (1927)	Holmes	A state law excluding African Americans from voting in Democratic primaries was unconstitutional.
Nixon v. Administrator of General Services	433 U.S. 425 (1977)	Brennan	Federal law giving the General Services Administration control of the papers of President Richard Nixon was not unconstitutional.
Nixon v. Condon	286 U.S. 73 (1932)	Cardozo	State law that gave party officials power to determine voting

Case Name	Case Citation and Date	Author of Court's Opinion	Case Summary
			qualifications for primaries was unconstitutional where officials determined that only whites could vote in primaries.
Nollan v. California Coastal Commission	483 U.S. 825 (1987)	Scalia	The just compensation clause barred a state from attempting to condition the award of a building permit on an owner's conveying an easement to the state across the owner's property.
Ogden v. Saunders	25 U.S. 213 (1827)	seriatim opinions	A state insolvency law did not violate the contracts clause when it applied only to contracts entered into subsequent to the law's passage.
Oklahoma City Board of Education v. Dowell	498 U.S. 237 (1991)	Rehnquist	Desegregation remedies for school districts should be terminated when districts have complied with desegregation orders in good faith for a reasonable time and when effects of past discrimination have been eliminated insofar as is practicable.
Olmstead v. United States	277 U.S. 438 (1928)	Taft	So long as use of a wiretap did not require entry of private premises, it was not an unreasonable search and seizure.
Osborne v. Ohio	495 U.S. 103 (1990)	White	Freedom of speech did not prevent punishing the possession or viewing of child pornography.
Pacific Mutual Life Insurance Company v. Haslip	499 U.S. 1 (1991)	Blackmun	Award of punitive damages in a civil case did not violate due process of law.
Palko v. Connecticut	302 U.S. 319 (1937)	Cardozo	The double jeopardy limitation of the Fifth Amendment was not applicable to states.
Palmer v. Thompson	403 U.S. 217 (1971)	Black	Decision by public officials to close public swimming pools rather than integrate them did not violate the equal protection clause.

Case Name	Case Citation and Date	Author of Court's Opinion	Case Summary
Pasadena Board of Education v. Spangler	427 U.S. 424 (1976)	Rehnquist	Federal court did not have power to order yearly adjustments to maintain racial balance in public schools after official racial segregation had been remedied.
Payne v. Tennessee	501 U.S. 808 (1991)	Rehnquist	The Constitution did not bar the use of victim impact evidence during the sentencing phase of a capital murder case.
Personnel Administrator of Massachusetts v. Feeney	442 U.S. 256 (1979)	Stewart	State statute that gave an employment preference to veterans did not violate the equal protection clause, even though it had the effect of favoring men more often than women.
Pierce v. Society of Sisters	268 U.S. 510 (1925)	McReynolds	A state law requiring children to be educated in public schools violated due process.
Planned Parenthood v. Casey	505 U.S. 833 (1992)	O'Connor, Kennedy, and Souter	A state law requiring women seeking an abortion to notify their spouses violated the right to an abortion, but a 24-hour waiting period, informed consent, and reporting requirements did not.
Planned Parenthood v. Danforth	428 U.S. 52 (1976)	Blackmun	The right to abortion was violated by state spousal and parental notification requirements and by the requirement that physicians attempt to save the lives of aborted fetuses.
Plessy v. Ferguson	163 U.S. 537 (1896)	Brown	A state law requiring separate railway facilities for black and white passengers did not violate the equal protection clause.
Plyler v. Doe	457 U.S. 202 (1982)	Brennan	A state violated the equal protection clause by denying a public education to children of illegal aliens.
Pointer v. Texas	380 U.S. 400 (1965)	Black	The right of criminal defendants to confront their accusers is applicable to state as well as federal criminal proceedings.

Case Name	Case Citation and Date	Author of Court's Opinion	Case Summary
Pollock v. Farmers' Loan & Trust Co.	157 U.S. 429 (1895)	Fuller	Federal income tax was unconstitutional.
Powell v. Alabama	287 U.S. 45 (1932)	Sutherland	Criminal defendants in rape cases are entitled to court-appointed attorneys.
Powell v. McCormack	395 U.S. 486 (1969)	Warren	Refusal of Congress to seat one of its members who met constitutional requirements for membership in Congress but who had allegedly committed various improprieties was unconstitutional.
Powers v. Ohio	499 U.S. 400 (1991)	Kennedy	Prosecutors in a criminal trial may not exclude potential jurors on account of their race, whether or not potential jurors are the same race as the defendant.
Prigg v. Pennsylvania	41 U.S. 539 (1842)	Story	Fugitive Slave Law of 1793 was constitutional.
Printz v. United States	521 U.S. 898 (1997)	Scalia	Congress lacked authority under the commerce clause to require local law enforcement officials to conduct background checks on persons seeking to purchase guns.
Prize Cases	67 U.S. 635 (1863)	Grier	At the outset of the Civil War, President Lincoln's order of a blockade of Southern ports prior to Congress's declaration of war was constitutional.
R.A.V. v. City of St. Paul	505 U.S. 377 (1992)	Scalia	A municipal "hate speech" ordinance violated freedom of speech.
Raines v. Byrd	521 U.S. 811 (1997)	Rehnquist	Six members of Congress who challenged the Line Item Veto Act had not suffered the kind of individual injury that would entitle them to press their claim in federal court.
Reed v. Reed	404 U.S. 71 (1971)	Burger	A state law that gave preference to fathers over mothers as executors of their children's estates violated the equal protection clause.

Case Name	Case Citation and Date	Author of Court's Opinion	Case Summary
Regents of the University of California v. Bakke	438 U.S. 265 (1978)	Powell	The equal protection clause barred a state from using racial quotas for medical school admissions but not from a more informal consideration of race as a factor in the admissions process.
Reitman v. Mulkey	387 U.S. 369 (1967)	White	Equal protection was violated by a state constitutional provision that prohibited the state from interfering with racial discrimination by private individuals in sale or lease of property.
Reno v. ACLU	521 U.S. 844 (1997)	Stevens	A federal law that regulated indecent material on the Internet violated freedom of speech.
Renton v. Playtime Theaters	475 U.S. 41 (1986)	Rehnquist	The free speech clause did not prevent a local community from prohibiting adult theaters from operating near residential areas, churches, parks, or schools.
Reynolds v. Sims	377 U.S. 533 (1964)	Warren	Equal protection required voting districts to be draw up according to the "one person, one vote" standard.
Reynolds v. United States	98 U.S. 145 (1879)	Waite	A federal antibigamy law did not violate free exercise rights of Mormons who wished to engage in the practice o polygamy.
Rhodes v. Chapman	452 U.S. 337 (1981)	Powell	Prison arrangement that housed two inmates in a cell designed for one was not unconstitutional.
Richmond v. J. A. Croson Co.	488 U.S. 469 (1989)	O'Connor	A municipal affirmative action program involving public works contracts violated the equal protection clause.
Roberts v. United States Jaycees	468 U.S. 609 (1984)	Brennan	State statute that required Jaycees to admit women did not violate the First Amendment associational rights of the organization.

Case Name	Case Citation and Date	Author of Court's Opinion	Case Summary
Robinson v. California	370 U.S. 660 (1962)	Stewart	The Eighth Amendment's cruel and unusual punishments clause prohibited classification of drug addiction as a crime.
Roe v. Wade	410 U.S. 113 (1973)	Blackmun	Women have a right to abortion that can only be restricted beginning in the second trimester to protect a woman's health or in the third trimester to protect the fetus.
Romer v. Evans	116 S. Ct. 1620 (1996)	Kennedy	A Colorado constitutional amendment that barred state laws from affording homosexuals protection against discrimination violated the equal protection clause.
Rosenberger v. Rector & Visitors of the University of Virginia	515 U.S. 819 (1995)	Kennedy	A public university's refusal to allow a religious student organization the same right to have printing expenses reimbursed as enjoyed by other student organizations violated freedom of speech.
Rostker v. Goldberg	453 U.S. 57 (1981)	Rehnquist	A federal law excluding women from the draft was not unconstitutional.
Roth v. United States	354 U.S. 476 (1957)	Brennan	Obscenity was not protected by the First Amendment.
Rummel v. Estelle	445 U.S. 263 (1980)	Rehnquist	The imposition of a life sentence for a defendant convicted of the third of relatively minor offences was not unconstitutional.
Runyon v. McCrary	427 U.S. 160 (1976)	Stewart	Refusal of private school to admit black students violated federal law prohibiting racially discriminatory contracts.
Rust v. Sullivan	500 U.S. 173 (1991)	Rehnquist	Neither freedom of speech nor the right to an abortion were infringed by federal regulations that prohibit federally funded clinics from providing abortion counseling or referrals.
Rutan v. Republican Party of Illinois	497 U.S. 62 (1990)	Brennan	Denying low-level government jobs on partisan grounds

Case Name	Case Citation and Date	Author of Court's Opinion	Case Summary
			violated the First Amendment rights of applicants.
Saenz v. Roe	526 U.S. 489 (1999)	Stevens	State welfare law that limited new residents, for the first year they lived in the state, to the welfare benefits they would have received in their former state violated the right to travel.
San Antonio Independent School District v. Rodriguez	411 U.S. 1 (1973)	Powell	Reliance on the property tax as part of a state's system for supporting public education did not violate the equal protection clause.
Santa Fe School District v. Doe	530 U.S. 290 (2000)	Stevens	School's arrangement to let students vote on whether to have prayers before football games violated the establishment clause.
Santobello v. New York	404 U.S. 257 (1971)	Burger	A defendant who entered a guilty plea based on a prosecutor's commitment to recommend a particular sentence was entitled to a remand when the prosecutor violated the commitment.
Scales v. United States	367 U.S. 203 (1961)	Harlan	The conviction of a criminal defendant for "active" membership in the Communist Party did not violate the First Amendment.
Schall v. Martin	467 U.S. 253 (1984)	Rehnquist	A state could detain a suspect before trial who posed a substantial risk of committing a serious crime.
Schechter Poultry Corp. v. United States	295 U.S. 495 (1935)	Hughes	National Industrial Recovery Act exceeded Congress's power under the commerce clause.
Schenck v. United States	249 U.S. 47 (1919)	Holmes	The prosecution of protests against the draft did not violate the First Amendment.
Seminole Tribe of Florida v. Florida	517 U.S. 44 (1996)	Rehnquist	The Eleventh Amendment prevented Congress from allowing Indian tribes to sue states to force them to negotiate concerning gambling issues.

Case Name	Case Citation and Date	Author of Court's Opinion	Case Summary
Shapiro v. Thompson	394 U.S. 618 (1969)	Brennan	A durational residency requirement for the receipt of welfare benefits violated the right to travel.
Shaw v. Reno	509 U.S. 630 (1993)	O'Connor	A redistricting plan adopted solely to maximize minority voting strength violated the equal protection clause.
Shelley v. Kraemer	334 U.S. 1 (1948)	Vinson	The enforcement of a racially restrictive real estate covenant by a state court violated the Fourteenth Amendment.
Sheppard v. Maxwell	384 U.S. 333 (1966)	Clark	Excessive pretrial publicity violated a criminal defendant's right to a fair trial.
Sherbert v. Verner	374 U.S. 398 (1963)	Brennan	The free exercise clause was violated by the refusal of a state to grant unemployment benefits to a Seventh Day Adventist fired for refusing to work on Saturday, her Sabbath.
Shreveport Rate Cases	234 U.S. 342 (1914)	Hughes	Congress had power under the commerce clause to establish a commission to set intrastate rates of interstate carriers.
Skinner v. Oklahoma	316 U.S. 535 (1942)	Douglas	State law requiring compulsory sterilization of certain habitual offenders violated the equal protection clause.
Skinner v. Railway Labor Executives' Association	489 U.S. 602 (1989)	Stevens	The Constitution did not prevent drug testing for railroad workers after major accidents.
Slaughterhouse Cases	83 U.S. 36 (1873)	Miller	A state law that awarded a monopoly to one slaughterhouse did not violate the Fourteenth Amendment.
Smith v. Allwright	321 U.S. 649 (1944)	Reed	The exclusion of blacks from party primaries for state and national offices violated the Fourteenth and Fifteenth Amendments.
Solem v. Helm	463 U.S. 277 (1983)	Powell	The cruel and unusual punishments clause barred a state from imposing a life sentence

Case Name	Case Citation and Date	Author of Court's Opinion	Case Summary
			for the last of a series of nonviolent crimes.
South Carolina v. Katzenbach	383 U.S. 301 (1966)	Warren	Congress had power to pass the Voting Rights Act of 1965 under its constitutional power to enforce the Reconstruction Amendments.
South Dakota v. Dole	483 U.S. 203 (1987)	Rehnquist	It was permissible for Congress to condition receipt of federal highway funds on states raising the legal drinking age to 21.
Standard Oil v. United States	221 U.S. 1 (1911)	White	The Sherman Antitrust Act prohibits only "unreasonable" restraints on trade.
Stanford v. Kentucky	492 U.S. 361 (1989)	Scalia	Capital punishment imposed for a crime committed while the defendant was a minor did not necessarily violate the cruel and unusual punishments clause.
Stanley v. Georgia	394 U.S. 557 (1969)	Marshall	A state may not punish the private possession of obscene materials in a home.
Sternberg v. Carhart	530 U.S. 914 (2000)	Breyer	State law criminalizing "partial birth abortions" violated the right to an abortion.
Steward Machine Co. v. Davis	301 U.S. 548 (1937)	Cardozo	The payroll tax used to fund the Social Security unemployment compensation program was constitutional.
Strauder v. West Virginia	100 U.S. 303 (1880)	Strong	Exclusion of blacks from jury service violated the equal protection clause.
Stromberg v. California	283 U.S. 359 (1931)	Hughes	State law prohibiting the display of a red flag was unconstitutional.
Sturges v. Crowninshield	17 U.S. 122 (1819)	Marshall	A state law discharging previously existing debts violated the contracts clause.
Swann v. Charlotte-Mecklenburg Board of Education	402 U.S. 1 (1971)	Burger	A district court had authority to make flexible use of racial quotas and could order busing to integrate a public school district that had previously segregated students by race.

Case Name	Case Citation and Date	Author of Court's Opinion	Case Summary
Sweatt v. Painter	339 U.S. 629 (1950)	Vinson	A state's denial of admission for a black applicant to the state law school violated equal protection.
Taylor v. Louisiana	419 U.S. 522 (1975)	White	Exclusion of women from jury service was unconstitutional.
Tennessee v. Garner	471 U.S. 1 (1985)	White	Police could not use deadly force to stop a fleeing felon except to prevent death or serious injury to a bystander.
Terminiello v. Chicago	337 U.S. 1 (1949)	Douglas	Speech cannot be punished simply because it provokes anger in an audience.
Terry v. Ohio	392 U.S. 1 (1968)	Warren	The Fourth Amendment did not prohibit "stop and frisk" searches.
Texas v. Johnson	491 U.S. 397 (1989)	Brennan	A state statute providing for punishment of flag desecration infringed on the freedom of speech.
Thornburgh v. American College of Obstetricians and Gynecologists	476 U.S. 747 (1986)	Blackmun	The right to an abortion was violated by certain informed consent and reporting requirements relating to abortions and to a requirement that physicians attempt to preserve lives of aborted fetuses.
Thornhill v. Alabama	310 U.S. 88 (1940)	Murphy	Peaceful labor picketing is protected by the First Amendment's free speech clause.
Tilton v. Richardson	403 U.S. 672 (1971)	Burger	The establishment clause was not violated by a state's grant of construction funds to religious colleges for buildings to be used for secular purposes.
Tinker v. Des Moines School District	393 U.S. 503 (1969)	Fortas	Freedom of speech protected the right of students to wear black armbands in protest of the Vietnam War.
Tison v. Arizona	481 U.S. 137 (1987)	O'Connor	An accomplice to murder could be sentenced to death if the accomplice participated in the crime in a major way and displayed a reckless indifference to human life.

Case Name	Case Citation and Date	Author of Court's Opinion	Case Summary
Troxel v. Granville	530 U.S. 57 (2000)	O'Connor for the plurality	State law that permitted a court to order visitation rights for grandparents of children violated parents' fundamental right to control the upbringing of their children.
United States v. Alvarez-Machain	504 U.S. 655 (1992)	Rehnquist	It was not unconstitutional for a federal court to try a Mexican national kidnapped and brought to the United States for trial.
United States v. Armstrong	517 U.S. 456 (1996)	Rehnquist	Criminal defendants were not entitled to pretrial discovery to support their claims that the government had prosecuted them because of their race without showing initially that the government had declined to prosecute suspects of other races.
United States v. Butler	297 U.S. 1 (1936)	Roberts	A federal law designed to decrease agricultural production by levying a tax on processors of agricultural products and using tax revenues to pay benefits to farmers who agreed to limit production was unconstitutional.
United States v. California	332 U.S. 19 (1947)	Black	Federal government owned submerged lands between the low-water mark and the three-mile offshore limit.
United States v. Classic	313 U.S. 299 (1941)	Stone	Congress had authority to regulate primary elections when such elections were an important part of the election process for federal office.
United States v. Cruikshank	92 U.S. 542 (1876)	Waite	White mob that killed more than a hundred blacks in Louisiana in the 1873 Colfax Massacre could not be prosecuted under a federal law that prohibited conspiracies to deny the constitutional rights of citizens, since no constitutional violation was properly alleged.

Case Name	Case Citation and Date	Author of Court's Opinion	Case Summary
United States v. Curtiss-Wright Export Corporation	299 U.S. 304 (1936)	Sutherland	Embargo against arms shipments to certain warring countries in South America ordered by the president pursuant to a congressional resolution authorizing him to do so was not an unconstitutional delegation to the president of a legislative function.
United States v. Darby Lumber Company	312 U.S. 100 (1941)	Stone	Under the commerce clause, Congress had authority to regulate wages and hours of workers who manufactured products shipped interstate.
United States v. Eichman	496 U.S. 310 (1990)	Brennan	A federal law prohibiting the mutilation of a U.S. flag violated freedom of speech.
United States v. Lanza	260 U.S. 377 (1922)	Taft	Prosecution of individual under state law and then subsequently federal law did not amount to unconstitutional double jeopardy.
United States v. Leon	468 U.S. 897 (1984)	White	Illegal obtained evidence may be used at trial so long as police had a search warrant and believed they were acting legally.
United States v. Lopez	514 U.S. 549 (1995)	Rehnquist	Congress did not have authority under the commerce clause to criminalize the possession of firearms near schools.
United States v. Monsanto	491 U.S. 600 (1989)	White	Federal drug forfeiture statute may be used to freeze criminal defendant's assets before trial even when the defendant seeks to use the assets to hire an attorney.
United States v. Morrison	529 U.S. 598 (2000)	Rehnquist	Congress lacked power to make domestic violence a federal crime.
United States v. Nixon	418 U.S. 683 (1974)	Burger	The president was not immune from a subpoena issued by a special prosecutor directing him to turn over White House tapes.

Case Name	Case Citation and Date	Author of Court's Opinion	Case Summary
United States v. O'Brien	391 U.S. 367 (1968)	Warren	Federal law that prohibited destruction of draft cards did not violate the free speech rights of draft protestors who wished to burn or otherwise destroy their cards as an act of political protest.
United States v. Playboy	529 U.S. 803 (2000)	Kennedy	Federal law that required cable television operators primarily dedicated to sexually oriented programming to either block those channels or limit their transmission to hours when children are unlikely to be viewing violated freedom of speech.
United States v. United States District Court	407 U.S. 297 (1972)	Powell	Government surveillance of domestic groups without a warrant was unconstitutional.
United States v. Virginia	518 U.S. 515 (1996)	Ginsburg	The exclusion of women from a public military academy violated the equal protection clause.
United States v. Wong Kim Ark	169 U.S. 649 (1898)	Gray	Persons born in the United States are U.S. citizens in spite of their ethnic backgrounds.
United Steelworkers of America v. Weber	443 U.S. 193 (1979)	Brennan	Employers could adopt voluntary affirmative action programs without violating federal laws prohibiting racial discrimination.
U.S. Term Limits, Inc. v. Thorton	514 U.S. 779 (1995)	Stevens	State constitutional provision that limited the number of terms of persons elected to Congress in the state was unconstitutional.
Vance v. Bradley	440 U.S. 93 (1979)	White	The equal protection clause did not prohibit mandatory retirement for foreign service officials.
Wallace v. Jaffree	472 U.S. 38 (1985)	Stevens	A state violated the establishment clause when it enacted a moment-of silence-statute for the purpose of restoring prayer to public schools.

Case Name	Case Citation and Date	Author of Court's Opinion	Case Summary
Wards Cove Packing Co. v. Atonio	490 U.S. 642 (1989)	White	A reasonable business justification may excuse the underrepresentation of racial minorities when challenged under civil rights laws.
Ware v. Hylton	3 U.S. 199 (1796)	Chase	A Virginia law regarding the payment of debts to the British was invalid because it was contrary to the terms of the 1783 Treaty of Paris.
Washington v. Davis	426 U.S. 229 (1976)	White	Requirement that police officer candidates take aptitude test did not violate the equal protection clause even though more black than white candidates failed the test.
Washington v. Glucksberg	521 U.S. 702 (1997)	Rehnquist	A state law banning assisted suicide did not violate due process.
Webster v. Reproductive Health Services	492 U.S. 490 (1989)	Rehnquist for the plurality	The right to abortion did not prohibit state from banning state employees from performing abortions or from requiring physicians to perform a test to determine the viability of a fetus.
Weeks v. United States	232 U.S. 383 (1914)	Day	Evidence obtained in an illegal search must may not be used in a subsequent criminal prosecution.
Wesberry v. Sanders	376 U.S. 1 (1964)	Black	Equal protection required that congressional districts not have substantial disparities in population.
West Coast Hotel Co. v. Parrish	300 U.S. 379 (1937)	Hughes	The due process clause did not prevent a state from regulating the minimum wages for women and children.
West Virginia State Board of Education v. Barnette	319 U.S. 624 (1943)	Jackson	The First Amendment prohibited schools from compelling Jehovah's Witness children to salute the flag and recite the pledge of allegiance.

Case Name	Case Citation and Date	Author of Court's Opinion	Case Summary
Wickard v. Filburn	317 U.S. 111 (1942)	Jackson	Congress had power under the commerce clause to regulate a farmer's consumption of wheat for personal use.
Wisconsin v. Mitchell	508 U.S. 476 (1993)	Rehnquist	Freedom of speech did not bar a law that punished crimes motivated by racial hatred more severely than crimes without this motivation.
Wisconsin v. Yoder	406 U.S. 205 (1972)	Burger	The free exercise clause entitled Amish parents to an exemption from a school attendance law that required children to attend school past the eighth grade.
Witherspoon v. Illinois	391 U.S. 510 (1968)	Stewart	A prosecutor in a murder case could not exclude potential jurors who expressed general objections to the death penalty.
Wolf v. Colorado	338 U.S. 25 (1949)	Frankfurter	Due process did not require states to exclude illegally obtained evidence from use in criminal proceedings.
Yates v. United States	354 U.S. 298 (1957)	Harlan	Freedom of speech prohibited government from prosecuting advocacy of forcible overthrow of government without proof of advocacy of specific acts to accomplish this end.
Yick Wo v. Hopkins	118 U.S. 356 (1886)	Matthews	Zoning laws administered in a racially discriminatory fashion violated the equal protection clause.
Young v. American Mini Theatres, Inc.	427 U.S. 50 (1976)	Stevens for plurality	Use of zoning ordinance to disperse adult theaters did not violate freedom of speech.
Youngstown Sheet & Tube Co. v. Sawyer	343 U.S. 579 (1952)	Black	President Harry S. Truman's seizure of steel mills during the Korean War was unconstitutional.
Zorah v. Clauson	343 U.S. 306 (1952)	Douglas	School program that released students from public school to attend religious classes away from school did not violate the establishment clause.

APPENDIX 4
THE CONSTITUTION OF THE UNITED STATES

We the people of the United States, in order to form a more perfect union, establish justice, insure domestic tranquility, provide for the common defense, promote the general welfare, and secure the blessings of liberty to ourselves and our posterity, do ordain and establish this Constitution for the United States of America.

Article I

Section 1. All legislative powers herein granted shall be vested in a Congress of the United States, which shall consist of a Senate and House of Representatives.

Section 2. The House of Representatives shall be composed of members chosen every second year by the people of the several states, and the electors in each state shall have the qualifications requisite for electors of the most numerous branch of the state legislature.

No person shall be a Representative who shall not have attained to the age of twenty five years, and been seven years a citizen of the United States, and who shall not, when elected, be an inhabitant of that state in which he shall be chosen.

Representatives and direct taxes shall be apportioned among the several states which may be included within this union, according to their respective numbers, which shall be determined by adding to the whole number of free persons, including those bound to service for a term of years, and excluding Indians not taxed, three fifths of all other Persons. The actual Enumeration shall be made within three years after the first meeting of the Congress of the United States, and within every subsequent term of ten years, in such manner as they shall by law direct. The number of Representatives shall not exceed one for every thirty thousand, but each state shall have at least one Representative; and until such enumeration shall be made, the state of New Hampshire shall be entitled to choose three, Massachusetts eight, Rhode Island and Providence Plantations one, Connecticut five, New York six, New Jersey four, Pennsylvania eight, Delaware one, Maryland six, Virginia ten, North Carolina five, South Carolina five, and Georgia three.

When vacancies happen in the Representation from any state, the executive authority thereof shall issue writs of election to fill such vacancies.

The House of Representatives shall choose their speaker and other officers; and shall have the sole power of impeachment.

Section 3. The Senate of the United States shall be composed of two Senators from each state, chosen by the legislature thereof, for six years; and each Senator shall have one vote. Immediately after they shall be assembled in consequence of the first election, they shall be divided as equally as may be into three classes. The seats of the Senators of the first class shall be vacated at the expiration of the second year, of the second class at the expiration of the fourth year, and the third class at the expiration of the sixth year, so that one third may be chosen every second year; and if vacancies happen by resignation, or otherwise, during the recess of the legislature of any state, the executive thereof may make temporary appointments until the next meeting of the legislature, which shall then fill such vacancies.

No person shall be a Senator who shall not have attained to the age of thirty years, and been nine years a citizen of the United States and who shall not, when elected, be an inhabitant of that state for which he shall be chosen.

The Vice President of the United States shall be President of the Senate, but shall have no vote, unless they be equally divided.

The Senate shall choose their other officers, and also a President pro tempore, in the absence of the Vice President, or when he shall exercise the office of President of the United States.

The Senate shall have the sole power to try all impeachments. When sitting for that purpose, they shall be on oath or affirmation. When the President of the United States is tried, the Chief Justice shall preside: And no person shall be convicted without the concurrence of two thirds of the members present.

Judgment in cases of impeachment shall not extend further than to removal from office, and disqualification to hold and enjoy any office of honor, trust or profit under the United States: but the party convicted shall nevertheless be liable and subject to indictment, trial, judgment and punishment, according to law.

Section 4. The times, places and manner of holding elections for Senators and Representatives, shall be prescribed in each state by the legislature thereof; but the Congress may at any time by law make or alter such regulations, except as to the places of choosing Senators.

The Congress shall assemble at least once in every year, and such meeting shall be on the first Monday in December, unless they shall by law appoint a different day.

Section 5. Each House shall be the judge of the elections, returns and qualifications of its own members, and a majority of each shall constitute a quorum to do business; but a smaller number may adjourn from day to day, and may be authorized to compel the attendance of absent members, in such manner, and under such penalties as each House may provide.

Each House may determine the rules of its proceedings, punish its members for disorderly behavior, and, with the concurrence of two thirds, expel a member.

Each House shall keep a journal of its proceedings, and from time to time publish the same, excepting such parts as may in their judgment require secrecy; and the yeas and nays of the members of either House on any question shall, at the desire of one fifth of those present, be entered on the journal.

Neither House, during the session of Congress, shall, without the consent of the other, adjourn for more than three days, nor to any other place than that in which the two Houses shall be sitting.

Section 6. The Senators and Representatives shall receive a compensation for their services, to be ascertained by law, and paid out of the treasury of the United States. They shall in all cases, except treason, felony and breach of the peace, be privileged from arrest during their attendance at the session of their respective Houses, and in going to and returning from the same; and for any speech or debate in either House, they shall not be questioned in any other place. No Senator or Representative shall, during the time for which he was elected, be appointed to any civil office under the authority of the United States, which shall have been created, or the emoluments whereof shall have been increased during such time: and no person holding any office under the United States, shall be a member of either House during his continuance in office.

Section 7. All bills for raising revenue shall originate in the House of Representatives; but the Senate may propose or concur with amendments as on other Bills.

Every bill which shall have passed the House of Representatives and the Senate, shall, before it become a law, be presented to the President of the United States; if he approve he shall sign it, but if not he shall return it, with his objections to that House in which it shall have originated, who shall enter the objections at large on their journal, and proceed to reconsider it. If after such reconsideration two thirds of that House shall agree to pass the bill, it shall be sent, together with the objections, to the other House, by which it shall likewise be reconsidered, and if approved by two thirds of that House, it shall become a law. But in all such cases the votes of both Houses shall be determined by yeas and nays, and the names of the persons voting for and against the bill shall be entered on the journal of each House respectively. If any bill shall not be returned by the President within ten days (Sundays excepted) after it shall have been presented to him, the same shall be a law, in like manner as if he had signed it, unless the Congress by their adjournment prevent its return, in which case it shall not be a law.

Every order, resolution, or vote to which the concurrence of the Senate and House of Representatives may be necessary (except on a question of adjournment) shall be presented to the President of the United States; and before the same shall take effect, shall be approved by him, or being disapproved by him, shall be repassed by two thirds of the Senate and House of Representatives, according to the rules and limitations prescribed in the case of a bill.

Section 8. The Congress shall have power to lay and collect taxes, duties, imposts and excises, to pay the debts and provide for the common defense and general welfare of the United States; but all duties, imposts and excises shall be uniform throughout the United States;

To borrow money on the credit of the United States;

To regulate commerce with foreign nations, and among the several states, and with the Indian tribes;

To establish a uniform rule of naturalization, and uniform laws on the subject of bankruptcies throughout the United States;

To coin money, regulate the value thereof, and of foreign coin, and fix the standard of weights and measures;

To provide for the punishment of counterfeiting the securities and current coin of the United States;

To establish post offices and post roads;

To promote the progress of science and useful arts, by securing for limited times to authors and inventors the exclusive right to their respective writings and discoveries;

To constitute tribunals inferior to the Supreme Court;

To define and punish piracies and felonies committed on the high seas, and offenses against the law of nations;

To declare war, grant letters of marque and reprisal, and make rules concerning captures on land and water;

To raise and support armies, but no appropriation of money to that use shall be for a longer term than two years;

To provide and maintain a navy;

To make rules for the government and regulation of the land and naval forces;

To provide for calling forth the militia to execute the laws of the union, suppress insurrections and repel invasions;

To provide for organizing, arming, and disciplining, the militia, and for governing such part of them as may be employed in the service of the United States, reserving to the states respectively, the appointment of the officers, and the authority of training the militia according to the discipline prescribed by Congress;

To exercise exclusive legislation in all cases whatsoever, over such District (not exceeding ten miles square) as may, by cession of particular states, and the acceptance of Congress, become the seat of the government of the United States, and to exercise like authority over all places purchased by the consent of the legislature of the state in which the same shall be, for the erection of forts, magazines, arsenals, dockyards, and other needful buildings;—And

To make all laws which shall be necessary and proper for carrying into execution the foregoing powers, and all other powers vested by this Constitution in the government of the United States, or in any department or officer thereof.

Section 9. The migration or importation of such persons as any of the states now existing shall think proper to admit, shall not be prohibited by the Congress prior to the year one thousand eight hundred and eight, but a tax or duty may be imposed on such importation, not exceeding ten dollars for each person.

The privilege of the writ of habeas corpus shall not be suspended, unless when in cases of rebellion or invasion the public safety may require it.

No bill of attainder or ex post facto Law shall be passed.

No capitation, or other direct, tax shall be laid, unless in proportion to the census or enumeration herein before directed to be taken.

No tax or duty shall be laid on articles exported from any state.

No preference shall be given by any regulation of commerce or revenue to the ports of one state over those of another: nor shall vessels bound to, or from, one state, be obliged to enter, clear or pay duties in another.

No money shall be drawn from the treasury, but in consequence of appropriations made by law; and a regular statement and account of receipts and expenditures of all public money shall be published from time to time.

No title of nobility shall be granted by the United States: and no person holding any office of profit or trust under them, shall, without the consent of the Congress, accept of any present, emolument, office, or title, of any kind whatever, from any king, prince, or foreign state.

Section 10. No state shall enter into any treaty, alliance, or confederation; grant letters of marque and reprisal; coin money; emit bills of credit; make anything but gold and silver coin a tender in payment of debts; pass any bill of attainder, ex post facto law, or law impairing the obligation of contracts, or grant any title of nobility.

No state shall, without the consent of the Congress, lay any imposts or duties on imports or exports, except what may be absolutely necessary for executing its inspection laws: and the net produce of all duties and imposts, laid by any state on imports or exports, shall be for the use of the treasury of the United States; and all such laws shall be subject to the revision and control of the Congress.

No state shall, without the consent of Congress, lay any duty of tonnage, keep troops, or ships of war in time of peace, enter into any agreement or compact with another state, or with a foreign power, or engage in war, unless actually invaded, or in such imminent danger as will not admit of delay.

Article II

Section 1. The executive power shall be vested in a President of the United States of America. He shall hold his office during the term of four years, and, together with the Vice President, chosen for the same term, be elected, as follows:

Each state shall appoint, in such manner as the Legislature thereof may direct, a number of electors, equal to the whole number of Senators and Representatives to which the State may be entitled in the Congress: but no Senator or Representative, or person holding an office of trust or profit under the United States, shall be appointed an elector.

The electors shall meet in their respective states, and vote by ballot for two persons, of whom one at least shall not be an inhabitant of the same state with themselves. And they shall make a list of all the persons voted for, and of the number of votes for each; which list they shall sign and certify, and transmit sealed to the seat of the government of the United States, directed to the President of the Senate. The President of the Senate shall, in the presence of the Senate and House of Representatives, open all the certificates, and the votes shall then be counted. The person having the greatest number of votes shall be the President, if such number be a majority of the whole number of electors appointed; and if there be more than one who have such majority, and have an equal number of votes, then the House of Representatives shall immediately choose by ballot one of them for President; and if no person have a majority, then from the five highest on the list the said House shall in like manner choose the President. But in choosing the President, the votes shall be taken by States, the representation from each state having one vote; A quorum for this purpose shall consist of a member or members from two thirds of the states, and a majority of all the states shall be necessary to a choice. In every case, after the choice of the President, the person having the greatest number of votes of the electors shall be the Vice President. But if there should remain two or more who have equal votes, the Senate shall choose from them by ballot the Vice President.

The Congress may determine the time of choosing the electors, and the day on which they shall give their votes; which day shall be the same throughout the United States.

No person except a natural born citizen, or a citizen of the United States, at the time of the adoption of this Constitution, shall be eligible to the office of President; neither shall any person be eligible to that office who shall not have attained to the age of thirty five years, and been fourteen Years a resident within the United States.

In case of the removal of the President from office, or of his death, resignation, or inability to discharge the powers and duties of the said office, the same shall devolve on the Vice President, and the Congress may by law provide for the case of removal, death, resignation or inability, both of the President and Vice President, declaring what officer shall then act as President, and such officer shall act accordingly, until the disability be removed, or a President shall be elected.

The President shall, at stated times, receive for his services, a compensation, which shall neither be increased nor diminished during the period for which he shall have been elected, and he shall not receive within that period any other emolument from the United States, or any of them.

Before he enter on the execution of his office, he shall take the following oath or affirmation:—"I do solemnly swear (or affirm) that I will faithfully execute the office of President of the United States, and will to the best of my ability, preserve, protect and defend the Constitution of the United States."

Section 2. The President shall be commander in chief of the Army and Navy of the United States, and of the militia of the several states, when called into the actual service of the United States; he may require the opinion, in writing, of the principal officer in each of the executive departments, on any subject relating to the duties of their respective offices, and he shall have power to grant reprieves and pardons for offenses against the United States, except in cases of impeachment.

He shall have power, by and with the advice and consent of the Senate, to make treaties, provided two thirds of the Senators present concur; and he shall nominate, and by and with the advice and consent of the Senate, shall appoint ambassadors, other public ministers and consuls, judges of the Supreme Court, and all other officers of the United States, whose appointments are not herein otherwise provided for, and which shall be established by law: but the Congress may by law vest the appointment of such inferior officers, as they think proper, in the President alone, in the courts of law, or in the heads of departments.

The President shall have power to fill up all vacancies that may happen during the recess of the Senate, by granting commissions which shall expire at the end of their next session.

Section 3. He shall from time to time give to the Congress information of the state of the union, and recommend to their consideration such measures as he shall judge necessary and expedient; he may, on extraordinary occasions, convene both Houses, or either of them, and in case of disagreement between them, with respect to the time of adjournment, he may adjourn them to such time as he shall think proper; he shall receive ambassadors and other public ministers; he shall take care that the laws be faithfully executed, and shall commission all the officers of the United States.

Section 4. The President, Vice President and all civil officers of the United States, shall be removed from office on impeachment for, and conviction of, treason, bribery, or other high crimes and misdemeanors.

Article III

Section 1. The judicial power of the United States, shall be vested in one Supreme Court, and in such inferior courts as the Congress may from time to time ordain and establish. The judges, both of the supreme and inferior courts, shall hold their offices during good behavior, and shall, at stated times, receive for their services, a compensation, which shall not be diminished during their continuance in office.

Section 2. The judicial power shall extend to all cases, in law and equity, arising under this Constitution, the laws of the United States, and treaties made, or which shall be made, under their authority;—to all cases affecting ambassadors, other public ministers and consuls;—to all cases of admiralty and maritime jurisdiction;—to controversies to which the United States shall be a party;—to controversies between two or more states;—between a state and citizens of another state;—between citizens of different states;—between citizens of the same state claiming lands under grants of different states, and between a state, or the citizens thereof, and foreign states, citizens or subjects.

In all cases affecting ambassadors, other public ministers and consuls, and those in which a state shall be party, the Supreme Court shall have original jurisdiction. In all the other cases before mentioned, the Supreme Court shall have appellate jurisdiction, both as to law and fact, with such exceptions, and under such regulations as the Congress shall make.

The trial of all crimes, except in cases of impeachment, shall be by jury; and such trial shall be held in the state where the said crimes shall have been committed; but when not committed within any state, the trial shall be at such place or places as the Congress may by law have directed.

Section 3. Treason against the United States, shall consist only in levying war against them, or in adhering to their enemies, giving them aid and comfort. No person shall be convicted of treason unless on the testimony of two witnesses to the same overt act, or on confession in open court.

The Congress shall have power to declare the punishment of treason, but no attainder of treason shall work corruption of blood, or forfeiture except during the life of the person attainted.

Article IV

Section 1. Full faith and credit shall be given in each state to the public acts, records, and judicial proceedings of every other state. And the Congress may by general laws prescribe the manner in which such acts, records, and proceedings shall be proved, and the effect thereof.

Section 2. The citizens of each state shall be entitled to all privileges and immunities of citizens in the several states.

A person charged in any state with treason, felony, or other crime, who shall flee from justice, and be found in another state, shall on demand of the executive authority of the state from which he fled, be delivered up, to be removed to the state having jurisdiction of the crime.

No person held to service or labor in one state, under the laws thereof, escaping into another, shall, in consequence of any law or regulation therein, be discharged from such service or labor, but shall be delivered up on claim of the party to whom such service or labor may be due.

Section 3. New states may be admitted by the Congress into this union; but no new states shall be formed or erected within the jurisdiction of any other state; nor any state be formed by the junction of two or more states, or parts of states, without the consent of the legislatures of the states concerned as well as of the Congress.

The Congress shall have power to dispose of and make all needful rules and regulations respecting the territory or other property belonging to the United States; and nothing in this Constitution shall be so construed as to prejudice any claims of the United States, or of any particular state.

Section 4. The United States shall guarantee to every state in this union a republican form of government, and shall protect each of them against invasion; and on application of the legislature, or of the executive (when the legislature cannot be convened) against domestic violence.

Article V

The Congress, whenever two thirds of both houses shall deem it necessary, shall propose amendments to this Constitution, or, on the application of the legislatures of two thirds of the several states, shall call a convention for proposing amendments, which, in either case, shall be valid to all intents and purposes, as part of this Constitution, when ratified by the legislatures of three fourths of the several states, or by conventions in three fourths thereof, as the one or the other mode of ratification may be proposed by the Congress; provided that no amendment which may be made prior to the year one thousand eight hundred and eight shall in any manner affect the first and fourth clauses in the ninth section of the first article; and that no state, without its consent, shall be deprived of its equal suffrage in the Senate.

Article VI

All debts contracted and engagements entered into, before the adoption of this Constitution, shall be as valid against the United States under this Constitution, as under the Confederation.

This Constitution, and the laws of the United States which shall be made in pursuance thereof; and all treaties made, or which shall be made, under the authority of the United States, shall be the supreme law of the land; and the judges in every state shall be bound thereby, anything in the Constitution or laws of any State to the contrary notwithstanding.

The Senators and Representatives before mentioned, and the members of the several state legislatures, and all executive and judicial officers, both of the United States and of the several states, shall be bound by oath or affirmation, to support this Constitution; but no religious test shall ever be required as a qualification to any office or public trust under the United States.

Article VII

The ratification of the conventions of nine states, shall be sufficient for the establishment of this Constitution between the states so ratifying the same.

Amendment I

Congress shall make no law respecting an establishment of religion, or prohibiting the free exercise thereof; or abridging the freedom of speech, or of the press; or the right of the people peaceably to assemble, and to petition the government for a redress of grievances.

Amendment II

A well regulated militia, being necessary to the security of a free state, the right of the people to keep and bear arms, shall not be infringed.

Amendment III

No soldier shall, in time of peace be quartered in any house, without the consent of the owner, nor in time of war, but in a manner to be prescribed by law.

Amendment IV

The right of the people to be secure in their persons, houses, papers, and effects, against unreasonable searches and seizures, shall not be violated, and no warrants shall issue, but upon probable cause, supported by oath or affirmation, and particularly describing the place to be searched, and the persons or things to be seized.

Amendment V

No person shall be held to answer for a capital, or otherwise infamous crime, unless on a presentment or indictment of a grand jury, except in cases arising in the land or naval forces, or in the militia, when in actual service in time of war or public danger; nor shall any person be subject for the same offense to be twice put in jeopardy of life or limb; nor shall be compelled in any criminal case to be a witness against himself, nor be deprived of life, liberty, or property, without due process of law; nor shall private property be taken for public use, without just compensation.

Amendment VI

In all criminal prosecutions, the accused shall enjoy the right to a speedy and public trial, by an impartial jury of the state and district wherein the crime shall have been committed, which district shall have been previously ascertained by law, and to be informed of the nature and cause of the accusation; to be confronted with the witnesses against him; to have compulsory process for obtaining witnesses in his favor, and to have the assistance of counsel for his defense.

Amendment VII

In suits at common law, where the value in controversy shall exceed twenty dollars, the right of trial by jury shall be preserved, and no fact tried by a jury, shall be otherwise reexamined in any court of the United States, than according to the rules of the common law.

Amendment VIII

Excessive bail shall not be required, nor excessive fines imposed, nor cruel and unusual punishments inflicted.

Amendment IX

The enumeration in the Constitution, of certain rights, shall not be construed to deny or disparage others retained by the people.

Amendment X

The powers not delegated to the United States by the Constitution, nor prohibited by it to the states, are reserved to the states respectively, or to the people.

Amendment XI (1798)

The judicial power of the United States shall not be construed to extend to any suit in law or equity, commenced or prosecuted against one of the United States by citizens of another state, or by citizens or subjects of any foreign state.

Amendment XII (1804)

The electors shall meet in their respective states and vote by ballot for President and Vice-President, one of whom, at least, shall not be an inhabitant of the same state with themselves; they shall name in their ballots the person voted for as President, and in distinct ballots the person voted for as Vice-President, and they shall make distinct lists of all persons voted for as President, and of all persons voted for as Vice-President, and of the number of votes for each, which lists they shall sign and certify, and transmit sealed to the seat of the government of the United States, directed to the President of the Senate;—The President of the Senate shall, in the presence of the Senate and House of Representatives, open all the certificates and the votes shall then be counted;—the person having the greatest number of votes for President, shall be the President, if such number be a majority of the whole number of electors appointed; and if no person have such majority, then from the persons having the highest numbers not exceeding three on the list of those voted for as President, the House of Representatives shall choose immediately, by ballot, the President. But in choosing the President, the votes shall be taken by states, the representation from each state having one vote; a quorum for this purpose shall consist of a member or members from two-thirds of the states, and a majority of all the states shall be necessary to a choice. And if the House of Representatives shall not choose a President whenever the right of choice shall devolve upon them, before the fourth day of March next following, then the Vice-President shall act as President, as in the case of the death or other constitutional disability of the President. The person having the greatest number of votes as Vice-President, shall be the Vice-President, if such number be a majority of the whole number of electors appointed, and if no person have a majority, then from the two highest numbers on the list, the Senate shall choose the Vice-President; a quorum for the purpose shall consist of two-thirds of the whole number of Senators, and a majority of the whole number shall be necessary to a choice. But no person constitutionally ineligible to the office of President shall be eligible to that of Vice-President of the United States.

Amendment XIII
(1865)

Section 1. Neither slavery nor involuntary servitude, except as a punishment for crime whereof the party shall have been duly convicted, shall exist within the United States, or any place subject to their jurisdiction.

Section 2. Congress shall have power to enforce this article by appropriate legislation.

Amendment XIV
(1868)

Section 1. All persons born or naturalized in the United States, and subject to the jurisdiction thereof, are citizens of the United States and of the state wherein they reside. No state shall make or enforce any law which shall abridge the privileges or immunities of citizens of the United States; nor shall any state deprive any person of life, liberty, or property, without due process of law; nor deny to any person within its jurisdiction the equal protection of the laws.

Section 2. Representatives shall be apportioned among the several states according to their respective numbers, counting the whole number of persons in each state, excluding Indians not taxed. But when the right to vote at any election for the choice of electors for President and Vice President of the United States, Representatives in Congress, the executive and judicial officers of a state, or the members of the legislature thereof, is denied to any of the male inhabitants of such state, being twenty-one years of age, and citizens of the United States, or in any way abridged, except for participation in rebellion, or other crime, the basis of representation therein shall be reduced in the proportion which the number of such male citizens shall bear to the whole number of male citizens twenty-one years of age in such state.

Section 3. No person shall be a Senator or Representative in Congress, or elector of President and Vice President, or hold any office, civil or military, under the United States, or under any state, who, having previously taken an oath, as a member of Congress, or as an officer of the United States, or as a member of any state legislature, or as an executive or judicial officer of any state, to support the Constitution of the United States, shall have engaged in insurrection or rebellion against the same, or given aid or comfort to the enemies thereof. But Congress may by a vote of two-thirds of each House, remove such disability.

Section 4. The validity of the public debt of the United States, authorized by law, including debts incurred for payment of pensions and bounties for services in suppressing insurrection or rebellion, shall not be questioned. But neither the United States nor any state shall assume or pay any debt or obligation incurred in aid of insurrection or rebellion against the United States, or any claim for the loss or emancipation of any slave; but all such debts, obligations and claims shall be held illegal and void.

Section 5. The Congress shall have power to enforce, by appropriate legislation, the provisions of this article.

Amendment XV
(1870)

Section 1. The right of citizens of the United States to vote shall not be denied or abridged by the United States or by any state on account of race, color, or previous condition of servitude.

Section 2. The Congress shall have power to enforce this article by appropriate legislation.

Amendment XVI
(1913)

The Congress shall have power to lay and collect taxes on incomes, from whatever source derived, without apportionment among the several states, and without regard to any census of enumeration.

Amendment XVII
(1913)

The Senate of the United States shall be composed of two Senators from each state, elected by the people thereof, for six years; and each Senator shall have one vote. The electors in each state shall have the qualifications requisite for electors of the most numerous branch of the state legislatures.

When vacancies happen in the representation of any state in the Senate, the executive authority of such state shall issue writs of election to fill such vacancies: Provided, that the legislature of any state may empower the executive thereof to make temporary appointments until the people fill the vacancies by election as the legislature may direct.

This amendment shall not be so construed as to affect the election or term of any Senator chosen before it becomes valid as part of the Constitution.

Amendment XVIII
(1919)

Section 1. After one year from the ratification of this article the manufacture, sale, or transportation of intoxicating liquors within, the importation thereof into, or the exportation thereof from the United States and all territory subject to the jurisdiction thereof for beverage purposes is hereby prohibited.

Section 2. The Congress and the several states shall have concurrent power to enforce this article by appropriate legislation.

Section 3. This article shall be inoperative unless it shall have been ratified as an amendment to the Constitution by the legislatures of the several states, as provided in the Constitution, within seven years from the date of the submission hereof to the states by the Congress.

Amendment XIX
(1920)

The right of citizens of the United States to vote shall not be denied or abridged by the United States or by any state on account of sex.

Congress shall have power to enforce this article by appropriate legislation.

Amendment XX
(1933)

Section 1. The terms of the President and Vice President shall end at noon on the 20th day of January, and the terms of Senators and Representatives at noon on the 3d day of January, of the years in which such terms would have ended if this article had not been ratified; and the terms of their successors shall then begin.

Section 2. The Congress shall assemble at least once in every year, and such meeting shall begin at noon on the 3d day of January, unless they shall by law appoint a different day.

Section 3. If, at the time fixed for the beginning of the term of the President, the President elect shall have died, the Vice President elect shall become President. If a President shall not have been chosen before the time fixed for the beginning of his term, or if the President elect shall have failed to qualify, then the Vice President elect shall act as President until a President shall have qualified; and the Congress may by law provide for the case wherein neither a President elect nor a Vice President elect shall have qualified, declaring who shall then act as President, or the manner in which one who is to act shall be selected, and such person shall act accordingly until a President or Vice President shall have qualified.

Section 4. The Congress may by law provide for the case of the death of any of the persons from whom the House of Representatives may choose a President whenever the right of choice shall have devolved upon them, and for the case of the death of any of the persons from whom the Senate may choose a Vice President whenever the right of choice shall have devolved upon them.

Section 5. Sections 1 and 2 shall take effect on the 15th day of October following the ratification of this article.

Section 6. This article shall be inoperative unless it shall have been ratified as an amendment to the Constitution by the legislatures of three-fourths of the several states within seven years from the date of its submission.

Amendment XXI
(1933)

Section 1. The eighteenth article of amendment to the Constitution of the United States is hereby repealed.

Section 2. The transportation or importation into any state, territory, or possession of the United States for delivery or use therein of intoxicating liquors, in violation of the laws thereof, is hereby prohibited.

Section 3. This article shall be inoperative unless it shall have been ratified as an amendment to the Constitution by conventions in the several states, as provided in the Constitution, within seven years from the date of the submission hereof to the states by the Congress.

Amendment XXII
(1951)

Section 1. No person shall be elected to the office of the President more than twice, and no person who has held the office of President, or acted as President, for more than two years of a term to which some other person was elected President shall be elected to the office of the President more than once. But this article shall not apply to any person holding the office of President when this article was proposed by the Congress, and shall not prevent any person who may be holding the office of President, or acting as President, during the term within which this article becomes operative from holding the office of President or acting as President during the remainder of such term.

Section 2. This article shall be inoperative unless it shall have been ratified as an amendment to the Constitution by the legislatures of three-fourths of the several states within seven years from the date of its submission to the states by the Congress.

Amendment XXIII
(1961)

Section 1. The District constituting the seat of government of the United States shall appoint in such manner as the Congress may direct:

A number of electors of President and Vice President equal to the whole number of Senators and Representatives in Congress to which the District would be entitled if it were a state, but in no event more than the least populous state; they shall be in addition to those appointed by the states, but they shall be considered, for the purposes of the election of President and Vice President, to be electors appointed by a state; and they shall meet in the District and perform such duties as provided by the twelfth article of amendment.

Section 2. The Congress shall have power to enforce this article by appropriate legislation.

Amendment XXIV
(1964)

Section 1. The right of citizens of the United States to vote in any primary or other election for President or Vice President, for electors for President or Vice President, or for Senator or Representative in Congress, shall not be denied or abridged by the United States or any state by reason of failure to pay any poll tax or other tax.

Section 2. The Congress shall have power to enforce this article by appropriate legislation.

Amendment XXV
(1967)

Section 1. In case of the removal of the President from office or of his death or resignation, the Vice President shall become President.

Section 2. Whenever there is a vacancy in the office of the Vice President, the President shall nominate a Vice President who shall take office upon confirmation by a majority vote of both Houses of Congress.

Section 3. Whenever the President transmits to the President pro tempore of the Senate and the Speaker of the House of Representatives his written declaration that he is unable to discharge the powers and duties of his office, and until he transmits to them a written declaration to the contrary, such powers and duties shall be discharged by the Vice President as Acting President.

Section 4. Whenever the Vice President and a majority of either the principal officers of the executive departments or of such other body as Congress may by law provide, transmit to the President pro tempore of the Senate and the Speaker of the House of Representatives their written declaration that the President is unable to discharge the powers and duties of his office, the Vice President shall immediately assume the powers and duties of the office as Acting President.

Thereafter, when the President transmits to the President pro tempore of the Senate and the Speaker of the House of Representatives his written declaration that no inability exists, he shall resume the powers and duties of his office unless the Vice President and a majority of either the principal officers of the executive department or of such other body as Congress may by law provide, transmit within four days to the President pro tempore of the Senate and the Speaker of the House of Representatives their written declaration that the President is unable to discharge the powers and duties of his office. Thereupon Congress shall decide the issue, assembling within forty-eight hours for that purpose if not in session. If the Congress, within twenty-one days after receipt of the latter written declaration, or, if Congress is not in session, within twenty-one days after Congress is required to assemble, determines by two-thirds vote of both Houses that the President is unable to discharge the powers and duties of his office, the Vice President shall continue to discharge the same as Acting President; otherwise, the President shall resume the powers and duties of his office.

Amendment XXVI
(1971)

Section 1. The right of citizens of the United States, who are 18 years of age or older, to vote, shall not be denied or abridged by the United States or any state on account of age.

Section 2. The Congress shall have the power to enforce this article by appropriate legislation.

Amendment XXVII
(1992)

No law varying the compensation for the services of the Senators and Representatives shall take effect until an election of Representatives shall have intervened.

BIBLIOGRAPHY

General Materials Concerning the Supreme Court

Abraham, Henry Julian. *The Judiciary: The Supreme Court in the Governmental Process*. New York: New York University Press, 1996.

———. *Justices, Presidents, and Senators: A History of the U.S. Supreme Court Appointments from Washington to Clinton*. 4th ed. Lanham, Md.: Rowman & Littlefield Publishers, 1999.

Atkinson, David N. *Leaving the Bench: Supreme Court Justices at the End*. Lawrence: University Press of Kansas, 1999.

Baum, Lawrence. *The Supreme Court*. 6th ed. Washington, D.C.: CQ Press, 1998.

Bickel, Alexander M. *The Least Dangerous Branch: The Supreme Court at the Bar of Politics*. Indianapolis: Bobbs-Merrill, 1962.

———. *The Supreme Court and the Idea of Progress*. New Haven: Yale University Press, 1978.

Birkby, Robert H. *The Court and Public Policy*. Washington, D.C.: CQ Press, 1983.

Biskupic, Joan & Elder Witt. *Guide to the U.S. Supreme Court*. 2 vols. Washington, D.C.: Congressional Quarterly, 3d ed. 1997.

Blandford, Linda A., and Patricia R. Evans, eds. *Supreme Court of the United States, 1789–1980: An Index to Opinions Arranged by Justice*. Millwood, N.Y.: Kraus International Publications, 1983; Supplement 1980–90, 1994.

Blaustein, Albert P., and Roy M. Mersky. *The First One Hundred Justices: Statistical Studies on the Supreme Court of the United States*. Hamden, Conn.: Archon Books, 1978.

Bogen, David S. *Bulwark of Liberty: The Court and the First Amendment*. Port Washington, N.Y.: Associated Faculty Press, 1984.

Braeman, John. *Before the Civil Rights Revolution: the Old Court and Individual Rights*. New York: Greenwood Press, 1988.

Brandwein, Pamela. *Reconstructing Reconstruction: The Supreme Court and the Production of Historical Truth*. Durham, N.C.: Duke University Press, 1999.

Brenner, Saul & Harold J. Spaeth. *Stare Indecisis: The Alteration of Precedent on the Supreme Court, 1946–1992*. New York: Cambridge University Press, 1995.

Bronner, Ethan. *Battle for Justice: How the Bork Nomination Shook America*. New York: W. W. Norton & Company, 1989.

Burger, Warren E. *It Is So Ordered: A Constitution Unfolds*. New York: William Morrow, 1995.

Campbell, Tom Walter. *Four Score Forgotten Men; Sketches of the Justices of the US Supreme Court:* Little Rock, Ark.: Pioneer Publishing, 1950.

Carson, Hampton Lawrence. *The History of the Supreme Court of the United States, With Biographies of all the Chief and Associate Justices*. 1902. Reprint. New York: B. Franklin, 1971.

Carter, Lief H. *Contemporary Constitutional Lawmaking: The Supreme Court and the Art of Politics*. New York: Pergamon Press, 1985.

Cheney, Timothy D. *Who Makes the Law: The Supreme Court, Congress, the States, and Society*. Upper Saddle River, N.J.: Prentice Hall, 1998.

Choper, Jesse H. *Judicial Review and the National Political Process: A Functional Reconsideration of the Role of the Supreme Court*. Chicago: University of Chicago Press, 1980.

Choper, Jesse H., ed. *The Supreme Court and Its Justices*. Chicago: American Bar Association, 1987.

Cooper, Phillip J. *Battles on the Bench: Conflict Inside the Supreme Court*. Lawrence.: University Press of Kansas, 1995.

Cox, Archibald. *The Court and the Constitution*. Boston: Houghton Mifflin, 1987.

Curie, David P. *The Constitution in the Supreme Court: The Second Century, 1888–1986*. Chicago: University of Chicago Press, 1990.

———. *The Constitution in the Supreme Court: The First Hundred Years, 1789–1888*. Chicago: University of Chicago Press, 1985.

Cushman, Clare, ed. *The Supreme Court Justices: Illustrated Biographies, 1789–1995*. 2d. ed. Washington, D.C.: Congressional Quarterly, 1995.

Dimond, Paul R. *The Supreme Court and Judicial Choice: The Role of Provisional Review in a Democracy*. Ann Arbor: University of Michigan Press, 1989.

Dunham, Allison, and Philip B. Kurland, eds. *Mr. Justice*. Chicago: University of Chicago Press, 1964.

Epstein, Lee & Thomas G. Walker. *Constitutional Law for a Changing America: Rights, Liberties, and Justice*. Washington, D.C.: CQ Press, 2d ed. 1995.

Faille, Christopher C. *The Decline and Fall of the Supreme Court: Living out the Nightmares of the Federalists*. Westport, Conn.: Praeger, 1995.

Flanders, Henry. *The Lives and Times of the Chief Justices of the Supreme Court of the United States*. 1881. Reprint. Buffalo: W. S. Hein, 1972.

Franck, Matthew J. *Against the Imperial Judiciary: The Supreme Court vs. the Sovereignty of the People*. Lawrence: University Press of Kansas, 1996.

Fridlington, Robert. *The Reconstruction Court, 1864–1888*. Millwood, N.Y.: Associated Faculty Press, 1969–1978.

Friedman, Leon & Fred L. Israel, eds. *The Justices of the United States Supreme Court: Their Lives and Major Opinions*, vols. 1–5. New York: Chelsea House, 1995.

Galloway, Russell. *Justice for All?: The Rich and Poor in Supreme Court History, 1790–1990*. Durham, N.C.: Carolina Academic Press, 1991.

Gerber, Scott Douglas. *Seriatim: The Supreme Court Before John Marshall*. New York: New York University Press, 1998.

Goldstein, Joseph. *The Intelligible Constitution: The Supreme Court's Obligation to Maintain the Constitution as Something We the People Can Understand*. New York: Oxford University Press, 1992.

Greenberg, Ellen. *The Supreme Court Explained*. New York: W.W. Norton, 1997.

Hall, Kermit L., ed. *The Oxford Companion to the Supreme Court of the United States*. New York: Oxford University Press, 1992.

Harrell, Mary Anne, and Burnett Anderson. *Equal Justice Under Law: The Supreme Court in American Life*. 6th ed. Washington, D.C.: Supreme Court Historical Society, with National Geographic Society, 1994.

Harrison, Maureen & Steve Gilbert, eds. *Landmark Decisions of the United States Supreme Court*. Beverly Hills, Calif.: Excellent Books, 1991.

———. *Landmark Decisions of the United States Supreme Court II*. Beverly Hills, Calif.: Excellent Books, 1992.

———. *Landmark Decisions of the United States Supreme Court III*. Beverly Hills, Calif.: Excellent Books, 1992.

History of the Supreme Court of the United States (The Oliver Wendell Holmes Devise). 9 vols. New York: Macmillan, 1971–1993.

Irons, Peter H. *A People's History of the Supreme Court*. New York: Viking, 1999.

Jacobs, Roger F., comp. *Memorials of the Justices of the Supreme Court of the United States*. Littleton, Colo.: Fred B. Rothman, 1981.

Jacobstein, J. Myron. *The Rejected: Sketches of the 26 Men Nominated for the Supreme Court but Not Confirmed by the Senate*. Milpitas, Calif.: Toucan Valley Publications, 1993.

Joseph, Joel D. *Black Mondays: Worst Decisions of the Supreme Court*. Bethesda, Md.: National Press, 1987.

Jost, Kenneth, ed. *The Supreme Court A to Z*. Washington, D.C.: Congressional Quarterly, 2d ed. 1998.

Karfunkel, Thomas & Thomas W. Ryley. *The Jewish Seat: Anti-semitism and the Appointment of Jews to the Supreme Court*. Hicksville, N.Y.: Exposition Press, 1978.

Katzmann, Robert A. *Courts and Congress*. Washington, D.C.: Brookings Institution Press/Governance Institute, 1997.

Lamb, Charles M., and Stephen C. Halpern, eds. *The Burger Court, Political and Judicial Profiles*. Champaign: University of Illinois Press, 1991.

Lankevich, George J., ed. *Supreme Court in American Life*. 9 vols. Millwood, N.Y.: Associated Faculty Press, 1986–.

Lasser, William. *The Limits of Judicial Power: The Supreme Court in American Politics*. Chapel Hill: University of North Carolina Press, 1988.

Leahy, James E. *Freedom Fighters of the United States Supreme Court: Nine Who Championed Individual Liberty*. Jefferson, N.C.: McFarland & Co., 1996.

———. *Supreme Court Justices Who Voted with the Government: Nine Who Favored the State over*

Individual Rights. Jefferson, N.C.: McFarland & Co., 1999.

Lemer, Max. *Nine Scorpions in a Bottle: Great Judges and Cases of the Supreme Court*. Edited by Richard Cummings. New York: Arcade Publishing, 1994.

Leuchtenburg, William Edward. *The Supreme Court Reborn: The Constitutional Revolution in the Age of Roosevelt*. New York: Oxford University Press, 1995.

Lewis, Frederick P. *The Context of Judicial Activism: The Endurance of the Warren Court Legacy in a Conservative Age*. Lanham, Md.: Rowman & Littlefield, 1999.

Lieberman, Jethro Koller. *A Practical Companion to the Constitution: How the Supreme Court Has Ruled on Issues from Abortion to Zoning*. Berkeley: University of California Press, 1999.

Maltese, John Anthony. *The Selling of Supreme Court Nominees*. Baltimore: Johns Hopkins University Press, 1995.

Marcus, Maeva, ed. *The Documentary History of the Supreme Court of the United States, 1789–1800*. 6 vols. New York: Columbia University Press, 1985.

Martin, Fenton S. *How to Research the Supreme Court*. Washington, D.C.: Congressional Quarterly, 1992.

Mason, Alpheus Thomas. *The Supreme Court From Taft to Burger*. Baton Rouge: Louisiana State University Press, 1979.

Mayer, Robert R. *The Court and the American Crises, 1930–1952*. Fort Washington, N.Y.: Associated Faculty Press, 1987.

McCloskey, Robert G. *The American Supreme Court*. Revised by Sanford Levinson. Chicago: University of Chicago Press, 2d ed. 1994.

Mersky, Roy M., comp. *The Supreme Court of the United States. Hearings and Reports on Successful and Unsuccessful Nominations of Supreme Court Justices by the Senate Judiciary Committee, 1916–1995*. 19 vols. Buffalo: W. S. Hein, 1977–1996.

O'Brien, David M. *Storm Center: The Supreme Court in American Politics*. 4th ed. New York: W. W. Norton, 1996.

Perry, Barbara A. *The Priestly Tribe: The Supreme Court's Image in the American Mind*. Westport, Conn.: Praeger, 1999.

Schwartz, Bernard. *A History of the Supreme Court*. New York: Oxford University Press, 1993.

———. *Decision: How the Supreme Court Decides Cases*. New York: Oxford University Press, 1996.

Semonche, John E. *Keeping the Faith: A Cultural History of the U.S. Supreme Court*. Lanham, Md.: Rowman & Littlefield Publishers, 1998.

Shnayerson, Robert. *The Illustrated History of the Supreme Court of the United States*. New York: Henry N. Abrams in association with the Supreme Court Historical Society, 1986.

Simon, James F. *The Center Holds: The Power Struggle Inside the Rehnquist Court*. New York: Simon & Schuster, 1995.

Simon, Paul. *Advice & Consent: The Senators and the Justices*. Bethesda, Md.: National Press Books, 1992.

Smolla, Rodney A. *A Year in the Life of the Supreme Court*. Durham, N.C.: Duke University Press, 1995.

Stephenson, D. Grier, Jr. *Campaigns and the Court: The U.S. Supreme Court in Presidential Elections*. New York: Columbia University Press, 1999.

Stevens, Richard G. and Matthew J. Franck, eds. *Sober as a Judge: The Supreme Court and Republican Liberty*. Lanham, Md.: Lexington Books, 1999.

The Supreme Court of the United States: Its Beginning & Its Justices, 1790–1991. Washington, D.C.: Commission on the Bicentennial of the United States Constitution, 1992.

Tribe, Laurence H. *God Save This Honorable Court: How the Choice of Supreme Court Justices Shapes Our History*. New York: Random House, 1985.

Umbreit, Kenneth Bernard. *Our Eleven Chief Justices: A History of the Supreme Court in Terms of Their Personalities*. 1938. Reprint. Port Washington, N.Y.: Kennikat Press, 1969.

Urofsky, Melvin I., ed. *The Supreme Court Justices: A Biographical Dictionary*. New York: Garland Publishing, 1994.

Van Santvoord, George. *Sketches of the Lives and Judicial Services of the Chief-Justices of the Supreme Court of the United States*. New York: C. Scribner, 1854.

Warren, Charles. *The Supreme Court in United States History*. Boston: Little, Brown, rev. ed. 1935.

Wasby, Stephen L. *The Supreme Court in the Federal Judicial System*. New York: Holt, Rinehart, and Winston, 2d ed. 1984.

Westin, Alan F., ed. *An Autobiography of the Supreme Court. Off-the-Bench Commentary by the Justices.* New York: Macmillan, 1963. Reprint. Westport, Conn.: Greenwood Press, 1978.

Wiecek, William M. *Liberty Under Law: The Supreme Court in American Life.* Baltimore: Johns Hopkins University Press, 1988.

White, G. Edward. *The American Judicial Tradition: Profiles of Leading American Judges.* New York: Oxford University Press, rev. ed. 1988.

Witt, Elder. *Guide to the U.S. Supreme Court.* 2d ed. Washington, D.C.: Congressional Quarterly, 1990.

Woodward, Bob and Scott Armstrong. *The Brethren.* New York: Simon & Schuster, 1979.

Yalof, David Alistair. *Pursuit of Justices: Presidential Politics and the Selection of Supreme Court Nominees.* Chicago: University of Chicago Press, 1999.

Materials Concerning Particular Cases or Subjects

Abraham, Henry Julian & Barbara A. Perry. *Freedom and the Court: Civil Rights and Liberties in the United States.* New York: Oxford University Press, 7th ed. 1998.

Alley, Robert S., ed. *The Supreme Court on Church and State.* New York: Oxford University Press, 1988.

Bybee, Keith J. *Mistaken Identity: The Supreme Court and the Politics of Minority Representation.* Princeton, N.J.: Princeton University Press, 1998.

Campbell, Douglas S. *Free Press v. Fair Trial: Supreme Court Decisions since 1807.* Westport, Conn.: Praeger, 1994.

Cortner, Richard C. *The Supreme Court and the Second Bill of Rights: The Fourteenth Amendment and the Nationalization of Civil Liberties.* Madison: University of Wisconsin Press, 1981.

Devins, Neal E. *Shaping Constitutional Values: Elected Government, the Supreme Court, and the Abortion Debate.* Baltimore: Johns Hopkins University Press, 1996.

Fairman, Charles. *Five Justices and the Electoral Commission of 1877.* New York: Macmillan Publishing Company, 1988.

Faux, Marian. *Roe v. Wade: The Untold Story of the Landmark Supreme Court Decision That Made Abortion Legal.* New York: Macmillan, 1988.

Friendly, Fred W. *Minnesota Rag: The Dramatic Story of the Landmark Supreme Court Case That Gave New Meaning to Freedom of the Press.* New York: Random House, 1981.

Graglia, Lino A. *Disaster by Decree: The Supreme Court Decisions on Race and the Schools.* Ithaca, N.Y.: Cornell University Press, 1976.

Harrison, Maureen & Steve Gilbert, eds. *Abortion Decisions of the United States Supreme Court.* Beverly Hills, Calif.: Excellent Books, 1993.

Howard, John R. *The Shifting Wind: The Supreme Court and Civil Rights from Reconstruction to Brown.* Albany: State University of New York Press, 1999.

Perry, Michael J. *We the People: The Fourteenth Amendment and the Supreme Court.* New York: Oxford University Press, 1999.

Polenberg, Richard. *Fighting Faiths: The Abrams Case, the Supreme Court, and Free Speech.* New York: Viking, 1987.

Sabin, Arthur J. *In Calmer Times: The Supreme Court and Red Monday.* Philadelphia: University of Pennsylvania Press, 1999.

Schwartz, Bernard. *Behind Bakke: Affirmative Action and the Supreme Court.* New York: New York University Press, 1988.

———. *Swann's Way: The School Busing Case and the Supreme Court.* New York: Oxford University Press, 1986.

Shapiro, Ian, ed. *Abortion: The Supreme Court Decisions.* Indianapolis, Ind.: Hackett Publishing Company, 1995.

Sullivan, Winnifred Fallers. *Paying the Words Extra: Religious Discourse in the Supreme Court of the United States.* Cambridge, Mass.: Distributed by Harvard University Press for the Harvard University Center for the Study of World Religions, 1994.

Westin, Alan F. *The Anatomy of a Constitutional Law Case: Youngstown Sheet and Tube Co. v. Sawyer: The Steel Seizure Decision.* New York: Macmillan, 1958.

Wilkinson, J. Harvie. *From Brown to Bakke: The Supreme Court and School Integration, 1954–1978.* New York: Oxford University Press, 1979.

Materials Concerning Individual Justices

Baldwin, Henry

Baldwin, Henry. *A General View of the Origin and Nature of the Constitution and Government of the United States.* 1837. Reprint. New York: Da Capo Press, 1970.

Gattell, Frank Otto. "Henry Baldwin." In *The Justices of the United States Supreme Court 1789–1969: Their Lives and Major Opinions,* vol. 1. Edited by L. Friedman and F. Israel. New York: R. R. Bowker Co., 1969.

Taylor, Flavia M. "The Political and Civil Career of Henry Baldwin." *Western Pennsylvania Historical Magazine* 24 (1941): 37–50.

Barbour, Philip Pendleton

Cynn, Paul P. "Philip Pendleton Barbour." *John P. Branch Historical Papers of Randolph-Macon College* 4 (1913): 67–77.

Gatell, Frank Otto. "Philip Pendleton Barbour." In *The Justices of the United States Supreme Court 1789–1969: Their Lives and Major Opinions,* vol. 1. Edited by Leon Friedman and Fred L. Israel. New York: R. R. Bowker Co., 1969.

Black, Hugo Lafayette

Ball, Howard. *Hugo L. Black: Cold Steel Warrior.* New York: Oxford University Press, 1996.

———. "Justice Hugo L. Black: a Magnificent Product of the South." *Alabama Law Review* 363 (1985): 791–834.

———. *The Vision and the Dream of Justice Hugo L. Black.* University: University of Alabama Press, 1975.

Ball, Howard & Phillip J. Cooper. *Of Power and Right: Hugo Black, William O. Douglas, and America's Constitutional Revolution.* New York: Oxford University Press, 1992.

Black, Elizabeth S. "Hugo Black: A Memorial Portrait." *Supreme Court Historical Society. Yearbook* (1982): 72–94.

Black, Hugo and Elizabeth. *Mr. Justice Black and Mrs. Black, the Memoirs of Hugo L. Black and Elizabeth Black.* New York: Random House, 1986.

Black, Hugo Jr. *My Father, A Remembrance.* New York: Random House, 1975.

Black, Hugo Lafayette. *"Sincerely Your Friend" . . . Letters of Mr. Justice Hugo L. Black to Jerome A. Cooper.* University: University of Alabama Press, 1973.

———. *A Constitutional Faith.* New York: Alfred A. Knopf, 1968.

Dennis, Everette E., Donald M. Gillmor, David L. Grey. eds. *Justice Hugo Black and the First Amendment: "'No Law' Means No Law."* Ames: Iowa State University Press, 1978.

Dunne, Gerald T. *Hugo Black and the Judicial Revolution.* New York: Simon & Schuster, 1977.

Edleman, Peter B. "Press v. Privacy: Haunted by the Ghost of Justice Black." *Texas Law Review* 68 (May 1990): 1195–1234.

Frank, John Paul. *Mr. Justice Black: The Man and His Opinions.* Westport, Conn.: Greenwood Press, 1948, Reprint 1977.

———. "The Shelf Life of Justice Hugo L. Black." Wisconsin Law Review (1997): 1–31.

Freyer, Tony and Oscar Handlin eds. *Hugo L. Black and the Dilemma of American Liberalism.* Glenview, Ill.: Scott, Foresman/Little, Brown Higher Education, 1990.

Freyer, Tony ed. *Justice Hugo Black and Modern America.* Tuscaloosa: University of Alabama Press, 1990.

Hackney, Sheldon. "The Clay County Origins of Justice Black: the Populist as Insider." *Alabama Law Review* 36 (1985): 835–843.

Hamilton, Virginia Van der Veer. "Lister Hill, Hugo Black, and the Albatross of Race." *Alabama Law Review* 36 (1985): 845–860.

———. *Hugo Black: The Alabama Years.* Baton Rouge: Louisiana State University Press, 1972.

Hockett, Jeffrey D. *New Deal Justice: The Constitutional Jurisprudence of Hugo L. Black, Felix Frankfurter, and Robert H. Jackson.* Lanham, Md.: Rowman & Littlefield Publishers, 1996.

Magee, James J. *Mr. Justice Black, Absolutist on the Court.* Charlottesville: University Press of Virginia, 1980.

Massaro, Toni M. "Reviving Hugo Black? The Court's 'Jot for Jot' Account of Substantive Due Process." *New York University Law Review* 73 (1998): 1086–1121.

Mauney, Connie Pat. *Justice Black and First Amendment Freedoms: Thirty-Four Influential Years.* Emporia, Kan.: Emporia State University, 1986.

Mauney, Constance. "Religion and 1st Amendment Protections: An Analysis of Justice Black's Constitutional interpretation." *Pepperdine Law Review* (1983): 377–420.

Meador, Daniel J. *Mr. Justice Black and His Books.* Charlottesville: University Press of Virginia, 1974.

Meese, Edwin. "A Tribute to Justice Hugo Black." *Saint Louis University Public Law Review* (1987): 187–195.

Newman, Roger K. "Black and *Brown.*" *University of San Francisco Law Review* (1995): 635–644.

———. *Hugo Black: A Biography.* New York: Pantheon Books, 1994.

Perry, Barbara A. "Justice Black and the 'Wall of Separation between Church and State.'" *Journal of Church and State* 31 (1989): 55–72.

Strickland, Stephen Parks, ed. *Hugo Black and the Supreme Court: A Symposium.* Indianapolis: Bobbs-Merrill, 1967.

Thorton, Mills J. "Hugo Black and the Golden Age." *Alabama Law Review* 36 (1985): 899–913.

Warren, Earl. "A Tribute to Hugo L. Black." *Harvard Law Review* 85 (1971): 1–2.

Yarbrough, Tinsley E. *Mr. Justice Black and His Critics.* Durham, N.C.: Duke University Press, 1988.

Blackmun, Harry A.

"The Changing Social Vision of Justice Blackmun." *Harvard Law Review* 96 (1983): 717–736.

Cleghorn, Amy S. "Justice Harry A. Blackmun: A Retrospective Consideration of the Justice's Role in the Emancipation of Women." *Seton Hall Law Review* 25 (1995): 1176–1218.

Coyne, Randall. "Marking the Progress of a Humane Justice: Harry Blackmun's Death Penalty Epiphany." *University of Kansas Law Review* 43 (1995): 367–416.

Hair, Penda D. "Justice Blackmun and Racial Justice." *Yale Law Journal* 104 (1994): 7–22.

"In Memorium: Harry A. Blackmun." *Harvard Law Review* 113 (1999): 1–25.

"In Memoriam: Justice Harry A. Blackmun, Principle and Compassion." *Columbia Law Review* 99 (1999): x–1412.

King, Jeffrey B. "Now Turn to the Left: The Changing Ideology of Justice Harry A. Blackmun." *Houston Law Review* 33 (1996): 277–297.

Koh, Harold Hongju. "Justice Blackmun and the 'World out There.'" *Yale Law Journal* 104 (1994): 23–31.

"Symposium: The Jurisprudence of Justice Harry A. Blackmun." *Hastings Constitutional Law Quarterly* 26 (1998): 1–305.

Wasby, Stephen L. "Justice Harry A. Blackmun: Transformation from 'Minnesota Twin' to Independent Voice." In *The Burger Court: Political and Judicial Profiles.* Edited by Charles M. Lamb and Stephen C. Halpern. Urbana: University of Illinois Press, 1991.

Blair, John

Drinard, J. Elliott. "John Blair." *Proceedings of the Virginia State Bar Association* 39 (1927): 436–449.

Holt, Wythe. "John Blair: 'A Safe and Conscientious Judge.'" In *Seriatim: The Supreme Court Before John Marshall.* Edited by Scott Douglas Gerber. New York: New York University Press, 1998.

Horner, Frederick. *History of the Blair, Banister and Braxton Families Before and After the Revolution.* Philadelphia: J. B. Lippincott Co., 1898.

Israel, Fred L. "John Blair, Jr." In *The Justices of the United States Supreme Court 1789–1969: Their Lives and Major Opinions,* vol. 1. Edited by Leon Friedman and Fred L. Israel. New York: R. R. Bowker Co., 1969.

Blatchford, Samuel

Hall, A. Oakey. "Justice Samuel Blatchford." *Green Bag* 5 (1893): 489–492.

"Honors to the Memory of Mr. Justice Blatchford." *Albany Law Journal* 48 (1893): 415–416.

Paul, Arnold. "Samuel Blatchford." In *The Justices of the United States Supreme Court 1789–1969: Their Lives and Major Opinions,* vol. 2. Edited by Leon Friedman and Fred L. Israel. New York: R. R. Bowker Co., 1969.

Bradley, Joseph P.

Bradley, Charles, comp. *Miscellaneous Writings of the Late Hon. Joseph P. Bradley, Associate Justice of the Supreme Court of the United States*. Reprint. Littleton, Colo: Fred B. Rothman, 1986.

Fairman, Charles. "The Education of a Justice: Justice Bradley and Some of His Colleagues." *Stanford Law Review* 1 (1949): 217–255.

———. "Mr. Justice Bradley." In *Mr. Justice*. Edited by Allison Dunham and Philip B. Kurland. Chicago: University of Chicago Press, 1964.

———. "What Makes a Great Justice: Mr. Justice Bradley and the Supreme Court, 1870–1892." *Boston University Law Review* 30 (1950): 423–485.

Friedman, Leon. "Joseph P. Badley." In *The Justices of the United States Supreme Court 1789–1969: Their Lives and Major Opinions,* vol. 1. Edited by Leon Friedman and Fred L. Israel. New York: R. R. Bowker Co., 1969.

Lurie, Jonathan. "Mr. Justice Bradley: A Reassessment." *Seton Hall Law Review* 16 (1986): 343–375.

Parker, Cortland. "Joseph P. Bradley." *American Law Review* 28 (1984): 481–509.

Pope, Dennis H. "Personality and Judicial Performance: A Psychobiography of Justice Joseph P. Bradley." Ph.D. diss., Rutgers Univ., 1988.

Brandeis, Louis Dembitz

Baker, Leonard. *Brandeis and Frankfurter: A Dual Biography*. New York: New York University Press, 1986.

Burt, Robert. *Two Jewish Justices: Outcasts in the Promised Land*. Berkeley: University of California Press, 1988.

Dawson, Nelson L., ed. *Brandeis and America*. Lexington: University Press of Kentucky, 1989.

Murphy, Bruce Allen. *The Brandeis/Frankfurter Connection: The Secret Political Activities of Two Supreme Court Justices*. New York: Oxford University Press, 1982.

Paper, Lewis J. *Brandeis*. Englewood Cliffs, N.J.: Prentice Hall, 1983.

Strum, Philippa. *Louis D. Brandeis: Justice for the People*. Cambridge, Mass.: Harvard University Press, 1984.

Urofsky, Melvin I. *Louis D. Brandeis and the Progressive Tradition*. Boston: Little, Brown, 1981.

Brennan, William J., Jr.

Eisler, Kim Isaac. *A Justice for All: William J. Brennan, Jr. and the Decisions That Transformed America*. New York: Simon & Schuster, 1993.

Friedelbaum, Stanley H. "Justice William J. Brennan, Jr.: Policy-making in the Judicial Thicket." In *The Burger Court: Political and Judicial Profiles*. Edited by Charles M. Lamb and Stephen C. Halpern. Urbana: University of Illinois Press, 1991.

George, B. Glenn. "Visions of a Labor Lawyer: The Legacy of Justice Brennan." *William and Mary Law Review* 33 (1992): 1123–1179.

"The Jurisprudence of Justice William J. Brennan, Jr." *University of Pennsylvania Law Review* 139 (1991): 1317–1371.

Marion, David E. *The Jurisprudence of Justice William J. Brennan, Jr.: The Law and Politics of "Libertarian Dignity."* Lanham, Md.: Rowman & Littlefield Publishers, 1997.

Mello, Michael. *Against the Death Penalty: The Relentless Dissents of Justices Brennan and Marshall*. Boston: Northeastern University Press, 1996.

Michelman, Frank I. *Brennan and Democracy*. Princeton, N.J.: Princeton University Press, 1999.

———. "Super Liberal: Romance, Community, and Tradition in William J. Brennan, Jr.'s Constitutional Thought." *Virginia Law Review* 77 (1991): 1261–1332.

Rosenkranz, E. Joshua & Bernard Schwartz, eds. *Reason and Passion: Justice Brennan's Enduring Influence*. New York: W. W. Norton & Company, 1997.

"A Tribute to Justice William J. Brennan, Jr." *Harvard Law Review* 104 (1990): xviii–39.

Brewer, David Josiah

Brodhead, Michael J. *David J. Brewer: The Life of a Supreme Court Justice, 1837–1910*. Carbondale, Ill.: Southern Illinois University Press, 1994.

Bergan, Francis. "Mr. Justice Brewer: A Perspective of a Century." *Albany Law Review* 25 (1961): 191–202.

Eitzen, D. Stanley. *David J. Brewer, 1837–1910: A Kansan on the United States Supreme Court*. Emporia: Kansas State Teacher's College, 1964.

Gamer, Robert E. "Justice Brewer and Substantive Due Process: A Conservative Court Revisited." *Vanderbilt Law Review* 18 (1964–65): 615–641.

Hylton, Joseph Gordon. "David Josiah Brewer: A Conservative Justice Reconsidered." *Journal of Supreme Court History* (1994): 45–64.

———. "The Judge Who Abstained in *Plessy v. Ferguson:* Justice David Brewer and the Problem of Race." *Mississippi Law Journal* 61 (1991): 315–364.

Lardner, Lynford A. "The Constitutional Doctrines of Justice David Josiah Brewer." Ph.D. diss., Princeton Univ., 1938.

Breyer, Stephen G.

Breyer, Stephen G. *Breaking the Vicious Circle: Toward Effective Risk Regulation.* Cambridge, Mass.: Harvard University Press, 1993.

Joyce, Walter E. "The Early Constitutional Jurisprudence of Justice Stephen G. Breyer: A Study of the Justice's First Year on the United States Supreme Court." *Seton Hall Constitutional Law Journal* 7 (1996): 149–163.

Brown, Henry Billings

Brown, Henry Billings. *Memoir of Henry Billings Brown: Late Justice of the Supreme Court of the United States: Consisting of an Autobiographical Sketch With Additions to His Life by Charles A. Kent.* New York: Duffield and Company, 1915.

Glennon, Robert J., Jr. "Justice Henry Billings Brown: Values in Tension." *University of Colorado Law Review* 44 (1973): 553–604.

Goldfarb, Joel. "Henry Billings Brown." In *The Justices of the United States Supreme Court 1789–1969: Their Lives and Major Opinions,* vol. 2. Edited by Leon Friedman and Fred L. Israel. New York: R. R. Bowker Co., 1969.

Burger, Warren Earl

Blasi, Vincent. *The Burger Court: The Counter-Revolution that Wasn't.* New Haven: Yale University Press, 1983.

Burger, Warren E. *It Is So Ordered: A Constitution Unfolds.* New York: William Morrow and Company, 1995.

Galub, Arthur L. *The Burger Court, 1968–1984.* Millwood, N.Y.: Associated Faculty Press, 1986.

"In Memoriam: A Tribute to My Predecessor." *Texas Law Review* 74 (1995): x–236.

"In Memoriam: Chief Justice Warren E. Burger." *William Mitchell Law Review* 22 (1996): 1–65.

Lamb, Charles M. "Chief Justice Warren E. Burger: a Conservative Chief for Conservative Times." In *The Burger Court: Political and Judicial Profiles.* Edited by Charles M. Lamb and Stephen C. Halpern. Urbana: University of Illinois Press, 1991.

Pfeffer, Leo. *Religion, State, and the Burger Court.* Buffalo, N.Y.: Prometheus Books, 1984.

Schwartz, Bernard. *The Ascent of Pragmatism: The Burger Court in Action.* Reading, Mass.: Addison-Wesley, 1990.

Schwartz, Bernard, ed. *The Burger Court: Counter-Revolution or Confirmation?* New York: Oxford University Press, 1998.

Schwartz, Herman. *The Burger Years: Rights and Wrongs in the Supreme Court, 1969–1986.* New York: Viking, 1987.

Starr, Kenneth W. "Chief Justice Burger's Contribution to American Jurisprudence." *Supreme Court Historical Society Yearbook* (1986): 18–23.

"A Tribute to Chief Justice Warren E. Burger." *Harvard Law Review* 100 (1987): 969–1001.

Zane, Phillip Craig. "An Interpretation of the Jurisprudence of Chief Justice Warren Burger." *Utah Law Review* (1995): 975–1008.

Burton, Harold Hitz

Atkinson, David N. "American Constitutionalism under Stress: Mr. Justice Burton's Response to National Security Issues." *Houston Law Review* 9 (1971): 271–288.

———. "Justice Harold H. Burton and the Work of the Supreme Court." *Cleveland State Law Review* 27 (1978): 69–83.

Burton, Harold H. *The Occasional Papers of Mr. Justice Burton.* Edited by Edward G. Hudon. Brunswick, Me.: Bowdoin College, 1969.

Berry, Mary Frances. *Stability, Security, and Continuity: Mr. Justice Burton and Decision-Making in the Supreme Court, 1945–1958.* Westport, Conn.: Greenwood Press, 1978.

Langram, Robert W. "Why Are Some Supreme Court Justices Rated as 'Failures'?" *Supreme Court Historical Society Yearbook* (1985): 8–14.

Butler, Pierce

Brown, Francis Joseph. *The Social and Economic Philosophy of Pierce Butler.* Washington, D.C.: Catholic University of America Press, 1945.

Cushman, Barry. "The Secret Lives of the Four Horsemen." *Virginia Law Review* 83 (1997): 559–645.

Danelski, David Joseph. *A Supreme Court Justice Is Appointed.* New York: Random House, 1964.

Byrnes, James Francis

Burns, Richard D. "James F. Byrnes (1945–1947)." In *An Uncertain Tradition: American Secretaries of State in the Twentieth Century.* Edited by Norman A. Graebner. New York: McGraw-Hill, 1961.

Burns, Ronald D. *James F. Byrnes.* New York: McGraw-Hill, 1961.

Byrnes, James F. *All in One Lifetime.* New York: Harper, 1958.

Clements, Kendrick A., ed. *James F. Byrnes and the Origins of the Cold War.* Durham, N.C.: Carolina Academic Press, 1982.

Langram, Robert W. "Why Are Some Supreme Court Justices Rated as 'Failures'?" *Supreme Court Historical Society Yearbook* (1985): 8–14.

Messer, Robert L. *The End of an Alliance: James F. Byrnes, Roosevelt, Truman, and the Origins of the Cold War.* Chapel Hill: University of North Carolina Press, 1982.

Partin, John William. "'Assistant President' for the Home Front: James F. Byrnes and World War II." Ph.D. diss., Univ. of Florida, 1977.

Robertson, David. *Sly and Able: A Political Biography of James F. Byrnes.* New York: Norton, 1994.

Ward, Patricia Dawson. *The Threat of Peace: James F. Byrnes and the Council of Foreign Ministers, 1945–1946.* Kent, Ohio: Kent State University Press, 1979.

Campbell, John Archibald

Connor, Henry Groves. *John Archibald Campbell, Associate Justice of the United States Supreme Court, 1853–1861.* Boston: Houghton Mifflin, 1920. Reprint. New York: Da Capo Press, 1971.

Holt, Thad, Jr. "The Resignation of Mr. Justice Campbell." *Alabama Law Review* 12 (1959): 105–118.

Jordan, Christine. "Last of the Jacksonians." *Supreme Court Historical Society Yearbook, 1980.* Washington, D.C.: Supreme Court Historical Society, 1980.

Mann, Justin S. "The Political Thought of John Archibald Campbell: The Formative Years, 1847–1851." *Alabama Law Review* 22 (1970): 275–302.

Saunders, Robert, Jr. *John Archibald Campbell: Southern Moderate, 1811–1889.* Tuscaloosa: University of Alabama Press, 1997.

Cardozo, Benjamin Nathan

Cardozo, Benjamin N. *Selected Writings of Benjamin Nathan Cardozo.* Edited by Margaret E. Hall. New York: Fallon Pub., 1947.

Hellman, George Sidney. *Benjamin N. Cardozo: American Judge.* New York: Whittlesey House, McGraw-Hill Book Company, 1940.

Kaufman, Andrew L. *Cardozo.* Cambridge, Mass.: Harvard University Press, 1998.

Pollard, Joseph Percival. *Mr. Justice Cardozo: A Liberal Mind in Action.* Westport, Conn.: Greenwood Press, 1970.

Polenberg, Richard. *The World of Benjamin Cardozo: Personal Values and the Judicial Process.* Cambridge, Mass.: Harvard University Press, 1997.

Posner, Richard A. *Cardozo: A Study in Reputation.* Chicago: University of Chicago Press, 1990.

Catron, John

Chandler, Walter. *The Centenary of Associate Justice John Catron of the United States Supreme Court.* Washington, D.C.: U.S. Government Printing Office, 1937.

Gattell, Frank Otto. "John McKinley." In *The Justices of the United States Supreme Court 1789–1969: Their Lives and Major Opinions,* vol. 1. Edited by Leon Friedman and Fred L. Israel. New York: R. R. Bowker Co., 1969.

Livingston, John. "Biographical Letter from Justice Catron." In *Portraits of Eminent Americans Now Living*. New York: R. Craighead, Printer, 1854.

Chase, Salmon Portland

Blue, Frederick J. *Salmon P. Chase: A Life in Politics*. Kent, Ohio: Kent State University Press, 1987.

Chase, Salmon Portland. *Inside Lincoln's Cabinet: The Civil War Diaries of Salmon P. Chase*. Edited by David Donald. New York: Longmans, Green, 1954.

Hart, Albert Bushnell. *Salmon P. Chase*. 1899. Reprint. New York: Chelsea House, 1980.

Middleton, Stephen. *Ohio and the Antislavery Activities of Attorney Salmon Portland Chase, 1830–1849*. New York: Garland Publishing: 1990.

Niven, John. *Salmon P. Chase: A Biography*. New York: Oxford University Press, 1995.

Schuckers, Jacob W. *The Life and Public Services of Salmon Portland Chase*. 1874. Reprint. New York: Da Capo Press, 1970.

Smith, Donnal Vore. *Chase and Civil War Politics*. 1930. Reprint. Freeport, N.Y.: Books for Libraries Press, 1972.

"A Symposium on Salmon P. Chase and the Chase Court: Perspectives in Law and History." *Northern Kentucky Law Review* 21 (1993): 1–252.

Chase, Samuel

Berger, Raoul. "The Transfiguration of Samuel Chase: A Rebuttal." *Brigham Young University Law Review* (1992): 559–596.

Chase, Samuel. *Trial of Samuel Chase, an Associate Justice of the Supreme Court of the United States, Impeached by the House of Representatives for High Crimes and Misdemeanors Before the Senate of the United States*. 1805. Reprint. New York: Da Capo Press, 1970.

———. *Exhibits, Accompanying the Answer and Plea of Samuel Chase, One of the Associate Justices of the Supreme Court of the United States*. Washington, 1805.

Elsmere, Jane Shaffer. *Justice Samuel Chase*. Muncie, Ind.: Janevar Pub. Co., 1980.

Haw, James. A., et al. *Stormy Patriot: The Life of Samuel Chase*. Baltimore: Maryland Historical Society, 1980.

Presser, Stephen B. "The Verdict on Samuel Chase and His 'Apologist.'" In *Seriatim: The Supreme Court Before John Marshall*. Edited by Scott Douglas Gerber. New York: New York University Press, 1998.

Presser, Stephen B. and Becky Bair Hurley. "Saving God's Republic: The Jurisprudence of Samuel Chase." *University of Illinois Law Review* (1984): 771–822.

Rehnquist, William H. *Grand Inquests: The Historic Impeachments of Justice Samuel Chase and President Andrew Johnson*. New York: William Morrow, 1992.

Clark, Thomas Campbell

Baier, Paul. "Justice Clark, the Voice of the Past, and the Exclusionary Rule." *Texas Law Review* 64 (1985): 415–419.

Dorin, Dennis D. "Tom C. Clark: The Justice as Administrator." *Judicature* 61 (Dec.–Jan. 1978): 271–77.

Frank, John P. "Justice Tom Clark and Judicial Administration." *Texas Law Review* 46 (1967): 5–56.

Gazell, James A. "Justice Tom C. Clark as Judicial Reformer." *Houston Law Review* 15 (1978): 307–329.

Kirkendall, Richard. "Tom C. Clark." In *The Justices of the United States Supreme Court 1789–1969: Their Lives and Major Opinions*, vol. 4. Edited by Leon Friedman and Fred L. Israel. New York: R. R. Bowker Co., 1969.

Mengler, Thomas M. "Public Relations in the Supreme Court: Justice Tom Clark's Opinion in the School Prayer Case." *Constitutional Commentary* 6 (Summer 1989): 331–349.

Srere, Mark. "Justice Tom C. Clark's Unconditional Approach to Individual Rights in the Courtroom." *Texas Law Review* 64 (1985): 421–442.

Clarke, John Hessin

Burner, David. "John H. Clarke" In *The Justices of the United States Supreme Court 1789–1969: Their Lives and Major Opinions*, Vol. 3. Edited by Leon Friedman and Fred L. Israel. New York: R. R. Bowker Co., 1969.

Levitan, David Maurice. "The Jurisprudence of Mr. Justice Clarke" *Miami Law Quarterly* 7 (1952): 44–72.

Warner, Hoyt Landon. *The Life of Mr. Justice Clarke: A Testament to the Power of Liberal Dissent in America*. Cleveland: Western Reserve University, 1959.

Wittke, Carl. "Mr. Justice Clarke in Retirement." *Western Reserve Law Review* 1 (1949): 28–48.

Clifford, Nathan

Chandler, Walter. "Nathan Clifford: A Triumph of Untiring Effort." *American Bar Association Journal* 11 (1925): 57–60.

Clifford, Philip Greely. *Nathan Clifford: Democrat, 1803–1881*. New York: Putnam's, 1922.

Clinton, Robert Lowry and Kevin Walsh. "Judicial Sobriety: Nathan P. Clifford." In *Sober as a Judge: The Supreme Court and Republican Liberty.* Edited by Richard G. Stevens and Matthew J. Franck. Lanham, Md.: Lexington Books, 1999.

Gillette, William. "Nathan Clifford." In *The Justices of the United States Supreme Court 1789–1969: Their Lives and Major Opinions,* vol. 2. Edited by Leon Friedman and Fred L. Israel. New York: R. R. Bowker Co., 1969.

Curtis, Benjamin Robbins

Curtis, Benjamin Robbins, ed. *A Memoir of Benjamin Robbins Curtis, LL.D., with Some of His Professional and Miscellaneous Writings*. 1879. Reprint. New York: Da Capo Press, 1970.

Gillette, William. "Benjamin R. Curtis." In *The Justices of the United States Supreme Court 1789–1969: Their Lives and Major Opinions,* vol. 2. Edited by Leon Friedman and Fred L. Israel. New York: R. R. Bowker Co., 1969.

Robbins, Chandler. "Memoir of the Hon. Benjamin Robbins Curtis, LL.D." *Proceedings of the Massachusetts Historical Society* 16 (1879): 16–35.

Leach, Richard H. "Benjamin R. Curtis: Case Study of a Supreme Court Justice." Ph.D. diss., Princeton Univ., 1951.

Cushing, William

Cushing, John D. "The Cushing Court and the Abolition of Slavery in Massachusetts." *American Journal of Legal History* 5 (1961): 118–544.

———. "A Revolutionary Conservative: The Public Life of William Cushing, 1732–1810." Ph.D. diss., Clark Univ., 1959.

Gerber, Scott Douglas. "Deconstructing William Cushing." In *Seriatim: The Supreme Court Before John Marshall.* Edited by Scott Douglas Gerber. New York: New York University Press, 1998.

Johnson, Herbert Alan. "William Cushing." In *The Justices of the United States Supreme Court 1789–1969: Their Lives and Major Opinions,* vol. 1. Edited by Leon Friedman and Fred L. Israel. New York: R. R. Bowker Co., 1969.

O'Brien, F. William. "Justice William Cushing and the Treaty Making Power." *Vanderbilt Law Review* 10 (1957): 351–367.

Rugg, Arthur P. "William Cushing." *Yale Law Journal* 30 (1920): 120–144.

Daniel, Peter Vivian

Burnette, Lawrence, Jr. "Peter V. Daniel: Agrarian Justice." *Virginia Magazine of History and Biography* 62 (1954): 289–305.

Frank, John Paul. *Justice Daniel Dissenting: A Biography of Peter V. Daniel, 1784–1860.* Cambridge, Mass.: Harvard University Press, 1964.

Gatell, Frank Otto. "Peter V. Daniel." In *The Justices of the United States Supreme Court 1789–1969: Their Lives and Major Opinions,* vol. 1. Edited by Leon Friedman and Fred L. Israel. New York: R. R. Bowker Co., 1969.

Davis, David

Dent, Thomas. "David Davis of Illinois: A Sketch." *American Law Review* 53 (1919): 535–560.

King, Willard Leroy. *Lincoln's Manager: David Davis.* Cambridge, Mass.: Harvard University Press, 1960.

Kutler, Stanley I. "David Davis." In *The Justices of the United States Supreme Court 1789–1969: Their Lives and Major Opinions,* vol. 2. Edited by Leon Friedman and Fred L. Israel. New York: R. R. Bowker Co., 1969.

Day, William Rufus

"Character of Mr. Justice Day." *American Law Review* 37 (1903): 402–403.

Duncan, George W. "The Diplomatic Career of William Rufus Day, 1897–1898." Ph.D. diss., Case Western Reserve Univ., 1976.

McLean, Joseph E. *William Rufus Day: Supreme Court Justice from Ohio.* Baltimore: The Johns Hopkins University Press, 1946.

Morris, Jeffrey B. "The Era of Melville Weston Fuller." *Supreme Court Historical Society Yearbook* (1981): 36–51.

Roelofs, Vernon R. "William R. Day and Federal Regulation." *Mississippi Valley Historical Review* 37 (1950): 39–60.

———. "William R. Day: A Study in Constitutional History." Ph.D. diss., Univ. of Michigan, 1942.

Douglas, William Orville

Ball, Howard. *Of Power and Right: Hugo Black, William O. Douglas, and America's Constitutional Revolution.* New York: Oxford University Press, 1992.

Cooper, Phillip J. "Justice William O. Douglas: Conscience of the Court." In *The Burger Court: Political and Judicial Profiles.* Edited by Charles M. Lamb and Stephen C. Halpern. Urbana: University of Illinois Press, 1991.

Countryman, Vern. *The Judicial Record of Justice William O. Douglas.* Cambridge, Mass.: Harvard University Press, 1974.

Douglas, William O. *The Court Years, 1939–1975: The Autobiography of William O. Douglas.* New York: Random House, 1980.

———. *The Douglas Letters: Selections from the Private Papers of Justice William O. Douglas.* Edited with an introduction by Melvin I. Urofsky with the assistance of Philip E. Urofsky. Bethesda, Md.: Adler & Adler, 1987.

———. *The Douglas Opinions.* Edited by Vern Countryman. New York: Random House, 1977.

———. *Go East, Young Man: The Early Years—The Autobiography of William O. Douglas.* New York: Random House, 1974.

———. *The Supreme Court and the Bicentennial: Two Lectures.* Rutherford, N.J.: Fairleigh Dickinson University Press, 1978.

Duram, James C. *Justice William O. Douglas.* Boston: Twayne Publishers, 1981.

Simon, James F. *Independent Journey: The Life of William O. Douglas.* New York: Harper & Row, 1980.

Duvall, Gabriel

Currie, David P. "The Most Insignificant Justice: a Preliminary Inquiry." *University of Chicago Law Review* 50 (1983): 466–480.

Dilliard, Irving. "Gabriel Duvall." In *The Justices of the United States Supreme Court 1789–1969: Their Lives and Major Opinions,* vol. 1. Edited by Leon Friedman and Fred L. Israel. New York: R. R. Bowker Co., 1969.

Ellsworth, Oliver

Brown, William G. *The Life of Oliver Ellsworth.* New York: Macmillan, 1905; New York: Da Capo Press, 1970.

Casto, William. "Oliver Ellsworth's Calvinism: A Biographical Essay on Religion and Political Psychology in the Early Republic." *Journal of Church and State* 36 (1994): 507–525.

———. *The Supreme Court in the Early Republic: The Chief Justiceships of John Jay and Oliver Ellsworth.* Columbia, S.C.: University of South Carolina Press, 1995.

———. "Oliver Ellsworth: I Have Sought the Felicity and Glory of Your Administration." In *Seriatim: The Supreme Court Before John Marshall.* Edited by Scott Douglas Gerber. New York: New York University Press, 1998.

Lettieri, Ronald John. *Connecticut's Young Man of the Revolution: Oliver Ellsworth.* Hartford: American Bicentennial Commission of Connecticut, 1978.

Field, Stephen Johnson

Bergan, Philip J., Owen M. Fiss, and Charles W. McCurd. *The Fields and the Law: Essays.* San Francisco: United States District Court for the Northern District of California Historical Society, 1986.

Black, Chauncey Forward, and Samuel B. Smith, eds. *Some Account of the Work of Stephen J. Field, as Legislator, State Judge, and Justice of the Supreme Court of the United States.* New York: S. B. Smith, 1895.

Field, Stephen Johnson. *Personal Reminiscences of Early Days in California*. 1893. Reprint. New York: Da Capo Press, 1968.

Kens, Paul. *Justice Stephen Field: Shaping Liberty from the Gold Rush to the Gilded Age*. Lawrence: University Press of Kansas, 1997.

McCurdy, Charles W. "Justice Field and the Jurisprudence of Government-Business Relations: Some Parameters of Laissez-Faire Constitutionalism, 1863–1897." *Journal of American History* 61 (1975): 970–1005.

———. "Stephen J. Field and Public Land Law Development in California, 1850–1866: A Case Study of Judicial Resource Allocation in Nineteenth-Century America." *Law and Society* 10 (1976): 235–266.

———. "The Roots of 'Liberty of Contract' Reconsidered: Major Premises in the Law of Employment, 1867–1937." *Yearbook of the Supreme Court Historical Society* (1984): 20–33.

Swisher, Carl Brent. *Stephen J. Field, Craftsman of the Law*. 1930. Reprint. Chicago: University of Chicago Press, 1969.

Fortas, Abe

Brennan, William J., Jr. "Abe Fortas." *Yale Law Journal* 91 (1982): 1049–1051.

Goldberg, Arthur J. "A Tribute to Justice Abe Fortas." *Hastings Constitutional Law Quarterly* 9 (1982): 458–461.

Handberg, Roger. "After the Fall: Justice Fortas' Judicial Values and Behavior after the Failure of His Nomination as Chief Justice." *Capital University Law Review* 15 (1986): 205–222.

Kalman, Laura. *Abe Fortas: A Biography*. New Haven: Yale University Press, 1990.

Lee, Rex. "In Memoriam: Abe Fortas." *Supreme Court Historical Society Yearbook* (1983): 6–9.

Murphy, Bruce Allen. *Fortas: The Rise and Ruin of a Supreme Court Justice*. New York: William Morrow, 1988.

Shogan, Robert. *A Question of Judgment: The Fortas Case and the Struggle for the Supreme Court*. Indianapolis: Bobbs-Merrill, 1972.

Silverstein, Mark. *Judicious Choices: The New Politics of Supreme Court Confirmations*. New York: W. W. Norton & Co., 1994.

Frankfurter, Felix

Baker, Leonard. *Brandeis and Frankfurter: A Dual Biography*. New York: New York University Press, 1986.

Burt, Robert. *Two Jewish Justices: Outcasts in the Promised Land*. Berkeley: University of California Press, 1988.

Frankfurter, Felix. *Felix Frankfurter on the Supreme Court: Extrajudicial Essays on the Court and the Constitution*. Edited by Philip B. Kurland. Cambridge, Mass.: Belknap Press of Harvard University Press, 1970.

Hockett, Jeffrey D. *New Deal Justice: The Constitutional Jurisprudence of Hugo L. Black, Felix Frankfurter, and Robert H. Jackson*. Lanham, Md.: Rowman & Littlefield Publishers, 1996.

Mennel, Robert M. & Christine L. Compston, eds. *Holmes and Frankfurter: Their Correspondence, 1912–1934*. Hanover, N.H.: Published by University Press of New England for University of New Hampshire, 1996.

Murphy, Bruce Allen. *The Brandeis/Frankfurter Connection: The Secret Political Activities of Two Supreme Court Justices*. New York: Oxford University Press, 1982.

William T. Coleman, Jr. "Mr. Justice Felix Frankfurter: Civil Libertarian as Lawyer and as Justice: Extent to Which Judicial Responsibilities Affected His Pre-court Convictions." In *Six Justices on Civil Rights*. Edited by Ronald D. Rotunda. London: Oceana Publications, Inc., 1983.

Fuller, Melville Weston

Ely, James W., Jr. *The Chief Justiceship of Melville W. Fuller, 1888–1910*. Columbia: University of South Carolina Press, 1995.

Furer, Howard B. *The Fuller Court*. Port Washington, N.Y.: Associated Faculty Press, 1986.

King, Willard Leroy. *Melville Weston Fuller: Chief Justice of the United States, 1888–1910*. New York: Macmillan, 1950.

Morris, Jeffrey B. "The Era of Melville Weston Fuller." *Supreme Court Historical Society Yearbook* (1981): 36–51.

Pratt, Walter F. "Rhetorical Styles on the Fuller Court." *American Journal of Legal History* 24 (1980): 189–220.

Umbreit, Kenneth Bernard. *Our Eleven Chief Justices: A History of the Supreme Court in Terms of Their Personalities.* New York: Harper, 1938.

Ginsburg, Ruth Bader

Baugh, Joyce Ann, Christopher E. Smith, Thomas R. Hensley, and Scott Patrick Johnson. "Justice Ruth Bader Ginsburg: A Preliminary Assessment." *University of Toledo Law Review* 26 (1994): 1–34.

Bayne, David Cowan. "Insider Trading: Ginsburg's *O'Hagan* Insider Trading Ignored." *University of Miami Law Review* 53 (1999): 423–503.

Berry, Dawn Bradley. *The 50 Most Influential Women in American Law.* Los Angeles: Lowell House; Chicago: Contemporary Books, 1996.

Confusione, Michael James. "Justice Ruth Bader Ginsburg and Justice Thurgood Marshall: A Misleading Comparison." *Rutgers Law Journal* 26 (1995): 887–907.

Davis, W. Kent. "Answering Justice Ginsburg's Charge That the Constitution Is 'Skimpy' in Comparison to Our International Neighbors: A Comparison of Fundamental Rights in American and Foreign Law." *South Texas Law Review* 39 (1998): 951–994.

Ellington, Toni J. "Ruth Bader Ginsburg and John Marshall Harlan: A Justice and Her Hero." *University of Hawaii Law Review* 20 (1998): 797–834.

Elington, Toni J., Sylvia K. Higashi, Jayna K. Kim, and Mark Murakami. "Justice Ruth Bader Ginsburg and Gender Discrimination." *University of Hawaii Law Review* 20 (1998): 699–796.

Gillman, Elizabeth E. and Joesph M. Micheletti. "Justice Ruth Bader Ginsburg." *Seton Hall Constitutional Law Journal* 3 (1993): 657–663.

Ginsburg, Ruth Bader. "Constitutional Adjudication in the United States as a Means of Advancing the Equal Stature of Men and Women under the Law." *Hofstra Law Review* 26 (1997): 263–271.

———. "On the Interdependence of Law Schools and Law Courts." *Virginia Law Review* 83 (1997): 829–836.

———. "Reflections on Way Paving Jewish Justices and Jewish Women." *Touro Law Review* 14 (1998): 283–294.

———. "Remarks on Judicial Independence." *University of Hawaii Law Review* 20 (1998): 603–609.

———. "Some Thoughts on Autonomy and Equality in Relation to *Roe v. Wade.*" *North Carolina Law Review* 63 (1985): 375–386.

Halberstam, Malvina. "Ruth Bader Ginsburg: The First Jewish Woman on the United States Supreme Court." *Cardozo Law Review* 19 (1998): 1441–1454.

Karst, Kenneth L. "'The Way Women Are': Some Notes in the Margin for Ruth Bader Ginsburg." *University of Hawaii Law Review* 20 (1998): 619–633.

King, Jody. "Dedication to Justice Ruth Bader Ginsburg." *Annual Survey of American Law* (1997): viii–x.

Kuo, Mei-Fei and Kai Wang. "When Is an Innovation in Order? Justice Ruth Bader Ginsburg and Stare Decisis." *University of Hawaii Law Review* 20 (1998): 835–894.

Merritt, Deborah Jones. "Hearing the Voices of Individual Women and Men: Justice Ruth Bader Ginsburg." *University of Hawaii Law Review* 20 (1998): 635–646.

Pressman, Carol. "The House That Ruth Built: Justice Ruth Bader Ginsburg, Gender and Justice." *New York Law School Journal of Human Rights* 14 (1997): 311–337.

"Ruth Bader Ginsburg: A Personal, Very Fond Tribute." *University of Hawaii Law Review* 20 (1998): 583–601.

Smith, Christopher E., Joyce Ann Baugh, Thomas R. Hensley, and Scott Patrick Johnson. "The First-term Performance of Justice Ruth Bader Ginsburg." *Judicature* 78 (1994): 74–80.

Smith, Sheila M. "Justice Ruth Bader Ginsburg and Sexual Harassment Law: Will the Second Female Supreme Court Justice Become the Court's Women's Rights Champion?" *University of Cincinnati Law Review* 63 (1995): 1893–1945.

Walsh, Amy. "Ruth Bader Ginsburg: Extending the Constitution." *John Marshall Law Review* 32 (1998): 197–225.

Yip, Elijah and Eric K. Yamamoto. "Justice Ruth Bader Ginsburg's Jurisprudence of Process and Procedure." *University of Hawaii Law Review* 20 (1998): 647–698.

Goldberg, Arthur Joseph

Goldberg, Arthur J. *The Defenses of Freedom: The Public Papers of Arthur J. Goldberg.* Edited by Daniel Patrick Moynihan. New York: Harper & Row, 1966.

———. *Equal Justice: The Warren Era of the Supreme Court.* Evanston, Ill.: Northwestern University Press, 1971.

Goldberg, Dorothy. *A Private View of a Public Life.* New York: Charterhouse, 1975.

"In Memoriam: Arthur J. Goldberg, 1908–1990." *Northwestern University Law Review* 84 (1992): x–831.

Lasky, Victor. *Arthur J. Goldberg: The Old and the New.* New Rochelle, N.Y.: Arlington House, 1970.

Stebenne, David L. *Arthur J. Goldberg: New Deal Liberal.* New York: Oxford University Press, 1996.

Van Tassel, Emily Field. "Justice Arthur J. Goldberg." In *The Jewish Justices of the Supreme Court Revisited: Brandeis to Fortas.* Edited by Jennifer M. Lowe. Washington, D.C.: Supreme Court Historical Society, 1994.

Gray, Horace

Filler, Louis. "Horace Gray." In *The Justices of the United States Supreme Court 1789–1969: Their Lives and Major Opinions,* vol. 2. Edited by Leon Friedman and Fred L. Israel. New York: R. R. Bowker Co., 1969.

Hoar, George F. "Memoir of Horace Gray." *Massachusetts Historical Society Proceedings* 18 (1904): 155–187.

Spector, Robert M. "Legal Historian on the United States Supreme Court: Justice Horace Gray, Jr., and the Historical Method." *American Journal of Legal History* 12 (1968): 181–210.

Williston, Samuel. "Horace Gray." In *Great American Lawyers,* Vol. 8. Edited by William D. Lewis. Philadelphia: J. C. Winston Company, 1907–1909.

Grier, Robert Cooper

Gatell, Frank Ott. "Robert C. Grier." In *The Justices of the United States Supreme Court 1789–1969: Their Lives and Major Opinions,* vol. 2. Edited by Leon Friedman and Fred L. Israel. New York: R. R. Bowker Co., 1969.

Jones, Francis R. "Robert Cooper Grier." *Green Bag* 16 (1904): 221–224.

Livingston, John. "Honorable Robert C. Grier." In *Portraits Of Eminent Americans Now Living.* New York: R. Craighead, Printer, 1854.

Harlan, John Marshall II

Baker, Liva. "John Marshall Harlan I and a Color Blind Constitution: The Frankfurter-Harlan II Conversations." *Journal of Supreme Court History* (1992): 27–37.

Dorsen, Norman. "John Marshall Harlan and the Warren Court." *Journal of Supreme Court History* (1991): 50–62.

———. "John Marshall Harlan, Civil Liberties, and the Warren Court." *New York Law School Law Review* 36 (1991): 81–107.

———. "The Second Mr. Justice Harlan: A Constitutional Conservative." *New York University Law Review* 44 (1969): 249–271.

Fried, Charles. "The Conservatism of Justice Harlan." *New York Law School Law Review* 36 (1991): 33–52.

Mendelson, Wallace. "Justice John Marshall Harlan: Non sub Homine . . ." In *The Burger Court: Political and Judicial Profiles.* Edited by Charles M. Lamb and Stephen C. Halpern. Urbana: University of Illinois Press, 1991.

O'Brien, David M. "John Marshall Harlan's Unpublished Opinions: Reflections of a Supreme Court at Work." *Journal of Supreme Court History* (1991): 27–49.

Shapiro, David L., ed. *The Evolution of a Judicial Philosophy: Selected Opinions and Papers of Justice John M. Harlan.* Cambridge, Mass.: Harvard University Press, 1969.

Van Alstyne, William W. "The Enduring Example of John Marshall Harlan: 'Virtue as Practice' in the Supreme Court." *New York Law School Law Review* 36 (1991): 109–126.

Vasicko, Sally Jo. "Justice Harlan and the equal protection clause." *Supreme Court Historical Society Yearbook* (1982): 46–56.

Wilkinson, J. Harvie. "Justice John Marshall Harlan and the Values of Federalism." *Virginia Law Review* 57 (1971): 1185–1221.

Yarbrough, Tinsley E. *John Marshall Harlan: Great Dissenter of the Warren Court.* New York: Oxford University Press, 1992.

Harlan, John Marshall

Clark, Floyd B. *The Constitutional Doctrines of Justice Harlan.* Baltimore: The Johns Hopkins Press, 1915.

Baker, Liva. "John Marshall Harlan I and a Color Blind Constitution: The Frankfurter-Harlan II Conversations." *Journal of Supreme Court History* (1992): 27–37.

Beth, Loren P. "Justice Harlan and the Uses of Dissent," *American Political Science Review* 49 (1955): 1085–1104.

———. *John Marshall Harlan: The Last Whig Justice.* Lexington: University Press of Kentucky, 1992.

Przybyszewski, Linda. *The Republic According to John Marshall Harlan.* Chapel Hill: University of North Carolina Press, 1999.

Yarbrough, Tinsley E. *Judicial Enigma: The First Justice Harlan.* New York: Oxford University Press, 1995.

Holmes, Oliver Wendell

Aichele, Gary Jan. *Oliver Wendell Holmes, Jr.: Soldier, Scholar, Judge.* Boston: Twayne Publishers, 1989.

Baker, Liva. *Justice from Beacon Hill: The Life and Times of Oliver Wendell Holmes.* New York: Harper Collins, 1991.

Biddle, Francis. *Justice Holmes, Natural Law and the Supreme Court.* New York: Macmillan, 1961.

Bowen, Catherine Drinker. *Yankee from Olympus: Justice Holmes and His Family.* Boston: Little, Brown, 1945.

Cohen, Jeremy. *Congress Shall Make No Law: Oliver Wendell Holmes, the First Amendment, and Judicial Decision-making.* Ames: Iowa State University Press, 1989.

Frankfurter, Felix. *Mr. Justice Holmes and the Supreme Court.* Cambridge, Mass.: Belknap Press of Harvard University Press, 2d ed. 1961.

Gordon, Robert W., ed. *The Legacy of Oliver Wendell Holmes, Jr.* Stanford, Calif.: Stanford University Press, 1992.

Hoffheimer, Michael H. *Justice Holmes and the Natural Law.* New York: Garland Publishing, 1992.

Holmes, Oliver Wendell. *The Collected Works of Justice Holmes: Complete Public Writings and Selected Judicial Opinions of Oliver Wendell Holmes.* Edited by Sheldon M. Novick. 3 vols. Chicago: University of Chicago Press, 1995.

———. *Touched with Fire: Civil War Letters and Diary of Oliver Wendell Holmes, Jr., 1861–1864.* Edited by Mark De Wolfe Howe. Cambridge, Mass.: Harvard University Press, 1947.

Howe, Mark De Wolfe. *Justice Oliver Wendell Holmes.* 2 vols. Cambridge, Mass.: Belknap Press of Harvard University Press, 1957.

Kelley, Patrick J. *Holmes on the Supreme Judicial Court: The Theorist as Judge.* Supreme Judicial Court Historical Society, 1992.

Mennel, Robert M. & Christine L. Compston, eds. *Holmes and Frankfurter: Their Correspondence, 1912–1934.* Hanover, N.H.: Published by University Press of New England for University of New Hampshire, 1996.

Novick, Sheldon M. *Honorable Justice: The Life of Oliver Wendell Holmes.* Boston: Little, Brown, 1989.

Pohlman, H. L. *Justice Oliver Wendell Holmes & Utilitarian Jurisprudence.* Cambridge, Mass.: Harvard University Press, 1984.

Rosenberg, David. *The Hidden Holmes: His Theory of Torts in History.* Cambridge, Mass.: Harvard University Press, 1995.

Shriver, Harry Clair. *What Gusto: Stories and Anecdotes about Justice Oliver Wendell Holmes.* Potomac, Md.: Fox Hills Press, 1970.

White, G. Edward. *Justice Oliver Wendell Holmes: Law and the Inner Self.* New York: Oxford University Press, 1993.

Hughes, Charles Evans

Friedman, Richard D. "Switching Time and Other Thought Experiments: The Hughes Court and Constitutional Transformation." *University of Pennsylvania Law Review* 142 (1994): 1891–1984.

Galloway, Gail. "Charles Evans Hughes: The Eleventh Chief Justice." *Supreme Court Historical Society Yearbook* (1981): 94–112.

Hendel, Samuel. *Charles Evans Hughes and the Supreme Court.* New York: King's Crown Press, 1951.

Hughes, Charles Evans. *The Supreme Court of the United States: Its Foundation, Methods and Achievements: An Interpretation.* New York: Columbia University Press, 1928.

Knox, John. "Some Comments on Chief Justice Hughes." *Supreme Court Historical Society Yearbook* (1984): 34–44.

Olken, Samuel R. "Charles Evans Hughes and the *Blaisdell* Decision: A Historical Study of Contract Clause Jurisprudence." *Oregon Law Review* 72 (1993): 513–602.

Perkins, Dexter. *Charles Evans Hughes and American Democratic Statesmanship.* Boston: Little, Brown, 1956.

Pusey, Merlo John. *Charles Evans Hughes.* New York: Macmillan, 1951.

———. "The Hughes Biography: Some Personal Reflections." *Supreme Court Historical Society Yearbook* (1984): 45–52.

———. "The Nomination of Charles Evans Hughes as Chief Justice." *Supreme Court Historical Society Yearbook* (1982): 95–99.

Hunt, Ward

Barnes, William Horatio. "Ward Hunt, Associate Justice." In *The Supreme Court of the United States.* Part 11 of Barnes's *Illustrated Cyclopedia of the American Government.* n.p.: 1875.

Kutler, Stanley I. "Ward Hunt." In *The Justices of the United States Supreme Court 1789–1969: Their Lives and Major Opinions,* vol. 2. Edited by Leon Friedman and Fred L. Israel. New York: R. R. Bowker Co., 1969.

Iredell, James

Connor, H. G. "James Iredell: Lawyer, Statesman, Judge." *University of Pennsylvania Law Review* 60 (1912): 225–253.

Fordham, Jeff B. "Iredell's Dissent in *Chisholm v. Georgia.*" *The North Carolina Historical Review* 8 (1931): 155–167.

Graebe, Christopher T. "The Federalism of James Iredell in Historical Context." *North Carolina Law Review* 69 (1990): 251–272.

Israel, Fred L. "James Iredell." In *The Justices of the United States Supreme Court 1789–1969: Their Lives and Major Opinions,* vol. 1. Edited by Leon Friedman and Fred L. Israel. New York: R. R. Bowker Co., 1969.

McRee, Griffith John. *Life and Correspondence of James Iredell: One of the Associate Justices of the Supreme Court of the United States.* New York: Appleton, 1857–1873.

Waldrup, John Charles. "James Iredell and the Practice of Law in Revolutionary Era North Carolina." Ph.D. diss., Univ. of North Carolina-Chapel Hill, 1985.

Whichard, Willis P. "James Iredell: Revolutionist, Constitutionalist, Jurist." In *Seriatim: The Supreme Court Before John Marshall.* Edited by Scott Douglas Gerber. New York: New York University Press, 1998.

Jackson, Howell Edmunds

Calvani, Terry. "The Early Career of Howell Jackson." *Vanderbilt Law Review* 30 (1977): 39–72.

Doak, Henry M. "Howell Edmunds Jackson." *Greenbag* (1893): 209–215.

Green, John W. "Judge Howell E. Jackson." In *Law and Lawyers: Sketches of the Federal Judges of Tennessee,* by John W. Green. Jackson, Tennessee: McCowat-Mercer Press, 1950.

Hardawy, Roger D. "Howell Edmunds Jackson: Tennessee Legislator and Jurist." *West Tennessee Historical Society Papers* 30 (1976): 104–119.

Phillips, Harry. "Tennessee Lawyers of National Prominence." *Tennessee Bar Journal* 17 (1981): 34–53.

Schiffman, Irving. "Howell E. Jackson." In *The Justices of the United States Supreme Court 1789–1969: Their Lives and Major Opinions,* vol. 2. Edited by Leon Friedman and Fred L. Israel. New York: R. R. Bowker Co., 1969.

"Two United States Circuit Judges." *Tennessee Law Review* 18 (1944): 311–322.

Jackson, Robert Houghwout

Gerhart, Eugene C. *America's Advocate: Robert H. Jackson.* Indianapolis: Bobbs-Merrill, 1958.

Hockett, Jeffrey D. *New Deal Justice: The Constitutional Jurisprudence of Hugo L. Black, Felix Frankfurter, and Robert H. Jackson.* Lanham, Md.: Rowman & Littlefield Publishers, 1996.

Kurland, Philip. "Justice Robert H. Jackson: Impact on Civil Rights and Civil Liberties." In *Six Justices on Civil Rights.* Edited by Ronald D. Rotunda. London: Oceana Publications, Inc., 1983.

Jackson, Robert Houghwout. *The Struggle for Judicial Supremacy: A Study of a Crisis in American Power Politics.* New York: Knopf, 1941.

———. *The Supreme Court in the American System of Government.* Cambridge, Mass.: Harvard University Press, 1955.

Prettyman, E. Barrett, Jr. "Robert H. Jackson: 'Solicitor General for Life.'" *Journal of Supreme Court History* (1992): 75–85.

Schwartz, Bernard. "Chief Justice Rehnquist, Justice Jackson, and the *Brown* Case." *Supreme Court Review* (1988): 245–267.

Jay, John

Casto, William. *The Supreme Court in the Early Republic: The Chief Justiceships of John Jay and Oliver Ellsworth.* Columbia, S.C.: University of South Carolina Press, 1995.

Jay, John. *The Correspondence and Public Papers of John Jay.* Edited by Henry P. Johnston. Reprint. New York: Da Capo Press, 1971.

———. *John Jay.* Edited by Richard B. Morris. New York: Harper & Row, 1975.

Jay, William. *The Life of John Jay: with Selections from his Correspondence and Miscellaneous Papers.* Freeport, N.Y.: Books for Libraries Press, 1972.

Johnson, Herbert Alan. *John Jay, Colonial Lawyer.* New York: Garland, 1989.

McLean, Jennifer P. *The Jays of Bedford: The Story of Five Generations of the Jay Family Who Lived in the John Jay Homestead.* Katonah, N.Y.: Friends of John Jay Homestead, 1984.

Morris, Richard Brandon. *Witnesses at the Creation: Hamilton, Madison, Jay, and the Constitution.* New York: Holt, Rinehart, and Winston, 1985.

———. *John Jay, the Nation, and the Court.* Boston: Boston University Press, 1967.

Pellew, George. *John Jay.* Boston, New York: Bobbs-Merrill, 1898. Philadelphia: Chelsea House, 1997.

Sirvet, R.B. Bernstein. "Documentary Editing and the Jay Court: Opening New Lines of Inquiry." *Journal of Supreme Court History* (1996): 17–22.

———. "John Jay: Judicial Independence, and Advising Coordinate Branches." *Journal of Supreme Court History* (1996): 23–29.

Smith, Donald L. *John Jay: Founder of a State and Nation.* New York: Teachers College Press, Columbia University, 1968.

VanBurkleo, Susan. "'Honour, Justice, and Interest': John Jay's Republican Politics and Statesmanship on the Federal Bench." In *Seriatim: The Supreme Court Before John Marshall.* Edited by Scott Douglas Gerber. New York: New York University Press, 1998.

Johnson, Thomas

Delaplaine, Edward S. *The Life of Thomas Johnson: Member of the Continental Congress, First Governor of Maryland, and Associate Justice of the United States Supreme Court.* New York: Grafton Press, 1927.

———. *Thomas Johnson, Maryland and the Constitution.* Baltimore: Maryland State Bar Association, 1925.

Johnson, Herbert Alan. "Thomas Johnson." In *The Justices of the United States Supreme Court 1789–1969: Their Lives and Major Opinions,* vol. 1. Edited by Leon Friedman and Fred L. Israel. New York: R. R. Bowker Co., 1969.

Johnson, William

Greenberg, Irwin F. "Justice William Johnson: South Carolina Unionist, 1823–1830." *Pennsylvania History* 36 (1969): 307–334.

Huebner, Timothy S. "Divided Loyalties: Justice William Johnson and the Rise of Disunion in South Carolina, 1822–1834." *Journal of Supreme Court History Annual* (1995): 19–30.

Kolsky, Meredith. "Justice William Johnson and the History of the Supreme Court Dissent." *Georgetown Law Journal* 83 (1995): 2069–2098.

Morgan, Donald. "Justice William Johnson and the Treaty-Making Power." *George Washington Law Review* 22 (1953): 187–215.

———. "Mr. Justice William Johnson and the Constitution." *Harvard Law Review* 57 (1944): 328–361.

———. *Justice William Johnson: The First Dissenter.* Columbia: University of South Carolina Press, 1954.

———. "The Origin of Supreme Court Dissent." *William and Mary Quarterly* 10 (1953): 353–377.

Schroeder, Oliver, Jr. "Life and Judicial Work of Justice William Johnson, Jr." *University of Pennsylvania Law Review* 95 (1946): 164–201; 344–386.

Kennedy, Anthony M.

Amar, Akhil Reed. "Justice Kennedy and the Idea of Equality." *Pacific Law Journal* 28 (1997): 515–532.

Friedman, Lawrence M. "The Limitations of Labeling: Justice Anthony M. Kennedy and the First Amendment." *Ohio Northern University Law Review* 20 (1993): 225–262.

Golden, Sue. "Justice Anthony M. Kennedy: A Trojan Horse Conservative." *Maryland Journal of Contemporary Legal Issues* 1 (1990): 229–246.

Gottlieb, Stephen E. "Three Justices in Search of a Character: The Moral Agendas of Justices O'Connor, Scalia and Kennedy." *Rutgers Law Review* 49 (1996): 219–283.

McArtor, Keith O. "A Conservative Struggles with *Lemon:* Justice Anthony M. Kennedy's Dissent in *Allegheny.*" *Tulsa Law Journal* 26 (1990): 107–133.

Melone, Albert P. "Revisiting the Freshman Effect Hypothesis: The First Two Terms of Justice Anthony Kennedy." *Judicature* 74 (1990): 6–13.

Smith, Christopher E. "Supreme Court Surprise: Justice Anthony Kennedy's Move Toward Moderation." *Oklahoma Law Review* 45 (1992): 459–476.

Lamar, Joseph Rucker

Dinnerstein, Leonard. "Joseph Rucker Lamar." In *The Justices of the United States Supreme Court 1789–1969: Their Lives and Major Opinions,* vol. 3. Edited by Leon Friedman and Fred L. Israel. New York: R. R. Bowker Co., 1969.

Lamar, Clarinda Pendleton. *The Life of Joseph Rucker Lamar, 1857–1916.* New York: Putnam, 1926.

O'Connor, Sandra Day. "Supreme Court Justices from Georgia." *Georgia Journal of Southern Legal History* 1 (1991): 395–405.

Sibley, Samuel Hale. *Georgia's Contribution to Law: The Lamars.* New York: Newcomen Society of England, American Branch, 1948.

Lamar, Lucius Quintus C.

Cate, Wirt Armistead. *Lucius Q.C. Lamar: Secession and Reunion.* Chapel Hill: The University of North Carolina Press, 1935.

Hoffheimer, Michael H. "L.Q.C. Lamar: 1825–1893." *Mississippi Law Journal* 63 (1993): 5–106.

Mayes, Edward. *Lucius Q. C. Lamar: His Life, Times, and Speeches. 1825–1893.* Nashville, Tenn.: Publishing House of the Methodist Episcopal Church, South, 1896.

Murphy, James B. *L. Q. C. Lamar: Pragmatic Patriot.* Baton Rouge: Louisiana State University Press, 1973.

Livingston, Henry Brockholst

Dunne, Gerald T. "Brockholst Livingston." In *The Justices of the United States Supreme Court 1789–1969: Their Lives and Major Opinions,* vol. 1. Edited by Leon Friedman and Fred L. Israel. New York: R. R. Bowker Co., 1969.

———. "The Story-Livingston Correspondence, 1812–1822." *American Journal of Legal History* 10 (1966): 224–236.

Livingston, Edwin Brockholst. *The Livingstons of Livingston Manor.* New York: The Knickerbocker Press, 1910.

Lurton, Horace Harmon

Green, John W. "Judge Horace H. Lurton." In *Law and Lawyers: Sketches of the Federal Judges of Tennessee, Sketches of the Attorneys General of Tennessee, Legal Miscellany, Reminiscences by John W. Green.* Jackson, Tenn.: McCowat-Mercer Press, 1950.

Phillips, Harry. "Tennessee Lawyers of National Prominence." *Tennessee Bar Journal* 17 (1981): 34–53.

Tucker, David M. "Justice Horace Harmon Lurton: The Shaping of a National Progressive." *American Journal of Legal History* 13 (1969): 223–232.

Watts, James F., Jr. "Horace H. Lurton." In *The Justices of the United States Supreme Court 1789–1969: Their Lives and Major Opinions,* vol. 3. Edited by Leon Friedman and Fred L. Israel. New York: R. R. Bowker Co., 1969.

Williams, Samuel C. "Judge Horace H. Lurton." *Tennessee Law Review* 18 (1944): 242–250.

Marshall, John

Baker, Leonard. *John Marshall: A Life in Law.* New York: Macmillan, 1974.

Brandow, James C. "John Marshall's Supreme Court Practice: A Letter Comes to Light." *Journal of Supreme Court History Annual* (1995): 73–76.

Campbell, A. I. L. "'It Is a Constitution We Are Expounding': Chief Justice Marshall and the 'Necessary and Proper' Clause." *Journal of Legal History* 12 (1991): 190–245.

Costa, Greg. "John Marshall, the Sedition Act, and Free Speech in the Early Republic." *Texas Law Review* (1999): 1011–1047.

Engdahl, David E. "John Marshall's 'Jeffersonian' Concept of Judicial Review." *Duke Law Journal* 42 (1992): 279–339.

Eisgruber, Christopher L. "John Marshall's Judicial Rhetoric." *Supreme Court Review Annual* (1996): 439–481.

Faulkner, Robert Kenneth. *The Jurisprudence of John Marshall.* Princeton, N.J.: Princeton University Press, 1968.

Haskins, George Lee and Herbert A. Johnson. *Foundations of Power: John Marshall, 1801–15.* New York: Macmillan, 1981.

Hobson, Charles F. *The Great Chief Justice: John Marshall and the Rule of Law.* Lawrence: University Press of Kansas, 1996.

Johnson, Herbert Alan. *The Chief Justiceship of John Marshall, 1801–1835.* Columbia: University of South Carolina Press, 1997.

Jones, William Melville, ed. *Chief Justice John Marshall: A Reappraisal.* Ithaca, N.Y.: Cornell University Press, 1956.

Loth, David Goldsmith. *Chief Justice: John Marshall and the Growth of the Republic.* 1949. Reprint New York: Greenwood Press, 1970.

Magruder, Allan Bowie. *John Marshall.* Boston: Houghton, Mifflin and Company, 1885.

Marshall, John. *The Constitutional Decisions of John Marshall.* New York: G. P. Putnam's Sons, 1905.

Newmyer, R. Kent. *The Supreme Court under Marshall and Taney.* New York: Crowell, 1968.

Rudko, Frances Howell. *John Marshall and International Law: Statesman and Chief Justice.* New York: Greenwood Press, 1991.

Shevory, Thomas C. *John Marshall's Law: Interpretation, Ideology, and Interest.* Westport, Conn.: Greenwood Press, 1994.

Siegel, Adrienne. *The Marshall Court, 1801–1835.* Port Washington, N.Y.: Associated Faculty Press, 1987.

Smith, Jean Edward. *John Marshall: Definer of a Nation.* New York: H. Holt and Co., 1996.

Stites, Francis N. *John Marshall, Defender of the Constitution.* Boston: Little, Brown, 1981.

Swindler, William Finley. *The Constitution and Chief Justice Marshall.* New York: Dodd, Mead, 1978.

Thayer, James Bradley. *John Marshall.* New York: Da Capo Press, 1974.

White, G. Edward. *The Marshall Court and Cultural Change, 1815–35.* New York: Macmillan, 1988.

Yoo, John Choo. "Marshall's Plan: The Early Supreme Court and Statutory Interpretation." *Yale Law Journal* 101 (1992): 1607–1630.

Marshall, Thurgood

Aldred, Lisa. *Thurgood Marshall.* New York: Chelsea House, 1990.

Arthur, Joe. *The Story of Thurgood Marshall: Justice for All.* Milwaukee: G. Stevens Pub., 1996.

Ball, Howard. *A Defiant Life: Thurgood Marshall and the Persistence of Racism in America.* New York: Crown Publishers, 1998.

Bland, Randall Walton. *Private Pressure on Public Law: The Legal Career of Justice Thurgood Marshall.* Port Washington, N.Y.: Kennikat Press, 1973.

Daniels, William J. "Justice Thurgood Marshall: The Race for Equal Justice." In *The Burger Court: Political and Judicial Profiles.* Edited by Charles M. Lamb and Stephen C. Halpern. Urbana: University of Illinois Press, 1991.

Davis, Michael D. and Hunter R. Clark. *Thurgood Marshall: Warrior at the Bar, Rebel on the Bench.* Secaucus, N.J.: Carol, 1992.

Fenderson, Lewis H. *Thurgood Marshall: Fighter for Justice*. New York: McGraw-Hill, 1969.

Goldman, Roger L. *Thurgood Marshall: Justice for All.* New York: Carroll & Graf, 1992.

Krug, Elisabeth. *Thurgood Marshall: Champion of Civil Rights*. New York: Fawcett Columbine, 1993.

Marshall, Thurgood. "Reflections on the Bicentennial of the United States Constitution." *Harvard Law Review* 101 (1987): 1–5.

Mello, Michael. *Against the Death Penalty: The Relentless Dissents of Justices Brennan and Marshall.* Boston: Northeastern University Press, 1996.

Rowan, Carl Thomas. *Dream Makers, Dream Breakers: The World of Justice Thurgood Marshall.* Boston: Little, Brown, 1993.

"Thurgood Marshall." *New York University Law Review* 68 (1993): vi–225.

"A Tribute to Justice Marshall." *Harvard Blackletter Journal* 6 (1989): 1–140.

Tushnet, Mark. *Making Civil Rights Law: Thurgood Marshall and the Supreme Court, 1936–1961.* New York: Oxford University Press, 1994.

———. *Making Civil Rights Law: Thurgood Marshall and the Supreme Court, 1961–1991.* New York: Oxford University Press, 1997.

Williams, Juan. *Thurgood Marshall: American Revolutionary.* New York: Times Books, 1998.

Matthews, Stanley

Filler, Louis. "Stanley Matthews." In *The Justices of the United States Supreme Court 1789–1969: Their Lives and Major Opinions,* vol. 2. Edited by Leon Friedman and Fred L. Israel. New York: R. R. Bowker Co., 1969.

Greve, Charles Theodore. "Stanley Matthews." In *Great American Lawyers,* Vol. 7. Edited by William Draper Lewis. Philadelphia: J. C. Winston Co., 1907–1909.

Helfman, Harold M. "The Contested Confirmation of Stanley Matthews to the United States Supreme Court." *Historical and Philosophical Society of Ohio* 8 (1958): 154–170.

Stevens, Richard G. "Due Process of Law: Stanley Matthews." In *Sober as a Judge: The Supreme Court and Republican Liberty.* Edited by Richard G. Stevens and Matthew J. Franck. Lanham, Md.: Lexington Books, 1999.

McKenna, Joseph

McDevitt, Matthew. *Joseph McKenna: Associate Justice of the United States.* Washington, D.C., The Catholic University of America Press, 1946.

Watts, James F., Jr. "Joseph McKenna." In *The Justices of the United States Supreme Court 1789–1969: Their Lives and Major Opinions,* vol. 3. Edited by Leon Friedman and Fred L. Israel. New York: R. R. Bowker Co., 1969.

McKinley, John

Gatell, Frank Otto. "John McKinley." In *The Justices of the United States Supreme Court 1789–1969: Their Lives and Major Opinions,* vol. 1. Edited by Leon Friedman and Fred L. Israel. New York: R. R. Bowker Co., 1969.

Hicks, Jimmie. "Associate Justice John McKinley: A Sketch." *Alabama Review* 18 (1965): 227–233.

Levin, H. "John McKinley." In *The Lawyers and Law Makers of Kentucky.* Chicago: Lewis Publishing Co., 1897.

Martin, John M. "John McKinley: Jacksonian Phase." *Alabama Historical Quarterly* 28 (1966): 7–31.

Whatley, George C. "Justice John McKinley." *North Alabama History Association Bulletin* 4 (1959): 15–18.

McLean, John

Gattel, Frank O. "John McLean." In *The Justices of the United States Supreme Court 1789–1969: Their Lives and Major Opinions,* vol. 1. Edited by Leon Friedman and Fred L. Israel. New York: R. R. Bowker Co., 1969.

Kahn, Michael A. "The Appointment of John McLean to the Supreme Court: Practical Presidential Politics in the Jacksonian Era." *Journal of Supreme Court History, Annual* (1993): 59–72.

Weisenburger, Francis Phelps. *The Life of John McLean: A Politician on the United States Supreme Court.* Reprint. New York: Da Capo Press, 1971.

McReynolds, James Clark

Bond, James E. *I Dissent: The Legacy of Justice James Clark McReynolds.* Fairfax, Va.: George Mason University Press, 1992.

Bruner, David. "James Clark McReynolds." In *The Justices of the United States Supreme Court*

1789–1969: Their Lives and Major Opinions, vol. 3. Edited by Leon Friedman and Fred L. Israel. New York: R. R. Bowker Co., 1969.

Cushman, Barry. "The Secret Lives of the Four Horsemen." *Virginia Law Review* 83 (1997): 559–645.

Fletcher, R. V. "Mr. Justice McReynolds: An Appreciation." *Vanderbilt Law Review* 2 (1948): 35–46.

Jones, Calvin P. "Kentucky's Irascible Conservative: Supreme Court Justice James Clark McReynolds." *Filson Club History Quarterly* 57 (1983): 20–30.

Langram, Robert W. "Why Are Some Supreme Court Justices Rated as 'Failures'?" *Supreme Court Historical Society Yearbook* (1985): 8–14.

Miller, Samuel Freeman

Fairman, Charles. *Mr. Justice Miller and the Supreme Court, 1862–1890.* Cambridge, Mass.: Harvard University Press, 1939.

Gillette, William. "Samuel Miller." In *The Justices of the United States Supreme Court 1789–1969: Their Lives and Major Opinions,* Vol. 2. Edited by Leon Friedman and Fred L. Israel. New York: R. R. Bowker Co., 1969.

Gregory, Charles Noble. *Samuel Freeman Miller.* Iowa City: State Historical Society of Iowa, 1907.

Miller, Samuel Freeman. *The Constitution and the Supreme Court of the United States of America: Addresses by the Hon. Samuel F. Miller.* New York: D. Appleton & Co., 1889.

———. *Lectures on the Constitution of the United States.* Littleton, Colo.: F. B. Rothman, 1980.

Palmer, Robert C. "The Parameters of Constitutional Reconstruction: *Slaughter-House, Cruikshank,* and the Fourteenth Amendment." *University of Illinois Law Review* (1984): 739–770.

Minton, Sherman

Atkinson, David N. "From New Deal Liberal to Supreme Court Conservative." *Washington University Law Quarterly* (1975): 361–394.

———. "Justice Sherman Minton and the Protection of Minority Rights." *Washington and Lee Law Review* 34 (1977): 97–117.

Gugin Linda C. and James E. St. Clair. *Sherman Minton: New Deal Senator, Cold War Justice.* Indianapolis: Indiana Historical Society, 1997.

Kirkendall, Richard. "Sherman Minton." In *The Justices of the United States Supreme Court 1789–1969: Their Lives and Major Opinions,* vol. 4. Edited by Leon Friedman and Fred L. Israel. New York: R. R. Bowker Co., 1969.

Radcliff, William Franklin. *Sherman Minton: Indiana's Supreme Court Justice.* Indianapolis: Guild Press of Indiana, 1996.

Wallace, Harry L. "Mr. Justice Minton: Hoosier Justice on the Supreme Court." *Indiana Law Journal* 34 (1959): 145–205; 377–424.

Moody, William Henry

Heffron, Paul T. "Profile of a Public Man." In *Supreme Court Historical Society Yearbook, 1980.* Washington, D.C.: Supreme Court Historical Society, 1980, 30–31, 48.

———. "Theodore Roosevelt and the Appointment of Mr. Justice Moody." *Vanderbilt Law Review* 18 (1965): 545–568.

McDonough, Judith R. "William Henry Moody." Ph.D. diss., Auburn Univ., 1983.

Moody, William Henry. "Constitutional Powers of the Senate: A Reply." *North American Review* 174 (1902): 386–94.

Watts, James F., Jr. "William Moody." In *The Justices of the United States Supreme Court 1789–1969: Their Lives and Major Opinions,* vol. 3. Edited by Leon Friedman and Fred L. Israel. New York: R. R. Bowker Co., 1969.

Moore, Alfred

Davis, Junius. *Alfred Moore and James Iredell, Revolutionary Patriots.* Raleigh: North Carolina Society of the Sons of the Revolution, 1899.

Friedman, Leon. "Alfred Moore." In *The Justices of the United States Supreme Court 1789–1969: Their Lives and Major Opinions,* vol. 1. Edited by Leon Friedman and Fred L. Israel. New York: R. R. Bowker Co., 1969.

Mason, Robert. *Namesake: Alfred Moore 1755–1810, Soldier and Jurist.* Southern Pines, S.C.: Moore County Historical Association, 1989.

Murphy, Frank

Fine, Sidney. *Frank Murphy.* Vol. 1, *The Detroit Years.* Vol. 2, *The New Deal Years.* Chicago: University of Chicago Press, 1979. Vol. 3, *The*

Washington Years. Ann Arbor: University of Michigan Press, 1975–84.

Howard, J. Woodford, Jr. *Mr. Justice Murphy: A Political Biography*. Princeton, N.J.: Princeton University Press, 1968.

Lunt, Richard D. *The High Ministry of Government: The Political Career of Frank Murphy*. Detroit: Wayne State University Press, 1965.

Potts, Margaret H. "Justice Frank Murphy: A Reexamination." *Supreme Court Historical Society Yearbook* (1982): 57–65.

Nelson, Samuel

"Biographical Sketch of Justice Samuel Nelson." *Central Law Journal* 1 (1874): 2–3.

Countryman, Edwin. "Samuel Nelson." *Green Bag* (1907): 329–334.

Gatell, Frank Otto. "Samuel Nelson." In *The Justices of the United States Supreme Court 1789–1969: Their Lives and Major Opinions,* vol. 2. Edited by Leon Friedman and Fred L. Israel. New York: R. R. Bowker Co., 1969.

Leach, Richard H. "Rediscovery of Samuel Nelson." *New York History* 34 (1953): 64–71.

"The Old Judge and the New." *Albany Law Journal* 6 (1872): 400–401.

O'Connor, Sandra Day

Behuniak-Long, Susan. "Justice Sandra Day O'Connor and the Power of Maternal Thinking." *The Review of Politics* (1992): 417–444.

Brown, Judith Olans, Wendy E. Parmet, and Mary E. O'Connell. "The Rugged Feminism of Sandra Day O'Connor." *Indiana Law Review* 32 (1999): 1219–1246.

Bruckmann, Barbara Olson. "Justice Sandra Day O'Connor: Trends Toward Judicial Restraint." *Washington and Lee Law Review* 42 (1985): 1185–1231.

Cook, Beverly B. "Justice Sandra Day O'Connor: Transition to a Republican Court Agenda." In *The Burger Court: Political and Judicial Profiles.* Edited by Charles M. Lamb and Stephen C. Halpern. Urbana: University of Illinois Press, 1991.

"The Emerging Jurisprudence of Justice O'Connor." *University of Chicago Law Review* 52 (1985): 389–459.

Horner, Matina S. *Sandra Day O'Connor.* New York: Chelsea House, 1990.

Maveety, Nancy. *Justice Sandra Day O'Connor: Strategist on the Supreme Court.* London: Rowman & Littlefield, 1996.

O'Connor, Sandra Day. "Madison Lecture: Portia's Progress." *New York University Law Review* 66 (1991): 1546–1548.

Riggs, Robert. "Justice O'Connor: First Term Appraisal." *Brigham Young University Law Review* (1983): 1–46.

Savage, David G. "Sandra Day O'Connor." In *Eight Men and a Lady: Profiles of the Justices of the Supreme Court.* Edited by J. Joseph. Bethesda, Md.: National Press, 1990.

Shea, Barbara. "Sandra Day O'Connor—Woman, Lawyer, Justice: Her First Four Terms on the Court." *University of Missouri-Kansas City Law Review* 55 (1986): 1–32.

Van Sickel, Robert W. *Not a Particularly Different Voice: The Jurisprudence of Sandra Day O'Connor.* New York: P. Lang, 1998.

Paterson, William

Amar, Akhil Reed. "Colloquy: Article III and the Judiciary Act of 1789: The Two-Tiered Structure of The Judiciary Act of 1789." *University of Pennsylvania Law Review* (1990): 1499–1567.

Degnan, Daniel A. "Justice William Paterson: Founder." *Seton Hall Law Review* 16 (1986): 313–338.

———. "William Paterson: Small States' Nationalist." In *Seriatim: The Supreme Court Before John Marshall.* Edited by Scott Douglas Gerber. New York: New York University Press, 1998.

Gibbons, John J. "A New Nation." *Seton Hall Law Review* 16 (1986): 309–338.

Hickox III, Charles F. and Andrew C. Laviano. "William Paterson." *Journal of Supreme Court History Annual* (1992): 53–61.

Holt, Wythe. "'To Establish Justice': Politics, The Judiciary Act of 1789, and the Invention of the Federal Courts." *Duke Law Journal* (1989): 1421–1531.

Laws of the State of New Jersey, Revised and Published under the Authority of the Legislature, by William Paterson. Newark: M. Day, 1800.

O'Connor, John E. *William Paterson, Lawyer and Statesman, 1745–1806.* New Brunswick, N.J.: Rutgers University Press, 1979.

Paterson, William. *Glimpses of Colonial Society and the Life at Princeton College, 1766–1773, by One of the Class of 1763.* Edited by W. Jay Mills. Philadelphia: Lippincott, 1903; Detroit: Grand River Books, 1971.

Peckham, Rufus Wheeler

Duker, William F. "Mr. Justice Rufus W. Peckham and the Case of *Ex parte Young:* Lochnerizing *Munn v. Illinois.*" *Brigham Young University Law Review* (1980): 539–558.

———. "Mr. Justice Rufus W. Peckham: The Police Power and the Individual in a Changing World." *Brigham Young University Law Review* (1980): 47–67.

Hall, A. Oakey. "The New Supreme Court Justice." *Green Bag* 8 (1896): 1–4.

Proctor, L. B. "Rufus W. Peckham." *Albany Law Journal* 55 (1897): 286–288.

Skolnik, Richard. "Rufus Peckham." In *The Justices of the United States Supreme Court 1789–1969: Their Lives and Major Opinions,* vol. 3. Edited by Leon Friedman and Fred L. Israel. New York: R. R. Bowker Co., 1969.

Pitney, Mahlon

Belknap, Michal R. "Mr. Justice Pitney and Progressivism." *Seton Hall Law Review* 16 (1986): 380–423.

Breed, Alan Ryder. "Mahlon Pitney: His Life and Career—Political and Judicial." B.A. thesis, Princeton University, 1932.

Israel, Fred. "Mahlon Pitney." In *The Justices of the United States Supreme Court 1789–1969: Their Lives and Major Opinions,* vol. 3. Edited by Leon Friedman and Fred L. Israel. New York: R. R. Bowker Co., 1969.

Levitan, David Maurice. "Mahlon Pitney, Labor Judge." *Virginia Law Review* 40 (1954): 733–770.

Powell, Lewis F., Jr.

Freeman, George Clemon, Jr. "Justice Powell's Constitutional Opinions." *Washington and Lee Law Review* 45 (1988): 411–465.

"In Memoriam: Lewis F. Powell, Jr." *Harvard Law Review* 112 (1999): x–610.

"In Memoriam: Writing for Justice Powell." *Columbia Law Review* 99 (1999): viii–551.

Jeffries, John Calvin, Jr. *Justice Lewis F. Powell, Jr.* New York: Charles Scribner's Sons, 1994.

Landynski, Jacob W. "Justice Lewis F. Powell, Jr.: Balance Wheel of the Court." In *The Burger Court: Political and Judicial Profiles.* Edited by Charles M. Lamb and Stephen C. Halpern. Urbana: University of Illinois Press, 1991.

"Symposium in Honor of Justice Lewis F. Powell, Jr." *Virginia Law Review* 68 (1982): 161–458.

"A Tribute to Justice Lewis F. Powell." *Seton Hall Law Review* 18 (1988): x–222.

"A Tribute to Justice Lewis F. Powell, Jr." *Harvard Law Review* 101 (1987): 395–420.

Reed, Stanley Forman

Boskey, Bennett. "Justice Reed and His Family of Law Clerks." *Kentucky Law Journal* 69 (1981): 869–876.

Burger, Warren. "Stanley F. Reed." *Supreme Court Historical Society Yearbook* (1981): 10–13.

Canon, Bradley C., Kimberly Greenfield, and Jason S. Fleming. "Justice Frankfurter and Justice Reed: Frienship and Lobbying on the Court." *Judicature* 78 (March-April 1995): 224–231.

Fassett, John D. "Mr. Justice Reed and *Brown v. Board of Education.*" *Supreme Court Historical Society Yearbook* (1986): 48–63.

———. *New Deal Justice: The Life of Stanley Reed of Kentucky.* New York: Vantage Press, 1994.

O'Brien, F. William. *Justice Reed and the First Amendment: The Religion Clauses.* Washington: Georgetown University Press, 1958.

Prickett, Morgan D.S. "Stanley Forman Reed: Perspectives on a Judicial Epitaph." *Hastings Constitutional Law Quarterly* 8 (1981): 343–369.

Rehnquist, William H.

Boles, Donald E. *Mr. Justice Rehnquist, Judicial Activist: The Early Years.* Ames: Iowa State University Press, 1987.

Davis, Derek. *Original Intent: Chief Justice Rehnquist and the Course of American Church-State Relations.* Buffalo, N.Y.: Prometheus Books, 1991.

Davis, Sue. *Justice Rehnquist and the Constitution.* Princeton, N.J.: Princeton University Press, 1989.

———. "Justice William H. Rehnquist: Right-Wing Ideologue or Majoritarian Democrat?" In *The Burger Court: Political and Judicial Profiles.* Edited by Charles M. Lamb and Stephen C. Halpern. Urbana: University of Illinois Press, 1991.

Maveety, Nancy. "The Populist of the Adversary Society: The Jurisprudence of Justice Rehnquist." *Journal of Contemporary Law* 13 (1987): 221–247.

Ray, Laura K. "A Law Clerk and His Justice: What William Rehnquist Did Not Learn from Robert Jackson." *Indiana Law Review* 29 (1996): 535–592.

Rehnquist, William H. *Civil Liberty and the Civil War.* Washington, D.C.: National Legal Center for the Public Interest, 1997.

———. *The Supreme Court: How It Was, How It Is.* New York: Morrow, 1987.

Savage, David G. *Turning Right: The Making of the Rehnquist Supreme Court.* New York: John Wiley and Sons, 1992.

Tucker, David F. B. *The Rehnquist Court and Civil Rights.* Brookfield, Vt.: Dartmouth, 1995.

Roberts, Owen Josephus

Fish, Peter G. "Spite Nominations to the United States Supreme Court: Herbert C. Hoover, Owen J. Roberts, and the Politics of Presidential Vengeance in Retrospect." *Kentucky Law Journal* 77 (1989): 545–576.

Frankfurter, Felix. "Mr. Justice Roberts." *University of Pennsylvania Law Review* 104 (1955–56): 311–317.

Friedman, Richard D. "A Reaffirmation: The Authenticity of the Roberts Memorandum, or Felix the Non-forger." *University of Pennsylvania Law Review* 142 (1994): 1985–1995.

———. "Switching Time and Other Thought Experiments: The Hughes Court and Constitutional Transformation." *University of Pennsylvania Law Review* 142 (1994): 1891–1984.

Griswold, Erwin N. "Owen J. Roberts as a Judge." *University of Pennsylvania Law Review* 104 (1955–56): 322–331.

Leonard, Charles A. *A Search for a Judicial Philosophy: Mr. Justice Roberts and the Constitutional Revolution of 1937.* Port Washington, N.Y.: Kennikat Press, 1971.

McCracken, Robert T. "Owen J. Roberts—Master Advocate." *University of Pennsylvania Law Review* 104 (1955–56): 332–349.

Pusey, Merlo J. "Justice Roberts' 1937 Turnaround." *Supreme Court Historical Society Yearbook* (1983): 102–107.

Rutledge, Wiley Blount

Brant, Irving. "Mr. Justice Rutledge—The Man." *Iowa Law Review* 35 (1950): 544–565.

Harper, Fowler V. *Justice Rutledge and the Bright Constellation.* Indianapolis: Bobbs-Merrill, 1965.

Mann, W. Howard. "Rutledge and Civil Liberties." *Indiana Law Journal* 25 (1950): 532–559.

Pollak, Louis H. "Wiley Blount Rutledge: Profile of a Judge." In *Six Justices on Civil Rights.* Edited by Ronald D. Rotunda. London: Oceana Publications, Inc., 1983.

Rockwell, Landon G. "Justice Rutledge on Civil Liberties." *Yale Law Journal* 59 (1949): 27–59.

Rutledge, Wiley. *A Declaration of Legal Faith.* Lawrence: University of Kansas Press, 1947.

Rutledge, John

Barry, Richard Hayes. *Mr. Rutledge of South Carolina.* New York: Duell, Sloan and Pearce, 1942.

Haw, James. *John & Edward Rutledge of South Carolina.* Athens: University of Georgia Press, 1997.

———. "John Rutledge: Distinction and Declension." In *Seriatim: The Supreme Court Before John Marshall.* Edited by Scott Douglas Gerber. New York: New York University Press, 1998.

Sanford, Edward Terry

Burner, David. "Edward Terry Sanford." In *The Justices of the United States Supreme Court 1789–1969: Their Lives and Major Opinions,* vol. 3. Edited by Leon Friedman and Fred L. Israel. New York: R. R. Bowker Co., 1969.

Fowler, James A. "Mr. Justice Edward Terry Sanford." *American Bar Association Journal* 17 (1931): 229–233.

Green, John W. "Judge Edward T. Sanford." In *Law and Lawyers: Sketches of the Federal Judges of Tennessee, Sketches of the Attorneys General of Tennessee, Legal Miscellany, Reminiscences by John W. Green*. Jackson, Tenn.: McCowat-Mercer Press: 1950.

Phillips, Harry. "Tennessee Lawyers of National Prominence." *Tennessee Bar Journal* 17 (1981): 34–53.

Scalia, Antonin

Boling, David. "The Jurisprudential Approach of Justice Antonin Scalia: Methodology over Result?" *Arkansas Law Review* 44 (1991): 1143–1205.

Brisbin, Richard A. *Justice Antonin Scalia and the Conservative Revival*. Baltimore: Johns Hopkins University Press, 1997.

Brock, Beau James. "Justice Antonin Scalia: A Renaissance of Positivism and Predictability in Constitutional Adjudication." *Louisiana Law Review* 51 (1991): 623–650.

Gerhardt, Michael J. "A Tale of Two Textualists: A Critical Comparison of Justices Black and Scalia." *Boston University Law Review* 74 (1994): 25–66.

"The Jurisprudence of Justice Antonin Scalia." *Cardozo Law Review* 12 (1991): 1593–1867.

Kannar, George. "The Constitutional Cathechism of Antonin Scalia." *Yale Law Journal* 99 (1990): 1297–1357.

King, Michael Patrick. "Justice Antonin Scalia: The First Term on the Supreme Court—1986–1987." *Rutgers Law Journal* 20 (1988): 1–77.

Nagareda, Richard. "The Appellate Jurisprudence of Justice Antonin Scalia." *University of Chicago Law Review* 54 (1987): 705–739.

Scalia, Antonin. "The Dissenting Opinion." *Journal of Supreme Court History* (1994): 33–44.

———. *A Matter of Interpretation: Federal Courts and the Law*. Princeton, N.J.: Princeton University Press, 1997.

———. "Originalism: The Lesser Evil." *University of Cincinnati Law Review* 57 (1989): 849–865.

———. "The Rule of Law as a Law of Rules." *University of Chicago Law Review* 56 (1989): 1175–1188.

Schultz, David Andrew. *The Jurisprudential Vision of Justice Antonin Scalia*. Lanham, Md.: Rowman & Littlefield Publishers, 1996.

Segall, Eric J. "Justice Scalia, Critical Legal Studies and the Rule of Law." *George Washington Law Review* 62 (1994): 991–1042.

Smith, Christopher E. *Justice Antonin Scalia and the Supreme Court's Conservative Moment*. Westport, Conn.: Praeger, 1994.

Spitko, Edward Gary. "A Critique of Justice Antonin Scalia's Approach to Fundamental Rights Adjudication." *Duke Law Journal* (1990): 1337–1360.

Sunderland, Lane V. "Steady, Upright, and Impartial Administration of Laws: Antonin Scalia." In *Sober as a Judge: The Supreme Court and Republican Liberty*. Edited by Richard G. Stevens and Matthew J. Franck. Lanham, Md.: Lexington Books, 1999.

Shiras, George, Jr.

Paul, Arnold. "George Shiras, Jr." In *The Justices of the United States Supreme Court 1789–1969: Their Lives and Major Opinions*, vol. 2. Edited by Leon Friedman and Fred L. Israel. New York: R. R. Bowker Co., 1969.

Shiras, George III. *Justice George Shiras, Jr., of Pittsburgh, Associate Justice of the United States Supreme Court, 1892–1903: A Chronicle of His Family, Life, and Times*. Edited and completed by Winfield Shiras. Pittsburgh: University of Pittsburgh Press, 1953.

Souter, David H.

Fliter, John A. "Keeping the Faith: Justice David Souter and the First Amendment Religion Clauses." *Journal of Church & State* 40 (1998): 387–409.

Gomperts, John S. and Elliot M. Mincberg. "A Review of Justice David Souter's Public Record: Questions about His Views on Constitutional Issues." *Maryland Journal of Contemporary Legal Issues* 1 (1990): 195–228.

Hanks, Liza Weiman. "Justice Souter: Defining 'Substantive Neutrality' in an Age of Religious Politics." *Stanford Law Review* 48 (1996): 903–935.

Kan, Liang. "A Theory of Justice Souter." *Emory Law Journal* 45 (1996): 1373–1427.

Koehler, David K. "Justice Souter's 'Keep-what-you-want-and-throw-away-the-rest' Interpretation of Stare Decisis." *Buffalo Law Review* (1994): 859–892.

Meese, Alan. "Will, Judgment, and Economic Liberty: Mr. Justice Souter and the Mistranslation of the due process clause." *William and Mary Law Review* 41 (1999): 3–61.

Powe, Lucas A., Jr. "From Bork to Souter." *Willamette Law Review* 27 (1991): 781–801.

Smith, Christopher E. and Scott P. Johnson. "Newcomer on the High Court: Justice David Souter and the Supreme Court's 1990 Term." *South Dakota Law Review* 37 (1992): 21–43.

Smith, Robert H. "Justice Souter Joins the Rehnquist Court: An Empirical Study of Supreme Court Voting Patterns." *University of Kansas Law Review* 41 (1992): 11–95.

Stevens, John Paul

Canon, Bradley C. "Justice John Paul Stevens: the Lone Ranger in a Black Robe." In *The Burger Court: Political and Judicial Profiles.* Edited by Charles M. Lamb and Stephen C. Halpern. Urbana: University of Illinois Press, 1991.

"Perspectives on Justice John Paul Stevens." *Rutgers Law Journal* 27 (1996): 521–661.

Sickels, Robert J. *John Paul Stevens and the Constitution: The Search for Balance.* University Park: Pennsylvania State University Press, 1988.

Stevens, John Paul. "The Bill of Rights: A Century of Progress." *University of Chicago Law Review* 59 (1992): 13–38.

———. "The Freedom of Speech." *Yale Law Journal* 102 (1993): 1293–1313.

———. "Is Justice Irrelevant?" *Northwestern University Law Review* 87 (1993): 1121–1130.

Stewart, Potter

Binion, Gayle. "Justice Potter Stewart: The Unpredictable Vote." *Journal of Supreme Court History* (1992): 99–108.

Bush, George. "In Memory of Justice Potter Stewart." *Hastings Constitutional Law Quarterly* 13 (1986): 171–72.

"In Tribute of Honorable Potter Stewart." *Yale Law Journal* 95 (1986): 1321–1333.

Marsel, Robert S. "Mr. Justice Potter Stewart: The Constitutional Jurisprudence of Justice Potter Stewart—Reflections on a Life of Public Service." *Tennessee Law Review* 55 (1987): 1–39.

Monsma, Stephen V. "Justice Potter Stewart on Church and State." *Journal of Church & State* 36 (1994): 557–576.

Powell, Lewis F., Jr. "In Memoriam: Justice Potter Stewart." *Supreme Court Historical Society Yearbook* (1986): 5–7.

Stewart, Potter. "Or of the Press." *Hastings Law Journal* 50 (1999): 705–710.

———. "The Road to *Mapp v. Ohio* and Beyond: The Origins, Development and Future of the Exclusionary Rule in Search-and-Seizure Cases." *Columbia Law Review* 83 (1983): 1365–1404.

Yarbrough, Tinsley E. "Justice Potter Stewart: Decisional Patterns in Search of Doctrinal Moorings." In *The Burger Court: Political and Judicial Profiles.* Edited by Charles M. Lamb and Stephen C. Halpern. Urbana: University of Illinois Press, 1991.

Stone, Harlan Fiske

Dowling, Noel T. "The Methods of Mr. Justice Stone in Constitutional Cases." *Columbia Law Review* 41 (1941): 1160–1189.

Givens, Richard A. "Chief Justice Stone and the Developing Function of Judicial Review." *Virginia Law Review* 47 (1961): 1321–1365.

Konefsky, Samuel Joseph. *Chief Justice Stone and the Supreme Court.* New York: Macmillan, 1945.

Mason, Alpheus Thomas. *Harlan Fiske Stone: Pillar of the Law.* New York: Viking Press, 1956.

Urofsky, Melvin I. *Division and Discord: The Supreme Court under Stone and Vinson, 1941–1953.* Columbia: University of South Carolina Press, 1997.

Wechsler, Herbert. "Stone and the Constitution." *Columbia Law Reviews* 45 (1946): 764–800.

Story, Joseph

Dunne, Gerald T. *Justice Joseph Story and the Rise of the Supreme Court.* New York: Simon and Schuster, 1970.

Eisgruber, Christopher L. "Justice Story, Slavery, and the Natural Law Foundations of American

Constitutionalism." *University of Chicago Law Review* 55 (1988): 273–327.

Finkelman, Paul. "Story Telling on the Supreme Court: *Prigg v. Pennsylvania* and Justice Joseph Story's Judicial Nationalism." *Supreme Court Review Annual* (1994): 247–294.

Hoffer, Peter Charles. "Principled Discretion: Concealment, Conscience, and Chancellors." *Yale Journal of Law & the Humanities* 3 (1991): 53–82.

Holden-Smith, Barbara. "Lords of Lash, Loom, and Law: Justice, Story, Slavery and *Prigg v. Pennsylvania*." *Cornell Law Review* 78 (1993): 1086–1151.

McClellan, James. *Joseph Story and the American Constitution: A Study in Political and Legal Thought with Selected Writings.* Norman: University of Oklahoma Press, 1971.

Newmyer, R. Kent. *Supreme Court Justice Joseph Story: Statesman of the Old Republic.* Chapel Hill: University of North Carolina Press, 1985.

Story, Joseph. *The Miscellaneous Writings of Joseph Story.* Edited by William W. Story. Boston: C. C. Little and J. Brown, 1852. Reprint New York: Da Capo Press, 1972.

———. *Joseph Story: A Collection of Writings by and about an Eminent American Jurist.* Edited by Mortimer D. Schwartz and John C. Hogan. New York: Oceana Publications, 1959.

Story, William Wetmore, ed. *Life and Letters of Joseph Story, Associate Justice of the Supreme Court of the United States, and Dane Professor of Law at Harvard University.* Freeport, N.Y.: Books for Libraries Press, 1971.

Woodard, Calvin. "Joseph Story and American Equity." *Washington and Lee Law Review* 45 (1988): 623–644.

Strong, William

Barnes, William Horatio. "William Strong, Associate Justice." In *The Supreme Court of the United States.* Part 11 of Barnes's *Illustrated Cyclopedia of the American Government.* n.p.: 1875.

Kutler, Stanley I. "William Strong." In *The Justices of the United States Supreme Court 1789–1969: Their Lives and Major Opinions,* Vol. 2. Edited by Leon Friedman and Fred L. Israel. New York: R. R. Bowker Co., 1969.

"Retirement of William J. Strong." *American Law Review* 15 (1881): 130–131.

Strong, William. "The Needs of the Supreme Court." *North American Review* 132 (1881): 437–450.

Sutherland, George

Arkes, Hadley. *The Return of George Sutherland: Restoring a Jurisprudence of Natural Rights.* Princeton, N.J.: Princeton University Press, 1994.

Cushman, Barry. "The Secret Lives of the Four Horsemen." *Virginia Law Review* 83 (1997): 559–645.

Mason, Alpheus Thomas. "The Conservative World of Mr. Justice Sutherland, 1883–1910." *American Political Science Review* 32 (1938): 443–447.

Paschal, Joel Francis. *Mr. Justice Sutherland: A Man Against the State.* Princeton, N.J.: Princeton University Press, 1951.

Swayne, Noah Haynes

Barnes, William Horatio. "Noah H. Swayne, Associate Justice." In *The Supreme Court of the United States.* Part 11 of Barnes's *Illustrated Cyclopedia of the American Government.* n.p.: 1875.

Gillette, William. "Noah H. Swayne." In *The Justices of the United States Supreme Court 1789–1969: Their Lives and Major Opinions,* vol. 2. Edited by Leon Friedman and Fred L. Israel. New York: R. R. Bowker Co., 1969.

Silver, David Mayer. *Lincoln's Supreme Court.* Urbana: University of Illinois Press, 1956.

Taft, William Howard

Anderson, Judith Icke. *William Howard Taft: An Intimate History.* New York: Norton, 1981.

Burton, David Henry. *Taft, Holmes, and the 1920s Court: An Appraisal.* Madison, N.J.: Fairleigh Dickinson University Press; Cranbury, N.J.: Associated University Presses, 1998.

Coletta, Paolo Enrico. *The Presidency of William Howard Taft.* Lawrence: University Press of Kansas, 1973.

Hicks, Frederick Charles. *William Howard Taft: Yale Professor of Law & New Haven Citizen.* New Haven: Yale University Press, 1945.

Mason, Alpheus Thomas. *William Howard Taft: Chief Justice.* New York: Simon and Schuster, 1965.

Pringle, Henry Fowles. *The Life and Times of William Howard Taft.* New York: Farrar & Rinehart, 1939.

Ragan, Allen E. *Chief Justice Taft.* Columbus, Ohio: The Ohio State Archeological and Historical Society, 1938.

Taft, William Howard. *The Collected Works of William Howard Taft.* Athens, Ohio: Ohio University Press, 2000.

Taney, Roger Brooke

Freedman, Suzanne. *Roger Taney: The Dred Scott Legacy.* Springfield, N.J.: Enslow Publishers, 1995.

Grimsted, David. "Robbing the Power to Aid the Rich: Roger B. Taney and the Bank of Maryland Swindle." *Supreme Court Historical Society Yearbook* (1987): 38–81.

Higginbotham, Jr., A. Leon. "The Ten Precepts of American Slavery Jurisprudence: Chief Justice Roger Taney's Defense and Justice Thurgood Marshall's Condemnation of The Precept of Black Inferiority." *Cardozo Law Review* (1996): 1695–1710.

Lewis, Walker. *Without Fear or Favor: A Biography of Chief Justice Roger Brooke Taney.* Boston: Houghton Mifflin, 1965.

Newmyer, R. Kent. *The Supreme Court under Marshall and Taney.* 1968. Reprint. Arlington Heights, Ill.: Harlan Davidson, 1986.

Palmer, Benjamin Whipple. *Marshall and Taney: Statesmen of the Law.* 1939. Reprint. New York: Russell and Russell, 1966.

Siegel, Martin. *The Taney Court, 1836–1864.* Millwood, N.Y.: Associated Faculty Press, 1987.

Smith, Charles W. *Roger B. Taney: Jacksonian Jurist.* 1936. Reprint. New York: Da Capo Press, 1973.

Steiner, Bernard Christian. *Life of Roger Brooke Taney, Chief Justice of the United States Supreme Court.* Westport, Conn.: Greenwood Press, 1970.

Swisher, Carl Brent. *Roger B. Taney.* New York: Macmillan Company, 1935.

Tyler, Samuel. *Memoir of Roger Brooke Taney.* 1872. Reprint. New York: Da Capo Press, 1970.

Thomas, Clarence

Black, Virginia. "Natural Law, Constitutional Adjudication and Clarence Thomas." *U.C. Davis Law Review* 26 (1993): 769–789.

Chrisman, Robert and Robert L. Allen, eds. *Court of Appeal: The Black Community Speaks out on the Racial and Sexual Politics of Clarence Thomas vs. Anita Hill.* New York: Ballantine Books, 1992.

Danforth, John C. *Resurrection: The Confirmation of Clarence Thomas.* New York: Viking, 1994.

Flax, Jane. *The American Dream in Black & White: The Clarence Thomas Hearings.* Ithaca, N.Y.: Cornell University Press, 1998.

Gerber, Scott Douglas. *First Principles: The Jurisprudence of Clarence Thomas.* New York: New York University Press, 1999.

Gerhardt, Michael J. "Divided Justice: A Commentary on the Nomination and Confirmation of Justice Thomas." *George Washington Law Review* 60 (1992): 969–996.

Levy, Jared A. "Blinking at Reality: The Implications of Justice Clarence Thomas's Influential Approach to Race and Education." *Boston University Law Review* 78 (1998): 575–619.

Marcosson, Samuel. "Colorizing the Constitution of Originalism: Clarence Thomas at the Rubicon." *Law & Inequality: A Journal of Theory and Practice* 16 (1998): 429–491.

Mayer, Jane and Jill Abramson. *Strange Justice: The Selling of Clarence Thomas.* New York: Plume, 1995.

Morrison, Toni, ed. *Race-ing Justice, En-gendering Power: Essays on Anita Hill, Clarence Thomas, and the Construction of Social Reality.* New York: Pantheon Books, 1992.

Muller, Eric L. "Where, but for the Grace of God, Goes He? The Search for Empathy in the Criminal Jurisprudence of Clarence Thomas." *Constitutional Commentary* 15 (1998): 225–250.

Nagel, Robert F. "The Thomas Hearings: Watching Ourselves." *Colorado Law Review* 63 (1992): 945–952.

Phelps, Timothy M. *Capitol Games: Clarence Thomas, Anita Hill, and the Story of a Supreme Court Nomination.* New York: Hyperion, 1992.

Ragan, Sandra L., ed. *The Lynching of Language: Gender, Politics, and Power in the Hill-Thomas Hearings.* Urbana: University of Illinois Press, 1996.

Roberts, Ronald Suresh. *Clarence Thomas and the Tough Love Crowd: Counterfeit Heroes and Unhappy Truths.* New York: New York University Press, 1995.

Siegel, Paul. *Outsiders Looking in: A Communication Perspective on the Hill/Thomas Hearings.* Cresskill, N.J.: Hampton Press, 1996.

Simon, Paul. *Advice & Consent: Clarence Thomas, Robert Bork, and the Intriguing History of the Supreme Court's Nomination Battles.* Washington, D.C.: National Press Books, 1992.

Smith, Christopher E. "Clarence Thomas: A Distinctive Justice." *Seton Hall Law Review* 28 (1997): 1–28.

———. *Critical Judicial Nominations and Political Change: The Impact of Clarence Thomas.* Westport, Conn.: Praeger, 1993.

Taylor, Kim A. "Invisible Woman: Reflections on the Clarence Thomas Confirmation Hearing." *Stanford Law Review* 45 (1993): 443–452.

Thomas, Clarence. *Clarence Thomas—Confronting the Future: Selections from the Senate Confirmation Hearings and Prior Speeches.* Introduction by Gordon Crovitz. Washington, D.C.: Regnery Gateway, 1992.

Thompson, Smith

Dunne, Gerald T. "Smith Thompson." In *The Justices of the United States Supreme Court 1789–1969: Their Lives and Major Opinions,* vol. 1. Edited by Leon Friedman and Fred L. Israel. New York: R. R. Bowker Co., 1969.

Hammond, J. *The History of Political Parties in the State of New York.* Albany: n.p., 1842.

Lobingier, Charles S. "The Judicial Opinions of Mr. Justice Thompson." *Nebraska Bar Bulletin* 12 (1924): 421–426.

Roper, Donald Malcolm. *Mr. Justice Thompson and the Constitution.* 1963. Reprint. New York: Garland, 1987.

Todd, Thomas

Currie, David P. "The Most Insignificant Justice: A Preliminary Inquiry." *University of Chicago Law Review* 50 (1983): 466–480.

Easterbrook, Frank H. "The Most Insignificant Justice: Further Evidence." *University of Chicago Law Review* 50 (1983): 481–503.

Gardner, Woodford L., Jr. "Kentucky Justices on the U.S. Supreme Court." *Register of the Kentucky Historical Society* 70 (1972): 121–142.

Israel, Fred L. "Thomas Todd." In *The Justices of the United States Supreme Court 1789–1969: Their Lives and Major Opinions,* vol. 1. Edited by Leon Friedman and Fred L. Israel. New York: R. R. Bowker Co., 1969.

Levin, H. "Thomas Todd." In *The Lawyers and Law Makers of Kentucky.* Chicago: Lewis Publishing Co., 1897.

O'Rear, Edward C. "Justice Thomas Todd." *Kentucky State Historical Society Record* 38 (1940): 112–119.

Trimble, Robert

Goff, John S. "Mr Justice Trimble of the United States Supreme Court." *Kentucky Historical Society Register* 58 (1960): 6–28.

Israel, Fred L. "Robert Trimble." In *The Justices of the United States Supreme Court 1789–1969: Their Lives and Major Opinions,* vol. 1. Edited by Leon Friedman and Fred L. Israel. New York: R. R. Bowker Co., 1969.

Schneider, Alan N. "Robert Trimble: A Kentucky Justice on the Supreme Court." *Kentucky State Bar Journal* 12 (1947): 21–30.

Van Devanter, Willis

Burner, David. "Willis Van Devanter." In *The Justices of the United States Supreme Court 1789–1969: Their Lives and Major Opinions,* vol. 3. Edited by Leon Friedman and Fred L. Israel. New York: R. R. Bowker Co., 1969.

Cushman, Barry. "The Secret Lives of the Four Horsemen." *Virginia Law Review* 83 (1997): 559–645.

Holsinger, M. Paul. "The Appointment of Supreme Court Justice Van Devanter: A Study of Political Preferment." *American Journal of Legal History* 12 (1968): 324–335.

———. "Willis Van Devanter: Wyoming Leader, 1884–1897." *Annals of Wyoming* 37 (1965): 170–206.

Nelson, Daniel A. "The Supreme Court Appointment of Willis Van Devanter." *Annals of Wyoming* 53 (1981): 2–11.

Van Devanter, Willis. "Justice Van Devanter's Remarks to the Montana and Wyoming Bar Associations in 1937." *Supreme Court Historical Society Yearbook* (1986): 64–76.

Vinson, Fred Moore

Bolner, James. "Mr. Chief Justice Vinson and the Communist Controversy: A Reassessment." *Register of the Kentucky Historical Society* 66 (1968): 378–391.

Franck, Matthew J. "The Last Justice Without a Theory: Fred M. Vinson." In *Sober as a Judge: The Supreme Court and Republican Liberty.* Edited by Richard G. Stevens and Matthew J. Franck. Lanham, Md.: Lexington Books, 1999.

Frank, John P. "Fred M. Vinson and the Chief Justiceship." *University of Chicago Law Review* 21 (1954): 212–46.

Langram, Robert W. "Why Are Some Supreme Court Justices Rates as 'Failures'?" *Supreme Court Historical Society Yearbook* (1985): 8–14.

Lefberg, Irving F. "Chief Justice Vinson and the Politics of Desegregation." *Emory Law Journal* 24 (1975): 243–312.

Palmer, Jan S. *The Vinson Court Era: The Supreme Court's Conference Votes: Data and Analysis.* New York: AMS Press, 1990.

Pritchett, C. Herman. *Civil Liberties and the Vinson Court.* Chicago: University of Chicago Press, 1954.

Symposium. "In Memoriam: Chief Justice Fred M. Vinson." *Northwestern University Law Review* 49 (1954): 1–75.

Urofsky, Melvin I. *Division and Discord: The Supreme Court under Stone and Vinson, 1941–1953.* Columbia: University of South Carolina Press, 1997.

Waite, Morrison Romick

Magrath, C. Peter. *Morrison K. Waite: The Triumph of Character.* New York: Macmillan, 1963.

Morris, Jeffrey Brandon. "Morrison Waite's Court." In *Supreme Court Historical Society Yearbook, 1980.* Washington, D.C.: Supreme Court Historical Society, 1980.

Stephenson, D. Grier, Jr. "The Chief Justice as Leader: The Case of Morrison Remick Waite." *William and Mary Law Review* 14 (1973): 899–927.

Trimble, Bruce Raymond. *Chief Justice Waite, Defender of the Public Interest.* 1938. Reprint. New York: Russell and Russell, 1970.

Warren, Earl

Cray, Ed. *Chief Justice: A Biography of Earl Warren.* New York: Simon & Schuster, 1997.

Horwitz, Morton J. *The Warren Court and the Pursuit of Justice.* New York: Hill and Wang, 1998.

Kurland, Philip B. *Politics, the Constitution, and the Warren Court.* Chicago: University of Chicago Press, 1970.

Lewis, Frederick P. *The Context of Judicial Activism: The Endurance of the Warren Court Legacy in a Conservative Age.* Lanham, Md.: Rowman & Littlefield, 1999.

Pollack, Jack Harrison. *Earl Warren: The Judge Who Changed America.* Englewood Cliffs, N.J.: Prentice Hall, 1979.

Schwartz, Bernard. *Inside the Warren Court.* Garden City, N.Y.: Doubleday, 1983.

———. *Super Chief: Earl Warren and His Supreme Court.* New York: New York University Press, 1983.

Schwartz, Bernard, ed. *The Warren Court: A Retrospective.* New York: Oxford University Press, 1996.

Tushnet, Mark, ed. *The Warren Court in Historical and Political Perspective.* Charlottesville: University Press of Virginia, 1993.

Warren, Earl. *The Memoirs of Earl Warren.* Garden City, N.Y.: Doubleday, 1977.

———. *The Public Papers of Chief Justice Earl Warren.* Edited by Henry M. Christman. New York: Simon & Schuster, 1959.

White, G. Edward. *Earl Warren: A Public Life.* New York: Oxford University Press, 1982.

Washington, Bushrod

Binney, Horace. *Bushrod Washington.* Philadelphia: C. Sherman & Son, 1858.

Blaustein, Albert P. and Roy M. Mersky. "Bushrod Washington." In *The Justices of the United States Supreme Court 1789–1969: Their Lives and Major Opinions,* vol. 1. Edited by Leon Friedman and Fred L. Israel. New York: R. R. Bowker Co., 1969.

Stoner, James R. Jr., "Heir Apparent: Bushrod Washington and Federal Justice in the Early Republic." In *Seriatim: The Supreme Court Before John Marshall.* Edited by Scott Douglas Gerber. New York: New York University Press, 1998.

Wayne, James Moore

Battle, George G. "James Moore Wayne: Southern Unionist." *Fordham Urban Law Journal* 14 (1964): 42–59.

Lawrence, Alexander A. *James Moore Wayne, Southern Unionist.* Westport, Conn.: Greenwood Press, 1943; Reprint 1970.

O'Connor, Sandra Day. "Supreme Court Justices from Georgia." *The Georgia Journal of Southern Legal History* 1 (Fall-Winter 1991): 395–405.

White, Byron Raymond

Hutchinson, Dennis J. *The Man Who Once Was Whizzer White: A Portrait of Justice Byron R. White.* New York: Free Press, 1998.

Ides, Allan. "The Jurisprudence of Justice Byron White." *Yale Law Journal* 103 (1993): 419–461.

Kramer, Daniel C. "Justice Byron R. White: Good Friend to Polity and Solon." In *The Burger Court: Political and Judicial Profiles.* Edited by Charles M. Lamb and Stephen C. Halpern. Urbana: University of Illinois Press, 1991.

Lee, Rex E. "On Greatness and Constitutional Vision: Justice Byron R. White." *Journal of Supreme Court History* (1993): 5–10.

Nelson, William E. "Justice Byron R. White: A Modern Federalist and a New Deal Liberal." *Brigham Young University Law Review* (1994): 313–348.

"A Tribute to Justice Byron R. White." *Harvard Law Review* 107 (1993): xii–26.

"A Tribute to Justice Byron R. White." *Yale Law Journal* 103 (1993): 1–56.

White, Edward Douglass

Cassidy, Lews C. "An Evaluation of Chief Justice White." *Mississippi Law Journal* 10 (1938): 136–153.

Fegin, Hugh E. "Edward Douglass White, Jurist and Statesman." *Georgetown Law Journal* 14 (1925): 1–21; and 15 (1926): 148–168.

Highsaw, Robert Baker. *Edward Douglass White: Defender of the Conservative Faith.* Baton Rouge: Louisiana State University Press, 1981.

Stevens, Dennis G. "Constitutional Jurisprudence at the Crossroads: Edward Douglass White." In *Sober as a Judge: The Supreme Court and Republican Liberty.* Edited by Richard G. Stevens and Matthew J. Franck. Lanham, Md.: Lexington Books, 1999.

Whittaker, Charles Evans

Berman, D.M. "Mr. Justice Whittaker: A Preliminary Appraisal." *Missouri Law Review* 24 (1959): 1–15.

Friedman, Leon. "Charles Whittaker." In *The Justices of the United States Supreme Court 1789–1969: Their Lives and Major Opinions,* vol. 4. Edited by Leon Friedman and Fred L. Israel. New York: R. R. Bowker Co., 1969.

Wilson, James

Conrad, Stephen A. "The Rhetorical Constitution of Civil Society at the Founding: One Lawyer's Anxious Vision." *Indiana Law Journal* 72 (1997): 335–373.

———. "James Wilson's 'Assimilation of the Common-Law Mind.'" *Northwestern University Law Review* 84 (1989): 186–219.

———. "Metaphor and Imagination in James Wilson's Federal Union." *Law and Social Inquiry* 13 (1988): 1–70.

———. "Polite Foundation: Citizenship and Common Sense in James Wilson's Republican Theory." *Supreme Court Review* (1984): 359–388.

Frohnen, Bruce. "The Bases of Professional Responsibility: Pluralism and Community in Early America." *George Washington Law Review* 63 (1995): 931–954.

Hall, Mark David. *The Political and Legal Philosophy of James Wilson 1742–1798.* Columbia: University of Missouri Press, 1997.

———. "James Wilson: Democratic Theorist and Supreme Court Justice." In *Seriatim: The Supreme Court Before John Marshall.* Edited by Scott Douglas Gerber. New York: New York University Press, 1998.

Hills, Roderick M., Jr. "The Reconciliation of Law and Liberty in James Wilson." *Harvard Journal of Law and Public Policy* 12 (1989): 891–940.

Pascal, Jean M. *The Political Ideas of James Wilson, 1742–1798.* New York: Garland Publishing, 1991.

Smith, Page. *James Wilson, Founding Father, 1741–1798.* Chapel Hill: University of North Carolina Press for the Institute of Early American History and Culture, 1956.

Wilson, James. *The Works of James Wilson, Associate Justice of the Supreme Court of the United States . . . Being His Public Discourses Upon Jurisprudence and the Political Science, Including Lectures as Professor of Law, 1790–2.* Edited by James DeWitt Andrews. Chicago: Callaghan and Company, 1896.

Woodbury, Levi

Bader, William D., Henry J. Abraham, and James B. Staab. "The Jurisprudence of Levi Woodbury." *Vermont Law Review* (1994): 261–312.

Woodbury, Charles Levi. *Memoir of Honorable Levi Woodbury, LL.D.* Boston: David Clapp and Son, 1894.

Woodbury, Levi. *Writings of Levi Woodbury, LL.D., Political, Judicial and Literary.* Boston: Little, Brown, 1852.

Woods, William Burnham

Baynes, Thomas E. "A Search for Justice Woods: Yankee from Georgia." *Supreme Court Historical Society Yearbook, 1978.* Washington, D.C.: Supreme Court Historical Society, 1978.

Filler, Louis. "William B. Woods." In *The Justices of the United States Supreme Court 1789–1969: Their Lives and Major Opinions,* vol. 2. Edited by Leon Friedman and Fred L. Israel. New York: R. R. Bowker Co., 1969.

INDEX

Locators for main entries are set in **boldface.** Locators for photographs are set in *italics*. Locators for glossary entries are followed by *g*, for chronology entries by *c*, and for material in the appendixes by *a*.

A

Abington School District v. Schempp 443*c*, 455*a*
 Warren Burger and 386
 Tom C. Clark and 343
 Earl Warren and 351
abortion rights. *See also Roe. v. Wade.*
 Harry A. Blackmun and 389–390
 Stephen G. Breyer and 430
 Warren Burger and 386
 Anthony Kennedy and 414, 415
 Sandra Day O'Connor and 406
 Lewis F. Powell, Jr., and 394
 William H. Rehnquist and 397
 Antonin Scalia and 410
 David H. Souter and 417, 418
 John Paul Stevens and 402
 Clarence Thomas and 422
 Byron R. White and 370
Abrams v. United States 455*a*
 John H. Clarke and 272
 Oliver Wendell Holmes, Jr., and 233
abstention 433*g*
accessory 433*g*
accused 433*g*
ACLU. *See* American Civil Liberties Union.
acquittal 433*g*
actionable 433*g*
activist judges. *See* judicial activism.
Adair v. United States 455*a*
Adams, John 439*c*
 and William Cushing 11–12
 and Oliver Ellsworth 38
 and John Jay 8
 and John Marshall 47
 and Alfred Moore 44
 and William Paterson 31
 and Bushrod Washington 40–41
Adams, John Quincy 440*c*
 and Philip Barbour 97
 and John McLean 79–80
 and Robert Trimble 75
Adams, Samuel 12
Adamson v. California 309, 455*a*
Adams v. Storey 57
Adarand Constructors, Inc. v. Pena 455*a*
 Ruth Bader Ginsburg and 426
 Anthony Kennedy and 414
 Sandra Day O'Connor and 406
 David H. Souter and 418
 Clarence Thomas and 423
 Adkins v. Children's Hospital 281, 282, 455*a*
admiralty law 191
affidavit 433*g*
affirmative action 433*g*
 William J. Brennan, Jr., and 361
 Ruth Bader Ginsburg and 426
 Anthony Kennedy and 414
 Sandra Day O'Connor and 406
 Lewis F. Powell, Jr., and 394
 William H. Rehnquist and 398
 David H. Souter and 418
 Clarence Thomas and 421–423
AFL. *See* American Federation of Labor.
aggravation 433*g*
Agnew, Spiro T. 444*c*
Agostini v. Felton 455*a*
Agricultural Adjustment Act 297
Akron v. Akron Center for Reproductive Health, Inc. 455*a*
Alabama
 Hugo Black and 304
 John A. Campbell and 128
 John McKinley and 104, 105
 William Woods and 179
Albertson v. Subversive Activities Control Board 456*a*
Alden v. Maine 430, 445*c*, 456*a*
Aldrich, James A. 324
Aldridge v. United States 264
Alexander v. Holmes County Board of Education 456*a*
Alien and Sedition Act 30–31, 440*c*
Allegheny County v. ACLU Greater Pittsburgh Chapter 456*a*
Allgeyer v. Louisiana 224, 456*a*
American Civil Liberties Union (ACLU) 425, 426
American Communications Association v. Douds 456*a*
American Federation of Labor (AFL) 373
American Revolution 439*c*
 Samuel Chase and 33
 William Cushing and 11
 Gabriel Duvall and 63
 James Iredell and 22
 John Jay and 6
 Thomas Johnson and 26
 H. Brockholst Livingston and 56
 John Marshall and 47
 Alfred Moore and 44
 John Rutledge and 19
 Thomas Todd and 60
 Bushrod Washington and 40
 James M. Wayne and 87
 James Wilson and 2
amicus curiae briefs 343, 433*g*
Amistad 456*a*
Anderson, Myers 421
Andrew, John A. 187
Antelope, The
 Joseph Story and 68
 Robert Trimble and 76
Anthony, Susan B. 165, 167
anti-Semitism 262, 264
antitrust cases 342, 401. *See also* Sherman Antitrust Act.
antitrust law 433*g*
Apodaca v. Oregon 456*a*–457*a*
appeal 433*g*
appellant 433*g*
appellee 433*g*
Application of Yamashita 332
Apprendi v. New Jersey 457*a*
Aptheker v. Secretary of State 457*a*
arbitration 433*g*
Argersinger v. Hamlin 457*a*
Arizona 405
Arizona v. Fulminate 457*a*
Arlington Heights v. Metropolitan Housing Development Corp. 457*a*
arraignment 433*g*
arrest 433*g*
Arthur, Chester A. 441*c*
 and Samuel Blatchford 191
 and David Brewer 203
 and David Davis 144
 and Horace Gray 188
 and Ward Hunt 167
Ashwander v. Tennessee Valley Authority 457*a*
assignment of error 433*g*
attempt 433*g*
Austin v. United States 457*a*

B

Babbit, Bruce 405
Bacon, Augustus O. 258
bail 433*g*
Bailey, James A. 244
Bailey, James E. 215
Bailey v. Drexel Furniture Co. 277, 457*a*–458*a*
Baker v. Carr 443*c*, 458*a*
 William J. Brennan, Jr., and 360
 Felix Frankfurter and 314
 Earl Warren and 351
Bakke case. *See Regents of the University of California v. Bakke.*
Baldwin, Henry *82*, **82–85,** 120, 447*a*
Ballard v. United States 458*a*

Ballew v. Georgia 458*a*
Bank of Augusta v. Earle 104–105, 458*a*
Bank of North America 2
Bank of the United States 440*c*
Henry Baldwin and 84
Philip Barbour and 97
John Marshall and 49
Roger Taney and 91
James M. Wayne and 87
Bank of the United States v. Deveaux 458*a*
bankruptcy 433*g*
Barbour, James 96
Barbour, Philip Pendleton *95,* **95–98,** 447*a*
and Gabriel Duvall 64
and Roger Taney 92
Barenblatt v. United States 458*a*
Barker v. Wingo 458*a*
Barnes v. Glen Theatre 458*a*
Barron v. Baltimore 176, 440*c*, 459*a*
Bas v. Tingy 45
Bates v. State Bar of Arizona 459*a*
Batson v. Kentucky 459*a*
Bay of Pigs 443*c*
Beal, Gen. W. N. R. 219
Belle Terre v. Boraas 459*a*
Bennis v. Michigan 459*a*
Benton v. Maryland 459*a*
Berman v. Parker 459*a*
Betts v. Brady 459*a*
beyond a reasonable doubt 433*g*
Bigelow v. Virginia 460*a*
bill of attainder 433*g*
Bill of Rights 433*g*, 439*c*, 509*a*–510*a*. *See also individual amendments.*
Hugo Black and 305
Benjamin N. Cardozo and 302
William O. Douglas and 317
Felix Frankfurter and 314
John Marshall Harlan and 176
Robert Jackson and 328
William Moody and 241
Edward T. Sanford and 288
Harlan Fiske Stone and 292
Birney, James G. 154
Bituminous Coal Act of 1935 297
Bivens v. Six Unknown Named Agents 460*a*
Black, Hugo Lafayette *303,* **303–306,** 449*a*
and William O. Douglas 315–317
and Felix Frankfurter 314
and Arthur J. Goldberg 373
and Robert Jackson 328, 329
and Sherman Minton 347
and Lewis F. Powell, Jr., 393
and Stanley Reed 309
and Owen J. Roberts 298
and Wiley Rutledge 332
and Harlan Fiske Stone 293
and Fred M. Vinson 338, 339
"Black Monday" 250
Blackmun, Harry Andrew *388,* **388–391,** 450*a*
and Stephen G. Breyer 430
and William H. Rehnquist 397
and John Paul Stevens 401, 402
Blair, John, Jr., 12, *14,* **14–16,** 446*a*
Blatchford, Samuel *190,* **190–193,** 448*a*
and Rufus Peckham, Jr., 223
and Edward Douglass White 220
blue laws 433*g*
BMW of North America, Inc. v. Gore 460*a*
Board of Education of Cincinnati v. Minor 183
Board of Education of Kiryas Joel Village School District v. Grumet 460*a*
Board of Regents of University of Wisconsin System v. Southworth 460*a*
Bolling v. Sharpe 460*a*
Bonus Bill of 1817 96
Boone, Thomas 18
Borden, Lizzie murder case 240
Bordley, Stephen 26
Bork, Robert
and Anthony Kennedy 412, 413
and David H. Souter 417
and Clarence Thomas 422
Boston Massacre 439*c*
Boston Tea Party 439*c*
Bowers v. Hardwick 444*c*, 460*a*
Lewis F. Powell, Jr., and 394
Byron R. White and 370
Bowsher v. Synar 460*a*
boycott 433*g*
Boy Scouts of America v. Dale 418, 460*a*
Bradley, Joseph P. *161,* **161–164,** 448*a*
and L. Q. C. Lamar 197
and George Shiras, Jr., 211
and William Strong 158, 159
and William Woods 179
Bradwell v. Illinois 163–164, 460*a*–461*a*
Brady Handgun Violence Prevention Act 402
Brady v. United States 461*a*
Brandeis, Louis Dembitz *267,* **267–270,** 449*a*
and David Brewer 205
and Benjamin N. Cardozo 301
and John H. Clarke 272, 273
and William O. Douglas 316
and Felix Frankfurter 312
and Horace Gray 187
and Oliver Wendell Holmes, Jr., 233
and Robert Jackson 327
and James C. McReynolds 263, 264
and Mahlon Pitney 261
and Owen J. Roberts 296
and Harlan Fiske Stone 292
and Willis Van Devanter 254
Brandenburg v. Ohio 444*c*, 461*a*
Branzburg v. Hayes 461*a*
breach of the peace 433*g*
Brecht v. Abrahamson 461*a*
Breedlove v. Suttles 461*a*
Brennan, Jr., William J. *358,* **358–361,** 450*a*
and Harold H. Burton 336
and Arthur J. Goldberg 373
and Thurgood Marshall 382
and Antonin Scalia 410
and David H. Souter 416–418
and John Paul Stevens 401
Brewer, David Josiah *202,* **202–205,** 448*a*
and Henry Brown 208
and Stephen J. Field 151
and John Marshall Harlan 176–177
and Charles Evans Hughes 249
and Howell E. Jackson 216
Breyer, Stephen G. 418, *428,* **428–431,** 451*a*
brief 433*g*
Briscoe v. Bank of the Commonwealth of Kentucky
Philip Barbour and 97
Roger Taney and 92
Bristow, Benjamin H. 174
Bronson v. Kinzie 461*a*–462*a*
Brown, Henry Billings *206,* **206–209,** 448*a*
and David Brewer 203
and John Marshall Harlan 176
and Howell E. Jackson 216
and Horace Lurton 245
and William Moody 241
Brown, James 75
Browning-Ferris Industries v. Kelco Disposal, Inc. 462*a*
Brown v. Board of Education 443*c*, 462*a*
Harold H. Burton and 336
John Marshall Harlan and 176
John Marshall Harlan II and 355–356
Robert Jackson and 329
Thurgood Marshall and 380–383
Sherman Minton and 345, 347
Lewis F. Powell, Jr., and 393
Stanley Reed and 309
William H. Rehnquist and 397
Earl Warren and 349, 351
Brown v. Maryland 462*a*
Brown v. Mississippi 462*a*
Bryan, William Jennings 272
Buchanan, James 440*c*
and John Catron 101
and Nathan Clifford 134
and Benjamin R. Curtis 126
and Robert C. Grier 121
and Stanley Matthews 183
and Roger Taney 93
Buchanan v. Warley 462*a*
Buckley v. Valeo 444*c*, 462*a*
Buck v. Bell 285–286, 462*a*
Budd v. New York 192, 462*a*
Bunting v. Oregon 462*a*
Burger, Warren Earl *384,* **384–387,** 444*c*, 450*a*
and Harry A. Blackmun 388, 389
and William J. Brennan, Jr., 358, 361
and Thurgood Marshall 382
and Sandra Day O'Connor 404
and William H. Rehnquist 397, 398
and Antonin Scalia 409
and John Paul Stevens 401
and Earl Warren 352
Burlington Industries, Inc. v. Ellerth 462*a*–463*a*
Burr, Aaron 440*c*
and Oliver Ellsworth 37
and H. Brockholst Livingston 56
Burton, Harold Hitz *334,* **334–336,** 450*a*
and Sherman Minton 347
and Potter Stewart 366
Burton v. Wilmington Parking Authority 463*a*

Bush, George Herbert Walker 444*c*
and William H. Rehnquist 398
and David H. Souter 416, 417
and Clarence Thomas 420, 422
Bush, George W. 445*c*
Bush v. Gore 445*c,* 463*a*
Bush v. Vera 463*a*
Butler, Pierce *283,* **283–286,** 449*a*
and James C. McReynolds 265
and Frank Murphy 321
and Harlan Fiske Stone 292
and George Sutherland 279
and Willis Van Devanter 254
Butz v. Economou 463*a*
Bylew v. United States 159
Byrnes, James Francis *323,* **323–325,** 331, 450*a*

C

C & A Carbone, Inc. v. Clarkstown 463*a*
Calder v. Bull 34, 463*a*
Calhoun, John C.
and Henry Baldwin 83
and John McLean 80
California
Stephen G. Breyer and 428–429
Stephen J. Field and 149–150
Anthony Kennedy and 413
Joseph McKenna and 227
Sandra Day O'Connor and 405
Earl Warren and 350
Cameron, James Donald 211
Cameron, Simon 154
Campbell, John Archibald *127,* **127–131,** 447*a*
and David Davis 146
and Samuel Miller 142
and Samuel Nelson 113
and James M. Wayne 88
and William Woods 179, 180
Cantwell v. Connecticut 297, 464*a*
capital crime 433*g*
capital punishment 433*g. See* death penalty.
Cardozo, Benjamin Nathan *299,* **299–302,** 449*a*
and Felix Frankfurter 312, 313
and James C. McReynolds 264
and Harlan Fiske Stone 292
Carmel v. Texas 464*a*
Carroll, Charles 26
Carroll v. United States 464*a*
Carswell, G. Harrold
and Harry A. Blackmun 389
and Lewis F. Powell, Jr., 393–394
Carter, Jimmy 444*c*
and Stephen G. Breyer 429
and Ruth Bader Ginsburg 426
and Arthur J. Goldberg 374
and Antonin Scalia 409
Carter v. Carter Coal Co. 297, 464*a*
case law 433*g*
case method of legal instruction 433*g*
cases, important 455*a*–503*a*
Cass, Lewis 117
Catron, John *99,* **99–102,** 447*a*
and John A. Campbell 128
and David Davis 146
and Robert C. Grier 121
cause of action 433*g*
centrist judges
Stephen G. Breyer **428–431**
David H. Souter **416–419**
certiorari, writ of 434*g*
chambers 434*g*
Chambers, Henry 104
Chambers v. Florida 305, 464*a*
Champion v. Ames 441*c,* 464*a*
Chaplinsky v. New Hampshire 464*a*
Charles River Bridge Co. v. Warren Bridge Co. 464*a*
Philip Barbour and 97
John McLean and 80
Roger Taney and 92
Chase, Jeremiah 91
Chase, Salmon Portland *153,* **153–156,** 441*c,* 448*a*
and Joseph P. Bradley 162
and Ward Hunt 166
and Samuel Miller 142
and William Strong 159
and Noah H. Swayne 137, 138
and Morrison Waite 168, 169
Chase, Samuel *32,* **32–35,** 446*a*
and Gabriel Duvall 63
and Thomas Johnson 26
Chauncey, Charles 87
Cherokee nation 87
Cherokee Nation v. Georgia 440*c,* 465*a*
Henry Baldwin and 84
John McLean and 80
Smith Thompson and 72–73
Chicago, Burlington & Quincy Railroad Company v. Chicago 465*a*
Chicago, Milwaukee & St. Paul Railway Company v. Minnesota 465*a*
Samuel Blatchford and 192
David Brewer and 204
L. Q. C. Lamar and 197
Chicago v. Morales 465*a*
Child Labor Act 237–238
child labor laws 277
Chimel v. California 465*a*
Chisholm v. Georgia 439*c,* 465*a*
John Blair, Jr., and 15–16
William Cushing and 12
James Iredell and 23–24
John Jay and 7
James Wilson and 3
chronology 439*c*–445*a*
church and state, separation of
Warren Burger and 386
Tom C. Clark and 343
Ruth Bader Ginsburg and 426
Anthony Kennedy and 414
Stanley Matthews and 183
Sandra Day O'Connor and 406
Wiley Rutledge and 332
David H. Souter and 418
John Paul Stevens and 402
Earl Warren and 351
Church of the Lukumi Babalu Aye v. Hialeah 465*a*
CIO. *See* Congress of Industrial Organizations.
Circuit Court of Appeals Act of 1891 200
circuit courts/circuit riding 434*g*
William Cushing and 12
Peter V. Daniel and 108
Melville W. Fuller and 200
Robert C. Grier and 121
James Iredell and 23
Howell E. Jackson and 216
John Jay and 7
Thomas Johnson and 27
John McKinley and 104–106
John McLean and 79
Alfred Moore and 45
Samuel Nelson and 112
William Paterson and 29–31
John Rutledge and 17, 19
Joseph Story and 68
Bushrod Washington and 41
James M. Wayne and 89
William Woods and 179
Circuit Courts of Appeals 167
circumstantial evidence 434*g*
citation 434*g*
City of Boerne v. Flores 399, 465*a*
City of Laude v. Gilleo 465*a*
civil action 434*g*
civil liberties
William J. Brennan, Jr., and 358
Pierce Butler and 285
William O. Douglas and 317
Abe Fortas and 377
Horace Gray and 188
John Marshall Harlan II and 356
Charles Evans Hughes and 250
Robert Jackson and 328, 329
Thurgood Marshall and 382
James C. McReynolds and 264
Frank Murphy and 319
Wiley Rutledge and 332
George Shiras, Jr., and 212
civil rights 443*c. See also specific headings.*
William J. Brennan, Jr., and 358
Henry Brown and 206, 208, 209
Harold H. Burton and 336
Pierce Butler and 285
Tom C. Clark and 343
William O. Douglas and 317
Stephen J. Field and 150–151
Ruth Bader Ginsburg and 427
John Marshall Harlan and 175–176
John Marshall Harlan II and 356
Charles Evans Hughes and 250
Ward Hunt and 166–167
Robert Jackson and 328
Thurgood Marshall and 380–382
Stanley Matthews and 184
James C. McReynolds and 264
Sherman Minton and 347
Frank Murphy and 319–321
Lewis F. Powell, Jr., and 393
Stanley Reed and 309
William H. Rehnquist and 397, 399
Owen J. Roberts and 297
Wiley Rutledge and 332
Potter Stewart and 366
William Strong and 159
Clarence Thomas and 420–422
Fred M. Vinson and 339–340
Morrison Waite and 170, 172
Earl Warren and 351

Byron R. White and 370
William Woods and 180
Civil Rights Act of 1866 159
Civil Rights Act of 1875
Joseph P. Bradley and 163
John Marshall Harlan and 175
Morrison Waite and 170
Civil Rights Cases 441*c*, 466*a*
Joseph P. Bradley and 163
John Marshall Harlan and 175
Morrison Waite and 170–171
civil service 434*g*
Civil War 441*c*
Henry Brown and 207
John A. Campbell and 127, 129–130
John Catron and 101–102
Salmon P. Chase and 154–155
David Davis and 146
Stephen J. Field and 150
Melville W. Fuller and 199
Robert C. Grier and 119, 121–122
John Marshall Harlan and 174
Oliver Wendell Holmes, Jr., and 231
Howell E. Jackson and 215
L. Q. C. Lamar and 196
Horace Lurton and 244
Stanley Matthews and 183
Samuel Miller and 141–142
Samuel Nelson and 113
Noah H. Swayne and 138
James M. Wayne and 86, 88
Edward Douglass White and 219
William Woods and 179
Clark, Thomas Campbell *341,* **341–344,** 450*a*
and Thurgood Marshall 382
and Sherman Minton 347
Clark, William Ramsey
and Tom C. Clark 343
and Thurgood Marshall 382
Clarke, John Hessin *271,* **271–273,** 281, 449*a*
class action suit 434*g*
Clay, Henry
and Philip Barbour 96
and John McKinley 104
and Bushrod Washington 40
Clayton Antitrust Act 281
Cleveland, Grover 441*c*
and Stephen J. Field 151
and Melville W. Fuller 200
and Howell E. Jackson 216
and L. Q. C. Lamar 196
and Horace Lurton 245
and Samuel Miller 143
and Rufus Peckham, Jr., 223, 224
and Edward Douglass White 220
Clifford, Nathan *132,* **132–135,** 187–188, 447*a*
Clinton, Bill 444*c*, 445*c*
and Stephen G. Breyer 428–430
and Ruth Bader Ginsburg 424, 426
impeachment 445*c*
and Byron Raymond White 370
Clinton v. City of New York 466*a*
Clinton v. Jones 466*a*
Clinton v. New York 445*c*
Cohens v. Virginia 466*a*
Cohen v. California 356, 466*a*
Coker v. Georgia 466*a*
cold war 347
Colegrove v. Green 466*a*
Coleman v. Miller 466*a*
Collector v. Day 466*a*
Colorado
Wiley Rutledge and 331
Byron R. White and 369
Columbus Board of Education v. Penick 467*a*
Commerce Clause cases 125
commercial cases 57
common law 434*g*
Common Law, The (Oliver Wendell Holmes, Jr.) 231–232
Communist Party v. Subversive Activities Control Board 467*a*
compensatory damages 434*g*
Compromise of 1850 154
Compromise of 1877
Stanley Matthews and 184
Edward Douglass White and 219
concurring opinion 434*g*
confession 434*g*
Congress of Industrial Organizations (CIO) 373
Conkling, Roscoe
and Samuel Blatchford 191
and Ward Hunt 166, 167
Connecticut
Henry Baldwin and 83
Henry Brown and 207
Oliver Ellsworth and 36–37
Stephen J. Field and 149
Ward Hunt and 166
William Strong and 158
Morrison Waite and 169
Connelly, W. B. 183
consent decree 434*g*
conservatism, judicial. *See* judicial conservatism.
conservative judges
David Brewer **202–205**
Warren Burger **384–387**
Pierce Butler **283–286**
Nathan Clifford **132–135**
Peter V. Daniel **107–110**
Melville W. Fuller and **198–201**
James C. McReynolds **262–265**
Sherman Minton **345–347**
Rufus Peckham, Jr., **222–225**
Mahlon Pitney **259–261**
William H. Rehnquist **396–399**
Antonin Scalia **408–411**
George Shiras, Jr., **210–212**
George Sutherland **279–282**
Clarence Thomas **420–423**
Willis Van Devanter **252–255**
Fred M. Vinson **337–340**
Edward Douglass White **218–221**
Constitutional Convention 439*c*
John Blair, Jr., and 15
Samuel Chase and 33–34
Gabriel Duvall and 63
Oliver Ellsworth and 37
James Iredell and 22
Alfred Moore and 44
William Paterson and 29
John Rutledge and 19
James Wilson and 2–3
"constitutional crisis"
James C. McReynolds and 265
Stanley Reed and 308, 309
Owen J. Roberts and 295
Willis Van Devanter and 252, 254
Constitution of the United States 504*a*–514*a*. *See also* Bill of Rights; *individual amendments.*
Oliver Ellsworth and 37
James Iredell and 22–23
William Paterson and 29
James Wilson and 2–3
Continental Congress 439*c*
Samuel Chase and 33
John Jay and 6
Thomas Johnson and 26
John Rutledge and 18, 19
James Wilson and 2
contraception. *See Griswold v. Connecticut.*
Contracts Clause
John McLean and 80
Roger Taney and 92
conviction 434*g*
Cooley, Thomas M. 280
Cooley v. Board of Wardens of the Port of Philadelphia 467*a*
Benjamin R. Curtis and 125, 126
Robert C. Grier and 120
John McLean and 80
James M. Wayne and 88
Coolidge, Calvin 442*c*
and Charles Evans Hughes 249
and Owen J. Roberts 296
and Harlan Fiske Stone 291
Cooper v. Aaron 467*a*
Coppage v. Kansas 260–261
court clerk 434*g*
"court-packing" 442*c*
Hugo Black and 304
Pierce Butler and 285
Benjamin N. Cardozo and 301
John H. Clarke and 273
Charles Evans Hughes and 250
James C. McReynolds and 265
Sherman Minton and 346
Stanley Reed and 308
William H. Rehnquist and 398
Owen J. Roberts and 297
Wiley Rutledge and 331
Harlan Fiske Stone and 292
George Sutherland and 279, 281, 282
Willis Van Devanter and 252, 254
Fred M. Vinson and 338
court reporter 434*g*
Cowan, Benjamin R. 169
Cox, Archibald 429
Cox v. New Hampshire 467*a*
Coyle v. Smith 467*a*
Craig v. Boren 444*c*, 467*a*
William J. Brennan, Jr., and 361
Ruth Bader Ginsburg and 426
creditor 434*g*
criminal defendant rights
Hugo Black and 305
Warren Burger and 385, 386
Pierce Butler and 285
Abe Fortas and 378

Felix Frankfurter and 314
Arthur J. Goldberg and 374
John Marshall Harlan II and 356
Sherman Minton and 347
Lewis F. Powell, Jr., and 394
Potter Stewart and 366
Earl Warren and 351
Byron R. White and 370
cross-examination 434*g*
Crowninshield, Jacob 66
cruel and unusual punishment 434*g*
Cruzan v. Director, Missouri Dept. of Health 468*a*
Cuba 441*c*, 443*c*
Cummings v. Missouri 468*a*
Salmon P. Chase and 155
Samuel Miller and 142
Noah H. Swayne and 138
James M. Wayne and 89
Cumming v. Richmond County Board of Education 468*a*
Curtis, Benjamin Robbins *123,* **123–126,** 447*a*
and John A. Campbell 128, 129
and Nathan Clifford 134
Cushing, Luther S. 187
Cushing, William *10,* **10–13,** 446*a*
and John Blair, Jr., 15
and Gabriel Duvall 63
and Oliver Ellsworth 38
and Joseph Story 66

D

Dana, Richard Henry 240
Dandridge v. Williams 468*a*
Dane, Nathan 68
Danforth, John 421
Daniel, Peter Vivian *107,* **107–110,** 447*a*
Darrow, Clarence 204
Dartmouth College v. Woodward 440*c*, 468*a*
Gabriel Duvall and 64
Levi Woodbury and 116
Daubert v. Merrell Dow 468*a*
Daugherty, Harry M.
and Edward T. Sanford 288
and Harlan Fiske Stone 291
Davie, William R. 44
Davis, David *144,* **144–147,** 448*a*
and Salmon P. Chase 155
and Melville W. Fuller 200
and John Marshall Harlan 174
Davis, Jefferson 195, 196
Davis v. Bandemer 468*a*
Davis v. Beason 469*a*
Day, William Rufus *235,* **235–238,** 449*a*
and Pierce Butler 284
and Horace Lurton 245
death penalty
Harry A. Blackmun and 390–391
Stephen G. Breyer and 430
Thurgood Marshall and 382
Lewis F. Powell, Jr., and 394
Potter Stewart and 366
Debs, Eugene 204, 442*c*
Declaration of Independence 439*c*
Samuel Chase and 33
Thomas Johnson and 26
declaratory judgment 434*g*
defamation 434*g*
default judgment 434*g*
defendant 434*g*
DeJonge v. Oregon 250, 469a
de minimus 434*g*
Democratic Party
Philip Barbour and 97
Hugo Black and 304
Pierce Butler and 284
Benjamin N. Cardozo and 300
John H. Clarke and 272
Nathan Clifford and 132, 134, 135
Stephen J. Field and 150
Melville W. Fuller and 199
Howell E. Jackson and 215
L. Q. C. Lamar and 195
Horace Lurton and 243
James C. McReynolds and 263
Sherman Minton and 346
Frank Murphy and 320
Rufus Peckham, Jr., and 223
Lewis F. Powell, Jr., and 394
William Strong and 158
Noah H. Swayne and 137
Roger Taney and 91
Byron R. White and 369
Edward Douglass White and 219
William Woods and 179
Democratic Republicans
H. Brockholst Livingston and 56
Joseph Story and 66
Robert Trimble and 75
Dennis v. United States 469*a*
William O. Douglas and 317
Fred M. Vinson and 339
deportation 434*g*
deposition 434*g*
derivative action 434*g*
desegregation. *See also* segregation.
James Byrnes and 325
Lewis F. Powell, Jr., and 393
Earl Warren and 349, 351
Dewey, Thomas E.
and John Marshall Harlan II 355
and Earl Warren 350
Dickerson v. United States 469*a*
Dickinson, John 2
dictum 434*g*
Dillon v. Gloss 469*a*
direct examination 434*g*
discovery, pretrial 434*g*
discrimination 434*g*. *See* civil rights; segregation.
dismissal 434*g*
disorderly conduct 434*g*
dissenting opinion 434*g*
district attorney 434*g*
Dodge v. Woolsey 128
Doe v. Bolton 469*a*
Dolan v. City of Tigard 470*a*
Dombrowski v. Pfister 470*a*
domicile 434*g*
Dorr Rebellion 133
double jeopardy 434*g*
Douglas, Stephen
and Melville W. Fuller 199
and L. Q. C. Lamar 195
Douglas, William Orville *315,* **315–318,** 449*a*
and James Byrnes 324
and Abe Fortas 377
and Arthur J. Goldberg 373
and Robert Jackson 328
and Sherman Minton 347
and Wiley Rutledge 332
and John Paul Stevens 401
and Harlan Fiske Stone 293
and Fred M. Vinson 338
and Charles Whittaker 363
Dred Scott v. Sandford 440*c*, 470*a*
Henry Brown and 209
John A. Campbell and 129
John Catron and 99–101
Salmon P. Chase and 155
Benjamin R. Curtis and 123, 125–126
Peter V.Daniel and 109
Robert C. Grier and 119, 121, 122
John McLean and 78, 80, 81
Samuel Miller and 142
Samuel Nelson and 111–113
Roger Taney and 90, 91, 93, 94
James M. Wayne and 86, 88
Duane, William J. 91
due process 434*g*
Duncan v. Louisiana 470*a*
Dunn v. Blumstein 470*a*
duress 435*g*
Durham, Monte 377
Duvall, Gabriel *62,* **62–64,** 447*a*
and Philip Barbour 97
and Joseph Story 67
and Roger Taney 91

E

E. C. Knight Co. v. United States 470*a*
economic conservatism 281
economic regulations
Louis D. Brandeis and 269
Harlan Fiske Stone and 292
Edmonson v. Leesville Concrete Co. 470*a*
Edwards v. Aguillard 470*a*
Edwards v. California 324, 470*a*
Edwards v. South Carolina 471*a*
EEOC. *See* Equal Employment Opportunity Commission.
Eighteenth Amendment 442*c*
Eighth Amendment 510*a*
William H. Rehnquist and 398
Potter Stewart and 366
Byron R. White and 370
Eisenhower, Dwight D. 443*c*
and Harry A. Blackmun 389
and William J. Brennan, Jr., 359–360
and Warren Burger 385
and John Marshall Harlan II 355–356
and Stanley Reed 309
and Potter Stewart 366
and Earl Warren 350–352
and Byron Raymond White 371
and Charles Whittaker 362, 363
Eisenstadt v. Baird 471*a*

election of 1876
Joseph P. Bradley and 163
Stanley Matthews and 184
Morrison Waite and 171
Eleventh Amendment 439*c*, 510*a*
John Blair, Jr., and 16
Stephen G. Breyer and 430
William Cushing and 12
James Iredell and 24
John Jay and 7
Stanley Matthews and 184
James Wilson and 3
Elfbrandt v. Russell 471*a*
Elkison v. Deliesseline 53
Ellsworth, Oliver *36,* **36–38,** 439*c*, 446*a*
and John Jay 8
and John Marshall 47
and William Paterson 29, 31
and Bushrod Washington 41
Elrod v. Burns 471*a*
Emancipation Proclamation 441*c*
David Davis and 145, 146
Melville W. Fuller and 199
John Marshall Harlan and 175
Emerson, Ralph Waldo 231
eminent domain 435*g*
Employer's Liability Case 241
Employment Division v. Smith 410, 471*a*
en banc 435*g*
Enforcement Act of 1870 166–167
Engel v. Vitale 443*c*, 471*a*
Warren Burger and 386
Earl Warren and 351
enjoin 435*g*
environmentalism 316, 317
Epperson v. Arkansas 378
Equal Employment Opportunity Commission (EEOC) 421–422
equal protection clause
Warren Burger and 386
Thurgood Marshall and 381
equal protection of the law 435*g*
equity 435*g*
Erie Railroad Co. v. Tompkins 68, 471*a*
Escobedo v. Illinois 374, 471*a*
establishment clause. *See* church and state, separation of.
Euclid v. Ambler Realty Co. 472*a*
Evans v. Abney 472*a*
Everson v. Board of Education 332, 472*a*
evolution, teaching of 378
exclusionary rule 435*g*
exemplary damages 435*g*
Ex parte Crow Dog 472*a*
Ex parte Garland
John A. Campbell and 130
Salmon P. Chase and 155
Samuel Miller and 142
Noah H. Swayne and 138
James M. Wayne and 89
Ex parte McCardle 155, 472*a*
Ex parte Milligan 472*a*
Salmon P. Chase and 155
David Davis and 146–147
Ex parte Virginia
Stephen J. Field and 150–151
Morrison Waite and 170
Ex parte Yarbrough 472*a*
ex post facto clause 34
ex post facto law 435*g*
extradition 435*g*

F

Fairfax, Thomas Lord 67
Fairfax's Devisee v. Hunter's Lessee 67–68
Fair Labor Standards Act 304
Fall, Albert B. 296
Fay v. Noia 472*a*
FDA v. Brown Williamson Tobacco Corporation 418, 472*a*–473*a*
Federal Bureau of Investigation 442*c*
federalism. *See also* states' rights.
Samuel Chase and 33–34
Gabriel Duvall and 63
John Marshall Harlan II and 356
James Iredell and 22–24
William Johnson and 52
H. Brockholst Livingston and 55
Alfred Moore and 44
William Paterson and 31
William H. Rehnquist and 398
Joseph Story and 68
Roger Taney and 92
James M. Wayne and 87–88
Federalist Papers 6
Federalist Party
John Marshall and 48, 49
Alfred Moore and 45
Federal Trade Commission Act 281
federal v. state power 398
Feiner v. New York 473*a*
felony 435*g*
fiduciary 435*g*
Field, Stephen Johnson *148,* **148–152,** 448*a*
and Samuel Blatchford 192
and David Brewer 202, 203
and L. Q. C. Lamar 197
and Joseph McKenna 228
and William Strong 159
Fifteenth Amendment 441*c*, 512*a*
Ward Hunt and 166–167
Samuel Miller and 142
Morrison Waite and 170
Fifth Amendment 510*a*
Louis D. Brandeis and 269
David Brewer and 204
Benjamin N. Cardozo and 302
William Moody and 241
Rufus Peckham, Jr., and 224
Stanley Reed and 309
Fillmore, Millard 440*c*
and John A. Campbell 128
and Benjamin R. Curtis 124–125
Finley v. Lynn 61
First Amendment 509*a*
Hugo Black and 303–305
Louis D. Brandeis and 269–270
William J. Brennan, Jr., and 361
Pierce Butler and 285
Tom C. Clark and 341, 343
Abe Fortas and 378
John Marshall Harlan II and 356
Oliver Wendell Holmes, Jr., and 233
Robert Jackson and 328
Anthony Kennedy and 414
William H. Rehnquist and 399
Owen J. Roberts and 297
Wiley Rutledge and 332
Edward T. Sanford and 288–289
Antonin Scalia and 410
John Paul Stevens and 402
Potter Stewart and 367
Harlan Fiske Stone and 292–293
Fred M. Vinson and 339
Earl Warren and 351
First English Evangelical Lutheran Church of Glendale v. County of Los Angeles 473*a*
First National Bank of Boston v. Bellotti 473*a*
Fisher's Negroes v. Dabbs 100, 101
flag desecration
William J. Brennan, Jr., and 361
Anthony Kennedy and 414
Antonin Scalia and 410
Flast v. Cohen 473*a*
Fletcher v. Peck 66, 440*c*, 473*a*
Foraker, Joseph B. 276
"force bill" 87
Ford, Gerald 444*c*
and William O. Douglas 317
and Antonin Scalia 409
and John Paul Stevens 401
Ford v. Wainwright 473*a*
foreclosure 435*g*
Fort, J. Franklin 260
Fortas, Abe *376,* **376–379,** 444*c*, 450*a*
and Harry A. Blackmun 389
and Warren Burger 385
and Arthur J. Goldberg 374
and Lewis F. Powell, Jr., 393
and Earl Warren 352
forum non conveniens 435*g*
Foster, Henry Clay 257
"Four Horsemen"
Pierce Butler and 283, 285, 286
James C. McReynolds and 265
Stanley Reed and 308–309
Owen J. Roberts and 296, 297
Harlan Fiske Stone and 292
George Sutherland and 279, 281, 282
Willis Van Devanter and 252, 254–255
Fourteenth Amendment 441*c*, 511*a*
Hugo Black and 305
Samuel Blatchford and 192
Joseph P. Bradley and 163
William J. Brennan, Jr., and 360
David Brewer and 204
Henry Brown and 208
Warren Burger and 386
Pierce Butler and 285
James Byrnes and 324
John A. Campbell and 130
Benjamin N. Cardozo and 302
Tom C. Clark and 343
Stephen J. Field and 150
Abe Fortas and 378
Felix Frankfurter and 314
Melville W. Fuller and 200
Ruth Bader Ginsburg and 426
Horace Gray and 188
John Marshall Harlan and 176
Oliver Wendell Holmes, Jr., and 232

Thurgood Marshall and 382
Stanley Matthews and 184
James C. McReynolds and 264
Samuel Miller and 142–143
Rufus Peckham, Jr., and 224
Mahlon Pitney and 261
Stanley Reed and 309
Owen J. Roberts and 297
Edward T. Sanford and 288
John Paul Stevens and 402
Harlan Fiske Stone and 292
Noah H. Swayne and 138
Roger Taney and 93
Willis Van Devanter and 254
Morrison Waite and 170, 171
William Woods and 179–180
Fourth Amendment 269, 510*a*
Frankfurter, Felix *311,* **311–314,** 449*a*
and Joseph P. Bradley 164
and Louis D. Brandeis 270
and Arthur J. Goldberg 373
and John Marshall Harlan II 356
and Charles Evans Hughes 250
and James C. McReynolds 265
and Harlan Fiske Stone 293
and Fred M. Vinson 338
fraud 435*g*
freedom of speech
Louis D. Brandeis and 269–270
William J. Brennan, Jr., and 360, 361
William O. Douglas and 317
Felix Frankfurter and 313–314
Robert Jackson and 328
Frank Murphy and 321–322
Antonin Scalia and 410
Harlan Fiske Stone and 292
free exercise clause 410
Free-Soil Party 154
Fries, John 34
Frontiero v. Richardson 473*a*
William J. Brennan, Jr., and 360
Ruth Bader Ginsburg and 425–426
William H. Rehnquist and 397
Fugitive Slave Act 183
Fugitive Slave Act of 1793
Salmon P. Chase and 154
and Levi Woodbury 117
Fugitive Slave Act of 1850 129
Fugitive Slave Law 85
Fuller, Melville Weston *198,* **198–201,** 441*c,* 448*a*
and Stephen J. Field 151
and Oliver Wendell Holmes, Jr., 232
and Charles Evans Hughes 249
and Edward Douglass White 220
Fullilove v. Klutznick 473*a*
fundamental right 402
Furman v. Georgia 397–398
Furman v. Georgia 444*c,* 474*a*
Thurgood Marshall and 382
Lewis F. Powell, Jr., and 394
William H. Rehnquist and 397–398
Potter Stewart and 366

G

gag order 435*g*
Galleried v. Greenman 188
Garcia v. San Antonio Metropolitan Transit Authority 474*a*
Garfield, James A. 441*c*
and Nathan Clifford 135
and David Davis 144
and Horace Gray 188
and John Marshall 46
and Stanley Matthews 184
Garner, William 166
garnishment 435*g*
gay rights
Anthony Kennedy and 414
David H. Souter and 418
Byron R. White and 370
Geduldig v. Aiello 474*a*
gender-based violence
Stephen G. Breyer and 430
Ruth Bader Ginsburg and 427
Anthony Kennedy and 414
Sandra Day O'Connor and 407
William H. Rehnquist and 398
David H. Souter and 418
gender discrimination
William J. Brennan, Jr., and 360
Warren Burger and 386
Ruth Bader Ginsburg and 424–426
William H. Rehnquist and 397
Georgia
Joseph Lamar and 257
L. Q. C. Lamar and 195
Clarence Thomas and 421
James M. Wayne and 87
Georgia v. McCollum 474*a*
Gettysburg Address 441*c*
Gibbons v. Ogden 474*a*
John Marshall and 49
Smith Thompson and 71
Gideon, Earl 377
Gideon v. Wainwright 443*c,* 474*a*
Hugo Black and 305
Warren Burger and 386
Abe Fortas and 377
Earl Warren and 351
Gilchrist, Adam 53
Gilchrist v. Collector of Charleston 53
Ginsburg, Douglas
and Anthony Kennedy 412–414
and David H. Souter 417
Ginsburg, Ruth Bader *424,* **424–427,** 451*a*
and Stephen G. Breyer 430
and David H. Souter 416, 418
Gitlow v. New York 288, 289, 474*a*
Glynn, Martin 300
Goldberg, Arthur Joseph *372,* **372–375,** 450*a*
and Stephen G. Breyer 429
and Abe Fortas 378
Goldberg v. Kelly 360–361, 475*a*
Gold Clause Cases 308, 474*a*
Goldfarb v. Virginia State Bar 475*a*
Goldwater, Barry 397
Gomillion v. Lightfoot 475*a*
Gompers v. Bucks Stove and Range Company 258
governors
James Byrnes 323
Charles Evans Hughes 248–249
Frank Murphy 320
Earl Warren as 350
Graham v. Richardson 475*a*
grand jury 435*g*
Granger laws
Samuel Blatchford and 192
David Brewer and 204
Grant, Ulysses S. 441*c*
and Joseph P. Bradley 162
and Henry Brown 207
and Ward Hunt 166
and Horace Lurton 244
and Samuel Miller 143
and Samuel Nelson 113
and William Strong 158, 159
and Noah H. Swayne 139
and Morrison Waite 168, 169
and William Woods 179
Graves v. New York ex rel. O'Keefe 475*a*
Gray, Horace *186,* **186–189,** 232, 448*a*
Greater New Orleans Broadcast Association v. United States 475*a*
Green v. County School Board of New Kent County 475*a*
Gregg v. Georgia 475*a*
Thurgood Marshall and 382
Lewis F. Powell, Jr., and 394
Grier, Robert Cooper *119,* **119–122,** 447*a*
and Joseph P. Bradley 162
and William Strong 158
Griffin v. Breckenridge 475*a*
Griffin v. California 476*a*
Griffin v. County School Board of Prince Edward County 476*a*
Griggs v. Duke Power Co. 476*a*
Griswold v. Connecticut 443*c,* 476*a*
Hugo Black and 306
Harry A. Blackmun and 389
Stephen G. Breyer and 429
Warren Burger and 386
William O. Douglas and 317
John Marshall Harlan II and 356
Potter Stewart and 366
Earl Warren and 351–352
Grosjean v. American Press Co. 281, 282, 476*a*
Grove City College v. Bell 476*a*
Groves v. Slaughter 476*a*
Henry Baldwin and 84
John McKinley and 105
Grovey v. Townsend 297, 476*a*
Guinn v. United States 476*a*
Gun Free Schools Zone Act
Stephen G. Breyer and 430
John Paul Stevens and 402

H

habeas corpus, writ of 435*g*
Hague v. Congress of Industrial Organizations 477*a*
Hall v. Decuir 477*a*
Hamilton, Alexander 440*c*
and Samuel Chase 33
and John Jay 6
and H. Brockholst Livingston 56

and John Marshall 48
and William Paterson 29
Hammer v. Dagenhart 442*c*, 477*a*
John H. Clarke and 272
William Day and 237–238
Hancock, John 12
handgun possession
Stephen G. Breyer and 430
Anthony Kennedy and 414
Sandra Day O'Connor and 407
Hanna, Mark 272
Harding, Warren G. 442*c*
and Pierce Butler 284, 285
and William Day 238
and Charles Evans Hughes 249
and Owen J. Roberts 296
and Edward T. Sanford 288
and George Sutherland 281
and William Howard Taft 277
Harlan, John Marshall *173*, **173–177**, 448*a*
and Stephen J. Field 151
and John Marshall Harlan II 354
and Mahlon Pitney 260
Harlan, II, John Marshall *354*, **354–357**, 397, 450*a*
Harmelin v. Michigan 477*a*
Harper v. Virginia State Board of Elections 317, 477*a*
Harrison, Benjamin 441*c*
and David Brewer 203
and Henry Brown 208
and William Day 236
and Howell E. Jackson 215, 216
and Joseph McKenna 227–228
and George Shiras, Jr., 211
and William Howard Taft 276
and Willis Van Devanter 253
Harrison, Robert H.
and John Blair, Jr., 15
and James Iredell 23
Harrison, William Henry 117, 440*c*
Harris v. Forklift Systems, Inc. 477*a*
Harris v. McRae 477*a*
Harris v. New York 477*a*
Harris v. United States 478*a*
hate crime statutes 435*g*
Hawaii Housing Authority v. Midkiff 478*a*
Hayburn's Case 478*a*
Hayes, Rutherford B. 441*c*
and Joseph P. Bradley 163
and Nathan Clifford 135
and Stephen J. Field 151
and John Marshall Harlan 174
and Ward Hunt 167
and Stanley Matthews 183, 184
and Samuel Miller 143
and Noah H. Swayne 139
and Morrison Waite 171
and Edward Douglass White 219
and William Woods 180
Haynsworth, Clement F.
and Harry A. Blackmun 389
and Lewis F. Powell, Jr., 393
hearing 435*g*
hearsay 435*g*
Heart of Atlanta Motel v. United States 343, 443*c*, 478*a*
Helvering v. Davis 478*a*
Henderson v. United States 336
Henry, Patrick 15, 439*c*
Hepburn, Hopewell 211
Hepburn v. Griswold
Joseph P. Bradley and 162–163
Salmon P. Chase and 155
William Strong and 158–159
Herndon v. Lowry 478*a*
Hill, Anita 420, 422
Hill, David B.
and Rufus Peckham, Jr., 223, 224
and Edward Douglass White 220
Hill v. Colorado 478*a*
Hirabayashi v. United States 478*a*
Hiroshima 442*c*
Hoar, E. Rockwood 162
Hoar, George 188
Hodgson v. Minnesota 478*a*–479*a*
Holden v. Hardy 208, 479*a*
holding 435*g*
Holmes, Jr., Oliver Wendell *230*, **230–233**, 449*a*
and Pierce Butler 285
and Benjamin N. Cardozo 301
and John H. Clarke 272
and Felix Frankfurter 312
and Melville W. Fuller 201
and Horace Gray 188
and John Marshall 46
and James C. McReynolds 264, 265
and William Moody 241
and Rufus Peckham, Jr., 225
and Mahlon Pitney 261
and Owen J. Roberts 296
and Antonin Scalia 411
and Harlan Fiske Stone 292
and George Sutherland 281
Home Building and Loan Association v. Blaidsell 250, 442*c*, 479*a*
homicide 435*g*
Hook, William C. 260
Hoover, Herbert 442*c*
and Benjamin N. Cardozo 301
and Charles Evans Hughes 249
and Stanley Reed 308
and Owen J. Roberts 296
Hoover, J. Edgar 291
Hornblower, William B. 223, 224
House, Edward M. 263
House of Representatives. *See* U.S. House of Representatives.
Hoyt v. Florida 479*a*
Hudson & Goodwin v. United States 479*a*
Hudson v. Palmer 479*a*
Hughes, Charles Evans *247*, **247–251**, 442*c*, 449*a*
and Pierce Butler 285
and Benjamin N. Cardozo 301
and John H. Clarke 272
and Felix Frankfurter 314
and Oliver Wendell Holmes, Jr., 232
and Robert Jackson 327
and James C. McReynolds 265
and Stanley Reed 308
and William H. Rehnquist 398
and Owen J. Roberts 296
and Harlan Fiske Stone 292
and George Sutherland 281
and William Howard Taft 276, 277
and Edward Douglass White 220–221
Hunt, Ward *165*, **165–167**, 191, 448*a*
Hurtado v. California 184, 479*a*
Hustler Magazine v. Falwell 479*a*
Hutchinson, Thomas 11
Hutchison v. Proxmire 479*a*–480*a*
Hutto v. Davis 480*a*
Hylton v. United States 480*a*

I

Ickes, Harold 377
Illinois
Harry A. Blackmun and 389
David Davis and 145
Melville W. Fuller and 199
Arthur J. Goldberg and 373
John Marshall Harlan II and 355
John Paul Stevens and 401
Illinois ex. rel. McCollum v. Board of Education 480*a*
Illinois v. Krull 480*a*
Immigration and Naturalization Service v. Chadha 480*a*
immunity 435*g*
impanelment 435*g*
impeach 435*g*
impeachment
Samuel Chase and 32, 34–35
William O. Douglas and 317
inalienable 435*g*
income tax
Henry Brown and 208
Melville W. Fuller and 200
Howell E. Jackson and 214, 216–217
Noah H. Swayne and 138
incriminate 435*g*
Indiana
Sherman Minton and 346
Willis Van Devanter and 253
indictment 435*g*
indigent 435*g*
individual rights
Harry A. Blackmun and 388
Arthur J. Goldberg and 373–374
in forma pauperis 435*g*
information 435*g*
injunction 435*g*
Innes, Harry 60
innocence, presumption of 435*g*
inquest 435*g*
In re Debs 204–205, 480*a*
In re Gault 378, 480*a*
In re Neagle 480*a*
Stephen J. Field and 151
L. Q. C. Lamar and 197
In re Winship 480*a*–481*a*
INS 435*g*
insanity defense 377
International Society for Krishna Consciousness, Inc. v. Lee 481*a*
International Union v. Johnson Controls, Inc. 481*a*
interstate commerce
Philip Barbour and 97–98
David Brewer and 204

Stephen G. Breyer and 430
Harold H. Burton and 336
James Byrnes and 324
Benjamin R. Curtis and 125
William Day and 237–238
Melville W. Fuller and 200
Ruth Bader Ginsburg and 427
Robert C. Grier and 120
Robert Jackson and 328
Anthony Kennedy and 414
John Marshall and 49
John McKinley and 104–105
John McLean and 80
Sandra Day O'Connor and 407
William H. Rehnquist and 398
Harlan Fiske Stone and 292
James M. Wayne and 88
Interstate Commerce Act of 1887 196
Intolerable Acts 439*c*
Iowa
Samuel Miller and 141
Wiley Rutledge and 331
Iredell, James *21,* **21–24,** 446*a*
and John Blair, Jr., 16
and John Jay 7
and Alfred Moore 44
and James Wilson 3, 4
IRS 436*g*

J

Jackson, Andrew 440*c*
and Henry Baldwin 83, 84
and Philip Barbour 96, 97
and John Catron 100–102
and Peter V. Daniel 108
and Gabriel Duvall 64
and John McKinley 104
and John McLean 78, 80
and Joseph Story 68
and Noah H. Swayne 137
and Roger Taney 91, 92
and Smith Thompson 73
and James M. Wayne 87
and Levi Woodbury 116
Jackson, Howell Edmunds *214,* **214–217,** 448*a*
and Henry Brown 208
and Horace Lurton 245
and Rufus Peckham, Jr., 224
and George Shiras, Jr., 212
Jackson, Robert Houghwout *326,* **326–329,** 450*a*
and James Byrnes 324
and John Marshall Harlan II 355
and Frank Murphy 321
and William H. Rehnquist 397
and Fred M. Vinson 338–339
Jackson v. Metropolitan Edison Co. 481*a*
Jacobellis v. Ohio 367
James, William
and Felix Frankfurter 312
and Oliver Wendell Holmes, Jr., 231
Japanese American internment 350
Jay, John *5,* **5–9,** 439*c,* 446*a*
and John Blair, Jr., 15, 16
and William Cushing 12
and Oliver Ellsworth 37–38
and James Iredell 23
and H. Brockholst Livingston 56
and John Marshall 47
and John Rutledge 19, 20
Jay Treaty 67
J.E.B. v. Alabama Ex Rel. T.B. 481*a*
Jefferson, Thomas 439*c,* 440*c*
and Philip Barbour 96
and Samuel Chase 34
and Gabriel Duvall 63
and John Jay 8
and William Johnson 51–53
and H. Brockholst Livingston 55, 57
and John Marshall 48
and Joseph Story 66, 67
and Thomas Todd 60
Jeffersonians 49
Jehovah's Witnesses 293
Johnson, Andrew 441*c*
and Joseph P. Bradley 162
and John A. Campbell 130
and Salmon P. Chase 155, 156
and Benjamin R. Curtis 126
and William Strong 158
Johnson, Lyndon B. 443*c*
and Warren Burger 385
and Tom C. Clark 343
and Abe Fortas 376–378
and Ruth Bader Ginsburg 424
and Arthur J. Goldberg 374
and Thurgood Marshall 380–382
and Earl Warren 352
Johnson, Samuel 22
Johnson, Thomas *25,* **25–27,** 446*a*
and H. Brockholst Livingston 57
and William Paterson 30
Johnson, William *51,* **51–54,** 446*a*
and John Marshall 48
and Smith Thompson 72
and James M. Wayne 87
Johnson v. Louisiana 481*a*
Johnson v. Santa Clara County 481*a*
Johnson v. Zerbst 481*a*
Joint Anti-Fascist Refugee Committee v. McGrath 481*a*
Jones Glass Co. v. Glass Bottle Blowers Association 260
Jones v. Alfred H. Mayer Co. 366, 481*a*
Jones v. Van Zandt 481*a*
Salmon P. Chase and 154
Levi Woodbury and 117
Judaism
Louis D. Brandeis and 269
Benjamin N. Cardozo and 301
Felix Frankfurter and 311
judicial activism
William J. Brennan, Jr., and 360
William O. Douglas and 317
Abe Fortas and 378
Felix Frankfurter and 313, 314
Ruth Bader Ginsburg and 427
Thurgood Marshall and 382
John Paul Stevens and 402
Potter Stewart and 366
Byron R. White and 370
judicial conservatism
Warren Burger and 385
Felix Frankfurter and 311, 313
John Marshall Harlan II and 356
Potter Stewart and 366
Morrison Waite and 172
Charles Whittaker and 363
judicial restraint
Harold H. Burton and 335–336
Ruth Bader Ginsburg and 426
John Marshall Harlan II and 354, 356
Robert Jackson and 327–328
Sherman Minton and 345–347
Byron R. White and 368, 370
judicial review 436*g*
Judiciary Act of 1787 30
Judiciary Act of 1789
Oliver Ellsworth and 36, 37
James Iredell and 23
John Jay and 7
Thomas Johnson and 26, 27
John Marshall and 48
William Paterson and 28–30
John Rutledge and 17, 19
Joseph Story and 67
Thomas Todd and 60
Judiciary Act of 1869 162
Judiciary Act of 1925 254
jurisdiction 436*g*
jurisprudence 436*g*
jurist 436*g*
justices (in general)
age vi
educational background vii
gender vi
intellectual abilities vii–viii
power in American political system viii–x
race vi
religious background vi–vii
table 446*a*–451*a*
juvenile delinquent 436*g*

K

Kansas
David Brewer and 203
Charles Whittaker and 363
Kansas v. Hendricks 481*a*–482*a*
Katzenbach v. McClung 343, 482*a*
Katzenbach v. Morgan 482*a*
Katz v. United States 482*a*
Keillor, Garrison 391
Kennedy, Anthony McLeod *412,* **412–415,** 451*a*
and Sandra Day O'Connor 406
and David H. Souter 417, 418
Kennedy, Edward
on Robert Bork 413
and Stephen G. Breyer 429, 430
Kennedy, John F. 443*c*
and Arthur J. Goldberg 372, 373
and Thurgood Marshall 381
and Earl Warren 352
and Byron Raymond White 368, 369, 371
Kennedy, Joseph P. 316
Kennedy, Robert 444*c*
and Arthur J. Goldberg 373
and Byron Raymond White 369
Kent, James 56

Kent State 444*c*
Kentucky
Louis D. Brandeis and 268
John Marshall Harlan and 173–174
Horace Lurton and 244
James C. McReynolds and 263
Samuel Miller and 141
Stanley Reed and 308
Wiley Rutledge and 331
Thomas Todd and 60
Robert Trimble and 75
Fred M. Vinson and 338
Ker v. California 482*a*
Keyes v. Denver School District No. 1 482*a*
Keyishian v. Board of Regents 482*a*
Kidd v. Pearson 482*a*
Kimel v. Florida Board of Regents 430, 483*a*
King, Jr., Martin Luther 443*c*, 444*c*
King, William 280, 281
Kissam, Benjamin 6
Kleindienst, Richard 397
Know Nothing Party
John Marshall Harlan and 175
Joseph McKenna and 227
Knox, Philander
and James C. McReynolds 263
and William Moody 241
Knox v. Lee
Joseph P. Bradley and 163
William Strong and 159
Korean War 443*c*
Harold H. Burton and 335
Tom C. Clark and 343
Fred M. Vinson and 339
Korematsu v. United States 442*c*, 483*a*
William O. Douglas and 317
Frank Murphy and 321, 322
Owen J. Roberts and 297
Ku Klux Klan 304
Ku Klux Klan Act of 1871 180
Kunz v. New York 483*a*

L

labor movement
Felix Frankfurter and 312
Arthur J. Goldberg and 373
Frank Murphy and 320
Mahlon Pitney and 259, 260
Lacey, John W. 253
La Follette, Robert 284
laissez-faire economics
Pierce Butler and 283
William Day and 237
Oliver Wendell Holmes, Jr., and 232
Rufus Peckham, Jr., and 224
George Sutherland and 281
Lamar, Joseph Rucker *256*, **256–258**, 449*a*
and Louis D. Brandeis 269
and William Howard Taft 276
Lamar, Lucius Quintus Cincinnatus *194*, **194–197**, 448*a*
and Henry Brown 208
and Howell E. Jackson 216
and Joseph Lamar 257
and William Woods 180
Lassiter v. Northampton County Board of Elections 483*a*
Lattimore, Owen 377
League of Nations 442*c*
John H. Clarke and 271, 273
Edward T. Sanford and 288
Lee, Robert E. 196, 197
Lee v. Weisman 483*a*
Anthony Kennedy and 414
Sandra Day O'Connor and 406
legal tender 436*g*
Legal Tender Act of 1862
Joseph P. Bradley and 162–163
Salmon P. Chase and 154–155
William Strong and 158–159
Lemon v. Kurtzman 444*c*, 483*a*
Warren Burger and 386
Antonin Scalia and 410–411
lesser included offense 436*g*
Levi, Edward 401
libel 436*g*
liberal judges
Harry A. Blackmun **388–391**
William J. Brennan, Jr., **358–361**
Ruth Bader Ginsburg and **424–427**
Arthur J. Goldberg **372–375**
Frank Murphy **319–322**
liberal nationalism 241
Licence Cases
John Catron and 101
Robert C. Grier and 120
Levi Woodbury and 117
Lincoln, Abraham 441*c*
and John A. Campbell 129
and Salmon P. Chase 153–155
and David Davis 144–146
and Stephen J. Field 150
and Melville W. Fuller 199
and Robert C. Grier 121, 122
and John Marshall Harlan 175
and Horace Lurton 244
and Stanley Matthews 183
and John McLean 81
and Samuel Miller 141, 142
and Samuel Nelson 113
and William Strong 158
and Noah H. Swayne 137–138
and James M. Wayne 88
Lindsey v. Normet 483*a*
"living Constitution" 410
Livingston, Henry Brockholst *55*, **55–58**, 71, 446*a*
Livingston v. Van Ingen 71
Lochner v. New York 441*c*, 483*a*
Hugo Black and 306
Louis D. Brandeis and 268
David Brewer and 205
Henry Brown and 208
Melville W. Fuller and 200
Oliver Wendell Holmes, Jr., and 232
Rufus Peckham, Jr., and 222, 224, 225
Edward Douglass White and 220
Loewe v. Lawlor 483*a*
long arm statute 436*g*
Longstreet, Augustus B. 195
Lopez v. United States 398
Louisiana 219
Louisiana ex rel. Francis v. Resweber 483*a*–484*a*
Louisiana Purchase 440*c*
Loving v. Virginia 484*a*
Lucas v. South Carolina Coastal Council 484*a*
Lurton, Horace Harmon *243*, **243–246**, 449*a*
and William Day 237
and James C. McReynolds 263
and William Moody 241
and William Howard Taft 276
Luther v. Borden 133, 484*a*
Lynch, William 236
Lynch v. Donnelly 484*a*
Lyon, Matthew 31

M

Madison, James 440*c*
and Philip Barbour 96
and John Blair, Jr., 15
and Gabriel Duvall 63
and John Jay 6
and William Johnson 52
and John Marshall 48
and Joseph Story 67
and Robert Trimble 75
and Levi Woodbury 116
magistrate 436*g*
Maher v. Roe 484*a*
Maine
Nathan Clifford and 133
Melville W. Fuller and 199
malice aforethought 436*g*
Malloy v. Hogan 241, 484*a*
mandamus 436*g*
"Manhattan well mystery" case 56
Mann Act 263, 442*c*
Mapp v. Ohio 443*c*, 484*a*
Warren Burger and 386
Tom C. Clark and 343
Earl Warren and 351
Marbury, William 48
Marbury v. Madison 440*c*, 484*a*
John Catron and 102
William Johnson and 52, 53
John Marshall and 48
Alfred Moore and 45
William Paterson and 30
Joseph Story and 68
Roger Taney and 93
maritime cases 57
maritime law 436*g*
Marshall, John *46*, **46–49**, 440*c*, 446*a*
and Henry Baldwin 82–85
and Philip Barbour 97
and Samuel Chase 35
and Gabriel Duvall 62–64
and Oliver Wendell Holmes, Jr., 230
and John Jay 8–9
and William Johnson 51–53
and H. Brockholst Livingston 55, 57, 58
and John McLean 78, 80
and Alfred Moore 44, 45
and William Paterson 31
and *seriatim* opinions 41

and Joseph Story 65–69
and Roger Taney 90, 92, 93
and Smith Thompson 70–73
and Thomas Todd 60–61
and Robert Trimble 74–76
and Earl Warren 352
and Bushrod Washington 39–42
and James M. Wayne 87, 89
and Levi Woodbury 116
Marshall, Thurgood *380,* **380–383,** 450*a*
and Ruth Bader Ginsburg 424
and Antonin Scalia 410
and John Paul Stevens 401
and Clarence Thomas 420, 422
Marshall Plan 442*c*
Marshall v. Baltimore and Ohio Railroad 128
Marsh v. Chambers 386
martial law 436*g*
Martin v. Hunter's Lessee 67, 484*a*
Maryland
Samuel Chase and 33
David Davis and 145
Gabriel Duvall and 63
Thomas Johnson and 25–26
Thurgood Marshall and 381
Roger Taney and 91
Maryland v. Craig 484*a*
Maryland v. Wilson 485*a*
Mason, George
and John Blair, Jr., 15
and James Iredell 22–23
Mason-Dixon Line 439*c*
Massachusetts
Henry Brown and 207
Harold H. Burton and 335
Benjamin R. Curtis and 124
William Cushing and 10–12
Horace Gray and 186–187
Oliver Wendell Holmes, Jr., and 230–231
William Moody and 240
David H. Souter and 417
Joseph Story and 66
Massachusetts Board of Retirement v. Murgia 485*a*
Massachusetts Constitutional Convention 12
Massachusetts v. Sheppard 485*a*
Massiah v. United States 485*a*
Matthews, Stanley *182,* **182–185,** 448*a*
and David Brewer 203
and Henry Brown 207
and Horace Gray 188
and Howell E. Jackson 216
Maxwell v. Dow 485*a*
McCarthy, Joseph 443*c*
and William J. Brennan, Jr., 359, 360
and Tom C. Clark 343
and Abe Fortas 377
McCleskey v. Kemp 485*a*
McColloch v. Maryland 48–49, 440*c*
McCullough v. Maryland 91, 485*a*
McKenna, Joseph *226,* **226–228,** 291, 448*a*
McKinley, John *103,* **103–106,** 447*a*
and John A. Campbell 128
and William Day 237
and Joseph McKenna 228
McKinley, William 441*c*
and William Day 235, 236
and Joseph McKenna 227
and William Howard Taft 276
and Willis Van Devanter 253
McLane, Louis 91
McLaurin v. Oklahoma State Regents for Higher Education 485*a*
Harold H. Burton and 336
Fred M. Vinson and 340
McLean, John *78,* **78–81,** 447*a*
and Philip Barbour 97
and Noah H. Swayne 137
McNutt, Paul 346
McPherson v. Buick Motor Company 300–301
McReynolds, James Clark *262,* **262–265,** 449*a*
and Pierce Butler 285
and James Byrnes 324
and John H. Clarke 273
and Harlan Fiske Stone 292
and George Sutherland 279
and Willis Van Devanter 254
Meese, Ed 413
Mellon, Andrew 327
mens rea 436*g*
Mercer, John 40
Metro Broadcasting v. Federal Communications Commission 361, 485*a*
Meyer v. Nebraska 264, 485*a*
Meyer v. United States 363
Miami Herald Publishing Co. v. Tornillo 486*a*
Michael M. v. Superior Court of Sonoma County 486*a*
Michigan
Henry Brown and 207
Frank Murphy and 320
Potter Stewart and 365
Miller, Samuel Freeman *140,* **140–143,** 448*a*
and Henry Brown 208
and Howell E. Jackson 216
and Noah H. Swayne 138, 139
Miller v. California 444*c*, 486*a*
Milligan, Lambdin P. *See Ex parte Milligan.*
Milliken v. Bradley 486*a*
Minersville School District v. Gobitis 486*a*
William O. Douglas and 317
Felix Frankfurter and 313
Robert Jackson and 328
Frank Murphy and 321
Harlan Fiske Stone and 292–293
minimum wage law
Stanley Reed and 308
Owen J. Roberts and 297
Minnesota
Harry A. Blackmun and 389
Warren Burger and 385
Pierce Butler and 283–284
William O. Douglas and 316
Minnick v. Mississippi 486*a*
minor 436*g*
Minor, John B. 263
Minor v. Happersett 486*a*
Minton, Sherman *345,* **345–347,** 359, 450*a*
Miranda rights 436*g*
Miranda v. Arizona 443*c*, 486*a*
Warren Burger and 386
Arthur J. Goldberg and 374
John Marshall Harlan II and 356
Potter Stewart and 366
Earl Warren and 351
Byron R. White and 370
misdemeanor 436*g*
Mississippi
L. Q. C. Lamar and 195
John McKinley and 105
Mississippi University for Woman v. Hogan 486*a*
Missouri
Clarence Thomas and 421
Charles Whittaker and 363
Missouri Compromise 440*c*
John Catron and 101
Benjamin R. Curtis and 125
Peter V. Daniel and 109–110
Robert C. Grier and 121
Samuel Nelson and 113
Roger Taney and 93
James M. Wayne and 88
Missouri ex rel. Gaines v. Canada 285, 487*a*
Missouri v. Jenkins 486*a*–487*a*
Mistretta v. United States 487*a*
mistrial 436*g*
Mitchell v. Helms 418, 487*a*
Mobile v. Bolden 487*a*
moderate judges
Stephen G. Breyer **428–431**
Tom C. Clark **341–344**
William Day **235–238**
Joseph McKenna **226–228**
Sandra Day O'Connor **404–407**
Lewis F. Powell, Jr., **392–395**
Stanley Reed **307–309**
John Paul Stevens **400–403**
Potter Stewart **365–367**
Monell v. Department of Social Services 487*a*
monopolies 263
Monroe, James 440*c*
and John McLean 79
and Smith Thompson 70–72
Moody, William Henry *239,* **239–242,** 245, 449*a*
Moose Lodge No. 107 v. Irvis 487*a*
Morehead v. New York ex rel. Tipaldo 254
Morgan, Gen. John Hunt 244
Morgan v. Virginia 336
Morrison v. Olson 487*a*
motion 436*g*
Mueller v. Allen 488*a*
Mueller v. Oregon
Louis D. Brandeis and 268–269
David Brewer and 205
Mulford v. Smith 297
Muller v. Oregon 441*c*, 488*a*
Munn v. Illinois 488*a*
Samuel Blatchford and 192
Joseph P. Bradley and 164
David Brewer and 204
Stephen J. Field and 150
Morrison Waite and 171
murder 436*g*

Murphy, Frank *319,* **319–322,** 450*a*
and Tom C. Clark 343
and Wiley Rutledge 332

N

NAACP. *See* National Association for the Advancement of Colored People.
NAACP v. Alabama 356
Nader, Ralph 430
Nagasaki 442*c*
National Association for the Advancement of Colored People (NAACP)
Thurgood Marshall and 381
Clarence Thomas and 422
National Association for the Advancement of Colored People v. Button 488*a*
National Labor Relations Board v. Jones & Laughlin Steel Corp. 488*a*
National League of Cities v. Usery 488*a*
William H. Rehnquist and 398
Potter Stewart and 366
National Organization of Women v. Scheidler 488*a*
National Recovery Act 297
National Treasury Employees Union v. Raab 488*a*
naturalization 436*g*
natural law 436*g*
Neagle, David 151
Near v. Minnesota 488*a*
Nebbia v. New York 296–297, 489*a*
Nebraska Press Association v. Stuart 489*a*
negligence 436*g*
Nelson, Samuel *111,* **111–114,** 447*a*
and Samuel Blatchford 191
and John A. Campbell 129
and Ward Hunt 166
Newberry v. United States 489*a*
New Deal 442*c*
James Byrnes and 324
William O. Douglas and 316
Abe Fortas and 377
Felix Frankfurter and 312–313
Sherman Minton and 346
Frank Murphy and 319, 320
Stanley Reed and 307
Wiley Rutledge and 331
Potter Stewart and 367
Fred M. Vinson and 338
New Deal legislation
Hugo Black and 304
Pierce Butler and 285
Benjamin N. Cardozo and 301
Charles Evans Hughes and 250
James C. McReynolds and 262, 265
Stanley Reed and 308
Owen J. Roberts and 295–297
Edward T. Sanford and 289
Harlan Fiske Stone and 292
George Sutherland and 281
Willis Van Devanter and 252, 254
New Federal Equity Rules 246
New Hampshire
Salmon P. Chase and 154
David H. Souter and 417
Harlan Fiske Stone and 291
Levi Woodbury and 116
New Jersey
Joseph P. Bradley and 162
William J. Brennan, Jr., and 359
John McLean and 79
William Paterson and 28–30
Mahlon Pitney and 259–260
Antonin Scalia and 409
New Jersey Plan 29
New Jersey v. T.L.O. 489*a*
New York Central Railroad Co. v. White 261
New York State
Samuel Blatchford and 191
Joseph P. Bradley and 162
Benjamin N. Cardozo and 300
Felix Frankfurter and 312
Ruth Bader Ginsburg and 425
John Marshall Harlan II and 355
Charles Evans Hughes and 248–249
Ward Hunt and 165–166
Robert Jackson and 327
John Jay and 5–6, 8
H. Brockholst Livingston and 56
Samuel Nelson and 112
Rufus Peckham, Jr., and 223
Smith Thompson and 71
New York State Club Association v. City of New York 489*a*
New York Times v. Sullivan 360, 443*c*, 489*a*
New York Times v. United States 489*a*
New York v. Ferber 489*a*
New York v. Herndon 489*a*
New York v. Miln 489*a*
Philip Barbour and 97–98
Roger Taney and 92
Nicholas, George 75
Nichols, Francis R. T. 219
Nineteenth Amendment 442*c*
Nixon, Richard M. 444*c*
and Hugo Black 306
and Harry A. Blackmun 389
and Warren Burger 384–386
impeachment 444*c*
and Lewis F. Powell, Jr., 393, 394
and William H. Rehnquist 396–399
and Antonin Scalia 409
and John Paul Stevens 401
and Potter Stewart 367
and Earl Warren 352
Nixon v. Administrator of General Services 489*a*
Nixon v. Condon 489*a*–490*a*
Nollan v. California Coastal Commission 490*a*
nominal damages 436*g*
Norman v. Baltimore & Ohio Railroad Co. See Gold Clause Cases.
Norris, George 284
North Carolina
James Iredell and 22
Alfred Moore and 43–44
Nortz v. United States. See Gold Clause Cases.
Nuremburg Trials 326–328, 442*c*

O

objection 436*g*
obscenity 436*g*
obscenity, definition of 367
obstruction of justice 436*g*
O'Connor, Sandra Day *404,* **404–407,** 451*a*
and Ruth Bader Ginsburg 424
and Anthony Kennedy 414
and William H. Rehnquist 397
and David H. Souter 418
Ogden v. Saunders 490*a*
Gabriel Duvall and 63–64
Smith Thompson and 72
Robert Trimble and 76, 77
Ohio
Harold H. Burton and 335
Salmon P. Chase and 154
John H. Clarke and 272
William Day and 236
Stanley Matthews and 182–183
John McLean and 79
Potter Stewart and 366
Noah H. Swayne and 137
William Howard Taft and 276
Morrison Waite and 169
William Woods and 179
Ohio Constitutional Convention of 1873 169
Ohio v. Carneal 79, 80
Oklahoma City Board of Education v. Dowell 490*a*
Oliver, Peter 11
Olmstead v. United States 490*a*
Louis D. Brandeis and 269
Pierce Butler and 285
Moore, Alfred *43,* **43–46,** 52, 446*a*
opinion 436*g*
ordinance 436*g*
original jurisdiction 436*g*
Osborne v. Ohio 490*a*
Oswald, Lee Harvey 352, 443*c*
overrule 436*g*

P

Pacific Mutual Life Insurance Company v. Haslip 490*a*
Palko v. Connecticut 302, 490*a*
Palmer v. Thompson 490*a*
Palsgraf v. Long Island Railroad Co. 301
Panama Canal 441*c*
Panama Refining Co. v. Ryan 297
Papachristou v. City of Jacksonville 317
Parker, John J. 296
Parker v. Davis
Joseph P. Bradley and 163
William Strong and 159
Pasadena Board of Education v. Spangler 491*a*
Passenger Cases
John Catron and 101
Peter V. Daniel and 109
Robert C. Grier and 120
Levi Woodbury and 117
patent 436*g*

patent law 191
Paterson, William *28*, **28–31,** 446*a*
and Oliver Ellsworth 37
and H. Brockholst Livingston 57
and John Marshall 47
Payne v. Tennessee 491*a*
Peckham, Jr., Rufus Wheeler *222*, **222–225,** 448*a*
and David Brewer 204
and Oliver Wendell Holmes, Jr., 232
and Horace Lurton 245
Peckham, Wheeler 223
Pennoyer v. Neff 166
Pennsylvania
Henry Baldwin and 83
Robert C. Grier and 120
Robert Jackson and 327
Joseph McKenna and 227
Owen J. Roberts and 295–296
George Shiras, Jr., and 210–211
William Strong and 158
James Wilson and 2
People for the American Way 422
peremptory challenge 436*g*
perjury 436*g*
Permanent Court of Arbitration in the Hague 201
Perry v. United States. See Gold Clause Cases.
personal property 436*g*
Personnel Administrator of Massachusetts v. Feeney 491*a*
Philippines 441*c*
Horace Lurton and 245
Frank Murphy and 320
William Howard Taft and 276
Pierce, Franklin 128, 440*c*
Pierce, William 19
Pierce v. Society of Sisters 264, 491*a*
Pinckney, Charles Cotesworth 52
Pitney, Mahlon *259*, **259–261,** 276, 449*a*
plain error rule 436*g*
plaintiff 436*g*
plain view doctrine 437*g*
Planned Parenthood v. Casey 491*a*
Harry A. Blackmun and 390
Anthony Kennedy and 414, 415
Sandra Day O'Connor and 406
David H. Souter and 418
John Paul Stevens and 402
Planned Parenthood v. Danforth 491*a*
Planters' Bank of Mississippi v. Sharp 109
plea 437*g*
plea bargain 437*g*
pleadings 437*g*
Plessy, Homer 208
Plessy v. Ferguson 441*c*, 491*a*
Henry Brown and 206, 208
John Marshall Harlan and 110, 175–176
William H. Rehnquist and 397
Plyler v. Doe 491*a*
Poe v. Ulman 356
Poindexter v. Greenhow 184
Pointer v. Texas 491*a*
Polk, James K. 440*c*
and Nathan Clifford 133–134
and Robert C. Grier 120
and Levi Woodbury 117
Pollock v. Farmers' Loan & Trust Co. 492*a*
David Brewer and 204
Henry Brown and 208
Stephen J. Field and 151
Melville W. Fuller and 200
Howell E. Jackson and 216–217
George Shiras, Jr., and 212
Noah H. Swayne and 138
Edward Douglass White and 220
Pomerene, Atlee 296
pornography, definition of 367
Porter, James G. 244
Porter, Paul 378
Potter, Charles N. 253
Powell, Jr., Lewis Franklin *392*, **392–395,** 450*a*
and Hugo Black 306
and Anthony Kennedy 413
and William H. Rehnquist 397
and John Paul Stevens 401
Powell v. Alabama 492*a*
Pierce Butler and 285
James C. McReynolds and 264
George Sutherland and 281, 282
Powell v. McCormack 492*a*
Powers v. Ohio 492*a*
precedent 437*g*
preemption 437*g*
preliminary hearing 437*g*
preponderance of the evidence 437*g*
presidents 275–278, 452*a*–454*a*
Presser v. Illinois 180
Prigg v. Pennsylvania 492*a*
Henry Baldwin and 85
James M. Wayne and 88
Levi Woodbury and 117
prima facie case 437*g*
Printz v. United States 402, 445*c*, 492*a*
privacy, right to
Hugo Black and 306
Harry A. Blackmun and 389–390
Louis D. Brandeis and 268, 269
Stephen G. Breyer and 429
Warren Burger and 386
William O. Douglas and 317
John Marshall Harlan II and 356
Potter Stewart and 366
Earl Warren and 351–352
privileged communication 437*g*
Prize Cases 492*a*
John Catron and 101–102
Robert C. Grier and 121, 122
Samuel Miller and 142
Samuel Nelson and 113
Noah H. Swayne and 138
James M. Wayne and 88
probable cause 437*g*
probate 437*g*
pro bono publico 267
process 437*g*
product liability law 300–301
Profiles in Courage (John F. Kennedy) 194
progressive judges
Louis D. Brandeis **267–270**
John H. Clarke **271–273**
pro-life movement 390
property rights
Joseph P. Bradley and 164
David Brewer and 203
Stephen J. Field and 149–151
Melville W. Fuller and 200
Mahlon Pitney and 260
William Strong and 157
Morrison Waite and 171
Proposition One (California) 413
pro se 437*g*
prosecutor 437*g*
Pullman strike 204
punitive damages 437*g*
Pure Food and Drug Act 284

Q

quasi-suspect classification 402
Quay, Matthew 211

R

racial discrimination 366. *See also Brown v. Board of Education.*
racial quotas 394. *See also* affirmative action.
racism
Pierce Butler and 285
James C. McReynolds and 264
Radical Republicans 155, 156
Railroad Pension Act 254
Railroad Retirement Act 297
Railroad Retirement Board v. Alton Railroad
Owen J. Roberts and 297
Willis Van Devanter and 254
Raines v. Byrd 492*a*
Randolph, Edmund
and John Blair, Jr., 15
and Peter V. Daniel 108
R.A.V. v. City of St. Paul 492*a*
Reagan, Ronald 444*c*
and Ruth Bader Ginsburg 424
and Anthony Kennedy 412, 413
and Sandra Day O'Connor 405
and William H. Rehnquist 396, 398
and Antonin Scalia 409
and David H. Souter 417
and Clarence Thomas 421
real property 437*g*
recess 437*g*
Reconstruction
David Davis and 146–147
Stanley Matthews and 184
Edward Douglass White and 219
Reconstruction Amendments 511*a*
Joseph P. Bradley and 163
John Marshall Harlan and 175
William Strong and 159
Morrison Waite and 170
William Woods and 180
Reconstruction Congress
John Marshall Harlan and 175
Samuel Miller and 142
Morrison Waite and 170, 171
Reconstruction Finance Corporation 308

recusal 437*g*
Red Scare
William J. Brennan, Jr., and 359
Tom C. Clark and 341, 343
Reed, Stanley Foreman *307,* **307–309,** 449*a*
and Robert Jackson 327
and Sherman Minton 347
and Charles Whittaker 363
Reed v. Reed 492*a*
Warren Burger and 386
Ruth Bader Ginsburg and 425
Regents of the University of California v. Bakke 444*c,* 493*a*
William J. Brennan, Jr., and 361
Lewis F. Powell, Jr., and 394
Rehnquist, William Hubbs *396,* **396–399,** 444*c,* 450*a,* 451*a*
and William J. Brennan, Jr., 358, 361
and Stephen G. Breyer 430
and Anthony Kennedy 414, 415
and Sandra Day O'Connor 404–406
and Antonin Scalia 409
and David H. Souter 418
and John Paul Stevens 401, 402
and Clarence Thomas 421
Reitman v. Mulkey 493*a*
religious freedom
William O. Douglas and 317
Felix Frankfurter and 313
Frank Murphy and 321
William H. Rehnquist and 399
Antonin Scalia and 410
remand 437*g*
removal 437*g*
Reno v. ACLU 493*a*
Renton v. Playtime Theaters 493*a*
repossession 437*g*
reproductive rights. *See* abortion rights; *Griswold v. Connecticut.*
Republicanism 67
Republican Party 440*c*
Joseph P. Bradley and 162
Warren Burger and 385
Harold H. Burton and 335
Salmon P. Chase and 154, 155
David Davis and 145
William Day and 236
John Marshall Harlan and 174
Charles Evans Hughes and 249
Ward Hunt and 166
Anthony Kennedy and 413
Joseph McKenna and 227
John McLean and 81
Samuel Miller and 141
William Moody and 240
Alfred Moore and 45
Sandra Day O'Connor and 405
Mahlon Pitney and 260
William H. Rehnquist and 397
Potter Stewart and 366
William Strong and 158
George Sutherland and 280
Noah H. Swayne and 137
William Howard Taft and 277
Willis Van Devanter and 253
Morrison Waite and 169
Earl Warren and 350
Charles Whittaker and 363
William Woods and 179
res judicata 437*g*
restrictive covenant 437*g*
reversible error 437*g*
Revolutionary War. *See* American Revolution.
Reynolds v. Sims 443*c,* 493*a*
William J. Brennan, Jr., and 360
John Marshall Harlan II and 356
Reynolds v. United States 441*c,* 493*a*
Rhode Island 133
Rhodes v. Chapman 493*a*
Richmond v. J. A. Croson Co. 444*c,* 493*a*
Anthony Kennedy and 414
Sandra Day O'Connor and 406
right of association 356
"rights revolution"
Arthur J. Goldberg and 373
John Marshall Harlan II and 357
Roberts, Owen Josephus *295,* **295–298,** 449*a*
and Harold H. Burton 335
and Pierce Butler 285
and Benjamin N. Cardozo 301
and James C. McReynolds 265
and Frank Murphy 321
and Stanley Reed 308
and Harlan Fiske Stone 292
and George Sutherland 281
and Willis Van Devanter 254
Roberts v. United States Jaycees 493*a*
Robinson v. California 370, 494*a*
Rodney, Caesar A. 53
Roe v. Wade 444*c,* 494*a*
Harry A. Blackmun and 389–391
Stephen G. Breyer and 430
Warren Burger and 386
Ruth Bader Ginsburg and 426
Anthony Kennedy and 414, 415
Sandra Day O'Connor and 406
Lewis F. Powell, Jr., and 394
William H. Rehnquist and 397
David H. Souter and 417, 418
John Paul Stevens and 402
Clarence Thomas and 422
Byron R. White and 370
Roman Catholicism
William J. Brennan, Jr., and 360
Pierce Butler and 284, 285
Joseph McKenna and 226–228
Frank Murphy and 320, 321
Antonin Scalia and 409
Roger Taney and 92
Edward Douglass White and 219
Romer v. Evans 414, 494*a*
Roosevelt, Franklin Delano 442*c*
and Hugo Black 304
and Louis D. Brandeis 270
and Harold H. Burton 335
and Pierce Butler 285
and James Byrnes 323–325
and Benjamin N. Cardozo 301
and Tom C. Clark 342
and John H. Clarke 273
and William O. Douglas 316, 317
and Abe Fortas 377
and Felix Frankfurter 312–313
and Charles Evans Hughes 248–250
and Robert Jackson 327
and James C. McReynolds 265
and Sherman Minton 346, 347
and Frank Murphy 320, 321
and Stanley Reed 307, 308
and William H. Rehnquist 398
and Owen J. Roberts 295, 297
and Wiley Rutledge 330–332
and Edward T. Sanford 289
and Potter Stewart 367
and Harlan Fiske Stone 290, 292, 293
and George Sutherland 279, 281, 282
and Willis Van Devanter 252, 254
and Fred M. Vinson 338, 339
and Earl Warren 350
Roosevelt, James 350
Roosevelt, Theodore 441*c*
and William Day 235, 237
and Horace Gray 188
and Oliver Wendell Holmes, Jr., 232
and Horace Lurton 245
and James C. McReynolds 263
and William Moody 239–241
and Edward T. Sanford 288
and William Howard Taft 276, 277
and Willis Van Devanter 253
Roosevelt v. Meyer 138
Rosenberger v. Rector & The Visitors of the University of Virginia 494*a*
Rostker v. Goldberg 494*a*
Roth v. United States 494*a*
Rowan, John 75
Rudman, Warren B. 417
"rule of reason" 221
ruling 437*g*
Rummel v. Estelle 494*a*
Runyon v. McCrary 494*a*
Rust v. Sullivan 494*a*
Rutan v. Republican Party of Illinois 494*a*–495*a*
Rutledge, John *17,* **17–20,** 446*a*
and John Blair, Jr., 15, 16
and William Cushing 12
and Thomas Johnson 26
and William Paterson 30
Rutledge, Wiley Blount *330,* **330–333,** 450*a*
and Sherman Minton 347
and John Paul Stevens 401

S

Saenz v. Roe 495*a*
San Antonio Independent School District v. Rodriguez 394, 495*a*
Sanborn, John 389
Sanford, Edward Terry *287,* **287–289,** 296, 449*a*
Santa Fe School District v. Doe 402, 495*a*
Santobello v. New York 495*a*
Scales v. United States 495*a*
Scalia, Antonin *408,* **408–411,** 451*a*
and Stephen G. Breyer 430
and Anthony Kennedy 414
and Sandra Day O'Connor 406
and William H. Rehnquist 398

and David H. Souter 418
and John Paul Stevens 402
and Clarence Thomas 421, 422
Schall v. Martin 495*a*
Schechter Poultry Corp. v. United States 495*a*
Charles Evans Hughes and 250
Owen J. Roberts and 297
Schenck v. United States 232–233, 495*a*
schools, local control of 394
Scott, Dred. *See Dred Scott v. Sandford.*
Scottsboro cases
Pierce Butler and 285
James C. McReynolds and 264
George Sutherland and 281, 282
search warrant 437*g*
Searight v. Stokes 109
Second Amendment 180, 509*a*
Securities Act of 1933 313
Securities and Exchange Commission 316
Securities Exchange Act of 1934 313
Sedition Act of 1798 34
Sedition Act of 1918 272
segregation
Harold H. Burton and 336
James Byrnes and 325
Thurgood Marshall and 380, 381
Sherman Minton and 345, 347
Stanley Reed and 309
William H. Rehnquist and 397
Fred M. Vinson and 339–340
Earl Warren and 349, 351
self-incrimination 437*g*
Seminole Tribe of Florida v. Florida 495*a*
Senate. *See* U.S. Senate.
senatorial courtesy 437*g*
sentencing 437*g*
"separate but equal" doctrine. *See Brown v. Board of Education.*
seriatim opinions 437*g*
seriatim opinions 41
John Marshall and 48
Alfred Moore and 45
Bushrod Washington and 41
service of process 437*g*
Seventeenth Amendment 281, 442*c*, 512*a*
1794 Treaty of Amity (Jay's Treaty) 8
Seward, William
and Samuel Blatchford 191
and John A. Campbell 129
and Salmon P. Chase 154
and John McLean 81
and Samuel Nelson 113
sexual discrimination
Joseph P. Bradley and 163–164
David Brewer and 203
Ward Hunt and 167
Shapiro v. Thompson 496*a*
Shaw v. Reno 496*a*
Shay, Daniel 12
Shay's Rebellion 12
Shelley v. Kraemer 496*a*
Tom C. Clark and 343
Fred M. Vinson and 339
Sheppard v. Maxwell 496*a*
Sherbert v. Verner 496*a*
Sherman, John
and William Day 236–237
and Stanley Matthews 184
Sherman, William 179, 180
Sherman Antitrust Act
Pierce Butler and 284
Melville W. Fuller and 200
William Moody and 241
Mahlon Pitney and 261
Edward Douglass White and 221
Shiras, Jr., George *210,* **210–212,** 237, 448*a*
Shreveport Rate Cases 496*a*
Sixteenth Amendment 442*c*, 512*a*
David Brewer and 204
Melville W. Fuller and 200
Howell E. Jackson and 217
George Shiras, Jr., and 212
Sixth Amendment 510*a*
Hugo Black and 305
Abe Fortas and 377
Arthur J. Goldberg and 374
Skinner v. Oklahoma 317, 496*a*
Skinner v. Railway Labor Executives' Association 496*a*
slander 438*g*
Slaughterhouse Cases 441*c*, 496*a*
John A. Campbell and 130
Stephen J. Field and 150
Samuel Miller and 142–143
Noah H. Swayne and 138
Morrison Waite and 170–171
William Woods and 179–180
slavery issue. *See also Dred Scott v. Sandford.*
Henry Baldwin and 84–85
Philip Barbour and 95
Joseph P. Bradley and 163
John A. Campbell and 129
John Catron and 100–102
Salmon P. Chase and 154, 155
Benjamin R. Curtis and 125–126
David Davis and 145
Robert C. Grier and 119, 121, 122
John Marshall Harlan and 175
Ward Hunt and 166
William Johnson and 53
Stanley Matthews and 183
John McKinley and 104, 105
John McLean and 79–81
Samuel Miller and 141–142
Samuel Nelson and 111–113
John Rutledge and 19
Joseph Story and 68
William Strong and 157
Roger Taney and 93
Robert Trimble and 76
Bushrod Washington and 41
James M. Wayne and 88
Levi Woodbury and 117
Smith, William French 405–406
Smith v. Allwright 496*a*
Thurgood Marshall and 381
Stanley Reed and 309
Socratic method 438*g*
Solem v. Helm 496*a*–497*a*
Solicitor General 438*g*
Souter, David H. *416,* **416–419,** 451*a*
and Stephen G. Breyer 430
and Anthony Kennedy 414
and Sandra Day O'Connor 406
South Carolina
James Byrnes and 324, 325
William Johnson and 52, 53
John Rutledge and 18–20
James M. Wayne and 87
South Carolina v. Katzenbach 497*a*
South Dakota v. Dole 497*a*
sovereign immunity 438*g*
Spain 56
Spanish-American War 236–237, 441*c*
speedy trial requirement 438*g*
Springer v. United States 138
Stamp Act 439*c*
John Blair, Jr., and 15
Samuel Chase and 33
Thomas Johnson and 26
John Rutledge and 18
Standard Oil v. United States 221, 497*a*
standing 438*g*
Stanford, Leland 227, 228
Stanford v. Kentucky 497*a*
Stanley v. Georgia 382, 497*a*
Stanton, Edwin M.
and Joseph P. Bradley 162
and Salmon P. Chase 156
and William Strong 158
stare decisis 438*g*
stare decisis 411, 438*g*
Stassen, Harold E. 385
states, claims against 430
states' rights. *See also* federalism.
Philip Barbour and 95–97
John A. Campbell and 128, 130
John Catron and 101
Nathan Clifford and 134
Peter V. Daniel and 108–109
Robert C. Grier and 120
William Johnson and 53
L. Q. C. Lamar and 195
John Marshall and 49
Samuel Nelson and 113
Joseph Story and 66–68
Roger Taney and 91
Robert Trimble and 75
James M. Wayne and 88
James Wilson and 3
Levi Woodbury and 117
State v. Mulger (Kansas) 203
State v. Smith 101
statute 438*g*
statutory rape 438*g*
Sternberg v. Carhart 497*a*
Stevens, John Paul *400,* **400–403,** 451*a*
and Stephen G. Breyer 430
and Sandra Day O'Connor 406
and David H. Souter 418
Steward Machine Co. v. Davis 497*a*
Stewart, Potter *365,* **365–367,** 450*a*
and Sandra Day O'Connor 405
and John Paul Stevens 401
Stimson, Henry Louis 312
Stone, Harlan Fiske *290,* **290–293,** 442*c*, 449*a*, 450*a*
and Harold H. Burton 335
and Felix Frankfurter 314
and Robert Jackson 327, 329
and James C. McReynolds 265
and Owen J. Roberts 296, 298
and Fred M. Vinson 338

Story, Joseph *65,* **65–69,** 447*a*
and Henry Baldwin 84
and Benjamin R. Curtis 124
and Gabriel Duvall 62, 63
and H. Brockholst Livingston 57
and John McKinley 105
and John McLean 80
and Robert Trimble 76
and Bushrod Washington 41
and Levi Woodbury 117
Strauder v. West Virginia 497*a*
William Strong and 159
Morrison Waite and 170
Stromberg v. California 497*a*
Pierce Butler and 285
Charles Evans Hughes and 250
Strong, William *157,* **157–160,** 448*a*
and Samuel Blatchford 192
and Joseph P. Bradley 163
and William Woods 180
Sturges v. Crowninshield 497*a*
H. Brockholst Livingston and 57
Smith Thompson and 72
Robert Trimble and 76
subpoena 438*g*
suffrage. *See* voting rights.
summary judgment 438*g*
summons 438*g*
Sumner, Charles 196
Sununu, John 417
susbstantive due process 305–306
suspect classification 402
Sutherland, George *279,* **279–282,** 449*a*
and John H. Clarke 271
and James C. McReynolds 265
and Stanley Reed 307, 309
and Harlan Fiske Stone 292
and Willis Van Devanter 254
Swann v. Charlotte-Mecklenburg Board of Education 444*c,* 497*a*
Swayne, Noah Haynes *136,* **136–139,** 184, 447*a*
Sweatt v. Painter 498*a*
Harold H. Burton and 336
Thurgood Marshall and 381
Fred M. Vinson and 340
Swift v. Tyson 68

T

Taft, William Howard *275,* **275–278,** 442*c,* 449*a*
and Pierce Butler 284
and John H. Clarke 273
and William Day 237
and Felix Frankfurter 312
and Oliver Wendell Holmes, Jr., 232
and Charles Evans Hughes 249
and Joseph Lamar 257–258
and Horace Lurton 243, 245
and Joseph McKenna 228
and James C. McReynolds 264
and Sherman Minton 346
and Mahlon Pitney 259, 260
and Edward T. Sanford 288, 289
and Harlan Fiske Stone 292
and Willis Van Devanter 254
and Earl Warren 352
and Edward Douglass White 220–221
Taney, Roger Brooke *90,* **90–94,** 440*c,* 447*a*
and Philip Barbour 97, 98
and John A. Campbell 129
and John Catron 99, 101, 102
and Salmon P. Chase 155
and Benjamin R. Curtis 123, 125, 126
and Peter V. Daniel 109
and Peter V. Daniel 108
and Gabriel Duvall 64
and Robert C. Grier 120, 121
and John McKinley 105
and John McLean 78, 80
and Samuel Miller 142
and Samuel Nelson 111–114
and Joseph Story 68
and Noah H. Swayne 138
and Smith Thompson 73
and James M. Wayne 86–89
and Levi Woodbury 115–117
tariffs 219
Taylor, Zachary 440*c*
Taylor v. Louisiana 498*a*
Teapot Dome Scandal 296
Tennessee
John Catron and 101–102
Abe Fortas and 377
Howell E. Jackson and 215
Horace Lurton and 244
James C. McReynolds and 263
Edward T. Sanford and 287–288
Tennessee v. Garner 498*a*
Tenth Amendment 297, 510*a*
Terminiello v. Chicago 498*a*
William O. Douglas and 317
Robert Jackson and 328
Terrell, J. S. 257
Terry, David S. 150, 151
Terry v. Ohio 498*a*
test case 438*g*
testimony 438*g*
Texas
Tom C. Clark and 342
Sandra Day O'Connor and 405
Texas v. Johnson 444*c,* 498*a*
William J. Brennan, Jr., and 361
Anthony Kennedy and 414
Antonin Scalia and 410
Thirteenth Amendment 441*c,* 511*a*
John Marshall Harlan and 175
Samuel Miller and 142
Potter Stewart and 366
Roger Taney and 93
Thomas, Clarence *420,* **420–423,** 451*a*
and Sandra Day O'Connor 406
and William H. Rehnquist 398
and Antonin Scalia 408
and John Paul Stevens 402
Thompson, Meldrin 417
Thompson, Smith *70,* **70–73,** 112, 447*a*
Thornburgh v. American College of Obstetricians and Gynecologists 498*a*
Thornhill v. Alabama 321–322, 498*a*
Thurman, Samuel R. 280
Tilden, Samuel
and Joseph P. Bradley 163
and Nathan Clifford 134–135
and Stephen J. Field 151
and Stanley Matthews 184
and Noah H. Swayne 137
and Morrison Waite 171
Tilton v. Richardson 498*a*
Tinker v. Des Moines School District 378, 498*a*
Tison v. Arizona 498*a*
tobacco cases 418
tobacco trust 263
Todd, Thomas *59,* **59–61,** 75, 447*a*
tort 438*g*
Totten, A. W. O. 215
Townshend Acts 439*c*
transcript 438*g*
treason 438*g*
Treaty of Ghent 440*c*
Treaty of Paris 439*c,* 441*c*
John Jay and 6
John Marshall and 47
Joseph Story and 67
Trillin, Calvin 371
Trimble, Robert *74,* **74–77,** 80, 447*a*
Troxel v. Granville 499*a*
Truman, Harry S. 442*c,* 443*c*
and Harold H. Burton 335
and James Byrnes 323, 325
and Tom C. Clark 341–343
and William O. Douglas 317
and Robert Jackson 329
and Sherman Minton 345–347
and Fred M. Vinson 338–340
"trust-busting" 241
Turner, William R. 149
Twelfth Amendment 440*c*
Twenty-fifth Amendment 443*c*
Twenty-first Amendment 442*c*
Twenty-fourth Amendment 443*c*
Twenty-second Amendment 443*c*
Twenty-seventh Amendment 444*c*
Twenty-sixth Amendment 444*c*
Twenty-third Amendment 443*c*
Twining v. New Jersey
John Marshall Harlan and 176
William Moody and 241
Tyler, John 440*c*
and Robert C. Grier 120
and Samuel Nelson 112

U

United Nations 374, 442*c*
United States v. Alvarez-Machain 499*a*
United States v. Armstrong 499*a*
United States v. Arredondo 84
United States v. Butler 499*a*
Owen J. Roberts and 297
Willis Van Devanter and 254
United States v. California 499*a*
United States v. Carolene Products 292
United States v. Classic 499*a*
United States v. Cruikshank 170, 499*a*
United States v. Curtiss-Wright Export Corporation 500*a*
United States v. Darby Lumber Company 500*a*
United States v. E. C. Knight Co.

David Brewer and 204
Melville W. Fuller and 200
United States v. Eichman 500*a*
William J. Brennan, Jr., and 361
Antonin Scalia and 410
United States v. Harris 180
United States v. Hudson & Goodwin 67
United States v. La Jeune Eugenie 68, 76
United States v. Lanza 500*a*
United States v. Leon 500*a*
United States v. Lopez 444*c*, 500*a*
Stephen G. Breyer and 430
Anthony Kennedy and 414
Sandra Day O'Connor and 407
David H. Souter and 418
John Paul Stevens and 402
United States v. Monsanto 500*a*
United States v. Morrison 500*a*
Stephen G. Breyer and 430
Ruth Bader Ginsburg and 427
Anthony Kennedy and 414
Sandra Day O'Connor and 407
William H. Rehnquist and 398
David H. Souter and 418
John Paul Stevens and 402
United States v. Nixon 386, 500*a*
United States v. O'Brien 501*a*
United States v. Playboy 430, 501*a*
United States v. Reese
Ward Hunt and 166–167
Morrison Waite and 170
United States v. Schwimmer 285
United States v. United States District Court 501*a*
United States v. Virginia 426, 445*c*, 501*a*
United States v. Wong Kim Ark 188, 501*a*
United Steelworkers of America v. Weber 501*a*
U.S. Civil Rights Commission 309
U.S. House of Representatives
Henry Baldwin and 83
Philip Barbour and 96–97
James Byrnes and 324
Nathan Clifford and 133
Joseph McKenna and 227
John McKinley and 104
John McLean and 79
Mahlon Pitney and 260
George Sutherland and 280
Fred M. Vinson and 338
James M. Wayne and 87
U.S. Senate
Hugo Black and 304
Salmon P. Chase and 154
Nathan Clifford and 134
David Davis and 144
Howell E. Jackson and 215–216
L. Q. C. Lamar and 196
John McKinley and 104
George Sutherland and 280
Edward Douglass White and 219
U.S. Term Limits, Inc. v. Thorton 501*a*
Utah 280

V

vacate 438*g*
Van Buren, Martin 440*c*
and Henry Baldwin 83
and Philip Barbour 97
and John Catron 101
and Peter V. Daniel 108
and Ward Hunt 166
and John McKinley 104
and Smith Thompson 71–72
Vance v. Bradley 501*a*
Van Devanter, Willis *252,* **252–255,** 449*a*
and Pierce Butler 284
and James C. McReynolds 265
and Stanley Reed 309
and Harlan Fiske Stone 292
and George Sutherland 279
and William Howard Taft 276
Van Horne's Lessee v. Dorrance 30
Van Zandt, John 154
venire 438*g*
venue, change of 438*g*
verdict 438*g*
Vietnam War 443*c*, 444*c*
Abe Fortas and 378
Arthur J. Goldberg and 374, 375
Vinson, Fred Moore *337,* **337–340,** 442*c*, 450*a*
and Tom C. Clark 343
and Felix Frankfurter 314
and Robert Jackson 329
and Sherman Minton 347
and Earl Warren 351
and Byron Raymond White 369
Violence Against Women Act
Stephen G. Breyer and 430
John Paul Stevens and 402
Virginia
Philip Barbour and 96
John Blair, Jr., and 14–15
Peter V. Daniel and 107–108
John Marshall and 47
Lewis F. Powell, Jr., and 392–393
Noah H. Swayne and 137
Thomas Todd and 60
Robert Trimble and 74
Virginia Military Institute (VMI) 426
Virginia Plan 29
visa 438*g*
VMI. *See* Virginia Military Institue.
voir dire 438*g*
Voorhees, Foster M. 260
voter districting 360
voting rights
William J. Brennan, Jr., and 360
Samuel Chase and 34
William O. Douglas and 317
John Marshall Harlan II and 356
Thurgood Marshall and 381
Earl Warren and 351
Byron R. White and 370

W

Waite, Morrison Remick *168,* **168–172,** 441*c*, 448*a*
and Joseph P. Bradley 164
and Salmon P. Chase 153
and Stephen J. Field 151
and Melville W. Fuller 200
and Ward Hunt 167
and Noah H. Swayne 139
Wallace v. Jaffree 501*a*
Wards Cove Packing Co. v. Atonio 502*a*
Ward v. Race Horse 253
Ware v. Hylton 502*a*
Samuel Chase and 34
John Marshall and 47
warrant 438*g*
Warren, Earl *349,* **349–352,** 443*c*, 450*a*
and William J. Brennan, Jr., 358, 361
and Warren Burger 384, 385
and Harold H. Burton 336
and William O. Douglas 317
and Abe Fortas 378
and Felix Frankfurter 314
and Arthur J. Goldberg 373
and John Marshall Harlan II 356
and Robert Jackson 329
and Thurgood Marshall 382
and Sherman Minton 347
and Frank Murphy 322
and Stanley Reed 309
and William H. Rehnquist 399
and Potter Stewart 367
and Byron Raymond White 368, 371
and Charles Whittaker 363
Warren, Francis E. 253
Warren Commission 352, 443*c*
Washington, Bushrod *39,* **39–42,** 446*a*
and Henry Baldwin 83
and Bushrod Washington 39, 40
Washington, George 439*c*
and John Blair, Jr., 15, 16
and Samuel Chase 34
and William Cushing 10, 12, 13
and Oliver Ellsworth 36–38
and James Iredell 23
and John Jay 6–8
and Thomas Johnson 26–27
and John Marshall 47
and William Paterson 29–31
and John Rutledge 18–20
and Bushrod Washington 39, 40
and James Wilson 3
Washington state 316
Washington v. Davis 502*a*
Washington v. Glucksberg 502*a*
Watergate 386, 444*c*. *See also United States v. Nixon.*
Watergate investigation 429
Wayne, Henry 88
Wayne, James Moore *86,* **86–90,** 113, 447*a*
Webster, Daniel
and Philip Barbour 98
and Benjamin R. Curtis 124, 125
and Gabriel Duvall 64
and John McKinley 105
Webster v. Reproductive Health Services 390, 502*a*
Weeks v. United States 502*a*
Weinberger v. Weisenfeld 426
welfare rights 360–361
Wesberry v. Sanders 502*a*
West Coast Hotel Co. v. Parrish 502*a*
Charles Evans Hughes and 250
Stanley Reed and 308
Owen J. Roberts and 297

Harlan Fiske Stone and 292
George Sutherland and 281
West Virginia State Board of Education v. Barnette 442*c*, 502*a*
William O. Douglas and 317
Felix Frankfurter and 313–314
Robert Jackson and 328, 329
Frank Murphy and 321
Harlan Fiske Stone and 293
Whig Party
Salmon P. Chase and 154
Benjamin R. Curtis and 124
Peter V. Daniel and 108
David Davis and 145
John Marshall Harlan and 174
Morrison Waite and 169
Whiskey Rebellion 439*c*
White, Byron Raymond *368,* **368–371,** 450*a*
and Stephen G. Breyer 429
and Ruth Bader Ginsburg 426
and Sandra Day O'Connor 406
and William H. Rehnquist 397
and John Paul Stevens 401, 402
White, Edward Douglass *218,* **218–221,** 442*c*, 448*a*, 449*a*
and Pierce Butler 284
and Oliver Wendell Holmes, Jr., 232
and Charles Evans Hughes 249
and Joseph Lamar 258
and Rufus Peckham, Jr., 224
and William Howard Taft 276
White House Tapes. *See United States v. Nixon.*
Whitney v. California 288, 289
Whittaker, Charles Evans *362,* **362–364,** 370, 450*a*
Wickard v. Filburn 328, 442*c*, 503*a*
Wickersham, George
and Pierce Butler 284
and James C. McReynolds 263
Wilkie, Wendell L. 346
Wilson, James *1,* **1–4,** 439*c*, 446*a*
and John Blair, Jr., 15
and William Cushing 12
and Bushrod Washington 40
Wilson, Woodrow 442*c*
and Louis D. Brandeis 269
and John H. Clarke 271–273
and Charles Evans Hughes 249
and Joseph Lamar 257, 258
and James C. McReynolds 262, 263
and Mahlon Pitney 260
and William Howard Taft 277
Wilson-Gorman Tariff Act 220
wiretaps
Louis D. Brandeis and 269
Pierce Butler and 285
Wisconsin 397
Wisconsin v. Mitchell 503*a*
Wisconsin v. Yoder 503*a*
Witherspoon v. Illinois 503*a*
witness 438*g*
Wolf v. Colorado 503*a*
women's rights 414. *See also* abortion rights; gender-based violence; gender discrimination.
Wong Wing v. United States 212
Woodbury, Levi *115,* **115–118,** 124, 447*a*
Woods, William Burnham *178,* **178–181,** 196, 448*a*
Worcester v. Georgia
Henry Baldwin and 84
John McLean and 80
Smith Thompson and 73
workers' compensation laws 261
World War I 442*c*
Harold H. Burton and 335
Oliver Wendell Holmes, Jr., and 233
Sherman Minton and 346
Frank Murphy and 320
Lewis F. Powell, Jr., and 393
Stanley Reed and 308
World War II 442*c*
William J. Brennan, Jr., and 359
Tom C. Clark and 342
Arthur J. Goldberg and 373
John Marshall Harlan II and 355
Robert Jackson and 328
Frank Murphy and 321
John Paul Stevens and 401
Fred M. Vinson and 338
Byron R. White and 369
Wright v. Moell (Kansas) 203
writ 438*g*
Wyoming 253
Wythe, George
and John Blair, Jr., 15
and John Marshall 47
and Bushrod Washington 40

X

XYZ Affair 47

Y

Yates, Peter 56
Yates v. United States 503*a*
Yick Wo v. Hopkins 184, 185, 503*a*
Youngstown Sheet & Tube Co. v. Sawyer 443*c*, 503*a*
Harold H. Burton and 335
Tom C. Clark and 343
Fred M. Vinson and 339
Young v. American Mini Theatres, Inc. 503*a*

Z

Zionism 269
Zorah v. Clauson 503*a*